In Defence of Lenin

Rob Sewell at the London office where
Lenin edited *Iskra* in 1902-3

Alan Woods speaking in
London in 2023

Rob Sewell and Alan Woods were brought up in South Wales in a Communist household. As young teenagers, they became committed Marxists and are now leading members of the International Marxist Tendency (IMT).

Rob Sewell is the political editor of *The Communist* (communist.red) – the organ of the British section of the IMT – and has written extensively on revolutionary theory and history. He is the author of *Socialism or Barbarism: Germany 1918-1933; Chartist Revolution; In the Cause of Labour – A History of British Trade Unionism; Revolution and Counter-revolution in Germany; What is Marxism?* with Alan Woods and *Understanding Marx's Capital: A Reader's Guide* with Adam Booth.

Alan Woods is the political editor of the IMT's flagship *In Defence of Marxism* website (marxist.com) and has written many books covering a wide spectrum of topics. These include *Lenin and Trotsky: What They Really Stood For* and *Reason in Revolt: Marxist Philosophy and Modern Science* – both in conjunction with the late Ted Grant; *Bolshevism: The Road to Revolution; Spain's Revolution Against Franco: The Great Betrayal; Marxism and the USA; Reformism or Revolution; The Ideas of Karl Marx* and *The Venezuelan Revolution: A Marxist Perspective*.

In Defence of Lenin

Rob Sewell *and* Alan Woods

Volume Two

Wellred Books
London

Dedicated to the memory of Steve Jones (1955 – 2022),
who devoted his life to the socialist revolution.

In Defence of Lenin
Rob Sewell and Alan Woods

Volume 2 of 2

First edition
Wellred Books, January 2024

UK distribution: Wellred Books Britain, wellredbooks.co.uk
152-160 Kemp House, City Road
London
EC1V 2NX
contact@wellredbooks.co.uk

USA distribution: Marxist Books, marxistbooks.com
WR Books
250 44th Street #208
Brooklyn
New York
NY 11232
sales@marxistbooks.com

DK distribution: Forlaget Marx, forlagetmarx.dk
Degnestavnen 19, st. tv.
2400 København NV
forlag@forlagetmarx.dk

Front cover: Lenin and his cat in Gorki, 1922
Back cover: Lenin in his office in the Kremlin, 1922
 – colour by Olga Shirnina

Cover design by Jesse Murray-Dean

Layout by Wellred Books

ISBN:
Volume 1 – 978 1 913026 95 0
Volume 2 – 978 1 913026 96 7

Contents

VOLUME ONE

VOLUME TWO

Preface to the Second Volume

At the time of the overthrow of the tsar in February 1917, Lenin is only nine months away from the Bolsheviks establishing a Soviet government. He is forty-six years old. He had behind him more than two decades of revolutionary work, involving imprisonment, internal exile, and exile abroad.

As a committed Marxist, his perspective was world revolution and the building of a revolutionary party. This constituted his life's work, which culminated in the October Revolution of 1917 and the founding of the Communist International, the world party of socialist revolution.

The second volume of Lenin will deal with these questions in some detail. It will trace the events up to the death of Lenin in January 1924 and will provide an explanation for the Stalinist political counter-revolution that followed it.

The world significance of October

For Marxists, the study of history is not a dry academic exercise. Still less is it a harmless source of entertainment, as it seems to be regarded by the postmodernist historians. We study history in order to draw practical conclusions from the past. In the words of the American philosopher George Santayana: "Those who cannot remember the past are condemned to repeat it."[1]

Nowadays, the enemies of communism try to paint the Russian Revolution in the darkest colours: a period of violence and bloodshed. In reality, it was the birth of a new power, and it was a tremendous source of inspiration for all the living forces of society.

It is difficult for us to imagine the colossal significance of those events. The spirit of that period was well expressed in the words of the French writer

Albert Camus: "Wonderful times, wonderful times, when the world seemed to be starting anew, when history was at last beginning afresh, on the ruins of an empire."[2]

Lenin is not a subject to be consigned to some dusty and airless library or museum. He is of colossal relevance for the here and now. A new epoch has opened up internationally, which is preparing the greatest of dramas, namely the downfall of a rotten social system, which has long outlived its usefulness and is ripe for overthrow.

In such a period, when new and exciting horizons open up before humanity, we would do well to recapture the spirit of those times, which bears a striking resemblance to our own. In these decisive moments, a return to Lenin is not a return to a long-forgotten past. The ideas of Lenin are for the present and the future. In writing a book about Lenin, we hope we have managed to do justice to the subject, which it so rightly deserves.

In the words of Edward Alsworth Ross, an American who visited Russia in 1923:

> The Russian Communists were men with a vision of a regenerated society which they sought to realise. All the party leaders who, in November 1917, laid rude hands on Russian society to remould it by force were sincere men, since, for the sake of their ideal, they had made themselves targets for the inhuman persecutions that went on under the Tsars. When freedom arrived in March, nobody had any standing with the Russian masses who had not stood up for them in those ghastly years when every spokesman for the robbed toilers had to skulk and run and burrow if he would remain at large. These fire-tested revolutionaries had behind them a record of personal disinterestedness and heroism, which should put to the blush our smug captains of conservative opinion, who have never risked their lives or freedom for others yet affect to dwell on a higher moral plane than the Russian fighters.[3]

Lenin left a rich legacy of ideas that retain all their relevance and vitality today. That is of immeasurable importance for the new generation, which is attracted to communism.

It is their task to complete the work Lenin and the Bolsheviks had begun more than a century ago. Armed with this knowledge, the workers and youth can change the world. It is to this new generation of class fighters that we dedicate the present work.

What Volume Two contains

The second volume of this book covers the period when the Bolsheviks took power in the October Revolution. From this 'besieged fortress', they proclaimed the fight for the world socialist revolution.

In October 1917, the old regime fell like a rotten fruit with hardly any resistance. Its inability to provide the masses with peace, bread and land completely eroded its base of support. In the words of Isaac Deutscher, the Provisional Government was "elbowed out of existence by a slight push."[4]

To go from a persecuted underground party to the successful conquest of power in a matter of months is an event unparalleled in history. However, surrounded by hostile forces, the problems faced by the Bolsheviks seemed almost insurmountable.

The material basis for a classless society did not exist in Russia, but only on a world scale. The Russian Revolution was therefore regarded as the first step in the world socialist revolution, and led to the creation of the Third (Communist) International in March 1919.

The book then deals with the period of the civil war, when the Soviet Republic was continuously fighting for its very survival, faced with armies of imperialist intervention. This was followed by the defeat of the German Revolution, leaving the Revolution isolated in conditions of frightful backwardness. This was the material basis for the rise of a privileged caste of bureaucrats that, in turn, was the basis for the political counter-revolution carried out by Stalin after Lenin's death.

Rob Sewell and Alan Woods
London, December 2023

22. Revolutionary Petrograd

In April and May 1917, Petrograd was awash with mass demonstrations and rowdy protests, as workers and soldiers gathered in huge numbers in avenues and on street corners. In 'normal' times, the masses are generally passive, when 'politics' is the preserve of the privileged elite of bourgeois politicians.

Now, with the fall of the old regime, they discovered for themselves newfound freedoms of political self-expression, ruthlessly denied under tsarism. They were engaged in heated discussions and debates on the streets, in the workplaces and in the endless food queues that snaked around the city. Those who had no interest in politics in the past now became the most enthusiastic participants.

Around half a million people, out of a city of 2 million inhabitants, would be talking, discussing, arguing, debating and simply milling around. The liberal paper *Rech* wrote in May 1917 that "Russia is being turned into a kind of lunatic asylum."[1] They were shocked at this popular 'madness', but it was simply the activity of the masses newly awakened by a revolution. Krupskaya recalls:

The streets in those days presented a curious spectacle: everywhere people stood about in knots, arguing heatedly and discussing the latest events. Discussion that nothing could interrupt! ... The house in which we lived overlooked a courtyard, and even here, if you opened the window at night, you could hear a heated dispute. A soldier would be sitting there, and he always had an audience – usually some of the cooks or housemaids from next door, or some young people. An hour after midnight you could catch snatches of talk – "Bolsheviks, Mensheviks..." At three in the morning: "Milyukov, Bolsheviks..." At five – still the same street-corner-

118. Petrograd, 12 March 1917

meeting talk, politics, etc. Petrograd's white nights are always associated in my mind now with those all-night political disputes.[2]

This revolution witnessed a colossal awakening in the masses. It was their grand entry onto the stage of history, a hallmark of the sharp changes in consciousness taking place. The masses began to feel their power and become aware of their strength. They were intoxicated with feelings of success as they threw aside their old conservatism and brought the regime crashing down. The revolution broke through the old barriers and forced the masses to rise up from their knees. "The history of a revolution", wrote Trotsky, "is for us

119. Demonstration on the Nevsky Prospect, Petrograd, in April

first of all a history of the forcible entrance of the masses into the realm of rulership over their own destiny."[3]

In a similar vein, Lenin also wrote about the sharp and sudden changes taking place in the revolution:

> During a revolution, millions and tens of millions of people learn in a week more than they do in a year of ordinary, somnolent life. For at the time of a sharp turn in the life of an entire people it becomes particularly clear what aims the various classes of the people are pursuing, what strength they possess, and what methods they use.[4]

The revolution had brought the masses to their feet, but the deteriorating economic situation was rapidly adding to their feelings of anger. Bread rations were continually being reduced in Petrograd and Moscow, and the queues were growing longer by the day. At the same time, prices rose rapidly for basic commodities, the scarcities only adding to a thriving black market.

Unemployment also rose and factories closed down, resulting in increasing hardship. 108 factories employing 8,701 workers were closed in May, 125 factories employing 38,455 workers in June, and 206 factories employing 47,754 workers in July. As the employers resorted to closures and lockouts, workers turned to factory occupations and, out of desperation, even kidnapped their bosses as ransom. In May, the Soviet Executive Committee spoke of a "general collapse of the country's economic life."

Along with the towns and cities, the countryside was also affected by the virus of revolution. There was increasing turmoil in the rural areas as land seizures multiplied and soviets sprang up in the villages. The class divide was as stark as ever, where one landowner had over 2,000 dessiatins,* while the poorest families held a mere 7.5 dessiatins.

The masses were constantly told to wait for the Constituent Assembly, where their problems would be resolved. But the peasants, desperate for the land, could no longer afford to wait and were taking matters into their own hands. The Mensheviks, now in positions of authority, warned against this 'anarchic' movement of the masses:

> … Agrarian disorders can benefit only the counter-revolution and not the peasants.
> It must be remembered that the power is now in the hands of the people, and the
> people will themselves settle the land question in the Constituent Assembly…[5]

Likewise, the Provisional Government continually talked of the "spread of anarchy" across the Russian countryside as the turmoil spread. But rather than supporting the peasants, the new authorities condemned their 'excesses' and sided with their enemies, the landlords.

Even after 'moderate' socialists entered the government, nothing changed. The Menshevik minister of the interior, Tsereteli, ordered government officials to "suppress with the utmost energy any attempt to sow disorder and anarchy, any arbitrary seizure of lands, any act of violence…"[6] But this simply added fuel to the fire and served to discredit them in the eyes of the poor peasants.

Many now began to look towards the Bolsheviks for salvation, with their slogan of 'Peace, Bread and Land' increasingly getting an echo.

---

* A dessiatin, used in tsarist Russia, was equivalent to 2.7 acres

120. Demonstration at Vosstaniya Square, Petrograd, in May

Winning the masses

Lenin had succeeded in conquering the Party, but the task now was to conquer the working class. He understood that the working class could only be won over to the Bolshevik programme on the basis of experience, explanation, and patient persuasion. There were no shortcuts. The revolution now allowed the Bolsheviks the freedom to organise openly and propagate their ideas.

Lenin rejected the idea of immediately 'seizing power', which he regarded as an adventure under the circumstances, but instead insisted upon the Soviets taking power through a *peaceful* transfer of power between parties within the Soviets.

The Bolshevik demands, simple and to the point, were now finding an echo among the masses. The Provisional Government was clearly incapable of solving their problems and became increasingly unpopular. Even within the army, officers were becoming alarmed at the increased presence of Bolsheviks in their regiments, who acted as a transmission belt for the discontent. A single Bolshevik, under the prevailing conditions, could become the catalyst for the subterranean revolt in all society.

Under such conditions, the Bolshevik Party began to grow, develop and adapt to the new conditions. The Party bore no resemblance to the malicious caricature, assiduously disseminated by the bourgeois historians, of a small, authoritarian, conspiratorial organisation under Lenin's iron grip. Rabinowitch explains:

> ... in 1917 Lenin's pre-revolutionary conception of a small, professional, conspiratorial party was discarded and the doors opened wide to tens of thousands of new members who were by no means without influence, so that to a significant degree the party was now both responsive and open to the masses [...][7]

> [The] relative flexibility of the party, as well as its responsiveness to the prevailing mass mood, had at least as much to do with the Bolshevik victory as did revolutionary discipline, organisational unity, or obedience to Lenin.[8]

Throughout 1917, the Party was navigating its way through the rapids of the revolution. Amongst the masses, there was a growing thirst for revolutionary ideas, with an immense demand for Party literature, newspapers, pamphlets and leaflets. Raskolnikov referred to the huge interest in Bolshevik ideas at Kronstadt:

> Our paper *Golos Pravdy* was distributed with hardly any copies left over. In addition, we subscribed to the leading Party papers in both Petrograd and Moscow. We circulated, besides newspapers, a large quantity of other Party literature and we also had to bring out pamphlets of our own. The thirst for literature was unprecedented in those days. Every ship, every regiment, every workshop sought to form a library of its own, however small this might be, and in those ship, regimental and work-shop libraries every political pamphlet was read literally to shreds. The February Revolution had aroused tremendous interest in politics and had thereby evoked an unprecedented demand for Bolshevik literature.[9]

'Honest defencists'

This change in Lenin's perspective for the socialist revolution, with the abandonment of the slogan of 'democratic dictatorship', also reflected itself in his new approach to the question of war. He was no longer simply educating the cadres, but was now looking to a mass audience.

While the Party was, of course, opposed to the imperialist war, the idea of regarding Russia's defeat in the war as the 'lesser evil' was put to one side. Rather than educating the cadres against social-chauvinism, the Party's propaganda was now aimed at winning the masses. As a result, it was now important to take account of their honest 'defencism' and separate out the progressive content from these feelings. Lenin explained:

> The slogan 'Down with the War!' is, of course, correct. But it fails to take into account the specific nature of the tasks of the present moment and the necessity of *approaching* the broad mass of the people *in a different way*. It reminds me of the slogan 'Down with the Tsar!' with which the inexperienced agitator of the 'good old days' went simply and directly to the countryside – and got a beating for his pains.[10]

The slant of the Bolshevik propaganda from the period of 1914-1916 needed to be modified in the light of the changed circumstances. Lenin now drew a sharp line of distinction between the social patriots who had abandoned the class standpoint and entered a bloc with the ruling class, and the many workers who, for honest reasons, had supported the war:

> The mass believers in revolutionary defencism are *honest*, not in the personal, but in the class sense, i.e. they belong to *classes* (workers and the peasant poor) which *in actual fact* have nothing to gain from annexations and the subjugation of other peoples. [...]
>
> The rank-and-file believer in defencism regards the matter in the simple way of the man in the street: "I don't want annexations, but the Germans are 'going for' *me*, therefore I'm defending a just cause and not any kind of imperialist interests at all." To a man like this it must be explained again and again that it is not a question of his personal wishes, but of mass, *class*, political relations and conditions, of the connection between the war and the interests of capital and the international network of banks, and so forth. Only such a struggle against defencism will be serious and will promise success – perhaps not a very rapid success, but one that will be real and enduring.[11]

The war itself was directly linked to this question of workers' power. 'Peace' was linked to 'bread' and 'land', but above all to the slogan 'all power to the Soviets'. Lenin underlined this point at the Petrograd City Conference at the end of April:

> When I spoke of the 'honest' mass of revolutionary defencists, I had in mind not a moral category, but a class definition. The classes represented in the Soviets of Workers' and Soldiers' Deputies have no interest in the predatory war. [...] In our country the Soviet of Workers' and Soldiers' Deputies pursues its policy of revolutionary defencism, not by violence, but because the masses trust it. [...]

In Russia the soldiers are armed; by agreeing only to 'defend themselves' against Wilhelm they allowed themselves to be peacefully deceived.[12]

He continued:

Here in Russia the power is in the hands of the soldiers, who are defencist-minded. The objective class position of the capitalists is one thing. They are conducting the war in their own interests. The soldiers are proletarians and peasants. This is another thing. Are they interested in seizing Constantinople? No, their class interests are opposed to war! That is why they can be made to see light, made to change their minds. The crux of the political situation at this moment is to be able to make the masses see the truth. […]

'Down with war' does not mean flinging the bayonet away. It means the transfer of power to another class. Everything must now be focused on making that clear. Blanquism was a striving to seize power with the backing of a minority. With us it is quite different. We are still a minority and realise the need for winning a majority.[13]

This change in Lenin's approach showed his great flexibility in the field of tactics. This was what allowed the Bolsheviks to connect with, and eventually win over, the broad mass of workers. In this way, in conquering power, they would become genuine 'defencists' of the revolution, and would be in favour of a revolutionary war when the working class was in power.

Dual power

Throughout this period, the authority of the Soviets within the working class – and the peasants – was continuing to increase exponentially. In April, a national All-Russian Conference of Workers' and Soldiers' Soviets was called to elect an All-Russian Central Executive Committee. In May, the Peasant Soviets also held an All-Russian Congress and likewise elected its own Executive. Then, as the next step, they elected a joint body which came to represent the great mass of Russian people.

The most influential Soviet in the land was naturally in Petrograd, which was the industrial centre as well as the seat of government. The problem was that it was dominated by the Mensheviks and SRs, the Compromisers who had capitulated to the bourgeoisie. But this was their Achilles heel and would eventually lead to their downfall.

The rise of the Soviets, alongside the Provisional Government, had produced a regime in Russia of 'dual power'. As Lenin explained:

Alongside the Provisional Government, the government of the *bourgeoisie*, *another government* has arisen, so far weak and incipient, but undoubtedly a government that actually exists and is growing – the Soviets of Workers' and Soldiers' Deputies. [...]

This power is of *the same type* as the Paris Commune of 1871.[14]

Lenin here is talking about a *workers' state*, or dictatorship of the proletariat, to use Marx's phrase.

Lenin attacked the Menshevik and SR leaders for refusing to recognise the real role of the Soviets as an alternative power. If left to these so-called 'moderates', the Soviets would have ended up in the same way as the workers' councils in Germany in 1918, where they were dissolved in favour of a bourgeois National Assembly. The Mensheviks and SRs, as with all the reformists, only sought to deceive the workers with their empty phrases, evasions, and subterfuge. As Lenin explained:

... they congratulate each other a thousand times upon the revolution, but refuse to *consider what* the Soviets of Workers' and Soldiers' Deputies *are*. They refuse to recognise the obvious truth that in as much as these Soviets exist, *in as much* as they are a power, we have in Russia a state of the *type* of the Paris Commune.

I have emphasised the words 'in as much as', for it is only an incipient power. By direct agreement with the bourgeois Provisional Government and by a series of actual concessions, it has itself *surrendered and is surrendering* its positions to the bourgeoisie.[15]

Lenin then went on to give the reasons for this state of affairs:

Why? Is it because Chkheidze, Tsereteli, Steklov and Co. are making a 'mistake'? Nonsense. Only a philistine can think so – not a Marxist. The reason is *insufficient class-consciousness* and organisation of the proletarians and peasants. The 'mistake' of the leaders I have named lies in their petty-bourgeois position, in the fact that instead of clarifying the minds of the workers, they are *befogging* them; instead of dispelling petty-bourgeois illusions, they are *instilling* them; instead of freeing the people from bourgeois influence, they are *strengthening* that influence.[16]

Lenin explains the real reason why the workers had not taken power. It was due to the lack of class consciousness and organisation. But this failure was reinforced by the petty-bourgeois leaders, who held the workers back. Only by removing these 'leaders' could the workers move to take power:

121. First Peasant Congress, May 1917

It should be clear from this why our comrades, too, make so many mistakes when putting the question 'simply': Should the Provisional Government be overthrown immediately?

My answer is: (1) it should be overthrown, for it is an oligarchic, bourgeois, and not a people's government, and *is unable* to provide peace, bread, or full freedom; (2) it cannot be overthrown just now, for it is being kept in power by a direct and indirect, a formal and actual *agreement* with the Soviets of Workers' Deputies, and primarily with the chief Soviet, the Petrograd Soviet; (3) generally, it cannot be 'overthrown' in the ordinary way, for it rests on the '*support*' given to the bourgeoisie by the *second* government – the Soviet of Workers' Deputies, and that government is the only possible revolutionary government, which directly expresses the mind and will of the majority of the workers and peasants. Humanity has not yet evolved and we do not as yet know a type of government superior to and better than the Soviets of Workers', Agricultural Labourers', Peasants', and Soldiers' Deputies.[17]

Again, Lenin underlines the point about the need for a peaceful revolution through the Soviets and is categorically against the methods of Blanquism:

To become a power the class-conscious workers must win the majority to their side. *As long as* no violence is used against the people there is no other road to power. We are not Blanquists, we do not stand for the seizure of power by a

122. Assembly of the Petrograd Soviet, March 1917

minority. We are Marxists, we stand for proletarian class struggle against petty-bourgeois intoxication, against chauvinism-defencism, phrase-mongering and dependence on the bourgeoisie.[18]

Lenin then concluded:

Let us create a proletarian Communist Party; its elements have already been created by the best adherents of Bolshevism; let us rally our ranks for proletarian class work; and larger and larger numbers from among the proletarians, from among the *poorest* peasants will range themselves on our side. For *actual experience* will from day to day shatter the petty-bourgeois illusions of those 'Social-Democrats', the Chkheidzes, Tseretelis, Steklovs and others, the 'Socialist-Revolutionaries', the petty bourgeois of an even purer water, and so on and so forth.[19]

While Lenin warned against premature actions, he also warned that this regime of dual power could not last or coexist with the bourgeois state. One or other of these powers had to give way. The bourgeoisie were plotting to rid themselves of the Soviets, which they understood posed a serious threat to their class rule.

The task of the Bolsheviks, on the other hand, was to call for the Soviets to take power, and sweep away the old order of landlords and capitalists. In raising this demand, they criticised and explained the shortcomings of the Menshevik and SR leaders. This work, said Lenin, was "nothing more" than propaganda, but was "in reality the most *practical revolutionary work*".[20]

Vilification campaign

As expected, the bourgeois newspapers began a campaign to vilify and discredit the Bolsheviks, accusing them above all of preaching violence. The bourgeois ministers also joined in on the attack. Lenin replied forcefully in an article in *Pravda*, 'A Shameless Lie of the Capitalists', which threw the allegations back in their face:

> You are lying, Mr Minister, worthy member of the 'people's freedom' party. It is Mr Guchkov who is preaching violence when he threatens to punish the soldiers for dismissing the authorities. It is *Russkaya Volya*, the riot-mongering newspaper of the riot-mongering 'republicans', a paper that is friendly to you, that preaches violence.
>
> *Pravda* and its followers do not preach violence. On the contrary, they declare most clearly, precisely, and definitely that our main efforts should now be concentrated on *explaining* to the proletarian masses their proletarian problems, as distinguished from the petty bourgeoisie which has succumbed to chauvinist intoxication.[21]

Nevertheless, the bourgeois newspapers continued their slander campaign, seeking to smear Lenin and the Bolsheviks as German agents for travelling back to Russia through Germany in April. These slurs, however, did not deter the Bolsheviks, whose ideas were gaining support.

In response to the charge that they were fermenting civil war, the Party's Central Committee instructed its propagandists to refute this slander. The resolution was drafted by Lenin:

> Party propagandists and speakers must refute the despicable lies of the capitalist papers and of the papers supporting the capitalists to the effect that we are holding out the threat of *civil war*. This is a despicable lie, for only at the present moment, as long as the capitalists and their government cannot and dare not use force against the masses, as long as the mass of soldiers and workers are freely expressing their will and freely electing and displacing *all* authorities – *at such a moment* any thought of civil war would be naïve, senseless, preposterous; at such a moment *there must be compliance with the will of the majority of the population* and free criticism of this will by the discontented minority;

should violence be resorted to, the responsibility will fall on the Provisional Government and its supporters.[22]

The radicalised masses were considerably further to the left than the 'Compromisers' in the Soviet. They had experienced three years of war, carnage, and hunger that had given rise to revolution on the streets in February. War-weary and hungry, they had certainly no appetite for military adventures.

It was Milyukov, the main bourgeois strategist, who formulated the war policy of the Provisional Government. In alliance with the Allies, his aim was to pursue the imperialist war to the bitter end. However, the 'moderate' socialist leaders of the Soviet, under intense pressure from the masses, felt that they had no alternative but to push for peace without annexations and indemnities. As a concession to the Soviet, the Provisional Government decided to inform the Allies of the text of the 'Appeal to the Citizens of Russia' of 9 April, which renounced any imperialist war aims. Milyukov opposed this concession, but agreed reluctantly to send the text to the Allies as long as he could write his own explanatory accompanying note.

But Milyukov's note simply reaffirmed that "the Provisional Government, while safeguarding the rights of our country, will fully observe the obligations assumed towards our Allies."[23] In other words, he was pledging that the government would continue with the imperialist war policy as before.

On slogans

As soon as Milyukov's note became public, it created a storm of opposition. On 3 May, spontaneous mass demonstrations, many armed, developed in Petrograd and other areas, in which the Bolsheviks fully participated. Banners appeared, under Bolshevik influence, with the slogans: 'Down with the Provisional Government!', 'Down with Milyukov!', 'Down with Imperialist policy!', and 'Milyukov, Guchkov, resign!'

The next day, demonstrators clashed in the streets with middle-class and upper-class supporters of the government. As a result, the bourgeois newspapers screamed about the "spectre of civil war". There was, it is true, some indiscriminate shooting and a few lives were lost, but this was far from a picture of civil war.

Up until now, the Bolsheviks had opposed the slogan 'Down with the Provisional Government'. It was premature, since they were still in a minority. This inopportune slogan was issued, not by the national party, but by the Petrograd Committee. Carried away by the mood of the advanced workers and sailors, the Petrograd Bolsheviks were marching too far ahead of the masses in the rest of Russia. That could only serve to play into the hands of the government.

In all revolutions, there are always moments when sections of workers, even within the revolutionary party, tend to move further ahead of the mass. They become impatient at the slow pace of events, or react to provocations and take an ultra-left stand. This was the case with a layer of Petrograd workers and also the sailors from Kronstadt. In fact, a number of Kronstadt sailors went to the street demonstrations in Petrograd with the express aim of overthrowing the Provisional Government. Raskolnikov describes the scene:

> We went first to the Naval College and then to Deryabinsk Barracks, in Galernaya Gavan. When our car appeared at the gates, the Kronstadters came running towards us from all directions. The vehicle was transformed into a tribune, from which we gave brief accounts of the political situation and the decision adopted by our Party. The comrades' morale was excellent. They were ready to begin an armed struggle for Soviet power, but the Bolshevik Party's authority obliged them to agree to our proposals… Only sailors were present. Placed as they were at the centre of military preparations and aroused by this atmosphere of a besieged camp, they naturally thirsted for battle, and their revolutionary impatience prompted in them the idea, senseless in the given circumstances, of an immediate seizure of power.[24]

The street demonstrations and clashes in Petrograd precipitated the most serious governmental crisis since the February Revolution. Panicked and under pressure, the Soviet Executive Committee issued a declaration that stating that anyone calling for armed demonstrations or so much as firing a gun into the air was a "traitor to the Revolution". This was followed by a ban on all meetings and demonstrations for a period of two days.

Under growing pressure, the Provisional Government was forced to repudiate Milyukov's provocative note. Shortly afterwards, Milyukov and Guchkov, the two key bourgeois ministers, decided to resign from the government.

Lenin predicted that this government crisis would be followed by others unless the Soviets took power. But he also warned that the Bolsheviks must not be provoked or thrown off course by premature adventures, which he saw as the biggest danger facing the Party. Lenin emphasised:

> The crisis cannot be overcome by violence practised by individuals against individuals, by the local action of small groups of armed people, by Blanquist attempts to 'seize power', to 'arrest' the Provisional Government, etc.[25]

At the All-Russia Party Conference in May (April, Old Style), he delivered a report on the current situation and the lessons to be drawn. He explained in an honest fashion that ultra-left mistakes had been made, which the Party must face up to and correct:

> We advanced the slogan for peaceful demonstrations, but several comrades from the Petrograd Committee issued a different slogan. We cancelled it, but were too late to prevent the masses from following the slogan of the Petrograd Committee. We say that the slogan 'Down with the Provisional Government' is an adventurist slogan, that the government cannot be overthrown now. That is why we have advanced the slogan for peaceful demonstrations. All we wanted was a peaceful reconnoitring of the enemy's forces; we did not want to give battle. But the Petrograd Committee turned a trifle more to the left, which in this case is certainly a very grave crime. Our organisational apparatus proved weak – our decisions are not being carried out by everyone.[26]

While the Bolsheviks were gaining ground in the capital, their support in the provinces and at the front was still lagging behind. Therefore, it was vital that the Bolsheviks were not provoked into taking premature actions, which could be ruinous. The Government, with the backing of the Soviet majority, still had reserves of support in the population, especially among the more inert layers.

Seeing the dangers implicit in this situation, Lenin devoted much of his time in June to restraining his comrades. He played the role of a 'firefighter'. The task of the Party was still to politically convince the majority of workers of the Bolshevik position, but until then, they were in a minority and had to act accordingly.

"Today's task is to explain more precisely, more clearly, more widely, the proletariat's policy", explained Lenin.[27] At this time, Lenin repeatedly warned against the danger posed by Blanquism, the tactics advocated by the French revolutionary Louis Auguste Blanqui, who believed that the workers could take power through the actions of a determined revolutionary minority. Lenin stood resolutely against these methods. Despite the allegation so persistently disseminated that the October Revolution was a 'coup', Lenin was implacably opposed to the idea of the seizure of power by a minority. That is the entire meaning of his slogan 'All Power to the Soviets'. On this, he wrote:

> There is a degree of freedom now in Russia that enables the will of the majority to be gauged by the make-up of the Soviets. Therefore, to make a serious, not a Blanquist, bid for power, the proletarian party must *fight for influence* within the Soviets.[28]

And he stressed:

> The government must be overthrown, but not everybody understands this correctly. So long as the Provisional Government has the backing of the Soviet of Workers' Deputies, you cannot 'simply' overthrow it. *The only way it can and must be overthrown is by winning over the majority in the Soviets.*[29]

'Down with the Ten Capitalist Ministers!'

The crisis resulted in a ministerial reshuffle in the Provisional Government. A new coalition was formed in early May, which for the first time brought into government a layer of moderate 'socialists', Mensheviks and SRs. These included Kerensky, Tsereteli, Chernov and Matvey Skobelev. Kerensky was now appointed Minister of War. The majority of the coalition – ten ministers in all – was still made up of representatives from the bourgeois and landlord parties.

Yet the Mensheviks and SRs, as expected, described the new ministry as a 'revolutionary' government. This class-collaborationist coalition was an anticipation of the later Popular Front governments of the 1930s, promoted by the Stalinists, which, under a 'left' cover, were to play a strike-breaking role. Lenin correctly described the new coalition government as a "shameful alliance [of Mensheviks and SRs] with *their* imperialist bourgeoisie".[30]

However, this reorganisation at the top was simply changing the pieces on the chessboard. Milyukov's departure, although a blow to the ruling class, would not change anything fundamental. As Lenin explained:

> It is a matter of class, not of persons. To attack Milyukov personally, to demand, directly or indirectly, his dismissal, is a silly comedy, for *no* change of personalities can change anything so long as the *classes* in power are unchanged.[31]

Faced with this new coalition, which included 'socialists', the Bolshevik Party raised the demand that the Mensheviks and SRs openly break with the bourgeois ministers, which they popularised with the slogan, 'Down with the Ten Capitalist Ministers!', linked to the demand, 'All Power to the Soviets!'

The Bolsheviks directed all their fire against the capitalists and their representatives. They skilfully placed the responsibility on the moderate 'socialists' to repudiate the capitalists. This slogan had a colossal educational significance for the masses. The obstinate refusal of the Soviet leaders to break with the bourgeoisie and take power into their hands would inevitably serve to create a wedge between them and their supporters.

This change of government was followed by another important turning point, which came some weeks later, in June. Throughout this time, amid growing food shortages, preparations for a new military offensive by the Provisional Government were giving rise to grave tensions.

The Allies were not only determined to keep Russia in the war, but also pressed the Provisional Government to step up their attack on the Central Powers. This meant curtailing the influence of the Bolsheviks and stiffening up the 'socialists' within the government. The Allied governments dispatched a number of Labour leaders, such as Arthur Henderson, the Foreign Secretary in the Lloyd George government, and Emile Vandervelde, the President of the Second International, to put pressure on their Russian counterparts to 'do as they were told'.

The bourgeoisie and the liberals were hell-bent on a new military offensive. This, they believed, would strengthen national unity and build up their support. But this was a delusion.

The Menshevik-SR majority, despite their pacifism, also favoured an offensive, believing that a strong and victorious Russia in the war would become a counterweight to the main imperialist powers. More importantly, they were also keenly aware that Russia needed to fulfil its wartime 'obligations', given that it was reliant on Western financial aid. Therefore, they believed there was no alternative but to prepare a military offensive.

While the Bolsheviks came out firmly against this military adventure, the Provisional Government rested on the majority support of the Menshevik and SR dominated Petrograd Soviet to push it through. In the end, a vote was taken in the Soviet that approved the Government's military plans by 472 votes to 271 with thirty-nine abstentions.

Kerensky, as Minister of War, became Supreme Commander, and in his new role boldly declared to the Russian troops heading for the front: "You will carry peace, truth and justice on the points of your bayonets." He went on: "I implore all of you to go forward, forward, in the struggle for liberty. You are not going to a banquet but to your death. We revolutionaries have the right to die."[32]

Of course, while Russian troops were dying in the trenches, the Minister of War himself had not the slightest intention of going to his death anytime soon. Having finished his inspiring speeches to the troops and calmly sent them off to meet their Maker, he would be far away, safe and sound, sitting comfortably behind his government desk and sleeping soundly in his bed.

Приказъ № 1.

1 марта 1917 года.

По гарнизону Петроградскаго Округа всѣмъ солдатамъ гвардіи, арміи, артиллеріи и флота для немедленнаго и точнаго исполненія, а рабочимъ Петрограда для свѣдѣнія.

Совѣтъ Рабочихъ и Солдатскихъ Депутатовъ постановилъ:

1) Во всѣхъ ротахъ, батальонахъ, полкахъ, паркахъ, батареяхъ, эскадронахъ и отдѣльныхъ службахъ разнаго рода военныхъ управленій и на судахъ военнаго флота немедленно выбрать комитеты изъ выборныхъ представителей отъ нижнихъ чиновъ вышеуказанныхъ воинскихъ частей.

2) Во всѣхъ воинскихъ частяхъ, которыя еще не выбрали своихъ представителей въ Совѣтъ Рабочихъ Депутатовъ, избрать по одному представителю отъ ротъ, которымъ и явиться съ письменными удостовѣреніями въ зданіе Государственной Думы къ 10 часамъ утра, 2-го сего марта.

3) Во всѣхъ своихъ политическихъ выступленіяхъ воинская часть подчиняется Совѣту Рабочихъ и Солдатскихъ Депутатовъ и своимъ комитетамъ.

4) Приказы военной комиссіи Государственной Думы слѣдуетъ исполнять только въ тѣхъ случаяхъ, когда они не противорѣчатъ приказамъ и постановленіямъ Совѣта Рабочихъ и Солдат. Депутатовъ.

5) Всякаго рода оружіе, какъ то: винтовки, пулеметы, бронированные автомобили и прочее должны находиться въ распоряженіи и подъ контролемъ ротныхъ и баталіонныхъ комитетовъ и ни въ коемъ случаѣ не выдаваться офицерамъ, даже по ихъ требованіямъ.

6) Въ строю и при отправленіи служебныхъ обязанностей солдаты должны соблюдать строжайшую воинскую дисциплину, но внѣ службы и строя, въ своей политической, общегражданской и частной жизни солдаты ни въ чемъ не могутъ быть умалены въ тѣхъ правахъ, коими пользуются всѣ граждане.

Въ частности, вставаніе во фронтъ и обязательное отданіе чести внѣ службы отмѣняется.

7) Равнымъ образомъ отмѣняется титулованіе офицеровъ: ваше превосходительство, благородіе и т. п., и замѣняется обращеніемъ: господинъ генералъ, господинъ полковникъ и т. д.

Грубое обращеніе съ солдатами всякихъ воинскихъ чиновъ и, въ частности, обращеніе къ нимъ на «ты», воспрещается и о всякомъ нарушеніи сего, равно какъ и о всѣхъ недоразумѣніяхъ между офицерами и солдатами, послѣдніе обязаны доводить до свѣдѣнія ротныхъ комитетовъ.

Настоящій приказъ прочесть во всѣхъ ротахъ, баталіонахъ, полкахъ, экипажахъ, батареяхъ и прочихъ строевыхъ и нестроевыхъ командахъ.

Петроградскій Совѣтъ Рабочихъ и Солдатскихъ Депутатовъ.

123. 'Order No. 1' of the Petrograd Soviet

'Order No. 1'

However, a much bigger problem was now facing the Provisional Government: the Russian army was in a state of disintegration. The peasants in uniform had lost their appetite for the hardships of trench warfare and the sight of blood. As mentioned, many simply deserted and returned home to work their land. The demoralisation at the front was compounded by the appalling lack of organisation, and the constant shortages of food, equipment and military supplies.

Worse still, the long-suffering soldiers were subjected to constant humiliation at the hands of arrogant officers, the pampered sons of the privileged classes. In 1915, the tsarist authorities, fearing the collapse of discipline in the army, reintroduced the cruel practice of punishment by flogging. This simply served to further embitter relations with the ordinary soldiers who yearned for an end to war and a parcel of land on which to work. This growing hatred among the troops was graphically expressed in the high, and rising, rate of desertions.

However, the revolution was having a dramatic effect on the armed forces. The question of democratic accountability over the military caste now became a burning issue in the ranks. In response, 'Order No. 1', was issued on 14 March (1 March, Old Style) by the Petrograd Soviet. Trotsky wrote that 'Order No. 1' was "the single worthy document of the February Revolution, a charter of the freedom of the revolutionary army".[33]

This Order granted a number of important rights to the ranks of all soldiers and sailors. These included the right to elect their own Soviet representatives and establish committees in the armed forces. All weapons would now be under the control of the regimental and battalion committees, and should "in no case be given up to the officer". The saluting off duty and titling of officers were abolished, and uncivil treatment of soldiers was forbidden. In other words, on duty, the strictest military discipline, but off duty, complete citizen's rights.

This decision transformed the role of the Soviet and tied the soldiers and sailors firmly to the revolution. The Order is therefore worth quoting in full:

Order No. 1

1 March 1917

To the garrison of the Petrograd area. To all soldiers of the guard, army, and artillery, and to the fleet for immediate and precise execution, and to the workers of Petrograd for their information.

The Soviet Workers' and Soldiers' Deputies has resolved:

1. Every company, battalion, regiment, depot, battery, squadron, branch of military administration and naval vessel shall immediately elect a committee of representatives of the lower ranks of the given unit.

2. All units of the armed forces, which have not yet elected their representatives to the Soviet of Workers' Deputies, shall elect one representative from each company, who shall present himself at the building of the State Duma with written credentials on the 2 March at 10 am.

3. In all their political actions military units shall obey the instructions of the Soviet of Workers' and Soldiers' Deputies and their own committees.

4. Orders of the Military Commission of the State Duma are to be obeyed only if they do not conflict with the orders and decisions of the Soviet of Workers' and Soldiers' Deputies.

5. Arms of all kinds, such as rifles, machine guns, armoured cars, etc. should be placed at the disposal and under the control of the company and battalion committees, and shall under no circumstances be issued to officers even on the demand of the latter.

6. Soldiers must observe strict military discipline when in military formation and when performing military duties, but when not performing military duties and when not in military formation – in their political, civil and private lives – soldiers may not be restricted in any of the rights enjoyed by all citizens.

    In particular, coming to attention and compulsory saluting when off-duty are abolished.

7. Similarly, officers titles, such as Your Excellency, Your Honour, etc. are abolished and are replaced by such forms of address as Mr general, Mr Colonel, etc.

Rudeness to soldiers on the part of officers and, in particular, addressing them in the second person singular is forbidden, and all infractions of this rule, as all misunderstandings between officers and soldiers in general, must be reported by the latter to the company committees.

This order shall be read in all companies, battalions and regiments on all ships, in all batteries and in all other combatant and non-combatant units.

[Signed] The Petrograd Soviet of Workers' and Soldiers' Deputies.[34]

Within days of 'Order No. 1' being introduced, under pressure from the General Staff, came the attempt to annul the first order with 'Order No. 2', but this was of no avail.

"Discipline declines daily", complained General Alekseyev, who saw 'Order No. 1' as a major part of the problem.[35] More correctly, it was the fact that war weariness and Bolshevik propaganda were having their effect. The soldiers simply did not want to fight.

This was the state of affairs just before the proposed offensive in June 1917. By any military standards, the Russian offensive was sheer folly. After an initial surge forward, the offensive collapsed. The bankruptcy of the Provisional Government and its war policies were exposed for all to see.

'We will assume power'

On 17 June, Lenin addressed the First All-Russian Congress of Soviets, attended by 1,000 delegates, in which the Bolshevik delegation numbered a little over 100. He made the uncompromising call for the Soviet majority to break with the capitalists and take power into its hands. This led to an altercation in the assembly. He stated that it had been a month since the new coalition had been formed with its 'near-socialist' ministers, but Russia was still faced with complete ruin.

Then, on the second day of the Congress, the new Menshevik Minister of Posts and Telegraphs, Tsereteli, delivered a speech in which he stated that there was no political party in Russia which could say that it was ready to assume full power. Lenin from his seat shouted out loudly: "There is. Our Party is ready to take over full power at any moment!" This announcement provoked applause from the left of the Soviet Congress and laughter and jeers from the right wing. Then Lenin stood up and addressed the Congress, in which he stated:

> He [Tsereteli] said there was no political party in Russia expressing its readiness to assume full power. I reply: "Yes, there is. No party can refuse this, and our Party certainly doesn't. It is ready to take over full power at any moment." (*Applause and laughter.*) You can laugh as much as you please, but if the Minister confronts us with this question side by side with a party of the Right, he will receive a suitable reply. No party can refuse this. [...] give us your confidence and we will give you our programme.

Lenin continued:

> With regard to the economic crisis, our programme is immediately – it need not be put off – to demand the publication of all the fabulous profits – running as high as 500 and 800 per cent – which the capitalists are making on war supplies, and not as capitalists in the open market under 'pure' capitalism. This is where workers' control really is necessary and possible. This is a measure which, if you call yourselves 'revolutionary' democrats, you should carry out in the name of the Congress, a measure which can be carried out overnight.

> It is not socialism. It is opening the people's eyes to the real anarchy and the real playing with imperialism, the playing with the property of the people, with the hundreds of thousands of lives that tomorrow will be lost because we continue to throttle Greece. Make the profits of the capitalists public, arrest fifty or a hundred of the biggest millionaires. Just keep them in custody for a few weeks, if only in the same privileged conditions in which Nicholas Romanov is being held, for the simple purpose of making them reveal the hidden springs, the fraudulent practices, the filth and greed which even under the new government are costing our country thousands and millions every day. That is the chief cause of anarchy and ruin. That is why we say that everything remains as of old, that the coalition government hasn't changed a thing and has only added a heap of declarations, of

pompous statements. However sincere people may be, however sincerely they may wish the working people well, things have not changed – *the same class* remains in power. The policy they are pursuing is not a democratic policy.[36]

Although the Bolsheviks were in a minority at the Congress, they received solid support from Trotsky, Lunacharsky and the ten delegates from the Mezhraiontsy throughout the three weeks of its proceedings.

Lenin still insisted that Russia was an exceptional case where a peaceful revolution was possible if the 'Compromisers' acted to take real power into their hands. But the ruling majority of Mensheviks and SRs, for fear of alienating their bourgeois allies, wanted nothing to do with such a programme.

Meanwhile, in Petrograd, the Bolsheviks were making consistent headway, with their numbers growing on a daily basis. In the workers' section of the Petrograd Soviet, a Bolshevik motion for transferring power to the Soviet was resoundingly passed. The same was true in the Petrograd garrison. As a result, the Bolsheviks called for a peaceful demonstration for 22 June, with the main slogans of: 'All power to the Soviets!', 'Down with the Ten Capitalist Ministers!', 'Workers' Control of Industry!' and 'Bread, Land and Peace!'

Several regiments in the capital announced their intention of joining the demonstration. This terrified the Menshevik-SR dominated Soviet Executive, which stepped in to ban the planned procession. The All-Russian Congress of Soviets then passed a resolution endorsing the ban on all street demonstrations, without exception, for three days, and another one condemning the provocative actions of the Bolsheviks. The reason given for the ban was the unsubstantiated claim that "concealed counter-revolutionaries want to take advantage of your demonstration", with a view of turning it into a confrontation.[37] But no facts were given to substantiate this claim.

The Menshevik and SR leaders were getting desperate. Under pressure from the bourgeoisie, the 'Compromisers' believed they had no alternative but to act against the Bolsheviks, who in any case were a constant thorn in their side. The official Menshevik paper hysterically declared: "It is high time to unmask the Leninists as criminals and traitors to the Revolution."[38] Tsereteli announced:

… what has taken place is nothing but a *conspiracy*, a conspiracy for the overthrow of the government and the seizure of power by the Bolsheviks, who know that they will never obtain power in any other way… Let the Bolsheviks not blame us if we now adopt other methods. Revolutionaries who cannot bear arms worthily should be deprived of arms. The Bolsheviks must be disarmed… Machine guns and rifles must not be left in their hands. We shall not tolerate conspiracies.[39]

This meant they were throwing down the gauntlet and preparing to wage a decisive blow against the revolutionary left, especially the Bolsheviks.

Tactical retreat

In response, the Bolsheviks, not wishing to go against the decision of the Soviet Congress, called off the demonstration and key Bolshevik speakers were dispatched to the factories to explain the decision. This retreat created problems for the Bolsheviks, but at least it served to hold the line. A member of the Vyborg Bolshevik Committee wrote: "we had to deploy a great deal of energy to calm the ruffled tempers."[40] Lenin recognised the disappointment, but under the circumstances, it was necessary to make a tactical retreat:

> Even in ordinary warfare, it sometimes happens that a planned offensive has to be cancelled for strategic reasons. This is all the more likely to occur in class warfare, depending on the vacillation of the middle, petty-bourgeois groups. We must be able to take account of the situation and be bold in adopting decisions.[41]

Then, two days later, the Soviet Congress decided to hold its own demonstration on 1 July, the day of the Russian military offensive. This, they thought, would allow the workers to display their patriotism as well as proof of the peoples' 'confidence' in the Provisional Government.

One day prior to the demonstration, Tsereteli announced: "Today we are not discussing plots hatched in some back parlour, but a test in the plain light of day. Tomorrow we shall see…"[42] The Soviet Executive Committee issued official slogans for the demonstration: 'Universal Peace', 'Immediate Convocation of a Constituent Assembly', and 'Democratic Republic'.

When the demonstration assembled, some half-a-million workers and soldiers answered the call in a massive display of strength. Petrograd was filled with working people, together with their banners and placards. However, to the utter shock of the Soviet 'Compromisers', the bulk of the demonstrators carried banners not with official slogans, but with Bolshevik ones: 'Down with the Ten Capitalist Ministers!', 'Down with the Offensive!', 'No separate peace with Germany, nor secret treaties with the Anglo-French capitalists!', 'Peace to the Hearth, War to the Castle!', and 'All power to the Soviets!'

The political tide had begun to turn. The subterranean mood among the masses had bubbled up to the surface, demonstrating a further shift to the left.

In May, Lenin replied to Maklakov, who had stated that as the government moved to the left, the 'country' moved to the right – by 'country' meaning 'the possessing classes'. Lenin stated on the contrary:

> … 'the country' of workers and poor peasants, I assure you, Citizen Maklakov, is a thousand times farther to the left than the Chernovs and Tseretelis, and a hundred times farther than we are.[43]

In making this observation, Lenin was reflecting the profound changes in the consciousness of the masses. He added: "The future will prove this to you."[44] This was soon proved to be entirely correct.

23. July Days

The 1 July demonstration proved to be a watershed. The advances made by the Bolsheviks graphically revealed the changed balance of forces in little more than three months following the February Revolution. According to *Novaya Zhizn*, the paper of Maxim Gorky, "the Sunday demonstration revealed the complete triumph of Bolshevism among the Petrograd proletariat and the garrison."[1]

"Every revolution, if it is a real revolution, amounts to a class shift", wrote Lenin.[2] And at this time, it was clear that a profound leftward shift was taking place in the psychology of the masses.

The massive outward display of support for Bolshevism took the Soviet Executive Committee completely by surprise. Their manoeuvre in calling their own demonstration had utterly backfired.

The Bolshevik success in the demonstration provoked a sharp reaction from the 'moderate' socialists, who immediately launched a ferocious attack on them, accusing Lenin of using the demonstration as a cover for an attempted coup d'état. They became hysterical and tried to blame the Bolsheviks for all their problems, representing them as a threat to the revolution itself. Tsereteli and other ministers charged the Bolsheviks with conspiracy. That was the signal for an all-out offensive against the Party.

This was the most serious situation ever faced by the Bolsheviks. Lenin responded boldly to the slanderers by declaring that the revolution was indeed in danger, but this was the result of the backsliding by the Mensheviks and SRs. He called on the working class to be vigilant.

At the beginning of July, social tensions increased still further as food shortages became more acute. Strikes hit Petrograd and the entire workforce of the Putilov factory of around 30,000 workers walked out. The mood began to affect the garrison. In response, the authorities began to transfer rebellious military units to the front. This only added petrol to the fire. Once again, the streets filled with demonstrations.

On 15 July, a further crisis hit the government as five Cadet ministers resigned in protest at concessions given to the Ukrainian Rada (parliament), which for them was the excuse to abandon the government.

If the Mensheviks and SRs had wished, they could have used the crisis to brush aside the other capitalist ministers and form a fully socialist government to consolidate their position. But instead, they preferred to continue to huddle together in a cosy coalition with the bourgeoisie. They hoped that the Cadets who had resigned would reconsider their hasty decision and, as honourable gentlemen, return to government.

This new crisis at the top served to stoke the fires of rebellion still further. The failure of the 'moderate' socialists to act added to the fury of those who swarmed into the streets. The 1st Machine-gun Regiment in Petrograd, sensing the mood, decided the time had come for a mass demonstration and called upon other military units to join them. Feelings were running high and the idea of armed action and even the overthrow of the government were being raised.

The Bolsheviks attempted to restrain the movement, fearing that it would lead to a premature showdown. However, they were unable to hold the Machine-gun Regiment back. The indignation of the soldiers was boiling over and the dam was about to break.

News of the ignominious collapse of Kerensky's offensive, launched on the same day as the July demonstration, further aroused the indignation of the capital. The government's talk of peace proved to be a sham, which also rebounded on the Executive Committee of the Soviets.

The situation was becoming critical. The Soviet Executive Committee, fearing the worst, once again ordered a ban on all demonstrations. However, given the situation, it was a ban that lacked any authority. This was followed by a banning order issued by General Polovtsev of the Petrograd Military District.

The Bolsheviks were in a very difficult position. Taking account of the balance of forces on a national scale, there could be no question of leading a successful insurrection against the government. On the other hand, the mood of the workers and sailors in Petrograd and Kronstadt had reached a point where the armed demonstration was now an inevitability.

124. Revolutionary sailors of battleship *Petropavlovsk* in Helsinki, summer 1917
The flag reads: "Death to the Bourgeois"

Lenin was away from Petrograd in Finland when the Bolsheviks were frantically discussing what should be done. Kamenev addressed the workers' section of the Petrograd Soviet: "We did not call the demonstration, but the masses themselves have come into the street, and once they have done so our place is among them. Our present task is to give the movement an organised character."[3]

The Bolsheviks therefore decided to go along with a demonstration that they were powerless to prevent, but at all costs to make sure it was peaceful and avoid a bloody collision.

Workers take to the streets

On the appointed day, tens of thousands of workers poured onto the streets of Petrograd, followed by hundreds of thousands of workers who flooded into the city. These were then joined by thousands of strikers from a string of factories. The feeling among the crowds became increasingly intense and extremely bitter against the Provisional Government.

The mutinous mood was openly displayed as machine guns were defiantly loaded onto trucks with placards on the sides bearing inscriptions, such as 'Let the Bourgeoisie Perish by Our Machine guns!' Once again, many of the 30,000 Putilov workers headed a march on the Palace, calling out factories and regiments on their way. They were followed by the Volhynian Regiment, then half the 180th Regiment and others followed suit. Huge crowds gathered outside the Bolshevik headquarters, at the Kshesinskaya, pressing the Party to take decisive action.

Lenin rushed back to Petrograd by the afternoon of 17 July. By this time, the Bolshevik building was surrounded by 10,000 revolutionary sailors from Kronstadt, mostly armed, looking for a lead from the Party, and demanding that Lenin speak to them. What was on his mind at this critical moment? He must have been conscious that a grave historical responsibility was weighing heavily on his shoulders.

The workers and sailors listening avidly to his every word wanted only one thing – to take power, not tomorrow or the day after, but right now. They eagerly awaited some word, some sign from their leader that this was also his wish. But far more difficult questions were occupying Lenin's thoughts. He knew what his audience did not know: that the moment for a decisive insurrection had not yet arrived; that there was no possibility of the workers taking power while the provinces still lagged behind.

Lenin must have realised that an armed insurrection in Petrograd had every possibility of success. But what then? If the workers and soldiers took power in the capital before the more backward provinces had enough time to draw all the necessary conclusions, Petrograd would be isolated.

And what of the soldiers at the front? They could be influenced by the lie that the Bolsheviks were German agents, *provocateurs*, enemies of the Revolution. The advanced guard in the capital could be attacked on all sides and massacred. Was it to be the fate of the Russian Revolution to enter the annals of history as just another heroic defeat, like the Paris Commune?

All these alarming thoughts must have crowded into Lenin's mind as he stepped out onto the balcony to address the expectant crowd in one of the most difficult and decisive speeches of his entire life. Hesitantly at first, weighing every word carefully, Lenin addressed the crowd.

Lenin began by expressing the need to fight for 'All Power to the Soviets'. So far, so good, the sailors must have thought. But they had not come here just to listen to general slogans and propaganda. And the words they were eagerly awaiting never came.

Lenin concluded his speech by calling on the sailors for restraint, steadfastness and vigilance. In other words, there was to be no armed insurrection, no arrests of ministers, no seizure of power!

125. Snipers opening fire on demonstrators on Nevsky Prospekt, Petrograd,
17 July 1917

The assembled workers and sailors listened respectfully, but they found it difficult to contain their disappointment and indignation. So this is all that the Bolsheviks have to offer: more empty words and phrases! Can we believe that they are just the same as all the others?

In order to provide the crowd with some kind of aim, Lunacharsky led the Kronstadters towards the city centre, while crowds of soldiers, sailors from Kronstadt and workers from Putilov made their way to the Tauride Palace, where the Soviet leaders were based, chanting 'All Power to the Soviets!'

The immediate danger had passed. But Lenin's fears proved to be justified. On the streets the situation had turned menacing as snipers opened fire on the demonstrators from rooftops on Nevsky Prospect. As a series of shots rang out, the demonstrators returned fire in self-defence and a gun battle ensued. There were rumours that hundreds were wounded and killed in a deliberate provocation to inflame the situation. Groups of workers began to break into houses and apartments to arrest suspects at random. The shootings were, in reality, a signal for the counter-revolution to move against the workers.

Just as Lenin had expected, the Executive Committee of the Soviet immediately seized the opportunity to call for loyal troops to be drafted into the capital under the pretext of disorder and anarchy on the streets. This was their only hope of putting an end to the demonstrations and 'restoring order'.

A large group of workers burst into the Tauride Palace. Mass meetings were taking place in the Catherine Hall. Such was the mood that the workers demanded to see the 'socialist' ministers. The Minister of Agriculture, Chernov, was sent out to pacify them, but they simply placed him under arrest. It took the intervention of Trotsky to finally release him.

One worker, armed with a rifle, burst into the main hall and confronted a meeting of the Executive Committee that was taking place. He bellowed:

Comrades, how long must we workers put up with this treachery? All of you are debating and making deals with the bourgeoisie and the landlords… You are simply betraying the working class.

Well then, let me tell you that the working class won't put up with it. There are 30 thousand workers all told here from the Putilov works. We are going to have our way. All power to the soviets! We have a firm grip on our rifles! Your Kerenskys and Tseretellis are not going to fool us![4]

Although Chkheidze, who chaired the meeting, was in a fluster, he managed to restore order and got the workers to withdraw. The crowd, fed up with waiting outside, eventually started to disperse. According to Sukhanov, the 'excesses' dissipated:

The blood and filth of this senseless day had had a sobering effect by evening, and evidently evoked a swift reaction. Nothing was heard of further demonstrations. The 'uprising' had definitely crumbled. There remained only the excesses of a wanton mob. There were some 400 killed and wounded.[5]

The Soviet sessions continued to meet into the evening. The speakers continued speaking as normal. As the Menshevik and SR leaders carried on with their deliberations, they suddenly heard the noise of heavy boots surrounding the building.

Fearing the worst, they were surprised that these troops were not coming to arrest them, as they thought, but to defend them. Suddenly, they all jumped for joy as the loyal regiments arrived. They could hardly contain themselves and started to sing the *Marseillaise*. The 14th Cavalry Division, the 14th Don Cossack Regiment, the 117th Izborsky Regiment and other units turned up to restore order in Petrograd and clear the streets of people.

In so doing, they would teach the workers a lesson. "A classic scene of the beginning of a counter-revolution!" exclaimed Martov, as the streets emptied and the forces of the armed counter-revolution took control of the capital.[6] The pendulum swung in the opposite direction.

At two o'clock in the morning of 18 July, a hastily convened meeting of the Bolshevik Central Committee resolved to call on the workers and soldiers to terminate the street demonstrations. But events had overtaken them.

'July Days' begin

With the troops at their back, the government now went onto the offensive and ordered the arrest of the Bolshevik leaders. On 18 July, the newspapers were full of stories of Lenin's treachery.

Thus began the July Days, the month of the great slander and repression of the revolutionary vanguard. The repression began with the unsubstantiated testimony, supplied by the Intelligence Service of the Russian General Staff, to 'prove' that Lenin was an agent, acting on behalf of the German military.

A document sent to Kerensky by an anonymous spy alleged that "military censorship has discovered a continuous exchange of telegrams of a political and financial nature between German agents and Bolshevik leaders." Raskolnikov recalls that "this crudely fabricated falsehood made me realise that what was hidden in it was a diabolical plan to blacken our Party morally and kill it politically."[7]

In a scandalous development, the accusations against the Bolsheviks as foreign agents were supported by none other than Plekhanov, who had travelled far to the right during the War, when he went over to the side of the most extreme social-patriotism. The old man, clearly motivated by spite against political opponents, wrote: "Apparently [!], the disruptions… were an integral part of a plan formulated by the foreign enemy to destroy Russia. Therefore stamping them out must be a constituent part of any plan for Russia's national defence." He concluded: "The revolution must crush everything in its way immediately, decisively, and mercilessly."[8]

Apart from Gorky's paper, the entire press was screaming for action against the Bolsheviks. Faced with a witch-hunt, they were driven underground. The Bolsheviks warned of a re-enactment of the Dreyfus frame-up.* Amid this

---

* The Dreyfus Affair began in 1894 when Captain Alfred Dreyfus, a Jewish officer, was convicted in a secret court martial of selling secrets to a foreign power, and sentenced to life on Devil's Island. This was a frame-up to protect another officer – a non-Jewish aristocrat – involving the General Staff. A scandal erupted that shook French society, pitting the army, clergy and aristocracy against the liberals led by Zola and the socialists

atmosphere of reactionary hysteria, military cadets and Cossacks broke in and ransacked the offices of *Pravda*, and its staff were beaten up and arrested.

In the attack, both *Pravda* and *Okopnaya Pravda* were shut down. Party members' homes were raided and searched, and a number of arrests were made. Armed detachments, complete with artillery, were sent to dislodge the Bolsheviks from their headquarters. The situation became so dangerous that they were forced to abandon the building. A new phase was now opening up as the revolution gave way to counter-revolution.

On the night of 18 July, following the orchestrated hysteria, the Bolsheviks' offices were wrecked. With *Pravda* now banned, they tried to produce a paper under another name, but that was also closed down. The Bolshevik organisation, under this rain of hammer blows, was in disarray. Party speakers, attempting to rally the workers, were beaten up, while their meetings attracted no more than a few hundred people. They were denounced as traitors to the revolution and hunted down like common criminals. "An immense torrent of abuse and slander is being poured on the Bolsheviks", wrote Lenin.[9] Kerensky announced:

> [Our] fundamental task is the defence of the country from ruin and anarchy. My government will save Russia, and if the motives of reason, honour, and conscience prove inadequate, it will beat her into unity with blood and iron.[10]

The British Ambassador, Sir George Buchanan, transmitted his feelings to the Minister of Foreign Affairs, Tereshchenko, of what should be done:

1. Re-establish the death penalty throughout Russia for all individuals subject to military and naval law.

2. Require all units who took part in the unlawful demonstration of the 16 and 17 [New Style] to give up agitators.[11]

The counter-revolution was baring its teeth. The July demonstrations were completely crushed and the Bolsheviks were driven underground, as hundreds of members, including sympathisers, were arrested or forced into hiding. Workers were being systematically disarmed by the loyalist forces and Kerensky called for the Bolshevik Party to be outlawed.

However, the 'left' parties were fearful of going that far. Nevertheless, the Menshevik Tsereteli, as newly appointed Minister of the Interior, took the lead in the repression against the Bolsheviks and their supporters. The

---

led by Jaurès. At its peak, Waldeck-Rousseau headed a government to pardon Dreyfus to "defend the Republic" and defuse the situation. Dreyfus was finally released from prison in 1899 and fully vindicated in 1906.

Executive Committee of the Soviet, caught up in the hysteria, fell into line and backed the witch-hunt.

The events provoked another government shake-up, with Prince Lvov stepping down as premier. On 21 July, the government was reorganised and Kerensky became Prime Minister, while retaining his post as Minister of War. This second coalition, unlike the first, was now made up of a majority of 'moderate' socialists, 'Compromisers', most of whom were from the right wing of their parties. They regarded themselves more as government statesmen than anything else.

One of the first measures announced by Kerensky was to re-introduce the death penalty at the front for "certain major crimes committed by men on military duty…"[12] He also ordered the disarming of the workers' militia, the Red Guards. The government was regarded by reactionaries and 'moderates' alike as a "government of the salvation of the revolution", and salvation lay in the destruction of the Bolsheviks.[13]

To begin with, the Mensheviks and SRs demanded the Bolshevik Soviet deputies repudiate their leaders, but this was rejected out of hand. The bourgeoisie, boosted by the repression, demanded that the government go much further. The reactionary bourgeois paper, *Novoye Vremya*, goaded the Mensheviks and SRs, demanding that they should take "decisive steps to dissociate themselves from criminal Bolshevism and to place themselves above the suspicion of according comradely protection to Lenin." In this way, they became direct accomplices of the counter-revolution.

Lenin hunted

The Soviet Executive Committee, in turn, bent over backwards to appease the reactionaries by characterising the July movement as "an adventurous, abortive armed uprising" organised by "anarcho-Bolshevik elements."[14] In the days that followed, the Public Prosecutor in Petrograd charged the leading Bolsheviks, including Lenin, with treason and being the ring leaders of an armed uprising. All the hatred of the ruling classes was now focused on Lenin.

In the middle of this turmoil, Lenin met Trotsky in the Tauride Palace. "Now they will shoot us all", said Lenin, "for them [it] is the best moment."[15] Buchanan wrote in his memoirs:

> The government had suppressed the Bolshevik rising and seemed at last determined to act with firmness… On my calling on him a few days later, Tereshchenko assured me that the government was now completely master of the situation.[16]

Fearing for Lenin's life, the Bolshevik leaders persuaded him to go into hiding. There was no way under such conditions that he would get a fair trial. In fact, it is likely that he would have been shot before any trial, 'trying to escape', as in the case of the murder of Rosa Luxemburg and Karl Liebknecht in 1919. General Polovtsev confirmed this very idea in his memoirs:

> The officer who set out for Terijoki in the hope of catching Lenin asked me whether I wanted this gentleman delivered whole or in pieces... I smiled and said that arrested men often attempted to escape.[17]

Zinoviev also went into hiding, but Kamenev was arrested on 25 July, as well as Lunacharsky ten days later. Trotsky issued an 'Open Letter' to the Provisional Government, expressing his solidarity with the Bolsheviks:

> I understand that you have decreed the arrest... of Comrades Lenin, Zinoviev, Kamenev, but that the writ of arrest does not concern me. I therefore think it necessary to bring these facts to your attention:
>
> 1. I share in principle the attitude of Lenin, Zinoviev, and Kamenev, and I have expounded it in the journal *Vperyod* and in all my public speeches.
>
> 2. My attitude towards the events of 3 and 4 July [16 and 17, New Style] was uniform with that of the above-mentioned Comrades.[18]

The government could not afford to ignore such an effrontery and Trotsky was duly arrested on 23 July, charged with receiving German money and transferred to the Kresty Prison. In fact, in 1915, instead of giving him any money, a German military tribunal had sentenced Trotsky in his absence to several months of imprisonment for revolutionary activities. He would remain in the Kresty until he was freed on bail to help against the attempted coup by General Kornilov.

At first, Lenin changed hiding places five times in three days to evade capture. He stayed first with the 'old Bolshevik' SY Alliluyev, but then moved outside of Petrograd. Soon afterwards, he fled to Sestroretsk, where he remained until 22 August and then moved to the Finnish village of Jalkala. Afterwards, along with Zinoviev, he moved across the border to Helsinki.

'Virtually a military dictatorship'

To begin with, Lenin drew the conclusion that the counter-revolution had completely taken over the state and the Bolshevik Party would be forced to operate underground for quite a long period. "At present, basic state power in Russia is virtually a military dictatorship", he wrote.[19] "All hopes for a

126. Lenin in disguise for his false passport to flee to Finland

peaceful development of the Russian revolution have vanished for good."[20] He went on:

> The slogan 'All Power to the Soviets!' was a slogan for peaceful development of the revolution which was possible in April, May, June, and up to 5-9 July, i.e. up to the time when actual power passed into the hands of the military dictatorship.

> This slogan is no longer correct, for it does not take into account that power has changed hands and that the revolution has in fact been completely betrayed by the SRs and Mensheviks.[21]

In the first half of 1917, Lenin and the Bolsheviks stressed the idea of a peaceful revolution in Russia. If power had been transferred to the Soviets, as they argued, then he explained:

> … the struggle of classes and parties within the Soviets could have assumed a most peaceful and painless form, provided full state power had passed to the Soviets in good time.

> That would have been the easiest and the most advantageous course for the people. This course would have been the least painful, and it was therefore necessary to fight for it most energetically.[22]

But that time had now passed, the turning point being the repression on 17-18 July. "A peaceful course of development has become impossible", he explained. "A non-peaceful and most painful course has begun."[23] Lenin believed that the power which had fallen into the hands of the Cavaignacs* could now only be overturned by force. "The present soviets have failed", he wrote. "… they are like sheep brought to the slaughterhouse, bleating pitifully under the knife."[24]

Given the treacherous role played by the reformist leadership of the Soviets, Lenin came to the conclusion that the slogan 'All Power to the Soviets' should be abandoned and replaced with 'All Power to the Factory Committees'. Under the leadership of the Mensheviks and SRs, the Soviets had now become obstacles to the revolution, whereas the factory committees were far closer to, and more representative of, the working class. It was also where the Bolsheviks had their greatest influence.

The slogan of 'All Power to the Factory Committees' was retained by the Bolsheviks up until late August, when Kornilov's attempted coup breathed new life into the Soviets. At that point, the Bolsheviks reverted to their original slogan.

'The State and Revolution'

It was an extremely difficult time for Bolshevism, with the Party driven underground, Lenin in hiding and other leaders in prison. It was from Finland that he helped direct the Party and took the opportunity to write *The State and Revolution*.

---

* Louis-Eugène Cavaignac was a reactionary French general who crushed the Parisian workers uprising in June 1848 and headed the counter-revolutionary government in France from June to December 1848.

He had gathered together notes on the state during the war, with the intention, when time permitted, of writing something substantial in defence of Marx and Engels' views on the state. Just before he left Switzerland, on 17 February 1917, he wrote to Kollontai from Zurich: "I am preparing (have almost got the material ready) an article on the question of the attitude of Marxism to the state."[25] These were the extensive notes which he used to complete *The State and Revolution* during August and September 1917.

It was this question of the state, above all, that separated the Marxists from the reformists and revisionists. Marxism views the question historically. The state, defined as 'armed bodies of men' in defence of private property, came into being as society divided into classes. It was an arbiter of power that stood above the classes, balancing between them, so as to keep the class struggle within safe bounds. However, as the state, in the final analysis, represented the interests of the ruling class, the working class could not simply take over and use the old bourgeois state machine for its own ends. The capitalist state could not be reformed, but needed to be smashed and replaced with a new state, a workers' state.

Unlike previous states, this workers' state would be a semi-state, which, with the development of the productive forces and the withering away of class antagonisms, would itself begin to wither away. For Lenin, in 1917, the embryo of the workers' state was represented by the Soviets, which, as mentioned, had parallels with the Paris Commune.

Lenin regarded his work on the state as so important that during the July Days, when things were very precarious, he wrote the following confidential note to Kamenev in the event of his murder:

Comrade Kamenev,

Entre nous: if they do me in, I ask you to publish my notebook: 'Marxism on the State' (it got left behind in Stockholm). It's bound in a blue cover. It contains a collection of all the quotations from Marx and Engels, likewise from Kautsky against Pannekoek. There are a number of remarks and notes, and formulations. I think it could be published after a week's work. I believe it to be important, because not only Plekhanov but also Kautsky has bungled things. The condition: all this is absolutely *entre nous*![26]

Fortunately, Lenin was not murdered and he managed to retrieve these notes and write the book. He intended to write a further chapter, 'The Experience of the Russian Revolutions of 1905 and 1917', but he had no time to do so due to the advent of the October Revolution. "It is more pleasant and useful", he explained with a touch of humour, "to go through the 'experience of the revolution' than to write about it."[27]

Demands to answer the critics

The crisis of Russia was growing ever-more severe as factories closed and economic life ground to a halt. Transport had become increasingly dislocated and paralysed, meaning that fuel was in desperately short supply. This, in turn, led to food shortages and longer bread queues. Lenin responded to this emergency situation with a programme in his pamphlet, *The Impending Catastrophe and How to Combat It.* He began by explaining the objective situation:

> Unavoidable catastrophe is threatening Russia. The railways are incredibly disorganised and the disorganisation is progressing. The railways will come to a standstill. The delivery of raw materials and coal to the factories will cease. The delivery of grain will cease. The capitalists are deliberately and unremittingly sabotaging (damaging, stopping, disrupting, hampering) production, hoping that an unparalleled catastrophe will mean the collapse of the republic and democracy, and of the Soviets and proletarian and peasant associations generally, thus facilitating the return to a monarchy and the restoration of the unlimited power of the bourgeoisie and the landowners.
>
> The danger of a great catastrophe and of famine is imminent. All the newspapers have written about this time and again. A tremendous number of resolutions have been adopted by the parties and by the Soviets of Workers', Soldiers' and Peasants' Deputies – resolutions which admit that a catastrophe is unavoidable, that it is very close, that extreme measures are necessary to combat it, that 'heroic efforts' by the people are necessary to avert ruin, and so on.
>
> Everybody says this. Everybody admits it. Everybody has decided it is so.
>
> Yet nothing is being done.
>
> Six months of revolution have elapsed. The catastrophe is even closer. [...] We are nearing ruin with increasing speed. The war will not wait and is causing increasing dislocation in every sphere of national life.[28]

With this economic catastrophe, Lenin outlined a set of concrete measures, transitional demands, that should be fought for by the working class to resolve the crisis:

> These principal measures are:

1. Amalgamation of all banks into a single bank, and state control over its operations, or nationalisation of the banks.

2. Nationalisation of the syndicates, i.e. the largest, monopolistic capitalist associations (sugar, oil, coal, iron and steel, and other syndicates).

3. Abolition of commercial secrecy.

4. Compulsory syndication (i.e. compulsory amalgamation into associations) of industrialists, merchants and employers generally.

5. Compulsory organisation of the population into consumers' societies, or encouragement of such organisation, and the exercise of control over it.[29]

This programme represented a call to action for the masses to take control of the situation, which, in turn, raised the question of power in society. The demands constituted a concrete plan to tackle the deteriorating situation, which served as a bridge to the socialist revolution.

While engaged in this struggle, the workers and poor peasants would see through the ineffective policies offered by the Mensheviks and SRs, and come to understand the need for bold measures to end capitalism. This transitional approach was a break from the old 'minimum' and 'maximum' programmes of the Social-Democracy, which divorced the immediate demands from the socialist revolution. Its whole approach showed the difference between that of piecemeal reformism and revolution, as Lenin explained:

> This reveals with great clarity the fact that the Socialist-Revolutionaries and Mensheviks have betrayed the people and the revolution, and that the Bolsheviks are becoming the real leaders of the masses, *even* of the Socialist-Revolutionary and Menshevik masses.
>
> For only the winning of power by the proletariat, headed by the Bolshevik Party, can put an end to the outrageous actions of Kerensky and Co. and *restore* the work of democratic food distribution, supply and other organisations, which Kerensky and his government are *frustrating*.[30]

Following the repression of the July Days, the Bolsheviks began to recover from the blows of reaction. "Arrests of our comrades were still taking place", wrote Raskolnikov, who had himself been arrested.[31] "But there was no depression in Party circles. On the contrary, everyone was looking ahead hopefully, reckoning that the repressions would only strengthen our Party's popularity and, in the end, work to the advantage of the revolution."[32]

Sixth Party Congress

The revival of Bolshevism was revealed at the Sixth Party Congress, held between 8-16 August, when the recorded membership of the Party had risen to around 240,000, triple the size of the April figure. The number of party organisations had grown from seventy-eight to 162, which was more than double. In Petrograd, the Party now had more than 40,000 members. According to Sverdlov's report, the Party had forty-one newspapers with a circulation of 320,000.

This was the first Party Congress ever held inside Russia and was attended by some 157 delegates, and a further 110 with voice but no vote. Krupskaya states: "The Sixth Congress welded the forces of the Bolsheviks still closer."[33]

Krupskaya only managed to write a single paragraph about this Congress, presumably because all the main leaders were absent. This semi-illegal gathering, which met in two working-class districts, was held amid great tension, as there were rumours about Kerensky being on the verge of dispersing the Congress. In reality, entering the Vyborg District would have proved too risky for the government.

After some opposition was raised by V Volodarsky and Mikhail Lashevich, who favoured Lenin appearing in court, the Congress unanimously endorsed the decision that it was correct for Lenin to go into hiding. The delegates then sent comradely greetings to "Lenin, Trotsky, Zinoviev, Lunacharsky, Kamenev, Kollontai and all other arrested and persecuted comrades..." All those who were named were then elected to the Congress's honorary presidium, with Lenin as its honorary chairman.

Although Lenin was not present, he had been heavily involved in its preparations and wrote all the drafts of the key resolutions, including 'The Political Situation' and *On Slogans*. The main point was to guide the Party from the perspective of a peaceful transformation of the Soviets to one of preparing for armed insurrection. The Soviets had abdicated their role and the period of dual power had been squandered. Nevertheless, even then, the Bolsheviks would not abandon the Soviets but still work within them, while also working towards an uprising.

The Congress also underlined the need to participate in the trade unions as well as the importance of winning the youth. This entailed the establishment of 'Youth Leagues':

Congress considers it one of the urgent tasks of the moment to secure the assistance of the class-conscious Socialist organisations of the young workers, and charges the Party organisations to devote the maximum possible attention to this work.[34]

With Lenin, Trotsky, Zinoviev and the other leading comrades in hiding or in prison, the main reports were given by Bukharin, Stalin and Sverdlov.

It was at this Congress that Trotsky and the 4,000 strong Mezhraiontsy formally joined the Bolshevik Party, which introduced a layer of important cadres to its ranks, such as Lunacharsky, Adolph Joffe, Konstantin Yurenev, Moisei Uritsky and Volodarsky. A note in the first edition of Lenin's *Collected Works* described the Mezhraiontsy in the following terms:

> On the war question, the Mezhraiontsy held an internationalist position and in their tactics they were close to the Bolsheviks.
>
> Among the leaders of the Mezhraiontsy there were a number of people destined to play a central role in the October Revolution and the Soviet regime following it: Trotsky, Lunacharsky, Joffe, Uritsky, Yurenev, Riazanov, Karakhan, Manuilsky and others.[35]

Lenin wrote the following:

> It goes without saying that from among the Mezhraiontsy who have been hardly tested in proletarian work in our Party's *spirit*, no one would contest the candidature of, say, Trotsky, for, first, upon his arrival, Trotsky at once took up an internationalist stand; second, he worked among the Mezhraiontsy for a merger; third, in the difficult July days he proved himself equal to the task and a loyal supporter of the Party of the revolutionary proletariat. Clearly, as much cannot be said about many of the new Party members entered on the list.[36]

The Congress elected a new Central Committee of twenty-one members and ten candidate members. Only the names of the four members elected who received the highest votes were announced: Lenin (133 votes, out of a possible 134), Zinoviev (132), Trotsky (131), and Kamenev (131).

In the three-page-long note in Lenin's current *Collected Works* dealing with the Sixth Congress, edited by the Stalinists, there is no mention whatsoever of the Mezhraiontsy or the fusion. Of those names recorded as elected to the Central Committee, Zinoviev, Trotsky and Kamenev, who had the highest votes along with Lenin, are missing.[37]

Events continued to move rapidly, but the repression continued. Support for the Mensheviks and SRs abruptly fell. A decisive shift was taking place. In government circles, the counter-revolution had emboldened Kerensky, who suddenly developed even greater dictatorial ambitions. As Claude Anet, the French journalist, put it:

> He sits in the imperial box, he lives in the Winter Palace or at Tsarskoe Selo. He sleeps in the bed of Russian emperors. A little too much vanity and vanity a little too conspicuous; that is shocking a country which is the simplest in the world.[38]

This made him an attractive figure to the forces of the bourgeoisie, who were looking for a 'strong man'. But he was considered to be too close to the Soviets, and with the failure of the military offensive, others developed the taste for an even stronger military figure to head an iron dictatorship so as to crush the Soviets and restore order.

Kornilov's coup

There was no shortage of other aspiring candidates for the role of 'dictator'. But when General Kornilov was appointed Supreme Commander, the search for the strong man ended. He suited the part perfectly. He demanded the death penalty not only at the front, but also in the rear. He was not renowned for his intellect, and, according to General Alekseyev, Kornilov was "a man with a lion's heart and the brain of a sheep."[39] According to General Brusilov, who knew Kornilov: "He would make a chief of a dashing partisan band – nothing more."[40] In other words, he was an ideal candidate for the role of a counter-revolutionary hangman.

Attempts by the Petrograd Soviet to dismiss Kornilov were met with threats of armed rebellion from the General Staff. Instead, Kerensky organised a Moscow State Conference to generate support for himself and his government. Everyone was present, from the far left to the far right – apart from the Bolsheviks, who boycotted the charade. For good measure, General Kornilov, encouraged by the military, decided to make an appearance. He became the star of the show. The wife of the millionaire Morozov fell on her knees, fainting before Kornilov. Showing how far he had travelled politically, Peter Struve declared that Kornilov was an 'honest man' and that he was prepared to lay down his life in Kornilov's defence. The Cadet Kodichev greeted him with the words: "All of us, all Moscow, are united by our faith in you."[41]

Kornilov was determined to put the 'democrats' out of their misery. Behind the scenes, he planned to establish an open military dictatorship, supported by the landlords and capitalists, and, of course, the military and the Allied Powers. "It is high time we seized all these German agents and spies with

127. General Kornilov

Lenin at their head", Kornilov confided to his chief aide, General Lukomsky. "And for the rest, we shall hit this Soviet of workers and soldiers so hard that it will never dare to come out again."[42]

He decided to entrust his sidekick, General Krymov, with the honourable task of hanging all the members of the Petrograd Soviet. The July Days set everything in train. Now the time had come for 'Order' and the jackboot. This, of course, meant the elimination of the Soviets and the miserable 'socialist' crowd composing the Provisional Government.

Kerensky, dubbed 'the little Napoleon', was well aware of Kornilov's plan to deal with the workers of Petrograd, but he baulked at the overthrow of the Provisional Government, with himself at the head. Two dictators in Russia would not do. So Kerensky demanded the General's resignation, which Kornilov, of course, steadfastly refused. Kornilov then began his rebellion. The Cadet ministers within Kerensky's government, as good 'democrats', immediately pledged their support for the General. Kornilov also claimed the backing of the Allies and the General Staff. With such support, at the end of August, he pursued his attack on Petrograd to crush the Bolshevik Party and destroy the Soviet. "All my sympathies were with Kornilov", writes Buchanan, the British Ambassador.[43]

However, the General's coup did not go as planned. Realising the mortal danger, the Soviet All-Russian Executive Committee passed a resolution calling for a 'Committee of Struggle Against the Counter-revolution'. However, the 'Compromiser' socialists realised that there could be no effective resistance without the Bolsheviks' full participation. They had no alternative but to reluctantly invite the Bolsheviks to join the 'Committee of Struggle', which they eagerly accepted, on one condition – that the workers were armed.

As a result, armed squads were established everywhere and millions of leaflets were distributed among the general population calling for resistance. With their revolutionary approach, the Bolsheviks soon spearheaded the whole operation, changing its name to 'Committee of Revolutionary Defence'. Under their pressure, the workers were armed and the Red Guards re-established. Within days, 25,000 armed workers joined the fight against Kornilov.

The Bolsheviks appealed to the masses to take action and the counter-revolution faced problems at the outset. Party speakers were mobilised in all the districts of Petrograd. As a result, railway workers sabotaged part of the train lines and paralysed troop movements.

The next day, workers from Petrograd fraternised with Kornilov's soldiers, who were immobilised, sowing doubts and exposing the lies of their commanders. Every division that was sent against them was met by revolutionary agitators and propaganda. Sukhanov states:

> That same night and early morning the Bolsheviks had begun to display a feverish activity in the workers' districts. Their military apparatus organised mass-meetings in all the barracks. Everywhere instructions were given, and obeyed, to remain under arms, ready to advance. By and large Smolensk was meeting Kornilov with all its lights blazing.[44]

Defending Kerensky?

Quite a number of Bolsheviks, however, felt uneasy about defending Kerensky and his government. A delegation of Kronstadt sailors visited Trotsky in prison to complain about having to fight Kornilov on behalf of Kerensky. But Trotsky argued it was important to defeat Kornilov first, and then deal with Kerensky later. Lenin wrote to the Central Committee, which summed up his thinking:

> It is possible that these lines will come too late, for events are developing with a rapidity that sometimes makes one's head spin. [...]
>
> The Kornilov revolt is a most unexpected (unexpected at such a moment and in such a form) and downright unbelievably sharp turn in events.
>
> Like every sharp turn, it calls for a revision and change of tactics. And as with every revision, we must be extra cautious not to become unprincipled.[45]

Lenin was resolutely opposed to any *political* bloc with the Provisional Government. However, he explained:

> *Even now* we must not support Kerensky's government. This is unprincipled. We may be asked: aren't we going to fight against Kornilov? Of course we must! But this is not the same thing; there is a dividing line here, which is being stepped over by some Bolsheviks who fall into compromise and allow themselves to be *carried away* by the course of events.
>
> We shall fight, we are fighting against Kornilov, *just as* Kerensky's *troops do*, but we do not support Kerensky. *On the contrary*, we expose his weakness. There is the difference. It is rather a subtle difference, but it is highly essential and must not be forgotten. [...]
>
> We shall not overthrow Kerensky right now. We shall approach the task of fighting against him *in a different way*, namely, we shall point out to the people (who are fighting against Kornilov) Kerensky's *weakness and vacillation*. That has been done in the past *as well*. Now, however, it has become the *all-important* thing and this constitutes the change.
>
> The change, further, is that the *all-important* thing now has become the intensification of our campaign for some kind of 'partial demands' to be presented to Kerensky: arrest Milyukov, arm the Petrograd workers, summon the Kronstadt, Vyborg and Helsingfors troops to Petrograd, dissolve the Duma, arrest Rodzianko, legalise the transfer of the landed estates to the peasants, introduce workers' control over grain and factories, etc., etc.[46]

Lenin continued:

> We must present these demands not only to Kerensky, and *not so much* to Kerensky, as to the workers, soldiers and peasants who have been *carried away* by the course of the struggle against Kornilov. We must keep up their *enthusiasm*, encourage

them to deal with the generals and officers who have declared for Kornilov, urge *them* to demand the immediate transfer of land to the peasants, suggest to *them* that it is necessary to arrest Rodzianko and Milyukov, dissolve the Duma, close down *Rech* and other bourgeois papers, and institute investigations against them. The 'Left' SRs must be especially urged on in this direction.[47]

Lenin went on to explain the need for a *united front* and a revolutionary war against Kornilov:

It would be wrong to think that we have moved farther away from the task of the proletariat winning power. No. We have come very close to it, *not directly*, but from the side. *At the moment* we must campaign not so much directly against Kerensky, as *indirectly* against him, namely, by demanding a more and more active, truly revolutionary war against Kornilov. The development of this war alone can lead *us* to power, but we must *speak* of this as little as possible in our propaganda (remembering very well that even tomorrow events may put power into our hands, and then we shall not relinquish it). It seems to me that this should be passed on in a letter (not in the papers) to the propagandists, to groups of agitators and propagandists, and to Party members in general. We must relentlessly fight against phrases about the defence of the country, about a united front of revolutionary democrats, about supporting the Provisional Government, etc., etc., since they are just empty *phrases*. We must say: now is the time for *action*; you SR and Menshevik gentlemen have long since worn those phrases threadbare. Now is the time for *action*; the war against Kornilov must be conducted in a revolutionary way, by drawing the masses in, by arousing them, by inflaming them (Kerensky is *afraid* of the masses, *afraid* of the people). In the war against the Germans, *action* is required right now; *immediate and unconditional peace must be offered* on *precise* terms. If this is done, either a speedy peace *can* be attained or the war can be turned into a revolutionary war; if not, all the Mensheviks and Socialist-Revolutionaries remain lackeys of imperialism.[48]

Like the emperor without clothes, Kornilov very soon found himself without an army. The soldiers had deserted him, infected by the skilful propaganda and fraternisation of the Bolsheviks. Very quickly, the Kornilov coup collapsed like a house of cards.

Quite predictably, Kerensky and the Provisional Government treated the counter-revolutionaries with kid gloves. Kornilov was sentenced to house arrest in the south of Russia until the Bolsheviks took power, and he immediately went over to the White Army. General Krymov, on the other hand, shot himself. At the General Headquarters, Generals Denikin, Martov,

Lukomsky, Romanovsky and others, who had openly supported Kornilov, were arrested by the orders of the army committees. The Red Guards also arrested a number of conspirators, some of whom were shot.

New lease on life

The revolution was given a new lease of life by the attempted coup. The Provisional Government had become increasingly exposed as impotent. The mood changed rapidly as the support for the Bolsheviks dramatically increased, while that of the Mensheviks and SRs rapidly declined. The masses had their eyes opened and were learning quickly from the experience of the counter-revolution. As Marx once aptly explained, the revolution sometimes needs the whip of the counter-revolution to drive it forward.

Out of this whole experience, the Soviets filled out and once again grew in authority. The shift in mood resulted in the Bolsheviks winning majorities not only in the Soviets, but also in the elections to the borough and city councils.

The Baltic Fleet, based at Kronstadt, also came out overwhelmingly in favour of the Bolsheviks. By September, the membership of the Bolshevik Party rose to around 400,000, as Bolshevik propagandists toured the country, speaking to eager audiences in the factories and barracks.

The Petrograd Soviet, now under Bolshevik control, had created a Red Guard, which began the systematic arming of the workers. Soon the Red Guard and the Petrograd garrison would be united in October under the command of the Soviet's Military Revolutionary Committee.

Despite the growing support for Bolshevism, Lenin, even at this late hour, made a compromise offer to the Mensheviks and SRs to ensure a peaceful transfer of power through the Soviets. He underlined the point:

> Now, and only now, perhaps *during only a few days* or a week or two, such a government could be set up and consolidated in a perfectly peaceful way. In all probability it could secure the peaceful *advance* of the whole Russian revolution, and provide exceptionally good chances for great strides in the world movement towards peace and the victory of socialism.
>
> In my opinion, the Bolsheviks, who are partisans of world revolution and revolutionary methods, may and should consent to this compromise only for the sake of the revolution's peaceful development – an opportunity that is *extremely* rare in history and *extremely* valuable, an opportunity that only occurs once in a while.[49]

So Lenin's position is quite clear. He pledged that once a government exclusively responsible to the Soviets was formed, "the revolution would proceed peacefully and party strife in the Soviets would be *peacefully overcome* thanks to really complete freedom of propaganda and to the immediate establishment of a new democracy in the composition of the Soviets (new elections) and in their functioning."[50]

He concluded: "Perhaps this is *already* impossible? Perhaps. But if there is even one chance in a hundred, the attempt at realising this opportunity is still worth while."[51] Again, Lenin stressed: "The Bolsheviks will do *everything* to secure this *peaceful* development of the revolution."[52] He reiterated: "Our business is to help get everything possible done to make sure the 'last' chance for a peaceful development of the revolution…"[53] Once again, at the end of September, he repeated the offer:

> By seizing power, the Soviets could still today – and this is probably their last chance – ensure the peaceful development of the revolution, peaceful elections of deputies, by the people, and a peaceful struggle of parties inside the Soviets; they could test the programmes of the various parties in practice and power could pass peacefully from one party to another.[54]

By early September, Trotsky, who had been released from prison on bail, now led the Bolsheviks in the Petrograd Soviet. On a vote of confidence, the old leadership of Mensheviks and SRs was defeated and the Soviet passed into the hands of the Bolsheviks, supported by the Left SRs* and Mensheviks-Internationalists. Following a decision of the Central Committee, Trotsky was elected as President of the Petrograd Soviet, a post that he had occupied in 1905.

The Bolsheviks also gained victories in the Moscow Soviet on 5 September, followed by Kiev, Kazan, Baku, Nikolaiev, Krasnoyarsk and a host of others. For the Bolsheviks, winning both capitals was decisive. This pushed Lenin towards the idea that the Soviets should immediately take power with the aid of an insurrection.

In the meantime, those in the camp of bourgeois 'democracy' tried to rally what was left of their forces in the form of a 'Democratic Conference'. This renamed itself as the 'Pre-Parliament', which became another talking shop. This time, the left parties participated, including the Bolsheviks. The Mensheviks and SRs believed this body was 'the voice of the people', until the creation of the Constituent Assembly. Lenin was, however, vehemently

---

* By this time, the SRs had split into two parties, between left and right.

opposed to this participation, seeing it as a dangerous distraction, as the masses were weary of such delays and vacillations. In the end, he had been overruled by the leadership on this question. "The Party allowed itself to be diverted, for the time being, into the trap of a despicable talking-shop", stated Lenin.[55]

Pre-Parliament walk-out

For Lenin, the question of participation in this Pre-Parliament was linked to the question of the insurrection. If insurrection was to be seriously prepared, then participation in this talking shop was clearly wrong. Everything for Lenin was subordinated to the insurrection. When Lenin heard of Trotsky's firm opposition to participation in the Pre-Parliament, he was full of admiration. "Trotsky was for the boycott", he wrote. "Bravo, Comrade Trotsky!"[56]

Following a Central Committee, where only Kamenev and Rykov were opposed to a boycott, Trotsky carried the day and led a dramatic walkout from the Pre-Parliament. He read out the following statement:

> We, the Bolshevik faction of the Social Democratic Party, announce that we have nothing in common with this government of treason to the people and with this council of counter-revolutionary connivance. We have nothing in common with that murderous intrigue against the people which is being conducted behind the official scenes. We refuse to shield it either directly or indirectly for a single day.[57]

He ended with the words: "Long live an immediate, honest, democratic peace! All power to the Soviets, all land to the people! Long live the constituent assembly!"[58]

This stand delighted Lenin, who now had all his thoughts directed towards power. But, still in hiding, he was very much reduced to writing. Following on from *The State and Revolution*, he wrote another important pamphlet called *Can the Bolsheviks Retain State Power?* This was aimed at the sceptics, including those within the Bolshevik leadership, who lacked confidence in the working class' ability to run society. Of course, he explained, there would be problems and challenges, and that was inevitable, but these could be overcome.

We are not Utopians, Lenin used to say. Mistakes would be made, but we would learn from them. The new workers' state would draw on the initiative and talent of the proletariat, and, with training and confidence in their ability, they would succeed. It was time to reject the wailings of the bourgeoisie, explained Lenin, and place our confidence in the oppressed class.

With the Bolsheviks now in a majority in the Soviets, especially in Petrograd and Moscow, Lenin was against any further prevarication and wrote a series of letters urging the Central Committee to make preparations to take power. They had consistently argued for 'all power to the Soviets' and now, having won a majority, was the time to put words into deeds. Lenin stated:

> The majority of the people are *on our side*. This was proved by the long and painful course of events from 6 May to 31 August and to 12 September. The majority gained in the Soviets of the metropolitan cities *resulted* from the people coming *over to our side*.[59]

He continued: "We must remember and weigh Marx's words about insurrection, 'Insurrection is an art', etc." And finally: "History will not forgive us if we do not assume power now."[60]

In a further letter, entitled 'Marxism and Insurrection', Lenin detailed the mechanics of an insurrection, which was the culmination of the revolutionary process. The masses were eager for change. They had been disappointed by the complete inaction of the Mensheviks and SRs and had turned in droves to the Bolsheviks. They were no longer satisfied with mere words, but looked to the Bolsheviks for action. But the reaction from the Bolshevik leadership to Lenin's demand to take power was one of astonishment. Bukharin recalled:

> We all gasped. Nobody had yet posed the question so abruptly… At first all were bewildered. Afterwards, having talked it over, we made a decision. Perhaps that was the sole case in the history of our party when the Central Committee unanimously decided to burn a letter of Lenin.[61]

Once again, and not for the last time, Lenin had found himself isolated at a critical juncture in the Central Committee. He sent further letters, urging, cajoling, and warning of the dire consequences if they failed to act. In this, he was reflecting the desire of the masses for decisive action. He was increasingly alarmed at the delays and the vacillations within the Bolshevik leadership, which seemed hostile to his proposals and were dragging their feet.

Fearing they risked losing this opportunity to strike, in an unprecedented move, on 9 October Lenin wrote a letter to Ivar Smilga, the chairman of the Regional Committee of the Soviets in Finland, who stood on the left of the Party, urging him to act.

"The general political situation causes me great anxiety", Lenin insisted, as the government prepared a counter-offensive. "And what are we doing? We are only passing resolutions. We are losing time. We set 'dates' (20 October, the Congress of Soviets – is it not ridiculous to put it off so long? Is it not ridiculous to rely on that?)."[62] He called on Smilga to prepare his military forces in Finland:

> History has made the *military* question now the fundamental *political* question. I am afraid that the Bolsheviks forget this, being busy with 'day-to-day events', petty current questions, and '*hoping*' that 'the wave will sweep Kerensky away'. Such hope is naive; it is the same as relying on chance, and may prove criminal on the part of the party of the revolutionary proletariat.[63]

Lenin demanded that they must agitate in the Party for an immediate armed insurrection, lest they let the situation slip through their fingers. "If we fail to do this, we may turn out to be consummate idiots, the owners of beautiful resolutions and of Soviets, but *no power!*"[64]

Lenin threatens resignation

Lenin invited Smilga and others to visit him personally for further face-to-face discussions. By this time, Lenin's nerves were at breaking point. The revolution was balanced on a knife edge, as he linked the fate of the Russian Revolution with the fate of the world revolution. Two days later, he wrote in the starkest language:

> The crisis has matured. The whole future of the Russian revolution is at stake. The honour of the Bolshevik Party is in question. The whole future of the international workers' revolution for socialism is at stake.
>
> The crisis has matured...[65]

Lenin then added a postscript for distribution to the Central Committee, the Petrograd Committee, the Moscow Committee, and the Soviets. He pointed to the opposition in the leadership who were opposed to an insurrection and wanted to delay matters. He condemned this as "utter idiocy" and "sheer treachery".[66] He also noted his articles that contained such criticisms were being censored.

> I am compelled to regard this as a 'subtle' hint at the unwillingness of the Central Committee even to consider this question, a subtle hint that I should keep my mouth shut, and as a proposal for me to retire.[67]

The leadership was lagging behind the membership, and the Party was in danger of lagging behind the needs of the revolution. Lenin then dropped a bombshell:

128. Ivar Smilga   129. Nikolai Podvoisky

I am compelled to *tender my resignation from the Central Committee*, which I hereby do, reserving for myself freedom to campaign among the *rank and file* of the Party and at the Party Congress.[68]

Lenin's threat to resign from the leadership demonstrated the extreme seriousness of the situation. Weeks, even days, could decide everything at a critical juncture. Instead, he was determined if all else failed to campaign for his position in the Party's rank and file. It was very similar to the April Days, where he came into opposition with the 'old Bolsheviks'.

In the end, Lenin did not withdraw from the Central Committee. As Trotsky explains:

Lenin had said more than once that the masses are to the left of the Party. He knew that the Party was to the left of its own upper layer of 'old Bolsheviks'. He was too well acquainted with the inner groupings and moods in the Central Committee to expect from it any hazardous steps whatever. On the other hand he greatly feared excessive caution, Fabianism, a letting slip of one of those historic situations which are decades in preparation. Lenin did not trust the Central Committee – without Lenin. In that lies the key to his letters from underground. And Lenin was not so wrong in his mistrust.[69]

23 October was the key date when conflict erupted between the Petrograd Soviet and the Provisional Government over its decision to transfer

130. Vladimir Antonov-Ovseenko   131. Mikhail Lashevich

revolutionary troops from the capital to the front. The Petrograd Soviet decided that all troops should remain. The garrison rallied to the Soviet and the Executive Committee. The 'Committee of Revolutionary Defence' was renamed as the 'Military Revolutionary Committee'. Its work was carried out by a smaller Bureau, largely run by the Bolsheviks, with Trotsky, the President, assisted by Nikolai Podvoisky (Vice-President), Vladimir Antonov-Ovseenko (Secretary), Mikhail Lashevich, Pavel Lazimir (a Left SR), AD Sadovsky and Konstantin Mekhonoshin. Together these leaders formed the General Staff of the October insurrection.

One might add as a footnote that the name of Stalin was conspicuous by its absence. In fact, he remained virtually invisible in the most critical moments of the October Revolution, and his name was totally unknown to the masses and even to the majority of Bolshevik activists outside the narrow circle of Party functionaries that was his natural – indeed, his sole – sphere of activity.

130. Vladimir Antonov-Ovseenko   129. Mikhail Lashevich

24. The October Revolution

By the end of September, the situation had undergone a complete transformation as the pendulum swung sharply to the left. The reformist leaders of the Mensheviks and SRs had – unsurprisingly – dismissed as 'fanciful' the Bolsheviks' offer of a peaceful transfer of power within the Soviets. There was no longer going to be any progress on that front. In the meantime, Kerensky and his 'socialist' government were becoming more unpopular by the day. The initiative was now firmly in the hands of the Bolshevik leadership. The fate of the insurrection hung in the balance.

Lenin made his way to Petrograd on 22 October. This was to be only a little over two weeks before the Bolshevik insurrection would take place, but few, apart from Lenin, realised the urgency of the situation.

The objective conditions had fully developed for a decisive showdown. Lenin now had to convince the Bolshevik leadership to draw the necessary conclusions and act accordingly. But even at this late stage, this proved to be no easy task.

On 23 October, Lenin was to attend the crucial meeting of the Central Committee where the insurrection was on the agenda. Ironically, the venue of this historic meeting was in the house of Sukhanov, the Left Menshevik, which had been made available by his wife, a Bolshevik sympathiser.

Lenin had not attended a single Central Committee meeting since first going into hiding in early July. That now seemed an eternity away. He had moved from Finland to live secretly in a suburb of Petrograd, in order to be closer to the centre of operations. He clearly saw that time was pressing and the insurrection could not be delayed any longer. Lenin's campaign of relentless pressure found its expression in a stream of letters to the leadership demanding an insurrection.

There are moments in which a few days, or even hours, can mean the difference between victory and defeat. This is just as true in a revolution as in normal warfare. The masses could not be kept permanently in a state of expectation. Further prevarication could lead to a fatal loss of impetus. The precise calculation of the right moment to launch a decisive offensive is the essence of what Trotsky called the art of insurrection. And Lenin, like Trotsky, was a master of that art.

Following a tense discussion, the Central Committee meeting adopted Lenin's proposal to prepare for an immediate armed insurrection by a majority of ten votes – Lenin, Trotsky, Sverdlov, Stalin, Uritsky, Felix Dzerzhinsky, Kollontai, Grigory Sokolnikov, Andrei Bubnov and Lomov (Georgy Oppokov). But two prominent members of the Central Committee voted against – Kamenev and Zinoviev. And quite a few others, though they voted for the resolution, did so with reservations.

"We are practically approaching the armed insurrection. But when will it be possible? Perhaps a year from now – one can't really tell", pondered Mikhail Kalinin. Vladimir Milyutin, a member of the Central Committee, also added his voice to the doubters: "We are not ready to strike the first blow. We are in no position to overthrow the government or stop its supporters in the days to come."[1]

Sukhanov was later briefed about the meeting. Referring to Lenin as the 'Thunderer', he commented about what had happened in the following terms:

> In the Central Committee of the Party this decision was accepted by all but two votes. The dissenters were the same as in June – Kamenev and Zinoviev... This of course could not confound the Thunderer. He had never been confounded even when he remained practically alone in his own party; now he had the *majority* with him. And, besides the majority, *Trotsky was with Lenin*. I don't know to what degree Lenin himself valued this fact, but for the course of events it had incalculable significance. I have no doubt of that...[2]

There were, nevertheless, still some loose ends and the exact date of the seizure of power was still left hanging in the air. The Second National Congress of Soviets was scheduled for 2 November (20 October, Old Style), where the Bolsheviks were guaranteed a majority. It was therefore assumed that an insurrection should begin sooner, certainly not later than around 28 October. But that schedule only gave them five days to finalise everything, which was deemed insufficient. It was therefore agreed that another Central Committee meeting would take place on 29 October to finalise matters.

Opposition of Kamenev and Zinoviev

Following the Central Committee of 23 October, Zinoviev and Kamenev sent a personal statement of their opposition to an insurrection to Central Committee members, while sending a circular, entitled 'On the Current Situation', to a number of Bolshevik organisations. This read:

> We are deeply convinced that to proclaim an armed insurrection now is to put at stake not only the fate of our Party but also the fate of the Russian and the international revolution.

> There is no doubt that historical circumstances do exist when an oppressed class has to recognise that it is better to go on to defeat than surrender without a fight. Is the Russian working class in just such a position today? *No, a thousand times no!!* [...]

> The influence of Bolshevism is growing. Whole sections of the working population are still only beginning to be swept up in it. With the right tactics, we can get a third of the seats in the Constituent Assembly, or even more.[3]

It was abundantly clear that Zinoviev and Kamenev simply envisaged the role of the Bolshevik Party as an opposition group in the Constituent Assembly. This statement, coming from leading members, led to some confusion within the ranks of the Party. To counter this, Lenin immediately wrote two letters directly to the membership over the following few days. In them, he attacked Zinoviev and Kamenev, but without naming them:

> Only a most insignificant minority of the gathering, namely, all in all two comrades, took a negative stand. The arguments which those comrades advanced are so weak, they are a manifestation of such an astounding confusion, timidity, and collapse of all the fundamental ideas of Bolshevism and proletarian revolutionary internationalism that it is not easy to discover an explanation for such shameful vacillations. The fact, however, remains, and since the revolutionary party has no right to tolerate vacillations on such a serious question, and since this pair of comrades, who have scattered their principles to the winds, might cause some confusion, it is necessary to analyse their arguments, to expose their vacillations, and to show how shameful they are.[4]

Lenin then answered the objections that somehow the uprising was hopeless, and that the Bolsheviks should therefore wait for the summoning of the

Constituent Assembly, so as to form a strong opposition, and so on. This 'peaceful' parliamentary perspective was wholly at odds with Lenin's perspective of taking power and therefore he felt the need to pose things very sharply: either they – the Bolsheviks – would immediately seize power or a military dictatorship, not a Constituent Assembly, would be established:

> Let us forget all that was being and *has been demonstrated* by the Bolsheviks a hundred times, all that the six months' history of our revolution has proved, namely, that there is no way out, that there is no objective way out and can be none *except* a dictatorship of the Kornilovites or a dictatorship of the proletariat.[5]

He then continued to ridicule the route of the Constituent Assembly:

> Let us forget this, let us renounce all this and wait! Wait for what? Wait for a miracle, for the tempestuous and catastrophic course of events from 20 April to 29 August to be succeeded (due to the prolongation of the war and the spread of famine) by a peaceful, quiet, smooth, legal convocation of the Constituent Assembly and by a fulfilment of its most lawful decisions. Here you have the 'Marxist' tactics! Wait, ye hungry! Kerensky has promised to convene the Constituent Assembly.[6]

In regard to the accusation of Blanquism made against the proposed insurrection, Lenin replied:

> Marxism is an extremely profound and many-sided doctrine. It is, therefore, no wonder that *scraps* of quotations from Marx – especially when the quotations are made *inappropriately* – can always be found among the 'arguments' of those who break with Marxism. Military conspiracy is Blanquism, *if* it is organised not by a party of a definite class, *if* its organisers have not analysed the political moment in general and the international situation in particular, *if* the party has not on its side the sympathy of the majority of the people, as proved by objective facts, *if* the development of revolutionary events has not brought about a practical refutation of the conciliatory illusions of the petty bourgeoisie, *if* the majority of the Soviet-type organs of revolutionary struggle that have been recognised as authoritative or have shown themselves to be such in practice have not been won over, *if* there has not matured a sentiment in the army (if in war-time) against the government that protracts the unjust war against the will of the whole people, *if* the slogans of the uprising (like 'All power to the Soviets', 'Land to the peasants', or 'Immediate offer of a democratic peace to all the belligerent nations, with an immediate abrogation of all secret treaties and secret diplomacy', etc.) have not become widely known and popular, *if* the advanced workers are not sure of the desperate situation of

the masses and of the support of the countryside, a support proved by a serious peasant movement or by an uprising against the owners and the government that defends the owners, *if* the country's economic situation inspires earnest hopes for a favourable solution of the crisis by peaceable and parliamentary means.[7]

Lenin ends his letter: "This is probably enough."[8] He had made everything clear.

With the Petrograd Military Revolutionary Committee under the control of the Bolsheviks, and Trotsky at its head, the pieces were being put into place for a successful insurrection. This was the situation facing the extended Central Committee meeting, held on 29 October, and attended by representatives from the Petrograd committee, the military organisation, and the factory committees.

At this meeting, Lenin once again forcefully argued for an insurrection without any delay. "The masses had put their trust in the Bolsheviks and demanded deeds from them, not words", he argued.[9] If we take power now, he said, "the Bolsheviks would have all proletarian Europe on their side", once again linking the Russian revolution to the European revolution.[10]

But Zinoviev and Kamenev pressed their opposition, demanding that the decision be postponed until after the Soviet Congress so as to 'confer' with delegates from the provinces. In any case, they believed the plans for the insurrection were not sufficiently serious, as little had been prepared. Kamenev stated:

> A week has passed since the resolution was adopted and this is also the reason this resolution shows how not to organise an insurrection: during that week, nothing was done; it only spoiled what should have been done. The week's results demonstrate that there are no factors to favour a rising now.[11]

Tempers became quite heated within the meeting. However, in the end, it was agreed by twenty-two votes in favour and two against – again the votes of Zinoviev and Kamenev – to endorse the resolution of the 23 October and proceed with the planned insurrection. But time was clearly running out.

Fortunately, unbeknown to them, the Mensheviks and SRs came to the rescue. For their own reasons, they decided to postpone the Soviet Congress until 7 November (25 October, Old Style). This extra week proved indispensable.

In the biography of Stalin prepared by the Marx-Engels-Lenin Institute in Moscow in 1940, a spurious claim is made: "On October 16 (29), the Central Committee elected a Party Centre, headed by Comrade Stalin, to direct the uprising."[12] While it is true that the Central Committee did elect a 'Centre' to assist the insurrection, this body *never actually met!* It was simply overtaken by events and relegated to the waste paper basket.

Control of the October insurrection was in the hands of the Military Revolutionary Committee, under Trotsky's direction.

'Strike-breaking'

At the end of the Central Committee of October 29, Kamenev, having opposed the insurrection, announced his resignation from the Central Committee. Two days later, on 31 October, Kamenev and Zinoviev attacked the whole idea of an insurrection publicly in an article in Maxim Gorky's paper, *Novaya Zhizn*.

When their fellow comrades heard this news, they were stunned. Not only was this a complete breach of discipline and trust, but it was a clear warning to the enemies of the Party of their plans for an insurrection. This was the worst kind of betrayal – a stab in the back on the eve of battle.

Once Lenin heard the news, he was beside himself with rage at this outrageous behaviour. He immediately wrote a letter to the membership denouncing it:

> This is a thousand times more despicable and a *million times more harmful* than all
> the statements Plekhanov, for example, made in the non-Party press in 1906-07,
> and which the Party so sharply condemned! At that time it was only a question
> of elections, whereas now it is a question of an insurrection for the conquest of
> power![13]

He then wrote in another letter to the Central Committee: "No self-respecting party can tolerate strike-breaking and blacklegs in its midst."[14] He then called for the expulsion of Zinoviev and Kamenev from the Party. The next day he wrote a further letter, elaborating on the first.

Up until this point, Kamenev and Zinoviev were the 'old Bolsheviks', Lenin's closest Party comrades, who had been with him for many years. Zinoviev was personally with Lenin throughout the war years. And yet, when faced with the decisive question of power, they politically collapsed.

In an attempt to limit the public damage, Trotsky tried to disguise the insurrection by refuting the allegations. However, in doing so, he also added that any attempt by the counter-revolution to disrupt the Soviet Congress would be met with the severest measures. In the end, Kamenev had no alternative but to go along with Trotsky's public explanation.

However, to add to the confusion, the *Pravda* editors, after publishing a brief statement by Zinoviev, added an extraordinary statement from themselves, downplaying the betrayal. It even criticised Lenin for his tone! "The matter may be considered closed. The sharp tone of comrade Lenin's article does not change the fact, fundamentally, we remain of one mind."[15] It turned out that it was Stalin, as one of the editors, who was responsible for this statement.

At the Central Committee meeting of 3 November, Lenin was not present. His letter, however, condemning Zinoviev and Kamenev, was read out. But those present took a very lenient view. Stalin immediately declared that as far as Lenin's proposal was concerned, "expulsion from the Party was no remedy, what is needed is to preserve Party unity..." Therefore, Kamenev and Zinoviev should not be expelled, but should remain as members of the Central Committee.[16]

After some discussion, Kamenev's resignation from the Central Committee was accepted and Zinoviev and Kamenev were simply instructed to make no further announcements. Following the objections from Stalin, Miliutin, Uritsky and Sverdlov, Lenin's proposal to expel Zinoviev and Kamenev was also turned down. This was an exceptionally mild rebuke under the circumstances!

Trotsky, however, not only denounced their strike-breaking behaviour in the meeting, but he also attacked Stalin's mealy-mouthed statement in *Pravda*. In response, Stalin offered his resignation, but this was brushed aside as the *Pravda* statement was deemed not to be from him personally, but from the *whole* editorial board and the meeting merely passed on to the next business.

When he heard all of this, Lenin, it should be noted, did not agree with these decisions, but accepted them so as to concentrate everything on the success of the impending insurrection.

The October insurrection

Despite the damage, it was agreed that the insurrection would still take place before the opening of the Second All-Russian Congress of Soviets. Nevertheless, Lenin was still opposed to linking the date of the insurrection to the Soviet Congress, fearing it would be postponed and the opportunity missed. Lenin's fears were not without foundation as the Menshevik leaders, who controlled the Soviet Executive Committee, were definitely seeking to delay matters. Morgan Price writes:

132. Red Guards from the Putilov Steel Works
– they played a key role in the storming of the Winter Palace forty-eight hours after
this photograph was taken

I found members of the Executive very depressed. Reports from the provinces showed that the Bolshevik agitation for an immediate summoning of a Second Congress had met with great response... They had done, said the Menshevik Central Executive, everything to prevent the summoning of this Second Soviet Congress because they considered it useless.[17]

In reality, they knew they were in a minority and were destined to lose their positions once the Congress took place.

Trotsky, however, was in favour of this date. Due to his pivotal position, he was more in tune with the situation than most. Given the pressure from below, he firmly believed the Congress would proceed as planned on 7 November, which would give the insurrection greater legitimacy in the eyes of the masses, a 'legality', than if the Party carried it out alone. In the end, Trotsky was proved to be correct as he energetically directed the military operations of the insurrection.

Up to the very last minute, Lenin was understandably on tenterhooks. He, more than anyone else, realised the importance of the moment. His whole life's work was concentrated in these days and hours. He understood that

133. Bolshevik sailors from the cruiser *Aurora* during the insurrection

any delay by the Party could end in ruin and that everything was now in the balance. "Now or never!" he repeated.

Even the day before the insurrection, Lenin was still pleading for the Central Committee to act! "The government is tottering", he wrote. "It must be given the death-blow at all costs. To delay action is fatal."[18] In fact, it was the Provisional Government that moved first by ordering two Bolshevik offices to be closed down. This played into the hands of the insurrectionists, who used this to go onto the offensive.

Lenin, feeling increasingly anxious, defied the orders of the Central Committee and made his way over to Smolny, the headquarters of the Soviet. However, by this time, Trotsky had things firmly in hand and the insurrection was well under way.

During the night of 6-7 November (24-25 October, Old Style), the Military Revolutionary Committee deposed the Kerensky Government and carried through a smooth and peaceful transition of power – just in time for the opening of the Soviet Congress. All the key points of Petrograd were occupied and members of the Provisional Government had been arrested or had fled the scene. "The city was absolutely calm", writes Sukhanov. "Both the centre and the suburbs were sunk in a deep sleep, not suspecting what was going on in the quiet of the cold autumn night."[19]

134. Baltic sailors checking documentation at a roadblock
during the insurrection

Once the Winter Palace had fallen, the old regime was finally at an end. "The operations, gradually developing, went so smoothly that no great forces were required", explains Sukhanov.[20] The insurrection was so peaceful, even compared to the February Revolution, that there were only five casualties, all from the ranks of the revolutionaries. This was the most bloodless revolution in history.

"The Provisional Government is deposed", read the statement issued by the Petrograd Soviet of Workers' and Soldiers' Deputies at ten o'clock in the morning of 7 November:

> The State Power has passed into the hands of the organ of the Petrograd Soviet of Workers' and Soldiers' Deputies, the Military Revolutionary Committee, which stands at the head of the Petrograd proletariat and garrison. [...]
>
> Long live the revolution of the workers, soldiers, and peasants![21]

According to one witness:

> All practical work in connection with the organisation of the uprising was done under the immediate direction of Comrade Trotsky, the President of the Petrograd

Soviet. It can be stated with certainty that the Party is indebted primarily and principally to Comrade Trotsky for the rapid going over of the garrison to the side of the Soviet and the efficient manner in which the work of the Military Revolutionary Committee was organised. The principal assistants of Comrade Trotsky were Comrades Antonov and Podvoisky.[22]

The writer was none other than Joseph Stalin. However, in a speech delivered to the Plenum of the Communist Fraction of the All-Union Central Council of Trade Unions six years later, Stalin paints a totally different picture:

> Comrade Trotsky, who was a relative newcomer in our Party in the period of October, did not, and could not have played any *special* role either in the Party or in the October uprising.[23]

Stalin's depiction of events had changed by 1924, as this was the year that an all-out struggle took place against Trotsky, to denigrate his achievements and prevent him from assuming the leadership after Lenin's death.

The Congress opens

From the early morning of 7 November, the Smolny Institute began to fill with delegates. As the opening of the Congress was continually delayed, caucus and faction meetings repeatedly took place throughout the day. By three o'clock in the afternoon, the Great Hall was full of representatives from all parts of the country waiting in anticipation for the grand opening. But there was a further delay, as the Winter Palace had not yet been taken. Then, at twenty to eleven at night, as the Red Guards stormed the Winter Palace, the Congress finally opened.

From the very outset, a packed Smolny resounded with rallying speeches and enthusiastic appeals. It became clear that the Bolsheviks and their allies were in a large majority. According to estimates, the Bolsheviks held 390 seats out of a total of 650. The SRs held between 160 to 190 seats, but they had already split into left and right factions. The Mensheviks, which in June had 200 delegates, were now reduced to less than half, with only sixty to seventy. It was certain that an overwhelming majority of delegates favoured the insurrection and the seizure of power by the Soviets.

But the old members of the Congress Executive Committee still reflected the previous balance of forces. This meant that the first part of the proceedings was presided over by the outgoing Committee, dominated by the Mensheviks and SRs, with Fyodor Dan in the chair. "We have met under the most peculiar circumstances", he said in his opening remarks. "On the eve of the elections for the National Assembly the Government has been arrested by one of the parties in this Congress. As a spokesman of the old Executive I declare this action to be unwarranted."[24] But his opinions fell on deaf ears.

The delegates moved to elect a new chairman, with the Bolshevik, Sverdlov, taking charge of proceedings. Suddenly, an SR member jumped up to protest that three comrades of his party were at that very instant under siege in the Winter Palace. "We demand their immediate release!" he proclaimed.

This was answered by Trotsky, who immediately went to the rostrum. He replied that the outburst was completely hypocritical, as it was the SRs who shared responsibility for the arrest of a number of Bolsheviks, as well as permitting the spying activities on the Bolshevik Party by the old secret police! With Trotsky's reply, the whole hall erupted in general tumult.

The Mensheviks and right-wing SRs were feeling the ground shifting under their feet. They therefore moved that negotiations be immediately opened by the Soviet with the Provisional Government to establish a new Coalition government. But they also made it clear that the Bolsheviks, who they accused of being responsible for the 'adventure', would never be allowed to share power.

As expected, this proposal fell flat, since the Mensheviks and SRs were in a small minority at the Congress. Despite appeals from Martov, the Mensheviks and the Bund delegates, realising their impotence, walked out, taking around 20 per cent of the hall with them. As they left, they were met with cat-calls and jeers from all sides. Everyone felt that with this action, the Rubicon had been crossed.

At that moment, the platform read out that the Provisional Government had been arrested, which provoked stormy jubilation. Then, with a sea of hands, the delegates ratified the transfer of state power to the Soviet, followed by ecstatic cheers of celebration. Amid the noise and commotion, Martov tried to speak as if nothing had happened. His proposal for a coalition of all socialist parties, including those opposed to the seizure of power, was again met with derision. Then Trotsky once again took the floor.

The masses of the people have followed our banner, and our insurrection was victorious. And now we are told: Renounce your victory, make concessions, compromise. With whom? I ask with whom ought we to compromise? With those wretched groups who have left us...? But we have seen through them completely. No one in Russia is with them any longer. Should those millions of workers and peasants represented in this Congress make a compromise, as between equals, with the men who are ready, not for the first time, to leave

135. After the capture of the Winter Palace

us at the mercy of the bourgeoisie? No, here no compromise is possible. To those who have left, and to those who suggest it to us, we must say: You are miserable bankrupts, your role is over; go where you ought to be – into the dustbin of history.[25]

Martov, angered by this intervention, shouted from the platform: "Then, we'll leave as well."[26] And so his supporters walked out.

"Lenin was not present at it", explained Trotsky, relating to the first session of the Congress.

He remained in his room at Smolny, which, according to my recollection, had no, or almost no furniture. Later someone spread rugs on the floor and laid two cushions on them. Vladimir Ilyich and I lay down to rest. But in a few minutes I was called: "Dan is speaking; you must answer." When I came back after my reply I again lay down near Vladimir Ilyich, who naturally could not sleep. It would not have been possible. Every five or ten minutes someone came running in from the session hall to inform us what was going on there...

It must have been the next morning, for a sleepless night separated it from the preceding day. Vladimir Ilyich looked tired. He smiled and said, "The transition from the state of illegality, being driven in every direction, to power

– is too rough." "It makes one dizzy", he at once added in German, and made the sign of the Cross before his face. After this one more or less personal remark that I heard him make about the acquisition of power he went about the tasks of the day.[27]

Lenin speaks

John Reed, the American journalist and Communist, was present at the Congress. He recalled the events in his celebrated classic, *Ten Days That Shook the World*, to which Lenin wrote a preface "recommending it to the workers of the world…" Reed described the scene at the second session of the Congress where Lenin was about to speak:

It was 8.40 when a thunderous wave of cheers announced the entrance of the praesidium, with Lenin – great Lenin – among them. A short, stocky figure, with a big head set down on his shoulders, bald and bulging. Little eyes, a snubbish nose, wide generous mouth, and heavy chin; clean-shaven now but already beginning to bristle with the well-known beard of his past and future. Dressed in shabby clothes, his trousers much too long for him. Unimpressed, to be the idol of a mob, loved and revered as perhaps few leaders in history have been. A strange popular leader – a leader purely by virtue of intellect; colourless, humourless, uncompromising and detached, without picturesque idiosyncrasies – but with the power of explaining profound ideas in simple terms, of analysing a concrete situation. And combined with shrewdness, the greatest intellectual audacity.

After some interventions, Lenin rose to speak. John Reed continues:

Now Lenin, gripping the edge of the reading stand, letting his little winking eyes travel over the crowd as he stood there waiting, apparently oblivious to the long-rolling ovation, which lasted several minutes. When it finished, he said simply, "We shall now proceed to construct the Socialist order!" Again that overwhelming human roar.

"The first thing is the adoption of practical measures to realise peace… We shall offer peace to the peoples of all belligerent countries upon the basis of Soviet terms – no annexations, no indemnities, and the right of self-determination of peoples. At the same time, according to our promise, we shall publish and repudiate the secret treaties… The question of War and Peace is so clear that I think that I may, without preamble, read the project of a Proclamation to the Peoples of All the Belligerent Countries…"

"No gestures. And before him, a thousand simple faces looking up in intent adoration", explained Reed. Lenin proceeded to read the proclamation, and ended with the words:

> The revolution has opened the era of Social Revolution... The labour movement, in the name of peace and Socialism, shall win, and fulfil its destiny...

Reed commented:

> There was something quiet and powerful in all this, which stirred the souls of men. It was understandable why people believed when Lenin spoke...[28]

This was the first time that Lenin had appeared or spoken in public for quite some time, having spent almost four months in hiding. What a transformation in the situation! From underground fugitive to becoming leader of the Russian Revolution.

The insurrection had been successful. In the words of Rosa Luxemburg later: "They dared!"[29] They dared and by their actions transformed the words of socialism into deeds. These events would 'shake the world' and make Lenin and the Bolsheviks a household name internationally.

The Soviet Congress continued with its revolutionary business. The results in the elections for a new Central Executive Committee or Presidium were announced: sixty-seven Bolsheviks were elected, together with twenty-nine Left SRs, with twenty other seats divided among smaller tendencies, including Maxim Gorky's group.

Council of People's Commissars

The newly elected Soviet Executive Committee then appointed a new government – to be called the Council of People's Commissars – to run the country in the name of the Soviet Republic. The following day it was announced, amid loud and prolonged cheers, that Lenin was chosen, without portfolio, as Chairman of the new government. The list of members of the new government was then read out by Kamenev, who had been newly elected as chairman of the Executive Committee, with bursts of applause after each name. The Left SRs were offered posts in the new government, but for the moment they refused to accept them. The bourgeois concept of 'Minister' was rejected in favour of a new, more revolutionary-sounding title of 'Commissar'.

Trotsky recalled a conversation with Lenin about the new revolutionary terminology to be adopted to describe members of the new government:

"What shall we call it?" asked Lenin, thinking aloud. "Only let us not use the word Minister: it is a dull, hackneyed title."

"Perhaps 'Commissars'", I suggested, "only there are too many Commissars just now. Perhaps Supreme Commissars? … No, 'Supreme' sounds wrong too. What about 'People's Commissars'?"

"People's Commissars? Well, this sounds alright. And the government as a whole?"

"Council of People's Commissars", picked up Lenin. "That's splendid; it smells of revolution."[30]

Apart from Lenin as Chairman of the Council, other appointments included:

People's Commissar of the Interior:	AI Rykov
Agriculture:	VP Milyutin
Labour:	AG Shlyapnikov
Army and Navy Affairs:	A committee consisting of: VA Ovseyenko (Antonov), NV Krylenko and PY Dybenko
Commerce and Industry:	VP Nogin
Education:	AV Lunacharsky
Finance:	II Skvortsov (Stepanov)
Foreign Affairs:	LD Bronstein (Trotsky)
Justice:	GI Oppokov (Lomov)
Food:	IA Teodorovich
Posts and Telegraph:	NP Avilov (Glebov)
Chairman for Nationalities' Affairs:	JV Dzhugashvili (Stalin)

The office of People's Commissar of Railways was left temporarily vacant, mainly as a result of the strained relations with the leadership of the Menshevik-controlled All-Russian Railway Workers' Union.

The Congress continued with a number of other sessions, accompanied by numerous intervals and breaks. It was, without doubt, a real proletarian revolutionary assembly, the likes of which nobody had ever witnessed before. Power was finally in the hands of the Soviets, in *their* hands, the hands of the representatives of the proletariat and poor peasants.

Every decision of the Congress was met with enormous enthusiasm, hurrahs, thunderous clapping and caps and hats thrown into the air. The delegates also sang the funeral march in memory of the martyrs of the war, as well as the *Internationale*. Everyone could sense that the working class was finally in power! This was the most democratic revolution in history.

Morgan Philips Price, *Manchester Guardian* journalist, was so astonished that he couldn't believe his eyes. He had never experienced anything like it:

> Soon I was beginning to feel that the whole thing might be a mad adventure. How could committees of workmen and soldiers, even if they had the passive consent of war-weary and land-hungry peasants, succeed against the whole of the technical apparatus of the still-functioning bureaucracy and the agents of the Western Powers? Splendid as was this rebellion of the slaves, as showing that there was still hope and courage in the masses, it was surely doomed in the face of these tremendous odds. Russia could hardly escape the fate of Carthage.[31]

But deep down, there was a feeling of hope for the future, born out of the horrors of war. "It seemed as if there was, for the first time for many months, a political force in the country that knew what it wanted", wrote Price: "This was clearly reflected in the common talk in the streets."[32] "Everything happened so simply and so naturally", wrote Victor Serge: "It was all quite unlike any of the revolutionary scenes we knew from history."[33]

History was being made – and the messes felt and participated in it. For the delegates in Smolny, celebrating their victory, their hearts were uplifted, their eyes fixed on the future, while their ears were still ringing with Lenin's immortal words: "We shall now proceed to construct the socialist order." With these simple words, Lenin announced the greatest event in history and the beginning of a revolutionary new era internationally.

25. Soviets in Power

While there was widespread jubilation in Russia, the victory of the Bolsheviks was naturally regarded with profound hostility among the capitalist classes of the West. For them, the idea of a proletarian democracy, based on the rule of the Soviets, was anathema. The very thought of the working class running society was unbelievable or simply 'madness', an affront to human nature.

This coincided with their view that such a regime could not possibly last long. In particular, the Allied High Command harboured the illusion that the Bolshevik government would simply collapse in days or maybe weeks, and everything would return to normal. This view was confirmed by Bruce Lockhart, British agent in Russia, who left an impressively honest account of the Revolution:

> I could not share the general belief, stimulated by the opinion of nearly all the Russian experts in London, that the Lenin regime could not last more than a few weeks and that then Russia would revert to Tsarism or a military dictatorship.[1]

This view was confirmed by Sukhanov:

> The sole argument heard from the Rightists was this: the Bolshevik adventure would be liquidated from one day to the next; the 'Soviet Government' would not hold out more than a few days...[2]

But even he harboured such illusions: "I too was convinced that the power of a Bolshevik regime would be ephemeral."[3]

However, the Bolshevik regime did not fall in a few days or weeks, but held on against all the odds. The Russian bourgeoisie, robbed of political power, now looked towards British and even enemy German troops (despite their previous attacks on Lenin as a German agent) to suppress Bolshevism and re-establish their rule in Russia. Such was the depth of their 'patriotism'.

The bourgeois historians, as they have repeated many times, are not prepared to describe the overthrow of the old regime as a popular revolution, but simply as a 'coup', carried out behind the backs of the masses. This is utterly false. The insurrection was carried out in the name of the Soviets and approved by the Second All-Russian Congress of Workers' and Soldiers' Deputies, and the Congress of Peasants' Deputies, *the real rulers of Soviet Russia*. They constituted the real majority and power in the land, namely the organised working class and peasants. Even Sukhanov, who was opposed to the Bolsheviks, states:

> To call it a military conspiracy rather than a national uprising is utterly absurd, since the [Bolshevik] Party was already the *de facto* power in the land, and since it enjoyed the support of the enormous majority of the people.[4]

And as Marcel Liebman points out:

> In October, the people did not come out in the streets – they did not need to, for there was no armed resistance to overcome. Once the insurrection had started, the working class already held the upper hand.[5]

Morgan Philips Price, who worked in Russia at this time, wrote: "The government of Kerensky fell before the Bolshevik insurgents because it had no supporters in the country."[6] He added that the government "fell like a house of cards."[7]

Following the insurrection, the new Soviet government immediately got down to work in the Smolny, taking steps to develop Soviet power and build up its support throughout the country. The Bolsheviks faced a mountain of tasks and there was no ready-made blueprint to follow. Special attention was given, in particular, to the peasantry and the land decree, which would help to consolidate support for the revolution in the countryside.

Lenin believed it was necessary for the government to put down clear markers for the future, since there was no guarantee that the government would not be overthrown by the counter-revolution. As a result, Lenin and the Council of People's Commissars rapidly introduced a series of decrees, covering a whole host of questions: peace, land reform, the right of nationalities to self-determination, workers' control, the right of recall, and many more.

On 25 October, Lenin drafted an urgent appeal, 'To The Citizens of Russia!', announcing the Soviet victory:

The Provisional Government has been deposed. State power has passed into the hands of the organ of the Petrograd Soviet of Workers' and Soldiers' Deputies – the Revolutionary Military Committee, which heads the Petrograd proletariat and the garrison.

The cause for which the people have fought, namely, the immediate offer of a democratic peace, the abolition of landed proprietorship, workers' control over production, and the establishment of Soviet power – this cause has been secured.

Long live the revolution of workers, soldiers and peasants!

[Signed] Revolutionary Military Committee of the Petrograd Soviet of Workers' and Soldiers' Deputies – 10 am, 25 October 1917[8]

First decrees

The following day, a decree on peace, regarded as the most important, was drafted by Lenin as an appeal to the world. It stated:

The workers' and peasants' government, created by the Revolution of October 24-25 and basing itself on the Soviets of Workers', Soldiers' and Peasants' Deputies, calls upon all the belligerent peoples and their governments to start immediate negotiations for a just, democratic peace. [...]

... by such a peace the government means an immediate peace without annexations (i.e. without the seizure of foreign lands, without the forcible incorporation of foreign nations) and without indemnities.

The Government of Russia proposes that this kind of peace be immediately concluded by all the belligerent nations, and expresses its readiness to take all the resolute measures now, without the least delay, pending the final ratification of all the terms of such a peace by authoritative assemblies of the people's representatives of all countries and all nations. [...]

It then continued, after the Bolsheviks had just opened the archives of the tsarist diplomatic service, to expose the secret treaties of the old regime:

The government abolishes secret diplomacy, and, for its part, announces its firm intention to conduct all negotiations quite openly in full view of the whole people. It will proceed immediately with the full publication of the secret treaties endorsed or concluded by the government of landowners and capitalists from February to 25 October 1917. The government proclaims the unconditional and immediate annulment of everything contained in these secret treaties insofar as it is aimed, as is mostly the case, at securing advantages and privileges for the Russian landowners and capitalists and at the retention, or extension, of the annexations made by the Great Russians.[9]

This was followed by another vital decree, also issued on the same day, dealing with the issue of land reform. This was urgent in a country like Russia, where the proletariat could only hold power with the aid of the peasantry. In contrast, while the Provisional government had simply talked about 'reform', the Bolsheviks acted immediately. This decree, too, was drafted by Lenin:

1. Landed proprietorship is abolished forthwith without any compensation.

2. The landed estates, as also all crown, monastery, and church lands, with all their livestock, implements, buildings and everything pertaining thereto, shall be placed at the disposal of the volost* land committees and the uyezd** Soviets of Peasants' Deputies pending the convocation of the Constituent Assembly.

3. All damage to confiscated property, which henceforth belongs to the whole people, is proclaimed a grave crime to be punished by the revolutionary courts. The uyezd Soviets of Peasants' Deputies shall take all necessary measures to assure the observance of the strictest order during the confiscation of the landed estates, to determine the size of estates, and the particular estates subject to confiscation, to draw up exact inventories of all property confiscated and to protect in the strictest revolutionary way all agricultural enterprises transferred to the people, with all buildings, implements, livestock, stocks of produce, etc.[10]

The decree on land was especially important in winning over the poor peasants, as was the decree on peace. 'Land to the peasants!' would be immediately carried out as promised. All large-scale private ownership of land was abolished forthwith, without compensation. The landlord's right to land was therefore abolished and hired labour was prohibited. The decree also meant that the peasants were freed from the heavy burden of mortgages and debts. This served to win them over to the side of the revolution.

There is an interesting example of this. A Soviet Commissar was sent to a rural district on the far eastern island of Sakhalin to explain the government decrees. There he met an old peasant who said to him:

---

* A small, administrative peasant division.
** The second-level administrative division.

136. Peasants working in the fields, 1920

See here, Mr Chief, we have heard rumours here that in Russia there is now war among the Russian people, between some that are called Bolsheviks and others that are called Whites. They say that the Bolsheviks fight for the people so that there should be no tsar anymore and so that the land shall be taken from the lords and given to the peasants; we understand a little of that. Will you tell us about it?[11]

Another peasant intervened and said:

It would have been fine if the tsar had given the land to the peasants. I remember that in my village in Russia in my time there used to be talk that land would be allotted any day, but we never got it.[12]

The fact that they were now being given the land made all the difference to these peasants. The Commissar went on to report: "There was a general excitement. Everybody talked, I could see that they thought something new had happened, from which they would live better."[13]

This small example also showed how slowly news travelled from the proletarian centres to the countryside and the far-flung villages. More importantly, it showed how the peasants could be won over to support the new Soviet government.

The land reform programme being offered was, in fact, copied from the SRs, who then complained bitterly that the Bolsheviks had stolen their clothes. But Lenin freely admitted this was the case, and he had no qualms doing so. "What of it? Does it matter who drew them up?", asked Lenin:[14]

> Experience is the best teacher [...] We trust that the peasants themselves will be able to solve the problem correctly, properly, better than we could do it. Whether they do it in our spirit or in the spirit of the Socialist-Revolutionary programme is not the point. The point is that the peasants should be firmly assured that there are no more landowners in the countryside, that they themselves must decide all questions, and that they themselves must arrange their own lives. (*Loud applause.*)[15]

Originally, the agrarian programme of the Bolsheviks was based on the nationalisation of all land, which was to be then allocated by the local Soviets of Peasants' and Agricultural Labourers' Deputies to develop large-scale collectivised farming, which would be much more productive than individual plots.

This collectivisation was to be achieved not by compulsion, but through 'force of example'. However, this programme ran counter to the immediate aspirations of the peasants, who desperately wanted a division of land and their own individual plots. These feelings were forcibly expressed by the Peasant Soviets.

Lenin was personally very impressed with the report from the Congress of Peasants' Deputies and outlined his thoughts on the matter:

> The peasants want to keep their small farms [...] Fine. No sensible socialist will differ with the peasant poor over this. [...]
>
> The crux of the matter lies in political power passing into the hands of the proletariat. When this has taken place, everything that is essential, basic, fundamental in the programme set out in the mandates *will become feasible*. Life will show what modifications it will undergo as it is carried out. This is an issue of secondary importance. We are not doctrinaires. Our theory is a guide to action, not a dogma.
>
> We do not claim that Marx knew or Marxists know the road to socialism down to the last detail. It would be nonsense to claim anything of the kind. What we know is the direction of this road, and the class forces that follow it; the specific,

practical details will come to light only through the *experience of the millions* when they take things into their own hands.[16]

These lines sum up Lenin's flexible approach to all questions. Rather than impose a blueprint on the peasants, he recognised their wishes and saw the need to go through the experience with them. In this way, they could draw their own conclusions as to the best way to organise the land and, by example, they would see the benefits of collectivisation. According to John Reed:

> ... at two o'clock the Land Decree was put to the vote, with only one against and the peasant delegates wild with joy... So plunged the Bolsheviki ahead, irresistible, overriding hesitation and opposition – the only people in Russia who had a definite programme of action while the others talked for eight long months.[17]

This measure, which they acted upon, was crucial in ensuring the viability of the regime.

After the October Revolution, some socialists, such as Rosa Luxemburg, criticised the Bolsheviks for their agrarian programme. They feared that the land-holding peasantry would be a conservative force and the division of land into individual plots would hinder industrialisation. However, to have simply ignored the demands of the peasants for land would have led to mass opposition and the overthrow of the Soviet government.

The Bolsheviks knew full well that the growth of peasant agriculture was the breeding ground for capitalism and would be a problem in the longer term. But they had no alternative. They put all their faith in the developing world revolution.

We will see that with the delay in the revolution, other concessions would need to be made, such as the New Economic Policy (NEP), to allow a 'breathing space'. But this would come later.

Decree on workers' control

A further decree enacted was the 'Draft Regulations on Workers' Control', once again written by Lenin. This was a move in the direction of the planning of the economy and placing greater power in the hands of the workers. The decree stated:

1. *Workers' control* over the production, storage, purchase and sale of all products and raw materials shall be introduced in all industrial, commercial, banking,

agricultural and other enterprises employing not less than five workers and office employees (together), or with an annual turnover of not less than 10,000 rubles.

2. Workers' control shall be exercised by all the workers and office employees of an enterprise, either directly, if the enterprise is small enough to permit it, or through their elected representatives, who shall be elected *immediately* at general meetings, at which minutes of the elections shall be taken and the names of those elected communicated to the government and to the local Soviets of Workers', Soldiers' and Peasants' Deputies.[18]

The idea of workers' control had been present in the Bolshevik programme for a long time, but it could only acquire a fully concrete content in 1917 when state power was in the hands of the Soviets. Lenin argued that every factory should be a "fortress of the revolution" and within the factories, the workers should exercise control.

In his 'Resolution on Measures to Cope with the Economic Disorganisation', written on 25 May 1917, he had already explained:*

3. The only way to avert disaster is to establish effectual workers' control over the production and distribution of goods. For the purpose of such control it is necessary, first of all, that the workers should have a majority of not less than three-fourths of all the votes in all the decisive institutions and that the owners who have not withdrawn from their business and the engineering staff should be enlisted without fail; secondly, the shop committees, the central and local Soviets, as well as the trade unions, should have the right to participate in this control, that all commercial bank books be open to their inspection, and that the management supply them with all the necessary information; third, that a similar right should be granted to the representatives of all the major democratic and socialist parties.

4. Workers' control, which the capitalists in a number of conflict cases have already accepted, should, by means of various well-considered measures introduced gradually but without any delay, be developed into full regulation of the production and distribution of goods by the workers.

5. Workers' control should similarly be extended to all financial and banking operations with the aim of discovering your true financial state of affairs; such control to be participated in by councils and conventions of bank, syndicate and other employees, which are to be organised forthwith.[19]

---

* Please note that we have quoted the following 'Resolution' from point 3, which is a different text to the 'Decree on Workers Control' quoted above.

Lenin constantly urged the workers to take control of their own lives themselves, and not to wait for anyone. This was the essence of the revolution. As Marx had explained, the task of the emancipation of the working class is wholly in their hands. A few days after the revolution, he issued an appeal, 'To The Population', in which he wrote:

> Comrades, working people! Remember that now *you yourselves* are at the helm of the state. No one will help you if you yourselves do not unite and take into *your* hands *all affairs* of the state. *Your* Soviets are from now on the organs of state authority, legislative bodies with full powers.

> Rally around your Soviets. Strengthen them. Get on with the job yourselves; begin right at the bottom, do not wait for anyone.[20]

This became increasingly urgent as the capitalists began to sabotage the factories. The Petrograd Factory-Owners' Association had called for the closure of all workplaces where workers demanded workers' control. The same call to shut down industry was made in early December 1917 by the Congress of the Manufacturers' Association.

Faced with this sabotage, Lenin argued that the widest initiatives should be taken by the masses in developing and defending *their* revolution.

Decree on national rights

Another important decree was the 'Declaration of Rights of the Peoples of Russia', issued by the government on 15 November.

This vital decree guaranteed equality to the peoples of Russia, including the right to self-determination, up to and including separation, abolition of any national or religious privileges, and the free development of national minorities and ethnic groups that inhabited Russia. The decree read as follows:

> Executing the will of these Congresses, the Council of People's Commissars has resolved to establish as a basis for its activity in the question of Nationalities, the following principles:

> 1. The equality and sovereignty of the peoples of Russia.

> 2. The right of the peoples of Russia to free self-determination, even to the point of separation and the formation of an independent state.

> 3. The abolition of any and all national and national religious privileges and disabilities.

4. The free development of national minorities and ethnographic groups inhabiting the territory of Russia.[21]

This was followed up a few weeks later with a special appeal, 'To All Muslim Toilers of Russia and the East', which also proclaimed without reservation the right of self-determination for all peoples.

After the revolution, the Soviet government carried this out by giving independence to Finland. In December 1917, the Soviet government also gave self-determination to Ukraine, even though the Ukrainian bourgeois government was hostile to the revolution and lent support to the White armies.

In the Baltic states of Estonia, Latvia and Lithuania, independent Soviet republics were recognised in 1918, and as bourgeois republics in 1920. As Soviet power extended eastwards, new republics were set up in Azerbaijan, Uzbekistan and Turkmenistan. In Georgia, a bourgeois republic was recognised in May 1920 and a Soviet republic in the following year.

The Bolsheviks stood firmly for the unity of all peoples in a Socialist Federation. Nevertheless, such unity could not be brought about by compulsion, but only by the free consent of the workers and peasants of the various countries.

The Bolsheviks' programme on the national question allowed them to win the confidence of the oppressed nationalities. "In general, the initial recognition of the right of self-determination and secession was accorded after 1917 willingly, sincerely and, on the whole, unreservedly", writes EH Carr, one of the very few bourgeois historians who tried to write objectively about the Russian Revolution.[22]

In January 1918 they were able to establish the Russian Federated Soviet Republic (RSFSR), although much of Russia was occupied by counter-revolutionary forces under the command of the German imperialists, reactionary bourgeois nationalist governments or White generals and Cossacks.

The harsh demands of civil war forced new priorities on the Bolshevik regime, which partially cut across their national policy, especially when Soviet Russia was invaded by twenty-one armies of foreign intervention. In order to defend itself, the Soviet Republic was forced to intervene militarily in Ukraine in 1919 and again in 1920. The same was true of Poland in 1920 and Georgia in 1921.

The Bolsheviks – especially Lenin – always showed the greatest sensitivity to the feelings of the oppressed nationalities. But, in times of civil war, when the very fate of the revolution was in the balance, the need to defend the revolution was paramount, and, at least for a time, the national question had to take second place.

Other decrees

In addition to the decrees already mentioned, the Soviet government passed numerous other measures. Here are just a few:[23]

11 November   Eight-hour day enforced on the railways

22 November   Warm clothes were requisitioned for the army

27 November   Decree on workers' control introduced

 4 December   Right of recall instituted

15 December   Supreme Economic Council established

17 December   Market in living accommodation abolished in cities

24 December   Education taken out of the hands of the Church and Commissariat of Public Education established

27 November   Decree on workers' control introduced

28 December   Putilov factories confiscated

29 December   Ranks in the army abolished

29 December   Divorce instituted

31 December   Civil marriage instituted and Institute for the Protection of Mothers and Children formed

28 January   Russian Federation of Soviet Republics established

28 January   Socialist Red Army formed

 3 February   Payment of interest and dividends on bonds ended

On 25 January 1918, the 'Declaration of Rights of the Working and Exploited People' was passed by the All-Russian Central Executive Committee of the Congress of Soviets and was published the next day in *Izvestia*. It formally declared that, throughout Soviet Russia, the Soviets now constituted the sovereign body. It also proclaimed the political and social equality of men and women in the new proletarian state.

The first decree announced by Kollontai, the Commissar of the Commissariat of Social Welfare, was for the protection of mothers. This

137. Young woodworkers in a Moscow school, 1920

allowed for sixteen weeks paid maternity leave, and nursing mothers would work no longer than four days a week and would be given crèche facilities at their workplace, with time off for breast-feeding. Family allowances were also introduced, while long hours and night work were forbidden for pregnant women and nursing mothers.

"In its initial stages", write John Peter Roberts and Fred Weston, "the Soviet regime was the most progressive on the planet in terms of its policy towards women."[24]

In November 1918, despite all the pressures of work, Lenin still found time to submit a draft decree for the 'Reorganisation of the Petrograd Public Library'. This would allow the exchange of books between Russian and foreign libraries, and ensure lecture halls and reading rooms would remain open until 11pm, including Sundays, to allow workers free access.

On 11 January 1918, the Soviet Central Executive Committee published a decree to allow the publishing of cheap books, including all the great classics of literature. This included the proposal, as far as possible, for books to be supplied to the public free of charge.

This emphasised the importance of raising the cultural level of the masses, to liberate them from ignorance and backwardness. Even in the midst of the

138. Drawing lessons in a Moscow kindergarten, 1920

civil war, 1,500 new schools were established. Everything was done, within the limits of the prevailing conditions, to raise the sights of the masses.

> I remember that in Smolny we passed as many as ten or twelve decrees at one sitting. That was an expression of our determination and desire to stimulate the spirit of experiment and initiative among the proletarian masses.[25]

Trotsky comments: "The collection of Soviet decrees forms in a certain sense a part, and not a negligible part, of the *Complete Works* of Vladimir Ilyich Lenin."[26]

Period of innocence

The weeks that followed the October Revolution can be described as the period of 'revolutionary innocence'. As soon as the new government was established, the forces of counter-revolution began to organise and pose an ever-present and serious danger.

Yet this was a time when the counter-revolutionaries were naively treated with exaggerated kindness. The workers had not yet understood that revolution is a serious business and that the hatred and cruelty of its enemies knew nothing of humanity and compassion. This important lesson had not yet been learned. The members of the Provisional Government who had been arrested and held in the Peter and Paul Fortress were simply released. This act of kindness, of course, did not prevent them from immediately conspiring to overthrow the Soviet regime.

The initial threat of counter-revolution came from the cadets at the military school, who were forced to surrender in the Winter Palace, but allowed to go free after giving assurances – which were naturally quite useless. These young gentlemen immediately broke their promise and staged an ill-starred uprising against the Bolsheviks. During the night of 11 November, they seized the telephone exchange and arrested Antonov-Ovseenko. They were only eventually subdued, not by appeals to their better nature, but with field guns.

The next counter-revolutionary threat came from Kerensky and the tsarist generals, who had managed to escape from the capital and regroup on the outskirts. Within hours of the Bolshevik victory, General Krasnov, who was in league with Kerensky, was marching his troops on Petrograd from Gatchina. But his men were faced with determined resistance from the revolutionary workers and soldiers, and were driven back. This marked the first military victory of the new regime – the first in the impending civil war.

Shortly afterwards, general Krasnov was captured and brought to the Smolny Institute. But instead of sending him to a firing squad, the prevailing naivety allowed this reactionary to be released after he gave his solemn promise not to take up arms against the new government. Naturally, Krasnov immediately broke his word and headed for Ukraine, and fomented a bloody uprising of the Don Cossacks. He became leader of the murderous Cossack White Army, which specialised in murder, torture, rape, arson, and pillage.

An anti-Bolshevik alliance was established with the name of the 'Committee to Save the Country and the Revolution', made up of Mensheviks, SRs and Cadets. They set up an interim government with headquarters in the offices of the State Duma and engaged in sabotage on a wide scale, hoping to bring down the Soviet government. The revolutionary workers and peasants paid dearly for this leniency, a product of the first easy victories over the counter-revolution.

In the days following the October victory, on Kamenev's initiative, it was announced that the death penalty was to be abolished. When Lenin heard about this, he was furious. He complained bitterly that the Bolsheviks were being too soft in subduing the old order, which was a serious business and not to be trifled with. Trotsky recalls:

139. Pyotr Krasnov

When he heard about this first piece of legislation, his anger was unbounded.

'Nonsense', he kept on repeating. 'How can one make a revolution without firing squads? Do you think you will be able to deal with all your enemies by laying down your arms? What other means of repression do you have? Imprisonment? To this no one attaches any importance during a civil war when each side hopes to win.'

'It is a mistake', he went on, 'an inadmissible weakness, a pacifist illusion.'

He proposed to rescind the decree straight away. But there was opposition, suggesting it could be used when there was no other way, and it was left.[27]

Lenin was quite right. In the conduct of a civil war, anything less than the threat of the death penalty was rarely a barrier. The fear of imprisonment for a traitor was hardly a deterrent, as he would either hope for victory from his own side, which would eventually reward him, or, if that did not happen, he would hope for an amnesty at the end of the hostilities. Either way, he saw a satisfactory outcome. Lenin fully understood that one of the reasons for the defeat of the Paris Commune in 1871 was that they were too forgiving and failed to crush the bourgeois resistance "decisively enough".*[28]

---

* Marx himself had defended the actions of the Paris Commune when faced with the onslaught of the counter-revolution. In a circular issued by the General Council of the

While victory in Petrograd was more or less straightforward, in Moscow the turnover was more hard-fought, bloodier, and took a further week to carry through. At the hands of the former tsarist generals, many Bolshevik workers had been executed by self-appointed court martials. However, when the agents of the counter-revolution were finally disarmed, they faced no reprisals. This leniency shown towards the representatives of class enemies only angered Lenin. If the revolution had shown less generosity from the very beginning, hundreds of thousands of lives would have been saved.

The malicious caricature of Lenin as a bloodthirsty monster who delighted in violence is a pure fiction. The reintroduction of the death penalty was an emergency measure, dictated by the exigencies of war. Such measures are routinely adopted by even the most democratic governments in time of war. And war between the classes is a war that knows no boundaries. That is shown by the entire historical record, from Spartacus to the Paris Commune.

The Communards were put down by the counter-revolution in the most ferocious manner, where up to 25,000 men, women and children were executed in the days following the defeat. Lenin had to remind his comrades:

> … if the bourgeoisie had triumphed, it would have acted as it did in 1848 and 1871. Who was there that believed that we would not meet the sabotage on the part of the bourgeoisie? This was clear to an infant. We, too, must apply force. We must arrest the bank directors and others […]

> In Paris, they [the revolutionaries] used the guillotine while we only take away the food cards of those who fail to obtain them from the trade unions.[29]

However, Lenin regarded the reintroduction of the death penalty as a temporary measure, which was to be withdrawn as soon as conditions permitted. He made this clear in his speech at the Fourth Conference of Gubernia Extraordinary Commissions on 6 February 1920:

> So though the death sentence, after the capture of Rostov, has been abolished on Comrade Dzerzhinsky's initiative, a reservation was made at the very beginning

---

First International, Marx states:

When Thiers, as we have seen, from the very beginning of the conflict, enforced the humane practice of shooting down the Communal prisoners, the Commune, to protect their lives, was obliged to resort to the Prussian practice of securing hostages. The lives of the hostages had been forfeited over and over again by the continued shooting of prisoners on the part of the Versaillese. How could they be spared any longer after the carnage with which MacMahon's praetorians celebrated their entry into Paris? Was even the last check upon the unscrupulous ferocity of bourgeois governments – the taking of hostages – to be made a mere sham of? (Marx, *MECW*, Vol. 22, p. 352)

that we do not by any means close our eyes to the possibility of restoring capital punishment. With us this is a matter of expediency. It goes without saying that the Soviet government will not keep the death penalty longer than is absolutely necessary, and by doing away with it, has taken a step that no democratic government of any bourgeois republic has ever taken.[30]

We should add that the death penalty remained in force all this time in Britain, France and other democratic countries, even when they did not face the exigencies of a war. It remains in force in 'democratic' America to this day. Yet, for some strange reason, in contrast to Lenin, no British Prime Minister or American president is ever portrayed as anything other than a model representative of Christian values and civilisation.

Bloodless revolution

There really is no end to the number of myths created about the allegedly violent character of the Russian Revolution. To this day, the bourgeois media is still obsessed with the idea that in October 1917, the streets were awash with blood. In reality, as we have explained, the October insurrection was practically a bloodless affair.

In fact, only five people lost their lives in Petrograd. Just over ten years later, in 1928, the great Soviet film director Sergei Eisenstein made a film called *October*. It is a very fine piece of cinema. If it sometimes departs from the historical record, that can be excused by the kind of artistic license that distinguishes a true work of art from a mere documentary. And such instances take nothing away from the outstanding merit of that masterpiece of cinematic art.

A case in point is the description of the storming of the Winter Palace. It is undoubtedly a thrilling scene, with armed workers and sailors climbing the palace gates, hurling bombs, shooting their rifles and falling dead. As a piece of cinema, it is second to none. However, it bears absolutely no relation to the actual events described. In fact, more people were killed in filming this scene than in the actual event. There was an accident in which some people lost their lives.

In the actual storming of the Winter Palace, by contrast, there was very little fighting – and not a single death. The defenders surrendered, mostly without firing a shot. The shots fired by the sailors from the cruiser *Aurora* – also depicted in the film – were actually blanks, intended to frighten, not to kill. The red sailors did not wish to damage an historical building! Far from bloodthirsty monsters, they were conscientious revolutionaries who evidently did not lack a sense of aesthetic value.

In most other areas also, the Bolsheviks took power with little or no resistance, for the simple reason that there were very few actually prepared to fight and die for the discredited old regime. The one notable exception was Moscow, where there was some fighting, mainly as a result of the mistakes of the local Bolsheviks.

According to Bruce Lockhart, life in Petrograd in the aftermath of the revolution was a rather carefree affair, which is not what is written in the history books. He wrote in 1932:

> The Bolsheviks had not succeeded in establishing the iron discipline which today characterises the regime. They had, in fact, made little attempt to do so. There was no terror, nor was the population particularly afraid of its new masters. The anti-Bolshevik newspapers continued to appear and to attack the Bolshevik policy with violent abuse. In particular, Gorky, then editor of *Novaya Zhizn*, excelled himself in denouncing the men to whom today he has given his whole-hearted allegiance. The bourgeoisie, still confident that the Germans would soon send the Bolshevik rabble about its business, was more cheerful than one might have expected in such disturbing circumstances. The population was starving, but the rich still had money. Restaurants and cabarets were open, and the cabarets at any rate were crowded [...][31]

> Prices were high, especially for champagne, but there seemed no lack of money among the guests, who nightly thronged the tables until the early hours.[32]

Such were the freedoms under Bolshevik rule that Lockhart remarked:

> During our first two months in Moscow, Robins and I enjoyed a privileged position. We had no difficulty in seeing the various Commissars. We were even allowed to be present at certain meetings of the Central Executive Committee. On one occasion we went to hear the debate on the new army.[33]

In fact, at this time, all parties, including the bourgeois parties, were allowed to operate quite freely and produce their own newspapers. The only exception was the fascist Black Hundreds, who were banned. Only when opposition parties openly sided with the forces of counter-revolution and imperialist intervention were measures taken against them. But this would have been the case in even the most democratic bourgeois regime. No government on earth can allow parties that are engaged in armed conspiracies and terrorist actions against it. They would soon feel the full force of the law. Such repression is regarded as quite natural for the bourgeoisie. But when a workers' government like the Soviet Republic takes measures of self-defence, that is another matter!

The bourgeois Cadets were the first to provoke a reaction from the state, when they directly conspired with Kornilov and Kaledin to overthrow the Soviet government. They were officially declared 'enemies of the people' on 25 December 1917. Even then, the Cadets were allowed to participate in the elections for the Constituent Assembly and captured twenty-four seats. After that, unable to reconcile themselves to the revolution, many fled abroad from where they continued to support the White armies and the armies of foreign intervention.

Sabotage

Within days of coming to power, the Soviet government faced a campaign of sabotage by former government white-collar employees, who, under the influence of the Mensheviks and SRs, went on strike or worked to sabotage the new ministries. On 10 November, a general strike of all state employees was called in Petrograd which completely paralysed the Soviet administration. Workers at the ministries of Labour, Agriculture, Foreign Affairs, Food, Finance and Posts and Telegraphs all withdrew their labour. Public employees and municipal workers, manipulated by bourgeois reactionaries, openly engaged in organised disruption.

When Trotsky turned up at the Commissariat of Foreign Affairs, the staff ridiculed him, and simply refused to recognise his authority. John Reed explains:

> Trotsky went to the Ministry of Foreign Affairs; the functionaries refused to recognise him, locked themselves in, and when the doors were forced, resigned. He demanded the keys of the archives; only when he brought workmen to force the locks were they given up. Then it was discovered that Neratov, former assistant Foreign Minister, had disappeared with the Secret Treaties...[34]

When Shlyapnikov, the Commissar of Labour, arrived at the ministry, the skeleton staff refused to show him to his office. Kollontai, the Commissar of Public Welfare, with tears streaming down her face, arrested the strikers until they gave up the keys to the safe – but the former minister, the Countess Panina, had absconded with the funds.

The bank workers, backed by big businesses, also went on strike, declaring they would only make payments to the Provisional Government and nobody else, placing the Soviet government in an impossible position. The telephonists and telegraphists – naive youths, in the main – again refused to work and walked out. As these constituted the main means of communication, this was a serious blow to the new government. Of course, the salaries and wages of the 'strikers' were covered by various bankers and industrialists, who were behind the sabotage. John Reed described what was happening at the Telephone Exchange:

> The employees of the building, the line-men and labourers – they stayed. But the switchboards must be operated – the telephone was vital… Only half a dozen trained operators were available. Volunteers were called for; a hundred responded, sailors, soldiers, workers. The six girls scurried backwards and forwards, instructing, helping, soldering… So, crippled, halting, but *going*, the wires began to hum. The first thing was to connect Smolny with the barracks and the factories; the second, to cut off the Duma and the *junker* schools…[35]

The bureaucratic apparatus of the trade unions lagged far behind the masses. In fact, most of the trade unions were under the control of the old compromiser-socialists and acted in unison to wreck the new revolution. The leaders of the Union of Railway Workers, under the control of the Mensheviks and SRs, refused to cooperate with the 'illegitimate' government.

The trade union leaders threatened to call a general strike unless a 'broad' coalition government was formed of all socialist parties – meaning that the Bolsheviks should surrender their victory. These so-called 'leaders' reflected the past. In fact, where mass meetings were called, as on the railways, workers from the workshops passed resolutions condemning the threats of their leaders. In the meantime, the scale of strikes and sabotage paralysed the functioning of the government.

Administrative staff and equipment were in short supply and the government was forced to work around the clock simply to hold things together. Lenin was on call practically twenty-four hours a day. The Bolshevik Party had already gone through a baptism of fire to take power in October, but now they faced mountainous logistical challenges simply to survive. Even the simplest things became a colossal trial.

With no experience of government, the new ministries were established with a great degree of improvisation. Stanisław Pestkowsky described the setting up of the Commissariat of Nationalities, explaining that this grand office of state was located in a corner of a room in the Smolny that was already occupied, with only a small table, two chairs and a piece of paper fixed on the wall which said: 'People's Commissariat for the business of Nationalities'.

This was typical of the way the new institutions were being brought into being, where improvisation was on the order of the day. When Bruce

Lockhart met with Lenin in the Smolny, he was shocked by the sparseness and even the complete lack of furniture: "He received me in a small room on the same floor as Trotsky's. It was untidy and bare of all trappings except a writing desk and a few plain chairs."[36]

Arthur Ransome, who was present in Russia in 1917 and 1918, and returned in 1919, visited the Smolny, where he described his experience in the canteen where commissars simply grabbed their meals:

> Dinner in Smolny was the same informal affair that it was in the old days, only with much less to eat. The Commissars, men and women, came in from their work, took their places, fed and went back to work again, Zinoviev in particular staying only a few minutes. The meal was extremely simple, soup with shreds of horseflesh in it, very good indeed, followed by a little kasha [boiled buckwheat] together with small slabs of some sort of white stuff of no particular consistency or taste. Then tea and a lump of sugar.[37]

The Bolsheviks were striving to create a new world out of the ashes of the old. But all the obstacles and powers of the old order were being amassed against them. In early December, a revolutionary organ was created to fight the sabotage called the 'All-Russian Extraordinary Commission to Fight Counter-revolution and Sabotage', commonly known as the Cheka. It had a small staff and few resources, but at its head was Dzerzhinsky, a stern but honest Bolshevik. Its role, however, was very limited until the outbreak of the White Terror much later in 1918.

The crisis over coalition

The demands of the Menshevik leaders of the Union of Railway Workers, that the Bolsheviks stand down in favour of a coalition government, provoked an unexpected crisis within the new Soviet government.

Those who stood on the right wing of Bolshevism – Zinoviev, Kamenev, Rykov, Viktor Nogin, and Lunacharsky – who had argued against the October insurrection for being premature, now championed the idea that the Bolsheviks would not be able to retain power unless they entered a coalition with the Mensheviks and SRs.

As a result of this pressure from the Right, Lenin agreed to open negotiations with the 'Compromiser' parties in the days following the seizure of power. But these parties were adamant that they should be given a majority in a new coalition government and that those responsible for the 'debacle', namely Lenin and Trotsky, be excluded. In reality, this meant nothing more than total surrender and the beheading of the revolution. In spite of this, the right-wing Bolsheviks were prepared to countenance these proposals.

While Lenin said he was not opposed to negotiations in principle, he believed it was essential that the Bolsheviks retain a majority in any new government. Furthermore, a new coalition would need to accept the Soviet state and its decrees on peace, land, the national question and so on. Knowing his Menshevik and SR opponents, Lenin believed that they would refuse these conditions and that nothing would come from the 'negotiations'. Nevertheless, Lenin hoped the experience of going through this farce would put an end to the vacillations within the Bolshevik camp.

At the following Central Committee, where both Lenin and Trotsky were absent, a vote was taken on the Railway Workers' ultimatum that contained the exclusion of Lenin and Trotsky from any future government. While there were seven votes against (Joffe, Dzerzhinsky, Vinter,* Kollontai, Sverdlov, Bubnov, Uritsky), there were still four votes in favour of the proposal (Kamenev, Milyutin, Rykov, Sokolnikov). This reflected the real balance of forces at the top of the Party. It was then agreed to appoint a delegation to meet and discuss with the rail union leaders, consisting of Kamenev, Sokolnikov and Riazanov – the Bolshevik conciliators.

On 14 November, the delegation reported back, but merely repeated what was already known: the Menshevik union leaders were determined to behead the revolution and overturn its victory. Dzerzhinsky criticised the delegates for overstepping their mandate and reiterated the opposition of the Central Committee. At this point, Lenin came out firmly against any further negotiations, which he regarded as futile. It was time, in his opinion, to end the vacillation and time-wasting.

It took Lenin's intervention to bring matters to a head, but he was strongly opposed by Zinoviev, Kamenev, and Rykov. "If we break them off, we will lose the groups who are supporting us as well and we will be in no position to keep power", stated Rykov.[38] But Lenin was unequivocally supported by Trotsky. "The parties which took no part in the insurrection", explained Trotsky plainly, "want to grab power from the people who overthrew them."[39]

It was at an enlarged Central Committee meeting that the majority finally agreed to a resolution that laid down strict conditions, which, if adhered to, would inevitably lead to an end to the negotiations. Sukhanov notes that "now Lenin and Trotsky were completely at one."[40] All the old disagreements had completely evaporated. It was at this meeting that Lenin remarked:

---

* Pseudonym of Latvian Bolshevik Jan Antonovich Berzin.

As for conciliation I cannot speak about that seriously. Trotsky long ago said that unification is impossible. Trotsky understood this and from that time on there has been no better Bolshevik.[41]

All references to this important Central Committee meeting were deleted from the records by the Stalinists. Nevertheless, Trotsky managed to get hold of a photocopy of the original galley proofs that had been set up, but then scrapped by the State Publishers in 1927, under the title *The First Legal Petrograd Committee of the Bolsheviks in 1917*. The verbatim report of the meeting and original photographs of the galleys were published in Trotsky's book, *The Stalin School of Falsification*.*

To add to the government's problems, Lunacharsky tendered his resignation as Commissar of Education over the supposed damage in Moscow of the Kremlin buildings and some churches, due to a Red Guard bombardment. In fact, the damage was largely a myth, and he soon returned to his old post having disrupted the government in the process. Then, having returned, Lunacharsky came out for a coalition government with the 'Compromisers'. Lenin was furious. "When you come out against us at the moment of sharp struggle, you weaken us", stated Lenin, who was scathing about this behaviour.[42]

The following day, on 15 November, matters came to a head. Lenin submitted a resolution – which was only narrowly accepted – that defended the idea of a purely Bolshevik government and refused to yield to any threats and ultimatums. Following this, the Central Committee decided to instruct the vacillators in the leadership to submit to Party discipline or put themselves outside of the Party. Lenin stated:

> It stands to reason, a split would be highly deplorable. But an honest and open split would now be incomparably better than internal sabotage, the thwarting of our own decisions, disorganisation and prostration.[43]

Desertion

In face of this ultimatum, five members resigned from the Central Committee: Kamenev, Zinoviev, Rykov, Milyutin and Nogin. The last three also resigned

---

* In 2017, the Russian Political Encyclopedia (ROSSPEN) published *Lenin's Unknown Documents, 1891-1922*, a substantive archival collection of previously unpublished material. It supplies cast iron proof that what Trotsky provided in his book was 100 per cent accurate.

See the minutes for the 14 November 1917 St. Petersburg Committee of the RSDLP(B) at docs.historyrussia.org/ru/nodes/30812-vystuplenie-na-zasedanii-peterburgskogo-komiteta-rsdrp-b-1-14-noyabrya-1917-g

from the Soviet Government, together with seven other members. This provoked an extremely deep governmental crisis, at a time when there was no room for weakness.

Lenin always said that a crisis brought the best and the worst out of people. This was one of those occasions. Many of the 'old Bolsheviks', who had been close to Lenin for years, simply collapsed under the pressure and placed the very survival of the revolution in doubt.

Lenin wrote a message on behalf of the Central Committee to the Bolshevik members about the deepening crisis. In it, he never hid anything, but simply faced up squarely to all the difficulties, which was always his method:

> Comrades, yesterday, 4 November [17, New Style], several members of the Central Committee of our Party and of the Council of People's Commissars – Kamenev, Zinoviev, Nogin, Rykov, Milyutin and a few others – resigned from the Central Committee of our Party, and the three last named from the Council of People's Commissars. In a large Party like ours, notwithstanding the proletarian and revolutionary line of our policy, it was inevitable that individual comrades should have proved to be insufficiently staunch and firm in the struggle against the enemies of the people. The tasks that now face our Party are really immense, the difficulties are enormous, and several members of our Party who formerly held posts of responsibility have flinched in face of the onslaught of the bourgeoisie and fled from our ranks. The bourgeoisie and all its helpers are jubilant over this fact and are maliciously rejoicing, clamouring about disintegration and predicting the fall of the Bolshevik government.

> Comrades, do not believe these lies. The comrades who have resigned have acted as deserters, since they not only quitted the posts entrusted to them, but violated the direct decision of the Central Committee of our Party binding them to delay their resignation at least until a decision was taken by the Petrograd and Moscow Party organisations. We strongly condemn this desertion. We are profoundly convinced that all class-conscious workers, soldiers and peasants who belong to or sympathise with our Party will condemn the actions of the deserters with equal severity.[44]

The role of Zinoviev and Kamenev in opposing the October insurrection was very fresh in Lenin's mind: "You must recall, comrades, that two of the deserters, Kamenev and Zinoviev, acted as deserters and blacklegs even before the Petrograd uprising…"[45] Despite their campaign against the Party, this, he said confidently, would prove to be "a storm in a teacup".[46] Lenin, however, refused to moderate his tone:

Shame on all the faint-hearted, all the waverers and doubters, on all those who allowed themselves to be intimidated by the bourgeoisie or who have succumbed to the outcries of their direct and indirect supporters![47]

The Bolsheviks had invited the Left SRs to join the Soviet government, offering them three portfolios, but they had refused. Lenin was in favour of a coalition with the Left SRs, but not at any price. And he was not giving in to blackmail:

> We agreed, and *still* agree, to share power with the minority in the Soviets, provided that minority loyally and honestly undertake to submit to the majority and carry out the programme, *approved by the whole* Second All-Russia Congress of Soviets, for gradual, but firm and undeviating steps towards socialism. But we shall not submit to any ultimatums of groups of intellectuals who are not backed by the people, and who *in actual fact* are backed only by the Kornilovites, the Savinkov men, the officer cadets, etc.

> Let the working people, therefore, remain calm and firm! Our Party, the party of the Soviet majority, stands solid and united in defence of their interests and, as before, behind our Party stand the millions of the workers in the cities, the soldiers in the trenches and the peasants in the villages, prepared at all costs to achieve the victory of peace and the victory of socialism![48]

In the end, Zinoviev was forced to accept the undertaking and was readmitted to the Central Committee. The opposition at the top of the Party collapsed when the Mensheviks and SRs continued to make further outrageous demands. By the end of the month, those who had resigned asked to return.

Despite Zinoviev and Kamenev's criminal role, then and in the past, they were not expelled, but actually promoted and given very responsible positions in the state and the Party when Lenin was alive. Kamenev was at first appointed as chairman of the Executive Committee of the Soviets, the highest state body of the land, then as deputy to Lenin, chairman of the Council of People's Commissars. He was also a member of the Politburo, the highest body in the Party between Central Committees. Zinoviev received the key appointment as editor of the official state newspaper of the Central Executive Committee, *Izvestiya*. He also became chairman of the Petrograd Soviet, later chairman of the Presidium of the Communist International, and also member of the Politburo.

140. Alexey Kaledin   141. Mikhail Alekseyev

A by-product of this crisis was an agreement finally reached with the Left SRs to join the Soviet government, who received seven People's Commissariats, as opposed to eleven held by the Bolsheviks, thereby turning the government into a Bolshevik-Left SR coalition. A Left SR was also appointed deputy-head of the Cheka, responsible for internal security.

But before the end of the year, new challenges faced the young Soviet Republic. Firstly, there was the problem of the Constituent Assembly and how to deal with it; secondly, and more importantly, how to answer the German military advance, which led to the thorny negotiations at Brest-Litovsk.

Despite these challenges, Lenin was pleased to announce at the Third All-Russia Congress of Soviets in January 1918 that the Soviet government had been in power for two months and fifteen days. That was, he said, five days *more* than the workers of Paris had held power in the Paris Commune. Lenin confidently predicted:

> The example of the Soviet Republic will stand before them for a long time to come. Our socialist Republic of Soviets will stand secure, as a torch of international socialism and as an example to all the working people. Over there – conflict, war, bloodshed, the sacrifice of millions of people, capitalist exploitation; here – a genuine policy of peace and a socialist Republic of Soviets.[49]

142. Anton Denikin   143. Alexander Lukomsky

But the counter-revolution was continuing to gather its forces, beginning in south-eastern Russia, with the full backing of the imperialist powers. The Cossacks had found their leader in General Kaledin, who had managed to assemble a fighting force of several thousand.

Other generals joined their ranks, Generals Alekseyev, Denikin, Krasnov, Kornilov and Lukomsky, all of whom held important military positions under the Provisional Government. Alekseyev had established a 'Volunteer Army', composed mainly of former tsarist officers. While the revolution had spread, the south remained a hotbed of counter-revolution, presenting a mortal threat to the young Soviet Republic.

142. Anton Denikin   143. Alexander Lukomsky

26. Brest-Litovsk

Under tsarism, the call for a Constituent Assembly had long been one of the demands put forward by the Bolsheviks. It was a democratic demand, along with the right to organise, strike and vote. In tsarist Russia, where there were no democratic rights, such a demand was a very important way of connecting with the democratic aspirations of the masses.

Even after the February Revolution, this democratic demand continued to feature in Bolshevik propaganda, and the Bolsheviks attacked the Provisional Government for failing to convene the Constituent Assembly. But they always linked this demand with the slogan 'All Power to the Soviets', since they argued that only the victory of Soviet power would bring a Constituent Assembly into being.

Following the October Revolution, the calling of a Constituent Assembly could therefore not be avoided. The problem was that the revolution had ushered in a new Soviet regime that was a much higher form of democracy than any bourgeois parliament or constituent assembly. As the working class had already created the Soviets, there was no longer any practical need for a new assembly, especially one that did not correspond to the new class relations established by the October Revolution. In other words, the Constituent Assembly had been superseded by the Soviets. Lenin put the issue frankly:

> At one time, we considered the Constituent Assembly to be better than tsarism and the republic of Kerensky with their famous organs of power, but as the Soviets emerged, they, being revolutionary organisations of the whole people, naturally became incomparably superior to any parliament in the world, a fact that I emphasised as far back as last April.[1]

However, the question of calling a Constituent Assembly sparked heated debate within the Soviet government. Lenin wanted to postpone the Constituent Assembly, at least until the elections could be properly prepared. This preparation would mean, among other things, lowering of the voting age to eighteen, updating of the electoral lists which were out of date, and banning the Kornilovite and Cadet parties from standing. A certain delay would also give time for the Soviet decrees, at least partially, to be put into practice. However, once again, Lenin was overruled by the Central Committee, which decided to proceed with the elections on the old basis.

Given the real situation, once the Constituent Assembly had been called into being, the only function it could possibly have would be to ratify Soviet power and endorse its decrees. There was nothing else left for it to do.

Soviet democracy

The Soviet form of democracy was far superior, as under this new democracy, every worker, soldier and peasant in Russia had the right to vote in the election of deputies to their local Soviet, whose numbers corresponded to the number of electors. Local Soviets then elected delegates to an All-Russian Congress of Soviet Deputies. This was on the basis of one deputy for every 25,000 inhabitants in towns and one deputy for every 125,000 in the countryside. This Congress then elected a Central Executive Committee, which, in turn, appointed, controlled and dismissed the People's Commissars, who constituted the Soviet Government. All decrees of state importance were passed by the Central Executive Committee, before being issued as laws by the Council of People's Commissars.

Under this system, the masses were not limited to voting in an election every five years, as in bourgeois parliaments, where promises are continually violated with impunity. And the buying of elections, so endemic in bourgeois democracy, where millions of dollars are spent to elect rich people to power, was completely ruled out in a Soviet democracy. In a formal bourgeois democracy, where anyone can say (more or less) whatever they wish, as long as the bankers and capitalists decide, the masses are effectively disenfranchised. Behind the façade of bourgeois democracy lies the dictatorship of capital, the real power.

Soviet democracy was a people's democracy, with its elected representatives from factories, workshops and barracks, and from which the bourgeois were by definition excluded. Moreover, every delegate was regularly elected and subject to the right of immediate recall. This was a truly proletarian form of democracy from the bottom upwards. "Proletarian democracy is a *million times* more democratic than any bourgeois democracy", explained Lenin. "Soviet power is a million times more democratic than the most democratic bourgeois republics."[2]

The rich and privileged hated, and feared, the Soviet Republic. They openly declared their support for the counter-revolution. Lenin explained this in his 1918 pamphlet, *The Proletarian Revolution and the Renegade Kautsky*:

... the disfranchisement of the bourgeoisie is not a necessary and indispensable feature of the dictatorship of the proletariat. And in Russia, the Bolsheviks, who long before October put forward the slogan of proletarian dictatorship, did not say anything in advance about disenfranchising the exploiters. *This* aspect of the dictatorship did not make its appearance 'according to the plan' of any particular party; it *emerged* of itself in the course of the struggle. [...] even when the Mensheviks (who compromised with the bourgeoisie) still ruled the Soviets, the bourgeoisie cut themselves off from the Soviets of their own accord, boycotted them, put themselves up in opposition to them and intrigued against them. The Soviets arose without any constitution and existed without one for *more than a year* (from the spring of 1917 to the summer of 1918). The fury of the bourgeoisie against this independent and omnipotent (because it was all-embracing) organisation of the oppressed; the fight, the unscrupulous, self-seeking and sordid fight, the bourgeoisie waged against the Soviets; and, lastly, the overt participation of the bourgeoisie (from the Cadets to the Right Socialist-Revolutionaries, from Milyukov to Kerensky) in the Kornilov mutiny – all this *paved the way* for the formal exclusion of the bourgeoisie from the Soviets.[3]

And again:

The old bourgeois apparatus – the bureaucracy, the privileges of wealth, of bourgeois education, of social connections, etc. (these real privileges are the more varied the more highly bourgeois democracy is developed) – all this disappears under the Soviet form of organisation. Freedom of the press ceases to be hypocrisy, because the printing-plants and stocks of paper are taken away from the bourgeoisie. The same thing applies to the best buildings, the palaces, the mansions and manor houses. Soviet power took thousands upon thousands of these best buildings from the exploiters at one stroke, and in this way made the right of assembly – without which democracy is a fraud – a *million times* more democratic for the people. Indirect elections to non-local Soviets make it easier to hold congresses of Soviets, they make the *entire* apparatus less costly, more flexible, more accessible to the workers and peasants at a time when life is seething and it is necessary to be able very quickly to recall one's local deputy or to delegate him to a general congress of Soviets. [...]

Is there a single country in the world, even among the most democratic bourgeois countries, in which the *average rank-and-file* worker, the average rank-and-file *farm labourer*, or village semi-proletarian generally (i.e. the representative of the oppressed, of the overwhelming majority of the population), enjoys anything approaching such *liberty* of holding meetings in the best buildings, such *liberty* of using the largest printing-plants and biggest stocks of paper to express his ideas and to defend his interests, such *liberty* of promoting men and women of his own class to administer and to 'knock into shape' the state, as in Soviet Russia? [...]

In Russia, however, the bureaucratic machine has been completely smashed, razed to the ground; the old judges have all been sent packing, the bourgeois parliament has been dispersed – and *far more accessible* representation has been given to the workers and peasants; *their* Soviets have replaced the bureaucrats, or *their* Soviets have been put in control of the bureaucrats, and their Soviets have been authorised to elect the judges.[4]

In addition, the Bolshevik government elaborated four fundamental safeguards against careerism and bureaucracy, the founding principles of a workers' democracy:

1. The election of all officials. No official was to receive a wage higher than the average of a skilled worker.

2. There would be no permanent bureaucracy. The administrative duties were to be rotated, involving the widest layers of the population.

3. All workers would bear arms to protect the revolution against internal or external threats.

4. All power was invested in the Soviets, elected by the masses and accountable to them.

Dissolution

The Soviet government pressed on with the Constituent Assembly elections in November 1917 based on the old, outdated electoral register. Moreover, the candidate lists of the parties standing were out of date and largely based on the situation prior to the revolution. Thus, the Socialist-Revolutionary Party was represented by one list, whereas this party had already split into two parties, one of which was deeply hostile to the revolution, while the other was close to the Bolsheviks.

The SRs traditionally had a base in the peasantry. But the peasants had not had time to digest the split and make a clear choice between the two parties. Furthermore, they had not had the time to absorb the decrees on land or peace by the time of the election. The creaking parliamentary machinery and procedures lagged far behind the changes being ushered in by the revolution, and the Constituent Assembly could not accurately reflect the genuine will of the Russian people.

The results of the elections were declared on 30 December 1917 (12 January 1918). According to Liebman, the voting figures were:[5]

Party	Number of votes	Percentage vote
Socialist-Revolutionaries	20,900,000	58
Bolsheviks	9,023,963	25
Bourgeois parties (Cadets, etc.)	4,600,000	13
Mensheviks	1,700,000	4

Therefore, the Mensheviks and Socialist-Revolutionaries got a combined vote of 22,600,000 votes, or 62 per cent of the total. While the rural areas voted for the SRs, the industrial cities voted solidly for the Bolsheviks. The Bolsheviks also won around two-thirds of the votes of soldiers on the Western Front. The Mensheviks got most of their votes from the Caucasus.

In terms of seats, out of a total of 707, the Socialist-Revolutionaries had 410 seats – of which 370 went to candidates on the single SR list from the right wing and forty to the Left SRs – while the Bolsheviks gained 175, the Mensheviks sixteen, and the Cadets seventeen seats. The parties representing the national minorities gained eighty-six seats. The Popular Socialists gained two, and an Unknown got one seat.

The only purpose of the Constituent Assembly, under the concrete circumstances, was simply as a rallying point for the counter-revolution. This was revealed on 18 January 1918. On that day, the Constituent Assembly met and elected Viktor Chernov, the Right SR, as President, with 244 votes against 153 for the Left SR's candidate, Maria Spiridonova. When Sverdlov proposed the motion on behalf of the Soviet government to endorse the Soviet power and its decrees, it was voted down. This vote sealed the fate of the Constituent Assembly.

The question of power was now posed in the starkest terms. It would soon be resolved in practice. The revolutionary workers rallied around Soviet power, while the counter-revolution rallied around the Constituent Assembly. The Bolsheviks and the Left SRs, resting on the authority of the Soviets, stepped in and dissolved the Constituent Assembly after only thirteen hours of existence. To have allowed it to remain sitting would have turned it into a rallying point for counter-revolution, nothing more.

This was precisely the lesson to come out of the German Revolution of 1918, where the embryo of workers' power in the Workers' and Soldiers' Councils was dissolved by the German Social-Democrats in favour of elections to the 'democratic' National Assembly and a bourgeois republic. The elections to the National Assembly represented the victory of the counter-revolution in a democratic form. Behind the German bourgeois republic stood the bourgeoisie and the reactionary officers of the general staff.

Fortunately, in Russia, the Bolsheviks did not allow this to happen. When the Constituent Assembly was dissolved, there was no resistance whatsoever. There was no uprising or mass protests in its defence except for a small crowd of petty-bourgeois protesters, but they were soon scattered to the four winds.

It was the same experience as when Oliver Cromwell dissolved the Rump of the Long Parliament: "You are no Parliament. I say you are no Parliament; I will put an end to your sitting." Afterwards, Cromwell stated: "When they were dissolved, there was not so much as the barking of a dog, or any general or visible repining at it."[6] The Constituent Assembly was as irrelevant as the Rump Parliament in England. Nobody mourned its passing. As the historian EH Carr explains:

> The SRs had gone to the polls as a single party presenting one list of candidates. Its election manifesto had been full of lofty principles and aims but, though published on the day after the October Revolution, had been drafted before that event and failed to define the party attitude towards it. Now three days after the election the larger section of the party had made a coalition with the Bolsheviks, and formally split away from the other section which maintained its bitter feud against the Bolsheviks. The proportion between Right and Left SRs in the Constituent Assembly – 370 to 40 – was fortuitous. It was entirely different from the corresponding proportion in the membership of the peasants' congress, and did not represent the views of the electors on a vital point which had not been before them. "The people", said Lenin, "voted for a party which no longer existed." Reviewing the whole issue two years later Lenin found another argument which was more cogent than it appeared at first sight. He noted that in the large industrial cities the Bolsheviks had almost everywhere been ahead of the other parties. They secured an absolute majority in the two capitals taken together, the Kadets here being second and the SRs a poor third. But in matters of revolution

the well-known principle applied: "the town inevitably leads the country after it; the country inevitably follows the town." The elections to the Constituent Assembly, if they did not register the victory of the Bolsheviks, had clearly pointed the way to it for those who had eyes to see.[7]

This view was endorsed by Arthur Ransome, who explained:

> The Bolsheviks were not afraid of responsibility, were not looking for easy ways out, were confident that the whole of the active, conscious population was behind them, and swept the Assembly aside. Not anywhere in Russia did the indifferent mass stir in protest. The Assembly died, like the Tsardom, and the coalition before it.[8]

Plekhanov had long ago justified such an action at the 1903 Party Congress, citing the example of Cromwell, but he had abandoned his previous radicalism and now came out sharply against the Bolsheviks.

Bourgeois democracy was stillborn in Russia. But the bourgeoisie and its hangers-on continued to rally the forces with the sole aim of overthrowing the Soviets and establishing a military dictatorship – even if it was one based on German bayonets. It is no accident that the White armies in the civil war adopted the battle cry of the 'Constituent Assembly', a deceptive mask behind which stood the dictatorship of the generals, capitalists and landlords.

Brest-Litovsk

Following the publication of the Decree on Peace, adopted by the Soviet Congress on 9 November, the Bolshevik government proposed a general democratic peace to end the war. This peace proposal was to be without annexations or indemnities and was broadcast by radio from Russia on 20 November.

The Allies, however, replied with a stark threat that any attempt to make a separate peace with Germany would be met with dire consequences. Faced with this ultimatum, the Soviet Government stopped all military operations. This was then followed by another appeal to the Allies to join Russia in peace negotiations. But once again, this appeal was ignored.

Therefore, the Bolsheviks had no alternative but to open peace talks separately with Germany. On 2 December, Soviet Russia sent a delegation to Brest-Litovsk (modern-day Brest, Belarus) to meet with representatives from the Austro-Hungarian alliance. This meeting led to a ceasefire between Germany and Russia. Once more, the Soviet government appealed to the Allies to join the peace negotiations, but was again cold-shouldered.

On 16 December, an armistice was signed between the Soviet government and the central powers. A week later, on 22 December, formal peace negotiations opened at Brest-Litovsk, where the Soviet side was led by Trotsky, the Commissar of Foreign Affairs, assisted by Karl Radek. Given the extreme weakness of Russia, the Soviet Government aimed to use the negotiations to appeal – over the heads of the German generals – to the workers in Germany, with the hope of stimulating revolution.

As soon as the Soviet delegation arrived at Brest-Litovsk, Radek began handing out revolutionary literature to the German soldiers, which struck alarm among the German officers and diplomats, unaccustomed as they were to such behaviour. General Max Hoffman immediately protested about this outrageous diplomatic infringement. But Trotsky continued to take full advantage of the negotiations in order to skilfully make revolutionary appeals aimed at the German working class. This propaganda certainly had its effect in Germany, as Karl Liebknecht, who was in prison at the time, later confirmed.

But, as the talks dragged on, the German generals grew increasingly irritated and impatient. In the middle of the negotiations, Hoffman placed his great leather boot on the table. He had had enough. "For our part", noted Trotsky, "we never for a moment doubted that in the negotiations Hoffman's boot was the only reality to take seriously."[9]

On 18 January, the generals, concerned by the Bolshevik propaganda, pressed home their military advantage and demanded the Soviets sign an immediate peace treaty, which claimed Poland, Lithuania, a part of Estonia and Latvia, and also sizable areas of the Ukraine and Belarus for Germany.

Faced by this *de facto* ultimatum, Trotsky had no alternative but to break off negotiations and return to Petrograd. "We will not sign your robber's peace, but we demobilise our army and declare Russia is no longer at war", announced Trotsky. "Will the German people allow you to advance on a defenceless revolution?"[10] This outcome, however, caused huge divisions within the top of the Bolshevik Party, which once again threatened the stability of the new regime.

Originally, based on the experience of the French Revolution, the Bolsheviks' idea was that once the Russian proletariat came to power, it would need to launch a *revolutionary war* against the imperialist powers, or suffer an invasion. They believed that in the ensuing revolutionary wave sweeping Europe, a Soviet Red Army would come to the assistance of the workers' insurrection and help to establish a Socialist United States of Europe.

144. Signing the German-Russian armistice of 15 December 1917

That was the theory. However, reality posed things differently. After three years of terrible war, the Russian army was incapable of fighting any war, let alone a revolutionary war. The army was rapidly disintegrating and the peasant troops were leaving the trenches in their droves.

'Left Communists'

However, within the Bolshevik Party, there was a groundswell of support for a revolutionary war, no matter the consequences. This shrill ultra-leftism became the battle-cry of the 'Left Communists' and the Left SRs, and was championed in the Bolshevik leadership by Bukharin. Support for this idea was not only confined to the top but was also prevalent within sections of the working class and in the ranks of the Party. They had clearly become intoxicated by the revolution and were failing to take account of the new realities on the ground, most notably the dissolution of the army.

Lenin was radically opposed to such a move. Under the conditions, such a policy would plunge the Soviet Republic into an unwinnable war that would wreck the revolution. He based himself on the cold facts. Rather than the folly of a revolutionary war, Lenin came out forcefully for an *immediate*

145. Hindenburg's officers meet the Soviet delegation at Brest-Litovsk

signing of the peace treaty with Germany, despite the harsh terms. As always, Lenin put things squarely:

> The socialist government of Russia is faced with the question – a question whose solution brooks no delay – of whether to accept this peace with annexations now, or to immediately wage a revolutionary war. In fact, no middle course is possible.[11]

This was the stark choice and Lenin demanded they accept the peace.

Bukharin and the 'Lefts' argued from on high that signing the treaty was a betrayal of socialism and internationalism, and was in effect giving support to the German imperialists. Lenin rejected this argument as false and told the 'Lefts' they needed to face the facts and base themselves on reality. Romantic arguments in favour of revolutionary war, he said, "might perhaps answer the human yearning for the beautiful, dramatic and striking, but […] it would totally disregard the objective balance of class forces and material factors at the present stage of the socialist revolution now under way."[12]

Lenin explained that the signing of a peace treaty, under the concrete conditions, was not a betrayal, just as workers who were defeated in a strike were forced to sign an agreement to return to work under worse conditions. It was a retreat, but a necessary one that faced up to reality. The striking workers needed to regroup, strengthen themselves, and prepare for the future. The

146. The Soviet delegation at Brest-Litovsk
Left to right: Vladimir Lipsky, Trotsky, Vasili Altfater, Kamenev

same thing applied to the Soviet state, which had an imperialist's boot on its neck. As Lenin pointed out:

> I want to yield territory to the present victor to gain time. That's what it's all about, and only that... Signing a treaty in defeat is a way of gathering strength... If we were to wage a revolutionary war, as Bukharin wants, it would be the best way to get rid of us right now.[13]

Lenin explained the simple truth that the Russian army was in no condition to fight the Germans, as it was completely exhausted and on its knees. It was unable to resist any new offensive. The old tsarist officers had deserted their posts in their thousands and a new Red Army did not exist at this point. "To ignore the objective balance of class forces on this issue would be a fatal error", warned Lenin:[14]

> If the German revolution were to break out and triumph in the coming three or four months, the tactics of an immediate revolutionary war might perhaps not ruin our socialist revolution.
>
> If, however, the German revolution does not occur in the next few months, the course of events, if the war is continued, will inevitably be such that grave defeats will compel Russia to conclude an even more disadvantageous separate peace...[15]

Lenin believed that it was impermissible to gamble on the hope of an immediate German revolution, which unfortunately was not guaranteed. "We have no right to take such risks", he said, which would be disastrous for the young Soviet Republic.[16]

But Bukharin was completely opposed to Lenin. He wanted to risk everything, including the Russian revolution, for the hope of stimulating a European conflagration. "The Russian revolution will either be saved by an international revolution, or it will perish under the blows of international capital", he proclaimed.[17] Lenin believed this to be preposterous.

When Lenin heard the news of mass strikes in Austria and Germany in January, he was delighted and regarded them as signs of the beginning of the German Revolution. He therefore believed that this was a time to drag out the negotiations. "This fact offers us the opportunity, for the time being, of further delaying and dragging out the peace negotiations", he explained.[18]

This idea of extending the negotiations was similar to Trotsky's original position. Trotsky, like Lenin, was adamantly opposed to the idea of a revolutionary war under these conditions. He wanted to string out the negotiations as long as possible to provide a platform for further revolutionary propaganda. This had been very successful to date, but still needed time to have its complete effect. His view was accepted by everyone.

"Our words will reach the German people over the heads of the German generals", stated Kamenev to the All-Russian Central Executive Committee, "our words will strike from the hands of the German generals the weapon with which they fool their people."[19]

In fact, this was later confirmed when General Erich Ludendorff published his memoirs, in which he devoted ten pages to Brest-Litovsk. Lenin related:

> When Kamenev and I read that chapter, we said: "This is the best justification of the Brest Treaty." He tells how Trotsky and others had driven them into a corner during the talks, how they were outwitted, and so on. We decided there and then that these pages had to be translated and published with a short preface...[20]

Whether this was done, we do not know.

Morgan Philips Price, in touch with what was happening, confirmed the fears of the imperialists: "The rulers of Germany are in terror that the infection of the Russian Revolution is spreading into their army."[21] The propaganda was working, but would take more time to come to fruition. How much more time exactly was a difficult question to answer. But time was in short supply.

However, Lenin and Trotsky both met with stiff resistance within the Bolshevik Party for their opposition to waging an immediate revolutionary war. A large majority of the Petrograd Committee was in favour of a revolutionary war, as was the Moscow Committee. But there was also a growing appetite for such a move even in the working class, influenced by the easy victory in October.

Three positions

At the end of the day, there were, in reality, three positions on this question: Bukharin was in favour of an all-out revolutionary war; Lenin was opposed to war and in favour of *immediately* signing a peace treaty; while Trotsky was opposed to war and arguing not to sign, but rather to drag out the negotiations. Trotsky added that if there was a new military advance by the Germans, then they should sign. In reality, Trotsky's formula of 'neither war nor peace' served as a bridge to Lenin's position.

However, at the Central Committee meeting on 22 January, Bukharin's position was overwhelmingly accepted. Lenin's position gained fifteen votes, Trotsky's position sixteen, while Bukharin's support for revolutionary war got a massive thirty-two votes, more than Lenin and Trotsky's votes combined. It was clear the Party stood for a revolutionary war.

In these arguments, we are dealing with serious *tactical* differences, but not any based on principles. If a Red Army of millions had existed at this time, the question would have been posed entirely differently: a revolutionary war would have been possible.

In 1920, for instance, the Red Army had over 5 million members and was strong enough to march all the way up to the gates of Warsaw, although, even then, it was overstretched. But, in January – February 1918, there was no such Red Army.

Shortly after the Central Committee, Lenin summed up the situation and drew a parallel from the history of Bolshevism:

The state of affairs now obtaining in the Party reminds me very strongly of the situation in the summer of 1907 when the overwhelming majority of the Bolsheviks favoured the boycott of the Third Duma and I stood side by side with Dan in favour of participation and was subjected to furious attacks for my opportunism. Objectively, the present issue is a complete analogy; as then, the majority of the Party functionaries, proceeding from the very best revolutionary motives and the best Party traditions, allow themselves to be carried away by a 'flash' slogan and *do not grasp the new* socio-economic and political situation, do not take into consideration *the change in the conditions* that demands a speedy and abrupt change in tactics.

Lenin revealed the attitude of the rank-and-file Bolsheviks, who defended the traditional line of revolutionary war:

"I stand by Lenin's old position", exclaimed one young Muscovite (youth is one of the greatest virtues distinguishing that group of speakers). And that same speaker reproached me for repeating the old arguments of the defencists about the improbability of a revolution in Germany.

The whole trouble is that the Muscovites want to stick to the old *tactical* position, and stubbornly refuse to see the *change* that has taken place, the *new objective* situation that has arisen.

The Muscovites, in their zealous repetition of old slogans, have not even taken into consideration the fact that we Bolsheviks have now all become defencists. Having overthrown the bourgeoisie, having denounced and exposed the secret treaties, having proposed peace to all peoples, actually… [the text breaks off][22]

A further Central Committee meeting was called on 24 January, where again a separate peace was discussed. This time, Lenin found two allies in Stalin and Zinoviev, but he was nevertheless forced to distance himself from them, as Stalin believed there was no revolutionary movement in the West, while Zinoviev believed making peace would strengthen chauvinism in Germany.

Lenin explained that if the Bolshevik leadership believed a German revolution was about to immediately develop, "then we must sacrifice ourselves, for the power of the German revolution will be much greater than ours." But this, he believed, was not the case. While, on the other hand, "over here it already has a newborn and loudly shouting infant, and unless we now say clearly that we agree to peace, we shall perish. It is important for us to hold out until the general socialist revolution gets under way…"[23]

Incidentally, the fact that Lenin was prepared to sacrifice the Russian Revolution for a successful German one is an extremely telling point, which shows his implacable commitment to internationalism.

Germans launch new offensive

In the end, Trotsky insisted that the revolutionary war position be once again put to the vote. This resulted in only two votes in favour, eleven against, and one abstention. Next, according to the minutes, Lenin proposed they vote "that we do everything to drag out signing the peace…"[24] The vote was taken, with twelve in favour and one against. Trotsky then suggested they vote on his formula: "we halt the war, do not conclude peace and demobilise the army."[25] This was passed with nine voting in favour and seven against.

This vote, however, did not put an end to the matter – far from it. The debate over Brest-Litovsk, and what position to take on it, continued to rage within the Party.

When a special conference was called on 3 February, a majority of the delegates abstained over whether to sign a peace agreement. On 10 February, after the Bolsheviks tried to prolong the negotiations as much as possible, they were abruptly broken off by the German generals, who had lost all patience.

Trotsky reported back to the Soviet Central Executive Committee and a resolution, moved by Sverdlov, was passed unanimously approving Trotsky's conduct at Brest-Litovsk.*

However, within a week, the Germans declared they were at war with Soviet Russia and launched a new offensive. Everyone suspected that the German imperialists had come to an agreement with the Allied imperialists to allow them to crush the Soviet Republic. On 18 February, the Bolshevik Central Committee met again to discuss the imminent danger. After a long discussion, the meeting adjourned until the evening, when, unexpectedly, the latest news arrived of further German advances.

This news turned the tide and Lenin's arguments now won the day: there was no alternative but to agree to the German demands and sign a damaging treaty. In the vote to send the German government an immediate offer to conclude peace, there were seven votes in favour, which included Trotsky's vote, with five votes against and one abstention. Lenin and Trotsky were then charged with drawing up the text to the Germans.

A few days later, an additional complication arose when Trotsky reported that Britain and France offered to supply military aid to Russia to continue its resistance against Germany. The proposal was made through the French Military Mission and was reported to the Central Committee on 22 February.

Bukharin and the 'Left Communists' were vehemently opposed to accepting *anything* from the imperialists on principle. According to the

---

* It should be noted that from this time, the Russian calendar changes. They adopted the New Style Gregorian calendar from 14 February 1918 onwards (which would have been 1 February in the Old Style). The New Style calendar has been used throughout this book.

minutes: "Comrade Bukharin believes that the 'allies' have a plan here to turn Russia into one of their colonies. He points out that it is unthinkable to accept support from imperialists of any sort."[26]

Trotsky, on the other hand, managed to convince the meeting to accept the military aid to assist their revolutionary army, even from the imperialist governments: "… we obtain them where we can, including therefore from capitalist governments."[27] Of course, he said, in doing so, there would be no strings attached and the Soviet government would retain its complete independence in its foreign policy. Trotsky's proposal was approved by six votes in favour and five votes against. Lenin, however, was absent.

When Lenin heard about the vote, he asked in his absence for the following statement to be appended to the minutes in support of Trotsky's proposal: "Please add my vote *in favour* of taking potatoes and weapons from the Anglo-French imperialist robbers."[28]

Although the Russians had accepted the German demands, on 22 February the German generals replied with even more draconian terms. Furthermore, they demanded such terms be signed within three days. Lenin stated unequivocally that the Soviet government had no alternative but to sign, even with this humiliating imposition. However, this provoked a further revolt in the Party, and the Petrograd and Moscow Party Committees denounced Lenin's proposal.

This served to deepen the rifts at the top of the Party. Bukharin immediately tendered his resignation from the Central Committee and the editorship of *Pravda*. This was followed by the joint resignations from all posts of Lomov, Uritsky, Bubnov, Smirnov, Pyatakov, Vasily Yakovlev, Stukov and Pokrovsky. They were also joined by Kollontai, who resigned in protest from the Central Committee and her government post.

Refusing to retreat, Lenin wrote an article called 'The Revolutionary Phrase', which argued against those who were getting carried away and intoxicated with revolutionary phrases, and specifically aimed at the advocates of revolutionary war. It was vital to face facts and not be swayed with abstract generalisations. The reality, he explained, was that the "old army does not exist. The new army is only just being born."[29]

The following day, Lenin wrote an article called 'The Itch', justifying the Party's decision to immediately sue for peace with the Germans. He believed that there was no other alternative but to take this road. To illustrate his reasoning, he told a story about Ivan Kalyayev, an old SR terrorist:

Let us suppose Kalyayev, in order to kill a tyrant and monster, acquires a revolver from an absolute villain, a scoundrel and robber, by promising him bread, money and vodka for the service rendered. Can one condemn Kalyayev for his 'deal with a robber' for the sake of obtaining a deadly weapon? Every sensible person will answer 'no'. If there is nowhere else for Kalyavev to get a revolver, and if his intention is really an honourable one (the killing of a tyrant, not killing for plunder), then he should not be reproached but commended for acquiring a revolver in this way.

But if a robber, in order to commit murder for the sake of plunder, acquires a revolver from another robber in return for money, vodka or bread, can one compare (not to speak of identifying) *such* a 'deal with a robber' with the deal made by Kalyayev?

No, everyone who is not out of his mind or infected by the itch will agree that one cannot. Any peasant who saw an 'intellectual' disavowing such an obvious truth by means of phrase-making would say: you, sir, ought not to be managing the state but should join the company of wordy buffoons or should simply put yourself in a steam bath and get rid of the itch.[30]

At the end of the article Lenin noted that in the American War of Independence, the American revolutionaries received help from Spain and France, who were just as much their enemies, a swipe against those 'Left Bolsheviks', such as Bukharin, who were against taking 'potatoes' from the robber imperialists.

On 23 February, to show how serious matters were, Lenin himself issued a threat at the Central Committee to resign from the government and the Central Committee if the 'Lefts' were to get the upper hand. He stated in *Pravda*: "… I personally, of course, would not remain for a second either in the government or in the Central Committee of our Party if the policy of phrase-making were to gain the upper hand." At a meeting of the Central Committee, he explained:[31]

Some have reproached me for coming out with an ultimatum. I put it as a last resort. It is a mockery for our Central Committee members to talk of an international civil war. There is a civil war in Russia, but not in Germany. Our agitation remains. We are agitating not by words, but by the revolution. That too remains. Stalin is wrong when he says that we need not sign. These terms must be signed. If you don't sign them, you will sign the Soviet power's death warrant within three weeks.[32]

Lenin wins majority

At the Central Committee, Trotsky coincided fully with Lenin's position. He said:

> We cannot fight a revolutionary war when the Party is split. It is not only international relations that have to be taken into account but, with conditions as they are, our Party is in no position to lead a war, especially as some of the supporters of war do not want the material means to wage it with.[33]

In the vote, those in favour of signing the harsher terms received seven votes, with four votes against and four abstentions, which included Trotsky's. Trotsky's abstention, which he announced in advance, was decisive in allowing Lenin's proposal to pass.

Once again, this decision provoked a number of resignations from all Party and Soviet positions. The situation facing the revolution was serious in the extreme. However, Lenin was not only able to keep his nerve, but to calmly assess the situation and face down his critics. In his article, 'A Painful, But Necessary Lesson', he spoke about the giant of world imperialism, namely Germany, which *must* be fought. But, he explained, "one must *know how* to fight him…"[34] He then went on to explain the harsh realities of life:

> A peasant country that has been subjected to unparalleled devastation by three years of war and that has begun the socialist revolution, must avoid armed conflicts – must avoid them while it is still possible, even at the cost of huge sacrifices – in order to be able to do something worthwhile before the 'last, decisive battle' begins.

> That battle will begin only when the socialist revolution breaks out in the leading imperialist countries. That revolution is undoubtedly maturing and growing stronger month by month, week by week. That growing strength *must* be helped. And we have to *know how* to help it. It would harm and not help that growing strength if we were to give up the neighbouring Soviet Socialist Republic to destruction at a moment when it obviously has no army.

> We must not turn into an empty phrase the great slogan 'We bank on the victory of socialism in Europe'. It is a true slogan if we have in mind the long and difficult path to the full victory of socialism. It is an indisputable philosophic-historical truth in respect of the entire 'era of the socialist revolution'. But any abstract truth becomes an empty phrase if it is applied to *any* concrete situation. It is indisputable that 'every strike conceals the hydra of the social revolution'. But it is nonsense to think that we can stride directly from a strike to the revolution. If we 'bank on

the victory of socialism in Europe' in the sense that we guarantee to the people that the European revolution will break out and is certain to be victorious within the next few weeks, certainly before the Germans have time to reach Petrograd, Moscow or Kiev, before they have time to 'finish off' our railway transport, we shall be acting not as serious internationalist revolutionaries, but as adventurers.[35]

In the middle of this crisis, the Moscow Bureau of the Party went so far as to pass a resolution *unanimously* expressing no confidence in the Soviet Government. It then went on to demand the election of a new Central Committee and refused in advance to abide by the peace terms with Germany. It went on to warn that it "considers a split in the Party in the very near future hardly avoidable."[36]

While Lenin was taken aback by this serious provocation, he nevertheless adopted a conciliatory tone to defuse the situation. In fact, faced with talk about a split, he showed remarkable restraint:

> There is nothing monstrous, nor even strange in all this. It is quite natural that comrades who sharply disagree with the Central Committee over the question of a separate peace should sharply condemn the Central Committee and express their conviction that a split is inevitable. All that is the most legitimate right of Party members, which is quite understandable.[37]

However, what really angered Lenin was the light-minded resolution from Moscow, where it stated it was prepared to risk everything:

> In the interests of the world revolution, we consider it expedient to accept the possibility of losing Soviet power, which is now becoming purely formal…[38]

Lenin regarded this view as the height of irresponsibility. He believed the very suggestion of abandoning the revolution was utterly outrageous. Behind this, Lenin detected a hopeless pessimism, as if the Soviet power had no choice but to engage in a fruitless struggle and go down to inevitable defeat. This he could never accept.

Soon afterwards, on 3 March, the peace treaty with Germany was signed. It was an extremely bitter pill to swallow, but a necessary one. Russia would lose around a quarter of her territory, with over a third of her population, 32 per cent of her agricultural land, 54 per cent of all industrial plants and 89 per cent of her coal mines. In addition, Russia was forced to recognise the independence of Ukraine and cede three districts in the Caucasus to Turkey. But the Soviet Republic had been saved from extinction and had gained time, which, for Lenin, was *the* main consideration.

At the Seventh Extraordinary Party Congress held on 6-8 March, Lenin gave the political report. He reviewed the achievements of the October Revolution, which also dealt with the immense difficulties that it faced. In the report, he stressed: "I repeat, our salvation from all these difficulties is an all-European revolution."[39] It was important that this statement was not turned into a mere phrase, he explained. Referring to the treaty of Brest-Litovsk, he believed that: "This crisis will be overcome. Under no circumstances will it break the neck of our Party, or of our revolution."[40]

Lenin nevertheless warned the Congress that it must be prepared to face extraordinary difficulties, and even severe setbacks. This would, he said, sometimes even mean "to crawl on your belly in the mud…"[41] However, he returned to the same point that the fate of the Russian revolution was tied to the fate of the European revolution, especially the German revolution. "At all events", he explained bluntly, "under all conceivable circumstances, if the German revolution does not come, we are doomed."[42]

Bukharin's opposition

Bukharin and the 'Left Communists' refused to accept the agreement and launched a daily newspaper, the *Kommunist* – the organ of the Petrograd Committee of the Party – to oppose the treaty with Germany. Led by Bukharin, the 'Lefts' now constituted the main opposition at the Party Congress. In the debate, Lenin replied to him in the bluntest language:

> Now that Bukharin is thundering against us for having demoralised the masses, he is perfectly correct, except that it is himself and not us that he is attacking. Who caused this mess in the Central Committee? – You, Comrade Bukharin. (*Laughter.*) No matter how much you shout "No", the truth will out; we are here in our own comradely family, we are at our own Congress, we have nothing to hide, the truth must be told.[43]

Lenin later criticised Trotsky's position, but in a far milder term, regarding it as a tactical difference:

> Now I must say something about Comrade Trotsky's position. There are two aspects to his activities; when he began the negotiations at Brest and made splendid use of them for agitation, we all agreed with Comrade Trotsky. He has quoted part of a conversation with me, but I must add that it was agreed between us that we would hold out until the Germans presented an ultimatum, and then we would give way. The Germans deceived us – they stole five days out of seven from us. Trotsky's tactics were correct as long as they were aimed at delaying

matters; they became incorrect when it was announced that the state of war had been terminated but peace had not been concluded. I proposed quite definitely that peace be concluded. We could not have got anything better than the Brest peace.[44]

Trotsky concurred they were forced to sign the treaty:

> Yes, we signed it, clenching our teeth, for we knew how weak we were. Is there anything shameful in the fact that we were too weak to tear away the noose that was being tightened round our neck? Yes, we agreed to make peace with German imperialism, just as a hungry worker, clenching his teeth, goes to a kulak employer and sells the labour of himself and his wife for half its worth, because he has no other means of existence.[45]

Lenin's resolution on the peace was passed at the Congress by thirty votes to twelve, with four abstentions. But, at Lenin's request, the resolution was never made public, given the sensitivities surrounding it. As an olive branch, the Congress then called upon those who had resigned from their government posts to withdraw their resignations. Furthermore, as a mark of good faith, members of the Opposition were also elected to the Central Committee and onto the Commission to revise the Party programme. It was with such a patient, and even painstaking, approach, pioneered by Lenin, that a split in the Party was avoided and the crisis overcome.

Bukharin and his supporters, however, still campaigned as an opposition within the Party, but they were soon reduced to a small grouping when the All-Russian Congress of Soviets, the highest body in the land, ratified the peace treaty. Bukharin's daily paper was reduced to a weekly by June, reflecting its declining influence.

It is worth noting that an opposition faction within the Party was allowed to produce a public daily paper to argue its case. The Party was now a mass party, and this reflects both the high degree of flexibility shown by Lenin and the Bolsheviks in organisational matters, and the levels of internal party democracy that operated within the Bolshevik Party, even in the most difficult circumstances.

However, the Brest-Litovsk affair was not yet at an end. Following the signing of the treaty with Germany, a new and even more dangerous governmental crisis erupted. On 19 March 1918, the Left SRs, who were vehemently opposed to the treaty, resigned *en bloc* from the Council of People's Commissars. The alliance of Bolsheviks and Left SRs had broken down irreparably.

After only three months, the coalition government of Bolsheviks and Left SRs came to an abrupt end, forcing the Bolsheviks to govern alone. The idea of a one-party regime had never been regarded as a principle for the Bolsheviks, and it was certainly not what they wanted now. The sudden departure of the Left SRs meant that the political base upon which the revolutionary government rested was weakened. And the consequences were extremely serious.

27. Fighting for Survival

The draconian terms of the Treaty of Brest-Litovsk were a devastating blow to the Soviet Republic. However, despite this humiliation, there was some hope that this agreement would lead to a certain respite, a period in which peaceful reconstruction could begin. "We have gained the possibility of a respite", reflected Lenin, "even if only for twelve days…"[1] He added: "Possibly it will be exceedingly brief because the imperialist robbers are bearing down on us […] We do not close our eyes to the fact that the country lies in ruins."[2]

As it turned out, there was little – if any – respite. There was no way of avoiding the fact that the Soviet government was facing a host of crises on a number of fronts: growing destitution, famine, a worthless paper currency, a restless peasantry, a White rebellion in the south, and the beginning of a ferocious civil war.

As a result of the Treaty of Brest-Litovsk, then the civil war, whole regions that produced and supplied grain were lost, and food became increasingly scarce. As a consequence, famine conditions developed in the towns and cities, compounded by the collapse of the transport system, especially the railways. In addition, factories were forced to close down for lack of coal and raw materials, leading to widespread lay-offs and rising unemployment. As conditions deteriorated, industrial unrest and food riots broke out in a number of areas. Out of sheer desperation, many workers fled from the towns to the countryside in search of food, as famine, pestilence and disease stalked the land.

"The whole of North Russia", wrote Morgan Price, "is in such a condition of famine and misery that […] the inhabitants of the towns have nearly all

147. White Guards at Tampere, Finland, 19 April 1918

gone to the villages to escape death from starvation."[3] Victor Serge witnessed a meeting addressed by Trotsky, who outlined the chronic situation facing the Soviet Republic:

> Speaking in Moscow before a popular meeting, Trotsky displayed a sheaf of telegrams: "Viksi, Nizhni-Novgorod province: the shops are empty, work is going badly, shortage of 30 per cent of the workers through starvation. Men collapsing with hunger at their benches." From Sergiev-Posada the telegram says: "Bread, or we are finished!" From Bryansk, 30 May: "Terrible mortality, especially of children, around the factories of Maltsov and Bryansk; typhus is raging." From Klin, near Moscow: "The town has had no bread for two weeks." From Paslov-Posada: "The population is hungry, no possibility of finding corn." From Dorogobuzh: "Famine, epidemics…"[4]

Finnish Civil War

Added to these problems, civil war had broken out in Finland, sharply increasing tensions with the Soviets.

In January 1918, the red flag had been hoisted in Helsinki and the bourgeois government fled. A new Social-Democratic government was thrust into power, but it failed to carry through the revolution to a conclusion. According to Otto Wille Kuusinen, "until they were defeated, most of the leaders of the

148. Tampere Red Guard at the front, 1918

revolution had no idea of the aims of the revolution."[5] This failure allowed time for the Finnish bourgeoisie to take the initiative and create a small White Army with the aim of restoring their power. The Soviet troops, who had long been stationed in Finland, were forced to withdraw under the terms of the Brest-Litovsk treaty and therefore could not render any assistance. Thus, the Brest-Litovsk treaty sealed the fate of the Finnish workers.

The newly proclaimed White government under Pehr Evind Svinhufvud was reinforced by 20,000 German troops, which allowed them to retake Helsinki after bitter street battles. They then carried out their savage, bloody revenge. The workers' districts were bombarded by artillery and destroyed.

The counter-revolution went on the rampage, killing and murdering indiscriminately. It was a complete bloodbath and a harbinger of what was to come in the Russian Civil War. The numbers struck down by the White Terror, either shot or given long prison sentences, numbered more than 100,000. Victor Serge writes:

> The victors massacred the vanquished. It has been known since antiquity that class wars are the most frightful. There are no more bloody or atrocious victories than those won by the propertied classes. Since the bloodbath inflicted on the Paris Commune by the French bourgeoisie, the world had seen nothing to compare in horror with what took place in Finland.[6]

149. White Army parade after the conquest of Helsinki, 16 May 1918

Serge continues:

One more observation. The butchery in Finland took place in April 1918. Up to this moment the Russian revolution had virtually everywhere displayed great leniency towards its enemies. It had not used terror. We have noted a few bloody episodes in the civil war in the south, but these were exceptional. The victorious bourgeoisie of a small nation which ranks among the most enlightened societies of Europe was the first to remind the Russian proletariat that *woe to the vanquished!* is the first law of social war.[7]

The Russian masses were quickly forced to learn a painful lesson: the ruthless counter-revolution shows no mercy.

There were growing concerns about the defence of the Soviet Republic. Decisive action was needed. And in its hour of need, the revolution turned to the man it trusted to lead it to victory. In March 1918, Leon Trotsky, who had successfully led the Bolshevik insurrection, was appointed Commissar of War. With this responsibility came the formidable task of arming the Soviet Republic against the combined threat of foreign intervention and internal counter-revolution. Despite having no experience in this field, Trotsky soon displayed outstanding qualities as a military leader. He became the Red Army's chief architect and organiser.

150. Two Reds being executed in Varkaus, Finland, 1918

'Muster our forces'

Given the continued danger from a German attack, and with conspiracies being hatched everywhere, the decision was taken to move the capital out of harm's way from Petrograd to Moscow, which took place on 12 March. The day before the move, Lenin wrote an article for *Izvestia*, in which he called on the communists to hold their nerve:

> Russia will become mighty and abundant if she abandons all dejection and all phrase-making, if, with clenched teeth, she musters all her forces and strains every nerve and muscle, if she realises that salvation lies *only* along that road of world socialist revolution upon which we have set out.[8]

Lenin often remarked that it was far easier for the Russian workers to take power than for the workers in the West, but it was far more difficult to hold on to power. He knew all too well the difficulties faced by an isolated Russia, overwhelmed by terrible backwardness. All hope rested on the perspective of world revolution. He stated:

> We continue to be a besieged fortress towards which the eyes of the world's workers are turned, for they know that their freedom will come from here, and

in this besieged fortress we must act with military ruthlessness, with military discipline and self-sacrifice.[9]

He repeated this fact many times over the coming years.

The spring and summer of 1918 were unusually hard. The dire situation imposed upon them by civil war was made immeasurably worse by an imperialist blockade and the intervention of armies of foreign intervention. Not only Germany and Austro-Hungary, but Britain, France, America, Japan, Poland and others all joined this armed crusade against Bolshevism. By the middle of 1918, some thirty different governments operated in the area that was once the Russian Empire.

The Bolsheviks were navigating an unprecedented situation, and this meant a great deal of experimentation and improvisation. There were no textbooks as such, to follow. There was no historical precedent, except for the short-lived Paris Commune, which indicated a broad outline. "We never claimed to know the exact road", stated Lenin.[10]

The Bolsheviks did their revolutionary duty in Russia in taking power. But one thing was absolutely clear, not just to Lenin, but to the entire leadership of the Bolshevik Party: without the victory of the socialist revolution in Europe, the Russian Revolution would perish. He said:

> I repeat, our salvation from all these difficulties is an all-European revolution. Taking this truth, this absolutely abstract truth, as our starting point, and being guided by it, we must see to it that it does not in time become a mere phrase...[11]

Lenin was well aware that in Russia, capitalism had broken at its 'weakest link'. Marx always envisaged that the socialist revolution would be started by the French, continued by the Germans and finished by the British. These were, at the time, among the most advanced capitalist countries with a developed working class. Semi-feudal Russia certainly did not enter into Marx's scheme of things. With little industry, low productivity of labour, mass illiteracy and with a per capita income of about one-tenth of that of the United States, Russia was one of the least equipped countries to take the path of socialism in terms of its industrial development. Less than 10 per cent of the population were wage earners and a much smaller proportion were industrial workers.

The victory of the revolution in an advanced country like Germany would have transformed the situation. The German workers would have broken the imperialist stranglehold over Soviet Russia and provided them with the lifeline of credit against future food and raw materials, much needed machinery and capital equipment, and highly skilled technicians and engineers.

151. Lenin and Sverdlov on the presidium of the Congress of Agricultural
Communes and Poor Committees, Moscow, December 1918

This perspective was no utopian dream. The victory of the German
Revolution after November 1918 was entirely possible. If the German workers
did not take power, it was not because they lacked the possibility to do so,
but because they were held in check by their leaders – the Social-Democrats
– who played exactly the same treacherous game as the Mensheviks in Russia.
They betrayed the revolution and handed power back to the bourgeoisie.
That destroyed the German Revolution and prepared the ground for the
later rise of Hitler. It also led to the isolation of the Russian Revolution under
conditions of frightful backwardness.

New challenges

Basing himself on the experience of the Paris Commune, Lenin explained
that the first act of the working class in taking power was to destroy the old
state apparatus and create a new workers' state. This work had begun in
Russia with the creation of the new regime of Soviet power. This would form
the transitional regime from capitalism to socialism, where, with the victory
of the European revolution, the state itself would begin to wither away as
classes disappeared and the productive forces advanced.

The initial steps, however, would be the immediate introduction of
measures to eliminate bureaucracy on the lines of the Paris Commune. This

would include, as stated, the election of all officials with the right of recall and to be paid the same wages as skilled workers. It also meant the immediate introduction of the eight-hour day to allow workers the necessary time to participate in the running of society and the state. Lenin explained in *The State and Revolution*:

> The workers, after winning political power, will smash the old bureaucratic apparatus, shatter it to its very foundations, and raze it to the ground; they will replace it by a new one, consisting of the very same workers and other employees, *against* whose transformation into bureaucrats the measures will at once be taken which were specified in detail by Marx and Engels: (1) not only election, but also recall at any time; (2) pay not to exceed that of a workman; (3) immediate introduction of control and supervision by *all*, so that *all* may become 'bureaucrats' for a time and that, therefore, *nobody* may be able to become a 'bureaucrat'.[12]

Marx explained that a workers' state would be a *semi-state*, not the massive bureaucratic state apparatus as under capitalism. Under such conditions, the state, as a repressive force, as well as all other aspects of class rule, would gradually disappear. The 'struggle for individual existence', prevalent under capitalism, would likewise disappear. Society would adopt the motto: 'From each according to his ability, to each according to his needs.'

However, Russia was a *very* long way from this. In fact, as Lenin admitted, the work had hardly begun, as a result of the enormous economic and cultural backwardness. From the very beginning, the Soviet Republic was engaged in a Herculean struggle, not to build socialism, but to drag Russia into the twentieth century.

The isolation of Russia confronted the Bolsheviks with a series of problems that were difficult, even impossible to solve. As a result, they were compelled to improvise in the period known as 'War Communism'. Unlike the utopian socialists, who wished to create the perfect individual, who in turn would then create a better society, Lenin understood that they could only build a new society with the human material bequeathed and shaped by capitalism.

To cite just one example: the lack of administrative personnel was crippling the functioning of the government. Given the high levels of illiteracy, the Bolsheviks were forced to rely upon those officials from the old tsarist state apparatus who they could persuade or bribe to cooperate with the regime. This layer was overwhelmingly hostile to socialism. Their constant sabotage posed a grave danger to the revolution. But the Bolsheviks had no alternative but to use the material at hand in order to survive.

152. Lenin making a speech in Red Square at the unveiling of a temporary monument to Stepan Razin, 1919

The relatively small numbers of workers involved in state administration were mainly dedicated men and women who constituted the thin red line of the revolution, upon which the Soviet state rested. But in the prevailing conditions, even they were in danger of becoming absorbed in the daily struggle simply to make things function.

This colossal burden on the shoulders of the working class became even heavier as time went on and as the tasks became greater. Faced with famine, the struggle to simply survive became a daily battle. This eventually led to the exhaustion and weakening of the working class. This, in turn, affected their ability to participate in the Soviets and the running of the workers' state.

Lenin recognised the problem and explained that the Soviets, as "organs of government *by the working people*, are in fact organs of government *for the working people* by the advanced section of the proletariat, but not by the working people as a whole."[13]

This would have grave consequences in the future as the world revolution was further delayed. Lenin never tried to hide this fact and always took a sober, down-to-earth view:

> We have only just taken the first steps towards shaking off capitalism altogether and beginning the transition to socialism. We do not know and we cannot know how many stages of transition to socialism there will be. That depends on when the full-scale European socialist revolution begins [...]
>
> In Russia this has scarcely begun and has begun badly. If we are conscious of what is bad in what we have begun we shall overcome it, provided history gives anything like a decent time to work on that Soviet power.[14]

While the revolution rested as its mainstay on the determination of the proletariat, in the period afterwards, the thin layer of industrial workers was stretched to the limit by the demands of the revolution. Every day, trains would leave Moscow carrying carriages of communists to the front (many of whom would perish), on grain rationing detachments, and to take up roles as organisers of Soviet power throughout the country.

Banks nationalised

Very soon after taking power, the Bolsheviks took measures to nationalise the banks, a key plank of the economy, which were to be combined into a state bank. They were determined not to repeat the mistake of the Communards, who failed to nationalise the Bank of France, a failure which prepared their downfall. The nationalisation would centralise finance in the hands of the state, allow a unified system of investments and credits, according to the needs of the economy.

The Soviet government then took further measures to abolish the national debt, which was an unbearable lead weight around their neck. This was a heavy blow against foreign finance and represented a decisive break with international capitalism. The imperialists, in retaliation, carried out a blockade of Russia.

While the Bolsheviks took over the banks and a few other industries, the bulk of the economy was left in private hands. They intended to nationalise the economy, but gradually. The stress was very much on workers' control as a stepping stone to workers' management to allow the workers time to learn how to run it for themselves. This was the reason for the early decree on workers' control.

The new relations that were replacing the old were being formed slowly and under exceptionally difficult conditions. Workers' control, where it was introduced locally, did not have the results expected given the lack of coordination; it was very anarchic and created its own problems. Nevertheless, the Bolsheviks were determined to forge ahead.

As we have explained, the Bolsheviks had to deal with the concrete situation that faced them, and Lenin never hid the grave difficulties facing the Soviet state: "We are building our state out of the elements left over by capitalism..."[15] He explained:

> The workers were never separated by a Great Wall of China from the old society. And they have preserved a good deal of the traditional mentality of capitalist society. The workers are building a new society without themselves having become new people, or cleansed of the filth of the old world; they are still standing up to their knees in that filth. We can only dream of clearing the filth away. It would be utterly utopian to think this could be done at once. It would be so utopian that in practice it would only postpone socialism to kingdom come. [...]
>
> We are building while still standing on the soil of capitalist society, combatting all those weaknesses and shortcomings which also affect the working people and which tend to drag the proletariat down.[16]

Many times, Lenin returned to the problems of building a new society with the material bequeathed by capitalism:

> The old utopian socialists imagined that socialism could be built by men of a new type, that first they would train good, pure and splendidly educated people, and these would build socialism. We always laughed at this and said that this was playing with puppets, that it was socialism as an amusement for young ladies, but not serious politics.
>
> We want to build socialism with the aid of those men and women who grew up under capitalism, were depraved and corrupted by capitalism, but steeled for the struggle by capitalism. There are proletarians who have been so hardened that they can stand a thousand times more hardship than any army.[17]

And again:

> We were never utopians and never imagined that we would build communist society with the immaculate hands of immaculate Communists, born and educated in an immaculately communist society. That is a fairy-tale. We have to build communism out of the debris of capitalism, and only the class which has been steeled in the struggle against capitalism can do that. The proletariat, as you are very well aware, is not free from the shortcomings and weaknesses of capitalist society. It is fighting for socialism, but at the same time it is fighting against its own shortcomings.[18]

Regulating capitalism

When the Bolsheviks came to power, Lenin had initially envisaged quite a lengthy period of economic reform and intervention by the workers' state. In this interval, the working class would learn to absorb the best capitalist technique. While the working class would hold state power through the Soviets, the economy, which still remained largely in private hands, would need to be placed under state control as far as possible.

Through these means, the workers' state would *regulate* private industry by encouraging foreign investment, granting 'concessions' to foreign capitalists, such as joint ventures, in order to build up its industrial base and consolidate its position. As explained, this would also mean engaging bourgeois specialists and managers, using the methods of Taylorism,* introducing one-man management, etc., to develop and restore the shattered economy.

Although Lenin had previously denounced the methods of Taylorism in the hands of the capitalists, such methods in the hands of Soviet power could help scientifically raise the productivity of labour.

In this way, the workers' state was attempting to regulate the levers of the largely capitalist economy to its own advantage, and, as such, would help to consolidate and strengthen the new regime. As Lenin explained:

> Without the guidance of experts in the various fields of knowledge, technology and experience, the transition to socialism will be impossible, because socialism calls for a conscious mass advance to greater productivity of labour compared with capitalism, and on the basis achieved by capitalism.

The regime would harness the methods and talents of capitalism, but would do so "*in its own way*, by its own methods – or, to put it more concretely, by *Soviet* methods", he added.[19]

Of course, there were clear dangers in this approach, as a certain number of these bourgeois specialists, with loyalties to the old order, would seek to undermine the revolution. As a result, the Soviet state would need to closely supervise them through workers' committees and the use of political commissars, in an attempt to prevent this from happening. Lenin explained:

> ... Soviet power appoints workers' Commissars or workers' committees who watch the manager's every step, who learn from his management experience and

---

* Taylorism was a system of scientific management that analysed work flows so as to improve efficiency and productivity. It was developed by Frederick W Taylor in his book, *The Principles of Scientific Management* (1909).

who not only have the right to appeal against his orders, but can secure his removal through the organs of Soviet power. [...]

We, the party of the proletariat, have *no other way* of acquiring the ability to organise large-scale production on trust lines, as trusts are organised, except by acquiring it from first-class capitalist experts.[20]

Lenin never tried to dress things up, but explained things clearly and honestly:

Socialism cannot be built unless we utilise the heritage of capitalist culture. The only material we have to build communism with is what has been left us by capitalism.[21]

These bourgeois specialists would, however, be willing to work for the Soviet state only if they were granted higher salaries (a 'capitalist differential'), which Lenin regarded as a compromise and a backward step. But there was little alternative, as without such incentives, these specialists would leave the country for better paid work elsewhere.

Over time, as the working class learned the skills of management, they would be able to dispense with the services of the bourgeois specialists completely, together with their high salaries.

'State capitalism'

This attempt by the regime to harness the know-how and technique of capitalism through regulation and incentive, while holding on firmly to the levers of power, was given the name of 'state capitalism' by Lenin.* He explained:

There were differences of opinion among us on particular questions, but fundamentally, there was no room for doubt. We availed ourselves of the assistance of bourgeois experts who were thoroughly imbued with the bourgeois mentality,

---

* Normally, the use of the term 'state capitalism' by Marxists refers to a subordinate, nationalised sector within a capitalist economy, which is used to supply cheap energy, transport, etc. to the private sector. This was the case, for instance, in Britain prior to Thatcher's privatisations, where about 20 per cent of the economy was nationalised, including coal, steel, railways, etc. and used to provide cheap materials and transport to the rest of the capitalist economy. Lenin, however, used it differently, to describe the use of capitalist measures by a workers' state.

Some on the left, such as Tony Cliff, the founder of the Socialist Workers Party in Britain, developed the theory that the Soviet Union after Lenin's death was 'state capitalist' and not a deformed workers' state. For an explanation as to why this was a serious theoretical error, see Ted Grant's reply to Cliff, 'Against the Theory of State Capitalism'.

who were disloyal to us, and will remain disloyal to us for many years to come. Nevertheless, the idea that we can build communism with the aid of pure Communists, without the assistance of bourgeois experts, is childish. [...]

... we have to build communist society with the aid of our enemies. This looks like a contradiction, an irreconcilable contradiction, perhaps. As a matter of fact, this is the only way the problem of building communism can be solved.[22]

Lenin believed this transitional form of 'state capitalism', as he called it, would be a step forward compared to the backward, barbaric, peasant conditions that prevailed. If handled properly, this transitional stage would act as a stepping stone to a future planned economy. While he recognised that such a transition entailed dangers, nevertheless, the whole process would be managed under the strict control of the Soviet government, which held state power.

Of course, it was not intended that this arrangement would last indefinitely. Sooner or later, the economic base would need to come into line with the superstructure, and private ownership would give way to social ownership and appropriation. But for the moment, given the prevailing backwardness, they needed to harness what was positive from the old capitalist methods until help arrived from the West.

Lenin viewed this policy of 'state capitalism' as part of the strategy of "manoeuvring and retreating" domestically and in international affairs, simply as a means of holding out until the victory of the world revolution.[23] It was the only realistic way forward under the circumstances. In replying to the Samarkand Communists, Lenin explained:

We have no fear of capitalism, because the proletariat has the power, transport and large-scale industry firmly in its hands and will succeed, through its control, in channelling it into state capitalism. Under these conditions, capitalism will help us to combat red tape and the scattering of the petty producers. *We shall win out because we know what we want.*[24]

Not only would the Soviets and workers' committees oversee this period of 'state capitalism', but through workers' control and supervision, the working class would obtain the necessary knowledge to run and manage industry themselves – and this could only be achieved through actual practice.

This was the original idea behind the introduction of workers' control. The working class would discover for themselves the way forward through trial and error. As Lenin explained:

In introducing workers' control, we knew that it would take much time before it spread to the whole of Russia, but we wanted to show that we recognise only one road – changes from below; we wanted the workers themselves, from below, to draw up the new, basic economic principles.[25]

This experimentation, stimulated by the ideals of the revolution, certainly gripped the imagination of large layers of the working class. According to Paul Avrich, during the first months of the Soviet regime, "the Russian working class enjoyed a degree of freedom and sense of power unique in its history."[26]

However, while there was an abundance of enthusiasm, the cultural backwardness of Russia erected objective barriers in front of the working class. While workers' control could be introduced locally, there were far-wider considerations, which Lenin alluded to in April 1918 at the All-Russian Soviet Central Executive Committee. At the meeting, he gave an example of workers who had asked for their factory to be expropriated. Lenin answered as follows:

That is not where the hitch lies. There is no difficulty whatsoever in that. (*Applause.*) That we have sufficiently demonstrated and proved.

I told every workers' delegation with which I had to deal when they came to me and complained that their factory was at a standstill: you would like your factory to be confiscated. Very well, we have blank forms for a decree ready, they can be signed in a minute. (*Applause.*)

Nevertheless, he asked a question:

But tell us: have you learnt how to take over production and have you calculated what you will produce? Do you know the connection between what you are producing and the Russian and international market? Whereupon it turns out that they have not learnt this yet...[27]

This was certainly a problem. The masses were confronted with the unique task of constructing a new state and running industry on their own, but they lacked the necessary experience. This was to lead to a chaotic situation, where workers in one factory would decide matters without any reference to the needs of other industries, or the economy in general. This could place one factory's interests in direct conflict with another, resulting in economic paralysis. A workers' leader at the time explained the problem:

... workers' control had turned into an anarchistic attempt to achieve socialism in one enterprise, but actually leads to clashes among the workers themselves, and to the refusal of fuel, metal, etc. to one another.[28]

Such problems could only be resolved through the introduction of workers' control across the entire economy, combined with workers' management, and coordinated through a national plan. But, in the concrete conditions of Russia, with the lack of planning and expertise, this was not immediately possible. It would take time and resources, which were also in short supply.

A year later, Lenin looked back at the experience of workers' control: "One has only to recall how clumsy, immature and casual were our first decrees and decisions on the subject of workers' control of industry", he admitted. "We thought that it was an easy matter…"[29]

But the problem was that there was no explanation as to *how* it was to be done. Faced with increased sabotage by the capitalist owners, workers spontaneously took over the factories themselves. However, the running of these newly nationalised industries required skills and knowledge which were lacking. Lenin admitted squarely:

> At first we regarded them in an entirely abstract way, like revolutionary preachers, who had absolutely no idea of how to set to work. There were lots of people, of course, who accused us – and all the socialists and Social-Democrats are accusing us today – of having undertaken this task without knowing how to finish it. But these accusations are ridiculous, made by people who lack the spark of life. As if one can set out to make a great revolution and know beforehand how it is to be completed! Such knowledge cannot be derived from books and our decision could spring only from the experience of the masses. And I say that it is to our credit that amidst incredible difficulties we undertook to solve a problem with which until then we were only half familiar, that we inspired the proletarian masses to display their own initiative, that we nationalised the industrial enterprises, and so forth. I remember that in Smolny we passed as many as ten or twelve decrees at one sitting. That was an expression of our determination and desire to stimulate the spirit of experiment and initiative among the proletarian masses.[30]

Despite all the shortcomings, it was precisely this spirit of initiative from the masses from below that was the mainstay of the revolution. It was on this that the Soviet regime rested.

In practice, simply for the revolution to hang on and survive, required titanic efforts from everyone. The urgent need to restore production necessitated increased centralisation, improved organisation, as well as a stricter labour discipline to increase the productivity of labour. Without this, there could be no way forward.

Lenin was keen to learn lessons from elsewhere. He pointed out that German industry was employing the most advanced techniques and skills, which vastly increased the productivity of labour. Lenin believed this was a model to emulate if the Soviet regime was to survive and eventually prosper. "Learn discipline from the Germans", he urged, "for, if we do not, we, as a people, are doomed, we shall live in eternal slavery."[31]

The task was to "spare *no effort* in copying it and not shrink from adopting *dictatorial* methods to hasten the copying of it."[32] He continued:

> Our task is to hasten this copying even more than Peter [the Great] hastened the copying of Western culture by barbarian Russia, and we must not hesitate to use barbarous methods in fighting barbarism. If there are anarchists and Left Socialist-Revolutionaries (I recall off-hand the speeches of Karelin and Ghe at the meeting of the Central Executive Committee) who indulge in Narcissus-like reflections and say that it is unbecoming for us revolutionaries to 'take lessons' from German imperialism, there is only one thing we can say in reply: the revolution that took these people seriously would perish irrevocably (and deservedly).[33]

Lenin saw that it was important to harness the expertise of the past, and introduce greater coordination of the different branches of industry. He was especially keen to promote businesslike methods throughout industry to increase efficiency, accounting and control.

One of these new measures was the introduction of one-man management, which would introduce more centralised direction to industry and overcome unnecessary dislocation. But this would be under the strict control and check of the workers, through their workers' committees, commissars and their trade unions.

These measures, if applied properly, would allow the productive forces to develop, to increase production and lay the basis for the transition to a fully nationalised planned economy. However, in order for this to succeed, it was necessary to take one step at a time. And for Lenin, the ultimate success of the revolution was always organically linked to the perspective of the world revolution.

Principal enemy

Lenin believed that the greatest danger facing the Soviet Republic was not the White generals, or even the threat of foreign imperialist intervention, but

153. Rail workers at Minsk Station in front of a propaganda train

Russia's backward economy, an anarchic structure dominated by a myriad of petty-bourgeois proprietors, traders, speculators, and kulaks.

Lenin explained that the socio-economic structure of Russia was made up of different elements, where the petty-bourgeois peasant economy overwhelmingly dominated. He outlines these elements:

1. The patriarchal peasant farming system, which is largely a natural economy;

2. The economy of the petty trader (which includes the majority of those peasants who sell their grain);

[...] Clearly in a small-peasant country, the petty-bourgeois element predominates and it must predominate, for the great majority of those working the land are small commodity producers.[34]

The life of these small producers was dominated by one simple idea: "I grab all I can – the rest can go hang", as Lenin put it:

The existence of a multitude of petty-bourgeois traders and middle-men, which exerted such a powerful influence over the economy, constituted the principal enemy of socialist construction in Russia. Everything needed to be done to modernise the economy and combat its chronic chaotic backwardness.

154. Propaganda train, *October Revolution*, at a station near Samara, 1919

But this produced a dangerous situation for the young workers' state, which was attempting to lean on capitalism to get things moving. He continued:

> The shell of our state capitalism (grain monopoly, state-controlled entrepreneurs and traders, bourgeois co-operators) is pierced now in one place, now in another by *profiteers*, the chief object of profiteering being *grain*.[35]

Lenin saw that this petty-bourgeois trader statum was exerting an influence more powerful than all the Kornilovs, Dutovs and Kaledins put together. They, in turn, provided the fertile ground for the internal counter-revolution, and their influence was growing. Lenin warned:

> We know that the million tentacles of this petty-bourgeois hydra now and again encircle various sections of the workers, that, instead of state monopoly, profiteering forces its way into every pore of our social and economic organism.[36]

These petty profiteering layers, through its speculation and hoarding, were choking the workers' state at every level and threatened to overwhelm it. The Soviet regime needed to take a much firmer line in dealing with the profiteers, racketeers and capitalists – who constantly violated and circumvented the measures passed by the Soviets.

155. Bolsheviks conducting propaganda among the peasants

Agrarian problems

The mass of Russian people were peasants who spent their whole lives toiling on the land. They were still working with the same primitive instruments and animals that were known to their grandparents – and to their grandparents before them – the wooden plough and the ox.

The revolution had suddenly thrust them into political life. They entered it, armed not only with hammers and scythes, but with their own aims, prejudices, interests and demands. Above all else, the landless peasants sought to break the stranglehold of landlordism, which oppressed them and bled them dry.

The peasants had traditionally looked to the party of the Socialist-Revolutionaries, which, from the time of the Narodniks, and through the influence of radically inclined village schoolteachers and similar semi-intellectuals, had sunk deep roots in the countryside. However, the failure of the Provisional Government, with its SR ministers, only alienated the peasants and threw the countryside into turmoil.

Feeling the pressure of the revolution, the old landlords sold their lands to the rich kulaks. Between these kulak landowners and the sea of poor land-hungry peasants stood the middle peasants, the aspiring petty bourgeoisie of the countryside.

The victory of the revolution gave land to the peasants. However, the gulf between the rich kulaks and poor peasants still prevailed. Lenin knew full well that the existence of Soviet power rested on the alliance between workers and peasants, cemented by the government's agrarian reforms.

The Bolsheviks viewed the poor peasants as the real allies of the working class. They therefore needed to tear the poor peasants away from the rich kulaks. That could only be achieved by promoting the class struggle in the rural areas.

To encourage this, in May 1918, they began to organise separate 'Committees of Poor Peasants'. In doing so, they hoped to increase support for the measures of the Soviet government amongst the poor peasants.

But relations with the peasants as a whole were complicated by the developing civil war, unremitting hardship, famine and the need to defend the revolution. The sabotage of the kulaks, who hoarded grain, combined with the imperialist blockade, had drastically limited the sowing of crops.

The relationship between the government and the peasantry was further disrupted by the depreciation of the rouble. Mistrust in the currency inevitably led to a revival of barter and payment in kind, in place of worthless paper money.

The conditions of generalised scarcity gave a powerful boost to speculation in grain, which pushed up its price on the black market by four or five times. Previously, the Kerensky Government had tried to curtail the speculation by introducing a state monopoly on the sale of grain. Faced with the same problem, the Bolsheviks were forced to continue this policy.

Under the terms of the state monopoly arrangement, all excess grain was supposed to be delivered to the state. And the intensification of the civil war forced the Soviet government to introduce food requisitioning to feed the hungry workers in the cities and the soldiers of the Red Army. Under such conditions, there was no time to haggle over the price of grain. Nor did the Soviet government have enough cash to pay for it.

Grain procurement

The months of April and May 1918 were marked by an extreme intensification of the food crisis. In May, faced with the immediate threat of famine, the Soviet government took emergency measures to procure grain stocks, issuing the following decree on food procurement:

156. Sleds carrying corn

A ruinous process of disintegration of the food procurement of the country, the heavy legacy of a four-year war, continues to extend and aggravate the existing distress.

While the consuming provinces are starving, great stocks of cereals [lie] in the producing provinces. These stocks are in the hands of rural kulaks and wealthy people, in the hands of the rural bourgeoisie. [...]

... the All-Russian Executive Central Committee has decreed:

1. By keeping firmly the grain monopoly and fixed prices and also carrying out a merciless struggle against grain speculators and bagmen, to compel each grain holder to declare the surrender of all surpluses, except the quantity needed for consumption on established norms until the next harvest, in one week after the notification of this decree in each volost. The rules applying to the orders will be defined by the local food procurement organs of Narkomprod [the People's Commissariat for Food Supplies].

2. To invite all toiling people and unpropertied peasants to unite immediately in a merciless struggle against the kulaks.

157. Peasants delivering corn on the Volga

3. To declare enemies of the nation all people having surpluses of grain and not handing them over to the station points and even dissipating the stocks of cereals for their own home brew instead of delivering them to the collecting stations; to bring them before the Revolutionary Courts, put them in jail for not less than ten years, confiscate all their belongings, banish them out of the *obshchina* and condemn the holders of home brew to forced labour in public works.

4. In the case of discovery of any surplus of grain which had not been declared for delivery, according to Point 1, grain will be requisitioned without payment, and half of the value which was due at fixed prices for the undeclared surplus will be paid to the people who took part in discovering the surpluses, after they have been in fact received in the collecting stations, and the other half to the Agricultural Community. Information about discovery of surpluses has to be reported to the local food procurement organs.[37]

The situation sharply deteriorated when the grain supplies from both the Volga and Siberia were completely cut off by the counter-revolution.

Therefore, these procurement measures became absolutely essential in the face of growing famine and the need to feed the cities.

The requisitioning was primarily aimed at the kulaks, as it was this grouping who tended to hoard the grain supplies. This led to enormous resistance, so that requisitioning had to be carried out with the use of armed workers' detachments. These measures were undoubtedly harsh, but the threat of mass starvation left the Bolsheviks with no other choice.

On 20 May, the 'Food Army' was formally established. The shortage of grain had the immediate effect of reducing the supply of bread. Therefore, in July 1918, the new two-day bread ration was introduced in Petrograd, which was divided into four categories:

1. For workers performing heavy physical labour, 200 grams;

2. For workers engaged in ordinary manual labour, 150 grams;

3. For clerical workers, 100 grams;

4. For capitalists, rentiers, and the unoccupied 50 grams.

This allocation was based upon the principle that those who contributed the most, received the most in rations, and 'he that does not work, neither shall he eat'.

The civil war, blockade and imperialist intervention had caused a terrible famine. Combatting it became the absolute priority, as Lenin points out:

> We are now facing the most elementary task of human society – to vanquish famine [...] All grain surpluses must be collected; we must see to it that all stocks are brought to the places where they are needed [...]
>
> Incredible difficulties face us here.
>
> We do not fear these difficulties. We were aware of them. We never said that the transition from capitalism to socialism would be easy.[38]

This was, in the most literal sense, a matter of life and death. In order to resolve this crisis, he called on the workers to come to the aid of the revolution:

> The workers must unite, workers' detachments must be organised, the hungry people from the non-agricultural districts must be organised – it is to them we turn for help, it is to them our Commissariat for Food appeals, it is they we call upon to join the crusade for bread, the crusade against the profiteers and the kulaks and for the restoration of order.[39]

However, the campaign for grain encountered serious problems. Thanks to the programme of land redistribution introduced by the revolution, the numbers of what were known as 'middle peasants' had grown considerably. These were small land owners, standing between the rich kulaks and the poor peasants. This meant that the requisitioning of grain was met with far greater resistance than had been expected. The campaign served to push this layer into the arms of the reactionary kulaks. In response to the grain seizures, the peasants only planted enough land to satisfy their own needs, resulting in a collapse in agricultural production.

Under these circumstances, the Bolsheviks had little choice but to take these drastic measures to feed the cities and the army. The whole policy was born out of necessity and the fight for survival. If there had been no civil war, things would have been entirely different. But for now, they were forced to face the reality that confronted them.

The policy of forced requisitions of grain seriously damaged relations between the peasants and the Bolsheviks. Some peasants took up arms and joined the Whites to fight the Soviets. But as soon as they saw that behind the White armies came the old landowning class, demanding the restitution of their estates, the peasant learned the hard way that he had backed the wrong side, and hastily swung back the other way.

And so, although there was opposition to requisitioning, there were still important reserves of support for the Bolshevik government in the countryside. No democratic republic had done so much for the peasants. And the peasants feared – not without reason – that the victory of the White Armies would mean the return of the old landlords and the loss of their lands.

Despite everything, many peasants still had a stake in defending the revolution. But as the requisitioning was stepped up, this loyalty was being stretched to breaking point and the hostility to such measures was growing, leading to a series of armed clashes. This posed a grave and growing danger to the revolution.

'Left Communists'

The concessions to capitalism that were forced upon the Soviet government were repeatedly denounced by the 'Left Communists', who voiced their criticisms both inside and outside of the Party. Following on from their opposition to the Brest-Litovsk treaty, they proceeded to accuse Lenin of backsliding, giving in to capitalism and betraying the revolution.

Their paper, *Kommunist*, was used to full effect in denouncing what they called 'pro-capitalist' measures. They were particularly opposed to any measures to increase labour discipline, such as Taylorism, the employment of bourgeois managers, higher salaries for specialists and all such manifestations of 'state capitalism'.

One of these 'Lefts', David Ryazanov, poked fun at Lenin's leadership and accuse him of becoming an old maid:

> The English Parliament can do anything except change a man into a woman. Our Central Committee is more powerful – it has already changed more than one extremely revolutionary man into [an old] woman, and the number of these [old] women has increased incredibly.[40]

Lenin brushed aside such remarks, saying that where the objective situation demanded certain concessions, especially where the fate of the revolution was concerned, they would make them. The 'Left Communists' were very good at talking in abstractions, he maintained, but little else. Words like 'retreat' or 'compromise' did not enter their vocabulary. But a general who only knew one word of command – attack! – would soon break his army into pieces.

Unlike the 'Lefts', Lenin had his feet planted firmly on the ground. He displayed an unyielding frankness in telling the truth to the working class. And he firmly believed that, with all the precautions and checks in place, these short-term retreats were manageable and provided a temporary, but valuable, breathing space. Above all, decisive control of the economy would still remain in the hands of the Soviet state.

The Left SRs now launched off on a completely adventurist course that led them into a headlong conflict with the Soviet power. Their leader, Maria Spiridonova, joined in the attack with a wild tirade against the Bolshevik leaders. She accused them of betraying Ukraine, ruining the peasantry and sending the Germans secret trains loaded with gold, while also being in the pay of the Germans.

Spiridonova was no doubt sincere – as were many of the 'Lefts' – but she had never freed herself from the psychological traits of petty-bourgeois radicalism. Lenin merely shook his head and replied to Spiridonova's assault, simply saying: "It must be a bad party indeed whose best spokesmen stoop to spreading fairy-tales."[41]

Lenin answered that he refused to gamble with the future of the revolution. He based himself on what was possible, and not on subjective wishes. He regarded the 'Lefts' as utopian dreamers who were out of touch with reality.

158. Maria Spiridonova   159. Yevgeni Preobrazhensky   160. Georgy Pyatakov

They reminded him of the Polish nobleman, "who, dying in a beautiful pose, sword in hand, said: 'Peace is disgraceful, war is honourable'."[42] They had a great taste for the 'revolutionary phrase', paying no attention to actual conditions.

But, asked Lenin, did not Marx himself raise the possibility of the British workers reaching a compromise with the bourgeoisie in offering to peaceably 'buy them out'? Marx certainly did not rule out such a 'compromise'. In fact, he thought it a good thing if a peaceful transition was possible, given certain unique features of British capitalism at that time. Lenin explained in a reply to Bukharin:

> Marx taught that (as an exception, and Britain was then an exception) the idea was conceivable of *paying the capitalists well,* of buying them out, if the circumstances were such as to compel the capitalists to submit peacefully and to come over to socialism in a cultured and organised fashion, provided they were paid well.[43]

Lenin asked why it was impermissible for Marx's method to be applied to Russia with the payment of high salaries to bourgeois specialists. Were they not being 'bought out'? For Lenin, the task was to look at things concretely and soberly, not to proceed on the basis of abstractions. To adopt the slogan of the 'Lefts' of 'no compromise' would have quickly shipwrecked the revolution.

But the 'Left Communists' were far from convinced and engaged in continuous outbursts against Lenin. These attacks were led by Bukharin and Radek, but were also joined by Preobrazhensky, Pyatakov, Kollontai and others. They continued to publish *Kommunist* from the time of their opposition to the Brest-Litovsk treaty, which now campaigned against the 'right-wing deviation' at the top and fears of a retreat 'back to capitalism'.

The workers had been worn down by years of war and were exhausted. They were naturally suspicious of the idea of increased labour discipline. Lenin was well aware of this difficulty. However, now that the working class was at the helm in Russia, the only way they were ever going to escape from their dire situation was precisely by raising the productivity of labour.

But the 'Left Communist' opposition would have none of this and complained bitterly about 'dictatorship'. Their infantile language became increasingly violent towards these necessary measures. Lenin ridiculed their arguments:

> A rifle was a very good thing when the capitalist who was waging war against us had to be shot, when thieves had to be caught at their thievery and shot. But when Comrade Bukharin said there were people who were receiving salaries of 4,000 [roubles] and they ought to be put up against a wall and shot, he was wrong. We have got to *find* such people.[44]

Opposition to the Railway Decree

In particular, the 'Left Communists' opposed the 'draconian' railway decree of March 1918, which was simply an attempt by the Soviet government to bring order to the chaotic railway system and get it functioning again. Without a railway, in the words of Lenin, there would be no socialism or Russian revolution. This required increased centralisation and labour discipline, as well as ending chaotic workers' control on the railways. The 'Lefts' attacked this as the 'road to dictatorship'. He went on to expose their fallacies:

> Both Comrade Bukharin and Comrade Martov have got on their hobby horse – the railway decree – and are riding it to death. They talk about the dictatorship of Napoleon III, Julius Caesar and so on, providing material for a hundred issues that no one will read. But this is a little nearer the point. This is about the workers and the railways. Without railways not only will there be no socialism but everyone will starve to death like dogs while there is grain to be had close by. Everyone knows this perfectly well. Why don't you answer? You are closing your eyes. You are throwing dust in the eyes of the workers – the adherents of *Novaya Zhizn* and the Mensheviks deliberately, Comrade Bukharin by mistake. You are concealing the main issue from the workers when you talk of construction. What can be constructed without railways?[45]

The 'Lefts' attacked the railway decree with all kinds of empty phrases and accusations about a revolution in retreat. They argued that "the introduction of labour discipline coupled with the restoration of the leadership of the capitalists in production… threatens the enslavement of the working class" and was the road to ruin.[46] But when these critics were asked to put forward a concrete alternative of their own, they remained utterly silent, which exposed the hollowness of their arguments.

Novaya Zhizn, the paper of the Menshevik-Internationalists and edited by Gorky, was also continually hurling thunderbolts at Lenin and the Government:

> Lenin, Trotsky and their disciples are already intoxicated with the poison of power, as is proved by their shameful attitude towards liberty of speech, personal freedom, and all the rights for which Democracy has fought.[47]

Such criticisms are always quoted by the bourgeois historians to attack Lenin. But what has to be understood is that Gorky, although a talented writer and friend of Lenin, was politically very muddled and detested the 'chaos' of the revolution, which he couldn't reconcile himself to. Given his literary connections, he acted as the attorney between the Soviet regime and the old bourgeois intellectuals. Gorky was, therefore, a continual thorn in Lenin's side during these years. Only later on, when the lava of revolution had cooled, did he finally reconcile himself to it. But this was after Lenin's death.

Gorky's vitriolic attacks were now joined by those of the 'Left Communists' inside the Party. Lenin took time out to write a reply to the 'Lefts' in some detail, which appeared under the title of *Left-Wing Childishness*, published in early May 1918. It was a forerunner of his later broader work, *'Left-Wing' Communism: An Infantile Disorder*. Lenin remarked:

> What a frame of mind these people have and how their psychology coincides with the sentiments of the petty bourgeoisie: let us overthrow the rich, but there is no need for control. That is how they look at it...[48]

He went on:

> Comrades, I shall not touch on further details and quotations from the newspaper *Levi Kommunist*, but I shall say briefly: it is time to cry out when people have gone so far as to say that the introduction of labour discipline will be a step back. And I must say that I regard this as such an unheard-of reactionary thing, such a threat to the revolution, that if I did not know that it was said by a group without any influence, and that it would be refuted at any class-conscious meeting of workers, I would say: the Russian revolution is lost.[49]

Never impulsive, Lenin was not one who minced his words, especially when straight talking was required. This was one of those times.

28. The Civil War Begins

While the dispute over the employment of bourgeois specialists persisted over the next few years, events pushed the controversy into the background. The revolution would go through a number of key turning points and the summer of 1918 was one of them. It was a time when the civil war commenced in earnest.

Within days of the Bolshevik victory in October 1917, the generals Kaledin and Alexander Dutov, the Atamans of the Don, and the Orenburg Cossacks raised the standard of revolt against the Soviets. General Kornilov abandoned the monastery where he had been interned, placed himself at the head of his squadron and made for the Don to join the Whites. They were joined by General Alexeyev, who founded the 'Volunteer Army'.

These three generals, Alexeyev, Kornilov and Kaledin, formed the leading military triumvirate of counter-revolution. Behind the White generals stood the imperialist powers.

In Ukraine, the Rada, the bourgeois Ukrainian National Assembly, had declared its opposition to the Bolsheviks. While it refused free passage to Red Army troops across the Ukraine, it granted permission to the Whites. Given this duplicity and the dangers posed in the Ukraine, the Rada was overthrown by Soviet forces, but French imperialists quickly stepped in to support the Rada, as did the Central Powers.

On 30 April, the Soviets were driven out and replaced by the Germans, who occupied Kiev and set up a military dictatorship under their puppet, Pavlo Skoropadsky. The Germans had already seized large swathes of territory, including the Ukraine, and cut off Transcaucasia from Soviet Russia. Behind

161. Czech Legion's armoured train, Ufa, July 1918

the scenes, they too supplied the Whites with arms. Generals Krasnov and Mamontov, secretly supported by the Germans, organised the rebellion of the Don Cossacks against the Soviet Republic.

The British government immediately announced support for "any responsible body in Russia" which would "actively" oppose the Bolsheviks. The British and French imperialists quickly came to an accord to provide the White Armies with money, weapons and advisers. In addition, the SRs and Mensheviks, acting as shadows of the bourgeois reaction, joined in the attack on Soviet Russia by raising the counter-revolutionary slogan 'All Power to the Constituent Assembly!'

In June 1918, the Czech Legion, backed by Entente diplomats and officers, seized control of the Trans-Siberian railway line leading to the east. This large armed force was made up mainly of prisoners of war from the Austro-Hungarian army, numbering about 45,000 men, and under the control of French officers. The Soviet government, realising the danger, demanded the Czechs disarm, but was powerless to do much about it. This completed the encirclement of the Soviet Republic.

This planned revolt was confirmed by a former officer from the French Military Mission in Russia, Pierre Pascal, who later became a revolutionary:

The insurrection at Yaroslavl and the Czechoslovak rising were organised with the direct collusion of the agents of the French Mission and of M Noulens. The Mission was in constant relations with the Czechs, to whom it sent officers and funds ... The counter-revolutionaries were to seize Yaroslavl, Nizhni-Novgorod, Tambov, Murom and Voronezh in order to isolate and starve out Moscow. This plan began to be implemented with the insurrections in Yaroslavl, Murom, Tambov, etc. I can still see General Lavergne sketching a large circle with his finger on the map around Moscow and saying, "That's what Noulens wants. But I shall feel guilty because, if our plan succeeds, the famine in Russia will be terrible..."[1]

The Czech revolt provided the signal for the Allied intervention. On 2 July, the Anglo-French expedition landed in Murmansk, and a series of White-SR puppet governments were established in the Volga, Samara and Omsk, all under the protection of White bayonets.

'Nicholas the Bloody'

There was an event at this time that has drawn much attention from bourgeois historians. This was the shooting of the Tsar and his family by the Bolsheviks at Ekaterinburg on the night of 16-17 July 1918. The reason for this was the fear that the Tsar and family would fall into the hands of the advancing White Army.

The former Tsar had already been arrested by the Provisional Government, first held in Petrograd and then moved to Tobolsk, in Siberia, together with a treasure-trove of jewellery in trunks. The fate of the Tsar and his family was dictated by the exigencies of the civil war.

As Tobolsk was a rural area and very vulnerable to attack, the Soviet government had transported the Tsar and his family to Ekaterinburg in the Urals. The original intention of the Bolsheviks was to put Tsar Nicholas on public trial, where Trotsky would act as the public prosecutor. However, the advance of the Czechoslovak forces towards Ekaterinburg, where the royals were housed, ruled this out.

The decision was therefore taken by the local Bolsheviks to execute them. It was taken as an emergency measure. The Tsar and his family could not be allowed to fall into the hands of the White generals, as they would provide a valuable rallying point for the counter-revolution. Ten days later, the Czechs captured the town. A decree was then issued on 19 July by the Soviet government confiscating the property and all the ill-gotten gains of the Romanovs. The whole episode was described by Trotsky much later:

162. Location of the Romanovs' execution at Ekaterinburg

During one of my short visits to Moscow – I think a few weeks before the execution of the Romanovs – I incidentally mentioned in the Politburo that considering the bad situation in the Urals, it would be expedient to accelerate the Tsar's trial. I proposed that we hold an open court trial which would reveal a picture of the whole reign, with its peasant policy, labour policy, national minority and cultural policies, its two wars, etc. The proceedings of the trial would be broadcast throughout the country by radio; in the volosts [districts including several villages], accounts of the proceedings would be read and commented upon every day. Lenin replied to the effect that it would be very good if it were feasible, But … there might not be enough time … No debate took place, since I did not insist on my proposal, being absorbed in other work.

And in the Politburo, as I remember, there were just three or four of us: Lenin, myself, Sverdlov … Kamenev, as I recall, was not there. At that period Lenin was in a rather gloomy mood and did not feel very confident that we would succeed in building an army … My next visit to Moscow took place after the fall of Ekaterinburg. Talking to Sverdlov, I asked in passing: "Oh yes, and where is the Tsar?" "It's all over", he answered, "he has been shot." "And where is the family?" "And the family along with him." "All of them?" I asked, apparently with a touch of surprise. "All of them!" replied Sverdlov, "What about it?" He was waiting to see my reaction. I made no reply. "And who made the decision?" I asked. "We decided it here. Ilyich believed that we shouldn't leave the Whites a live banner to rally around, especially under the present difficult circumstances…" I did not ask any further questions, and considered the matter closed.[2]

Trotsky continues:

> Actually, the decision was not only expedient but necessary. The severity of this
> summary justice showed the world that we would continue to fight on mercilessly,
> stopping at nothing. The execution of the Tsar's family was needed not only in
> order to frighten, horrify, and dishearten the enemy, but also in order to shake up
> our own ranks, to show them that there was no turning back, that ahead lay either
> complete victory or complete ruin. In the intellectual circles of the Party there
> probably were misgivings and shakings of heads. But the masses of workers and
> soldiers had not a minute's doubt. They would not have understood and would
> not have accepted any other decision. *This* Lenin sensed well. The ability to think
> and feel for and with the masses was characteristic of him to the highest degree,
> especially at the great political turning points…
>
> When I was abroad I read in *Poslednie Novosti* a description of the shooting, the
> burning of the bodies, etc. How much of all this is true and how much is invented,
> I have not the least idea, since I was never curious about how the sentence was
> carried out and, frankly, do not understand such curiosity.[3]

Of course, today books are written to describe in fiendish detail how the
royals were murdered in cold blood. Little, however, is written of how
Bolshevik men and women were mercilessly butchered during this time by
the imperialists and their reactionary agents, or of the brutalities, pogroms
and atrocities carried out by the Tsar and his cronies. All we can say is that
the Bolsheviks had correctly followed the advice of Marat, the French
revolutionary: "Woe to the revolution which has not enough courage to
behead the symbol of the *Ancien Régime*."

The execution of Nicholas created a storm in the ruling classes, as had
the beheadings of Charles I and Louis XVI during the English and French
revolutions. But, in the scale of things, this was a trifle. Some 350,000 were
to die in combat during the civil war and more than 7 million perished from
disease and famine provoked by the capitalists and landlords, in collaboration
with foreign imperialism. If among them were members of the Romanov
dynasty, it would be hard not to view this as a small price for all the crimes
inflicted on the Russian people by the tsarist monarchy.

In the context of those times, this event hardly aroused the attention of
anyone inside Russia. There is plenty of evidence to support this assertion.
Bruce Lockhart, the British agent who broke the story to the outside world,
writes: "I am bound to admit that the population of Moscow received the
news with amazing indifference."[4] He added in passing: "Their apathy

is extraordinary."[5] A great deal of indignation towards this event is quite artificial. That is especially the case as far as the British were concerned.

As a matter of fact, the British monarchy had an important part to play in the deaths of Nicholas and his family. The British Government had originally agreed to the Provisional Government's request to give the Romanovs asylum in Britain, but King George V, the Tsar's cousin, objected, and the offer was rescinded. Lord Stamfordham, the Private Secretary to the king, wrote a letter on 30 March 1917 to the Foreign Secretary, Arthur Balfour:

> The king has a strong personal friendship for the emperor and would be glad to do anything to help him. But His Majesty cannot help doubting, not only on account of the dangers of the voyage, but on general grounds of expediency, whether it is advisable that the imperial family take up residence in this country. [...]
>
> As you know from the first the King has thought the presence of the Imperial Family (especially the Empress) in this country would raise all sorts of difficulties, and I feel sure that you appreciate how awkward it will be for our Royal Family.[6]

He asked the government to "make some other plan..." Later that day, the king requested that Balfour tell the Russians, "we must be allowed to withdraw..."[7]

Thus, "on general grounds of expediency", the doors of Buckingham Palace were firmly shut in the face of the unfortunate Tsar of all the Russias and his family. On the grounds of "expediency", they were to be kept at arm's length. The British monarchy politely suggested that his government make "some other plans". But no suggestions were ever made as to what those hypothetical plans might be.

Once the Romanovs had been executed, the British royals pretended to be most concerned. But it is clear from the correspondence that they were less concerned with them, and more worried about the outrage the British Royal Family would face over the unwanted presence of Nicholas the Bloody in Britain. The truth is that a dead tsar in Russia was of far more use to the imperialists than a live one in Britain.

It is very clear from the correspondence that King George was far more concerned about the security of his own throne than he was over the safety of his royal cousins in Russia. By refusing to grant them refuge in London, he effectively sealed their fate. He was just as responsible for what happened to them as if he had signed their death warrant himself. But about this dirty little secret, the bourgeois historians who rant about the alleged crimes of the Bolsheviks have draped an impenetrable veil of silence.

163. Nestor Makhno   164. Makhno with his lieutenants, 1919

Nestor Makhno

It should be noted that the Germans did not control the entire area of Ukraine. Part of the region was controlled by the forces of Nestor Makhno and his 'Ukrainian Army of Insurgent Peasants', who launched a guerrilla war against the German occupiers. His forces marched under the anarchist black flag and carried out attacks on the Whites and the Germans, but they also resisted the Reds.

His army was based on the property-owning peasant strata – the ones who could afford a horse. This gave it an unstable character that could veer towards either side. In the end, he lent his hesitant support to the Soviets against Denikin and Wrangel as their interests coincided.

Victor Serge gives a very idealised and overly romanticised description of Makhno, as "boozing, swashbuckling, disorderly and idealistic":

> Sometimes his insurgents marched into battle with one rifle for every two or three men: a rifle which, if any soldier fell, would pass at once from his still-dying hands into those of his alive and waiting neighbour.[8]

Makhno came from peasant stock and reflected their interests and psychology. He took part in the 1905 Revolution and became an anarchist. He was arrested in 1908 but was released by the February Revolution and returned home to the Ukraine, where he founded his anarchist Black Army.

He built up a peasant fighting force varying in size at different times from a few hundred to many thousands. They were mobilised against any threat to peasant lands granted by the revolution, especially from a return to landlordism. In September 1919, having pushed back the Germans, he inflicted a heavy defeat on General Denikin in Uman, from which the General never recovered.

With the threat of the return of landlordism removed, his peasant base shrank, and he rested increasingly on the kulak elements who wanted a free market in grain. Therefore, Makhno's main enemy from then on became the Bolsheviks and he created problems for the Red Army by obstructing its operations. In doing so, he declared that there were no differences between the Whites and the Bolsheviks.

There are many legends about Makhno, spread by anarchist sources, which have little or nothing to back them up. Within his own army, he was a tyrant despite the façade of 'elections', and was usually under the influence of alcohol. He burned down the villages of peasants who refused to support him.

While there was still an agreement between Soviet forces and Makhno in May 1919, he deliberately prevented grain collection in areas he controlled. In October 1920, another treaty of alliance was signed between the Soviets and Makhno to defeat Wrangel. But on both occasions, the treaties broke down as a result of Makhno's manoeuvring. Relations between the two sides were quite fragile after previous betrayals and Makhno's opposition to the 'state' socialism of the Bolsheviks.

Once Wrangel was routed, Makhno's forces suffered a steep decline. This was especially the case after the introduction of the New Economic Policy (NEP), which gave concessions to the peasants. Increasingly, Makhno's ragged army resembled gangs of bandits. At the end of the civil war, it was absurd for the Soviet Republic to allow unreliable anarchist bands to roam in southern Ukraine when the country was still surrounded by hostile imperialist forces. Under pressure, Makhno therefore fled Ukraine into exile with some of his supporters. He finally escaped to Romania and ended his life as a factory worker in Paris.

Although they disagreed politically with anarchism, both Lenin and Trotsky considered giving the anarchists of Ukraine an autonomous region where they could experiment with their utopian ideas. Unfortunately, the civil war and the economic calamity cut across this plan.

Despite Kropotkin's previous pro-war views, Lenin remained in touch with the old anarchist until his death in February 1921. While he disagreed with Kropotkin's anarchism, Lenin was a great admirer of his book on the French Revolution and wanted it republished and placed in all libraries. The government offered him extra rations due to his ill health, but he refused them as he didn't want any privileges.

165. Peter Kropotkin

166. Kropotkin's coffin in transit at the railway station in Dmitrov on its way to Moscow for the funeral

When Kropotkin died, he was given a state funeral addressed by Mostovenko, from the Central Committee, and Alfred Rosmer, the Executive Committee of the International, and laid to rest in the Hall of the Columns in the House of the Trade Unions. It was the last state funeral of a non-Bolshevik. To show his appreciation for the old anarchist, Lenin's government founded a Kropotkin Museum, endowed a number of schools with Kropotkin's name, and promised to publish his collected works. However, in 1938, after the death of Kropotkin's widow, Stalin closed the Museum and its contents were dispersed and lost.

Economy nationalised

In the summer of 1918, the policy of 'state capitalism' and the 'compromise' with the industrialists had to be abruptly abandoned. On 28 June, the Soviet Government was forced to carry through the widespread expropriation of the capitalist class. A decree was passed carrying through the wholesale nationalisation of the economy, as "a decisive struggle against disorganisation in production and supply…"[9] This involved heavy industry, most notably manufacturing and engineering. This abrupt turn was due to widespread capitalist sabotage, by which the capitalist owners had hoped the Bolshevik regime would collapse.

In fact, much of the initiative for these expropriations came from below, such as the miners in the Donets Basin, whose managers abandoned the mines and joined the Whites.

By August 1918, over 3,000 enterprises had been taken over by the state, either nationally or by local soviets. As the year progressed, the remaining sectors of the economy were taken over as, due to the advancing civil war, the centralisation of the economy became a military necessity. The Supreme Council of the Economy was placed in charge of the administration of the nationalised industries, which created plant managements, composed of representatives from the Economic Councils, the trade unions and those chosen by the workers within the industries.

1918 was the first year of the imperialist blockade, resulting in the collapse of imports and exports. Some 60 per cent of the railway lines were under the control of the Whites, who choked off supplies. As a result, there was a continual decline in production in the face of the famine. Absenteeism became widespread. Inflation became endemic as the burden of the civil war began to increase.

As a result of the nationalisations, economic life took on a dual form: a socialised sector and an anarchic peasant sector. In these conditions, the state sought to organise social production and distribution. Given the needs of self-defence and the war effort, the system evolved towards what became known as 'War Communism'. In reality, this had little to do with communism in the true sense of that word, but *everything* to do with survival. As Henry Brailsford correctly noted: "Russia has hardly yet begun to create her dream of a Communist economy. She has only struggled to survive amid war, civil war and blockade."[10]

This policy, which began in 1918, attained its fullest development in 1919-20. But the 'Left Communists' were never satisfied. In response to the widespread nationalisations, they called for more local autonomy, decentralisation and workers' control. These demands were not merely impractical. They were the direct opposite of what was required. In the given chaotic circumstances, what was needed was greater measures of centralisation, stricter organisation and stricter control of all branches of the economy. The tendency towards centralisation increased as the pressures of the civil war mounted, and the trade unions were also drawn into the tasks of economic planning. The whole economy became increasingly centred on military defence.

A dramatic turn of events occurred in the summer of 1918, when the Left SRs organised an armed revolt against the government. Ever since they resigned from the government in protest at the Brest-Litovsk treaty, they strove by any means to provoke war with Germany, beginning with the assassination of Count Mirbach, the German Ambassador. Although they still occupied important posts in the Cheka, they reacted violently towards the establishment of Poor Peasant Committees and the requisitioning of foodstuffs. This resulted in a complete breakdown in relations with the Bolsheviks. Then, in conjunction with some anarchist groups, they attempted to topple the government in Moscow. But the Left SRs lacked sufficient forces to succeed. They had no more than 2,000 men, sixty machine guns, half a dozen field guns and three armoured cars at their disposal. On the following day, the Left SR revolt had been crushed by midday.

They had, by now, clearly crossed the line and had ended up in the camp of the counter-revolution. Some 300 insurgents were arrested and a number of these were executed for their role in the uprising. "The Left SR party had committed suicide", wrote Victor Serge.[11]

Imperialists intervene

Hoping to capitalise on a weakened Russia, the Allies had devised an elaborate plan to support the internal counter-revolution. They believed that, following their military intervention, the Bolshevik regime would rapidly collapse.

In anticipation, the British and French governments had already planned the carving up of the Russian Empire into 'spheres of influence' according to their economic interests. The British zone, which reflected heavy investments in Russian oilfields, included the Caucasus, Armenia, Georgia and Kurdistan; the French, which had mainly investments in coal and iron in the Ukraine, carved out Ukraine, Bessarabia and Crimea. The British would also occupy the port of Baku, the centre of the Russian oil industry, while the French, together with Greeks and Poles, would seize the Black Sea ports of Odessa and Sevastopol. Others, like Japan, had their eyes on the resources of eastern Siberia.

The imperialists described their military intervention as 'an operation', to cover up the scale of their war on the Soviet state. As planned, the British, French and Canadians occupied Archangel and Murmansk, and established a 'Government of North Russia' as a rallying point for counter-revolution. The Japanese attacked Siberia, seized Vladivostok and Primorsky Krai, and immediately set about suppressing the local soviets. American troops also landed in Vladivostok in August. Meanwhile, private banks in the United States poured in money to help finance the war against the Soviet Republic.

In the North Caucasus, the White generals Kornilov, Alexeyev and Denikin, with the backing of the French and British, formed their 'Volunteer

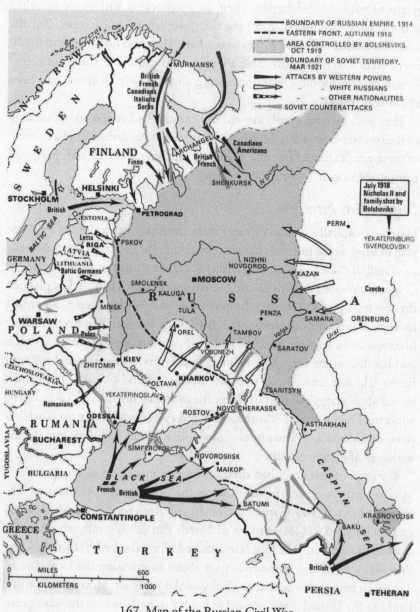

167. Map of the Russian Civil War

168. Allies' Parade in Vladivostok, Russia, September 1918

Army', attracting the support of the Junkers and other counter-revolutionary elements. This 'Volunteer Army' began its life by putting down workers' uprisings in Rostov and Taganrog and helping to establish a series of 'autonomous' (i.e. anti-Bolshevik) governments.

Within a few weeks, the Don Cossacks and the Czech forces advanced northward up the Volga, and Denikin controlled most of the territory between the Black Sea and the Caspian. At this point, only a narrow strip of land lay between these two White forces.

The Soviet Republic found itself between hammer and anvil. The military situation was dire. Morgan Philips Price was in Moscow in August 1918 when the Allied landing took place in Archangel and Murmansk. Many of Price's eyewitness reports sent to the *Manchester Guardian* were either censored or blocked. Price recalled that he was so fraught with anxiety that he could hardly bring himself to look at the maps displayed in Moscow shop windows showing the military situation on the different fronts, for fear of losing hope.

By this time, inspired by the ideals of the Russian Revolution, Price had thrown his lot in with the Soviet government. In May, he had written to his aunt in England that "most of the newspaper correspondents began to leave

Russia, Ransome and I decided to stick to our guns and sink or swim with the Russian Revolution."[12] In August 1918, he wrote his piece, *The Truth About the Allied Intervention in Russia*:

> One of the deadliest weapons wielded by the ruling classes of all countries is their power to censor the press; for thereby they are able to create under the pretext of military necessity an artificial public opinion with the object of hiding their fell designs. Never was this fact more clearly demonstrated than at the present moment; never was it more obvious that the governments of the Central Powers and the Allies, in order to suppress the workers' and peasants' Revolution in Russia, must hide from their own people the truth about this Revolution, must represent it to the proletariat of the West as the work of a gang of robbers.[13]

He continues:

> Just as the criminal or weak-minded man, after having committed some offence against public law, tries to shift the blame on to any person he finds handy, so the ruling classes of Europe, after butchering their people in a cruel four-year war, now in terror before the judgement of humanity and the inner prickings of conscience try to create for themselves pleasant illusions and find convenient scapegoats on which to vent their wrath.
>
> One cannot be surprised, of course, that the governments of England, France and Germany should, through the official agencies and their press censors, endeavour to blacken the work of the Russian Revolution. Living here in the besieged castle of the Russian Workers' and Peasants' Soviets, surrounded by the armed hosts of the European warlords, I am in a position to see more clearly than those outside this iron ring the power possessed by the ruling classes, whose fell designs include the strangling of this youngest of the governments of the toiling masses. For this is what I have to face day after day.[14]

A few months earlier, Arthur Ransome had written *The Truth About Russia*, a pamphlet for an American audience, which explained what was happening in simple language. He concluded:

> No one contends that the Bolsheviks are angels. I ask only that men shall look through the fog of libel that surrounds them and see that the ideal for which they are struggling, is among those lights which every man of young and honest heart sees before him somewhere on the road, and not among those other lights from which he resolutely turns away. These men who have made the Soviet government in Russia, if they fail, will fail with clean shields and clean hearts, having striven

for an ideal which will live beyond them. Even if they fail, they will nonetheless have written a page of history more daring than any other which I can remember in the history of humanity. They are writing it amid slinging of mud from all the meaner spirits in their country, in yours and in my own.[15]

The situation was becoming increasingly precarious for the Soviet Republic, threatened on the one hand with this foreign intervention, on the other with the danger of a further German advance. By this time, Soviet Power was confined to Petrograd and Moscow, with a small area surrounding them. But Lenin remained steadfast. He insisted that the revolution must show absolute determination in face of adversity. Whatever the cost, the Soviet regime was going to succeed:

We must be prepared for extraordinary difficulties, for extraordinarily severe defeats, which are inevitable because the revolution in Europe has not yet begun...[16]

In a discussion with Trotsky, Lenin revealed what might happen if things got so desperate that they were forced to abandon both Petrograd and Moscow. Trotsky asked: "And if the Germans maintain their offensive? And if they march on Moscow?" To which Lenin replied:

Then we shall withdraw further east, to the Urals, all the time declaring our readiness to conclude peace. The Kuznets Basin is rich in coal. We shall set up an Uralo-Kuznets Republic based on the regional industry and the Kuznets coal and, supported by the proletariat of Ural and by as many workers as we shall manage to move with us from Moscow and Petrograd, we shall hold out. If need be, we shall retreat even deeper, beyond the Urals. We may reach Kamchatka, but we shall hold out. The international situation will be changing a dozen times; from the redoubt of our Uralo-Kuznets Republic, we shall spread out again and we shall return to Moscow and Petersburg. But now, if we senselessly involve ourselves in a revolutionary war, if we let the elite of our working class and our party perish, then, of course, we shall return nowhere.[17]

"At that time", commented Trotsky, "the Uralo-Kuznets Republic formed an important part of Lenin's arguments."[18] Lenin pointed out that the coal reserves in the Kuznets Basin were enormous, and together with the iron ore in the Urals and grain in Siberia, this would be a base from which to advance. This was the worst-case scenario, but it needed to be considered just in case there was a turn for the worst. For Lenin, in such a situation, there could be no room for despair or pessimism.

Here, yet again, is displayed Lenin's realism, his courage, but also his optimism in the future, whatever may happen. For now, in this 'besieged fortress', they would have to do everything in their power to keep the revolution alive.

The revolt of the Czech Legion, followed by the Allied intervention, resulted in the complete encirclement of the young Soviet Republic, which was now fighting on all sides for its very survival. The Great French Revolution faced a hostile foreign intervention, numbering fourteen armies. The Allied intervention to crush the Soviet Republic involved twenty-one foreign armies.

While the Soviets lacked basic supplies and even an effective army, they bravely faced up to the combined weight of world imperialism. What they lacked in arms and weapons, they made up for in revolutionary élan and a solid revolutionary conviction. They issued appeals in many different languages addressed to the workers in uniforms in the interventionist armies. And they appealed for support from the international working class.

These bold appeals did not fall on deaf ears. In a short space of time, there were mutinies in virtually all the foreign armies, which had to be withdrawn from Russia.

An attempt on Lenin's life

The imperialists and the counter-revolution had continually thought of nothing else but beheading the revolution. In this, they were assisted by the actions of the Left SRs who, having failed in their attempt to win the support of the masses for an anti-Bolshevik uprising, resorted to the method of individual terrorism.

At the end of August 1918, Lenin was leaving a meeting at the Michelson factory in Moscow, where he had been addressing the workers. In those days, the leaders of the revolution walked the streets alone and unarmed, unaccompanied by the squads of armed bodyguards that have since become the norm in all countries.

On May Day, for instance, his car was stopped by demonstrators and he was lifted and carried shoulder high. No special security was established to protect Lenin's life. Like every other Bolshevik leader, Lenin had no fear for his own safety. He placed his faith wholly in the working class. So it was on that fateful day.

As he stepped out onto the street, he was confronted by a woman, a member of the Left SRs, who pulled out a revolver and fired three shots at

169. Lenin and his sister walking in Moscow without guards

him. One bullet penetrated his lung above the heart and lodged in his breast bone, another entered his neck close to the main artery and shattered his shoulder blade, while a third missed him.

After being shot, Lenin returned to the Kremlin but refused to be carried in a stretcher, and walked with assistance up three flights of stairs for medical attention. "It's nothing; it's only my arm", he said.[19] In fact, it was a narrow escape. If one of the bullets had hit him a little lower, he would have died. And it was not until 23 April 1922, over three years later, that one of the bullets was finally removed from his body. The other remained inside him, as it considered too dangerous to extract.

This was actually the second attempt on Lenin's life. The first was on 1 January 1918, when he was returning from a meeting in his car. When he turned off the Simeonovski Bridge onto the Fontanka, his car came under fire, bullets piercing the windscreen and hood. According to Fritz Platten, who was present and shielded Lenin with his body: "Lenin noted, no Russian Bolshevik can avoid such peril today."[20]

Another incident took place in January 1919, when his car was held up at gunpoint by robbers. They forced Lenin to hand over his wallet and the vehicle, leaving both him and his driver with no option but to walk back to the Kremlin on foot. He alluded to this episode about bandits just over a year later in an example referring to 'compromises', when he wrote *'Left-Wing' Communism: An Infantile Disorder.*[21]

But the most serious attempt was that of August 1918. Fanny Kaplan, the assailant, made a statement soon after her attempt to kill Lenin:

My name is Fanny Kaplan. Today I shot at Lenin. I did it on my own. I will not say from whom I obtained my revolver. I will give no details. I had resolved to kill Lenin long ago. I consider him a traitor to the Revolution.[22]

For this attempt on Lenin's life, Kaplan was duly executed.

At that precise moment, a change occurred in the psychology of the revolution. Gone were all the old peaceful illusions. The naivety that allowed counter-revolutionary generals to be released on parole no longer existed. In its place, a new spirit had arisen: an iron spirit that was utterly implacable in its will to conquer all obstacles, to defeat all enemies and to crush them without mercy.

It is the spirit that acts as a spur to action – the spirit that can be seen in every great revolution in history. It is the ferocious spirit that drove the French Revolution into battle against all the combined powers of monarchist Europe and drove the English Puritans to cut off the head of a king. Here we have the true genesis of what became known as the Red Terror. The justification of terror was again outlined by Trotsky in 1920 in his book *Terrorism and Communism*, which was a reply to Karl Kautsky:

The Red terror is not distinguishable from the armed insurrection, the direct continuation of which it represents. The state terror of a revolutionary class can be condemned 'morally' only by a man who, as a principle, rejects (in words) every form of violence whatsoever – consequently, every war and every rising...

The terror of tsarism was directed against the proletariat. The gendarmerie of tsarism throttled the workers who were fighting for the socialist order. Our Extraordinary Commissions shoot landlords, capitalists, and generals who are striving to restore the capitalist order. Do you grasp this... distinction? Yes? For us communists it is quite sufficient.[23]

The attempt on Lenin's life provoked a furious reaction in the working class. "Each drop of Lenin's blood must be paid for by the bourgeoisie and the

170. Fanny Kaplan | 171. Kaplan's gun

Whites in hundreds of deaths", wrote the Petrograd *Krasnaya Gazeta* a day later, on 31 August. "The interests of the revolution demand the physical extermination of the bourgeoisie. They have no pity: it is time for us to be pitiless."[24] Only those who showed positive loyalty to the regime deserved mercy, it said.

At this time, members of the Left SRs also tried to blow up Trotsky's train, but failed as he had taken a different route. However, they did succeed in assassinating Moisei Uritsky, the chief of the Petrograd Cheka, on the same day as Lenin was shot. These murders and attempted murders led to the launch of the 'Red Terror', the revolution's act of self-defence.

This began on a day of reckoning, where the authorities carried out widespread arrests and took bourgeois hostages into custody. It was clear that the revolution was now in mortal danger and all measures would be taken to defend it. Soon afterwards, on 20 August 1918, Lenin wrote a 'Letter to American Workers' defending these measures:

Their servants accuse us of resorting to terror… The British bourgeoisie have forgotten their 1649, the French bourgeoisie have forgotten their 1793. Terror was just and legitimate when the bourgeoisie resorted to it for their own benefit against feudalism. Terror became monstrous and criminal when the workers and poor peasants dared to use it against the bourgeoisie! Terror was just and legitimate when used for the purpose of substituting one exploiting minority for another exploiting minority. Terror became monstrous and criminal when it began to be used for the purpose of overthrowing *every* exploiting minority, to be used in the interests of the vast actual majority, in the interests of the proletariat and semi-proletariat, the working class and the poor peasants!

The international imperialist bourgeoisie have slaughtered ten million men and maimed twenty million in 'their' war, the war to decide whether the British or the German vultures are to rule the world.

If our war, the war of the oppressed and exploited against the oppressors and the exploiters, results in half a million or a million casualties in all countries, the bourgeoisie will say that the former casualties are justified, while the latter are criminal.

The proletariat will have something entirely different to say.[25]

On 1 September 1918, the British agent Bruce Lockhart was arrested on suspicion of being complicit in these terrorist acts, although he was then discharged. A few days later, the newspapers were full of accounts of an Allied conspiracy, orchestrated by Lockhart. On 4 September, Lockhart was again detained, but this time he was held for a month in the Lubyanka, the Cheka headquarters, before being released.

Cheka

For the revolution to defend itself, the Extraordinary Commission, or Cheka, had been established under Felix Dzerzhinsky. This Commission was to be responsible for internal security, and swung into action against the threats of counter-revolution. The Chekists were mostly men of high moral calibre, fearless fighters, totally dedicated to the cause of October. These shock troops of the revolution acted decisively and showed no signs of mercy to the enemies of the revolution.

On 7 September, the Petrograd Cheka had announced that 512 counter-revolutionaries had been shot, including ten Right SRs. Hostages were also taken, including Grand Dukes, aristocrats, officers, industrialists, financiers and other reactionaries, who would be shot if any revolutionaries were harmed. At Kronstadt, 500 counter-revolutionaries were shot. In the first ten days of the operation, in Moscow some sixty were executed. Similar retribution was carried out in the provinces. Such measures were designed to strike fear into the counter-revolutionaries. They were a warning of what they could expect in response to any future attacks.

After 5 September, the Party leadership made efforts to limit the terror. The *Krasnaya Gazeta* wrote:

The bourgeoisie has been taught a cruel lesson… Let our enemies leave us in peace to build a new life. If they do so, we shall ignore their simmering hatred and stop hunting them out. The Red terror is over, until the White terror begins again.[26]

172. Felix Dzerzhinsky

173. Mikhail Tukhachevsky

These deadly blows against the counter-revolution showed that there was no going back. The Soviet regime was prepared to go to whatever lengths were needed to defend the revolution and its leaders. It now fully understood that only by showing complete resolve could it hope to succeed.

In August, the Soviets faced another deadly threat. In the face of a further advance by the Czech Legion, the Red Army had withdrawn in a panic from Kazan in the upper Volga. It was clear that if the Czechs were allowed to cross the river, they would have a direct path towards Moscow. As a result, Trotsky took command and left for this front in his armoured train. "The Republic is in peril!" he declared: "Woe to those who directly or indirectly aggravate the peril."[27]

The front at Kazan was in a state of collapse and there were mass desertions. To restore discipline, Trotsky reorganised and reinforced the command structure. Other more worthy and determined officers were promoted. The discipline of the Red Army was based on class solidarity and loyalty to the revolution. But in this life and death struggle, severe methods were also required. The stern order went out that there would be no retreat of the Red Army on pain of death. The line would be held, come what may.

On 10 September, Red Army soldiers stormed and seized back Kazan. Days later, despite a growing threat from Czech forces, Mikhail Tukhachevsky, Commander of the Eastern Front, won a decisive victory at Simbirsk.

This success had an electrifying effect on the fighting spirit in the Red Army. By the beginning of October, the whole of the Volga region had once

174. Liebknecht speaking at a rally in Berlin, December 1918

again come under Soviet control. Thanks largely to the audacious leadership
of Trotsky, the immediate threat subsided.

But many new dangers had yet to be overcome. Only a revolutionary
breakthrough in Europe could come to the aid of the Soviet power. All eyes
were now fixed on the unfolding revolutionary situation in Germany.

German Revolution

The removal of General Ludendorff from the German government revealed
the cracks at the top of the regime. This gave way to the government of
Prince von Baden, which included the Social-Democrat Scheidemann. It was
a cosmetic manoeuvre, nothing more. Lenin was to grasp its significance. On
1 October 1918, in a letter to Trotsky and Sverdlov, Lenin wrote:

> Things have so 'accelerated' in Germany that we must not fall behind either. But
> today we are already behind. [...]
>
> The international revolution has come so close in *one week* that it has to be
> reckoned with as an event of the *next few days*. [...]
>
> We are all ready to die to help the German workers advance the revolution which
> has begun in Germany.

The conclusion:

1. Ten times more effort to secure grain (clean out *all* stocks both for ourselves *and for the German workers*).

2. Ten times more *enrolments* for the army. We must have *by the spring* an army of three millions to help the international workers' revolution."[28]

In early November 1918, revolution finally broke out in Germany. Workers' and soldier's councils were thrown up and the fate of the old regime hung in the balance.

A red flag flew over every barracks and over every ship in the Imperial Navy. It had all the parallels with the February Revolution in Russia, with the absolutism of the Hohenzollerns, following the Romanovs, reduced to rubble. It created, as in Russia between February and October, a situation of dual power. The hope now was for a German October. Lenin wrote:

News came from Germany in the night about the victory of the revolution there. First Kiel radio announced that power was in the hands of a Council of Workers and Sailors. Then Berlin made the following announcement:

"Greetings of peace and freedom to all. Berlin and the surrounding districts are in the hands of a Council of Workers' and Soldiers' Deputies. [...]"

Please take every step to notify German soldiers at all border points. Berlin also reports that German soldiers at the front have arrested the peace delegation from the former German Government and have begun peace negotiations themselves with the French soldiers.[29]

As the news spread, tens of thousands of Russian workers took to the streets in jubilation. Their isolation had surely been broken and the world revolution was advancing, beginning in mighty Germany! Karl Radek recalled:

From every corner of the city demonstrations were marching towards the Moscow Soviet ... Tens of thousands of workers burst into wild cheering. Never have I seen anything like it. Until late in the evening workers and Red Army soldiers were filing past. The world revolution had begun. The mass of people heard its iron tramp. Our isolation was over.[30]

However, like the Mensheviks and SRs in Russia, the old Social-Democratic leaders – Gustav Noske, Friedrich Ebert and Philipp Scheidemann – betrayed the revolution by handing power back to the frightened bourgeoisie. The Workers' and Soldiers' Councils were sidelined and, in their place, National

175. Spartacist barricade in Berlin

Assembly elections were called for January 1919. Liebknecht and Luxemburg were released from prison and went on to establish a Communist Party at the end of December. However, given its inexperience, the young Party took a very ultra-left line on most things and allowed itself to be dragged along by events.

The so-called Spartacist Uprising, in early January 1919, had all the hallmarks of the July Days in Russia. Its defeat led to a witch-hunt of the Spartacist leaders, as with the Bolsheviks previously. But whereas Lenin had gone into hiding, Liebknecht and Luxemburg failed to do so. They were hunted down and brutally murdered by the counter-revolutionary officers, with the full connivance of the Social-Democratic leaders.

The German workers could have taken power. The crucial factor that led to the defeat of the revolution was the lack of a Bolshevik Party. Lenin had built such a party before 1917, while the newly-formed German Communist Party was only days old and too weak to alter the course of events. This was a vital lesson for the future.

The tragic murder of Liebknecht and Luxemburg beheaded the German Revolution. A period of revolution and counter-revolution now spread throughout Germany. The workers came to power in Bavaria, under Kurt

Eisner and then Eugen Leviné, but this was soon drowned in blood. The Hessian Soviet Republic experienced a similar fate.*

Revolutionary ferment gripped the armed forces in France and Britain, with mutinies in Calais and elsewhere. The virus of revolution was also sweeping through the troops of the Allied intervention. Lenin's famous appeal, 'Why Have You Come to Murmansk?', was translated into English by Morgan Philips Price to great effect.

Despite the initial setbacks, the revolutionary events in Germany and elsewhere had shown that the world revolution had arrived. It was just a matter of time before there would be a decisive breakthrough in one key country or another.

The current of history was flowing fast. Everything seemed to indicate that the decisive moment that Lenin and the Bolsheviks had been expecting and preparing for had finally arrived.

---

* See Rob Sewell, *Germany 1918-1833: Socialism or Barbarism*, Wellred Books, 2018.

29. Founding the Comintern

The coming to power of the Bolsheviks in October 1917 unleashed a revolutionary wave throughout Europe and placed workers' power firmly on the agenda. Lenin believed that it was essential to take advantage of this situation, which, if handled correctly, would provide a starting point for world revolution. For Lenin, the key to this was Germany, a country that dominated Central Europe.

Lenin was not the only one who held this perspective. More than anything else, Lloyd George, the British Prime Minister, feared a potential alliance between Soviet Russia and a victorious Soviet Germany. The British ruling class was terrified the country was teetering on the edge of proletarian revolution. On 25 March 1919, Lloyd George was already envisaging the worst scenario:

> The greatest danger I perceive in the present situation is the possibility of Germany uniting her destiny with that of the Bolshevists and placing her wealth, intellect and great organising capacity at the disposal of the men who dream of conquering the world for Bolshevism by force of arms. This danger is no idle fancy. If Germany goes over to Spartacism, she will inevitably link her fate with that of the Bolshevists. If that takes place, all Eastern Europe will be drawn into the maelstrom of the Bolshevist Revolution, and a year hence we shall find ourselves opposed by nearly 3,000,000 men who will be welded by German generals and German instructors into a gigantic army equipped with German machine guns and ready to undertake an offensive against Western Europe.[1]

Tragically, it was not to be. The German Revolution in November 1918, the most important breakthrough after Russia, was betrayed by the Social-Democrats. Although the revolutionary possibilities in Germany were greater than they had been in Russia, it lacked a mass Communist Party comparable to the Bolshevik Party.

In order to rectify this, the founding of a new Third International was seen by Lenin as an absolutely crucial measure. Its overriding aim was to build Communist Parties in all countries, to sweep aside the social-traitors and prepare the overthrow of capitalism by the working class.

To this end, on 21 January 1919, a meeting of representatives from a number of small communist parties and left-wing socialist groups came together to discuss a manifesto drafted by Trotsky, entitled 'For the First Congress of the Communist International'. In the same month, Radio Moscow, in the name of the Executive Committee of the Russian Communist Party, called on "all parties hostile to the Second international" to hold a conference with a view to establishing a new Third Communist International.[2] The founding Congress would take place in Moscow in early March.

This appeal constituted a direct challenge to the efforts of the Social-Democrats and centrists who were trying desperately to breathe life into the corpse of the old Second International. They had held their own conference in Bern in February.

1919 was the high point of the revolutionary tide. The revolution was advancing on all sides. In March, the same month as the founding Congress of the Third Communist International, a Soviet Republic was declared in Hungary and in early April, another Soviet Republic was announced in Bavaria.

Lloyd George wrote a confidential memorandum to his French counterpart, Clemenceau, during the Versailles Peace Conference:

> The whole of Europe is filled with the spirit of revolution. There is a deep sense not only of discontent but of anger and revolt amongst the workmen against pre-war conditions. The whole existing order in its political, social and economic aspects is questioned by the masses of the population from one end of Europe to the other.[3]

The Communist International, also known as the Comintern, stood firmly on the principles of the First International, established by Marx and Engels. These ideas flowed from the position of the working class internationally and the fact that the common class interests of working people transcended national boundaries. They were then carried over into the Second (Socialist)

International, founded in July 1889 and composed of mass parties wedded to the ideas of Marxism.

But, as we have seen, the Second International developed in a period of capitalist upswing, which had a profound effect on its outlook. The upswing had created reformist illusions in the tops of the trade unions and socialist parties, who began to adapt to capitalism. The labour leaders began to accept the view that capitalism had solved its inner contradictions, and that revolution was unnecessary.

These were the objective conditions that led to the reformist and nationalist degeneration of the old International. This eventually found its expression in the betrayal of August 1914. The Second International was infected with the fatal disease of opportunism. It had therefore ceased to be a vehicle for the achievement of socialism.

The revolutionary mantle of Marxism now passed to the Communist International, which aimed to rescue and re-establish its original revolutionary principles, purged of opportunism. The new organisation would contain all the best traditions of the First and Second internationals, newly enriched and perfected by the experience of the Zimmerwald Left and Bolshevism.

The Second International had ceased to function during the war. But long before that, it had ceased to function as a genuine revolutionary international. The spirit of narrow nationalism that was spreading in its leading ranks was reflected in its organisational looseness. The national leaders paid lip-service to the International, but jealously guarded their own independence.

The semi-federal character of the International led to the adoption of all kinds of opportunist compromises, for instance, on the national and colonial question. In this opportunism and these concessions to nationalism, we already see the outlines of the betrayal of August 1914. Each national section was largely allowed to do as they pleased, and the others were informed of their activities.

Lenin commented ironically that it acted more like a post office than a revolutionary centre. In complete contrast, the new International was created as a single unified world party of socialist revolution.

The First Congress

The First Congress of the new International was held in Moscow over a four-day period between 2 and 6 March 1919. It was attended by fifty-one delegates, representing organisations and trends from more than two dozen countries, including Russia, Germany, Austria, Hungary, Poland, Ukraine,

176. Lenin in the presidium of the First Congress of the Comintern

Latvia, Lithuania, Estonia, Finland, Sweden, Switzerland, countries in the Balkans and others.

Because of the imperialist blockade and the post-war hazards and restrictions, no representatives were able to make it from Italy, France, or Britain. Many delegates who made their way illegally arrived late during the Congress. SJ Rutgers from the United States had to travel by way of Japan, and Hugo Eberlein, the sole German delegate, had to cross the front lines in Lithuania where German troops were still fighting the Red Army.

Tragically, only six weeks prior to the Congress, Rosa Luxemburg and Karl Liebknecht – the genuine leaders of the German Revolution – had been assassinated by the Freikorps,* with the complicity of the Social-Democratic leaders.

Arthur Ransome was present in Moscow at this time and was invited to attend its founding sessions. His fresh impressions are very illuminating:

The founding of the Third International had been proclaimed in the morning papers, and an extraordinary meeting in the Great Theatre announced for the

---

* The Freikorps ('Free Corps') were volunteer forces from the reactionary dregs in society. They were ultra-reactionary gangs of White-Guardist elements whose officers were drawn from the pro-monarchist military and sons of the aristocracy.

177. Another photo of the presidium
From left to right: Gustav Klinger, Hugo Eberlein, Lenin, Friz Platten

evening. I got to the theatre at about five, and had difficulty in getting in, though I had a special ticket as a correspondent. There were queues outside all the doors. The Moscow Soviet was there, the Executive Committee, representatives of the Trade Unions and the Factory Committees, etc. The huge theatre and the platform were crammed, people standing in the aisles and even packed close together in the wings of the stage. Kamenev opened the meeting by a solemn announcement of the founding of the Third International in the Kremlin. There was a roar of applause from the audience, which rose and sang the *Internationale* in a way that I have never heard it sung since the All-Russian Assembly, when the news came of the strikes in Germany during the Brest negotiations.

Kamenev then spoke of those who had died on the way, mentioning Liebknecht and Rosa Luxembourg, and the whole theatre stood again while the orchestra played *You Fell As Victims*. Then Lenin spoke.

If I had ever thought that Lenin was losing his personal popularity, I got my answer now. It was a long time before he could speak at all, everybody standing and drowning his attempts to speak with roar after roar of applause. It was an extraordinary, overwhelming scene, tier after tier crammed with workmen, the parterre filled, the whole platform and the wings. A knot of working women were close to me, and they almost fought to see him, and shouted as if each one were determined that he should hear her in particular. He spoke as usual, in the simplest way, emphasising the fact that the revolutionary struggle everywhere was forced to use the Soviet forms. "We declare our solidarity with the aims of the Sovietists", he read from an Italian paper, and added, "and that was when they did not know what our aims were, and before we had an established programme ourselves."[4]

Lenin attended the entire Congress, listening and intervening in the key debates. This honoured leader of the Russian Revolution opened the proceedings on 2 March with a brief explanation of the International's great historical significance.

On behalf of the Central Committee of the Russian Communist Party I declare the First Congress of the Communist International open. First I would ask all present to rise in tribute to the finest representatives of the Third International: Karl Liebknecht and Rosa Luxemburg. (*All rise.*)

Comrades, our gathering has great historic significance. It testifies to the collapse of all the illusions cherished by bourgeois democrats. Not only in Russia, but in the most developed capitalist countries of Europe, Germany for example, civil war is a fact.

The bourgeoisie are terror-stricken at the growing workers' revolutionary movement. This is understandable if we take into account that the development of events since the imperialist war inevitably favours the workers' revolutionary movement, and that the world revolution is beginning and growing in intensity everywhere.[5]

Lenin went on to criticise the slavish approach of the reformist leaders towards the bourgeois state, their utter subservience to the bourgeois and everything they stood for. He then drew out the lessons of the Paris Commune and the importance of Soviet power.

He attacked the spurious idea that Soviet power and the Constituent Assembly could coexist, as the centrists, such as Kautsky and the Mensheviks, argued. Such a regime of 'dual power' could not last. Either the Soviets or the bourgeois state would emerge victorious. There was no middle road.

Lenin attacked the counter-revolutionary role played by the Mensheviks in the civil war that was raging. While they passed solemn resolutions criticising their earlier support for the counter-revolution, the Mensheviks continued to ally themselves with the tsarist White Guards, intrigued with foreign powers, and then attempted to cover up their treacherous role.

But, explained Lenin, in such a civil war, nobody can sit on the fence and those who allied themselves with the counter-revolution would be dealt with firmly:

> The majority of the Mensheviks went over to the bourgeoisie and fought against us during the Civil War. We, of course, persecute Mensheviks, we even shoot them, when they wage war against us, fight against our Red Army and shoot our Red commanders. We responded to the bourgeois war with the proletarian war – there can be no other way. Therefore, from the political point of view, all this is sheer Menshevik hypocrisy. Historically, it is incomprehensible how people who have not been officially certified as mad could talk at the Bern Conference, on the instructions of the Mensheviks and Socialist-Revolutionaries, about the Bolsheviks fighting the latter, yet keep silent about their own struggle, in alliance with the bourgeoisie, against the proletariat.

> All of them furiously attack us for persecuting them. This is true. But they do not say a word about the part they themselves have taken in the Civil War![6]

He went on to conclude his speech with the following remarks:

> Of course, we are not in a position to prescribe the path of development. It is quite likely that the revolution will come very soon in many West-European countries, but we, as the organised section of the working class, as a party, strive and must strive to gain a majority in the Soviets. Then our victory will be assured and no power on earth will be able to do anything against the communist revolution.[7]

An interview with Lenin

Arthur Ransome noted that the business and speeches at the Congress were communicated in many languages, though, where possible, German and French were used:

> This was unlucky for me … Fineberg spoke in English, Rakovsky in French, Sadoul also. Skrypnik, who, being asked, refused to talk German and said he would speak in either Ukrainian or Russian, and to most people's relief chose the latter … Trotsky, in a leather coat, military breeches and gaiters, with a fur hat with the sign of the Red Army in front, was looking very well, but a strange figure for those who had known him as one of the greatest anti-militarists in Europe. Lenin sat quietly listening, speaking when necessary in almost every European language with astonishing ease… I could not help realising that I was present at something that will go down in the histories of socialism, much like that other strange meeting convened in London in 1848.[8]

178. May Day rally, 1919

There was a debate at the Congress about the status and timing of the launch of the new Third International. When she was alive, Rosa Luxemburg had felt that the launch of a new International might be premature on such precarious foundations, and therefore the sole German delegate, Hugo Eberlein, had a mandate to oppose its immediate founding. He argued that it was more appropriate instead to regard the gathering as a preliminary conference.

Others, however, were very eager to proceed with the founding of the Third International and opposed any further delay. After a lengthy debate, which included Lenin, and given the strength of feeling, Eberlein was convinced to abstain in the vote to allow the launch of the International to proceed with no votes against. When Eberlein returned home, the German Communist Party accepted the decision and agreed to affiliate to the new International.

All the principal resolutions which were passed at this Founding Congress were drafted by Lenin and Trotsky, the key political figures of the world movement. These resolutions highlighted the essential nature of the proletarian revolution and the principles of Soviet power. This was vital in drawing a sharp line between the revolutionary internationalists and the social chauvinists and centrists of the old International.

179. Lenin addressing troops, May 1919

Following the Congress, Arthur Ransome interviewed Lenin on the day of a holiday proclaimed in honour of the founding of the International. He wrote down his impressions:

More than ever, Lenin struck me as a happy man. Walking home from the Kremlin, I tried to think of any other man of his calibre who had a similar joyous temperament. I could think of none. This little, bald-headed, wrinkled man, who tilts his chair this way and that, laughing over one thing or another, ready any minute to give serious advice to any who interrupt him to ask for it, advice so well reasoned that it is to his followers far more compelling than any command, every wrinkle is a wrinkle of laughter, not of worry. I think the reason must be that he is the first great leader who utterly discounts the value of his own personality. He is quite without personal ambition. More than that, he believes, as a Marxist, in the movement of the masses which, with or without him, would still move. His whole faith is in the elemental forces that move people, his faith in himself is merely his belief that he justly estimates the direction of those forces. He does not believe that any man could make or stop the revolution which he thinks inevitable. If the Russian revolution fails, according to him it fails only temporarily, and because of forces beyond any man's control. He is consequently free with a freedom no other great man has ever had. It is not so much what he says that inspires confidence. It is this sensible freedom, this obvious detachment. With his philosophy he cannot for a moment believe that one man's mistake might ruin all. He is, for himself at any rate, the exponent not the cause of the events that will be forever linked with his name.[9]

In the spring of 1919, mass parties joined the Third International, such as the Norwegian Labour Party and the Italian Socialist Party. Other parties, such as the British Independent Labour Party, the French Socialist Party and the German Independent Social Democratic Party, all voted to leave the Second International and opened negotiations to join the Communist International. These were mass workers' organisations moving towards communism.

In 1919, the British government had ordered a slowdown in demobilisation, and instead looked to greater conscription for a fresh war against Russia. Churchill was determined to use British troops to overthrow Lenin and the Soviet government. But thousands of armed soldiers, determined to put an end to the fighting and the carnage of the trenches, marched on Whitehall demanding to be demobilised. They had been promised a 'land fit for heroes', and they were demanding such. British troops had also been affected in Calais, where soldiers proved unwilling to fight and to obey orders.

Towards the end of January 1919, the men of the Army Ordnance and Mechanical Transport sections at the Val de Lièvre camp organised a mass meeting, which took the decision to mutiny. The fraught nerves of the General Staff were clearly affected by these mutinies and revolts. "We are sitting on top of a mine which may go up at any moment", stated General Wilson to Churchill. Even the bone-headed Churchill feared that the unrest would spread and that "widespread disobedience would encourage Bolshevism in Britain."[10]

Throughout the year, 'Hands Off Russia' committees were established in Britain, America, and many other countries. This resulted in London dockers halting the *Jolly George* cargo vessel in May 1920, which was carrying munitions to fight the Soviet Republic.

In August, the British Labour Party and Trades Union Congress issued instructions to all Trades Councils and local Labour Parties urging "the whole industrial power of the organised workers" to be used to prevent war with Russia.[11] Up and down the country 'Councils of Action' were formed. Faced with this situation, the British government was forced to back down.

180. Aleksandr Kolchak

Civil war intensifies

The year 1919 was the most critical time for the Russian Revolution. The Soviet Republic was in deep peril, as multiple civil war fronts raged all around them. The threat of counter-revolution had never been greater. By this time, the Germans had occupied the vast bulk of Ukraine, the Don Cossacks had succeeded in clearing out the Soviet forces in their region, while further military advances were being made by the Kuban Cossacks.

By the summer of 1919, the military forces of Kolchak* made initial advances towards the Volga and Moscow. General Denikin and his White army had pushed further south and took Odessa, then swept up through the Don and Ukraine, swelling its ranks, and advancing north, taking Kursk and Orel. Denikin then threatened Tula, which was only a short distance from Moscow.

Simultaneously, General Yudenich, who had been made Commander-in-chief of the North-western army of the Whites, carried out an offensive in the west that approached the gates of Petrograd. The British Navy, which

---

* Another principal leader of the White Armies. He established a White government in Omsk, in south western Siberia. He was caught and shot on 6 February 1920.

was present in the Gulf of Finland, promised Yudenich's forces its support. Yudenich's stated aim was to take Petrograd and then meet Denikin in Moscow. This plan placed the fate of the revolution in the balance.

Added to the military threat, the rich kulaks continued to hide their grain, intensifying the famine and starving the cities. Such was the scarcity of bread and basic foods that food riots broke out across the country. The desperate plight of workers was summed up by the following comments from a worker-militant:

> In this period, hardly any horses were to be seen in Petrograd; they were either dead, or eaten, or requisitioned, or sent off into the countryside. Dogs and cats were no more visible either ... People lived on tea and potato-cakes made with linseed oil. As a member of the EC of the Vyborg Soviet I know that there were *whole weeks* in which no issues of bread or potatoes were made to the workers; all they got was sunflower seeds and some nuts... The balance of forces consisted of starving towns face to face with a hundred million hostile peasants. Soviet power seemed to be in a desperate position.[12]

This was the most difficult year of all for the revolution. The Soviet government tried to alleviate the burden by establishing communal kitchens in Petrograd, Moscow and other cities, where regular meals were supplied to those most in need. The priority of the Soviet government was to feed the children and feed its soldiers, the very defence of the revolution. Others would have to wait until their most urgent needs could be attended to. There was simply nothing available to feed them, so many went hungry. Lenin initiated decrees providing free meals for children, for which he had a particular concern:

> We, adults, will go hungry, but we shall give the last pinch of flour, the last lump of sugar and the last piece of butter to the children. It is better for the burden of these hard times to be borne by adults; the children must be spared in every possible way.[13]

Hunger is a weapon of war, just as much as bullets, bombs and poison gas. The imperialist powers used the blockade of Russia in a pincer movement to grind the population into submission. All sea routes and other lines of communication with the rest of the world were severed. Russia was completely isolated, while continuing to face ferocious internal counter-revolution in the form of the Whites, with the tacit support of the SRs and Mensheviks.

The leaders of these 'socialist' parties, who opposed the revolution, were watching to see which way the wind was blowing. But in a civil war, when

181. Armoured White Army train on its way to Tsaritsyn, June 1919

Russia was surrounded by the ravenous wolves of world imperialism, there was no room for half-measures or neutrality. The Soviet regime was fighting for its life. In the midst of all this, Lenin remained absolutely resolute. He did not hesitate to take whatever decisive action was needed to defend the revolution. And he became increasingly scathing in remarks directed against the cowardly 'socialists':

> Martov, Volsky and Co. fancy themselves 'superior' to both contending sides; they fancy themselves capable of creating a 'third side'.

> This desire, even when it is sincere, still remains the illusion of the petty-bourgeois democrat, who to this day, seventy years after 1848, has still not learned the most elementary thing, namely, that in a capitalist environment only the dictatorship of the bourgeoisie or the dictatorship of the proletariat is possible, and that no third course can exist. [...] in practice vacillations on the part of these people are inevitable, today in the direction of Denikin, tomorrow in the direction of the Bolsheviks.[14]

As always, Lenin put things squarely:

182. Workers at dinner

Our task is to put the question bluntly. What is better? To ferret out, to imprison, sometimes even to shoot hundreds of traitors from among the Cadets, non-party people, Mensheviks and Socialist-Revolutionaries, who 'come out' (some with arms in hand, others with conspiracies, others still with agitation against mobilisation, like the Menshevik printers and railwaymen, etc.) *against* Soviet power, *in other words, in favour of Denikin?* Or to allow matters to reach such a pass that Kolchak and Denikin are able to slaughter, shoot and flog to death tens of thousands of workers and peasants? The choice is not difficult to make.

That is how the question stands, and not otherwise.[15]

Petrograd threatened

In the spring of 1919, Lenin wrote:

The Soviet Republic, in the harsh but glorious struggle it is waging at the head of all peoples, is entering the most difficult period of its existence. The next few months will be months of crisis. The Entente is making its last, desperate effort

183. Lunchtime at a Moscow kindergarten

to crush us by force of arms. The food situation is becoming extremely acute. The transport system is in a serious state.

Only the greatest effort can save us. Victory is nevertheless fully possible.[16]

In October, with the army of General Yudenich approaching the gates of Petrograd, the Seventh Army was caught off balance and was withdrawing. Given the precarious military situation elsewhere, it was not possible to denude the other fronts. The problem was that Petrograd was under the leadership of Zinoviev.

Zinoviev's character was inherently unstable. He continually experienced the sharpest psychological reverses, typically being either absolutely ecstatic or deeply depressed. Now, with Yudenich's forces fast approaching, he succumbed to a deep depression, which soon turned, first to panic, then to hysteria. In Zinoviev, hysteria was the most obvious manifestation of cowardice. On the eve of the October Revolution, he was driven by panic to demand that the insurrection be called off. Now, he urgently put pressure on Lenin to abandon Petrograd, insisting that there was no way to defend it.

184. Barricades being built in Petrograd during Yudenich's offensive, 1919

The surrender of Red Petrograd would have been a catastrophic blow to the Revolution. Decisive action was needed. And that was least of all to be expected from Zinoviev. When Trotsky arrived in Moscow and became aware of what was being proposed, he was resolutely opposed to abandoning Petrograd. If that revolutionary bastion fell, there would be a bloodbath, and Moscow would be next.

Trotsky believed everything should be done to turn Petrograd into a military camp. He would take personal command to rally the workers and soldiers for a revolutionary defence of Petrograd. He also intended to exploit the antagonisms between the Cossacks and Yudenich's 'Voluntary Army', in an attempt to divide these forces.

After a discussion in the Politburo, Trotsky's proposal was accepted. Everything would be done to defend the city, including fighting street by street, if necessary. The enemy was already at the gates and emergency measures were demanded.

Under Trotsky's leadership, the Petrograd workers rallied to its defence, as the fate of the city hung in the balance. Such was the fierce resistance displayed by the workers that Yudenich was stopped in his tracks. As Trotsky had predicted, Yudenich's failure to involve the Cossacks had left Denikin fatally split and exposed. The personal intervention of Trotsky served to turn the situation around, defeat Yudenich's offensive, and save Petrograd.

The Soviet state had managed to hang on, but only by the skin of its teeth. The territory of the Soviet Republic shrank in the summer to dimensions not much greater than those of the Grand Duchy of Moscow of six centuries before.

Earlier in 1919, Lenin had accurately summed up the situation facing the Soviet state:

> *The primary task in a ruined country is to save the working people. The primary productive force of human society as a whole, is the workers, the working people.* If they survive, we shall save and restore *everything*.
>
> We shall have to put up with many years of poverty, retrogression to barbarism. The imperialist war has thrown us back to barbarism; but if we save the working people, if we save the primary productive force of human society – the workers – we shall recover everything, but if we fail to save them, we shall perish, so that those who are now shouting about 'consumers', or 'soldiers', communism, who look down upon others with contempt and imagine that they are superior to these Bolshevik Communists, are, I repeat, absolutely ignorant of political economy, and pick out passages from books like a scholar whose head is a card index box filled with quotations from books, which he picks out as he needs them; but if a new situation arises which is not described in any book, he becomes confused and grabs the wrong quotation from the box.[17]

Lenin had nothing but contempt for such so-called revolutionaries. He operated in a world of real workers, real civil war, real isolation, but at the same time, he had great faith in the world revolution, the real saviour of the Russian revolution and everything else.

Greater equality

Thus far, we have concentrated on the retreats and concessions that the Soviet regime was forced to make in this period. However, this should not overshadow the great achievements being made in many fields, notably in achieving equality between women and men. From the very beginning, there was a conscious drive to create a greater equality in society. In this regard, the People's Commissars themselves set an example.

Unlike the pampered bourgeois ministers in the West, the Soviet Commissars led a very austere life. This fact clearly goes against the 'narrative' of bourgeois historians, such as Volkogonov, who peddled the lie that, while

185. Lenin speaking in Moscow, 1919

preaching equality, the Communist leaders made sure of their privileged position. In this completely twisted view of reality, Lenin is transformed from a man living on humble means into a rich bureaucrat, who supposedly talked of wage 'equality' while apparently earning many times the wage of an industrial worker. This is utterly false.

Professor Richard Stites also promoted this false idea in his book, *Revolutionary Dreams: Utopian Vision and Experimental Life in the Russian Revolution*. While Stites was forced to recognise the egalitarian principles of the time, he states without any evidence that the party leaders, in particular, were filling their pockets: "Side by side with the augmentation of power among revolutionary leaders came the accretion of wealth – goods, services, wages, and privileges – for themselves and for designated 'specialists'". He continues: "Within the working class as well as between it and the leaders and specialists, stratification of wages continued as of old."[18]

The truth was completely different. Rather than seeking wealth and privileges for themselves, Lenin and the Bolsheviks took as their model the example of the Paris Commune, where deputies and officials received no more than the average workers' wage. Lenin elevated this important principle in his book, *The State and Revolution*, as a means of fighting bureaucracy. Therefore, when the Bolsheviks came to power, they introduced a wage rate for officials and ministers as no more than the average wage of a skilled worker.

On 1 December 1917 Lenin drafted a decree on 'The Salaries of High-Ranking Office Employees and Officials', which was approved with only small amendments by the Council of People's Commissars. It reads as follows:

> Recognising the need for energetic measures to reduce the salaries of high-ranking office employees and officials in all state, public and private institutions and enterprises, the Council of People's Commissars decrees:
>
> 1. that the salary limit for people's commissars be fixed at 500 rubles a month where there are no children, and 100 rubles extra for each child; housing to be at the rate of not more than one room for each member of the family;
>
> 2. that all local Soviets of Workers', Soldiers' and Peasants' Deputies be asked to prepare and carry out revolutionary measures to impose special taxes on high-ranking employees;
>
> 3. that the Ministry for Finance be instructed to draft a general law concerning this reduction;
>
> 4. that the Ministry for Finance and all the respective commissars be instructed to immediately study the estimates of the ministries and cut all excessively high salaries and pensions.[19]

During the first months of the Soviet Republic, the salaries of members of the government, including Lenin, were no more than 2:1 of the wage of ordinary workers. They were earning the same level as a skilled worker. Again, this stands out sharply with the bloated salaries, outside jobs and excessive expenses and perks received by present-day bourgeois politicians.

Wages of People's Commissars

Marcel Liebman, in his book *Lenin Under Leninism*, also showed the egalitarian principles that underpinned the ideals and practice of Lenin's Russia:

> In this matter the example was set from the top by Lenin in particular, who took the initiative in fixing the monthly wage for the highest in the land, the People's Commissars, at 500 rubles, comparable to the earnings of a skilled worker.
>
> Party members were obliged to pay over to the Party any income received in excess of that figure. This was no mere demagogic gesture. When a decision was taken in May 1918 to increase the wages of People's Commissars from 500 to 800 rubles, Lenin

wrote a letter, not intended for publication, to the office manager of the Council of People's Commissars, in which he protested against "the obvious illegality of this increase", which was "in direct infringement of the decree of the Council of People's Commissars [...]", and inflicted "a severe reprimand" on those responsible.[20]

This was Lenin's real attitude, who led by example, and refused wage increases above that of a skilled worker, which he regarded as "illegal", and reprimanded those who suggested such a rise. Stites' crude attempt to link the wages of Soviet leaders with "specialists", who received a lot more, is again completely false. As Liebman again explains:

> The 'specialists' to whom the new regime felt compelled to make concessions were paid a wage 50 per cent higher than that received by the members of the government.[21]

Any Communist Party members who were specialists and entitled to higher wages were banned from taking these higher sums. It was a strict rule of the Party that any excess was to be paid back to the state. This much higher rate paid to specialists was fully discussed by Lenin at the Petrograd Soviet in March 1919:

> The next question is about wages; the specialist gets 3,000, he goes from place to place and is difficult to catch. I say this about the specialists – they are people who have a knowledge of bourgeois science and engineering at a higher level than the overwhelming majority of workers and peasants; such specialists are needed and we say that at the moment we cannot introduce equalitarian wages, and are in favour of paying more than 3,000. Even if we pay several million a year in wages it will not be too much as long as we learn to work well with their help. We do not see any other way of arranging things so that they do not work under the lash, and as long as there are few specialists we are compelled to retain high wages.[22]

Lenin went on:

> I recently had a talk on this question with Schmidt, the Commissar for Labour, and he agrees with our policy and says that formerly, under capitalism, the wages of an unskilled worker were 25 rubles a month and those of a good specialist not less than 500 rubles, a ratio of 20:1; now the lowest wages amount to 600 rubles and the specialists get 3,000, a ratio of 5:1. We have, therefore, done a lot to equalise low and high wages and we shall continue in the same vein.[23]

This maximum wage differential of 5:1 was standard under Lenin. Another measure that limited wage differentials at this time was the fact that a growing number of services were provided free of charge, such as post, public transport, electricity, child care, and others.

With the introduction of the NEP at the end of 1921, the ratio between the highest paid specialists and lowest paid unskilled workers rose to 8:1. However, this did not apply to Party members, who received much lower rates. Interestingly, in March 1926, the average wage was 58.64 chervonets roubles, while factory managers received 189.90 chervonets roubles if they were a Party member, and 309.50 chervonets roubles if they were not.[24]

According to the *Statistical Handbook of the USSR 1926*, between 1926-27 the annual average income of manual workers in pre-war roubles was 465, and the maximum allowed to specialists was 1,811. Excluding the bourgeoisie, the NEPmen* and kulaks, there were only 114,000 people who earned this maximum, comprising a mere 0.3 per cent of all earners, and their income made up only 1 per cent of the national income.[25]

The rule limiting the income of Party members was modified in 1929 and later abolished. The general differentials were retained until 1931, when they were done away with by Stalin.

Lenin's lifestyle

The lack of privileges or special treatment for those at the top while Lenin was still alive was graphically shown in the account by Victor Serge, who worked as a government official during 1919:

> The eldest son of my friend Yonov, Zinoviev's brother-in-law, an Executive member of the Soviet and founder and director of the State Library, died of hunger before our eyes. All this while we were looking after considerable stocks, and even riches, but on the State's behalf and under rigorous control. Our salaries were limited to the 'Communist maximum', equal to the average wage of a skilled worker.[26]

Stites attempts to besmirch Lenin's honour by saying, "he dined on leftover imperial table service adorned with the Romanov eagle, rode in a chauffeured car, and possessed a library of 10,000 books."[27] Victor Serge counters these slurs by describing Lenin's meagre lifestyle as head of the Soviet government:

> In the Kremlin he [Lenin] still occupied a small apartment built for a palace servant. In the recent winter he, like everyone else, had had no heating. When he went to the barber's he took his turn, thinking it unseemly for anyone to give way to him.[28]

---

* These were rich speculators who had grown wealthy as a result of the NEP concessions.

The photographs of Lenin's flat in the Kremlin reveal a very modest affair indeed, made up of a table, six chairs, a clock and a sideboard.

Not only did Lenin dress modestly, he even continued to wear the overcoat that had bullet holes in it from the assassination attempt in August 1918, which had been patched over. This stands in marked contrast to the privileged lifestyle of our pampered bourgeois politicians today.

There was no special treatment for Lenin or the rest of the government, far from it. Krupskaya used to go to the common restaurant in the Kremlin to bring back dinner. She was often seen walking along with a large chunk of black bread and a pot of soup. This is hardly the lifestyle of a man accused of living on many times the income of an industrial worker. Clara Zetkin recorded the following picture when she visited Lenin:

> His private dwelling was of the utmost simplicity and unpretentiousness. I have seen more than one worker's home furnished much more richly than that of the 'all-powerful Muscovite dictator'. I found Lenin's wife and sister at supper, which I was immediately and heartily asked to share. It was a simple meal, as the hard times demanded: tea, black bread, butter, cheese. Later the sister tried to find something 'sweet' for the 'guest of honour' and discovered a small jar of preserves.[29]

Lenin's eating habits were as humble as those of any worker in Moscow. It consisted basically of soup, bread, fish and tea. The gifts of food he received from workers and peasants he donated to childcare institutions. His humble way of life was based on an egalitarian view, which "did not permit him to eat, while others starved..." Angelica Balabanoff described a characteristically frugal dinner she shared with Lenin:

> I should describe what I called 'dinner' with Lenin. On a little covered balcony, together with half a dozen scrawny peasant children in rags and two cats, we ate a bit of bread, a tiny slice of meat, and some cheese – which I had brought from Sweden – and drank a glass of tea with a small piece of sugar. Pointing at the food, Lenin said to me with a smile – pleased with the proofs of solidarity and desiring to justify the 'privileges' he enjoyed: "They have brought me the sugar from the Ukraine, the bread from central Russia, the meat was prescribed by the physician, and I don't know where it might have come from." I remember he was not easily persuaded to accept the cheese the comrades from Stockholm had sent him. "Give it to the children in Moscow", he said, and he accepted it only after my assurance that half of it had already been distributed to them and that I brought him only the part that was meant for him.[30]

186. Lenin at his desk in the Kremlin

When the workers at the Klintsy Cloth Mill announced they were going to call their factory 'Lenin', in honour of the fifth anniversary of the October Revolution, they offered to send him a new suit made of their cloth. Lenin answered the letter on 26 February 1919 with his customary combination of firmness and tact:

> Dear comrades.
>
> I thank you sincerely for your good wishes and your gift. But I'll tell you in secret that presents should not be given [to] me. I very much ask you to spread the secret request of mine as widely as you can among all the workers.
>
> With my best, thanks, regards and wishes, yours, V Ulyanov (Lenin).[31]

The common dining room in the Kremlin was created on Lenin's initiative, as he was always concerned about the health of his comrades. One night at a meeting at the headquarters, Alexander Tsiurupa, the People's Commissar for Food, fainted. The doctor who was called in put it mainly down to hunger. After that, Lenin told his secretary: "watch the comrades well. Some of them are so emaciated, they look simply awful. Start a dining room to feed about thirty to begin with, and include the most emaciated, the most famished."[32] That was when the dining room was established. Even Stites is forced to admit shamefacedly:

> ...his [Lenin's] immediate surroundings were modest and he amassed no personal fortune. He also waited his turn in the barber shops and pitched in for a while on voluntary work days, carrying logs for firewood or cleaning up Red Square.[33]

But he adds for good measure that "this was symbolic", as if to cast doubt on what he has just written.

Due to hyperinflation during the 1920s, the rouble suffered from redenomination in January 1922, January 1923, and again in March 1924. With each redenomination, the old currency was recalled and a new, revalued rouble put in their place.* While the currency was ravaged by inflation in these years, Lenin still made sure that the ratio between the lowest and the highest paid officials was strictly adhered to.

The notion, so assiduously cultivated by the bourgeois historians, of Lenin's alleged callousness and indifference to human suffering, is flatly contradicted by all the known facts. Although he always looked at things soberly, Lenin was deeply affected by the suffering of the Russian people.

On one occasion, in January 1919, he reacted furiously when he heard of the treatment of starving workers at the hands of a 'Communist' bureaucrat. He sent a telegram to the state security, the Kursk Cheka, requesting that they arrest a certain official named Kogan, who was a member of the Kursk Central Purchasing Board, for the crime of refusing to help the pleas of 120 starving workers from Moscow. The bureaucrat had simply sent these workers away empty-handed. An angry Lenin wrote:

> This to be published in the newspapers and by leaflet, so that all employees of the central purchasing boards and food organisations should know that formal and bureaucratic attitudes to work and incapacity to help starving workers will earn severe reprisals, up to and including shooting.[34]

It was signed, "Lenin, Chairman, Council of People's Commissars". This little episode reveals the real Lenin, a man whose implacable revolutionary firmness was tempered by a profoundly humanitarian spirit, a deep concern for the sufferings of the poor and downtrodden, and a hatred for all forms of bureaucratic arbitrariness and arrogance.

---

* This explains the introduction of the chervonets ruble.

30. The Red Army

With the enemy advancing and civil war raging all around, defence was now the most pressing necessity. The Whites had colossal resources supplied by the imperialists. Their armies were swelled by the adherence of thousands of experienced tsarist officers. Under these circumstances, it was clear that the methods of partisan warfare, conducted by mainly untrained or semi-trained Red Guard militias, were hopelessly inadequate.

What was needed was a Red Army – a centralised, professional army composed of millions of trained, disciplined and well-armed soldiers. But such an army did not exist. It needed to be created from scratch, as Lenin explained:

> The organisation of a Red Army was an entirely new question which had never been dealt with before, even theoretically. [...] We did not doubt that we should have to experiment, as Comrade Trotsky expressed it. We undertook a task which nobody in the world has ever attempted on so large a scale.[1]

He went on:

> We proceeded from experiment to experiment; we endeavoured to create a volunteer army, feeling our way, testing the ground and experimenting to find a solution to the problem in the given situation.[2]

Trotsky, as President of the Supreme War Council, was charged with the responsibility of building up a professional fighting force. The decree approved in December 1917, which vested all power within the army in the soldiers' committees and required the election of all officers, was no longer fit for purpose. It needed to be dramatically modified if the Red Army was to become a truly effective battle-ready weapon. To begin with, in order to build a centralised fighting force of millions, mass conscription would need to be introduced to swell the 100,000 volunteers who had already joined the Red Army since February 1918.

The main core of the new Army was its working-class base, recruited from the factories and proletarian centres of Petrograd, Moscow and elsewhere. Within this solid core, the Communists provided a firm and dedicated backbone.

However, the bulk of the new conscripts were inevitably drawn from the peasants. The prime motivation of these peasant soldiers was hatred towards the Whites, as behind them stood the power of the landlords, who they feared would return. Unlike the workers, their morale and fighting spirit tended to oscillate according to the vagaries of the civil war.

As a result, they were prone to desertion, and even mass desertions were not uncommon. The figures for desertion during the civil war are quite revealing, showing the sharp ebb and flow of the struggle. While around 2,846,000 deserted the Red Army in the period from January 1919 to January 1920, in the same period some 1,753,000 deserters were re-recruited into its ranks.

Despite the waverings, millions of peasants who joined the Red Army were imbued for the first time with ideas of world revolution under the influence of the propaganda of the Bolsheviks. As a result, the majority remained loyal. As for those who did not, Trotsky would often address them, referring to them as 'Deserter Comrades', using his considerable powers of persuasion to win them back to the Red Army.

In the early stages of the civil war, the soldiers' committees had played an important role. However, as the war became more intense and complex, the weaknesses in the command structure of the Red Army were beginning to show. The soldiers' committees lacked the necessary specialised military knowledge possessed by well-trained professionals. These weaknesses often gave the advantage to the Whites. If the Soviet Republic was to be saved, and the Red Army placed on a solid professional basis, it had to find a large number of reliable military specialists who had actually learned the art of warfare and knew how to conduct it. But where were such men to be found?

The only pool from which these specialists could be drawn was from former tsarist officers trained in the military schools. As we have seen, many officers had deserted to the Whites, but there were others who, although they were far from being convinced communists, or even sympathetic to

187. Trotsky addresses recruits to the newly formed Red Cavalry, 1918

the Bolsheviks, were at least neutral or could be persuaded to help the fight to defend the Soviet Republic. A plan was therefore devised to recruit them into the service of the Red Army and place them under the political control of Soviet commissars. These commissars, in turn, would be drawn from the most dedicated and trustworthy revolutionary workers and Communists.

Trotsky, like all the great military strategists, understood the colossal significance of morale in war. His greatness as a military leader consisted in his ability to make full use of morale and political ideas to motivate the worker and peasant soldiers of the Red Army. However, the fighting spirit of the troops was insufficient to triumph over a professional army. It had to be combined with the strictest military discipline, just as steam has to be concentrated by an iron piston box.

Trotsky unequivocally stood for a centralised, professional Red Army that made use of the best of the former tsarist officers as instructors, in the same way as bourgeois specialists were employed in industry. These officers had to be kept firmly under political control by the Red Commissars.

While the military leadership and military questions were to be left in the hands of the military commander, the political and propaganda work was firmly in the hands of the commissar, who had final overall control. The commissar was to be the direct political representative of Soviet power within the army. This meant that in practice, the commissar was invested with enormous powers, and in turn, was held highly responsible – the position came with a heavy price if they failed to carry out their duties.

This method of political control was not unique. It had existed within the French Revolutionary Army and also within Cromwell's New Model Army in the form of its Agitators. Kerensky himself had appointed political commissars within the Russian army, but their role was vague and was confined to the General Staff. Trotsky simply adopted the idea and placed the Soviet Commissars at every level of the army, from company commander to Commander-in-Chief.

Military opposition

Without this specialist military knowledge, the Red Army would have had to learn everything from scratch, and there was simply no time for such luxuries. The war would have been lost long before such an army could have been built.

Despite this, there was considerable opposition to such measures, partly born out of the natural hatred of the soldiers for the old army and its officer caste. But there were also other motives, not all of them very healthy: factionalism, clique considerations and all kinds of petty jealousy and personal resentment.

Those who were opposed to the new policy included, predictably, the Left SRs. But there was also an opposition within the Bolshevik Party, involving the 'Left Communists'. They became known as the 'Military Opposition', who, on dogmatic grounds, wanted nothing to do with old generals and tsarist officers, no matter what military skills or personal talent they might possess. "The curses against the old discipline were still ringing in our ears when we began to introduce the new", writes Trotsky, who faced the brunt of the attacks.[3]

The 'Military Opposition' was headed by Bukharin, Smirnoff, Radek and Bubnov – mainly individuals from the 'Left Communists' faction, who, as we saw, had opposed the Brest-Litovsk treaty and much else besides. They were joined by what became known as the 'Tsaritsyn Opposition'. The public faces of this faction were second-rate opportunists like Kliment Voroshilov, Sergo Ordzhonikidze and Sergei Gusev, who vehemently opposed all attempts to professionalise the army, in particular, the employment of specialists.

But the main moving force behind the Tsaritsyn Opposition was operating in the shadows. Behind the scenes, the man known as Stalin was playing a most active role in stoking the fires of resentment against the specialists, using it as a convenient weapon in the clandestine struggle he was already waging

188. Kliment Voroshilov   189. Sergei Gusev

against Trotsky. He systematically groomed and cultivated their grievances, flattered their vanity and encouraged their petty ambitions.

By such dishonest and underhand manoeuvres, Stalin was creating an invisible web of support, a nest of cronies and yes-men that would faithfully back him in all his future intrigues. In fact, the Tsaritsyn Opposition became the preparatory school for Stalin's intrigue against Trotsky – it was a vital component of his bureaucratic ascent through the apparatus that would eventually culminate in the complete destruction of Lenin's Party.

This opposition rested on the petty-bourgeois tendencies that favoured irregular guerrilla detachments, decentralisation and a looser army structure. Mikhail Lashevich, a Central Committee member and oppositionist, boasted that the Party would use the old generals, only to "squeeze them like lemons and throw them away..."[4]

Trotsky, as leader of the Red Army, came into head-on collision with these oppositionists and stubbornly resisted their demands. He explained:

> To train the Red Army we are enlisting former generals. Naturally, we are choosing these among the more decent and honest of them. Some people say: "How can you enlist generals? Surely, that's dangerous?" Of course, everything under the sun has its dangerous side. But, you see, we need instructors who know about military matters. Of course, we say frankly to these generals: "There is a new master in the land, the working class: it needs instructors to train the workers in the art of war so as to fight the bourgeoisie..."

190. Sergo Ordzhonikidze 191. Stalin in 1918

Of course, the Soviet power does not reject the services of the specialists in science and technique. It says: "Welcome, Messrs engineers: please come along to the factory and teach the workers there how to run factories. The workers don't know much about that: help them, come on to their payroll, into their service, the service of the workers. Up to now you have served the bourgeoisie: now enter into the service of the working class." To the generals the Soviet power says: "You have studied the art of war, and learnt it well. You have been on courses at the military academy. The art of war, that's a complex subject, involving intricate work, especially when it's directed against the Germans, whose enormous machinery for killing and destroying functions wonderfully well. We now need to prepare ourselves in military matters, and for that we need to learn: but, in order to learn, we must have specialists. If you please, Messrs specialists, former generals and officers, we will assign you to the appropriate places."

Trotsky then added:

But hardly had the thing got that far than certain comrades began to have doubts: if we take generals into our service, suppose they start to engage in counter-revolutionary activity? I don't know, some of them may wish to. It is quite possible that some may even try it; but, as the saying goes: "If you're afraid of wolves, don't go into the forest."[5]

192. Trotsky in intense discussion with Red Army officers and soldiers

While a number of former generals, to be sure, betrayed their trust, this was certainly not true in the majority of cases. In the end, such officers provided the Red Army with talented leaders, schooled in military warfare, such as the great Mikhail Tukhachevsky. Their considerable military skill and training were vital to the success of the Red Army and the promotion of new military commanders.

Most of these officers served the revolution well. Yet their loyalty was ultimately to be rewarded by the vilest disloyalty and treachery – most of them were brutally murdered by Stalin in the Great Purge Trials of the 1930s, an act that struck a deadly blow against the defences of the USSR and prepared the way for the military catastrophe that befell the Soviet Union in the summer of 1941.

Lenin's view

In order to save the revolution, it was essential to overcome the old prejudices towards the officer corps. In order to succeed, old ways needed to be uprooted, and a bold new course had to be followed with the necessary decisiveness. Lenin, who tended to leave military matters to Trotsky, was initially unsure of

193. Trotsky at the ceremony presenting the Honorary Revolutionary Red Banner
to the 51ˢᵗ Division, Crimea 1921

how far tsarist officers could be used. This, after all, was a new question, and
he wanted to reserve judgement and see how things developed. But Trotsky
was absolutely convinced.

When Lenin asked Trotsky in August 1918 about a proposal from Larin to
replace all officers with Communists, Trotsky ridiculed the idea as complete
nonsense. Lenin, who raised the point, was clearly probing the ground to see
Trotsky's reaction.

By the beginning of March 1919, it was clear that Lenin was now totally
convinced of Trotsky's position. Trotsky wrote about an interesting exchange
with Lenin at that time:

> During our reverses in the East, when Kolchak was approaching the Volga, at
> one of the meetings of the Soviet of Commissaries to which I had come straight
> from the train, Lenin wrote me a note: "What if we fire all the specialists and
> appoint Lashevich as commander-in-chief?" Lashevich was an old Bolshevik who
> had earned his promotion to the rank of a sergeant in the 'German' war. I replied
> on the same note: "Child's play!" Lenin looked slyly at me from under his heavy
> brows, with a very expressive grimace that seemed to say: "You are very harsh
> with me." But, deep down, he really liked abrupt answers that left no room for

194. Trotsky walking with the Red Army

doubt. We came together after the meeting. Lenin asked me various things about the front.

"You ask me", I said, "if it would not be better to kick out all the old officers? But do you know how many of them we have in the army now?"

"No."

"Not even approximately?"

"I don't know."

"Not less than thirty thousand."

"What?"

"Not less than thirty thousand. For every traitor, there are a hundred who are dependable; for every one who deserts, there are two or three who get killed. How are we to replace them all?"

A few days later, Lenin was making a speech on the problems of constructing the socialist commonwealth. This is what he said: "When Comrade Trotsky recently informed me that in our military department the officers are numbered in tens of thousands, I gained a concrete conception of what constitutes the secret of making proper use of our enemy, of how to build communism out of the bricks that the capitalists had gathered to use against us."[6]

Military specialists

While the element of morale is very important in a battle, enthusiasm and determination are not, in themselves, enough to win a war. War is not an exact science, but an art based on experience, which nevertheless requires knowledge in several sciences.

As industry needs engineers, and farming needs qualified agronomists, so military tactics and strategy need military specialists, as Lenin and Trotsky well understood. Only armed with such specialist knowledge, and with a solid core of dedicated and self-sacrificing Communists, could the army be bound together as a cohesive fighting force.

The Red Army was created in the heat of the battle. Through a combination of political persuasion and appeals to a sense of duty, eventually the best elements of the old officer corps were successfully drawn into military work, where they played a very important role. Gradually, the doubts were overcome and the Military Opposition fell silent – the best of them were sincerely convinced, the remainder acquiesced reluctantly but remained sullen and resentful. They were to raise their heads a few years later when the struggle against 'Trotskyism' began to take place.

Trotsky, as always, led from the front. He personally travelled the length and breadth of the different fronts in an armoured train, stopping to rally the troops, building their morale and driving home the message that this was a life-and-death struggle, but victory was at hand. In one reckoning, within a three-year period, Trotsky had covered a distance in his train equal to circumnavigating the globe five-and-a-half times.

The cream of the Communists and workers enlisted for the front, fighting for a cause they believed in, prepared to make the ultimate sacrifice for the revolution. They were spearheaded by volunteers from the Soviets of Petrograd and Moscow. An iron discipline existed in the new army. This was absolutely necessary in order to create a centralised body capable of delivering victory. But it was a discipline built on political inspiration, revolutionary fervour, and faith in socialism and world revolution. Indeed, every Red Army soldier made a solemn pledge to fight for the world revolution.

In this all-important struggle, no Red Army unit could make an unauthorised retreat or they would face serious consequences. On pain of death, no Soviet unit was allowed to desert a town threatened by counter-revolutionary forces. The workers' and peasants' deputies had a duty to remain and fight to the last soldier if necessary. If there was a display of cowardice or a dereliction of duty, the military commander and political commissar would answer with their lives. All deserters who offered resistance would be shot.

But the same Red Army that knew how to punish cowardice severely also knew how to pardon and redeem. Those deserters who immediately presented themselves and pledged to fight with honour for the revolution would be pardoned. Those soldiers who came over voluntarily from the White Armies would be given a place within the ranks of the Red Army to prove their loyalty.

These high standards of absolute dedication defined the moral fibre of the Red Army. This revolutionary discipline of the Red Army was not the same as the old bourgeois army. It was a conscious, collective spirit, based on revolutionary enthusiasm and a clear revolutionary duty to their class. Despite all the inadequacies, the shortages of guns, munitions, uniforms and boots, despite the hunger and disease, the forces of the Red Army stood the test of time.

By the end of the civil war, those officers of tsarist origin made up only one-third of the commanding staff of the army. In other words, two-thirds had been promoted through the ranks, a truly amazing accomplishment.

Within a relatively short period of time, the Red Army was built into a revolutionary force of more than 5 million. In the words of Karl Radek:

> Our party will go down in history as the first proletarian party which succeeded in creating a great army, and this bright page in the history of the Russian revolution will always be bound up with the name of Leon Davidovitch Trotsky, with the name of a man whose work and deeds will claim not only the love, but also the scientific study of the young generation of workers preparing to conquer the whole world.[7]

A life-and-death struggle

In the war between the classes, there exists no equivalent of the Geneva Convention. For the young Soviet state, the civil war became a life-or-death struggle with world imperialism and its agents, the White Armies. The war aims in this civil war, as in all wars, can be simply stated. It was to defeat and crush the enemy by force of arms. This meant annihilating the greater part and demoralising and disarming the rest.

For the imperialists and their allies, *all* means were considered permissible, in order to drown the revolution in blood. The Soviets had to fight fire with fire in a battle to the death. They made no apologies for this, as Victor Serge put it:

On all these points, civil war anticipates the code of war between states. It recognises no non-belligerents; it searches everywhere, without quarter, for the living strength of the hostile classes. Before a social class can be struck to the heart and admit its own defeat, terrible losses must be inflicted on it. Its sturdiest, bravest, most intelligent sons must be cut down. The best of its life-blood must be drained… That is how it has always been in the past… Nonetheless, let us have confidence in the power of the proletariat to spare humanity, in the social wars of the future, from too great a blood-letting.

He concluded:

Proletarian organisation; class consciousness; fearless and implacable revolutionary will; active international solidarity; these, we believe, are the factors which, if they are present in a certain degree of strength, may make the Red terror superfluous in the future.[8]

On many occasions during the civil war, the Bolshevik Revolution stood on the very edge of an abyss. The human cost was enormous, and not just on the field of battle. Up to 9 million people perished through warfare, famine, disease and freezing conditions. This was a fight to the finish: a struggle for survival. And the most desperate methods were called for.

Bruce Lockhart, the British representative who was no friend of Bolshevism, nevertheless honestly and correctly blamed the Allied intervention for the ferocity of the civil war. He recalled how free the atmosphere had been after the Bolsheviks came to power, but how the imperialists' intervention and civil war had put an end to it. Lockhart wrote:

I mention this comparative tolerance of the Bolsheviks, because the cruelties which followed later were the result of the intensification of the civil war. For the intensification of that bloody struggle Allied intervention, with the false hopes it raised, was largely responsible. I do not say that a policy of abstention from interference in the internal affairs of Russia would have altered the course of the Bolshevik revolution. I do suggest that our intervention intensified the terror and increased the bloodshed.[9]

Lockhart explains that it was the imperialists who gave life to the White generals, since the support for them within the Russian population hardly existed.

Without strong foreign aid they [the White Generals] were not powerful enough for this task. Outside the officer class – and it, too, was demoralised – they had no support in the country.[10]

195. Execution of the members of Alexandrovo-Gaysky Soviet by cossacks under the command of Alexander Dutov, 1918

Without the backing of the imperialists, there would not have been a bloody, protracted civil war, with all the death and destruction this entailed. Trotsky wrote:

> In October, we conquered power almost without a fight. Kerensky's attempt to reconquer it evaporated as a dewdrop falling on a red-hot stone. So mighty was the driving power of the masses that the older classes hardly dared to resist.

He concluded:

> The number of the victims would have been not ten times, but a hundred or a thousand times smaller but for British guineas, British monitors, British tanks, British officers, and British food supplies.[11]

The White Terror

A victory for the White generals would not have meant the arrival of 'democracy'. On the contrary, it would have meant the installation of a vicious, bloody regime of counter-revolution, a monstrous foretaste of the future fascist reaction. As in Finland, they would have carried out bloody revenge with impunity on the workers and peasants for their efforts to abolish

196. Symon Petliura in front of Ukrainian Army troops, Kiev, May 1920

capitalism and landlordism. A jack-boot regime, stamping on the faces of the working class, would have been a nightmare of untold misery, including economic and social collapse.

To prove this assertion, we need do no more than examine the actions of the White counter-revolution. Wherever they gained ground, they carried out the most horrific atrocities to root out the red viruses of revolution. General Kornilov had already attempted to install a military dictatorship in August 1917 to suppress the Soviets and eliminate the Kerensky government. Likewise, Kolchak had no qualms about dissolving the remains of the Constituent Assembly in Siberia and shooting its members.

According to Kerensky in the summer of 1919, in an interview with foreign journalists:

> …there is no crime the [White] agents of Admiral Kolchak would not commit… Executions and torture have been committed in Siberia, and often the population of whole villages have been flogged, including the teachers and intellectuals.[12]

The American interventionist forces meted out their fair share of brutality in the Murmansk area. In January 1919, British, Canadian and American forces were under pressure from the Red Army. In retribution, they set about destroying the town of Shenkursk to prevent the Reds from taking it. "We started burning the houses", says one US veteran.[13] As the flames spread, they withdrew to the edge of the town and systematically opened fire on the people left inside, who they presumed were Bolsheviks:

197. Excavations of Petrovsk residents killed by Denikin's soldiers, 1920

We killed so many that day it was unbelievable. I sat there with a machine gun, and poured bullets into that town just continually. It was not over a quarter of a mile away, so with a good machine gun you can do good work in there. They were scattered in between those houses, you could see them, they could not get in or out of a house, there was no cover for them.[14]

But when it comes to atrocities, nothing could compare with the methods of the White General Baron Roman von Ungern-Sternberg. He was a German Balt born in Estonia, who claimed to be nothing less than the reincarnation of Genghis Khan. A fanatical antisemite, he declared his intention in 1918 to exterminate all the Jews and commissars in Russia. His speciality was slaughtering Jews and skinning people alive. He enjoyed setting towns on fire, roasting 'Red' children alive in bakery ovens, strangling old women and raping young girls. He was also noted for leading his men in nocturnal rides on horseback, dragging burning bodies across the steppe at full gallop and for pledging to "make an avenue of gallows that will stretch from Asia across Europe…"[15]

Ungern-Sternberg was finally abandoned by his own mutinous troops and captured by the Bolsheviks, who had him executed.

In Ukraine, following the withdrawal of the Germans, Symon Petliura became Chief Ataman and Supreme Commander of the Ukrainian People's Republic. He supported the Polish dictator Józef Piłsudski and became renowned for his anti-Jewish pogroms. He was responsible for a detachment of the Ukrainian Army which carried out the massacre of around 1,500 Jews in the town of Proskuriv, where they were accused of 'Judeo-Bolshevism'. It was one of the bloodiest pogroms of the civil war.

When the Ministry of Jewish Affairs asked the Ministry of Justice to investigate Ukrainian units spreading antisemitic leaflets and propaganda, the Justice Ministry accused them of wanting to "take under its wing all Jews, even if they are Bolsheviks and even Trotskii-Bronshteins [sic]". It attacked the Ministry of Jewish Affairs, which, it claimed, "insults our army, insults our national feeling, and without doubt underlines its hostile relationship to our national cause."[16]

Today, these antisemites have been rehabilitated in Ukraine. On 14 October 2017, the recently created 'Day of the Defender of Ukraine', the municipal government of the city of Vinnytsia erected a statue to Symon Petliura. There was also an official national minute's silence held in memory of this murdering antisemite.

Antisemitism was rife in the White camp. They regularly exploited Trotsky's Jewishness in their propaganda and put up posters depicting Trotsky as the Jewish ogre of the Kremlin. This was reflected in Isaac Babel's story, *Salt*, which describes a peasant woman under the influence of these ideas accusing a Red soldier: "Don't give me that about saving Russia – all you care about is saving those Yids, Lenin and Trotsky!" To which he replies: "…a about Lenin I don't really know, but Trotsky is the dashing son of the Governor of Tambov who, turning his back on his high social rank, joined the working classes."[17]

From January 1918, General Kornilov ordered Soviet prisoners to be slaughtered. Captured Red soldiers, and those deemed sympathetic to them, were cruelly tortured, mutilated, shot and hanged. They faced mass executions. Some were skinned alive, burned alive or buried alive. Others were decapitated. Women and girls were stripped naked, raped repeatedly, and some whipped to within an inch of their lives. Irina Astashkevich writes:

> The Whites, like the Ukrainian soldiers and bandits, gang raped Jewish women publicly, and did so with exceeding brutality and visceral hatred. Even contemporary observers recognized that the Cossacks and officers had raped their victims in the manner that would inflict the most suffering, both physical and emotional.[18]

"My soldiers are embittered against Communists, and all the Communists are Jewish. We can't allow a Jewish kingdom in Russia", boasted General Markevich.[19] When Rabbis argued that young Jewish girls had nothing to do with politics, the general replied:

The first four or five days my boys need to unwind. There is nothing to be done about that, my Cossacks are good fighters but also good looters. If you just killed Trotsky all that would end.[20]

In response to this barbarism, the Bolsheviks intensified the Red Terror as a means of self-defence. The Cheka was given wide-ranging powers to carry out its duties, which were to defend the revolution against the agents of counter-revolution. One of the men who directed the terror wrote:

The Extraordinary Commission is neither an investigating commission nor a tribunal. It is an organ of struggle, acting on the home front of the civil war by the methods of investigation, the tribunal and armed force. It does not judge the enemy, it strikes him.[21]

The stench of antisemitism hung over every counter-revolutionary force in the anti-Bolshevik crusade. It was certainly present at the highest levels of the British establishment. The British War Secretary Winston Churchill, who was an ardent advocate of military intervention in Russia to 'break up' Bolshevik power, wrote in February 1920:

From the days of Spartacus-Weishaupt to those of Karl Marx this world-wide conspiracy for the overthrow of civilization and for the reconstitution of society on the basis of arrested development, of envious malevolence and impossible equality, has been steadily growing…

There is no need to exaggerate the part played in the creation of Bolshevism and in the actual bringing about of the Russian Revolution, by these international and for the most part atheistical Jews; it is certainly a very great one; it probably outweighs all others. With the exception of Lenin, the majority of leading figures are Jews.[22]

Scale of the Red Terror

Victor Serge, in his book, *Year One of the Russian Revolution*, considered the scale of the Red Terror. He explains:

All that we have available to answer this question is very incomplete data. No regular statistics were issued in the first months; the official figures published by Latsis are based on information often of a random character. With these reservations in mind, let us examine them. The Extraordinary Commissions were set up, as we know, in December 1917. In the first six months of their activity they executed only twenty-two people. In the last six months of 1918 more than 6,000 executions were proceeded with. The monthly average of executions for 1918 is: counter-revolutionaries, 380; dishonest and criminal officials, fourteen; speculators, three. The Red Terror, in four years of revolution, perhaps spilt less blood than what flowed on certain days during the battle of Verdun.[23]

Most of those executed were seized at or behind the front. Some were military deserters, while others were marauders and bandits. Some of these were guilty of pilfering and corruption, which was a terrible crime in a hunger-stricken country, while others were spies and active agents of foreign and domestic enemies in the middle of a civil war. No doubt some were victims of class hatred, but very few were executed for hostile political opinions.

While Serge gives some evidence for the scale of the Red Terror, he honestly qualifies his remarks by pointing to the lack of reliable statistics. Orlando Figes, by contrast, has no need of such details. For him, everything is as clear as day. "Nobody will ever know the exact number of people repressed and killed by the Cheka in these years", writes Figes, before adding without any hesitation whatsoever that "... *it was certainly several hundred thousand*, if one includes all those in the camps and prisons as well as those who were executed or killed by the Cheka's troops in the suppression of strikes and revolts."

The only thing that is *certain* here is that our old friend Figes attempts to *vastly inflate* the statistics by lumping together all the people held in "camps and prisons" at that time. He produces these figures out of thin air. "Although no one knew the precise figures, it is possible that more people were murdered by the Cheka than died in the battles of the civil war", claims Figes.[24]

So, without producing a single shred of evidence, he resorts to the simple trick of presenting something that is merely *possible* as a *certain fact*. By the same logic, one might assert that since there are at present over 1,200,000 prisoners in the United States, this means that over one million people are regularly executed in that country – a conclusion that one somehow suspects cannot altogether be correct...

What is an undeniable fact, as Bruce Lockhart stated, is that the blame for the terrible carnage in Russia lies fully with the imperialists and their allies. The imperialists' blockade of Russia – mostly carried out by the British Royal Navy – prevented urgently needed medical supplies and food from reaching a starving population. That alone resulted in the deaths from hunger and disease of up to 9 million people.

Were there excesses? Without doubt, in the situation of civil war, excesses were inevitable. That is the nature of war. There has never been a war in history, nor a revolution, without terror perpetrated by the ruling classes.

But when the oppressed rise up and fight back, they are condemned for resorting to 'terrorism' by the privileged classes and their apologists. The Red Terror was simply born out of the reaction to the White Terror of the counter-revolution.

The Cheka was involved in a pitiless war against a cruel enemy. It recruited many enthusiastic young people, most of them inexperienced and untrained, some of whom, no doubt, were not of the best quality, including a number of dubious elements from alien classes who had joined for entirely the wrong reasons.

Given the appalling nature and scale of White atrocities, some excesses were unavoidable. Lenin was aware of this problem and tried his best to prevent and curb such excesses. In fact, he frequently demanded limits on the use of terror and the abuse of power that went with it, including the Cheka. According to the historian, Tamás Krausz:

A plethora of documents indicate that the leader of the Revolution often took measures, even at the peak of the civil war, against Chekhist or bureaucratic abuses of power.[25]

He continues:

To Lenin, mass terror counted as the most extreme instrument of struggle against the enemy and was to be applied (and often demanded by him in vain), on a case-by-case basis… He frequently demanded curbs on the use of terror and even the elimination of concrete abuses of power, and advocated punishing Cheka employees. For instance, he protested in horror against the "evil bleakness" of some Ukrainian representatives of the Cheka:

"Kamenev says – and declares that several most prominent Cheka men confirm it – that the Chekas in the Ukraine have brought a host of evils, having been set up too early and having allowed a mass of hangers-on to get in… It is necessary at all costs to discipline the Cheka men and throw out the alien elements."

He knew that illiterate or semi-literate, politically unschooled youth were in the majority in the Cheka, including the type of "careerist people without any ideals" who showed up wherever power offered an opportunity for domination and good living.[26]

He goes on:

Under the pressure of escalating terror, Lenin was forced – though historians like Volkogonov, Pipes, and Felshtynsky are silent on this point – to bring corrective measures against the Cheka and the courts, as they did not heed laws or regulations.[27]

Trotsky explained what they were fighting for, and what was necessary in order to win that fight:

> Now that the workers are being charged with committing cruelties in the civil war, we must reply, instructed by our experience: the only unpardonable sin which the Russian working class can commit at this moment is that of indulgence towards its class enemies. We are fighting for the sake of the greatest good of mankind, for the sake of the regeneration of mankind, to drag it out of the darkness, out of slavery…[28]

Relations between Lenin and Trotsky

Trotsky had played an absolutely crucial role in building and leading the Red Army. Following the Stalinist counter-revolution, Trotsky was demonised and his role was completely erased. The Stalinists even went as far as to deny his leading role in the October Revolution. In August 1940, Leon Trotsky was finally assassinated by a Stalinist agent under the direct orders of Stalin.

The Soviet Union's official biography of Stalin, issued in 1940, the same year as Trotsky's assassination, states categorically:

> It was the Bolshevik Party, headed by Lenin and Stalin, that created the Red Army – the first Red Army in the world… *And it was Stalin who directly inspired and organised the major victories of the Red Army.* Wherever the destinies of the Revolution hung in the balance, the Party sent him to the front. It was he who drew up the most important strategic plans and personally directed the decisive military operations… And, finally, it was he who trained and led the military commissars, without whom, Lenin said, there would have been no Red Army, so that his name is forever linked with the most glorious victories of our Red Army.[29]

Added to this utter falsification, another Stalinist 'outline history' by Nicolai Popov, written in the mid-1930s, states the following:

> The Party won its victories in the Civil War over the principal enemies of the Soviet under Lenin's leadership and against the advice contained in Trotsky's plans. We are not going to deny that Trotsky played a certain role in the Civil War as an agitator and as an executor of the decisions of the Central Committee, when he did carry them out. But Trotsky's whole policy and strategy suffered from a number of organic defects, which would have had disastrous consequences had not the Central Committee, under the leadership of Lenin, corrected Trotsky at every step.

198. Soviet leaders celebrating the second anniversary of the October Revolution
at Red Square, Moscow, 7 November 1919
Lenin and Trotsky are side by side in the centre

The most characteristic feature of Trotsky's policy and strategy was a profound
mistrust in the power of the proletariat to lead the peasantry and in the power
and ability of the Party to lead the Red Army. Hence his policy based exclusively
on formal discipline, on methods of compulsion similar to the bourgeois armies.
Hence his efforts to keep the Party away from the army. Hence his excessive
confidence in bourgeois specialists, his underestimation of the strength of the
Red Army as against the White Guard armies – tendencies which reflected the
psychology of the former tsarist generals who were serving on our staff.[30]

This Stalinist version contrasts with Maxim Gorky's account of Lenin's
appraisal of Trotsky contained in his *Reminiscences of Lenin*, published soon
after Lenin's death in 1924. In a conversation between Gorky and Lenin,
where Gorky mentioned the hostility shown by certain Bolsheviks towards
Trotsky, Lenin banged the table with his fist and said:

> Show me another man who could have practically created a model army in a year
> and won the respect of the military specialists as well. We have got such a man!
> We have got everything. And we shall work wonders.[31]

Lenin adds, "Yes, yes, I know they lie a lot about my relations with him." These lies were already in circulation when the Bolshevik Party was universally known as 'the Party of Lenin and Trotsky'. Balabanoff wrote:

> When speaking of Lenin and the mastermind and chief exponent of the Soviet Russian regime, one must also speak of Trotsky. In the most difficult and crucial moments, in tragedy or triumph, their names were united.[32]

But after the death of Lenin, the campaign of lies and slander grew to a deafening crescendo. One of the slanders most often repeated by the Stalinists was the completely unfounded claim that Trotsky was against the peasants and 'underestimated the peasantry'.

In February 1919, Lenin deals with the baseless rumours about the relationship between himself and Trotsky in a letter to *Pravda*, in a reply to a peasant concerning the subject of the middle peasantry. In it, he writes the following:

> *Izvestia* of 2 February carried a letter from a peasant, G Gulov, who asks a question about the attitude of our Workers' and Peasants' Government to the middle peasantry, and tells of rumours that Lenin and Trotsky are not getting on together, and that there are big differences between them on this very question of the middle peasant.
>
> Comrade Trotsky has already replied to that in his 'Letter to the Middle Peasants', which appeared in *Izvestia* of 7 February. In this letter Comrade Trotsky says that the rumours of differences between him and myself are the most monstrous and shameless lie, spread by the landowners and capitalists, or by their witting and unwitting accomplices. For my part, I entirely confirm Comrade Trotsky's statement. There are no differences between us, and as regards the middle peasants there are no differences either between Trotsky and myself, or in general in the Communist Party, of which we are both members.
>
> In his letter Comrade Trotsky has explained clearly and in detail why the Communist Party and present Workers' and Peasants' Government, elected by the Soviets and belonging to that Party, do not consider the middle peasants to be their enemies. I fully subscribe to what Comrade Trotsky has said.[33]

This letter from Lenin clearly showed the real relationship between him and Trotsky. He clearly states that *"there are no differences between us"*, including on the question of the middle peasants. This serves to refute the allegations made repeatedly by the Stalinists. However, in the footnote to this letter in Lenin's *Collected Works*, Volume 36, pages 696-7, the editors did not fail to repeat the old slanders.

In reality, there was a close political bond and working relationship between the two men. The revolution of 1917 had brought them together. Their paths had crossed and there was a meeting of minds. Nothing remained of the differences that had kept them apart in the past. Lenin often expressed the warmest praise for Trotsky's military achievements, and many of Trotsky's operational instructions carry a note of Lenin's approval.

One example of their complete solidarity and mutual trust is particularly striking. At a Politburo meeting, in the middle of the civil war, Trotsky defended the court marshalling and shooting of a commander and commissar, who, in an act of mutiny, had withdrawn their regiment, seized a steamer by threat of arms and were preparing to sail to Nizhny-Novgorod. Trotsky's critics eagerly seized on this incident to denounce his allegedly harsh methods. But when Lenin was asked whether he approved of Trotsky's action, he replied "absolutely".[34]

Lenin then took an unprecedented step. He halted the Politburo meeting and wrote his signature on a blank piece of paper that bore the seal of the Soviet of People's Commissars and handed it to Trotsky. The note reads as follows:

> Comrades: knowing the strict character of Comrade Trotsky's orders, I am so convinced, so absolutely convinced, of the correctness, expediency, and necessity for the success of the cause of the order given by Comrade Trotsky, that I unreservedly endorse this order.[35]

And Lenin assured Trotsky: "I will give you as many forms like this as you want."[36]

This close identification of the two men was very much the case in the ranks of the Communist International. As late as 1925, JT Murphy, a leading member of the British Communist Party wrote:

> Comrade Trotsky's name had always been associated in our minds with Comrade Lenin. 'Lenin and Trotsky!' These were the names with which we conjured in all our thoughts and feelings about the Russian Revolution and the Communist International...[37]

Paradoxically, these lines were written in the foreword to a book that opened up the campaign against 'Trotskyism' in Britain. Murphy, a supporter of Stalin, was no friend of Trotsky. In fact, he was the person who moved Trotsky's expulsion from the Communist International. However, that didn't save him from meeting a similar fate, as within a few years, Murphy himself would be driven out.

By 1925, a year after Lenin's death, the campaign against 'Trotskyism' was in full swing. Trotsky was removed as Commissar for War by manoeuvres of the *troika* – the secret faction formed by Stalin, Zinoviev and Kamenev – in order to oust Trotsky from the leadership. The spool of revolution began to unwind rapidly. The historian Volkogonov, who had access to the Party and state archives, was correct when he stated:

> The relations between Lenin and Trotsky are revealed in their correspondence. It is certain that many letters in which Lenin expressed a favourable attitude towards Trotsky were destroyed.[38]

Even today, the conspiracy continues. The real relationship between Lenin and Trotsky remains buried, hidden, or distorted beyond recognition. It is our task to rescue the reputation of two great leaders of the world proletariat. In the words of Trotsky: the locomotive of history is truth, not lies.

31. War Communism

The years 1919 and 1920 proved to be a turning point, not only militarily, but economically. The country had been laid to waste by war, then ravaged by civil war. "The all-powerful Entente was marching against us, was at our throats", stated Lenin.[1]

On the economic front, a deepening crisis was revealed by the collapse of industrial output. The stocks of raw materials, vital for industrial production, were almost exhausted, while the imperialist blockade prevented any further replenishment. Russia was being squeezed in a vice. Arthur Ransome wrote: "Russia produced practically no manufactured goods (70 per cent of her machinery she received from abroad), but great quantities of food. The blockade isolated her."[2]

With civil war raging, the areas producing cotton and flax were completely cut off from the Soviet Republic. Oil from Baku and the Caucasus was also lost, as were iron and coal from the Ukraine. This resulted in a terrible fuel crisis, which caused many industries to grind to a halt.

A major factor in the economic dislocation was the collapse of the rail system, which played a key role in communications for Russia over its vast distances. Half the rolling stock was in need of desperate repair. Many of the locomotives were inoperable and lacked spare parts, turning the train depots into a graveyard of broken-down engines.

By the end of 1919, more than 60 per cent of a total of 16,000 locomotives were out of service. Of the 75,000 kilometres of railway in European Russia, only 16,000 kilometres had remained intact. By 1920, Russia possessed only 20 per cent of the locomotives from 1914. Without transport, the distribution of grain and essential goods ground to a halt, and with it the rest of the economy. Brailsford, who visited Russia in the autumn of 1920, wrote:

> Sóbinka depends for its cotton on the supplies of Turkestan, and these had varied with the vicissitudes of the civil war. First the Czechoslovaks and then Denikin had occupied the railways and the rivers which should have carried its supplies, and even after their defeat the broken bridges and the wrecked traffic yards had first to be repaired. The result of this isolation was that Turkestan, during the civil war, ceased to grow its unmarketable cotton. The area sown fell in 1919 to less than one-eighth of what it was in 1916.[3]

This situation fed on itself in a vicious circle. The breakdown of production led many factories to compete with one another for scarce raw materials, fuel and components. In 1919, the factories received only one-tenth of the fuel they needed to function. Many desperately tried to convert their reliance on coal burning to wood burning to survive.

Such was the dire situation that there were reports of workers breaking up machinery to sell, sometimes intact, sometimes as scrap metal. Transmission belts, tools, nails, anything that could be sold, were pilfered.

As a result of these chronic conditions, absenteeism from work reached unprecedented levels. In a coal mine near Simbirsk, 25 per cent of workers were regularly absent and the mine only worked seventeen or eighteen days a month. Lenin reported: "… industry is at a standstill. There is no food, no fuel, no industry."[4] Under such conditions, the working class was in a wretched state, especially in the winter months. Ransome explains:

> People living in rooms in a flat, complete strangers to each other, by general agreement bring all their beds into the kitchen. In the kitchen, soup is made once a day. There is a little warmth there beside the natural warmth of several human beings in a small room.[5]

In face of these freezing conditions, everything people could get their hands on was burned as fuel in an attempt to survive. People burned books and the floorboards in their flats. Entire libraries vanished as a result. It was either that or freeze and starve to death, while praying for the spring to come early.

As food became scarce, horses vanished from the streets, followed by dogs, cats and birds. Streets became cluttered with debris as there was nowhere else people could dump their rubbish, which attracted rats and other vermin. Work brigades were organised, involving reluctant bourgeois elements, in a desperate effort to clear the mess.

Effect on the working class

Calculations based upon trade union statistics for the area under Soviet control in 1919 showed that the number of industrial workers had fallen to 76 per cent of the 1917 level. In construction, it had fallen to 66 per cent and on the railways to 63 per cent. EH Carr explains:

> The figures seemed catastrophic enough. But since the productivity of labour declined even more steeply than its numerical strength, the fall in actual production was far greater than the decrease in the number of workers would by itself have warranted. Published statistics showed that production in all branches of industry declined continuously till 1920.[6]

The industrial working class numbered just over 3 million in 1917. Between then and 1922, it suffered a massive decline:[7]

Year	1918	1919	1920-21	1922
Number of industrial workers	2,486,000	2,035,000	1,480,000	1,243,000

The dictatorship of the proletariat was resting on a very thin layer, which continued to narrow. This collapse in the productive forces resulted in the breakdown of relations between town and country. The towns had little to exchange for grain, except credit notes, which people understandably regarded with deep suspicion. They were unable to supply even basic things the peasants needed, such as salt, sugar, paraffin, soap, boots and warm clothes.

The expanding demands of the Red Army only served to compound such problems. This burden is graphically illustrated with figures from the following year, 1920, when the Red Army absorbed half of all industrial production, 60 per cent of the sugar, 40 per cent of fats, 90 per cent of footwear, 40 per cent of soap and 100 per cent of tobacco. As Lenin honestly explained:

> ... consider this carefully – our proletariat has been largely declassed; the terrible crises and the closing down of the factories have compelled people to flee from starvation. The workers have simply abandoned their factories; they have had to settle down in the country and have ceased to be workers. Are we not aware of the fact that the unprecedented crises, the civil war, the disruption of proper relations between town and country and the cessation of grain deliveries have given rise to a trade in small articles made at the big factories – such as cigarette lighters – which are exchanged for cereals, because the workers are starving, and no grain is being

delivered? Have we not seen this happen in the Ukraine, or in Russia? That is the economic source of the proletariat's declassing and the inevitable rise of petty-bourgeois, anarchist trends.[8]

As a consequence of the crisis, the cities began to empty. Driven by freezing temperatures and gnawing hunger, many workers had been forced to abandon their workplaces and return to the countryside to scavenge for food. Petrograd had lost nearly three-quarters of its population between 1918 and 1920. Moscow's population was almost halved in the same period. It lost a third of its working population in one year. In the autumn of 1920, the population of forty provincial capitals had declined by a third since 1917. The larger the city, the greater the fall.

All this naturally led to a dramatic decline in the political activity of the working class. Under such conditions, the Soviets were withering away. It was not that the workers did not control the factories, but the factories simply did not function. They were not abolished or closed down, but workers abandoned them, either to fight in the Red Army or to forage for food in the countryside.

As a result, the working class, which was hanging on by the skin of its teeth, was not in a position to exercise genuine power.

It was these realities of life that the Workers' Opposition under Shlyapnikov and Kollontai failed to take into consideration. How were alternative proposals of control by producers' committees going to operate when the 'producers' themselves were disappearing? It was a question they could not answer. Emma Goldman, the American anarchist, returned to Petrograd in 1920 and described the scene:

> It was almost in ruins, as if a hurricane had swept over it. The houses looked like broken old tombs upon neglected and forgotten cemeteries. The streets were dirty and deserted; all life had gone from them. The population of Petrograd before the war was almost 2 million; in 1920 it had dwindled to 500,000. The people walked about like living corpses; the shortage of food and fuel was slowly sapping the city; grim death was clutching at its heart. Emaciated and frostbitten men, women, and children were being whipped by the common lash, the search for a piece of bread or a stick of wood. It was a heart-rending sight by day, an oppressive weight at night. Especially were the nights of the first month in Petrograd dreadful. The utter stillness of the large city was paralysing. It fairly haunted me, this awful oppressive silence broken only by occasional shots.[9]

Henry Brailsford also visited Petrograd in the autumn of 1920 and wrote down his impressions:

> To be sure, Petrograd looks at first glance like a dead city. Grass grows literally in the streets... only about 600,000 remain of its former 2 million inhabitants. The mortality must have been heavy, but on the whole most of the vanished population has returned to its native villages. The old wooden houses of the slums, infested with vermin and reeking of disease, have been pulled down, partly as a sanitary measure and partly to furnish fuel. Here and there in the wood-paved streets one even noticed holes where the blocks had been stolen for fuel. One rarely saw horses in the streets, probably because they had been eaten.[10]

With hunger came epidemics, especially typhus, which affected millions and killed untold numbers. Between 1917 and 1922, around 22 million people contracted typhus, and in 1918-19, 1.5 million perished from the disease. Cholera and scarlet fever killed 7 or 8 million. Lenin wrote about the desperate conditions – the hunger, the scourge of lice and the typhus that was mowing down the population, including the troops:

> Comrades, it is impossible to imagine the dreadful situation in the typhus regions, where the population is broken, weakened, without material resources, where all life, all public life ceases. To this we say, "Comrades, we must concentrate everything on this problem. *Either the lice will defeat socialism, or socialism will defeat the lice!*"[11]

The hospitals were at breaking point, dealing with casualties and the spread of infections, but lacking basic medicines and equipment due to the blockade. Walter Meakin, who was part of the British 1920 Labour-TUC delegation to Russia, wrote:

> On this subject Dr Semashko, Commissary for Public Health, gave me yesterday some illuminating information. With the co-operation of the medical service generally, he is working heroically to cope with the adverse conditions, but the task of the doctors in the hospitals is rendered extremely difficult owing to the lack of soap, disinfectants...[12]

In winter, the water and sewage pipes inside buildings froze. There was no fuel, water, light, no drugs, and no nourishing foods. So intense was the suffering, and the hunger so acute, that many Russian people perished during the winter months amidst freezing conditions.

War Communism

The country had faced more than two years of War Communism, in which the entire economy was turned towards the needs of defence and sustaining the Red Army.

The depreciation of the currency encouraged a general tendency towards exchanges in kind and a barter economy. Money had become increasingly worthless by 1920, and, as a result, all public services were free, rent was abolished, theatres were free, post and trams were mostly free. In 1919, free meals had been introduced.

"In both cities [Petrograd and Moscow]", explained Henry Brailsford, "there is a free dinner available for every citizen, man or woman."[13] Despite the scarcity, the card system ensured equal rations and distribution of food according to need. The authorities also had seized the empty and under-used properties of the rich and well-to-do for allocation to the homeless. Housing space, dwellings and rooms were allocated by neighbourhood committees on the basis of need. "Rooms are distributed on much the same plan as clothes", wrote Ransome.[14]

Private industrial, commercial and real-estate were expropriated. One commentator remarked that the bourgeoisie has been transformed into an ex-bourgeoisie in rags or "lumpen ex-bourgeoisie".[15] Many were reduced to selling off any valuables at huge illegal markets.

Relations with the country were based mainly on requisition to feed the towns in exchange for promissory notes. The few manufactured goods that could be spared were given to poor peasants as an inducement to support the government's confiscation of kulak grain. Speculation was met with repression, although an estimated two-thirds of the towns' food supplies were furnished by the illegal market.

It was under these conditions that the state sought to organise socialist production and distribution. But it was a system born out of the needs of civil war. And it had very little to do with real socialism, still less communism.

This gave rise to quite a few utopian illusions, especially on the part of Bukharin and the 'Left Communists', who imagined that such things as the collapse of the currency heralded the abolition of money, and the state distribution of goods meant that they could simply proceed directly into communism.

That was quite simply absurd. To talk of building socialism – or even communism – in such conditions was completely utopian. The immediate task was not to build a higher stage of human society, for which the material conditions were entirely absent, but, on the contrary, to prevent society from falling to pieces altogether and sinking into barbarism.

Faced with such a devastating picture, the Soviet government needed to take drastic measures simply to survive until help finally came from the West in the form of a victorious socialist revolution. Looking back at that period, Lenin frankly admitted that they had made many mistakes and even stupidities in the past:

> We expected – or perhaps it would be truer to say that we presumed without having given it adequate consideration – to be able to organise the state production and the state distribution of products on communist lines in a small-peasant country directly as ordered by the proletarian state. Experience has proved that we were wrong.[16]

Furthermore, explained Lenin:

> The peasant knows and is accustomed to the market and trade. We were unable to introduce direct communist distribution. We lacked the factories and their equipment for this. That being the case, we must provide the peasants with what they need through the medium of trade, and provide it as well as the capitalist did, otherwise the people will not tolerate such an administration. This is the key to the situation…[17]

Lenin never had the idea that it was possible to build socialism in one country – least of all a backward country like Russia. As we have seen, he always tied the fate of the revolution to the perspective of the world revolution.

The idea of completely bypassing the market was based on the prospect of the victory of the European revolution. In this event, Socialist Europe would supply all the needs of the Russian economy and much more. Along with the workers of Europe, they would advance with giant leaps forward. Even then, however, given Russia's backwardness and the weight of the peasant economy, it would still be necessary to rely upon some aspects of the market. It would not be possible to jump over this stage immediately.

But by the beginning of 1920, the only respite was the news coming from the civil war fronts. The imperialist-backed White Armies, facing a revolutionary Red Army of more than 5 million at its height, were finally routed. With their defeat, the foreign intervention simply collapsed.

In January, the imperialists were alarmed by news of mutinies of their soldiers in Russia. The red light was flashing. One by one, the British, French,

American, Italian, then Japanese imperialists, were forced to withdraw from Russia with their tails between their legs.

The remnants of the White armies fled to Estonia, where they were interned. That finally put an end to General Denikin's exploits. He first fled to London, then France, then emigrated to the United States in 1945, where he died two years later.* General Yudenich had been arrested by another White Russian general in 1920, released after Allied intervention, and died in England in 1933. Others were not so fortunate. In early 1920, the Red Army had suppressed the 'Government of the North', which had been established in Archangel and Murmansk, under the protection of the British and Americans. After this, the only significant anti-Soviet forces remaining in Russia were in the last holdout in Crimea, under General Wrangel. This too would not last long. The other enclave was Vladivostok, which was retaken in October 1922. To all intents and purposes, the civil war was over.

Ninth Party Congress

Despite the enormous difficulties faced by the Soviet Republic, the Ninth Party Congress took place in March 1920. In his opening speech, Lenin began by looking at the world situation, which he regarded as their only saviour. In his report, he pointed to the revolutionary situation in Germany following the defeat of the counter-revolutionary putsch of General Kapp, as a result of an all-out general strike.

He explained that, from an international point of view, the position had never been more favourable. Once again, power was within the sights of the German working class. This, explained Lenin, "gives us the assurance that the time is not far off when we shall be marching hand in hand with a German Soviet government."[18]

At the Congress, Lenin paid tribute to Sverdlov, who had tragically died the previous year. He had played the role within the Party of general secretary, in helping to administer things, although the title did not enter the Party's vocabulary until later. Sverdlov had the great ability to choose the right person for the right responsibility. His role was mostly behind the scenes, but it was essential work. Lenin stated:

> No one has been able to combine organisational and political work in one person so successfully as Comrade Sverdlov did and we have been obliged to attempt to replace his work by the work of a collegium.[19]

---

* In 2005, Denikin's remains were transferred from the US to Moscow on the authority of Vladimir Putin.

199. Yakov Sverdlov

He went on to report on the work of the Central Committee, which covered both domestic and foreign policy. The fundamental change compared to the previous year was the Soviet victory in the bitter two-year civil war.

It was remarkable that Soviet Russia, a weak, exhausted and backward country, had been able to defeat the united onslaught of the most powerful countries in the world. This was primarily due, he explained, to the adoption of the strictest centralism, sacrifice and discipline. As a result of this great success, Lenin was able to claim that "Bolshevism has become a world-wide phenomenon, the workers' revolution has raised its head."[20]

However, the Soviet victory came at a terrible cost and incredible sacrifices were made by the masses. Now, with the end of the civil war, it was necessary to concentrate their minds on economic recovery, especially the rebuilding of the basic industries of rail, fuel, iron and steel. This also included an ambitious plan for the electrification of the economy, which Lenin regarded as vital and even coined the slogan: 'Communism is Soviet power plus electrification'.[21]

200. The presidium of the Ninth Party Congress, 1920
Sitting (from left): Yenukidze, Kalinin, Bukharin, Tomsky, Lashevich, Kamenev,
Preobrazhensky, Serebryakov, Lenin and Rykov
Standing: Krestinsky, Milyutin, Smilga

At the Congress, Lenin spoke plainly about the new exertions that still
needed to be made to accomplish this task. If they were going to turn the
situation around, it would require further superhuman sacrifices and even
greater discipline than before. "We must create a different kind of discipline,
a different source of discipline and unity", he stated.[22]

The Polish War

With the end of the civil war, as previously explained, the counter-revolution
was not defeated by a superior force of arms. Although the Red Army played
an indispensable role, what really saved the Russian Revolution were the
mass desertions, mutinies, sabotage and risings in the occupied areas, and
the international solidarity of the working class – all of which served to
undermine the Whites and the Allied intervention.

In September 1919, for instance, dockers in Seattle identified huge
crates labelled 'sewing machines'. When examined, they discovered stacks
of rifles bound for Kolchak's counter-revolutionary government. The cargo
was immediately banned by the workers and they notified other ports. The
Central Labour Council backed the actions of the dockers.

201. Pyotr Wrangel

As a result of such solidarity, the imperialists were forced to leave as their forces were infected with revolution, fed by Bolshevik propaganda and the class sympathy of the workers back home.

With the civil war finally at an end, things appeared to stabilise. Then, out of a clear blue sky, in April 1920, Poland launched an unprovoked attack against Russia, marched into Soviet Ukraine and seized Kiev. Simultaneously, encouraged by the Poles, General Wrangel also threatened the Donets Basin in the south. Once again, the imperialists' hopes were raised and they rushed to supply munitions to the Piłsudski dictatorship. But this attack rallied the whole of Russia, as well as workers internationally.

The Red Army, partially demobilised, was brought back into action. As already mentioned, in Britain, dockers refused to load the *Jolly George* with munitions planned for Poland, Councils of Action were formed and the Labour-Trade Union Congress threatened a general strike if British troops intervened. This threat paralysed the hands of the British imperialists.

The initial victories of Piłsudski's forces soon gave way to defeats, and his armies were forced to retreat. By mid-July, the counter-offensive of the Red Army had not merely recovered Kiev and driven the Poles out of White

202. Józef Piłsudski

Russia (Belarus), but had advanced so far that its troops reached the gates of Lvov (modern-day Lviv) and then approached Warsaw. This was the first time the Red Army had penetrated Europe. Tukhachevsky's order on 2 July read:

> To the West! … The time of reckoning has come. Over the corpse of White Poland shines the road to world-wide conflagration. On our bayonets we shall bring happiness and peace to toiling humanity… On to Vilna, Minsk, Warsaw! March![23]

Some units covered nearly thirty kilometres a day for twelve days in a row. As a result, Lenin was in favour of not only driving back the Polish attack, but for the Red Army to push on and take Warsaw, establishing another bastion of the world revolution. The war of defence should now be turned into a revolutionary war of advance. If successful, such a victory would have broken the Soviet Republic's isolation and transformed the entire situation.

However, Trotsky was opposed to the idea. He was fearful that the Red Army's supply lines were overstretched and, more importantly, the Polish workers showed no sign of a revolutionary uprising.

203. Polish troops enter Kyiv, 7 May 1920

In the end, Trotsky was proved correct and the Russian offensive floundered, without ammunition and reduced rations, and began to fall back in the face of Piłsudski's counter-attack.* In the end, an armistice came into force in October 1920 and a peace treaty was signed in March 1921. Following this, the Red Army turned its attention to fighting Wrangel, whose troops were cornered in the Crimea and eventually defeated.

In relation to the war with Poland, Lenin and Trotsky's positions had been reversed compared to the Treaty of Brest-Litovsk. It was now Trotsky who argued for the signing of a peace treaty and Lenin against. Lenin was forced to recognise his mistake and referred to it on several occasions. At the Tenth Party Congress, he explained:

> Our offensive, our too swift advance almost as far as Warsaw, was undoubtedly a
> mistake. I shall not now analyse whether it was a strategic or a political error, as

---

* Stalin and Voroshilov played a fatal role in undermining Tukhachevsky's assault on Warsaw. They deliberately disobeyed an order to unite with the army outside Warsaw, instead, ordering the 1st Cavalry Army to march on Lvov in a fruitless adventure. This was part of their old vendetta against Tuchachevsky and Trotsky, as well as an attempt to enhance their own prestige.

204. Communists before being sent to the Polish Front, 1920

this would take me too far afield. Let us leave it to future historians, for those of us who have to keep beating off the enemy in hard struggle have no time to indulge in historical research. At any rate, the mistake is there, and it was due to the fact that we had overestimated the superiority of our forces. [...] But the fact remains that we had made a definite mistake in the war with Poland.[24]

Mensheviks and SRs

After much hesitation, given their involvement in terrorism against the Soviet regime during the civil war, the newspapers of the Mensheviks and SRs were periodically closed down, and some of their members were arrested for espionage. These defensive measures increased as the civil war intensified. "Those who are not for us", warned Lenin, "are against us." This view certainly echoed the feelings within the working class, who were more determined than ever to hold out and safeguard what they had conquered.

Despite these measures, these 'socialist' parties continued to function in one way or another. Even the bourgeois Cadet party, which was openly restorationist, was initially allowed to exist, and even won seven seats in the Constituent Assembly, but it was eventually outlawed when it supported

205. The Red Army celebrating victory over Wrangel in Crimea, 1920

sabotage and the activities of Kornilov. Despite this, the newspaper of the Cadets continued to be published in Moscow up until the summer of 1918, while the civil war was taking off.

Both the Mensheviks and SRs were certainly involved with the counter-revolution. The SRs, for instance, gave support to the rising of the Czech Legion. In a number of areas, these parties entered reactionary governments set up by the counter-revolution. For example, the SRs were at the head of the Samara government. In 1918, together with the other White military governments, they formed the Ufa Directorate of five persons, with the SR Avksentyev as chairman.* The Mensheviks in the Volga and Ural regions supported the Samara Committee of the Constituent Assembly and also participated in the Ufa Directorate. However, having fulfilled its purpose in bolstering the counter-revolution, this Directorate was suppressed two months later by General Kolchak, who had no need for these formal trappings of government.

From this alone, it can be seen that both the Mensheviks and SRs were a direct part of the counter-revolution. It was this, and solely this, that led to their suppression. Despite this, the Mensheviks' paper was still being

---

* The Ufa Directorate was the informal name given to the Provisional All-Russian Government, the government of the counter-revolution.

206. Lenin addressing the Sverdlov Square rally on 5 May 1920
Trotsky is standing to the right, with Kamenev behind him

published from time to time, as were the anarchist papers. In fact, they were still bringing out their papers and were allowed to function in 1920.

But throughout this time, these parties also played a double game. The Menshevik Central Committee in Moscow attempted to pursue a policy of 'neutrality', while those involved with the Whites began to fear their extremism, as demonstrated by the actions of Kolchak. The Whites, after all, paid little attention to the differences between the 'socialists', whether Menshevik or Bolshevik.

As a result of these vacillations between the two poles of revolution and counter-revolution, the Mensheviks and SRs tended to fragment. Matters escalated when the Left SRs carried out assassinations against the Bolsheviks, such as Volodarsky in June 1918, then made attempts against the lives of Lenin and Trotsky. Such actions could not be tolerated, and arrests soon followed as an elementary measure of defence.

Decisions were taken to exclude the Mensheviks and SRs from the Soviets as agents of the counter-revolution. Even then, at the Sixth All-Russian Congress of Soviets in November 1918, which was almost exclusively Bolshevik, an amnesty was approved. This called for the release of all those

207. Lenin, Trotsky and Kamenev after the rally

"detained by the organs combatting counter-revolution" unless a definite charge of counter-revolutionary activity was offered against them within two weeks of their arrest, and of all hostages except those held by the central Cheka as a specific guarantee for "comrades in enemy hands".[25]

When the Mensheviks adopted resolutions in October 1918 recognising the October Revolution as "historically necessary" and promising "direct support of the military actions of the Soviet Government against foreign intervention", Lenin declared that nothing more would be asked of the Mensheviks and SRs than "neutrality and good-neighbour relations".[26] In February 1919, a conference of SRs in Petrograd "decisively rejected any attempt to overthrow the Soviet power by way of armed struggle…"[27]

Given this change, in December 1919 the SRs attended the All-Russian Congress of Soviets as visitors, and the Menshevik Fyodor Dan spoke, welcoming the Soviet victories. In the summer of 1920, Brailsford reported:

> … the Left Social Revolutionaries have a monthly organ and the Jewish parties, not yet wholly absorbed, have several weekly organs. The Menshevik leaders told me of their difficulties. They can get no paper, which is a Government monopoly, for pamphlets or leaflets at election time. They can rarely hire a hall for public

meetings, though they can and do speak at meetings called by the various bodies of electors (e.g. Soviet employees),... They are nonetheless a tolerated and legal opposition. Other parties, notably the Right Social Revolutionaries and the 'Cadets' (Liberals), which openly support the 'Whites' in the civil war, are, of course, not tolerated at all as organised parties.[28]

Arthur Ransome met with Martov in Moscow in the summer of 1919. While Martov opposed the foreign intervention, he produced his own newspaper highly critical of the government:

I saw Martov at the offices of his newspaper, which had just been suppressed on account of an article, which he admitted was a little indiscreet, objecting to the upkeep of the Red Army. He pointed eloquently to the seal on some of the doors, but told me that he had started a new paper, of which he showed me the first number, and told me that the demand for it was such that although he had intended that it should be a weekly he now expected to make it a daily.[29]

Despite all the restrictions imposed on the opposition parties, the 'moderate' socialist parties continued to operate in one form or another. In May 1920, members of the British Labour delegation visiting Moscow, most of whom opposed the Bolsheviks, "were allowed complete freedom to see politicians of opposition parties", and even attended a session of the Menshevik Central Committee.[30]

In August 1920, with the end of the civil war, the Mensheviks openly held their own national conference in Moscow, which was even reported in the Soviet press – such were the liberties they were allowed. In December, Mensheviks and SRs attended the Congress of Soviets, from which they had been previously debarred, but without voting rights.

Nevertheless, the Cheka kept its eyes on the Mensheviks, who were constantly urging workers to go on strike against the Bolshevik government. In 1920, Brailsford wrote:

There was a 'round up' of Mensheviks in Moscow... About 700 were imprisoned for no reason that I could ascertain, kept for a few days, and then, with some few exceptions, released.[31]

While the civil war had just ended, this was at a time when war raged with Poland, following the aggression from the Piłsudski regime that was backed by the imperialists. The Cheka was therefore on the lookout for potential internal dangers, which included their old adversaries.

These were emergency measures in an emergency situation. Lenin envisaged that as the crisis subsided, these defensive measures would be relaxed and eventually lifted. But everything depended upon the situation.

Nevertheless, there was a certain toleration. For instance, the anarchist press that was hostile to the Soviet regime, as well as that of the Maximalists – a split-off from the SRs, formed in 1906 – continued to appear up to 1921. That of the Left SRs continued later still.

All this shows how opposition groups still operated in the middle of a civil war, and how lenient the Bolsheviks were at this time.

It should also be noted that in the 'democratic' capitalist countries, workers, trade unionists, communists and socialists were being arrested, banned, framed, jailed, deported and assassinated. In the United States, during the notorious Palmer Raids, 10,000 'suspected Reds' were arrested, and many deported. From the declaration of the First World War, the British government had imprisoned around 10,000 conscientious objectors who were considered a threat to the war effort.

Lenin answers his critics

Despite their apparent change of tune, Lenin did not fully trust the opposition parties. "When the Mensheviks announced that they were opposed to the intervention of the Entente, we invited them to work with us, and they willingly accepted our invitation", said Lenin to a plenary meeting of the Moscow Soviet.[32] But he went on to warn:

> If you have come here to help us, then do so, but if you are going to publish newspapers and incite the workers to strike, and these strikes cause the death of our Red Army men at the front, and every day of a strike causes tens of thousands of our factory workers to suffer privations, pangs of hunger – the pangs which are causing us so much concern – then you may be right from the Constituent Assembly point of view, but from the standpoint of our struggle and the responsibility we bear, you are wrong, you cannot help us, so get out, go to Georgia, go to Kolchak, or else you will go to prison.[33]

As expected, the way the Bolsheviks dealt with the opposition parties was met with repeated howls of protest from the leaders of the Second International, as well as the bourgeois hypocrites. Lenin confronted the arguments of his accusers and defended the revolution, together with its shortcomings. In his 'Letter to American Workers', he explained:

The contours of a new world, the world of socialism, are rising before us in the shape of the Soviet Republic. It is not surprising that this world does not come into being ready-made, does not spring forth like Minerva from the head of Jupiter. [...][34]

Let the corrupt bourgeois press shout to the whole world about every mistake our revolution makes. We are not daunted by our mistakes. People have not become saints because the revolution has begun. The toiling classes who for centuries have been oppressed, downtrodden and forcibly held in the vice of poverty, brutality and ignorance cannot avoid mistakes when making a revolution. And, as I pointed out once before, the corpse of bourgeois society cannot be nailed in a coffin and buried. The corpse of capitalism is decaying and disintegrating in our midst, polluting the air and poisoning our lives, enmeshing that which is new, fresh, young and virile in thousands of threads and bonds of that which is old, moribund and decaying.[35]

He went on to say that:

Mistakes are being committed in the course of their revolutionary work by our peasants, who at one stroke, in one night, 25-26 October 1917, entirely abolished the private ownership of land, and are now, month after month, overcoming tremendous difficulties and correcting their mistakes themselves, solving in a practical way the most difficult tasks of organising new conditions of economic life, of fighting the kulaks, providing land for the *working people* (and not for the rich), and of changing to *communist* large-scale agriculture.

Mistakes are being committed in the course of their revolutionary work by our workers, who have already, after a few months, nationalised almost all the biggest factories and plants, and are learning by hard, everyday work the new task of managing whole branches of industry, are setting the nationalised enterprises going, overcoming the powerful resistance of inertia, petty-bourgeois mentality and selfishness, and, brick by brick, are laying the foundation of *new* social ties, of a *new* labour discipline, of a new influence of the workers' trade unions over their members.

Mistakes are committed in the course of their revolutionary work by our Soviets, which were created as far back as 1905 by a mighty upsurge of the people. The Soviets of Workers and Peasants are a *new* type of state, a new and higher *type* of democracy, a form of the proletarian dictatorship, a means of administering the state *without* the bourgeoisie and *against* the bourgeoisie. For the first time democracy is here serving the people, the working people, and has ceased to be democracy for the rich as it still is in all bourgeois republics, even the most democratic. For the first time, the people are grappling, on a scale involving one hundred million, with the problem of implementing the dictatorship of the proletariat and semi-proletariat – a problem which, if not solved, makes socialism *out of the question*.[36]

Lenin concluded:

We are now, as it were, in a besieged fortress, waiting for the other detachments of the world socialist revolution to come to our relief. These detachments *exist*, they are *more numerous* than ours, they are maturing, growing, gaining more strength the longer the brutalities of imperialism continue.[37]

In 1920, a visiting Labour delegation from Britain raised matters of deep concern with Lenin about the repression and Red Terror, to which he replied in a 'Letter to the British Workers':

Several members of your delegation questioned me with surprise about the Red terror, about the absence of freedom of the press in Russia, of freedom of assembly, about our persecution of Mensheviks and pro-Menshevik workers, etc. My reply was that the real cause of the terror is the British imperialists and their 'allies', who practised and are still practising a White terror in Finland and in Hungary, in India and in Ireland, who have been supporting Yudenich, Kolchak, Denikin, Piłsudski and Wrangel. Our Red terror is a defence of the working class against the exploiters, the crushing of resistance from the exploiters with whom the Socialist-Revolutionaries, the Mensheviks and an insignificant number of pro-Menshevik workers have sided. Freedom of the press and assembly under bourgeois democracy is freedom for the wealthy to conspire against the working people, freedom for the capitalists to bribe and buy up the press. I have explained this in newspaper articles so often that I have derived no pleasure in repeating myself.[38]

Many of the members of the Labour delegation were vehemently opposed to Bolshevism, but were nevertheless given free access to wherever and whomever they wished. Most sought out the enemies of the Soviet regime, but there were others like the journalist Walter Meakin, who was determined to tell the truth, and wrote several honest reports of what he saw and experienced. These reports, together with his pictures, have been republished by *In Defence of Marxism* and certainly provide the reader with an antidote to the lies that were being spread at the time about the situation in Russia.*

---

* Many of Meakin's photographs are included in this book – see the image credits on page 974. For the full reports and photographs, see 'Russian Revolution as Never Seen Before:

Georgia

Georgia had long been the base of Menshevism. They had managed to form a Georgian government soon after the overthrow of tsarism. But, given their vehement hostility to the new Soviet government, they soon began to collaborate with its enemies. They first conspired with the Germans, and then the Whites. Soon afterwards, the Menshevik government under Noe Zhordania banned the Communist Party and repressed its activities.*

In May 1920, the Soviet Republic decided to recognise the independence of Georgia after it promised to legalise the Georgian Communist Party. In the end, however, the Georgian Mensheviks reneged on their promise and instead continued their intrigues with Britain and other capitalist powers against the Soviet Republic. Despite these hostilities, for reasons of expediency, the Bolsheviks decided not to take action against Georgia.

However, the Party's representative in Georgia was Ordzhonikidze and behind him stood Stalin. Both Ordzhonikidze and Stalin were Georgians. They were irritated by the Georgian Mensheviks and conspired to engineer a clash. An uprising was therefore orchestrated in Tbilisi, which demanded the active intervention by the Red Army to secure its success.

In February 1921, the Red Army intervened in Georgia on Stalin's initiative. Lenin was very reluctant to support the occupation of Georgia. Trotsky was away in Ukraine when the decision was taken to invade. Although opposed, once the deed had been done, he felt that there was no point in going back. Lenin was extremely anxious that any military action should not be seen as the annexation of Georgia by Russia, thus identifying the Soviet state with the tsarist oppressors. Stalin and Ordzhonikidze, on the other hand, had no such qualms.

Increasingly concerned by reports of the heavy-handed methods of Stalin and Ordzhonikidze, Lenin wrote letters instructing Ordzhonikidze to pursue a "policy of concessions in relation to the Georgian intelligentsia and small traders", and to advocate the setting up of a "coalition with Zhordania or similar Georgian Mensheviks."[39] But this advice was ignored and Lenin sent a further telegram to Ordzhonikidze:

> In view of the fact that units of the 11th Army are on the territory of Georgia, you are instructed to establish complete contact with the Revolutionary Committee

---

The real story, told by an eyewitness', *In Defence of Marxism*, 5 November 2021, available on marxist.com.

* Noe Zhordania was President of the Menshevik Georgian Republic from 1920 to 1922. After the Soviet invasion he went into exile and died in 1953.

of Georgia and to abide strictly by the directives of the Revolutionary Committee, undertaking no measures which might affect the interests of the local population [...] to observe particular respect for the sovereign bodies of Georgia; to display particular attention and caution in regard to the Georgian population. [...] Hold to account all those who infringe this directive.[40]

As one might expect, the reformist leaders of the Second International raised a strident outcry against the Bolsheviks over the Red Army's invasion of Georgia. In Britain, the Labour leader Arthur Henderson and Prime Minister Lloyd George suddenly became champions of self-determination for Georgia, conveniently forgetting about India or Ireland, where British troops were holding down a population of millions of colonial slaves using methods of extreme violence.

The Second International waged a noisy campaign demanding the withdrawal of Soviet forces from Georgia. In reply, Trotsky wrote a small book answering the hypocrisy and lies of the Social-Democrats, called *Between Red and White*. The Social-Democrats wanted the Soviets to leave Georgia, but were perfectly content for the warships of the Entente, including the British, to remain in the Black Sea with their eyes on Baku oil. In the end, despite all the protests, the Soviets remained firmly in control in Georgia.

32. A School of Communism

The global impact of the Russian Revolution created favourable conditions for the Communist International. Its call to establish Communist Parties was enthusiastically taken up by the most radical layers of the workers and youth. Over the following twelve months since its foundation, the new International established mass organisations in a whole series of countries.

This growth and influence of communism was reflected in the increased attendance at the Second World Congress, which lasted from 19 July to 7 August 1920, and was held in Petrograd and Moscow. On this basis, the birth of the Third International and the world revolution looked secure.

Under Lenin, even in the darkest days of the civil war, the World Congresses were held on an annual basis. Here, the leading communists of many lands gathered to collectively work out the programme, policy, tactics and strategy of the world movement. These congresses acted as a 'school of communism' for all the national sections, preparing them for the tasks that lay ahead.

The opening session of the Second Congress was held in the Smolny in Petrograd – in a country, we should remember, that was still at war with Poland. It was attended by over 200 delegates, representing organisations from thirty-seven countries.

Apart from the established Communist Parties, delegates also attended from the German Independents (USPD), the Socialist Parties from Italy and France, the Industrial Workers of the World (IWW) from America and other organisations which were considering affiliation. Brailsford provided a glimpse of the optimistic mood at that time:

208. Delegates to the Second Congress of the Comintern, Petrograd
Amongst those pictured are: Radek (second from the left), Bukharin (to his right,
with hands visible), Lenin, Gorky (behind Lenin), Zinoviev and Maria Ulyanova
(wearing white, centre right)

It was a time of high hopes and excitement, and as these foreign delegates, all
optimists, all enthusiasts, made their presence felt, the world revolution looked
imminent to the more visionary Russian Communists.[1]

Alfred Rosmer recalled:

A few days after we [the delegates] had arrived in Moscow we received two books
that had just been published by the Communist International. They were *'Left-
Wing' Communism: An Infantile Disorder* by Lenin, and *Terrorism and Communism*,
a reply by Trotsky to a work of Kautsky's which appeared with the same title. The
two books formed a sort of introduction and commentary on the *Theses* prepared
for the Congress.[2]

A large map of Russia was displayed in the Congress hall, where delegates
could follow the regular progress of Tukhachevsky's march on Warsaw,
accompanied by a great deal of interest and enthusiasm. Given the
progress of the International, it looked as if communism was on the march
everywhere.

209. Lenin's opening speech at the Congress

At the opening session of the Congress, Lenin gave the main political report on the international situation and the fundamental tasks facing the communist movement. He dealt with the aftermath of the world war and the growing contradictions of imperialism, including the harsh consequences of the Versailles Peace Treaty:

By means of the Treaty of Versailles, the war imposed such terms upon these countries that advanced peoples have been reduced to a state of colonial dependence, poverty, starvation, ruin, and loss of rights: this treaty binds them for many generations, placing them in conditions that no civilised nation has ever lived in. [...]

Today, after this 'peaceful' period, we see a monstrous intensification of oppression. [...]

Not only have the colonial and the defeated countries been reduced to a state of dependence; within each victor state the contradictions have grown more acute; all the capitalist contradictions have become aggravated.[3]

210. Smolny Institute in 1920, where the Congress was held in Petrograd

In his speech, Lenin quoted from John Maynard Keynes, the British diplomat and author of *The Economic Consequences of the Peace*, who had been present at the Versailles peace treaty negotiations. He remarked that Keynes, a well-known bourgeois economist and implacable enemy of Bolshevism, had "arrived at conclusions which are more weighty, more striking and more instructive than any a Communist revolutionary could draw…"[4]

Keynes believed that, following Versailles, the whole world, and especially Europe, was heading for bankruptcy. As a result, he had resigned in disgust from the Paris Peace Conference. Lenin went on to quote Keynes' figures on the mountain of debts that had been built up, including the astounding depreciation of the different national currencies.

"This fact shows that the 'mechanism' of the world capitalist economy is falling apart", remarked Lenin.[5] The contradictions of world capitalism were aggravated to unprecedented levels, "this being the origin of the intense revolutionary ferment that is ever growing."[6]

On the one hand, bourgeois economists depict this crisis simply as 'unrest', to use the elegant expression of the British. On the other hand, revolutionaries sometimes try to prove that the crisis is absolutely insoluble.[7]

211. Lenin delivering a speech at the Congress, 19 July 1920

"This is a mistake", stated Lenin. "There is no such thing as an absolutely hopeless situation."[8] He went on:

> The bourgeoisie are behaving like barefaced plunderers who have lost their heads; they are committing folly after folly, thus aggravating the situation and hastening their doom. All that is true. But nobody can 'prove' that it is absolutely impossible for them to pacify a minority of the exploited with some petty concessions [...] To try to 'prove' in advance that there is 'absolutely' no way out of the situation would be sheer pedantry, or playing with concepts and catchwords.[9]

Lenin then went on to state that the only 'proof' of capitalism's doom was the actual overthrow of capitalism, and that was precisely why they were gathered at this Congress. The capitalist system will not fall under its own contradictions but needs to be consciously overthrown. He concluded his speech by saying:

> Today the advanced proletariat is everywhere with us. A proletarian army exists everywhere, although sometimes it is poorly organised and needs reorganising. If our comrades in all lands help us now to organise a united army, no shortcomings will prevent us from accomplishing our task. That task is the world proletarian revolution, the creation of a world Soviet republic.[10]

This speech was followed by prolonged enthusiastic applause.

'Left-Wing' Communism

The Communist International had succeeded in drawing into its ranks the most militant sections of the working class, the most determined opponents of opportunism and reformism. The bulk of these new recruits came from the centrist parties that had evolved towards Bolshevism. However, among these layers were politically inexperienced militants who were deeply influenced by ultra-leftism. In fact, ultra-leftism was widespread among the young Communist Parties at this time.

Many young and inexperienced members, who had not passed through the long experience of the Bolsheviks, believed that simply adopting an intransigent revolutionary stance and refusing to compromise were sufficient qualities for a revolutionary leadership.

Throughout the Congress, Lenin intervened to counter this ultra-leftist tendency and clarify the genuine approach and tactics of Bolshevism. That was why, as part of this education, copies of Lenin's 'Left-Wing' Communism: An Infantile Disorder were translated and given to every delegate to read.

Lenin's pamphlet is one of his most important works. It sums up the entire history of Bolshevism in the field of revolutionary tactics and explains in a concise manner the lessons that had been accumulated over the previous twenty years. In doing so, Lenin based himself on that rich experience in order to educate the young cadres of the new International. He explained:

> At the present moment in history, however, it is the Russian model that reveals to *all* countries something – and something highly significant – of their near and inevitable future.[11]

Lenin stressed the vital need to build a disciplined and theoretically steeled party based on Bolshevism:

> Only the history of Bolshevism during the *entire* period of its existence can satisfactorily explain why it has been able to build up and maintain, under most difficult conditions, the iron discipline needed for the victory of the proletariat.[12]

Ultimately, the success of Bolshevism rested on the granite foundation of Marxist theory. The unique challenges faced by the revolutionary movement in Russia allowed Bolshevism to build upon that sound foundation, but also to learn to apply it in a flexible manner, as dictated by the concrete circumstances at any given time. He went on to explain:

Russia achieved Marxism – the only correct revolutionary theory – through the *agony* she experienced in the course of half a century of unparalleled torment and sacrifice, of unparalleled revolutionary heroism, incredible energy, devoted searching, study, practical trial, disappointment, verification, and comparison with European experience. Thanks to the political emigration caused by tsarism, revolutionary Russia, in the second half of the nineteenth century, acquired a wealth of international links and excellent information on the forms and theories of the world revolutionary movement, such as no other country possessed.[13]

This wealth of experience, combined with Marxist theory, served to train up and educate a whole generation in the ideas, tactics and methods of revolutionary Marxism. In the hard school of the class struggle, the Bolsheviks learned how to combine legal and illegal work. They also learned that one must know how to attack, but also – and equally importantly – one must know how to retreat in good order.

The experiences of the Russian movement were in complete contrast to those of the bankrupt reformist leaders of the Second International, who had completely embraced opportunism and adapted themselves fully to capitalism.

The Party must have a correct programme and policy, but that is not sufficient. It also has to learn how to connect this programme with the working class. The Party must learn to go through the experiences of the class struggle alongside the workers, teaching them to reject reformism and uniting them in the struggle for power.

This, in turn, requires flexible tactics, and the ability to take into consideration the national peculiarities and traditions of the labour movement in each country. They must not, Lenin stressed, speak to the workers of their country "in Russian", but translate the ideas of Bolshevism into a language that will be acceptable and understandable to them. That was excellent advice. Unfortunately, it was not always followed.

Tactical flexibility

The task of Bolshevism, Lenin explained, was to defend the fundamentals of Marxism and launch an offensive against both opportunism and anarchism, which were really two sides of the same coin.

Lenin described anarchism (and ultra-leftism) as the penalty the workers' movement paid for the opportunism of its leaders. Bolshevism also meant a struggle against the petty-bourgeois ideas of individual terrorism and for the construction of a mass revolutionary party based on the working class.

In the past, Lenin had modelled himself on the German Social-Democracy, which, when combatting Bernsteinism, "*came closest* to being the party the revolutionary proletariat needs to achieve victory…"[14] Despite the leaders eventually succumbing to opportunism, the German movement had nevertheless given birth to the revolutionary currents of the Spartacists as well as the leftward-moving USPD, which were soon to become the basis of a mass Communist Party in Germany.

Lenin gave many examples of the tactical flexibility of Bolshevism, citing the tactics of boycott during the first Russian Revolution, the experience of Brest-Litovsk and the mistakes of the 'Left Communists'.

Lenin dismissed the demands of the 'Lefts' for 'no compromises' as 'childish innocence'. Any militant who has been involved in a strike should know that it is sometimes necessary to compromise, *depending upon the concrete circumstances*. It is absurd to see the demand of 'no compromises' as a general principle, applicable to all occasions.

He explained that the compromise (and retreat) that had to be made over Brest-Litovsk in early 1918 had nothing in common with the betrayals carried out by the labour bureaucracy using the excuse of the 'compromise':

> One must learn to distinguish between a man who has given up his money and firearms to bandits so as to lessen the evil they can do and to facilitate their capture and execution, and a man who gives his money and firearms to bandits so as to share in the loot.[15]

Unfortunately, the 'Lefts' had not understood, or more likely were not acquainted with the history of Bolshevism, which freely changed its tactics and made 'compromises', depending on the realities facing the Party. In the class war, as in war generally, flexible tactics are essential to succeed.

Lenin sharply criticised the ultra-left trends within the German Communist movement, which he saw as a prime example of the "infantile disorder of Leftism".[16] However honest, sincere and revolutionary they might be, the 'Lefts' were committing very serious mistakes. Of course, they were correct to conduct an implacable struggle against reformist opportunism and to emphasise the revolutionary class struggle, soviets and so on. But to reject participating in the parliamentary struggle and refuse to conduct work in reformist trade unions – even those that were dominated by the right-wing leaders – was a mistake that risked isolating the communist advance guard from the mass of the workers, who were still under the influence of the reformist leaders.

Regarding the trade unions, Lenin explained that even those controlled by reactionaries were still the basic organisations of the working class that embraced millions of workers. They were mass organisations of the workers and, no matter how bureaucratic they were, could not be ignored or boycotted.

The real task of communists was to break the grip of these reformist leaders over the unions. However, that could not be achieved from outside their ranks. It was therefore important for the communists to "work wherever the masses are to be found", however difficult that might be.[17]

Communists must learn the methods needed to overcome the obstacles and barriers placed in their way by the reformist leaders. In this way, they would be able to find a road to the masses and carry out genuine communist work among them. To boycott the unions would simply strengthen the grip of the right-wing leaders over the membership. They would in effect be boycotting themselves and assisting the bureaucracy.

To show how far the Bolsheviks went in carrying out this work, Lenin pointed to the involvement of the Russian Marxists in the Zubatov unions at the turn of the century, which had been established by the tsarist police to cut across the formation of radical trade unionism. In Russia, where there were no legal trade unions, the Bolsheviks made use of, and worked within, the Zubatov unions, an example that showed audacity and the greatest flexibility when faced with a difficult situation.

Compared to this, the conditions for work in the unions in Europe were far easier. Following the First World War, the workers were now pouring into the trade unions, and the communists needed to orientate towards these workers and not remain aloof.

On the question of participation in bourgeois parliaments, there was further disagreement. The 'Lefts' regarded such institutions as 'obsolete', along with bourgeois democracy. Consequently, they believed such bodies should be boycotted. Lenin replied that, while parliament may be "historically obsolete" as compared to the Soviet system, the masses did not yet see it that way.[18] In Germany, in particular, millions of workers actively participated in national elections. It had been a grave mistake for the newly formed Communist Party, under the influence of the 'Lefts', to boycott the National Assembly elections in January 1919. This was the first ever election held under universal suffrage, in which the Social-Democrats won 11.5 million votes. Lenin wrote:

> It is obvious that the 'Lefts' in Germany have mistaken *their desire*, their politico-ideological attitude, for objective reality. That is a most dangerous mistake for revolutionaries to make.[19]

It was vital to see reality not as what the communists would like it to be, but through the eyes of the workers. It was now essential to learn from these mistakes and expose the bourgeois and reformist politicians by using the parliamentary struggle and other means to enlighten the masses about communism.

> We Bolsheviks participated in the most counter-revolutionary parliaments, and experience has shown that this participation was not only useful but indispensable to the party of the revolutionary proletariat…[20]

He went on:

> It is very easy to show one's 'revolutionary' temper merely by hurling abuse at parliamentary opportunism, or merely by repudiating participation in parliaments; its very ease, however, cannot turn this into a solution of a difficult, a very difficult, problem.[21]

Marxism, Lenin repeated, was not a lifeless dogma but a guide to action. Lenin argued that the revolutionary party must be prepared, when necessary, to take any measures needed to win the masses, otherwise these workers would be left at the mercy of their right-wing leaders. If the Bolsheviks had refused to work within the Menshevik-SR dominated Soviets, for example, there would have been no October Revolution.

Although the Bolsheviks relentlessly condemned bourgeois liberalism, under tsarism, they were prepared to make tactical agreements with the liberals for *concrete practical ends*, when it was advantageous. In the struggle against tsarism, they sometimes formed a tactical bloc with the petty-bourgeois SRs and the Trudoviks against the openly bourgeois Cadets.

Furthermore, the Bolsheviks operated within the same party, the RSDLP, as the opportunist Mensheviks from 1903 until 1912, which did not prevent them from waging a struggle against Menshevism. After the October Revolution, they adopted the agrarian programme of the SRs, taking into consideration the concrete desires of the peasantry. This showed how flexible the Bolsheviks were in relation to tactics *before* and *after* the October Revolution.

'Leftism' in Britain

In Britain, where there was an attempt to found a communist party, many of those who participated in it were very much influenced by sectarianism and lacked any real knowledge of Marxist theory.

212. Parade for the arrival of the 1920 British Labour delegation to Russia

They were very sincere people, but they were very far from being steeled in the ideas of Marxism, and also suffered from the infantile disease of ultra-leftism. 'Left' tendencies were reflected in such individuals as Sylvia Pankhurst, who led the militant Workers' Socialist Federation, and Willie Gallacher from the Clyde Shop Stewards' Committee in Scotland.

Many of the leading shop stewards were also infected with syndicalism, the idea that militant trade union struggle alone was enough to overthrow capitalism, reacting against the opportunist policies of the reformist Labour leaders.

Lenin took a very patient approach to these manifestations of ultra-leftism, which he recognised as an expression of the "highly gratifying" temper of young workers who were just beginning to accept communism. But he also warned:

At the same time, we must tell them openly and frankly that a state of mind is *by itself* insufficient for leadership of the masses in a great revolutionary struggle, and that the cause of the revolution may well be harmed by certain errors that people who are most devoted to the cause of the revolution are about to commit, or are committing.[22]

Lenin agreed wholeheartedly that the leaders of the British Labour movement, such as Henderson, Philip and Ethel Snowden, JR Clynes and Ramsay MacDonald were class traitors. However, he explained that in advocating communist propaganda, it was necessary to distinguish carefully between the open representatives of capitalism, the Conservatives, and the reformist Labour Party, which rested on a working-class base, namely the trade unions.

It was important to give critical support to the Labour Party, even when led by these reactionaries, to defeat the likes of Lloyd George, Churchill and the bourgeois parties, while at the same time, putting forward a communist programme as the only genuine answer to the problems of the working class.

After all, the Bolsheviks did not initially call for the overthrow of the Provisional Government. That would have been premature. Instead, they called on the leaders of the Soviets – the reformist Mensheviks and SRs – to break with the ten capitalist ministers and to take power, which they refused to do. Basing themselves on the slogan 'All power to the Soviets', the Bolsheviks skilfully used this approach to expose the cowardly vacillations of the Soviet leaders and win support, eventually achieving a majority in the Soviets and the working class. Lenin gave the inexperienced cadres sound advice on how work in elections should be conducted along principled communist lines:

> We would put up our candidates in a very few but absolutely safe constituencies, namely, constituencies where our candidatures would not give any seats to the Liberals at the expense of the Labour candidates. We would take part in the election campaign, distribute leaflets agitating for communism, and, in *all* constituencies where we have no candidates, we would urge the electors to *vote for the Labour candidate and against the bourgeois candidate*.[23]

He continued:

> Comrades Sylvia Pankhurst and Gallacher are mistaken in thinking that this is a betrayal of communism, or a renunciation of the struggle against the social-traitors. On the contrary, the cause of communist revolution would undoubtedly gain thereby.[24]

Labour Party affiliation debate

A very heated debate was raging in Britain about whether a new communist party should affiliate to the reformist Labour Party. The British Socialist Party, which was already affiliated to the Labour Party, now wanted to become part of the British Communist Party. The question of the Labour Party was therefore a live issue.

This question, however, was not left to the British alone to decide, but was referred to the Second Congress, a far higher and more experienced body. The International as a whole would debate and decide. As Lenin explained: "We cannot, however, say that this question concerns Britain alone – that would mean copying the worst habits of the Second International."[25]

After a lot of discussion, Lenin made up his mind to support the British Communist Party affiliating to the Labour Party, as long as they were allowed to conduct their own independent propaganda. Again, Lenin hoped that this move would help them break from their old sectarianism and allow the communists to influence the best radicalised workers in the Labour Party.

This debate was taking place at a time when the Labour Party was undergoing a great ferment. It had just opened up to individual membership and adopted its socialist aims as encapsulated in the Clause 4 of the Party's Constitution. Nevertheless, this proposal to affiliate aroused heated controversy at the Second Congress, especially on the part of some of the British delegates. While William McLaine from the British Socialist Party was in favour of affiliation, those attached to the Shop Stewards movement were very much opposed. Jack Tanner, from the Shop Stewards movement, put the argument forcefully against affiliation:

> The Shop Stewards have always propagated 'direct action,' and the political parties are beginning to understand its implications and adopt its methods. Now efforts are being made again to get the workers to resort to Parliament, though all are agreed that it must be abolished as soon as possible. The workers are losing faith in parliamentary action; strong efforts will have to be made to revive their faith – only to destroy it again later. You will get nothing but antagonism from the class-conscious workers on the question of affiliation to the Labour Party.[26]

Lenin intervened in this debate, saying he had no regrets in repeating arguments as long as it served to clarify matters. While Lenin was in favour of affiliation to Labour, he disagreed with the intervention of William McLaine from the BSP, who said the Labour Party was the political organ of the trade unions:

> Of course, most of the Labour Party's members are working men. However, whether or not a party is really a political party of the workers does not depend solely upon a membership of workers, but also upon the men that lead it, and the

content of its actions and its political tactics. Only this latter determines whether we really have before us a political party of the proletariat. Regarded from this, the only correct point of view, the Labour Party is a thoroughly bourgeois party, because, although made up of workers, it is led by reactionaries, and the worst kind of reactionaries at that, who act quite in the spirit of the bourgeoisie. It is an organisation of the bourgeoisie, which exists to systematically dupe the workers with the aid of the British Noskes and Scheidemanns.[27]

Nevertheless, having outlined the Labour Party's class character in relation to its leaders, Lenin went on to explain that the Labour party was a "*highly original type of party, or rather, it is not at all a party in the ordinary sense of the word*", as it was made up of workers and trade unions.[28]

Lenin thought that a more correct description would be a 'bourgeois-workers party'. He drew the clear distinction between this strange hybrid Labour Party, based on the working class, and the bourgeois Liberals and Tories. Therefore, as quoted previously, he said the British communists should, where they are not standing candidates, urge "electors *to vote for the Labour candidate and against the bourgeois candidate.*"[29]

More importantly, as far as communist affiliation was concerned, the Labour Party allowed a certain internal freedom of debate and criticism, which provided opportunities to openly argue for communist policies. The British Socialist Party, for instance, already affiliated to the Labour Party, was able to conduct its own independent propaganda.

"In such circumstances", concluded Lenin, "it would be a mistake not to join this party."[30] Nevertheless, Lenin also added that even if they were expelled, it would be a victory:

If the British Communist Party starts by acting in a revolutionary manner in the Labour Party, and if the Hendersons are obliged to expel this Party, that will be a great victory for the communist and revolutionary working-class movement in Britain.[31]

In the end, when the Communist Party requested affiliation to the Labour Party, it was declined, not least because of the ultra-left way the application was framed.

By 1924, the right-wing Labour leaders had succeeded in banning all communists from individual membership, including as delegates from affiliated trade unions. The Communist Party had nevertheless established a basis within Labour's rank and file. However, this support was later squandered by the Stalinists.

213. Sylvia Pankhurst 214. Willie Gallacher

Gallacher on Lenin

Willie Gallacher, a supporter of the 'Left', attended the Second Congress and personally discussed these issues with Lenin. "I was an outstanding example of the 'Left' sectarian and as such had been referred to by Lenin in his book *Left-Wing Communism: An Infantile Disorder*", explained Gallacher:

> But here I was in the company of Lenin himself and other leading international figures, arguing and fighting on the correctness or otherwise of these views. I was hard to convince. I had such disgust at the leaders of the Labour Party and their shameless servility that I wanted to keep clear of contamination.
>
> Gradually, as the discussions went on, I began to see the weakness of my position. More and more the clear simple arguments and explanations of Lenin impressed themselves in my mind…
>
> The more I talked with Lenin and the other comrades, the more I came to see what the party of workers meant in the revolutionary struggle. It was in this, the conception of the party, that the genius of Lenin had expressed itself. A Party of revolutionary workers, with its roots in the factories and in the streets, winning the Trade Unions and the Co-operatives with the correctness of its working-class policy, a party with no other interests but the interests of the working class and the peasant and petty-bourgeois allies of the working class, such a Party, using every avenue of expression, could make an exceptionally valuable parliamentary platform for arousing the great masses of workers to energetic struggle against the capitalist enemy.

Before I left Moscow I had an interview with Lenin during which he asked me three questions.

1. "Do you admit you were wrong on the question of Parliament and affiliations to the Labour Party?"

2. "Will you join the Communist Party of Great Britain when you return?" (A telegram had arrived a couple of days before, informing us of the formation of the Party.)

3. "Will you do your best to persuade your Scottish comrades to join it?"

To each other these questions I answered "yes". Having given this pledge freely I returned to Glasgow.[32]

Throughout his interventions, Lenin rejected not only right-wing doctrinairism, but also its left-wing counterpart, both of which had the potential to cause a lot of damage. He was confident that with the development of the world revolution and the lessons that had been learned, the newly-formed communist movement would fully recover from this bout of "infantile disorder".

The debates and discussions at the Second Congress served to raise the political and theoretical level of the entire movement. It was a genuine forum and 'school' of communism, which was on a far higher political level than the conferences of the national sections. This is what established its colossal importance and authority internationally.

The twenty-one conditions

The very success of the Communist International was also accompanied by its own special problems. "The Communist International is, to a certain extent, becoming the vogue", remarked Lenin.[33] The International had become so successful, so 'fashionable', that it attracted not only the cream of the working class but also a layer of opportunists and centrists from the old organisations, especially from its old leaders, who were determined to keep a grip on a leftward-moving membership.

These people still clung to their reformist baggage, and so special measures were needed to keep such elements out of the International. The Bolsheviks wanted to build a genuine revolutionary International and not simply a rehash of the old one, as Lenin pointed out:

Aware that the Second International is beyond hope, the intermediate parties and groups of the 'Centre' are trying to lean on the Communist International, which is steadily gaining in strength.[34]

He went on to warn about the dangers of reformism:

> No Communist should forget the lessons of the Hungarian Soviet Republic. The Hungarian proletariat paid dearly for the Hungarian Communists having united with the reformists.*

> In view of all this, the Second World Congress deems it necessary to lay down absolutely precise terms for the admission of new parties, and also to set forth the obligations incurred by the parties already affiliated.[35]

The founding Congress consisted mostly of communist trends and small groupings, and had not drawn up any precise conditions for affiliation. This task now fell to the Second Congress. A list of nineteen conditions were proposed, drawn up by Lenin, to prevent an influx of unwanted centrist or reformist elements into the International. This even included a list of specifically named individuals, social-traitors, who were debarred from joining, such as Kautsky, Ramsay MacDonald and Filippo Turati, amongst others.

During the Congress two further conditions were added, making the famous 'Twenty-one Conditions' for affiliation to the Third International. The last condition stated: "Party members who reject in principle the conditions and theses laid down by the Communist International shall be expelled from the party."[36] These conditions were then voted on and adopted unanimously. Zinoviev quipped that just as a camel could not pass through the eye of a needle, so the centrists would not pass through these conditions.

The new 'Twenty-one Conditions' were accepted by the German USPD (except for a small minority), the French Socialist Party (again apart from a small number), the Socialist Party of Czechoslovakia, a minority of the Italian Socialist Party, the Norwegian, Yugoslav, Bulgarian, Austrian, Dutch and Hungarian parties, as well as others. This development was especially important in Germany, given its strategic position.

Such safeguards showed that the International was not interested in short-term gains. In fact, to maintain its principle as a 'World Party of Socialist Revolution', it was prepared in 1923 to accept the disaffiliation of the Norwegian Labour Party, though this meant the loss of its mass membership, for its failure to fully adopt the 'Twenty-one Conditions'. This was also the case with the Italian Socialist Party, where a minority split away to form the Communist Party.

---

* The topic of the Hungarian Revolution goes beyond the scope of this book. See Alan Woods' 'The Hungarian Soviet Republic of 1919: The Forgotten Revolution', *In Defence of Marxism*, 21 March 1917, available on marxist.com.

This defence of principles allowed the Communist International under Lenin to remain a genuine revolutionary International. On this basis, the Third International became a mass force in many countries.

National and colonial questions

The impact of the Russian Revolution throughout Asia and Latin America laid the groundwork for the creation of Communist Parties among the colonial peoples. The Second Comintern Congress was attended by thirty delegates from several of these colonial and semi-colonial countries, representing parties in Iran, Turkey, Indonesia (Dutch East Indies), Palestine, Mexico, India, China, Korea and elsewhere.

This was in sharp contrast to the old Socialist International, which, according to the Congress resolution, "in reality recognised the existence only of people with white skin."[37]

The success of the October Revolution meant that there was widespread recognition in these countries of the role and significance of the Soviet system. This enriched and added a new dimension to the discussions at the Congress on the important national and colonial questions.

The Congress elected a number of Commissions to consider and draft theses on different questions, which would then be referred back to the delegates for further debate and approval. The Commission's report on the national and colonial question was given by Lenin.

He expressed delight that the Commission members had reached unanimity on all the major issues involved. He then proceeded to outline the role of imperialism and the effects of the world war on the underdeveloped countries. Lenin drew out the revolutionary implications for their respective bourgeois-democratic movements and their struggle against imperialism. In the Commission's deliberations, they decided to speak *not* of the 'bourgeois-democratic' movement, but of the 'national-revolutionary' movement, so as to emphasise its revolutionary character.

Although the most immediate tasks in these countries (national liberation and the solution of the land problem) would objectively have a bourgeois-democratic character, it was evident that a rapprochement between the imperialists and the national bourgeoisie in different countries had taken place. This meant that communists should not support all bourgeois national liberation movements, but only those which were genuinely revolutionary. In fact, the main task of communists must be to combat any illusions in the treacherous national bourgeoisie.

215. Turkestani delegation at the First Congress of the Peoples of the East

This was one of the main lessons of the cowardly role of the bourgeois liberals in Russia, which had overshadowed the debates between the Bolsheviks and Mensheviks in the pre-October period.

At this point in time, the proletariat was practically non-existent in many of these underdeveloped colonial or semi-colonial countries. Nevertheless, the Communist Party should not simply subordinate itself to other classes, but must strive to assume the role of leadership of the national struggle and campaign for soviets of working people, or peasants' soviets, with the aim of establishing a Soviet republic. Lenin explained:

> The question was posed as follows: are we to consider as correct the assertion that the capitalist stage of economic development is inevitable for backward nations now on the road to emancipation and among whom a certain advance towards progress is to be seen since the war? We replied in the negative. [...] it will be mistaken to assume that the backward peoples must inevitably go through the capitalist stage of development.[38]

He continued:

> ... the Communist International should advance the proposition, with the appropriate theoretical grounding, that with the aid of the proletariat of the advanced countries, backward countries can go over to the Soviet system and,

216. Eastern Orchestra performing at the Congress

through certain stages of development, to communism, without having to pass through the capitalist stage.[39]

In the colonial revolution the Communist Party must pursue its own independent class line in arguing for soviets and the perspective of socialist revolution. This, after all, was the lesson of the Russian Revolution, which had occurred in backward, semi-feudal Russia.

In Lenin's conception, there is not a trace of a two-stage theory, where the 'democratic' stage is separated from the 'socialist' stage, as later advocated by the Stalinists. Rather, he came very close to Trotsky's idea of permanent revolution, which was already anticipated by Marx, who argued that, on the basis of international revolution, colonial and semi-colonial countries could leap over the capitalist stage. It is no accident that Trotsky's celebrated book on the permanent revolution, *Results and Prospects*, was republished in 1919 by the State Publishing House and issued in many languages by the Communist International.

The debate on the national and colonial question, which lasted two full days, was extremely wide-ranging. There was also considerable discussion about the tactics to be employed by the Communist Parties in the different anti-imperialist struggles.

The closing ceremony took place in Moscow at the Bolshoi Theatre. On the stage sat Zinoviev, the President of the Comintern, together with the entire Executive Committee. The hall was decorated with banners and packed with hundreds of members of the trade unions and the Soviets. The closing speech was given by Trotsky, presenting the *Manifesto of the World Congress*. His inspiring speech lasted a little more than an hour, was delivered without notes, and was met with stormy applause.

Many of the European delegates at the Congress, along with John Reed, then travelled to Baku, the capital of Soviet Azerbaijan, to attend the First Congress of the Peoples of the East, the first attempt by the communist movement to build support for the Asian socialist revolution. The Congress was attended by nearly 2,000 delegates and was the largest gathering the Comintern had ever organised. It opened on 1 September 1920 under the presidency of Zinoviev, who delivered the opening speech amid scenes of wild enthusiasm, which was captured in the well-known film *Reds*.

33. Limits of War Communism

To assist the war effort, the Soviet government had encouraged the establishment of special labour armies, a voluntary scheme in which able-bodied men and women were asked to perform unpaid work in addition to their regular employment. These volunteers became known as 'subbotniks' and performed these duties normally on Saturdays (the term subbotnik is derived from the Russian word for Saturday).

The first example of this voluntary labour was undertaken by workers on the Moscow railway system, but their efforts were soon followed by other workers, especially in the autumn of 1918, in an attempt to alleviate the growing fuel crisis.

Eventually, as the subbotnik idea spread, all-Russia events were organised, which involved the voluntary labour of hundreds of thousands of workers on specific days. Lenin himself, despite his heavy work schedule, personally participated in these special activities. The enthusiasm displayed for such events was witnessed by HN Brailsford when he was in Russia:

> Then, from a side street, came the sound of singing, and a procession swung into view, advancing rapidly. They carried a banner with the familiar motto, 'Workers of all lands unite', and their song was the most popular and arresting of the Red Army's marching choruses. There were old and young among them, but chiefly young, and many were women. I remembered that it was Saturday afternoon. They were Communists evidently going to a 'Saturdaying' – a half-day of voluntary physical work done without payment, to carry help where help is needed. I followed them, and presently came on a group just starting operations. They broke step, ran to their places and took off their coats without the loss of

217. A May Day subbotnik on the Kremlin grounds
– Lenin (not pictured) took part in this subbotnik

a moment. The girls even took off their shoes and stockings, and presently were carrying bricks with rapidity and method. I stood and watched them … this scene of hard work and social zeal before me. Half amused, half annoyed, a working woman remarked, as she brushed past me, "It's easily seen that you're a *bourjóee*.* You look on while others work."[1]

In early 1920, although the civil war had come to an end, the system of War Communism was still very much in place. The idea quickly developed that the Red Army should now be used to deal with the massive task of economic reconstruction.

On 15 January 1920, a decree was passed to transform the army of the Urals into the first revolutionary labour army. Similar decrees in the Caucasus and the Ukraine were issued instructing armies to assist in the labour front. Alongside the subbotniks, the army was therefore drafted in to carry out essential work in rebuilding the country, by replacing broken rail tracks, mending roads and restoring collapsed and destroyed bridges.

---

* Russian pronunciation of 'bourgeois'.

218. Subbotnik volunteers

One army unit was dispatched to assist the construction of railroads in Turkestan, while another was sent to work the Donets coal mines. Those workers not involved in military service were conscripted to the 'Front of Labour'. The stage was set for the development of the 'militarisation of labour' and labour armies began to appear everywhere.

The 'militarisation of labour' was discussed at the Ninth Party Congress at the end of March and agreed without any dissent. Lenin and Trotsky were great believers in this policy and behind them stood the authority of the Central Committee and the Politburo. Opposition, however, arose a few weeks later at the Third All-Russia Congress of Trade Unions, where a small vocal minority of Mensheviks argued against 'abhorrent militarisation' and for the 'freedom of labour'. This sounded very noble, but the workers' state was on its knees. The crisis could only be overcome by the introduction of emergency measures, one of which was the militarisation of labour.

The arguments of the Mensheviks were demagogic in the extreme, and it was left to Trotsky to answer them. The leader of the Red Army was a firm supporter of central planning as a means to restore the battered

219. Another picture of subbotnik volunteers

Russian economy. Given his abilities, at the end of March 1920 Trotsky was appointed as Commissar for Transport by the Ninth Party Congress and was made responsible for restoring the vital transport links in the economy. With this position, he was made a member of the Supreme Council of National Economy.

The 'trade union controversy'

However, by November 1920, after an armistice was signed with Poland, Trotsky had become increasingly irritated by the lacklustre role of the trade unions in the Supreme Economic Council. Earlier, at the Ninth Party Congress that took place from March to April, he had raised complaints over the lack of a national plan and insufficient guidance from the centre.

Frustrated with the lack of progress, he advanced proposals to shake up the trade unions, insisting that they must take greater responsibilities in the running of the economy. This, however, led to a violent clash, in which Trotsky was accused of destroying the independence of the trade unions and introducing 'militarisation of labour', despite the fact that this already existed. This opened up a heated dispute that became known as the 'trade union controversy'.

Some say it was a mistake for Trotsky to have raised his criticisms, but that would have meant ignoring the terrible impasse facing the Soviet Republic. Later, the Stalinists unscrupulously used the dispute to manufacture 'principled' differences between Lenin and Trotsky. This was completely false.

In reality, the dispute had little to do with the trade unions, and everything to do with the general impasse of the current economic policy of War Communism, which had held the country in a colossal straitjacket. It was this that was creating a whole series of insoluble contradictions, which Trotsky was expected to solve. Under the given conditions, it was an impossible task.

Trotsky understood that administrative methods were not enough to bring the economy out of this impasse. But that was the point. As long as the Party firmly clung to the methods of War Communism, there were no other methods that could be adopted except purely administrative ones. This is where the apparent differences centred.

Trotsky had already seen the limits of War Communism as early as February 1920, sharply thrown into prominence by the growing resistance to requisitioning and state compulsion. As a way out of the impasse, he proposed replacing the policy of forcible requisitioning with a system based on a tax-in-kind on agricultural products. But this was rejected, even by Lenin. The 'crime' later attributed to Trotsky was only this: he was guilty of being consistent, nothing more. Being compelled to carry out a policy in which he no longer believed, Trotsky concluded that if the policies of War Communism were going to work, they needed to be applied more consistently and uniformly.

But there was a problem. The trade unions had to be brought into line with the policy of strict central control. This touched a raw nerve and set off a heated controversy. This policy was vociferously opposed by Tomsky, the Bolshevik who was responsible for the trade unions. A sharp debate opened up, which began to focus all the frustrations of the period on this one issue.

The dispute became so overheated and fractious that it led to the crystallisation of five different factions, fiercely battling it out within the Party. Their arguments and counter-arguments were then carried over into the press on a daily basis, and the pages of *Pravda* were filled with the whole affair. That only served to intensify the dispute.

This violent eruption was, on the one hand, the result of the growing objective problems facing the country and, on the other, the impasse of the old policy of War Communism. Everyone's nerves were on edge. After a period of sacrifices, struggle and regimentation, people were exhausted, frustrated and at the end of their tether. These frustrations soon spilled over into this fractious dispute, in which all the accumulated tensions were expressed in a wildly exaggerated form. All the separate streams of discontent found their expression in this 'trade union controversy'.

The whole affair was exacerbated by the irresponsible actions of 'Left Communists' and the vicious intrigues of the Mensheviks, who joined in the fray, loudly demanding the 'freedom of labour'. Once again, Bukharin became the champion of the 'Lefts'.

Lenin was very alarmed at this turn of events. He believed that the debate, which centred around a caricature of a discussion, was only serving to drive the Party into a blind alley and raise the danger of a split. As a result of this, Lenin criticised both Trotsky and Bukharin. He blamed Trotsky for mixing up issues, while he attacked Bukharin's position for light-mindedly playing with 'left' sounding slogans, which only served to confuse and polarise the dispute.

They were, in effect, debating in a closed circle hemmed in by an objective situation not of their making. It was this that coloured the whole controversy and became the lightning-rod for everyone's frustrations.

Lenin saw the whole affair as an enormous waste of time and energy, generating a colossal amount of heat and very little light, when far more important things were at stake. He viewed the runaway debate as an illness that had suddenly gripped the Party: "The Party is sick", he complained. "The Party is down with the fever."[2]

Faced with an exceptionally difficult situation, Lenin correctly felt that a debate over the trade unions was an entirely avoidable and inadmissible luxury.

In reality, the whole business was leading nowhere, which only served to obscure the impasse over economic policy. Even Lenin admitted that the debate had got the better of him and he was drawn into the arguments. He said that he "allowed himself in the course of the dispute certain obviously exaggerated and therefore erroneous sallies…"[3]

Lenin therefore chose the Tenth Party Congress in March 1921 to criticise everyone involved for an irresponsible, two-month-long, so-called 'discussion' which was consuming the Party:

> I must add, for my part, that I think it was quite an impermissible luxury, and we certainly made a mistake when we allowed it, for we had failed to realise that we were pushing into the forefront a question which for objective reasons cannot be there. We allowed ourselves to indulge in this luxury, failing to realise how much

attention we distracted from the vital and threatening question before us, namely, this question of the crisis.[4]

During this polemic, many sharp words were exchanged on all sides. These remarks were later torn out of context and used by the Stalinists in a dishonest attempt to create an artificial wedge between Lenin and Trotsky. But Lenin's admiration for Trotsky during these crucial years is shown by the fact that Trotsky was often assigned the most difficult and arduous tasks, from building and leading the Red Army, to organising an economy that had been completely shattered by the civil war.

The problem we have just examined was merely a reflection that the policy of War Communism – 'Communism in a besieged fortress' – had reached its limits and was breaking down. Neither Trotsky nor anyone else could have made it work. A complete change of course was necessary. That came with the introduction of the New Economic Policy (NEP).

In the end, these 'differences' over the trade unions proved ephemeral. As soon as the NEP was introduced, they rapidly melted away. Such was the essence of the so-called 'trade union controversy'. As Trotsky wrote a few years after the dispute:

> ... in the light of subsequent experience, we can record that the discussion in no way revolved around the trade unions, or even workers' democracy: what was expressed in these disputes was a profound uneasiness in the party, caused by the excessive prolonging of the economic regime of War Communism. The entire country was in an economic vice. The discussion on the role of the trade unions and of workers' democracy covered up the search for a new economic road. The way out was found in the elimination of the requisitioning of food products and of the grain monopoly, and in the gradual liberation of state industry from the tyranny of the central economic managements. These historical decisions were taken unanimously and completely overshadowed the trade union discussion...[5]

'Order No. 1042'

A very alarming case of the economic debacle facing the country was the chaotic state of the railway system, which was at the point of collapse. These were the main arteries of the economy making it a matter of life and death for the Soviet state. Without railways, there could be no recovery. As EH Carr explains:

> In the winter of 1919-1920 the conditions of the railways had become catastrophic and the economy was threatened with a breakdown owing to complete chaos in

220. A May Day subbotnik repairing the railways

transport and Lenin telegraphed to Trotsky, then in the Urals, asking him to take charge of the question.[6]

At the Ninth Congress, on Lenin's initiative, Trotsky was asked to take charge of rebuilding the rail network. Trotsky accepted the challenge and, as always, applied himself energetically to the task at hand. He established a transport commission, which issued its famous 'Order No. 1042' on 20 May 1920, to restore the locomotives crippled during the war and civil war to working condition within four years. Trotsky's method was to personally intervene, raising the political sights of those involved, and introduce centralised direction in the repair of locomotives.

As a result, he was able to report to the All-Russian Congress of Soviets in December 1920 (by which time a plan for restoring the wagons had been added) that the original five-year plan could be fulfilled in three-and-a-half years. Under his leadership, the number of locomotives under repair fell from 60 per cent to 20 per cent. EH Carr comments: "This success at once enhanced the popularity of planning. Where Lenin and Trotsky led the way, imitators were quickly found."[7]

221. Another picture from a May Day railway subbotnik

Lenin was so impressed with Trotsky's method of centralised planning that he praised it as a model which should be generally replicated. At the Eighth All-Russian Congress of Soviets in December 1920, Lenin explained:

> You have already seen from the theses of Comrades Yemshanov and Trotsky that in this field we have a real plan worked out for a number of years. Order No. 1042 was designed for a period of five years; in five years we can restore our transport and reduce the number of broken-down locomotives.[8]

He went on:

> An extra hundred or thousand machines and locomotives are of tremendous importance to us, for it will mean that transport repairs, which Trotsky planned over a period of four and a half years and reduced to three and a half, will be reduced by another year. Reducing the economic chaos and famine by a year is of colossal importance to us.[9]

Trotsky's efforts to bring about increased coal production also drew Lenin's approval at the Congress:

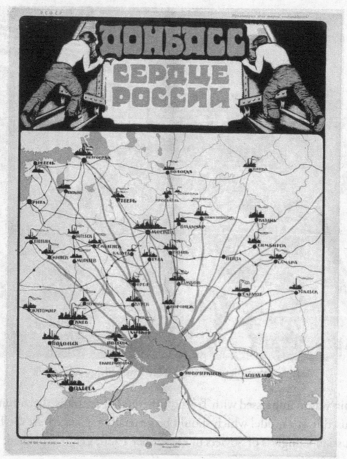

222. "The Donets Basin is the heart of Russia" – 1921 poster

Coal deliveries from the Donets Basin are being increased from 25,000,000 poods to 50,000,000 poods per month, thanks to the work of the authorised commission, which was sent there under the chairmanship of Comrade Trotsky.[10]

Brailsford noted the rising coal production in the Donetsk region at this time, which had mostly been ruined by Denikin and Makhno:

The low output estimated for 1920 has been greatly exceeded and the daily average has risen steadily, month by month. The number of miners is also growing, and here also the administration is at work on electrification and housing. Trotsky spent some time lately on the spot and started a big scheme of improvements, beginning with the food and clothing of men. While an output of only 40 million poods was estimated for 1920, the estimate made by the miners themselves for 1921 is 450 million.[11]

In continuing his report to the Soviet Congress, Lenin outlined the key plan for electrification of the economy over the next ten years. In it, he once again referred to Trotsky's successful method employed in mining and transport:

> We have an established plan of electrification, but the fulfilment of this plan is designed to cover a number of years. We must fulfil this plan at all costs, and the period of its fulfilment must be reduced. Here we must have the same thing as was the case with one of our first economic plans, the plan for the restoration of transport – Order No. 1042 – which was designed to cover a period of five years, but has now been reduced to three and a half years because we are ahead of the schedule.[12]

This success would lead Lenin to support Trotsky's demand for increased powers for Gosplan, the State Planning Committee.

The Kronstadt rebellion

By early 1921, with the end of the civil war, the strains of War Communism had become intolerable. Unrest flared up in open rebellion in some regions, and the regime was teetering on the verge of collapse. The proletariat was utterly exhausted and showed alarming signs of disintegration.

Lenin had compared the situation in Russia to a man beaten to within an inch of his life, but the beating had gone on for several years, and it was a wonder that he could still hobble about on crutches. This was a most dangerous state of affairs for the revolution. In Lenin's words:

> ... [the industrial working class] in our country, owing to the war and to the desperate poverty and ruin, has become declassed, i.e. dislodged from its class groove, and has ceased to exist as a proletariat. The proletariat is the class which is engaged in the production of material values in large-scale capitalist industry. Since large-scale capitalist industry has been destroyed, since the factories are at a standstill, the proletariat has disappeared. It has sometimes figured in statistics, but it has not been held together economically.[13]

But Lenin was a realist and was not afraid to explain or confront any difficulties, however extreme:

> No such problems have ever arisen in history before. We tried to solve this problem straight out, by a frontal attack, as it were, but we suffered defeat. Since the frontal

223. Red Army soldiers attack Kronstadt on the ice of the Gulf of Finland

attack failed, we shall make a flanking movement and also use the method of siege and undermining.[14]

The winter of 1920-21 had been horrendous. Relations with the peasantry had broken down, and the countryside was in a state of open revolt. The Kronstadt rebellion was a direct result of this. Discontent had turned to violence. In March 1921, the Kronstadt Fortress was seized by mutinous sailors, who raised a number of demands, including 'Soviets without Communists'.

Innumerable myths have been spread about Kronstadt by bourgeois apologists, reformists and anarchists, in an attempt to portray Bolshevism as the true source of the crimes of Stalinism. This view is entirely without foundation.

The first myth is to present the Kronstadt mutineers of 1921 as the same red sailors who have a special place in the history of the Russian Revolution. But that was in 1917, and much had changed between 1917 and 1921. The majority of Kronstadt sailors of 1917 were drawn from the ranks of the industrial proletariat. They were Bolsheviks, who comprised most of the garrison. Most of them later volunteered to fight in the civil war or go where they were most needed. They were dispersed to the four winds, never

224. Shelling of the Kronstadt forts

to return. As dedicated communists, the best of them became Red Army volunteers and lost their lives fighting for the revolution.

By 1921, the composition of the Kronstadt garrison had been completely transformed. It was now made up mainly of raw recruits from the Black Sea Fleet, mostly Ukrainians from peasant families who faithfully reflected the ideas, interests, and prejudices of that stratum. The names published on the list of mutineers bear witness to their Ukrainian origins. Kronstadt had ceased to be the proletarian bastion it once was.

The crisis of War Communism produced a serious and growing rift between the peasant masses, the proletariat, and its state. And these peasant sailors reflected the growing discontent of their class. The influence of anti-Bolshevik parties began to grow. SRs, Mensheviks and other elements began to get an echo, feeding anti-Bolshevik moods and creating conditions for an open rebellion against the government. The growing disillusionment and despair over the effects of War Communism first and foremost affected the peasants, but it increasingly involved a section of workers, exhausted by years of war, civil war and famine.

Kronstadt was one of many disturbances at this time, which affected Samara, Saratov, Tsaritsyn, Astrakhan, and Siberia. The largest and most dangerous peasant uprising was in Tambov, 480 kilometres south-east of

225. Lenin and Trotsky in the Kremlin, surrounded by a delegation of Red troops
who had taken part in the suppression of the Kronstadt rebellion

Moscow. However, the significance of Kronstadt was its position as a fortress
which defended Petrograd's Baltic coast. If it fell into enemy hands, red
Petrograd would be placed in extreme danger.

The rebellion took place during a period when the civil war had all but
finished. However, White troops still occupied the shores of the Black Sea
and Georgia, and there were remnants elsewhere in the country. Discontent,
especially amongst the peasantry, had reached boiling point. The workers
in the towns were hungry and strikes broke out in Petrograd over bread
shortages. This provided the chaotic background to the Kronstadt rebellion
of 1921. There was a danger that counter-revolutionary elements could try
to take advantage of the situation. And the British and French imperialists
were watching the situation closely.

On 2 March, the mutineers seized the fleet commanders and contacted key
foreign powers, who promised military and financial aid. As expected, the
international bourgeois press gave support to the mutiny, while a reactionary
émigré organisation in Finland appealed for funds, rations and support.

White émigrés were in contact with the French government and the right-wing Finnish authorities. Plans for counter-revolution were later discovered in a top-secret document called 'Memorandum on the Organisation of an Uprising in Kronstadt', written several weeks before the uprising, a copy of which is in the archives of Columbia University.

The main fear of the Bolsheviks was that Britain and France would use their naval forces to occupy the Kronstadt base, using the mutiny as a pretext. Given that whoever controlled Kronstadt controlled Petrograd, the revolt placed the Soviet state in extreme danger. If the peasant sailors had succeeded in consolidating their hold, it would have been a short step toward a reactionary bourgeois regime.

It is true that the negotiations between the Government and the garrison were badly handled by the Bolshevik negotiating delegation led by Mikhail Kalinin, who only inflamed an already tense situation. But once the mutineers had seized the most important naval base in Russia, there was no room for compromise. Within a few weeks, the ice would have melted around the Kronstadt fortress and hostile ships would have arrived from Europe. It would have begun a new Allied intervention.

Time was pressing. Therefore, the Bolsheviks, after some desultory negotiations which led nowhere, were left with no other option but to attack the fortress. Army units under the command of Tukhachevsky, joined by over 300 delegates from the Tenth Party Congress who had military experience, stormed Kronstadt and put down the revolt.

Trotsky's role

Trotsky did not play a direct role in this battle, although as Commissar for War and a member of the Government, he fully accepted the political responsibility for this action. As he later explained to the Dewey Commission:*

> For three years I directly led the Civil War. In this harsh work I was obliged to resort to drastic measures. For these I bear full responsibility before the world working class and before history. The justification of rigorous measures lay in their historical necessity and progressive character, in their correspondence with the fundamental interests of the working class. To all repressive measures dictated by the conditions of civil war, I gave their real designation, and I have given a public

---

* The Commission of Inquiry into the charges made against Trotsky in the Moscow Trials was called the Dewey Commission after its chairman John Dewey, the American philosopher. The Commission conducted its hearings over 10-17 April 1937 in Mexico, and issued the verdict that Trotsky and his son, Lev Sedov, were not guilty of the charges against them.

accounting for them before the working masses. I had nothing to hide from the people, as today I have nothing to hide from the Commission.[15]

The Kronstadt rebellion occurred as the Tenth Party Congress was taking place. Lenin explained to the delegates:

> I have not yet received the latest news from Kronstadt, but I have no doubt that this mutiny, which very quickly revealed to us the familiar figures of white guard generals, will be put down within the next few days, if not hours.[16]

Congress sessions were interrupted to allow delegates to participate in the attack on the fortress. Among those who volunteered for this dangerous enterprise were members of the Workers' Opposition, a semi-anarcho-syndicalist tendency. This fact serves to cut across another fable, which attempts to establish an amalgam between Kronstadt, anarchism, and the Workers' Opposition, when, in reality, they have absolutely nothing in common.

Victor Serge, who was won over from anarchism to Bolshevism, and remained in contact with the anarchists, wrote the following about Kronstadt:

> 'The Third Revolution!' it was called by certain anarchists whose heads were stuffed with infantile illusions. However, the country was absolutely exhausted, and production practically at a standstill; there were no reserves of any kind, not even reserves of stamina in the hearts of the masses. The working-class élite that had been moulded in the struggle against the old regime was literally decimated. The Party, swollen by the influx of power-seekers, inspired little confidence. Of the other parties, only minute nuclei existed, whose character was highly questionable. It seemed clear that these groupings could come back to life in a matter of weeks, but only by incorporating embitterness, malcontent and inflammatory elements in their thousands, no longer, as in 1917, enthusiasts for the young revolution. Soviet democracy lacked leadership, institutions and inspiration; at its back there were only masses of starving and desperate men.
>
> The popular counter-revolution translated the demand for freely-elected soviets into one for 'Soviets without Communists'. If the Bolshevik dictatorship fell, it was only a short step to chaos, and through chaos to a peasant rising, the massacre of the Communists, the return of the émigrés, and in the end, through the sheer force of events, another dictatorship, this time anti-proletarian. Dispatches from Stockholm and Tallinn testified that the émigrés had these very perspectives in mind: dispatches which, incidentally, strengthened the Bolshevik leaders' intention of subduing Kronstadt speedily and at whatever cost. We were not reasoning in the

abstract. We knew that in European Russia alone there were at least fifty centres of peasant insurrection. To the south of Moscow, in the region of Tambov, Antonov, the Right Social Revolutionary school teacher, who proclaimed the abolition of the Soviet system and the re-establishment of the Constituent Assembly, had under his command a superbly organised peasant army, numbering several tens of thousands. He had conducted negotiations with the Whites. (Tukhachevsky suppressed this Vendée around the middle of 1921.)[17]

One of the demands of the leaders of the mutineers was 'Soviets without Communists'. This was one of the rallying calls of the counter-revolutionaries. It was a call, in effect, to behead the Revolution. But the thing that gives the clearest proof of the class nature of the uprising was the demand for a free market in grain. This demand reflected the interests of the speculators and kulaks.

It is no accident that once the free market in grain was granted under the NEP, there were no more Kronstadts and no more Tambovs. The peasants were satisfied. But the NEP – although it was a necessary concession – represented a gigantic step back for the revolution.

Lenin's punishing schedule

Throughout this stormy period, Lenin kept up a punishing schedule, addressing meetings, writing articles, reviewing decrees, keeping abreast of events, chairing the Council of People's Commissars and much more besides, all of which placed intolerable strain on his physical constitution. These extreme pressures drained his energies and wore him down, resulting in severe headaches coupled with bouts of insomnia.

While Lenin spent most of his time on Party and government work, he did take some time out to relax whenever there was a chance. He would take recreational walks in the grounds of the Kremlin and would take trips with Krupskaya and his sister to the Vorobyovy Hills and the country around Moscow.

One of his favourite places to visit was a wood on the bank of the River Moskva, near Barvikha. His sister recalled:

> We would choose an out-of-the-way spot on a hill with a good view of the river and the surrounding fields, and would pass the time there till evening... Sometimes, when we were driving through a village a bunch of fair-headed peasant children would come rushing up to our car begging to be taken for a ride. Vladimir Ilyich, who was very fond of children, would ask Gill [Lenin's chauffeur] to pull up and

226. Lenin at work, 6 January 2021

the car would fill to overflowing with noisy jubilant youngsters. After driving a mile or so, we would let the children get out and they would run shouting and laughing back to their village.

This kind of recreation was a bit primitive, but it was impossible to arrange any other at the time and we always came home refreshed and satisfied and with happy memories.[18]

But such recreation was limited by the pressures of work. And these pressures increased remorselessly. On 2 February 1921, with the end of the civil war, a schedule recorded by his secretaries saw Lenin attend four separate meetings that day, which was typical.

Firstly, he presided over the Economic Commission that sat from 11 am to 2 pm, followed by the Politburo meeting from 2 pm to 4 pm, with an agenda which usually contained between twenty and forty different items. Then, in the middle of the meeting at 3 pm, Lenin was handed a telephone message about the precarious situation in Petrograd as regards to food shortages. This was followed by an interval before the evening session of the Central Committee that began at 6 pm, called to discuss the reorganisation of the Commissariat of Education.

227. Lenin with his family, 1920
Seated (left to right): Lenin, Krupskaya, Anna Ulyanova
Standing: Maria Ulyanova, Dmitry Ulyanov, Georgy Lozgachev

But in the 'interval', Lenin would use the time to write or dictate notes to various departments, during which he again was handed an urgent note to telephone Sokolov, from the Siberian Revolutionary Committee, that he arranged to make when he became free between 9 pm and 10 pm.

Numerous letters were written by Lenin each day on a host of different questions. During the course of that single day, 2 February, he wrote, read, made notes on or signed no less than forty documents, not counting the papers discussed at meetings over which he presided. Added to this, Lenin also chaired sessions of the government, which usually took place in the evenings and which supervised the affairs of state. The burden of work on Lenin's shoulders was truly immense.

Such was the weight of the business, Lenin complained about the procedure where every item raised on the Council of People's Commissars was then brought to the attention of the Politburo, which simply duplicated matters unnecessarily. "I, too, am greatly to blame for this, for to a large extent contact between the Council of People's Commissars and the Political Bureau was maintained through me", explained Lenin to the Eleventh Party Congress.[19] "But we must put a stop to the habit of bringing every petty matter before the Central Committee..."[20]

This growing workload, with its various duplications, certainly helped to undermine Lenin's increasingly poor health. He was forced to deal with a host of questions, ranging from issues of world politics to a mass of trivial, routine, daily matters. "Clever saboteurs are deliberately luring us into this paper swamp", he would complain.[21]

The number of reports, documents and minutes reaching the Central Committee from local Party organisations totalled 470 in May 1919. By the summer of 1920, they averaged 4,000 a month.[22]

Lenin's writings at this time were full of such concerns. He was busy chasing up all kinds of things. "In essence, I have not received an exhaustive reply to a single one of the five tasks which I laid down", he wrote to Dmitry Kursky, the Commissar of Justice, on 17 January 1922.[23] "Please inform me of further developments [in engineering] in writing through Comrade Gorbunov, Office Manager of the CPC (Council of People's Commissars). In the event of any obstacles arising, inform me immediately through the same channel", wrote Lenin to Bogdanov, with copies to five Commissars and the Soviet Central Executive.[24] These instructions to different individuals could be multiplied on a daily basis.

Lenin, although burdened with stress, was nevertheless very concerned about the health of those around him. He badgered Tsiurupa: "You look ill. Without loss of time, take two months' holiday. If you do not promise this definitely, I shall complain to the Central Committee."[25]

Again, he wrote a note to the superintendent of the All-Russian Central Executive Committee Houses:

> Please be sure to make available a room in the 1st House of Soviets to Comrade Cecilia Samoilovna Bobrovskaya, whom I knew very well as an old Party worker. She is now living in absolutely intolerable conditions, and the doctors have ordered her to be transferred at once to one of the Houses of Soviets.
>
> Inform my secretariat of execution.
>
> [Signed] Lenin, Chairman, Council of People's Commissars
>
> PS: I have known Bobrovskaya since the epoch *before* 1905, and know that she is capable of living in great hardships and be reticent about it exclusively. That is why she needs urgent help.[26]

Lenin had no time for time-wasters or ditherers. Time is precious, he would say, not only his own, but that of others too. With regard to the running of all meetings, Lenin was a strict chairman and was eager to promote greater

228. Vladimir Mayakovsky   229. Alexander Pushkin

efficiency in the work of government, as elsewhere. He even introduced a rule that if anyone was ten minutes late for a session, they should pay a fine. He frowned on unnecessary, long-winded speeches, which simply wasted time. For Lenin, there was a desperate need for greater order and efficiency in all things, starting at the top. He therefore wrote in early April 1919 to Kursky proposing the introduction of timings into all procedures:

1. For those making reports – *10* minutes

2. For speakers, the first time *5* minutes, the second time *3* minutes.

3. To speak not more than twice.

4. On a point of order, 1 for and 1 against, each for one minute.

5. Exceptions by *special* rulings of the CPC.[27]

Sometimes it was difficult for speakers to keep to the allocated time and they would request an extension for 'the order of the agenda'. Lenin tended to oppose such extensions unless they were vital, replying with his usual sense of humour, that such 'order' requests would only lead to greater 'disorder'.[28]

Nevertheless, Lenin did, at times, clutch his head at the incessant meetings and commissions that were taking place. On one occasion, he wrote to Tsiurupa about the workings of government, urging him "to fight the outrageous abundance of commissions [...] which are *killing all of us*."[29]

There was one funny episode when Lenin visited a group of students and chatted about literature. He asked them to name their favourite poet, to which they replied as one: "Mayakovsky". He laughed and said he preferred

Pushkin. Lenin was not an admirer of Mayakovsky, but he was very taken with one of his poems that was published in *Izvestia*, called 'Incessant Meeting Sitters', which poked fun at the communists' obsession with meetings. It ends with:

> Can't sleep for suspense.
> I meet the dawn with frenzied senses.
> 'Oh for just
> one
> more conference
> regarding the eradication of all
> conferences!'

The sentiments of this poem certainly struck a chord with Lenin.[30]

34. New Economic Policy and its Implications

With the rebellion at Kronstadt now over, Lenin's attention turned once again to repairing relations with the peasantry and resuscitating the economy. While he regarded the rebellion as an 'episode', he was keen to draw the lessons from the event. "Our position in February and March was grave", Lenin wrote to Zetkin and Paul Levi in April. "This is a peasant country, with a peasant economy – the vast majority of the population. They vacillate, they are ruined and are disgruntled."[1]

He saw that the troubles expressed the breakdown in relations between the proletariat and peasantry due to the strains of War Communism. This event signalled that an urgent change of policy was required, along with the introduction of concessions to the peasants to avert a complete rupture.

As a result, the policy originally put forward by Trotsky a year earlier, and rejected, was now adopted. Requisitioning was to be scrapped in favour of a tax on the food produced by the peasants, allowing them to dispose of any surplus on the open market as they saw fit. This would then give the peasants an incentive to produce more. This policy – called the New Economic Policy (NEP) – was outlined in Lenin's pamphlet, *The Tax in Kind*, which he championed at the Tenth Party Congress in March 1921.

In his notes for his speech at the Congress, Lenin wrote a heading "The lesson of 'Kronstadt'". He gave two replies: "in politics: more unity (and discipline) within the Party, more struggle against the Mensheviks and Socialist-Revolutionaries"; and "in the economy: to *satisfy* the *middle* peasantry as fully as possible."[2] These were the prime tasks of the Tenth Congress. On this occasion, Lenin outlined the difficulties that the revolution still faced:

> In such a country, the socialist revolution can triumph only on two conditions. First, if it is given timely support by a socialist revolution in one or several advanced countries. As you know, we have done very much indeed in comparison with the past to bring about this condition, but far from enough to make it a reality.
>
> The second condition is agreement between the proletariat, which is exercising its dictatorship, that is, holds state power, and the majority of the peasant population.[3]

These two pillars of the international revolution and the relationship with the peasantry were themes that were constantly stressed by Lenin, as the bedrock of the isolated revolution. The fracture of relations between town and country had to be immediately repaired, or the revolution would be in danger of breaking up on class lines. He explained:

> We know that so long as there is no revolution in other countries, only agreement with the peasantry can save the socialist revolution in Russia. And that is how it must be stated, frankly, at all meetings and in the entire press. [...]
>
> The state of affairs that has prevailed so far cannot be continued any longer.[4]

In his usual honest fashion, Lenin admitted things were taken to extremes, especially in the policies of War Communism:

> In this respect, we are very much to blame for having gone too far; we overdid the nationalisation of industry and trade, clamping down on local exchange of commodities. Was that a mistake? It certainly was.[5]

"The 'rope' can be given *more* slack, *without allowing any break* in it; it can be 'slackened', 'eased out'", noted Lenin.[6] Trotsky writes:

> Lenin explained the necessity of restoring the market by the existence in the country of millions of isolated peasant enterprises, unaccustomed to defining their economic relations with the outside world except through trade. Trade circulation would establish a 'connection', as it was called, between the peasant and the nationalised industries.[7]

This "connection" would enable the nationalised industries to supply the rural areas with the goods they needed at prices that would eradicate the need to carry out the forcible requisition of grain to feed the towns.

In hindsight, it would be true to say that the government hesitated too long before ending the period of War Communism and implementing this new policy. But this delay was based on the expectation of the rapid spread of revolution to key European countries, such as Germany. Now, with the increase of peasant uprisings, together with the rebellion in Kronstadt, there could be no further delay; it was time to act. This meant giving significant concessions to the middle peasants, in particular the granting of a free market in grain. Lenin explained:

> Basically the situation is this: we must satisfy the middle peasantry economically and go over to free exchange; otherwise it will be impossible – economically impossible – in view of the delay in the world revolution, to preserve the rule of the proletariat in Russia. We must clearly realise this and not be afraid to say it.[8]

The adoption of the NEP was the only possible road under the circumstances. In appeasing the interests of the middle peasants it was a step backwards for the revolution. However, it was only by allowing them to dispose of agricultural surpluses on the open market that relations could be re-established in the countryside, and the peasants pacified. From their profits, it was believed that the peasants would be able to earn money to buy manufactured goods from the cities. This growth in trade would then lead to industrial expansion.

Although the NEP was a step in the direction of capitalism, there was no denying that it meant granting the revolution a new, temporary lease of life. As long as the state controlled heavy industry, transport, foreign and wholesale trade, it had little to fear from such a development.

This was not a return to capitalism, as some ultra-lefts argued, but simply a means of stimulating the peasant economy while retaining the 'commanding heights' of the economy in the hands of the state. As Lenin honestly explained: "the New Economic Policy is, under Soviet power, a form of capitalism that is deliberately permitted and restricted by the working class."[9]

Lenin was not unaware of the dangers inherent in the NEP. Market relations would lead to increased class differentiation and create a sizable capitalist private sector – and with it, the growth in power and influence of the kulaks and an emerging class of speculators, the NEPmen. However, it was a price they were prepared to pay for an 'economic breathing space' before the success of the socialist revolution in Europe, which was regarded as imminent.

Lenin believed that it was vital to hold these negative features in check, given that the workers' state had control over the dominant sectors of the

230. Food distribution to children from railway carriages in Samara, 1921

economy, state banking and the monopoly over foreign trade. Certainly, it was not the best position to be in, but again, the overriding benefit was that it provided some valuable relief in those circumstances.

Povolzhye famine

1921 certainly had its fair share of problems. Prior to the NEP and the improvement in agricultural production, grain production suffered a collapse between 1920-21. The dislocation of the civil war, combined with a series of natural disasters, had resulted in a widespread famine in the spring of 1921, known as the Povolzhye famine. Millions lost their lives during this period. In some areas, there was a total crop failure, especially in those areas where the armies of Denikin and Wrangel were active. Approximately one-quarter of all grain and cereal crops perished in the ground before harvesting. This was particularly the case in Crimea, northern Caucasus and southern Ukraine. As a result, famine swept the Volga and Ural River regions.

According to the All-Russian Congress of Soviets in December 1921, the number of those in need was estimated at 22 million, but Kalinin thought that this figure was an underestimate and there was a further 5 million on top of this.

231. A temporary camp where farmers with their families and livestock wait on the banks of the Volga for transport away from the famine areas

This was a horrendous time in the famine-stricken areas, where men, women and children abandoned their villages and were reduced to eating weeds, bark, acorns or the flesh of rotting animals. Such was the desperation that the dried bones of dead animals were dug up and ground down to make flour, producing a foul smelling and tasting 'bread'. Others were reduced to living off a diet of clay and leather scrapings.

People were reduced to such levels of inhuman depravity in order to survive, that reports of cannibalism emerged in a number of areas. Moreover, about a quarter of a million people are believed to have trekked out of the stricken regions to Siberia, a journey taking weeks or months.

These unspeakable conditions were followed in tandem by widespread epidemics of typhus, typhoid fever, smallpox, influenza, dysentery, cholera, and even bubonic plague, which killed swathes of people.

To help relieve this truly horrific situation, government-organised evacuations took children out of the famine-stricken areas, while aid was raised elsewhere and dispatched to the regions most in need.

Bourgeois historians blame the Bolsheviks for this calamity, but in reality the blame lies with the imperialist blockade and intervention. Had the foreign armies not intervened, the White armies could have been swiftly dealt with

232. Two children's coffins being taken to cemetery in the Volga

and the rich resources of Russia could have been used to develop the economy and to improve living conditions. Instead, the Soviet Republic was forced to defend itself and focus on defeating the ruinous counter-revolutionary armies and their imperialist backers.

The situation became so desperate that the Soviet government appealed for international aid to alleviate the famine. Lenin and Maxim Gorky issued an open letter to "all honest European and American people" to "give bread and medicine". In response, relief was forthcoming from a number of countries and organisations, including the United States, through its American Relief Administration, which concluded an official agreement with the Russian government.

Communist and trade union organisations everywhere helped to raise aid for Russia through the International Workers' Aid. This organisation, under its chairperson Clara Zetkin, was active in collecting money, provisions and medical supplies, as well as providing care for malnourished children.

In contrast, the reactionary London *Daily Express* first denied the severity of the famine in Russia, then argued that the money raised for famine relief would be better spent in Britain, a fact ignored by bourgeois historians. Not surprisingly, the *Express* also supported military intervention to overthrow Bolshevism.

233. Distribution of clothes at a camp for starving people

Over a period, the introduction of the NEP certainly helped to improve matters and restore relations with the countryside. The peasants were satisfied with these concessions and there were no more peasant risings. In December 1921, the All-Russian Congress of Soviets announced the start of "the agricultural campaign of 1922", in which "the whole party organisation from top to bottom" was called upon to play its part.[10] This campaign, together with the NEP measures to stimulate agricultural production, meant that the harvest in 1922 was very successful compared to the past. This was a great relief and showed that things were moving in the right direction.

However, there were other complications. As agricultural prices fell and as more foodstuffs came onto the market, industrial prices actually rose. This was due to increased demand and the scarcity of industrial products, which in turn created the danger of a 'scissors' effect of diverging prices of agricultural and industrial products.

With the high price of industrial goods, many of the items were out of reach and resulted in a further disruption between town and country. This, in turn, added to the abysmal state of industry, which was increasingly starved of credits and materials. As a result, industrial output lagged far behind other sectors. The railway system was still suffering from considerable dislocation. As a consequence, industrial stocks were completely exhausted, which forced factories to shut down production. This disorganisation resulted in unemployment remaining high.

By the time the Tenth Congress convened, industrial output was less than a fifth of pre-war levels. The coal industry produced only a tenth of pre-war output, while the iron industries only reached one-fourteenth of pre-war figures. Only an economic revival that included industry could alleviate this desperate state of affairs.

This problem provoked a heated debate within the Party over the merits of a coordinated national plan, to balance the growth in different sectors of the economy. Trotsky, in particular, championed this idea and the need to strengthen the State Planning Commission (Gosplan), but found little support at that time in the Politburo.

'Workers' Opposition'

Throughout these testing times, opposition currents arose within the Party. The main one was the Workers' Opposition group founded in 1919, which was led by Shlyapnikov, Sergei Medvedev, Kollontai and Lutovinov, and had a certain basis in the trade unions. Another opposition grouping was the Democratic Centralism group, led by Valerian Osinsky, Bubnov and Sapronov, which opposed what it called 'bureaucratic centralism' and warned of government policies creating a 'bureaucratic dictatorship'.

Of the two groups, the Workers' Opposition was the more prominent. It had emerged in opposition to many of the harsh policies associated with War Communism. But these measures were born of necessity, nothing more, to guarantee the survival of the workers' state. To abandon them prematurely, as suggested by the Opposition, would have placed the whole revolution in jeopardy.

As always, the 'Lefts' lacked a sense of reality or proportion and failed to understand what was possible and what was not possible. Nevertheless, they were free to express their views. In March 1921, on the eve of the Tenth Congress, they published a platform, written by Kollontai, that was issued by the Party leadership in *Pravda*, so as to receive the widest circulation, as well as being printed as a separate pamphlet in 250,000 copies.*

The Opposition proposed that the national economy be run by an All-Russia Congress of Producers organised into industrial trade unions. Furthermore, all economic bodies should be elected by the trade unions.

---

* An English translation of Kollontai's pamphlet was published in London in 1921, under the title *The Workers' Opposition in Russia*.

This sounded very radical – the only problem was that under conditions of an economic collapse, these ideas were utopian and bore no relation to the actual state of affairs on the ground. The 'producers' – that is, the working class – were in a state of atomisation. Rather than 'producers' control' and decentralisation, centralised direction was needed to pull the economy out of its dire situation. In reality, the Workers' Opposition reflected the emergence of an anarcho-syndicalist tendency within the Party.

Nevertheless, the Workers' Opposition had tapped into those layers within the Party who had grown weary of the impositions of War Communism and were increasingly frustrated. This allowed the Opposition to gain sizable support.

For example, in the Moscow Party Conference in November 1920, it won the support of a significant 124 delegates out of 278. Again, in the Communist group meeting of the Second All-Russian Congress of Miners in early 1921, the Opposition gained 30 per cent of the vote. It dominated the Party in Samara and had considerable support in the Ukraine and among the metalworkers' organisation.

However, by the time of the Tenth Party Congress, when the NEP was adopted, the Opposition's support had dropped substantially. It only managed to gain around fifty delegates out of 694.

Precisely because of the growing atomisation of the proletariat at this time, Lenin warned of the dangers of petty-bourgeois influences among the workers, that would also be reflected within the Party. At this time, he explained that the danger of counter-revolution was assuming an anarchist, petty-bourgeois form, which posed "a far greater danger than all the Denikins, Kolchaks and Yudeniches put together. It would be fatal to be deluded on this score!"[11]

The problem was that as factories closed down and workers were compelled to flee to the countryside to avoid starvation, the proletariat had not simply become weak, but 'declassed'. The workers who abandoned the factories had, in effect, ceased to be proletarians.

This atomisation meant that the social weight of the working class had become notably weaker, while that of the petty bourgeoisie increased enormously. The decline of industry and the productivity of labour was, according to Lenin, "the economic source of the proletariat's declassing and the inevitable rise of petty-bourgeois, anarchist trends."[12]

With the bourgeois parties banned and the Mensheviks and SRs marginalised, Soviet power rested upon a single party. In such a situation, the pressures of alien class forces were beginning to find their expression *within*

the Bolshevik Party. Lenin believed that the groups, such as the Workers'
Opposition and Democratic Centralism, were a manifestation of these
outside pressures. He also regarded this Leftist deviation as part of a wider
problem of ultra-leftism within the ranks of the Communist International:

> The deviation we are discussing is identical with the anarchist deviation of the
> German Communist Workers' Party, the fight against which was clearly revealed
> at the last Congress of the Communist International.[13]

He feared that under these grave conditions, the danger of a split in the
Communist Party along class lines was entirely possible and warned the ranks
of the Party:

> We are not children, we have gone through some hard times, we have seen splits
> and have survived them; we know what a trial they are and are not afraid of giving
> the danger its proper name.[14]

Such a split – if it came about – would, in all probability, lead to the collapse
of the Soviet regime and the victory of counter-revolution.

He believed that in normal times, the Party had nothing to fear from
syndicalist or semi-anarchist deviations, which could be corrected over time.
However, at this time, the Soviet Republic was facing an *existential* crisis.
As the Soviet state did not exist in a vacuum, under such conditions the
existence of these opposition groupings became a transmission belt for alien
class pressures.

At this time, Lenin even pondered the dangers of a Thermidorian reaction
in Russia, as happened to the French Revolution. He wrote in his notes for
the Tenth Party Conference in 1921: "Thermidor?* Logically one has to say:
it's possible, isn't it? Will it arrive? We will see…"[15]

---

* Here Lenin is using the term 'Thermidor' in the sense of a possible victory of the counter-
revolution. It is derived from an analogy with the French Revolution of 1789-94.

According to the new French revolutionary calendar with its different months and
names, 9 Thermidor Year II was 27 July 1794, when the revolutionary dictatorship of
Robespierre's Committee of Public Safety was overthrown by a more conservative group in
the Convention (constituent assembly), which then instigated a White Terror against the
radical sans-culottes.

After having passed the Constitution of the Year III (1795), which overturned many of the
most democratic elements of the previous Constitution (1973), the Convention dissolved
itself in favour of a new government, calling itself the Directory.

This in turn was supplanted by the military dictatorship of Napoleon Bonaparte, who
made himself Emperor. Nevertheless, his regime based itself on the new bourgeois property
relations.

All these dangers, as Lenin stressed, were due to the isolation of the socialist revolution in a chronically backward peasant country, with a low cultural level, surrounded by hostile imperialist powers. Even with the end of the civil war, as one problem was solved, another problem emerged. The demobilisation of the Red Army added to the general instability. It led to the release of hundreds of thousands of former peasant soldiers "who have nothing to do, whose only accustomed occupation is war and who breed banditry", warned Lenin.[16]

This was extremely dangerous, but the Party still allowed itself for several months to "wallow in the luxury of studying shades of opinion", explained Lenin, a reference to the 'trade union controversy'.[17] He regarded this as completely unacceptable under the circumstances.

After Kronstadt and the peasant mutinies, Lenin believed action was needed to halt the situation from deteriorating further. As a result, in an unprecedented move, he proposed a resolution to the Tenth Party Congress, 'On Party Unity', which ordered the immediate dissolution of all factions based on a platform within the Party.

This proposed ban on factions did not arise from any 'theory' of Bolshevism, but was simply a defensive measure to protect the Soviet Republic at this time of acute crisis. Prior to the prohibition, the Party had existed for two decades without such a ban. It was in these years that Bolshevism was trained and educated. The measure proposed was regarded as a temporary and exceptional one until the danger had passed and the situation had stabilised.

Groups were allowed to operate within the Party as temporary tendencies that naturally arise in the process of Party life, but not as 'organised factions' based on a platform. Non-observance of this ban, according to the resolution, could ultimately lead to expulsion from the Party, although this was more intended as a warning than a serious intention. It would be interpreted fairly under Lenin's leadership.

It should also be noted that in Point 7 of the resolution on factions, the final paragraph about the threat of expulsion from the Party came with all kinds of qualifications, involving the control commission and "a two-thirds majority", and warned against any hasty action.[18] This, according to EH Carr, was "evidence of the reluctance with which the congress adopted this

---

Despite the limitations of historical analogies, the shift towards Stalinism and the degeneration of the revolution followed a similar pattern. The year of Lenin's death in 1924 marked the beginning of the Soviet Thermidor, which would end with the proletarian Bonapartist regime of Stalin. All elements of workers' democracy were eliminated, but the Stalinist regime retained the nationalised planned economy.

minatory measure."[19] In fact, the resolution added that "place should be found in special publications, miscellanies, etc. for the most detailed exchange of opinions among members of the Party on all the questions concerned."[20]

Lenin treated the opposition groups, which operated as factions, as mistaken comrades and certainly not as enemies. The latter approach was to become the classic feature of Stalinism. The ban was not introduced to bring about a monolithic party or to strangle Party life. It was left to Stalin, at a later date, to carry out what amounted to a counter-revolution that completely destroyed Lenin's party and transformed it into something entirely different, alien – a monstrous caricature of Bolshevism.

Syndicalism and anarchism

The Congress went on to adopt Lenin's draft resolution, which characterised the petty-bourgeois views of the Workers' Opposition and the Democratic Centralism group, as representing a syndicalist and anarchist deviation within the Party. Under the circumstances, the propagation of such views was now regarded as incompatible with Party membership, although little was done to rigidly enforce this.

Lenin understood that it was not possible, or desirable, to eliminate all opposition views simply by passing a resolution. In fact, at the same Congress, two members of the Workers' Opposition were elected to the Central Committee, the Party's highest body, with Lenin's full support. Lenin, as always, was prepared to show flexibility in relation to organisational matters. He said:

> I, for one, have publicly urged that it would be desirable to have representatives of the Workers' Opposition and Democratic Centralism groups on the Central Committee.[21]

This recognition of the need to build bridges, to show patience and to forge maximum unity in the Party, was in marked contrast to the future regime of Stalinism, where all oppositionists were crushed. EH Carr commented that in the Bolshevik Party there was "a freedom and publicity of discussion rarely practised by any party on vital issues of public policy."[22] Furthermore, he explained:

> Beyond question Lenin desired in principle, and even strove in practice, to initiate the rank and file of the Party, and subsequently of the proletariat, into active participation in the affairs of the Party and of the nation.[23]

Although factions were formally banned, Lenin did not intend to behave in a heavy handed manner against all opposition. Far from it. His intention was not to crush dissent, but to manage it. In fact, there was wide freedom of criticism within the Party, even in public. After all, the manifesto of the Workers' Opposition had been widely published in *Pravda* for everyone to read. In the run-up to the Congress, Lenin explained:

> It is, of course, quite permissible (specially before a congress) for various groups to form blocs (and also to go vote chasing). But this should be done within the framework of communism (and not syndicalism) and in such a way as to avoid being ridiculous.[24]

On the final day of the Tenth Congress, Lenin reassured delegates that political opposition was certainly tolerated within the Bolshevik Party. Given the deep democratic traditions of the Party, this was taken for granted. As a result, he moved a motion that the Congress should reject an amendment from Ryazanov, who wanted to ban the election of delegates to congresses on the basis of political platforms:

> We cannot deprive the Party and the members of the Central Committee of the right to appeal to the Party in the event of disagreement on fundamental issues. *I cannot imagine how we can do such a thing!*[25]

He continued:

> Supposing we are faced with a question like, say, the conclusion of the Brest peace? Can you guarantee that no such question will arise? No, you cannot. In the circumstances, the elections may have to be based on platforms. (*Ryazanov:* "On one question?") Certainly. But your resolution says: No elections according to platforms. I do not think we have the power to prohibit this. If we are united by our resolution on unity and, of course, the development of the revolution, there will be no repetition of elections according to platforms. The lesson we have learned at this Congress will not be forgotten. *But if the circumstances should give rise to fundamental disagreements, can we prohibit them from being brought before the judgement of the whole Party? No, we cannot! This is an excessive desire, which is impracticable, and I move that we reject it.*[26]

This shows Lenin's tolerance and flexibility. Even at the time of the ban's implementation, as the above shows, he fought against those who interpreted it as ending minority or tendency rights within the Party. Groupings and political blocs were allowed to operate after the Tenth Congress. This was also the case with the 'banned' Workers' Opposition, with Kollontai speaking as the leader of a left-wing minority at the 1922 Congress. Shlyapnikov also continued his opposition activities. Several leaders of the Workers' Opposition even appealed to the Communist International in 1922, a year after the ban, under the 'Letter of the Twenty-two', outlining grievances about how they were being handled.

Bolshevik traditions

The idea that Bolshevism did not tolerate factions is a complete myth. Invented by the Stalinists, it goes against the whole history of Bolshevism. From its very origins, Bolshevism was a struggle of factions and tendencies, as can be seen in the many disputes over the years. As we have seen, Lenin was not always in a majority in these disputes.

The idea that there could be no ideological debate or conflict with the emergence of groupings to defend them within the party was unthinkable. Again, the proposed ban on factions was a temporary measure taken in response to an emergency situation.

During the civil war, those who joined the Communist Party knew that they could expect nothing but hard sacrifice and perhaps lose their lives battling with the counter-revolution. There was, therefore, a kind of natural selection at work, which was a sufficient safeguard against corruption. But after the civil war had ended, and the Party had consolidated itself in power, the situation changed radically. A new breed of opportunists and careerists flocked to join the Party.

With the introduction of the NEP, the Party increasingly came under the pressure of alien classes: the speculators and kulaks were pushing their own agenda. As we have seen, there was a serious risk that, under certain circumstances, the Party could split along class lines. Lenin was well aware of that danger and was determined to take all the necessary steps to prevent it from happening. It is in that light that we must see the ban on factions.

It was, without doubt, a dangerous move. But the danger arose not from the doctrine or the tactics, but from the material weakness of the proletarian dictatorship and the problems that arose from the isolation of the revolution, in conditions of extreme economic and cultural backwardness. The survival of the Soviet Republic ultimately depended on the victory of the proletarian revolution in the more advanced countries of Europe – especially Germany.

In the meantime, the main thing was to hold onto power, and that depended above all on the Bolshevik Party. In that situation, preventing a dangerous split became an urgent task. The task of the leadership was to try to soften internal disputes and reduce any conflicts to a minimum, as well as reducing the period of factional debate. For this, Lenin's role was an absolutely decisive factor. This was to be fatally undermined after his death.

A very negative role was played by Zinoviev in this. Zinoviev had undoubted talents, especially as a public speaker. He had been at Lenin's side for several years before the revolution, and he saw himself as Lenin's closest colleague and disciple. But politically, he was very shallow, and he was never a theoretician, a fact to which his few surviving writings bear eloquent witness.

Far from enriching him, closeness to Lenin robbed him of any capacity for individual thought or originality. In left-wing exile circles, he had been regarded as something of a joke. Whenever he entered a room, they would whisper: "here comes Lenin's shadow."

The year 1917 had cruelly exposed both his political weakness and personal cowardice. As we have seen, together with Kamenev, who became his inseparable companion and, eventually, his fellow victim, he not only opposed the October Revolution, but actually published the plans for the insurrection – a crime for which Lenin angrily denounced him as a strike-breaker and demanded his expulsion from the Party.

Nevertheless, Zinoviev was accepted back into the ranks (as was Kamenev), and held positions of responsibility, including president of the Communist International, where, once again, his weak side was glaringly revealed. His character was marked by egotism, boundless ambition, and thirst for personal prestige. To compensate for his inability to persuade with political arguments, he was strongly inclined to resort to administrative methods to resolve differences.

Politically weak, he was not averse to utilising unscrupulous methods and underhand intrigues in the International to bolster his own position. He secretly backed a bureaucratic manoeuvre to remove the leadership of the German Communist Party and handed it over to the ultra-left faction, which led it on an adventurist course. That had the most disastrous results.

Lenin did not approve of anything that smelled of bureaucratic arbitrariness. He sternly warned both Bukharin and Zinoviev against their intrigues, saying that if they simply imposed 'loyal' people in positions, they would end up with obedient fools. As long as Lenin lived, Zinoviev had to constantly look nervously over his shoulder. But Lenin's death removed all constraints.

He proclaimed these bureaucratic methods in the name of 'Bolshevisation', but in fact, they had nothing in common with the traditions of Lenin. These alien methods were used against Trotsky and the 1923 Opposition and they prepared the ground for the later degeneration into the openly gangster methods of Stalinism.

Under Lenin's leadership, every care was taken to preserve the democratic rights within the Party. Tendencies and groupings would inevitably emerge, as was the case with the Workers' Truth and the Workers' Group, who published their own manifestos prior to the Party Congress in 1923. In late 1922, Lenin himself would form a 'bloc' with Trotsky over the monopoly of foreign trade and the national question, as well as the fight against bureaucracy, as we will see. In late 1923, the Left Opposition was created by Trotsky and other leaders, followed by the United Opposition of 1926-27. At the time, these were largely regarded as a legitimate means of carrying out a political struggle for influence within the Party.

With the death of Lenin in early 1924, these rights were gradually stripped away. By 1927, with the expulsion of the Left Opposition and with the capitulation of the Right Opposition of Bukharin at the end of 1929, they were effectively liquidated by the Stalinist apparatus. Trotsky wrote in hindsight:

> Not until the Tenth Party Congress, held under conditions of blockade and famine, growing peasant unrest, and the first stages of the NEP – which had unleashed petty-bourgeois tendencies – was consideration given to the possibility of resorting to such an exceptional measure as the banning of factions.
>
> It is possible to regard the decision of the Tenth Congress as a grave necessity. But in light of later events, one thing is absolutely clear: the banning of factions brought the heroic history of Bolshevism to an end and made way for its bureaucratic degeneration.[27]

The ban on factions at the Tenth Party Congress became permanent under Stalin and was used as a weapon of the Party bureaucracy to silence any opposition. Under this regime, the inner life of the Party was viewed exclusively from the point of view of bureaucratic convenience. Democratic centralism gave way to bureaucratic centralism. All opposition was banned and Oppositionists were expelled, as the Party was turned into a monolith, where dissent was completely crushed. The same methods were then applied to the young sections of the Communist International, all of which eventually suffered the same bureaucratic degeneration.

Lenin's personal authority had been firmly established through decades of impeccable revolutionary work and transparent honesty. That priceless conquest was systematically eroded and undermined under the tutelage of Zinoviev, then Stalin. In place of honesty and dedication to principles, the meanest motivation had become the norm: petty jealousy, ambition for position and rank. This was the way to obtain certain material privileges. Initially, these privileges were small things, which in conditions of great scarcity assumed a considerable importance.

At a later date, these privileges grew to the far greater rewards of a ruling clique: chauffeur-driven cars, servants, luxurious apartments in Moscow and Leningrad and country houses (*dachas*). The irresistible rise of the Stalinist bureaucracy had a material base. But this process was, as yet, only at a very incipient stage.

Stalin had been elected general secretary of the Party at the plenary meeting of the Central Committee immediately after the Eleventh Party Congress at the end of March 1922. At that time, this was still regarded as purely an administrative post. As Elizaveta Drabkina wrote in her memoirs: "It is one of a number of such events to which no one ascribed any special significance, and even in Party circles no one paid any attention to it."[28]

The work of a general secretary had been done by Sverdlov, although the post did not formally exist at that time. He was an honest man, a dedicated Bolshevik and a brilliant organiser. His death in 1919 was a colossal blow to the Party. In his place, a collegium of three people was appointed to carry out the work. Significantly, Stalin was not included.

It was Zinoviev and his allies who pressed for Stalin's candidature as general secretary at the Eleventh Congress, not without a hidden thought of a struggle against Trotsky. In fact, it was Kamenev, as chairman, who proposed Stalin at the Central Committee. Lenin had nothing to do with it and was presented with a *fait accompli*. While he valued Stalin's firmness and stubbornness in certain administrative matters, he was very uneasy about Stalin's appointment as general secretary. When he found out about it, he uttered the words: "This cook will prepare only peppery dishes."[29] However, given the purely administrative nature of the post, Lenin did not carry this objection to the point of suggesting someone else and yielded on his point. "We will try it and see", he said.[30]

Stalin was no Sverdlov. Within less than a year, in early 1923, Lenin's view had hardened and he was calling for Stalin's removal as general secretary.

35. The Impact of World Events

The Third Congress of the Communist International took place from 22 June to 12 July 1921. The Congress was especially important, as it was clear by now that the world revolution had been delayed, with the revolutionary wave of 1917-21 coming to an end.

The objective situation had changed and produced a temporary stabilisation. Therefore the main task of the Third Congress was to draw up a balance sheet, digest the experience of the previous two years and adjust the tactics of the Communist movement to the new situation.

The Third Congress was attended by 605 delegates (291 with voice and vote, and 314 with voice only) representing 103 organisations from fifty-two countries, namely forty-eight Communist Parties, eight Socialist Parties, twenty-eight Youth Leagues, four syndicalist organisations, two opposition Communist Parties (the Communist Workers' Party of Germany and the Workers' Communist Party of Spain) and thirteen other organisations. The seventy-two-strong delegation from the Russian Communist Party was headed by Lenin.

The Congress opened with a discussion on the world economic crisis and the tasks of the Communist International; the report on the activity of the Executive Committee; the Communist Workers' Party of Germany; the Italian question; the tactics of the International; the Red International Council of Trade Unions; the struggle against the Amsterdam International; tactics of the Russian Communist Party; the Communist youth movement; the women's movement, and some other questions.

234. Lenin speaking at the Third Congress of the Comintern

The main political report was given by Trotsky, entitled 'The Economic Situation and the New Tasks of the Communist International', which set the tone of the discussions throughout the Congress. Trotsky stated:

> The first period of the revolutionary movement after the war is characterised by the elemental nature of the onslaught, by the considerable formlessness of its methods and aims and by the extreme panic of the ruling classes; and it may be regarded by and large as terminated.[1]

Trotsky's report apparently lasted for nine hours, as he personally translated it into French and German. In it, he outlined the fundamental developments in the world situation, the character of the period, the unstable nature of the present equilibrium, the boom and slump cycle and the way in which these impacted on the class struggle, dictating a necessary change in tactics.

Given that a certain stability had returned, this lead to a recovery of confidence among the bourgeoisie. It became obvious that the task of proletarian revolution had been more complicated than originally thought. But the ebb in the situation had only signified a delay in the world revolution. The main task of the International was the building of mass Communist Parties, and to win over a majority of the working class to their side.

Lenin gave the report on the situation in Russia arising from the devastation of the war, civil war, and the imperialist blockade. He outlined the difficulties

235. Lenin making notes on the steps of the tribune at a Congress session

facing the workers' state and the need to maintain the fraying alliance between the working class and the peasantry. Therefore, the New Economic Policy had been introduced, as Lenin explained:

> Since the state cannot provide the peasant with goods from socialist factories in exchange for all his surplus, freedom to trade with this surplus necessarily means freedom for the development of capitalism.

> Within the limits indicated, however, this is not at all dangerous for socialism as long as transport and large-scale industry remain in the hands of the proletariat. On the contrary, the development of capitalism, controlled and regulated by the proletarian state (i.e. 'state' capitalism in *this* sense of the term), is advantageous and necessary in an extremely devastated and backward small-peasant country (within certain limits, of course), inasmuch as it is capable of hastening the *immediate* revival of peasant farming. [...]

> The food policy pursued by Soviet Russia in 1917-21 was undoubtedly very crude and imperfect, and gave rise to many abuses. A number of mistakes were made in its implementation. But as a whole, it was the only possible policy under the

conditions prevailing at the time. And it did fulfil its historic mission: it saved the proletarian dictatorship in a ruined and backward country.[2]

The task now, explained Lenin, was to electrify the country – a ten-year project – and develop the industrial base of the economy. At the same time, it was essential for the Communist International to prepare for the world revolution.

The 'March Action'

On the international front, the most important issue facing the Third Congress was the experience of Germany. Having the largest Communist Party outside of Russia, composed of around half-a-million members, and from the point of view of the world revolution, Germany was the most important country in Europe. It was regarded as the key to the European revolution.

The Congress therefore needed to debate the tactics that had been pursued in Germany, especially the party crisis that had arisen out of the so-called 'March Action' of 1921. Germany had been in the grip of revolution and counter-revolution ever since 1918. However, the 'March Action' constituted an adventurist attempt by the German Communist Party (KPD) to artificially provoke revolution in Germany, with the aim of spreading the revolution elsewhere. The 'Action' was not connected in any way to the real movement of the working class and, therefore, turned into a catastrophic defeat.

The idea behind the 'March Action' was that Communist Parties should pursue 'offensive' tactics – regardless of the objective conditions – to provoke the working class into revolutionary deeds. But revolution cannot be artificially induced in this way.

The 'offensive' policy led to a terrible fiasco, where the Party was outlawed, thousands were arrested and its membership suffered a massive decline. If this policy was adopted as a model to follow internationally, it would serve to wreck the Communist movement.

Behind the ultra-left leaders of the German Communist Party stood the likes of Béla Kun (the leader of the failed Hungarian Soviet Republic), Karl Radek, Bukharin and Zinoviev, all of whom welcomed this 'theory of the offensive'. A 'Left' resolution was even passed on the International Executive Committee, under Zinoviev's guidance, *supporting* the adventurist actions of the German Party. "The Communist International says to you: You acted rightly!", stated their message to the Germans.[3] The 'theory of the offensive' also found its followers among the 'Leftists' in the Communist Parties in

236. Communists attacking railways during the 'March Action'

Hungary, Czechoslovakia, Italy, Austria and France, who rallied to defend the Germans' action, and who saw it as a heroic revolutionary example to follow.

Paul Levi, who became the leader of the German Communist Party following the death of Luxemburg and Liebknecht, had criticised the 'March Action' publicly and was expelled from the party for breaking discipline. Levi's position was a minority within the party, and the delegation from the KPD who attended the World Congress were looking for support for their 'March Action'.

Prior to the Congress, Lenin had been distracted from the March events in Germany by his preoccupation with the Kronstadt rebellion, which also occurred at this time, as well as the implementation of the NEP. However, Paul Levi and Clara Zetkin had written to Lenin about the March fiasco, to which he gave the following reply:

> Thank you very much for your letters, dear Friends. Unfortunately, I have been so busy and so overworked in the last few weeks that I have had practically no opportunity to read the German press. The only thing I have seen is the Open Letter, which I think is *perfectly correct* tactics (I have condemned the contrary opinion of our 'Lefts' who were opposed to the letter). As for the recent strike movement and the action in Germany, I have read absolutely nothing about it. I readily believe that the representative of the Executive Committee [of the Comintern] defended the silly tactics, which were too much to the left...[4]

237. Paul Levi   238. Béla Kun

The "Open Letter" Lenin referred to was the united front appeal issued a few months earlier by the German Party under Levi's leadership. The 'Letter' was issued to the SPD, the USPD, the Communist Workers' Party of Germany and all trade unions, calling on them to unite in combatting the offensive against the workers' basic rights.

Their programme of joint action included demands for higher pensions for disabled war veterans; elimination of unemployment; improvement of the country's finances at the expense of the monopolies, introduction of factory and plant committee control over all stocks of food, raw materials and fuel, restarting of all closed enterprises, and other measures.

This offer of united action demonstrated that the Communist Party was not sectarian but was prepared to unite with other working-class organisations on a joint programme to defend the working class.

If such an appeal was rejected by the reformist leaders, the Communists could approach the rank and file of these organisations, urging them to condemn these leaders for this failure. If the leaders accepted, then the Communists could show in action the superiority of their revolutionary methods and approach. In this way, they would extend their influence and build support.

This approach, endorsed by Lenin, constituted an important lesson of Bolshevism.

Lenin takes a stand

As soon as Lenin found out what was happening in the sectarian adventure of the 'March Action', which was a sharp contrast to the previous position for a United Front put forward by Levi, he intervened to correct the blunder. In his conversations with Clara Zetkin, Lenin reassured her: "Don't worry, the plant of the theory of the offensive will not take root at the Congress."[5]

With Trotsky's support, Lenin approached Kamenev, and with the three of them, they were able to secure a majority in the Russian Politburo for their views. The next step was to win over the whole Russian delegation, which included the pro-leftists Zinoviev, Bukharin and Radek, before the World Congress. Lenin was implacable: "Well, we are forming a faction", he remarked, to fight for the line against the adventurist "faction".[6]

Lenin and Trotsky made it clear inside the leadership that if their opposition to putschism failed at the Congress, they would launch an international struggle over the question. This threat to launch an international faction fight came only *three* months after the ban on factions at the Tenth Party Congress, again showing the flexibility of Lenin when it came to the defence of political principles. This was a stark warning to their opponents of just how seriously they regarded the issue.

On 1 June, Radek had sent Lenin a draft thesis with amendments from the 'Leftists' Thalheimer and Béla Kun regarding the 'March Action'. As a warning shot, Lenin wrote a strongly worded letter to Zinoviev outlining his position, saying that if he wanted to avoid an all-out fight at the Congress, then they needed to change their tune and retreat. Lenin held nothing back:

The crux of the matter is that Levi in very many respects is *right politically*. Unfortunately, he is guilty of a number of breaches of discipline for which the Party has expelled him.

Thalheimer's and Béla Kun's theses are politically utterly fallacious. Mere phrases and playing at Leftism.

Radek is vacillating and has spoilt his original draft by a number of concessions to 'Leftist' silliness. His first 'concession' is highly characteristic: in §1 of his theses *'Abgrenzung der Fragen'* he first had "winning the majority of the working class (*to the principles of communism*)" (mark this). Amended (*verballhornt*) to: "winning the *socially decisive sections* of the working class."

A gem! To weaken here, in such a context, the necessity of winning precisely the *majority* of the working class "to the principles of communism", is the height of absurdity.

To win power, you need, *under certain conditions* (even when the *majority* of the working class have already been won over *to the principles of communism*) *a blow* dealt at the decisive place by the majority of the socially decisive sections of the working class. […]

What's to be done? I don't know. So much time and effort wasted.

If you don't want an open fight at the congress, then propose:

1) that Thalheimer's and B Kun's theses be rejected by exact voting this very day (since Bukharin assures me that the basic points have to be settled not later than today: they were better postponed) as being basically erroneous. Have this recorded. You will spoil everything if you don't do this and show indulgence. […]

None of the Communist Parties anywhere have yet won the majority (of the working class), not only as regards organisational leadership, but to the principles of communism as well. This is the basis of everything. To 'weaken' this foundation of the only reasonable tactic is *criminal irresponsibility*.

Hence: revolutionary explosions are possible nevertheless very soon considering the abundance of inflammable material in Europe; an easy victory of the working class – in exceptional cases – is also possible. But it would be absurd now to base the tactics of the Communist International on this possibility; it is absurd and harmful to write and think that the propaganda period has ended and the period of action has started.

The tactics of the Communist International should be based on a steady and systematic drive to win the *majority of the working class*, first and foremost *within the OLD trade unions*. Then we shall win for certain, whatever the course of events. As for "winning" for a short time in an exceptionally happy turn of events – any fool can do that.[7]

Then Lenin went on to advise support for the 'Open Letter' and draw a line under this adventurism:

Hence: the tactic of the Open Letter should definitely be applied everywhere. This should be said straight out, clearly and exactly, because waverings in regard to the 'Open Letter' are extremely harmful, extremely shameful and *EXTREMELY WIDESPREAD*. We may as well admit this. All those who have failed to grasp the necessity of the Open Letter tactic should be *expelled* from the Communist International within a month after its Third Congress. I clearly see my mistake in voting for the admission of KAPD. It will have to be rectified as quickly and fully as possible.

Instead of spinning a long yarn like Radek, we had better have the whole text of the Open Letter translated (and in German quoted in full), its significance properly brought home and adopted as a model.

I would confine the *general* resolution on tactics to this. Only then will the *tone* be set. The central idea will be clear. There will be no woolliness.[8]

In this letter, Lenin was as sharp as a razor. He then went on to criticise the childish attitudes of the 'Lefts', who tried to mix things up by equating what Levi had done and the vacillations of Serrati in Italy:

To generalise Serrati and Levi into the same 'opportunism' is stupid. Serrati is guilty; of what? It should be said clearly and precisely – on the *Italian* question, and not on the question of general tactics. Of having split with the Communists and not having expelled the reformists, Turati & Co. Until you have carried this out, Italian comrades, you are *outside* the Communist International. We are expelling you.

And to the Italian Communists – serious advice and the *demand*: so long as you have not been able by persistence, patience and skill to *CONVINCE* and win over the majority of the Serratian *workers*, don't swagger, don't play at Leftism. 'Fall Levi'* is not in general tactics, but in the appraisal of Märzaktion,** on the German question. Brandler says: there was a defensive. The government provoked it.

Assuming that this is true, that it is a fact.

What deduction is to be drawn from this?

1. That all the shouting about an offensive – and there was any amount of it – was erroneous and absurd;

2. that it was a tactical *error* to call for a *general* strike once there was provocation on the part of the government, who *wanted* to draw the *small fortress* of communism into the struggle (the district in the centre where the Communists already had a majority).

3. Mistakes like this must be avoided in future, as the situation in *Germany* is a special one after the killing of 20,000 workers in the civil war through the skilful manoeuvres of the Right. [...]

((The July days of 1917 were not a Bakuninist putsch. For such an appraisal we would have expelled a person from the Party. The July days were an heroic

---

* The Levi case.
** The 'March Action'.

offensive. And the deduction we drew was that we would not launch the next heroic offensive *prematurely*. Premature acceptance of a general battle – that is what the Märzaktion really was. Not a putsch, but a *mistake*, mitigated by the heroism of a defensive by hundreds of thousands.))[9]

With this bold approach, Lenin and Trotsky were able to subdue Zinoviev and his supporters and win over the Russian delegation to their side. Following this victory, they drafted the 'Theses on Tactics', which in effect condemned adventurism and putschism of all kinds.

But they also recognised that it would not be an easy task to win a majority at the Congress, which could be impressed by "heroic actions". To do so, they would have to place their political authority on the line. The Third Congress was seen by them as an important opportunity to deal with this ultra-leftist mistake and nip this danger in the bud.

'To the masses!'

At the Congress, as expected, the German 'Lefts' attempted to justify the 'March Action', and had gained the support of the Austrian and Italian sections. After listening carefully to their arguments, Lenin took the floor to answer them, including those of Umberto Terracini, the Italian delegate.

Lenin adopted his usual pedagogical approach to explain their errors and point the way forward. At the same time, he was very firm. To soften his criticisms, he began with a humorous point:

> Comrades! I deeply regret that I must confine myself to self-defence. (*Laughter.*) I say deeply regret, because after acquainting myself with Comrade Terracini's speech and the amendments introduced by three delegations, I should very much like to take the offensive, for, properly speaking, offensive operations are essential against the views defended by Terracini and these three delegations. If the Congress is not going to wage a vigorous offensive against such errors, against such 'Leftist' stupidities, the whole movement is doomed. That is my deep conviction. [...] We Russians are already sick and tired of these Leftist phrases.[10]

He then took up the errors proposed by the 'Lefts', who argued to delete the word 'majority' from the resolution, saying that it was not necessary for the Communists to win a majority of the working class to its side. This view summed up their whole ultra-left outlook. This was the policy of Blanqui, not Marx. Lenin stated bluntly:

And so, they want the word 'majority' deleted. If we cannot agree on such simple things, then I do not understand how we can work together and lead the proletariat to victory. [...]

Even the German party – one of the best – does not have the majority of the working class behind it. That is a fact. We, who face a most severe struggle, are not afraid to utter this truth, but here you have three delegations who wish to begin with an untruth, for if the Congress deletes the word 'majority' it will show that it wants an untruth. That is quite clear.[11]

The 'Open Letter' had been issued by the German Party under Paul Levi's leadership, under whose guidance the German Party had recovered from the setback of early 1919. They had fused with the USPD in October 1920, which meant that the Party grew to around 500,000 members, transforming it into a truly mass party.

All was well with the German leadership until January 1921, when a split took place in the Italian Socialist Party at the Livorno conference, out of which a minority created the Italian Communist Party under the ultra-left Amadeo Bordiga. Levi had been present at this conference and was very unhappy about the split, which he considered forced and premature. He also had a personal attachment to Serrati, the centrist leader, with whom he had regular discussions, but who was firmly attached to Turati and the right wing. In part, as a result of his sharp criticisms of the Italian split, Levi foolishly resigned in protest from the German Central Committee, together with Clara Zetkin and a few supporters. This action had drastic consequences in tipping the balance within the German leadership.

With the help of Béla Kun, the leadership of the German Party fell into the hands of the ultra-lefts. This set in motion a fatal chain of events, leading to the disastrous 'March Action'. When Lenin found out that Levi and his supporters had resigned, he shook his head in complete disbelief. Lenin explained in a letter to Zetkin and Levi:

I consider your tactics in respect of Serrati erroneous. Any defence or even semi-defence of Serrati was a mistake. But to withdraw from the Central Committee!!?? That, in any case, was the biggest mistake! [...]

We are so short of tried and tested forces that I am really indignant when I hear comrades announcing their withdrawal, etc. There is need to do everything possible and a few things that are impossible to avoid withdrawals and aggravation of differences at all costs.[12]

When Lenin saw Clara Zetkin, he stated:

> Tell me, how could you commit such a capital stupidity, yes, indeed a capital stupidity, as to leave the Central Committee? Where was your understanding? I was angry about it, terribly angry.[13]

At the Third Congress, Lenin defended the 'Open Letter' as a model to be followed internationally:

> The 'Open Letter' is a model political step. This is stated in our theses and we must certainly stand by it. It is a model because it is the first act of a practical method of winning over the majority of the working class. In Europe, where almost all the proletarians are organised, we must win the majority of the working class and anyone who fails to understand this is lost to the communist movement; he will never learn anything if he has failed to learn that much during the three years of the great revolution.[14]

Trotsky then intervened very firmly at the Congress. He declared:

> It is our duty to say clearly and precisely to the German workers that we consider this philosophy of the offensive to be the greatest danger. And in its practical application to be the greatest crime.[15]

Clara Zetkin states that these interventions had a great effect:

> The theoreticians of the offensive had not won any success in the debates on Trotsky's incisive and brilliant report on 'The Economic Situation and the New Tasks of the Communist International', nor in the Commission discussions on the Plenum.[16]

In the end, Lenin and Trotsky won the majority and the 'theory of the offensive' was rejected. Lenin was nevertheless mindful of the need to win over the German membership, which led him to tone down his criticism at the Congress. "We shall put some balm on their wounds", Lenin told Clara Zetkin.[17]

Lenin famously said that Levi had lost his head, but that he had a head to lose, as opposed to the others – the 'others' being Béla Kun, Thalheimer and the other ultra-lefts. Lenin later admitted that he had proudly stood on the 'right wing' at the Congress.

Following the Congress, the International issued the slogan: 'To the Masses!' The task at this stage was not the conquest of power, but the conquest of the masses. This led directly to the policy of the United Front, by means of which the Communists would offer to enter temporary fighting agreements with the reformists on concrete questions facing the working class, while maintaining their political independence. This policy was translated into the slogan: 'March separately; Strike together!' The Communists were not to bury themselves politically within the united front, but remain an independent force. With these tactics, the Communist Parties everywhere could be built into a decisive mass force.

On 14 August, not long after the Congress, Lenin wrote a letter to the German Communists, drawing out its lessons:

> In the overwhelming majority of countries, our parties are still very far from being what real Communist Parties should be; they are far from being real vanguards of the genuinely revolutionary and only revolutionary class, with every single member taking part in the struggle, in the movement, in the everyday life of the masses. But we are aware of this defect, we brought it out most strikingly in the Third Congress resolution on the work of the Party. And we shall overcome this defect.[18]

The letter was aimed at curbing the ultra-lefts and putting an end to the internal strife within the party.

> What the German proletariat must and will do – and this is the guarantee of victory – is keep their heads; systematically rectify the mistakes of the past; steadily win over the mass of the workers both inside and outside the trade unions; patiently build up a strong and intelligent Communist Party capable of giving real leadership to the masses at every turn of events; and work out a strategy that is on a level with the best international strategy of the most advanced bourgeoisie, which is 'enlightened' by age-long experience in general, and the 'Russian experience' in particular. [...]
>
> Now, after the decisions of the Third Congress of the Communist International, we must forget about him [Paul Levi] and devote all our attention, all our efforts, to peaceful, practical and constructive work (without any squabbling, polemics, or bringing up of the quarrels of yesterday), in the spirit of the decisions of the Third Congress.[19]

In the months after the Congress, Lenin stated that events had settled the question about Levi, and that he had been proved wrong. Levi had developed a swelled head and his Menshevism had become organic. In the end, he would become an apologist for those who opposed communism.

But this was merely an episode. The main conclusion that Lenin drew was that the infantile disorder of 'Leftism', reflected in the 'March Action', was passing "and will pass away as the movement grows."[20]

36. Bureaucratic Deformations

Lenin's health became a serious concern from the second half of 1921, after years of enormous stress and overwork, especially in the years of unrelenting civil war and economic collapse. He suffered his first stroke in May of the following year. This could not have come at a worse time.

After the exhaustion of civil war, the workers' state was now resting upon a partially atomised and severely weakened working class, the cream of which had perished at the front. While the fighting was largely over, Lenin was clearly alarmed at the increased dangers of bureaucratism facing the young Soviet Republic.

Hordes of officials from the old tsarist apparatus had been drawn in to help run the state, which expanded enormously in these years. Many of them were neutral or even hostile toward the revolution. But in a country where illiteracy was widespread, the Bolsheviks had little choice.

Lenin was increasingly troubled by the influence of this layer of officials, who were often secretly working against the government. The problem of bureaucracy was not simply a problem of officialdom and red tape, but the growth of an alien caste that was crystallising at the heart of the regime. Hemmed in by imperialism, and plagued by chronic backwardness and a low cultural level, the dangers of a bureaucratic degeneration were ever present.

The Bolsheviks took measures to combat bureaucracy by attempting to ensure the election of officials, the right of recall, no wages higher than that of a skilled worker and the involvement of workers in running society. But the material conditions created insurmountable barriers to the full implementation of these measures.

The working day was not shortened, but lengthened, and the difficulties of holding on in a backward country, ravaged by several years of conflict, had taken their toll. The Soviets had largely withered, and the masses were completely exhausted. The vanguard of the working class had been stretched to the limit. The heroic workers of Petrograd, the most advanced layer of the Russian working class, volunteered whenever and wherever they were most needed, either dispatched to the front or absorbed in the tasks of administration.

This, in turn, produced new dangers as the advanced layers were increasingly absorbed into the state apparatus. This tended to divorce them from the workers and helped narrow their political horizons. Over time, such layers could begin to lose their revolutionary outlook and become enmeshed into the machine.

As Marx warned, where there is generalised want, all the old crap will inevitably revive. This is precisely what was happening. In Russia, this took the form of a bureaucratic reaction.

Russian backwardness

What emerged after the revolution was, in Lenin's words, "a workers' state with bureaucratic distortions."[1] The Soviet state, with its officials inherited from the old class society, was in reality a tsarist state "slightly anointed with soviet oil…"[2] As a consequence, there was always the danger that it would degenerate and rise above the class it was supposed to represent. This could only be checked by the pressure from the workers and their organisations, especially the trade unions. As a result, during the trade union controversy, Lenin emphasised that the working class needed to defend itself *from* its own state. Lenin formulated the question dialectically:

> We now have a state under which it is the business of the massively organised proletariat to protect itself, while we, for our part, must use these workers' organisations to protect the workers from their state, and to get them to protect our state.[3]

For Lenin, the working class was the real defender of the Soviet Republic and it was only the working class, under the leadership of the Party, that could ultimately defeat the evil of bureaucracy, *inside* and *outside* the Party. Lenin, as always, explained the problem squarely and openly:

> The tsarist bureaucrats began to join the Soviet institutions and practise their bureaucratic methods, they began to assume the colouring of Communists and,

to succeed better in their careers, to procure membership cards of the Russian Communist Party. And so, they have been thrown out of the door but they creep back in through the window. What makes itself felt here most is the lack of cultured forces. These bureaucrats may be dismissed, but they cannot be re-educated all at once. Here we are confronted chiefly with organisational, cultural and educational problems.

We can fight bureaucracy to the bitter end, to a complete victory, only when the whole population participates in the work of government... The best of the bourgeois republics, no matter how democratic they may be, have thousands of legal hindrances which prevent the working people from participating in the work of government. What we have done, was to remove these hindrances, but so far we have not reached the stage at which the working people could participate in government.[4]

Bureaucrats, under the guise of Communists, were creeping into positions in the soviet state, and Lenin warned of the dangers:

We threw out the old bureaucrats, but they have come back, they call themselves 'commonists' when they can't bear to say the word Communist, and they wear a red ribbon in their buttonholes and creep into warm corners.[5]

"What to do about it?" asked Lenin. "We must fight this scum again and again and if the scum has crawled back we must again and again clean it up, chase it out..."[6]

Lenin nevertheless understood that the only real way out of this desperate situation was the victory of the international revolution. He repeated this many times:

You must remember that our Soviet land is impoverished after many years of trial and suffering, and has no socialist France or socialist England as neighbours which could help us with their highly developed technology and their highly developed industry. Bear that in mind! We must remember that at present all their highly developed technology and their highly developed industry belong to the capitalists, who are fighting us.[7]

He continued:

Complete and final victory on a world scale cannot be achieved in Russia alone; it can be achieved only when the proletariat is victorious in at least all the advanced countries, or, at all events, in some of the largest of the advanced countries. Only then shall we be able to say with absolute confidence that the cause of the proletariat has triumphed, that our first objective – the overthrow of capitalism – has been achieved.[8]

Combatting careerism

As the Party held a monopoly of political power, the danger of careerists penetrating the Communist Party to further their own interests was a perpetual danger. With the end of the civil war, large numbers of people who had no connection with the revolution, as well as turncoat Mensheviks, tried to squirm their way into the Party.

The Party required only the most self-sacrificing and dedicated members of the working class, especially in this besieged proletarian fortress. The Party therefore opened its ranks to new members at times when the Soviet Republic was in serious danger. That is why the doors of the Party were thrown open wide for one week in the autumn of 1919, when Yudenich had almost taken Petrograd and Denikin had advanced to Orel, within striking distance of Moscow.

Given that the White Generals, if successful, would slaughter every Communist they could identify, anyone who joined the Party in this darkest hour was considered sincere and worthy of membership. Only those who were prepared to make the ultimate sacrifice were permitted to join. However, as soon as the danger had passed, and the regime began to consolidate itself, it began to attract all kinds of careerists in search of a secure position.

Lenin argued that the Party needed to rid itself of "those who have 'attached' themselves to us for selfish motives", including – which hit the nail on the head – the "puffed-up commissars" and "bureaucrats".[9] The reference to "commissars" is indicative that this careerist layer had penetrated the most important positions of authority. The Party had to combat this menace through a series of regular purges to root out any undesirable self-seekers, bureaucrats and careerist elements. Brailsford notes:

At intervals a regular purge, known as a 'revision', is carried out in the Party, and unworthy members are expelled. The reasons for keeping the party select are as potent as they ever were. The Revolution is still fighting for its life. When an army wavers, Communist volunteer battalions are thrown into the breach. When a regiment lacks steadiness, a stiffening of Communists is introduced into its ranks. When a factory works ill, a few Communist workmen are transferred to its staff. When a village is disaffected, one or two Communists are sent to live in it. They are the leaven, the active, nervous, conscious element, in the sluggish Russian body. They are the élite of the Revolution, and every man and woman among them is expected to have will and magnetism enough to infuse some of his zeal into others. If the party were to deteriorate, if it became less zealous, less self-sacrificing, less audacious, the Revolution itself would collapse.[10]

In the second half of 1921, on the basis of a resolution passed at the Tenth Party Congress, the Party was purged of nearly 170,000 people, almost 25 per cent of the Party, to preserve its traditions from the corrupting influence of careerism and bureaucracy.

Bourgeois historians habitually point to this purge as 'proof' of the alleged affinity of Bolshevism and Stalinism. But this cleansing of the Party cannot be compared in any shape or form to Stalin's monstrous Purge Trials in the 1930s. There were no police, no trials, no prison camps, no shootings; simply the rooting out of petty-bourgeois careerists and Menshevik elements.

Stalin's Purges, by contrast, constituted a bloody, one-sided civil war against Bolshevism, the aim of which was to physically exterminate the last vestiges of Lenin's Party. *This fact, in and of itself,* is sufficient proof that a river of blood separates Bolshevism and Stalinism.

Rabkrin established

Lenin understood that to clear out the careerists from the apparatus, the workers needed to use the force of their own organisations. But, he also believed that special measures were needed to deal with this problem. This resulted in the creation of the Peoples' Commissariat of Workers' and Peasants' Inspection ('Rabkrin', or 'WPI'), in February 1920. Its task was to oversee the functioning of the state, reduce bureaucracy and rapidly increase the participation of honest workers in the administration.

However, the person appointed to head Rabkrin was none other than Stalin, on Zinoviev's proposal. He was chosen not for his political qualities, but for his administrative ability and firmness. Stalin had a reputation for applying 'pressure' to get things done, which was an important quality during the years of civil war. But he was to emerge precisely as the figurehead and champion of this growing bureaucracy, which was to become evident later.

Lenin had high hopes for Rabkrin and he was keen to promote its work as a weapon in the fight against inefficiency and bureaucracy. On 6 March 1920, he stressed Rabkrin's importance and function at a meeting of the Moscow Soviet:

> The worker and peasant masses who have to build up our entire state must start by organising state control. You will obtain this apparatus from among the worker

239. Lenin among delegates of the Tenth Party Congress, Moscow, 1921

and peasant masses, from among the young workers and peasants who have been fired as never before with the independent desire, the readiness and determination to set about the work of administering the state themselves. [...] You must recruit the most diffident and undeveloped, the most timid of the workers for the workers' inspection and promote them. [...] We need tens of thousands of new advanced workers. [...] At a time when hostile elements are trying by every method of warfare, deceit and provocation to cling to us and to take advantage of the fact that membership of a government party offers certain privileges, we must act in contact with the non-party people. [...] This apparatus is one of the means whereby we can increase the number of workers and peasants who will help us to achieve victory on the internal front in a few years.[11]

Thus, Rabkrin was specifically created to identify and involve the untapped reservoir of independent initiative and talent within the working class, and then use this to combat the bureaucratic cancer in the state. In this way, a permanent bureaucracy would be eliminated, and increasingly, tasks of administration would be carried out by the workers themselves.

The Soviet bureaucrat

The struggle against bureaucracy was one of the two central problems discussed at the Tenth Party Congress, the other being the NEP, as we have seen. Lenin argued at the Congress that:

> ... the struggle against the evils of bureaucracy is absolutely indispensable, and that it is just as intricate as the fight against the petty-bourgeois element. The bureaucratic practices of our state system have become such a serious malaise that they are dealt with in our Party Programme, because they are connected with this petty-bourgeois element, which is widely dispersed.[12]

The proposal of Lenin to bring representatives from the Workers' Opposition onto the Central Committee was met with their resistance, but it was aimed specifically to help to fight against the bureaucracy:

> And now, since the Workers' Opposition has defended democracy, and has made some sound demands, we shall do our utmost to mend our fences with it; and the Congress as such should make a definite selection. You say that we are not doing enough to combat the evils of bureaucracy – come and help us, come closer and help us in the fight...[13]

He went on to warn that the working class, after all the exertions of war then civil war, needed to recuperate and regenerate, adding "the 'forces of the working class' are not unlimited":[14]

> Without a certain 'respite' these new forces will not be forthcoming [...]

> After an enormous, unparalleled exertion of effort, the working class in a small-peasant, ruined country, the working class which has very largely become declassed, needs an interval of time in which to allow new forces to grow and be brought to the fore, and in which the old and worn-out forces can 'recuperate'.[15]

Yet, despite everything, Rabkrin made very little progress under Stalin. On the contrary, the bureaucratic state machine continued to degenerate and was becoming increasingly alien to the working class. Lenin was angry at this failure and he wrote a strongly worded letter to Stalin in September 1921. In particular, Lenin criticised Rabkrin's methods, which were entirely wrong, insisting that one cannot fight bureaucracy with bureaucratic methods:

> It is more the duty of the Workers' and Peasants' Inspection to be able to improve things than to merely 'detect' and 'expose' [...]

Timely and skilful rectification – this is the prime function of the Workers' and Peasants' Inspection.[16]

He stated bluntly:

But it is exactly on this fundamental question that the Workers' and Peasants' Inspection cannot [...] confine itself to the 'thesis' that 'accounting is faulty, that there is no accounting'. What have the comrades of the Workers' and Peasants' Inspection done to *improve* those methods?

Has the Workers' and Peasants' Inspection carried out its task and done its duty? Does it properly understand its task? That is the main question. *The reply to this must be negative.*[17]

In his drive against bureaucracy, Lenin left no stone unturned. He waged war on "Communist conceit" and the "puffed up Commissar", who made their appearance at every turn. In a stern letter to Aron Sheinman in February 1922, Lenin spelled out the truth in the plainest language:

Your words that the State Bank is now a "powerful apparatus" (22 Feb) made me laugh. Let me say in confidence: this is the height of childishness, the height of Communist-mandarin childishness. [...]

At present the State Bank = a bureaucratic paper game. There is the truth for you, if you want to hear not the sweet communist-official lies (with which everyone feeds you as a high mandarin), but the *truth*.

And if you don't want to look at this truth with open eyes, through all the communist lying, you are a man who has *perished* in the prime of life in a swamp of official lying. Now that is an unpleasant truth, but it is the truth.[18]

The attempts to cover up the bitter truth with lies and sweet words, by which the guilty individuals attempted to protect their positions, were an even greater crime in Lenin's eyes. He wrote to Osinsky:

They are afraid of washing dirty linen in public, afraid of the naked truth, and brush it aside with a meaningful glance, taking a superficial attitude, as Comrade Trotsky correctly said.[19]

In the same month, he wrote to Alexander Tsiurupa, who was to take over from Stalin in Rabkrin, complaining that, "All of us are sunk in the rotten bureaucratic swamp of 'departments'... The departments are shit; decrees are shit. To find men and check up on their work – that is the whole point."[20] Only by openly exposing the danger could it be tackled.

A bureaucratic machine

Lenin forcefully took up the fight again at the Eleventh Party Congress in March 1922. At this gathering, he referred to the views of the *Smena Vekh* (Changing Landmarks) group, which had emerged among the Russian émigrés, and was led by Professor Ustryalov, a former Cadet minister in the Kolchak government. This émigré group had worked out a perspective that with the Soviet government's adoption of pro-capitalist policies in the NEP, bureaucratic-bourgeois tendencies would inevitably evolve, eventually leading to complete capitalist restoration.

"I am for the support of the Soviet power in Russia", wrote the bourgeois Ustryalov, "because it has taken the road that will lead it back to an ordinary bourgeois state."[21]

Lenin, who always tried to bring out the essence of things, gave *Smena Vekh* and Ustryalov credit for producing this analysis of the creeping Thermidorian counter-revolution that was implicit in the NEP. From his own class standpoint, Ustryalov displayed a remarkably clear insight into the processes taking place. Referring to this, Lenin explained:

> We, and I particularly, because of my position, hear a lot of sentimental communist lies; 'communist fibbing', every day, and sometimes we get sick to death of them.[22]

Speaking with a tone of heavy and pointed irony, Lenin expressed his satisfaction at hearing an honest viewpoint directly from the class enemy, which was infinitely preferable to listening to an endless series of 'communist' lies that were only meant to cover up the real situation:

> But now instead of these 'communist fibs' I get a copy of *Smena Vekh*, which says quite plainly: "Things are by no means what you imagine them to be. As a matter of fact, you are slipping into the ordinary bourgeois morass with communist flags inscribed with catchwords stuck all over the place." This is very useful. It is not a repetition of what we are constantly hearing around us, but the plain class truth uttered by the class enemy.[23]

Lenin praised the frankness of this bourgeois group, pointing out that history knows all kinds of transformations and asking the most important question of all – who will prevail?:

> It is very useful to read this sort of thing; and it was written not because the communist state allows you to write some things and not others, but because it really is the class truth, bluntly and frankly uttered by the class enemy. [...]

We must say frankly that such candid enemies are useful. We must say frankly that the things Ustryalov speaks about are possible. *History knows all sorts of transformations.* Relying on firmness of convictions, loyalty, and other splendid moral qualities is anything but a serious attitude in politics. A few people may be endowed with splendid moral qualities, but historical issues are decided by vast masses, which, if the few do not suit them, may at times treat them none too politely.

There have been many cases of this kind; that is why we must welcome this frank utterance of the *Smena Vekh* people. The enemy is speaking the class truth and is pointing to the danger that confronts us, and which the enemy is striving to make inevitable. *Smena Vekh* adherents express the sentiments of thousands and tens of thousands of bourgeois, *or of Soviet employees whose function it is to operate our New Economic Policy. This is the real and main danger.* And that is why attention must be concentrated mainly on the question: "Who will win?"[24]

Lenin was explaining that power was, in reality, slipping out of the hands of the Communists and passing into the hands of an alien bureaucracy, a parasitic dead weight around the necks of the workers, which acted as a transmission belt for alien classes. That was the meaning of Thermidor. Rather than a withering away of the state, the objective difficulties had resulted in a monstrous strengthening of bureaucracy.

Lenin hammered home the same point in a speech to the delegates of the Eleventh Party Congress:

If we take Moscow with its 4,700 Communists in responsible positions, and if we take that huge bureaucratic machine, that gigantic heap, we must ask: who is directing whom? I doubt very much whether it can truthfully be said that the Communists are directing that heap. To tell the truth they are not directing, they are being directed.[25]

Having made this damning criticism, Lenin went on to draw parallels with the cultural level of a conquered nation following a war.

Something analogous happened here to what we were told in our history lessons when we were children: sometimes one nation conquers another, the nation that conquers is the conqueror and the nation that is vanquished is the conquered nation. This is simple and intelligible to all. But what happens to the culture of these nations? Here things are not so simple. If the conquering nation is more cultured than the vanquished nation, the former imposes its culture upon the latter; but if the opposite is the case, the vanquished nation imposes its culture upon the conqueror.[26]

Lenin then asked if this was not analogous to the situation the Soviet Republic now faced:

> Has not something like this happened in the capital of the RSFSR [Russian Soviet Federative Socialist Republic]? Have the 4,700 Communists (nearly a whole army division, and all of them the very best) come under the influence of an alien culture? True, there may be the impression that the vanquished have a high level of culture. But that is not the case at all. Their culture is miserable, insignificant, but it is still at a higher level than ours. Miserable and low as it is, it is higher than that of our responsible Communist administrators, for the latter lack administrative ability. Communists who are put at the head of departments – and sometimes artful saboteurs deliberately put them in these positions in order to use them as a shield – are often fooled. This is a very unpleasant admission to make, or, at any rate, not a very pleasant one; but I think we must admit it, for at present this is the salient problem. I think that this is the political lesson of the past year; and it is around this that the struggle will rage in 1922.

> Will the responsible Communists of the RSFSR and of the Russian Communist Party realise that they cannot administer; that they only imagine they are directing, but are, actually, being directed? If they realise this they will learn, of course; for this business can be learnt. But one must study hard to learn it, and our people are not doing this. They scatter orders and decrees right and left, but the result is quite different from what they want.[27]

This whole approach again reflected Lenin's honesty in confronting the realities facing the working class and the Soviet state. It was an unpalatable truth, but truthful nonetheless. It was necessary to highlight the dangers, and not hide them in order to deal with them. He pointed to the miserably low cultural level of the Russian working class, which lacked the necessary skills to administer the state: "The state apparatus in general: *bad beyond description; lower than the bourgeois level of culture*", noted Lenin. "*Often*: this apparatus does not belong to us, we belong to it!"[28]

Engels once explained that where art, science and government are the exclusive privilege of a small minority, that minority will always use and abuse its position for its own ends. And this must be the case when the majority are forced to work long hours.

The economic collapse led to the exhaustion and atomisation of the working class. And under the NEP, the pressure from bourgeois and petty-bourgeois elements asserted itself at all levels of society. These pressures increasingly made themselves felt inside the state and even inside the Communist Party.

By the spring of 1922, Stalin had been appointed general secretary and, while he formally relinquished the Commissariat of Rabkrin, he remained largely responsible for its functioning. He had transformed Rabkrin from a weapon against bureaucracy, into a means to gather a layer of social climbers around him, placing them into positions of power and influence. It was also at this time, when Lenin was ill, that Zinoviev and Kamenev began to manoeuvre behind the scenes. They soon drew Stalin into a secret faction, operating behind the backs of the Party and unknown to it, which was called the Troika, or triumvirate.

This was the beginning of the rise of Stalin. But initially, he did not play the leading role. That was reserved for Zinoviev, who appeared to hold all the threads of the conspiracy in his hands. However, appearances can be deceptive.

Zinoviev and Kamenev chose Stalin precisely because they thought they could manipulate and control him. How could such a grey, apparently talentless apparatchik lead anybody? They underestimated Stalin, and he allowed them to underestimate him. In the end, it was not they who controlled him, but he who controlled them. This did not seem possible in the beginning.

Skilful in the black arts of intrigue, Stalin used the Troika's secret manoeuvres against Trotsky in order to further his own position. Stalin, the machine man par excellence, operated in the shadows. All his life he had learned the virtues of patience, and he was cautious, very cautious, like a cat stalking its prey. Only at the last moment, when the unsuspecting mouse is in a completely hopeless position, does the cat suddenly jump on it and tear it into pieces. So it was in Stalin's relation with Kamenev and Zinoviev.

Rather than combatting bureaucracy, Stalin, through a series of appointments, helped forge the bureaucratic apparatus in his image within the state and the Party. The bureaucracy was becoming more conscious of itself and its interests, and looked towards someone who could reflect its outlook. Stalin was the ideal candidate to fulfil this role.

He had constructed a powerful base in the organisational apparatus of the Party. He gradually began to pull the threads together in assembling a secret faction around himself. But he now faced a very serious problem. In early 1922, Lenin grew increasingly alarmed at the bureaucratic danger. At the Eleventh Congress, he warned the Party of its responsibilities, but also of how "responsible Communists" were being assimilated into the apparatus, and how corrupt elements stood behind them:

The key feature is that we have not got the right men in the right places; that responsible Communists who acquitted themselves magnificently during the revolution have been given commercial and industrial functions about which they know nothing; and they prevent us from seeing the truth, for rogues and rascals hide magnificently behind their backs. [...]

In the sea of people we are after all but a drop in the ocean, and we can administer only when we express correctly what the people are conscious of. Unless we do this the Communist Party will not lead the proletariat, the proletariat will not lead the masses, and the whole machine will collapse.[29]

Again, in a blunt letter to Sokolnikov, he wrote:

All the work of all our economic bodies suffer most of all from bureaucracy. Communists have become bureaucrats. If anything will destroy us, it is this.[30]

In the months following the Eleventh Congress, Lenin felt the need to personally intervene in the work of Rabkrin, again raising doubts about Stalin's role:

I very much regret that Tsyurupa did not manage to do any work in the Workers' and Peasants' Inspection. I am afraid that the work is not quite rightly organised. The *type* of work is *individual investigations and reports*. This is old hat. But there is no *reorganisation* of the machinery or its improvement. There are no model staffs composed entirely of Communists, [...] there are no systematically worked-out *rates* of work, which might be applied to other departments; there are no systematic statistical studies of what *Soviet employees* can do in this or that branch of government in the course of a week, and so forth.

I had constantly hoped that the influx of new people into the Collegium of the WPI [Rabkrin] would liven up the work, but from my questioning of Stalin I have not been able to see this.[31]

This 'questioning' by Lenin would have been a most painful experience for Stalin. It was a polite way of saying that he was subjected to a thorough interrogation, accompanied by a stern rebuke. Lenin was angry and determined to pursue the fight to the very end. And his focus was now very much centred on the role of Stalin.

Stalin must have emerged from this encounter shaking with rage and indignation. He will have felt humiliated and revengeful, but also extremely fearful. A clash with Lenin was no small matter. Would this lead to his removal? Would all his work of building his network of influence be wasted?

240. Lenin and Krupskaya on the drive to Gorki

That might well be the case. The red light was flashing before him. But fortunately, the hand of fate intervened to save him.

Lenin's health deteriorates

Inevitably, Lenin's punishing workload was taking its toll on him physically. When his health suddenly took a turn for the worse, he wrote to the Politburo on 7 December 1921:

> I am going away today. Despite my working less and resting more during recent days, the insomnia has grown hellishly worse. I am afraid that I shall not be able to make any reports either at the Party conference or at the Congress of Soviets.[32]

Lenin moved to a retreat in Gorki (modern-day Gorki Leninskie), a suburb of Moscow 10 kilometres south of the city centre, to get more rest. But he

241. Lenin with his sister Maria, his nephew Victor, and Krupskaya in
Gorki, 1922

continued to suffer headaches, which his doctors put down to the bullets
still lodged in his body following the assassination attempt. Lenin remarked:

> A night doomed to insomnia is a truly terrible thing when you have to be ready
> in the morning for work, work, work without end...[33]

According to Georg Klemperer, Lenin's German doctor, the bullets still
lodged in him would need to be removed to eradicate their toxic effects and
alleviate the headaches, although others disputed this. In the end, Klemperer
got his way, and it was decided to remove one of the bullets, but leave the
other inside him as the doctors felt the operation would be too risky. On 23
April, the operation was carried out successfully.

On 21 May, Lenin informed all the members of the government, the
Comintern and other key bodies that he was going on holiday to recuperate
for several months, but wanted to be kept informed of the most important
decisions and plans.

But scarcely a month after the operation, later in May he suffered his first
serious stroke, leaving the right side of his body paralysed and his speech

partially impaired. Trotsky wrote: "The blow was overwhelming. It seemed as if the revolution itself were holding its breath."[34]

Towards the middle of June, his health began to improve, and he was allowed visitors. He was able to read books, then later newspapers. In July, as he recovered, he wrote a short note to his secretary, Lydia Fotieva: "You can congratulate me on my recovery. The proof is my handwriting, which is *beginning* to look human again."[35]

It was, however, not until October that he was able to return to work. It was clear that his health had not completely recovered.

37. The Growing Menace of the Bureaucracy

In 1922, a number of other key issues emerged. Among them was the dispute over the state monopoly of foreign trade. The state monopoly was the basic defence mechanism which guarded Russia's backward economy against the pressures of its advanced capitalist rivals. Without it, Russia's industries would be dragged down by a flood of cheap imports from the West, and the economy would face certain collapse.

Ever since its introduction in April 1918, the Communist Party leadership had been unanimous in its support of the state monopoly. However, by May 1922, the mounting pressures of the NEP, and the increased power of the kulaks and the speculators, were having an effect within the Party.

This pressure found its expression in the leadership with the formation of a right-wing group, which was opposed to the continuation of the monopoly. "Politics is the most concentrated expression of economics", wrote Lenin.[1] In other words, economic interests sooner or later acquire a political expression. And that was the case in this dispute.

Bukharin, who had been the standard bearer for the 'Left', now suddenly swung sharply to the right. Along with Pyatakov and Sokolnikov, he argued for the abolition of the state monopoly and the opening up of the Russian economy to the world market. Later, Bukharin's swing to the right was expressed in his call for the kulaks to 'Enrich yourselves!' The former ultra-left, who saw in War Communism the road to a swift achievement of communism, now advised the Soviet government not to be in a hurry, but to advance to socialism "at a snail's pace".

His position reflected the pressures of the NEPmen, the market traders and kulaks, who had grown ever more prosperous under the NEP and were now seeking ways of translating their economic power into political influence over the state. Bukharin's right-wing deviation would open the door to them. It would place the Soviet power in extreme danger.

Stalin, Zinoviev and Kamenev, on the other hand, stood half-way. They limited themselves to calling for the *relaxing* of the state monopoly on foreign trade.

Lenin immediately saw that this cowardly evasion was only the slippery road to the inevitable abolition of the monopoly. He came down emphatically against any weakening. Instead, he argued for the opposite – a *strengthening* of the state monopoly.

In a letter on 15 May 1922 to Stalin and Frumkin, the deputy People's Commissar for Foreign Trade, who favoured relaxation, Lenin demanded "*an official ban* on all talks and conversations and commissions, etc., on weakening the foreign trade monopoly…"[2]

In response, Stalin, who always looked which way the wind was blowing, wrote in his own handwriting across Lenin's letter:

> I have no objections to a 'formal ban' on measures to *mitigate* the foreign trade monopoly at the *present* stage. All the same, I think that mitigation is becoming indispensable.[3]

For the time being, Lenin's intervention acted to check the actions of the right-wing elements within the leadership. But it was around this time that Lenin suffered a stroke, which, as we have seen, took him out of political work until the autumn.

In the ensuing period, Stalin moved over to support Bukharin, who again raised the idea of abolishing the state monopoly. Then, in the absence of both Lenin and Trotsky, the Central Committee meeting of 6 October, in an obvious manoeuvre, agreed to the relaxation of restrictions on the Soviet trading agencies. This measure was a clear step toward abolition of the monopoly on foreign trade. Once again, this pushed the whole issue to the forefront.

Following his return to work, Lenin reacted angrily with a letter on 13 October, which stated that this decision by the Central Committee "wrecks the foreign trade monopoly."[4] He went on:

I regret it very much that illness prevented me from attending the meeting on that day and that I am now compelled to seek an exception to the rule.

But I think that the question must be weighed and studied, that haste is harmful. I propose that the decision on this question be deferred for two months, i.e. until the next Plenary Meeting...[5]

On 16 October, under pressure from Lenin, it was agreed to postpone the issue until the full Central Committee Plenum. But this was simply a delay. The central problem remained unresolved.

Georgian troubles

In the meantime, trouble was brewing over relations with the Georgian Party leaders over the national question.

Problems with Soviet Georgia arose when Stalin, as Commissar of Nationalities, was appointed to draft relations between the Russian Federation and the independent Soviet Republics. Relations until now were largely determined by a series of bilateral treaties between the Republics and the Russian Federation. Stalin presented a draft resolution that attempted to bureaucratically integrate the three Caucasian republics, Azerbaijan, Armenia and Georgia, into the Federation.

In the eyes of the Georgian Communists, this amounted to little more than an annexation. While they accepted proposals for greater economic integration, they were opposed to Stalin's form of 'autonomisation',* as 'premature', and demanded 'all the attributes of independence'.

On 26 September, having read the draft proposals, Lenin wrote a letter to the Politburo opposing Stalin's autonomisation (i.e. integration) plans. He instead suggested an alternative, to unite the republics by creating an equal Union of Soviet Socialist Republics, with the right of the Republics to secede. He therefore wrote to Kamenev:

Comrade Kamenev, Stalin has probably already sent you the resolution of his commission on the entry of the independent republics into the RSFSR.

If he has not, please take it from the secretary at once, and read it. I spoke about it with Sokolnikov yesterday, and with Stalin today. Tomorrow I shall see Mdivani (the Georgian Communist suspected of 'independent' sentiments).

In my opinion the matter is of utmost importance. Stalin tends to be somewhat hasty.[6]

---

* 'Autonomisation' was the name given to Stalin's proposals for the unification of the Russian Soviet Socialist Federation with the other non-Russian Soviet Republics.

242. Lenin presiding over a meeting of the Soviet of People's Commissars during a remission from his illness, October 1922

But the "hasty" Stalin ignored Lenin's advice and rushed ahead with his proposals. Although Stalin was himself a Georgian, he had now adopted the approach of a Great Russian nationalist. He leaned on his collaborators in Georgia, especially Ordzhonikidze, to 'soften up' the opposition to his original proposals. By this time, after applying similar pressure, Azerbaijan and Armenia, the other republics involved in the changes, were now in 'safe hands', although they still harboured some objections.

Stalin operated in the shadows behind the backs of the Politburo and, especially, Lenin, feeding them with misleading reports about what was happening in the republics.

By this time, Stalin must have realised that a conflict with Lenin was inevitable. He would have been mortally offended by Lenin's accusation of Great Russian chauvinism. Stalin was not someone who accepted such things gracefully. He took careful note of each and every criticism, great or small, and memorised each and every personal slight, whether real or imaginary. And when the time was right, he would take his revenge on those who had belittled him.

But Lenin was no ordinary opponent. By his side, Stalin keenly felt his moral and intellectual inferiority: a miserable dwarf beside a giant. And he feared being drawn into a direct confrontation – one that he was bound to lose. But why should Lenin, the 'Old Man', interfere in his personal sphere of action? Why should he stick his nose into other people's business? Stalin was forced to swallow his own bile, at least for the time being.

He resorted to his usual tricks: appear to retreat, deceive the 'Boss' about what he was doing, and in the meantime carry on as before. In reality, Stalin stubbornly stuck to his original position that Georgia had to be bureaucratically 'absorbed' into the Russian Federation.

Stalin, with his bureaucratic mindset, was not interested in the political side of the question, but simply viewed the integration of Georgia as an administrative task. This only served to intensify the conflict with the Georgian leaders, who eventually succeeded in making Lenin aware of the real situation. But this was not an easy task. Stalin was making good use of his contacts in the state administration in order to cut off Lenin's contact with the outside world – even to other leaders of the Soviet state and Communist Party.

As always, Stalin was proceeding cautiously, feeling his way step by step. But all the time, he was growing bolder and more insolent. In brushing aside Lenin's concerns, he even felt confident enough to accuse Lenin of 'national liberalism' – a clear attempt to answer Lenin's criticism of his great Russian chauvinism.

Stalin's insolent attitude to Lenin in this affair did not go unnoticed, at least to one Soviet biography of Lenin:

> Stalin did not take Lenin's criticisms in the right spirit [!]. He was opposed to Lenin's suggestion of unifying the Soviet Republics on the basis of equality and sovereignty. His letter to that effect addressed to Lenin and other members of the Political Bureau on 27 September 1922, referred with intolerable rudeness to Lenin... Evidently Kamenev and Stalin exchanged notes at the time... In his reply to Kamenev, who wrote "Lenin has made up his mind to go to war on behalf of independence", Stalin said "In my opinion, we have to be firm against Lenin."[7]

In the end, realising he would be in a minority in the Central Committee meeting, Stalin cunningly glossed over the differences and quietly gave in to Lenin's amendments. Lenin did not take part in the meeting, but sent Kamenev a stern note on the same day, which revealed his determination on this question, entitled 'Memo to the Politburo on combatting dominant nation chauvinism':

243. Lenin and Krupskaya at Gorki, August 1922
The sinister, gun-like object is in fact a telescope

Comrade Kamenev! I declare war to the very death on dominant-nation chauvinism. I shall eat it with all my healthy teeth as soon as I get rid of this accursed bad tooth.

It must be *absolutely* insisted that the Union Central Executive Committee should be *presided over* in turn by a Russian, Ukrainian, Georgian, etc. *Absolutely!*[8]

Stalin retreated, but it would not be the end of the matter. He would seek to take revenge on the Georgian Communist leaders. This was a step too far, however, and it was the final straw that would finally expose to Lenin his scandalous role in this whole affair.

Fourth World Congress

Later that year, between 5 November and 5 December, the Fourth World Congress of the Communist International took place with sessions in Petrograd and Moscow. The Congress was attended by 408 delegates, 343 of whom had voting rights, representing fifty-eight Communist organisations from various countries and further representatives from the Italian Socialist Party and others.

Significantly, it was the last World Congress that Lenin would ever attend. Even then, due to his poor health, he was only able to be present and speak at one session, and he had to send his greetings to the opening session in writing.

At the session in which he spoke, Lenin was met with a prolonged and stormy applause, and greeted with a general ovation, as delegates spontaneously rose to their feet to sing the *Internationale*. He opened his speech by saying:

> I am down in the list as the main speaker, but you will understand that after my lengthy illness I am not able to make a long report. I can only make a few introductory remarks on the key questions. My subject will be a very limited one.[9]

"Undoubtedly, we have done, and will still do, a host of foolish things. No one can judge and see this better than I", said Lenin, with a wry smile. This provoked some laughter in response. But Lenin was making a very serious point. He asked the delegates:

> Why do we do these foolish things? The reason is clear: firstly, because we are a backward country; secondly, because education in our country is at a low level; and thirdly, because we are getting no outside assistance. Not a single civilised country is helping us. On the contrary, they are all working against us.

He went on to explain that the subject he had been given to speak about, 'Five Years of the Russian Revolution and the Prospects of the World Revolution', was too broad and too large for one speaker to deal with in a single speech. Instead, he decided to concentrate on developments in Russia and proceeded to outline the progress of the NEP following the eighteen months of its implementation.

He referred to his previous idea of state capitalism, which he said would have been a step forward, in the context of a backward peasant economy like Russia. He realised this was a very strange idea when the working class had already established a socialist republic. But isolation in a backward country had meant a conscious retreat from socialist planning. Such a retreat was not realised beforehand, but forced upon them by the delay of the world revolution.

The civil war and the wrecking of the economy changed everything. By February 1921, this had led to a deep crisis and forced them to retreat. "We felt the impact of a grave – I think it was the gravest – internal political crisis in Soviet Russia", explained Lenin. "The reason for it was that in our economic offensive we had run too far ahead."[10]

The 'struggle for individual existence' not only did not disappear, but assumed an extremely exaggerated form. Lenin admitted that the early phase of War Communism or "purely socialist distribution, was beyond our available strength…"[11] The adoption of the NEP marked a serious retreat, but it served to placate the peasantry. He noted that: "Peasant uprisings, which previously, before 1921, were, so to speak, a common occurrence in Russia, have almost completely ceased."[12]

But while there had been progress in the light industries under the NEP, Russian heavy industry was still in a grave condition. He again pointed to the difficulties arising from isolation, economic backwardness, and the low cultural level. But he also made particular mention of the wretched condition of the state machinery.

This part of the speech merits special attention. It was certainly no accident that it occupied a prominent place in a very concise address, where he was choosing his expressions very carefully, weighing every word:

> We took over the old machinery of state, and that was our misfortune. Very often this machinery operates against us. In 1917, after we seized power, the government officials sabotaged us. This frightened us very much and we pleaded: "Please come back." They all came back, but that was our misfortune. We now have a vast army of government employees, but lack sufficiently educated forces to exercise real control over them. In practice it often happens that here at the top, where we exercise political power, the machine functions somehow; but down below government employees have arbitrary control and they often exercise it in such a way as to counteract our measures. At the top, we have, I don't know how many, but at all events, I think, no more than a few thousand, at the outside several tens of thousands of our own people. Down below, however, there are hundreds of thousands of old officials whom we got from the tsar and from bourgeois society and who, partly deliberately and partly unwittingly, work against us.[13]

Having underlined the seriousness of the problem of bureaucracy in the Soviet state, Lenin went on to issue a stern warning about the organisational resolution that had been adopted a year before at the Third Congress. Lenin felt that, while "excellent", it had been based almost entirely on the Russian experience:

This is its good point, but it is also its failing. It is its failing because I am sure that no foreigner can read it. I have read it again before saying this. In the first place, it is too long, containing fifty or more points. Foreigners are not usually able to read such things. Secondly, even if they read it, they will not understand it because it is too Russian. Not because it is written in Russian – it has been excellently translated into all languages – but because it is thoroughly imbued with the Russian spirit. And thirdly, if by way of exception some foreigner does understand it, he cannot carry it out. This is its third defect. I have talked with a few of the foreign delegates and hope to discuss matters in detail with a large number of delegates from different countries during the Congress, although I shall not take part in its proceedings, for unfortunately it is impossible for me to do that.

I have the impression that we made a big mistake with this resolution, namely, that we blocked our own road to further success. As I have said already, the resolution is excellently drafted; I am prepared to subscribe to every one of its fifty or more points. But we have not learnt how to present our Russian experience to foreigners. All that was said in the resolution has remained a dead letter. If we do not realise this, we shall be unable to move ahead.[14]

Lenin concluded his speech to the World Congress on 15 November. Despite the concise and extremely concentrated nature of his remarks – the inevitable constraints imposed on him by his illness – Lenin was laying down a series of markers. These had a vital importance for the future of the International and the world Communist movement. He was warning them not to blindly follow what later became known as 'the Moscow line', but to think for themselves and not merely repeat slogans handed down from above.

He explained that, while the experiences of Russian Bolshevism were of colossal importance, they were not necessarily applicable to every concrete case in other countries. And it was, above all, necessary for Communists to find a road to the mass of workers in their own country, who still had many illusions in reformism.

But how many delegates really understood the meaning of his words, couched, as they were, in fairly diplomatic language? How many were really listening to what Lenin was saying to them and merely being carried away by their enthusiasm for the undisputed leader of the world revolution? The answer only became clear by subsequent events, which showed that, while many paid tribute to Lenin, few had really taken the trouble to understand his ideas. Sadly, that remains the case even today.

The Congress went on to debate many of the questions raised by Lenin, including an extension to the United Front tactic, with the adoption of the slogan of the 'workers' government' or 'workers' and peasants' government', that could arise out of the struggles of the working class. Such a government would inevitably come into conflict with the bourgeoisie and, therefore, had the potential to unleash a revolutionary struggle. The Communists should be willing to participate in such a government, as long as it was prepared to conduct a real struggle against capitalism.

The Party, however, must also be alert to the possible dangers of such a government. The successful application of the policy of the United Front was dependent on one principle: keep one eye on your enemy, but always keep the other eye on your 'ally', who is liable to abandon you at any moment.

The World Congress during Lenin's lifetime was always full of life, characterised by an atmosphere of free and democratic debate. The Fourth Congress was an entirely typical example of a genuine Leninist International. But it was to be the last of its kind. The later Stalinist Congresses – the few times they were actually held – were a bureaucratic caricature: heavily controlled and regimented affairs in which everything was decided by the Party bosses in advance and no dissent of any sort was allowed. The real Communist International died together with its founder, Vladimir Ilyich Lenin.

Lenin's fight over foreign trade

Having made his position clear over the national question in Georgia, and with the Fourth World Congress over, Lenin turned his attention once again to the forthcoming Central Committee meeting in December, where the state monopoly of foreign trade was to be re-discussed. As there was some doubt around whether Lenin would be able to attend the meeting on health grounds, Lenin turned again to Trotsky for help.

On 12 December, Lenin wrote to Trotsky, asking: "I am going to fight for the monopoly. What about you?" The next day, 13 December, Lenin wrote again to Trotsky:

I think that you and I are in maximum agreement [...]

... it is my request that at the forthcoming plenary you should undertake the defence of our common standpoint on the unquestionable need to maintain and consolidate the foreign trade monopoly. Since the preceding plenum passed a decision in this respect which runs entirely counter to the foreign trade monopoly, and since there can be no concessions on this matter, I believe, as I say in my letter to Frumkin and Stomonyakov,* that in the event of our defeat on this question we must refer the question to a Party Congress.[15]

On the same day, Lenin dictated a further letter to Stalin, for the attention of the Central Committee Plenum, outlining his defence of the monopoly of foreign trade. His prime target in this case was Bukharin, the main spokesman for abolishing the monopoly:

> Bukharin does not see – this is his most amazing mistake, and a purely theoretical one at that – that no tariff system can be effective in the epoch of imperialism when there are monstrous contrasts between pauper countries and immensely rich countries. Several times Bukharin mentions tariff barriers, failing to realise that under the circumstances indicated any of the wealthy industrial countries can completely break down such tariff barriers. To do this it will be sufficient for it to introduce an export bounty to encourage the export to Russia of goods upon which we have imposed high import duties. All of the industrial countries have more than enough money for this purpose, and by means of such a measure any of them could easily ruin our home industry.
>
> Consequently, all Bukharin's arguments about the tariff system would in practice only leave Russian industry entirely unprotected and lead to the adoption of free trading under a very flimsy veil. We must oppose this with all our might and carry our opposition right to a Party Congress, for in the present epoch of imperialism the only system of protection worthy of consideration is the monopoly of foreign trade.[16]

Then Lenin went straight to the point, accusing Bukharin of becoming an agent of the NEPmen profiteers and kulaks:

> In practice, Bukharin is acting as an advocate of the profiteer, of the petty bourgeois and of the upper stratum of the peasantry in opposition to the industrial proletariat, which will be totally unable to build up its own industry and make Russia an industrial country unless it has the protection, not of tariffs, but of the monopoly of foreign trade.[17]

If Bukharin's proposal was implemented – which was supported by Stalin – it would have wrecked the Russian economy and guaranteed the restoration of capitalism in Russia in the early 1920s.

At this time, as Lenin's health had deteriorated, his doctors ordered him again to move to Gorki to take a rest. Two days after his agreed bloc with

---

* According to the editors of Lenin's *Collected Works*, the letter has not been found.

Trotsky on the foreign trade question, Lenin wrote a further note to Stalin as secretary of the Central Committee revealing his plans, as well as his agreement with Trotsky. This must have rattled Stalin:

> I have now finished winding up my affairs and can leave with my mind at peace. I have also come to an agreement with Trotsky on the defence of my views on the monopoly of foreign trade. Only one circumstance still worries me very much; it is that it will be impossible for me to speak at the Congress of Soviets. My doctors are coming on Tuesday and we shall see if there is even a small chance of my speaking.[18]

Lenin then wrote a personal note to Stalin on the same day, with a far sharper tone, revealing his cards and his determination to fight:

> I am emphatically against any procrastination of the question of the monopoly of foreign trade. If any circumstance (including the circumstance that my participation is desirable in the debate over this question) gives rise to the idea to postpone it to the next Plenary Meeting, I would most emphatically be against it because, firstly, I am sure Trotsky will uphold my views as well as I; secondly, the statements that you, Zinoviev and, according to rumours, Kamenev have made prove that some members of the CC have already changed their minds; thirdly, and most important, any further vacillation over this extremely important question is absolutely impermissible and will wreck all our work.[19]

Lenin again wrote to Trotsky, fearing a possible manoeuvre by the abolitionists and threatening to refer the entire dispute to a Party Congress:

> Comrade Trotsky:
>
> I consider that we have quite reached agreement. I ask you to declare our solidarity at the Plenum. I hope that our decision will be passed, because some of those who had voted against it in October have now partially or altogether switched to our side. [...]
>
> If this question should be removed from the present Plenum (which I do not expect, and against which you should, of course, protest as strongly as you can on our common behalf), I think that we should apply to the group of the Congress of Soviets anyway, and demand that the question be referred to the Party congress, because any further hesitation is absolutely intolerable.[20]

On the same day, Lenin, who was becoming increasingly agitated, sent another urgent letter to Trotsky:

Comrade Trotsky:

I am sending on to you Frumkin's letter which I have received today. I also think that it is absolutely necessary to have done with this question once and for all. If there are any fears that I am being worried by this question and that it could even have an effect on my health, I think that this is absolutely wrong, because I am infinitely more worried by the delay which makes our policy on one of the most basic questions quite unstable. That is why I call your attention to the enclosed letter and ask you to support an immediate discussion of this question.[21]

He continued:

I am sure that if we are threatened with the danger of failure, it would be much better to fail before the Party congress, and at once to apply to the group of the congress, than to fail after the congress. Perhaps, an acceptable compromise is that we pass a decision just now confirming the monopoly, and still bring up the question at the Party Congress, making an arrangement about this right away. I do not believe that we could accept any other compromise either in our own interests or the interests of the cause.[22]

The final sentence, "I do not believe that we could accept any other compromise either *in our own interests* or the interests of the cause", certainly appears to refer to the "bloc against bureaucracy" that Lenin and Trotsky had agreed upon at an earlier private meeting.

What we see is a line up of political forces, with Lenin and Trotsky against the 'old Bolsheviks', Stalin, Bukharin and the Party's right wing. The members of the Central Committee were well aware that Lenin was standing firm on this question. As a result of the pressure from the political bloc of Lenin and Trotsky, the Central Committee was forced to back down.

On 18 December 1922, the Central Committee Plenum rescinded the decision taken by the previous meeting in October and reaffirmed "the absolute need to maintain and effect the organisational strengthening of the foreign trade monopoly".[23]

Following the defeat of the pro-kulak elements in the Bolshevik leadership, a delighted Lenin wrote to Trotsky a few days later:

It looks as though it has been possible to take the position without a single shot, by a simple manoeuvre. I suggest that we should not stop and should continue the offensive, and for that purpose put through a motion to raise at the Party Congress the question of consolidating our foreign trade, and the measures to improve its implementation. This to be announced in the group of the Congress of Soviets. I hope that you will not object to this, and will not refuse to give a report in the group.[24]

Following this victory, and fearing an alliance between Lenin and Trotsky, increased factional manoeuvres began to take place behind the scenes between members of the secret triumvirate. A day later, on 22 December, Kamenev wrote to Stalin informing him of the latest developments:

Dear Joseph,

Tonight Trotsky phoned me, saying that he had received a note from Starik,* who, though he is happy with the congressional resolution on Vneshintorg [The Commissariat of Foreign Trade], wants Trotsky to deliver a report on this question to a faction of the Congress and to prepare the ground to put this question to the Party Congress. Apparently, he means to strengthen his position. Trotsky did not offer his opinion, but he asked that this matter be handed over to the section of the Central Committee responsible for the conduct of the Congress. I promised him to tell you about it, and I am doing this.

I could not reach you on the phone.

In my report I am going to present the resolution of the Central Committee Plenum with fervour. I shake your hand.

L Kamenev[25]

Stalin replied immediately, fearing the contact between Lenin and Trotsky, and in the process giving the game away about the existence of a secret "faction":

Comrade Kamenev!

I have received your note. I think we should confine ourselves to the statement in your report without bringing this up *in the faction*. How did Starik [Lenin] manage to organise this correspondence with Trotsky? Foerster [one of Lenin's doctors] utterly forbade him to do it.

J Stalin[26]

The secret faction was even more alarmed when Lenin now openly supported Trotsky's proposal to strengthen the powers of the State General Planning Commission (Gosplan). In a letter to the Congress, dated 23 December, Lenin wrote:

---

* Russian word meaning 'The Old Man' – a nickname for Lenin.

... I intend to propose that the Congress should on certain conditions invest the decisions of the State Planning Commission with legislative force, meeting, in this respect, the wishes of Comrade Trotsky – to a certain extent and on certain conditions.[27]

Four days later, Lenin again took up Trotsky's proposal:

This idea was suggested by Comrade Trotsky, it seems, quite a long time ago. I was against it at the time, because I thought that there would then be a fundamental lack of coordination in the system of our legislative institutions. But after closer consideration of the matter I find that in substance there is a sound idea in it, namely: the State Planning Commission stands somewhat apart from our legislative institutions, although, as a body of experienced people, experts, representatives of science and technology, it is actually in a better position to form a correct judgement of affairs. [...]

In this respect I think we can and must accede to the wishes of Comrade Trotsky...[28]

What is remarkable about this correspondence is that the first of Lenin's letters, dated 23 December, was deliberately doctored by Stalin! This was discovered decades later by Yuri Buranov, a professor of history and head of research at the former Central Archives of the CPSU. He explains in the introduction to his 1994 book, *Lenin's Will*:

There has been and still is speculation that Lenin's dictations during that period, particularly his will, were later edited and altered by Joseph Stalin. I have found, in the top-secret archives of the Central Committee of the Communist Party, one of the original manuscripts, which, I submit, proves that Lenin's works were partly altered. The changes were made so skilfully that, for example, to the end of his life, Lev D Trotsky never knew he dealt with the edited, not the original, text of the first and most important of Lenin's dictations, that of 23 December 1922. Stalin's art of falsifying and misinformation surprises historians again and again.[29]

According to Buranov, this original letter of 23 December, which is in the Central Archives, does not contain the words "to a certain extent and on certain conditions", which were deliberately inserted by Stalin to weaken Lenin's support for Trotsky's idea.

The failure of Rabkrin

With his health failing, Lenin was unfortunately unable to attend the Twelfth Party Congress, but instead wrote a letter to the Congress in which he

244. Vyacheslav Molotov   245. Valerian Kuibyshev

raised the dangers of bureaucracy, with Rabkrin (the Workers' and Peasants' Inspection) being one of his main bones of contention. Lenin wrote:

> It is beyond question that the Workers' and Peasants' Inspection is an enormous difficulty for us, and that so far this difficulty has not been overcome. I think that the comrades who try to overcome the difficulty by denying that the Workers' and Peasants' Inspection is useful and necessary are wrong. But I do not deny that the problem presented by our state apparatus and the task of improving it is very difficult, that it is far from being solved, and is an extremely urgent one.[30]

Lenin contrasted the work of Rabkrin with the methods employed by the Red Army, under Trotsky's leadership, which must have grated on Stalin's ears:

> With the exception of the People's Commissariat of Foreign Affairs, our state apparatus is to a considerable extent a survival of the past and has undergone hardly any serious change. It has only been slightly touched up on the surface, but in all other respects it is a most typical relic of our old state machine. And so, to find a method of really renovating it, I think we ought to turn for experience to our Civil War.

> How did we act in the more critical moments of the Civil War?

> We concentrated our best Party forces in the Red Army; we mobilised the best of our workers; we looked for new forces at the deepest roots of our dictatorship. I am convinced that we must go to the same source to find the means of reorganising the Workers' and Peasants' Inspection.[31]

246. Alexei Rykov   247. Mikhail Kalinin

Lenin reserved his sharpest blows against Rabkrin for his famous last article, 'Better Fewer, But Better'. However, there was a massive delay in getting it published.

Things now came to a head in the run-up to the Twelfth Party Congress. The negative effects of the NEP were beginning to reveal themselves.

The failings of Rabkrin had now become much clearer to Lenin, who had been somewhat removed from its work due to illness. Rabkrin's standard of work was shoddy, if not a hindrance, to say the least. Absolutely nothing had been done to draw workers with potential into the administration. Stalin's time and energy was only spent in building up his supporters and cronies within the state and Party apparatus.

Instead of purging the Soviet state of alien elements, careerists and other disreputable characters, Stalin had spent all his time surrounding himself with creatures of his own type. He was able to draw upon his old cronies of the Tsaritsyn Opposition, who he had become acquainted with during the civil war. These were the people who, like himself, held grudges – small people with small minds, greedy for personal advancement and positions of power.

Lenin wrote an article, 'How We Should Reorganise the Workers' and Peasants' Inspection', demanding a complete reorganisation of Rabkrin and the Central Control Commission: expanding the latter, cutting back on the former, and assigning different roles to these bodies. The article was eventually published in *Pravda* on 25 January 1923, after a long delay.

The reason for the delay was the hostile resistance to its content from within the Politburo and especially the Secretariat. Lenin, through Krupskaya, telephoned Trotsky, asking him to intervene to help get the article published. But when Trotsky raised the matter at the Politburo, he was met with a wall of opposition not only against the reorganisation, but against even publishing the article, from Bukharin, Stalin, Molotov, Valerian Kuibyshev, Rykov, Kalinin and others.

Kuibyshev even proposed that a single special number of *Pravda* should be printed with Lenin's article and then shown to him to placate him, but not made available to the Party. Trotsky argued against, with the support of only Kamenev. Eventually, after a long delay, the majority relented. The new balance of forces that was emerging in the leading body of the Party was becoming clearer by the day.

Lenin's article eventually appeared in *Pravda* a month later, on 4 March 1923. It came as a personal blow to Stalin. Although the article does not mention Stalin's name, it was obvious to whom the remarks were directed:

> In the matter of improving our state apparatus, the Workers' and Peasants' Inspection should not, in my opinion, either strive after quantity or hurry. […]
>
> Our state apparatus is so deplorable, not to say wretched, that we must first think very carefully how to combat its defects […]
>
> The most harmful thing here would be haste. The most harmful thing would be to rely on the assumption that we know at least something, or that we have any considerable number of elements necessary for the building of a really new state apparatus, one really worthy to be called socialist, Soviet, etc.
>
> The conclusions to be drawn from the above are the following: we must make the Workers' and Peasants' Inspection a really exemplary institution, an instrument to improve our state apparatus. […]
>
> We have been bustling for five years trying to improve our state apparatus, but it has been mere bustle, which has proved useless in these five years, or even futile, or even harmful. […]
>
> It is high time things were changed.
>
> We must follow the rule: Better fewer, but better.[32]

Lenin went on to the attack:

> Let us say frankly that the People's Commissariat of the Workers' and Peasants' Inspection does not at present enjoy the slightest authority. Everybody knows that

no other institutions are worse organised than those of our Workers' and Peasants' Inspection, and that under present conditions nothing can be expected from this People's Commissariat. [...]

Indeed, what is the use of establishing a People's Commissariat which carries on anyhow, which does not enjoy the slightest confidence, and whose word carries scarcely any weight? [...]

But I ask any of the present chiefs of the Workers' and Peasants' Inspection, or anyone associated with that body, whether they can honestly tell me the practical purpose of a People's Commissariat like the Workers' and Peasants' Inspection. [...] Either it is not worth while having another of the numerous reorganisations that we have had of this hopeless affair, the Workers' and Peasants' Inspection, or we must really set to work...[33]

Lenin's bloc with Trotsky, his support for Trotsky's economic proposals, and his severe criticisms of Rabkrin, were clear warnings to Stalin.

And as on so many other occasions, Lenin linked the fate of the Russian Revolution with that of the world revolution:

It is not easy for us, however, to keep going until the socialist revolution is victorious in more developed countries merely with the aid of this confidence, because economic necessity, especially under NEP, keeps the productivity of labour of the small and very small peasants at an extremely low level.[34]

However, Lenin was hopeful of the immediate prospects, stating:

We have the advantage that the whole world is now passing to a movement that must give rise to a world socialist revolution.[35]

Once again, the Georgian question

Around this time, Lenin had also become gradually aware of the events involving the Georgian Communist Party leadership, who had again clashed with Stalin and his henchmen over the national question.

At first, Lenin had no idea what was going on in Georgia, after being kept in the dark by Stalin. In fact, his initial response was to support Stalin against the allegations of the Georgians. But this did not last long. In Georgia, matters had been pushed to a breaking point by the actions of Stalin's supporters.

In an unprecedented incident, Ordzhonikidze lost his temper and physically struck Kabanidze, one of the Mdivani group, who he had been trying to intimidate. The criminal assault took place at a private session held

248. Anastas Mikoyan, Stalin and Ordzhonikidze
in Tiflis (modern-day Tbilisi), Georgia, 1925

at Ordzhonikidze's residence, where a bitter row took place. Rykov, Lenin's deputy and member of the Politburo was also present.

As a result of this and other provocations, the Central Committee of the Georgian Party resigned en bloc on 22 October 1922. This simply played into Ordzhonikidze's hands. He immediately appointed a new, more pliant Central Committee in its place. Stalin and his henchmen had in effect carried through a coup d'état against the Georgian leadership.

When this matter was reported to the Politburo, it was decided to establish a commission of inquiry about the dispute in Georgia. The three members chosen for this task were Dzerzhinsky, Solomon Lozovsky and Vincas Mickevičius-Kapsukas, all of whom, incidentally, had been proposed by Stalin.

Lenin was deeply suspicious and asked Rykov to find out what was going on. But things were being deliberately kept from him. Given the constant delays, he grew impatient to find out the facts. The Dzerzhinsky commission report turned out to be a complete whitewash, which put the blame for the strained relations on the Georgian leadership's supposed nationalist deviations.

When Lenin heard a report from Dzerzhinsky, he was shaken. Lenin dictated a note to his secretary:

249. Polikarp Mdivani   250. Solomon Lozovsky   251. Vincas Mickevičius-Kapsukas

> I suppose I have been very remiss with respect to the workers of Russia for not having intervened energetically and decisively enough in the notorious question of autonomisation...[36]

He justified this by his illness when this question first arose in the summer. He was then preoccupied with his recovery and was not able to attend the meetings where national questions were being discussed. Lenin admits "the question passed me by almost completely..."[37] But he went on:

> From what I was told by Comrade Dzerzhinsky, who was at the head of the commission sent by the CC to 'investigate' the Georgian incident, I could only draw the greatest apprehensions. If matters had come to such a pass that Ordzhonikidze could go to the extreme of applying physical violence, as Comrade Dzerzhinsky informed me, we can imagine what a mess we have got ourselves into. Obviously the whole business of 'autonomisation' was radically wrong and badly timed.[38]

According to Fotieva, when Lenin heard Dzerzhinsky's account, he said it "had a very painful effect on me."[39]

It was clear that Ordzhonikidze had been behaving criminally like a governor-general in Georgia, bureaucratically riding roughshod over the opinions of the Georgians. The assault was a brutal expression of the regime he was running. This was being done with the full support of Stalin, who was engaged in a vendetta against the Georgian leaders.

When Lenin found out about what had happened, he was furious. He treated these crimes against national minorities as an abomination and

252. Lenin with Rykov, 3 October 1922

immediately connected this incident to the growing bureaucratic menace within the Party and state apparatus.

Disgusted, he proposed taking measures to provide the non-Russian nationalities with real safeguards "against the truly Russian bully…"[40] Then he went on to indict Stalin, highlighting the role of personal spite, which motivated the General Secretary, in this most heinous crime:

I think that Stalin's haste and his infatuation with pure administration, together with his spite against the notorious 'nationalist-socialism', played a fatal role here.[41]

Lenin then added: "In politics spite generally plays the basest of roles".[42] And spitefulness was one of the most obvious characteristics of Stalin, and it played a prominent role in his relations with others. Lenin concluded:

I also fear that Comrade Dzerzhinsky, who went to the Caucasus to investigate the 'crime' of those 'nationalist-socialists', distinguished himself there by his truly Russian frame of mind (it is common knowledge that people of other nationalities

253. Dzerzhinsky with Stalin, June 1924

who have become Russified overdo this Russian frame of mind) and that the impartiality of his whole commission was typified well enough by Ordzhonikidze's 'manhandling'. I think that no provocation or even insult can justify such Russian manhandling and that Comrade Dzerzhinsky was inexcusably guilty in adopting a light-hearted attitude towards it.[43]

Having chastised these comrades for their Russian chauvinism (incidentally, Dzerzhinsky was Polish, while Stalin was Georgian), Lenin went on to ask the question: who was this Russian bureaucrat? He answers:

…that really Russian man, the Great-Russian chauvinist, in substance a rascal and a tyrant, such as the typical Russian bureaucrat is.

He warned:

There is no doubt that the infinitesimal percentage of Soviet and sovietised workers will drown in that tide of chauvinistic Great-Russian riff-raff like a fly in milk.[44]

Lenin then stated "exemplary punishment must be inflicted on Comrade Ordzhonikidze" for his unforgivable crime, which meant his expulsion from the Party. He then nailed his colours to the mast:

The political responsibility for all this truly Great-Russian nationalist campaign must, of course, be laid on Stalin and Dzerzhinsky.[45]

This was a devastating blow to Stalin, the Great Russian nationalist and so-called Commissar for Nationalities. For Lenin, the whole Georgian affair had shown Stalin in his true colours, as an archetypal bureaucrat, an intriguer, a bully and a tyrant. It was this more than anything that convinced Lenin of the need to remove him as general secretary. It was clear that the fight against bureaucracy needed to be urgently stepped up.

This fight would open up the final chapter in Lenin's political life. It was to be the most difficult fight of his entire life, undertaken in the most painful of circumstances.

38. Clash with Stalin

It was towards the end of 1922 when everything became clear to Lenin. All the pieces began to fall into place.

Following his period of recovery after the stroke, Lenin returned to the Kremlin. He was shocked by the changes he witnessed and alarmed at the growth of bureaucracy. He could see for himself how things had deteriorated. He realised that, given his state of health, he needed to act without any further delay.

It was also clear to him after the experience of the October Revolution, the civil war, and the backsliding of many of the 'old Bolsheviks', he needed to turn to Trotsky in what would be the final political battle of his life against bureaucracy. This faith in Trotsky had been borne from common work in defending and building the Soviet state. Once again, they were united in struggle.

Lenin's bloc with Trotsky against bureaucracy was cemented as soon as Lenin had returned to work in early October. In his meeting with Trotsky, he began by asking Trotsky to join Rabkrin so as to strengthen the struggle against bureaucracy, but Trotsky was not in favour of the proposal. He explained that the bureaucracy had the backing of certain Party leaders, a reference to Stalin, and therefore felt unable to accept the assignment. Trotsky recalled Lenin's response:

> Then Vladmir Ilyich reflected for a moment and – here I quote him practically verbatim – said: "That is, I propose a struggle with Soviet bureaucratism, and you want to add to that the bureaucratism of the Organisation Bureau of the Party."

I laughed at the unexpectedness of this, because no such finished formulation of the idea was in my head. I answered, "I suppose that's it."

Then Vladimir Ilyich said: "Well, all right, I propose a bloc", and I said: "I'm always ready to form a bloc with a good man."[1]

This was nothing less than a declaration of all-out war against bureaucracy and Stalin. Lenin had stressed the danger of a bureaucracy, not only within the state apparatus, but within the Party in his article, 'Better Fewer, But Better', where he states: "Let it be said in parentheses that we have bureaucrats in our Party offices as well as in the Soviet offices."[2] Stalin understood very well such language, and whom it was directed at.

However, Lenin never fully regained his health. He was frequently absent from meetings and his headaches still plagued him. He was continually tired and needed to rest. His first public appearance was a great trial for him. Rosmer recalls the moment he spoke at the Fourth World Congress in Moscow:

> Those who were seeing him for the first time said: "It's still the same Lenin." But the others could not allow themselves such illusions. Instead of the alert Lenin they had known, the man they had before them was deeply marked by paralysis. His features remained fixed and he walked like a robot. His usual simple, rapid, self-confident speech had given way to a haunting, hesitant delivery. Sometimes he couldn't find the words he wanted. Nonetheless, his mind remained unshaken, and the main ideas were presented and developed with skill.[3]

It was this speech in which Lenin said: "We took over the old machinery of state, and that was our misfortune. Very often this machinery operates against us."[4]

At the beginning of December 1922, as part of their common struggle against bureaucratism, Lenin insisted that Trotsky become his deputy in the Council of People's Commissars. The task was to carry out this battle with the least possible number of shocks and convulsions. This seemed optimistic, but certainly a combined bloc of Lenin and Trotsky would have been a formidable force.

Unfortunately, 12 December 1922 proved to be the last day Lenin spent working in his office. The following day, he suffered a further two strokes. On this day, he had wrote to Kamenev, Rykov and Tsiurupa:

> Owing to a recurrence of my illness I must wind up all political work and take a holiday again. [...]

> But please bear in mind that I give my consent to your proposed distribution, not for three months (as you suggest), but pending my return to work, should this take place earlier than within three months.[5]

But Lenin was never to return to work. His doctors ordered him to take a complete break from his work. Despite this advice, he was very reluctant to do so, painfully aware of the problems that were assailing him on all sides and his pressing responsibilities. His sister Maria wrote later:

> The doctors had great difficulty in persuading Vladimir Ilyich to drop work altogether and go out into the country. Meanwhile he was to lie down for as long as possible and not go for walks. In the end Vladimir Ilyich agreed to leave town and said "I'll start winding up my affairs this very day".[6]

As it turned out, Lenin spent several days at home, dictating letters and giving various instructions, anxious to fully wind up his affairs. It is no wonder that he often complained about the strain on his nerves, contributing to his headaches and anxiety. However, up until this point, to all those around him, Lenin always appeared active and good-humoured. To them, he seemed incombustible.

Lenin wrote to Stalin about his steps to retire, and it was at this point that he told him he had concluded an agreement with Trotsky to defend their common position on the monopoly of foreign trade. As we have seen, within days, the Central Committee had rescinded its decision about the monopoly and adopted the line advocated by Lenin and Trotsky.

However, despite the fact that he was still struggling with the effects of his second series of strokes, Lenin was increasingly alarmed at what was taking place and asked his secretaries to quietly gather information. He again turned his attention to the leadership and the danger of a split in the Party along class lines. He believed it best to keep the struggle over bureaucracy confined to the leadership if at all possible.

This was the purpose of the proposals in what became known as Lenin's *Testament*, his assessment of the key leaders of the party.

Behind the scenes, it was clear that the succession was being discussed among the 'old Bolsheviks', who were secretly resentful of Trotsky's success and popularity. They could not stomach the idea that this 'newcomer' should occupy a more prominent place in the Party and state than them – the old Bolshevik veterans. And they were mortified by the idea that he could take Lenin's place in the future.

Feelings of jealousy gradually turned to dislike, spite, and even hatred. This was the poisonous cement that brought together the triumvirate of Stalin, Zinoviev and Kamenev, whose single, overriding aim was to block Trotsky's rise.

254. Stalin, Rykov, Zinoviev and Bukharin in 1924

Trotsky's authority was becoming stronger as time passed. And the news of the existence of a bloc between Lenin and Trotsky only served to heighten the fears of the Troika about Lenin's succession. They therefore plotted to ensure Trotsky would never become the successor of Lenin. Zinoviev was determined to make use of every episodic conflict, every controversy like the one over the trade unions, to gather up ammunition for a future struggle with Trotsky, who he saw as his greatest rival. He saw Stalin as the most suitable man for this behind-the-scenes work.

This kind of plot was Zinoviev's speciality. In fact, it was not Stalin, who, for the time being, was content to play a secondary role in the Troika, but Zinoviev who would invent the term 'Trotskyism' in opposition to 'Leninism'. As we have already noted, he was profoundly convinced of his personal ability and leadership qualities. And he firmly believed that he was Lenin's true heir. This conviction of superiority meant that he alone was destined to occupy the leading role in the Troika.

Kamenev's character did not qualify him for it. He was, by nature, suited to play second fiddle to Zinoviev, who was intellectually far inferior to him, but possessed a far stronger character. As for Stalin, Zinoviev had no fears on his account. After all, if it hadn't been for him, Stalin would never have been general secretary. No, he was no leader, but a mere apparatchik – a machine man, fit only to press buttons and move the cogs. Zinoviev never suspected what hidden power lay in that machine, which in the hands of Stalin would one day crush him between its steel cogs.

Stalin's abuse

On 21 December 1922, Lenin dictated a further note to Trotsky on the monopoly of foreign trade. It was in this note, dictated to his wife Krupskaya, Lenin triumphantly hailed their victory at the Central Committee, which they had won "without a single shot".[7]

When Stalin heard about this 'infringement' he exploded. He immediately phoned Krupskaya and abused her using the foulest language, attacking her for allowing this contact without his permission, and mocking her childless marriage for good measure. He even had the audacity to threaten to take her before the Party's Control Commission. On 23 December, Krupskaya reported Stalin's abuse to Kamenev:

Lev Borisovich!

Because of a short letter which I had written in words dictated to me by Vladimir Ilych by permission of the doctors, Stalin allowed himself yesterday an unusually rude outburst directed against me. This is not my first day in the Party. During all these thirty years I have never heard from any comrade one word of rudeness... What one can and what one cannot discuss with Ilyich I know better than any doctor, because I know what makes him nervous and what does not, in any case I know better than Stalin. I am turning to you and Gregory [Zinoviev] as closer comrades of VI [Lenin] and I beg you protect me from rude interference with my private life from vile invective and threats... I am a living person and my nerves are strained to the utmost.

[Signed] N Krupskaya[8]

This letter was kept under lock and key, hidden from Communist Party members for more than thirty years and was only released with Khruschev's 'Secret Speech' to the Twentieth Party Congress in 1956. The then General Secretary of the CPSU listed the bloody crimes of Stalin and added, if this was the case, "we can easily imagine how Stalin treated other people."[9]

This incident sheds much light on Stalin's real attitude towards the dying Lenin, a clear example of his vicious and treacherous nature. So as to shield the sick Lenin, Krupskaya did not tell him the details of what Stalin said to her, for fear of distressing him further. Lenin only found out about Stalin's abuse against his wife more than two months later. That was the final straw for him – a clear and irrefutable confirmation of Stalin's disloyal and repulsive character.

Stalin now felt threatened by the mortally sick Lenin. And he immediately took measures to protect himself and isolate the dying man. His plans received a boost when, at the very same December Central Committee meeting where Lenin and Trotsky scored their victory over the monopoly of foreign trade, the decision was taken to make Stalin responsible for Lenin's medical supervision. That decision came directly from the Politburo, which was controlled by a secret faction. The undeclared aim was to manage and limit all access to the seriously ill Lenin.

This fatal move gave Stalin all he needed to secure control over Lenin's closest staff, even his doctors. He could receive regular reports about everything Lenin was saying or doing, the state of his health – was he getting better or worse? Above all, was he going to be in a fit state to address the forthcoming Party Congress? That was something Stalin had good reason to fear. And what communications was he having with other people? Stalin used his position to deliberately isolate Lenin. He pressed the doctors to pronounce that all visits to Lenin were forbidden, apart from Krupskaya, his sister Maria, his secretaries and the doctors.

Under Stalin's urgent pressure, the doctors repeatedly forbade Lenin to do any work or contact anybody. This was supposed to be in the interests of his health – to stop him from coming under stress. But, as Lenin complained many times, it was the lack of information that was causing him more psychological distress than anything else.

Lenin was, in effect, being held prisoner by Stalin. His secretaries were specifically forbidden by Stalin to give Lenin information about the current state of affairs. "To avoid giving him food for thought and alarm neither his friends nor members of his family should tell Vladimir Ilyich any political news", stated the directive.[10]

Lenin was increasingly aware and became suspicious of Stalin's motives. Lenin's secretary, Lydia Fotieva, related in her entries in the *Journal of Lenin's Duty Secretaries*:

> Vladimir Ilyich had the impression that it was not the doctors who gave instructions to the Central Committee, but the Central Committee that gave instructions to the doctors.[11]

Of course, it was Stalin, the General Secretary, who acted as the voice of the Central Committee, and through them the doctors. In fact, for Fotieva, it was not a question of probability but certainty.*

---

* See Lydia Fotieva's *Journal* entries on 1 and 3 February 1923, *LCW*, Vol. 42, pp. 485-7.

While Stalin continued his manoeuvres to strengthen his personal position, it was necessary to keep Lenin completely in the dark. As a result, Stalin continually pestered and hounded Lenin's secretaries, fearing they were giving him information behind his back. Lenin, on the other hand, was engaged in a battle to get as much information as possible.

In Fotieva's entry to the *Journal* on 16 December 1922, she relates a discussion with Krupskaya, in which Lenin asks for notes about the speeches of certain Central Committee members:

> She [Krupskaya] also asked [Fotieva], on his [Lenin's] instructions, to phone Yarovslavsky secretly and ask him to make notes of the speeches of Bukharin and Pyatakov, and if possible others at the plenum, on the question of foreign trade.[12]

He was worried that they were conspiring behind his back to once again weaken the monopoly of foreign trade. He could no longer trust them in his absence. With every passing day, Lenin's illness worsened, while his anxiety concerning the activities of Stalin and those around him increased. Lenin was clearly feeling the isolation. It was for this reason that his letter to Trotsky was dictated not to one of his secretaries, but to his wife, Krupskaya.

In the meantime, on the night of 22-23 December, Lenin suffered further paralysis.

Lenin's 'Testament'

According to Fotieva, on 23 December Lenin asked his doctors for permission to dictate for five minutes about matters that troubled him and robbed him of his sleep. After some resistance, they reluctantly complied, and Lenin began to dictate his last notes and letters to the Congress from that time onwards.

Everything now became extremely urgent for Lenin, who feared he was running out of time. According to the entry of MA Volodicheva, another of Lenin's secretaries, he said: "I want to dictate to you a letter to the Congress. Take it down." He then dictated for four minutes. "Dictated quickly, but his sick condition was obvious", commented Volodicheva.[13]

> After he stopped dictating he asked me what day it was. He also asked me why I looked so pale and why I was not at the Congress. He regretted having kept me from attending it. I received no other instruction.[14]

The following day, she wrote:

> Warned me that what he had dictated yesterday (23 December) and today (24 December) was *strictly* confidential. He emphasised this again and again.

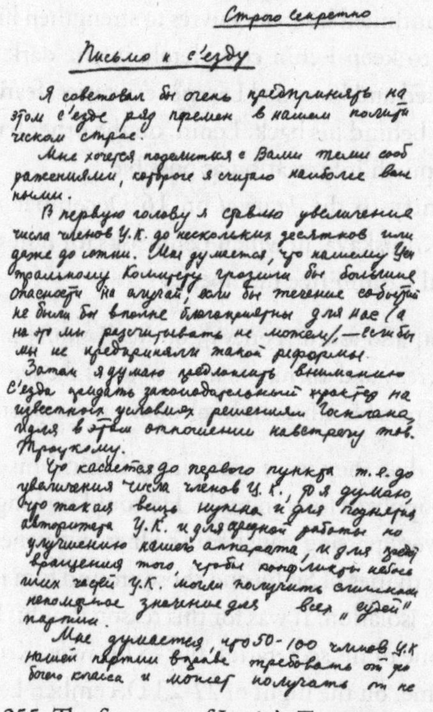

[Handwritten Russian text of Lenin's Testament, first page]

255. The first page of Lenin's *Testament*

Demanded that *everything* he was dictating should be kept in a special place under special responsibility and to be considered *categorically* secret.[15]

Lenin was dictating his famous *Testament*, also known as his 'Letters to the Congress', which, in the event of his death, should be read to the Congress. Contained in the *Testament* was a recognition of the dangers of a split in the Party and a detailed account of the qualities of six members of the leadership: Trotsky, Stalin, Zinoviev, Kamenev, Bukharin and Pyatakov. Lenin dictated the following over 24 and 25 December:

By stability of the Central Committee, of which I spoke above, I mean measures against a split, so far as such measures can at all be taken. [...]

Our Party relies on two classes and therefore its instability would be possible and its downfall inevitable if there were no agreement between those two classes. In that event this or that measure, and generally all talk about the stability of our CC, would be futile. No measures of any kind could prevent a split in such a case. But I hope that this is too remote a future and too improbable an event to talk about.

I have in mind stability as a guarantee against a split in the immediate future, and I intend to deal here with a few ideas concerning personal qualities.

I think that from this standpoint the prime factors in the question of stability are such members of the CC as Stalin and Trotsky. I think relations between them make up the greater part of the danger of a split, which could be avoided, and this purpose, in my opinion, would be served, among other things, by increasing the number of Central Committee members to 50 or 100.[16]

Lenin then went on to draw out both the relevant strengths and weaknesses of the individuals:

Comrade Stalin, having become Secretary-General, has unlimited authority concentrated in his hands, and I am not sure whether he will always be capable of using that authority with sufficient caution. Comrade Trotsky, on the other hand, as his struggle against the CC on the question of the People's Commissariat for Communications has already proved, is distinguished not only by outstanding ability. He is personally perhaps the most capable man in the present CC, but he has displayed excessive self-assurance and shown excessive preoccupation with the purely administrative side of the work.

These two qualities of the two outstanding leaders of the present CC can inadvertently lead to a split, and if our Party does not take steps to avert this, the split may come unexpectedly.

I shall not give any further appraisals of the personal qualities of other members of the CC. I shall just recall that the October episode with Zinoviev and Kamenev was, of course, no accident, but neither can the blame for it be laid upon them personally, any more than non-Bolshevism can upon Trotsky.

Speaking of the young CC members, I wish to say a few words about Bukharin and Pyatakov. They are, in my opinion, the most outstanding figures (among the youngest ones), and the following must be borne in mind about them: Bukharin is not only a most valuable and major theorist of the Party; he is also rightly considered the favourite of the whole Party, but his theoretical views can be classified as fully Marxist only with great reserve, for there is something scholastic about him (he has never made a study of dialectics, and, I think, never fully understood it).

As for Pyatakov, he is unquestionably a man of outstanding will and outstanding ability, but shows too much zeal for administrating and the administrative side of the work to be relied upon in a serious political matter.

Both of these remarks, of course, are made only for the present, on the assumption that both these outstanding and devoted Party workers fail to find an occasion to enhance their knowledge and amend their one-sidedness.[17]

These brief characterisations of the leading Party figures are written out of necessity in a highly concentrated manner, given the precarious state of Lenin's health. Furthermore, he clearly felt it necessary to express himself in the most diplomatic language. His main concern was to avoid a dangerous split in the Party.

At this point, Lenin was still struggling to hold things together. He therefore expressed himself very cautiously. He was reluctant to act against Stalin, and held back. To have gone ahead would have meant pointing to Trotsky as his favoured successor. He made some mild criticisms of Trotsky ("excessive self-assurance" and "excessive preoccupation with the purely administrative side of the work"), but these were of an entirely secondary nature. On the other hand, Lenin clearly states that he was the most capable member of the Central Committee and was a man of outstanding ability.

It would be a further ten days before Lenin made up his mind and came out openly against Stalin.

Remove Stalin!

As we have seen, Stalin's role in the 'Georgian affair' was, by now, clear to Lenin. All the disparate elements had come together, and Lenin had made up his mind. It was now time to lance the poisonous bureaucratic boil – to strike at the head of the monster.

Realising that his time was running out, Lenin displayed no hesitation. It was time for a complete break with Stalin. This was the moment that Stalin dreaded. On 4 January 1923, Lenin wrote an addition to his *Testament*:

Stalin is too rude and this defect, although quite tolerable in our midst and in dealings among us Communists, becomes intolerable in a Secretary-General. That is why I suggest that the comrades think about a way of removing Stalin from that post and appointing another man in his stead who in all other respects differs from Comrade Stalin in having only one advantage, namely, that of being more tolerant, more loyal, more polite and more considerate to the comrades, less capricious, etc. This circumstance may appear to be a negligible detail. But I think that from the standpoint of safeguards against a split and from the standpoint of what I wrote above about the relationship between Stalin and Trotsky it is not a detail, or it is a detail which can assume decisive importance.[18]

It is clear that the measures Lenin saw to prevent a split in the Party included the removal and replacement of Stalin, who "has unlimited authority concentrated in his hands", with someone "more tolerant, more loyal, more polite and more considerate…" In regard to both Stalin and Trotsky, Lenin proposes removing Stalin. *His instruction is clear and was evidently intended as a political death sentence for Stalin.*

This was Lenin's last word; it was the final entry by Lenin in his 'Letters' or *Testament* to the Congress. If this had become public, it would have meant the end for Stalin. But that was not to be. Stalin's influential allies in the leadership closed ranks to protect him. At the instigation of Zinoviev, the Politburo took the decision to keep Lenin's *Testament* secret.

Only five copies were made and placed in wax-sealed envelopes, one for Lenin, three for Krupskaya and one for his secretariat, labelled 'strictly secret'. The *Testament* was only to be opened by Krupskaya after his death and was intended to be read to delegates at the Party Congress. However, Fotieva, who had taken down the note, mentioned their contents to Stalin. Alarmed and furious, he began to prepare the ground, together with Zinoviev and Kamenev, to frustrate Lenin's wishes.

But for as long as his health held out, Lenin would continue the fight against this bureaucratic cancer within the Party, epitomised by the 'Georgian affair'. He was preparing a 'bomb' against Stalin, with all the necessary materials, which he hoped to deliver, depending on his health, at the forthcoming Party Congress, scheduled for 17 April 1923. As Trotsky explained:

> Lenin was now preparing not only to remove Stalin from his post of General Secretary, but to disqualify him before the Party as well. On the question of monopoly of foreign trade, on the national question, on questions of the regime in the party, of the worker-peasant inspection, and of the commission of control, he was systematically preparing to deliver at the Twelfth Congress a crushing blow at Stalin as personifying bureaucracy, the mutual shielding among officials, arbitrary rule and general rudeness.[19]

Lenin was hoping, against all the odds, to participate in the Twelfth Congress, but his doctors were less convinced. It was clear that if he managed to attend, the bloc of Lenin and Trotsky against bureaucracy would be invincible. Lenin held an exceptional position within the Party.

However, if he was absent and the fight was left up to Trotsky, it would be more complicated, given that Kamenev and Zinoviev, the other members of the triumvirate, stood behind Stalin. Everything depended on whether Lenin would recover sufficiently to participate.

Lenin proceeded tirelessly to make his preparations, gathering material for his assault. Every step he took drew him closer to Trotsky, in whom he had developed enormous confidence. His health appeared to improve, and he was allowed to read the newspapers and receive visits.

He was now especially concerned about the impartiality of the commission established by the Politburo to investigate the 'Georgian affair', headed by Dzerzhinsky. The Politburo had received and approved the conclusions of the report, which, in reality, white-washed Ordzhonikidze and condemned the Georgian opposition. It even suggested that the leaders of the Georgian opposition, Polikarp Mdivani, Filipp Makharadze and Kote Tsintsadze, be recalled to Moscow.

This endorsement rang alarm bells for Lenin and reinforced his suspicions about Stalin. He was determined to get to the bottom of it. Fotieva's entry in the *Journal* for 30 January 1923 states:

> On 24 January Vladimir Ilyich sent for Fotieva and gave instructions to ask Dzerzhinsky or Stalin for the materials of the commission on the Georgian question and to make a detailed study of them. This assignment was given to Fotieva, Glyasser and Gorbunov. Object – report to Vladimir Ilyich, who wanted this for the Party congress. Apparently, he did not know the question was up at the Politbureau. He said: "Just before I got ill Dzerzhinsky told me about the work of the commission and about the 'incident', and this had a very painful effect upon me." [...]

> On Saturday I asked Dzerzhinsky, he said Stalin had the materials. I sent Stalin a letter, but he was out of town. Yesterday, 29 January, Stalin phoned saying he could not give the materials without the [agreement of the] Politbureau.[20]

Lenin's distrustful attitude to the commission of Dzerzhinsky and the behaviour of the Central Committee is reflected in his instructions and probing questions to his secretaries:

1. Why was the old CC of the CP [Communist Party] of Georgia accused of deviationism.

2. What breach of Party discipline were they blamed for.

3. Why is the Transcaucasian Committee accused of suppressing the CC of the CP of Georgia.

4. The physical means of suppression ('biomechanics').

5. The line of the CC [of the RCP(B)] in Vladimir Ilyich's absence and in his presence.

6. Attitude of the Commission. Did it examine only the accusations against the CC of the CP of Georgia or also against the Transcaucasian Committee? Did it examine the 'biomechanics' incident?

7. The present situation (the election campaign, the Mensheviks, suppression, national discord).[21]

Fotieva took down Lenin's last notes on the Georgian question, which were evidently preparation for a speech at the Congress on this issue. He wanted to let it be known that he stood firmly behind the old Georgian leadership:

> Vladimir Ilyich's instructions that a hint be given to Soltz* that he (Lenin) was on the side of the injured party. Someone or other of the injured party to be given to understand that he was on their side.
>
> Three moments: 1) One should not fight. 2) Concessions should be made. 3) One cannot compare a large state with a small one. Did Stalin know? Why didn't he react? The name 'deviationist' for a deviation towards chauvinism and Menshevism proves the same deviation with the dominant nation chauvinists.
>
> Collect printed matter for Vladimir Ilyich.[22]

Lenin was planning to intervene publicly "on the side of the injured party" at the forthcoming Congress. And as soon as Stalin got a hint of what was going on, he immediately accused Fotieva of smuggling information to Lenin, as she explains in the *Journal*:

> Asked whether I had not been telling Vladimir Ilyich things he was not to be told – how was it he was posted about current affairs? For instance, his article about the WPI [Workers' and Peasants' Inspectorate] showed that certain circumstances were known to him. I answered that I had not been telling anything and had no reason to believe he was posted about affairs. Today Vladimir Ilyich sent for me to learn the answer and said that he would fight to get the materials.[23]

Stalin specifically had in mind the 'Georgian affair', which he knew Lenin wanted more information about. He suspected Lenin was preparing something important, and he was right. Fotieva repeated to Lenin what Stalin had told her about not speaking to him about "day-to-day matters". Lenin then remarked to her, "So the national affair is a day-to-day matter, is it?"[24] Fotieva wrote in the *Journal*:

---

* Aaron Soltz – a member of the praesidium of the Central Control Commission.

On January 24 Vladimir Ilyich said: "First of all, about this 'secret' job of ours – I know that you are deceiving me." To my assurances to the contrary, he answered: "I have my own opinion about that."[25]

That Lenin could sense a conspiracy against him, is shown by his suspicions that things were being deliberately withheld from him, especially by those who oversaw and managed his regime. These suspicions were well grounded. But this made him more determined to produce his own report on Georgia with the aid of a handful of loyal collaborators.

On 2 February 1923, Volodicheva commented about Lenin's health and how he was improving:

I had not seen him since 23 January. Outwardly, a considerable change for the better: fresh, cheerful looking. Dictates, as always, excellently: without halts, seldom at a loss for words, speaks, gesticulating, rather than dictates.[26]

On 5 February, Lenin asked for Fotieva, but she was indisposed, and so he was attended by Maria Glyasser, who commented:

I was with Vladimir Ilyich altogether twenty minutes. I was seeing him for the first time since his illness. I thought he looked well and cheerful, only slightly paler than before.[27]

Lenin immediately asked how the gathering of material for the Georgian commission was proceeding, and what date it would be finished. He was keen for it to be completed by the Congress in under two months time. He said that if more help was needed, Volodicheva and Shushanika Manucharyants could be used. He was desperate that the work should be completed in time. There was no time to lose. On 6 February Volodicheva wrote, "Vladimir Ilyich in a good humour":

He recollected how he tried to dictate an article of his to Trotsky's stenographer back in 1918, and how, when he felt himself getting "stuck", he "plunged" on in confusion with "incredible" speed, and how this led to his having had to burn the whole manuscript, after which he sat down to write himself and wrote 'The Renegade Kautsky', with which he was pleased.

Vladimir Ilyich talked about all this very gaily, laughing his infectious laugh. I had never seen him in such a mood."[28]

The next day, Fotieva reported:

Today Kozhovenikov said that there was a tremendous improvement in Vladimir Ilyich's health. He was now moving his arm and had begun to believe himself that he would regain the use of it.[29]

However, a week later his health once again began to deteriorate. On 10 February, Fotieva reported that Lenin: "Looks tired, speaks with great difficulty, losing the thread of his thoughts and confusing words."[30]

Relations break down

Volodicheva reported on 5 March:

Vladimir Ilyich did not send for me until round about 12. Asked me to take down two letters: one to Trotsky, the other to Stalin; the first letter to be telephoned personally to Trotsky and the answer given to him as soon as possible.[31]

This first letter was the request made to Trotsky to take up the fight over the Georgian case:

Dear Comrade Trotsky:

It is my earnest request that you should undertake the defence of the Georgian case in the Party CC. This case is now under 'prosecution' by Stalin and Dzerzhinsky, and I cannot rely on their impartiality. Quite to the contrary! I would feel at ease if you agreed to undertake its defence. If you should refuse to do so for any reason, return the whole case to me. I shall consider it a sign that you do not accept.

With best comradely greetings,

Lenin[32]

The purpose of this letter could not be clearer. Lenin was writing to Trotsky to act on his behalf, while explicitly stating that he had no confidence in Stalin and Dzerzhinsky.

Lenin had made sure through his secretaries that Trotsky remained firm over the Georgian question. He was completely reassured when he was told that Trotsky had accused Ordzhonikidze and the rest of trampling on the national question. Lenin's secretary then sent Trotsky a further note:

To Comrade Trotsky:

To his letter, sent to you by telephone, Vladimir Ilyich asks me to add for your information that comrade Kamenev is going to Georgia on Wednesday, and

Vladimir Ilyich asks me to find out whether you do not want to send something there from you.

M Volodicheva[33]

Kamenev was going to Georgia for the Party Conference. Having received Lenin's materials on Georgia, Trotsky suggested that he give them to Kamenev so as to acquaint him with the situation. Fotieva returned with a blunt message from Lenin:

Fotieva: Under no circumstances.

Trotsky: Why?

Fotieva: Vladimir Ilyich says: "Kamenev will immediately show everything to Stalin, and Stalin will make a rotten compromise and then deceive us."

Trotsky: Then the thing has gone so far that Vladimir Ilyich no longer thinks that we can compromise with Stalin even in the right lines?

Fotieva: Yes, he does not trust Stalin, and wants to come out against him openly before the entire Party. He is preparing a bomb.[34]

The word "bomb" was Lenin's. As for his second letter, which was to Stalin, Volodicheva reports:

... he asked it to be put off, saying that he was not very good at it that day. He wasn't feeling too good.[35]

By this time, Lenin had the full measure of Stalin. Krupskaya told him that Stalin had verbally abused her in the vilest language over the phone more than two months earlier. Lenin was outraged by Stalin's rudeness and disloyalty.

Although he was extremely ill, he dictated a letter to Stalin telling him in no uncertain terms what he thought of him, and breaking off relations with him. Copies of this letter were sent to Kamenev and Zinoviev.

Dear Comrade Stalin:

You have been so rude as to summon my wife to the telephone and use bad language. Although she had told you that she was prepared to forget this, the fact nevertheless became known through her to Zinoviev and Kamenev. I have no intention of forgetting so easily what has been done against me, and it goes without saying that what has been done against my wife I consider having been done against me as well. I ask you, therefore, to think it over whether you are prepared to withdraw what you have said and to make your apologies, or whether you prefer that relations between us should be broken off.

Respectfully yours,

Lenin[36]

This episode reflects the real situation between Lenin and Stalin prior to his death: a complete breakdown of personal and comradely relations. The unbearable stress brought on by the clash with Stalin must have helped to bring on a sudden and devastating deterioration in Lenin's already fragile health. On 6 March, a further stroke resulted in a complete loss of speech and paralysis down Lenin's right side.

On the very same day, prior to the stroke, Lenin had dictated another letter to the leaders of the Georgian opposition. He copied it to Trotsky and, this time, to Kamenev. According to Fotieva, "Evidently, Vladimir Ilyich is feeling worse and is in haste to do everything he can."[37]

This time Lenin informed Kamenev, with the clear assumption that he would inform Stalin and bring matters out into the open. Lenin could not have been more explicit.

Dear Comrades:

I am following your case with all my heart. I am indignant over Ordzhonikidze's rudeness and the connivance of Stalin and Dzerzhinsky. I am preparing for you notes and a speech.

Respectfully yours,

Lenin[38]

Lenin was now confined to bed; his health was in serious decline. He was being forced to come out fighting before it was too late. He felt he did not have much time left. Lenin now informed Trotsky that he could tell Kamenev everything.

According to Trotsky, when he did this, Kamenev was pale, very agitated, and did not know what to do. He then told Trotsky that Lenin had broken off all relations with Stalin. On that day, Krupskaya told Kamenev that Lenin had resolved to "crush Stalin politically".[39]

Trotsky surmised that the plans of the Stalin-Zinoviev-Kamenev triumvirate, who had planned Lenin's succession, were now in ruins. But the plotters were, as yet, far from defeated.

Fortunately for them, Lenin's health deteriorated even further, resulting in a third stroke, which lasted around two hours, again paralysing his right side and completely depriving him of his power of speech. This finally prevented him from preparing the promised materials for the Georgians. This setback must have caused him great distress.

Lenin had made up his mind to *declare* war on Stalin and the bureaucracy, but this decision was known only to a small group, and he was not able to carry this declaration through to the end. Soon after, Lenin suffered a further relapse that finally put an end to his political life.

Stalin, while formally retreating, replied to Lenin's letter, breaking off relations in a spiteful tone. The letter ends with:

> … my conversation with NK [Krupskaya] confirmed that my suspicions were groundless, nor could they be otherwise. Still, if you think that to maintain our 'relations' I should take my words back, then I can take them back, though I refuse to understand what the problem was, where my fault lay and what it is people want of me.[40]

Given Lenin's condition, it is extremely doubtful that this letter was ever read to him, and simply lay in Stalin's secret archive for decades. This was confirmed by Fotieva, who writes:

> Vladimir Ilyich was unable to read Stalin's answer because he had a bad attack of illness the day it arrived. That day marked a sharp change for the worse in Vladimir Ilyich's condition generally.[41]

This was further confirmed in the final entry of the secretaries' *Journal* on 6 March by Voldodicheva: "The letter has not yet been handed to Vladimir Ilyich, as he has fallen ill."[42]

On 16 March, Lenin's secretary wrote to Kamenev, but sent a copy to Trotsky:

> Leon Borisovich [Kamenev]:
>
> Supplementing our telephone conversation, I communicate to you as chairman of the Politburo the following:
>
> As I already told you, 31 December 1922, Vladimir Ilyich dictated an article on the national question.
>
> This question has worried him extremely and he was preparing to speak on it at the Party Congress. Not long before his last illness he told me that he would publish this article, but later. After that he took sick without giving final directions.
>
> Vladimir Ilyich considered this article to be a guiding one and extremely important. At his direction it was communicated to comrade Trotsky, whom

Vladimir Ilyich authorised to defend his point of view upon the given question at the Party Congress in view of their solidarity upon it.

The only copy of the article in my possession is preserved at the direction of Vladimir Ilyich in his secret archive.

I bring the above facts to your attention.

I could not do it earlier since I returned to work only today after a sickness.

L Fotieva
(Personal secretary of Comrade Lenin) [43]

These lines provided irrefutable proof that Lenin was preparing to launch an all-out struggle at the Twelfth Party Congress. This was now ruled out, given his condition. It would be down to Trotsky to carry forward the struggle.

However, without Lenin at his side, and with the triumvirate constantly manoeuvring behind his back, he was isolated. It posed a massive dilemma for Trotsky: it seemed to be a moment of decision.

39. Fighting for His Life

With Lenin incapacitated, 1923 was the year that Stalin and the triumvirate took control. Faced with Lenin's political attack, the Stalin faction closed ranks. Stalin knew full well what would happen if Lenin's health recovered. He would be removed from his position, disgraced and finished politically. It would be the end of the road for him, and so he did everything in his power to prevent it.

According to Volkogonov, Fotieva had informed Stalin and other members of the Politburo of the contents of Lenin's *Testament*, giving valuable time for them to neutralise its effects.[1] Volkogonov gives no references for this view. With Lenin completely debilitated, now was the opportune time to strike and open up the struggle against Trotsky.

By the time of Lenin's third stroke, Stalin had control over the central levers of power. To use Lenin's expression, he had "unlimited authority concentrated in his hands…"[2]

Three-quarters of the apparatus, centrally and in the regions, had now been hand-picked by Stalin and was ready to defend its interests. An artificial selection had taken place, not of the best cadres, but of the most adaptable and pliant elements: careerists and toadies, anxious to please their superiors in order to secure their positions to climb further up the bureaucratic ladder.

Independent thinkers and honest revolutionaries were replaced by mediocrities, loyalists, who owed their position to those in charge of the apparatus. Millions of bureaucrats came to regard Stalin, the 'old Bolshevik', as a figure who would best represent their interests.

256. Delegates at the Twelfth Party Congress
Middle row (left tt right): Bukharin, Rykov, Stalin
Ordzhonikidze is below Rykov

A similar process took place in the ebb tide of the French Revolution, when many Thermidorian reactionaries emerged from the former circle of the Jacobins, or semi-Jacobins of the Napoleon Bonaparte kind. "Every social epoch needs its great men, and when it does not find them, it invents them", explained Marx.[3] This is not a bad description of Stalin. Above all, these upstarts were ready to defend the interests of the apparatus and, when necessary, to crush all opposition.

When the Twelfth Congress finally arrived in the middle of April 1923, it fell to Trotsky to take up the fight in Lenin's absence. Lenin had provided Trotsky with his notes and materials beforehand.

But Trotsky hesitated and instead tried to buy time, hoping that Lenin would recover. He had therefore offered Stalin a compromise that included promises of a radical change on the national question, no persecution of the Georgians, no administrative repression in the Party, greater industrialisation and an honest cooperation at the top. Stalin should also apologise to Krupskaya, and there must be no more intrigues.

257. Lenin at Gorki, 1 July 1923

In the moment of extreme danger, Stalin resorted to the methods he knew best – deceitfulness, evasion, lying and bluff. He made use of all his skills to prevaricate, find excuses for himself, confuse the minds of his critics and deflect all suspicion away from the General Secretary.

Stalin therefore welcomed the compromise, which he then cynically turned to his own advantage. He agreed to everything, only to go back on this later. It was precisely the kind of "rotten compromise" that Lenin had warned against.[4]

Kamenev, who was the chair of the Congress, together with Zinoviev, presented the main report to the four hundred delegates, which poured praise on Lenin and called for unity and discipline. Stalin, on the other hand, held the reins of the machine. Behind the scenes, a whispering campaign had been initiated by them about Trotsky's 'Bonapartist ambitions' to replace Lenin. Their motto was 'we mustn't allow Trotsky, the newcomer, to take over the leadership'.

The Georgians were expecting support, as Lenin had promised. But it was Stalin who gave the report on the nationalities and he aimed to cover his tracks in another cynical manoeuvre, by precisely attacking the very tendency he represented, namely Great Russian chauvinism. Having thus covered his rear, he then struck a vicious blow against the Georgians, accusing them of local nationalism and "deviations" towards "Georgian chauvinism". Lenin's attack on Stalin and Ordzhonikidze was kept from the delegates. When the Georgians asked for Lenin's notes to be read out, they were simply brushed aside. Of the Russians, only Bukharin raised objections.

Stalin then went on to defuse any criticisms against Rabkrin by agreeing to Lenin's proposal to merge the body with an enlarged Central Control Commission. The proposal was then accepted unanimously. But Stalin would, in due course, ensure that Ordzhonikidze was not only allowed to remain in the Party, but was made head of the Control Commission, the body supposed to fight the growing bureaucracy.

When Trotsky spoke at the Congress, having agreed to the compromise, he limited himself exclusively to economic matters. The opportunity to launch an open attack (the "bomb") against Stalin was missed. There was no hint of any disagreements at the top. The Congress presented the appearance of complete unanimity.

The enlarged Central Committee that was elected by the Congress, as expected, reappointed Stalin as general secretary of the Party. Trotsky wrote about his reticence a few years later:

> I avoided entering the fight as long as possible, since its nature was that of an unprincipled conspiracy directed against me personally, at least in the first stages. It was clear to me that such a fight, once it broke out, would inevitably take on extremely sharp features and might under the conditions of the revolutionary dictatorship lead to dangerous consequences. This is not the place to discuss whether it was correct to try to maintain some common ground for collective work at the price of very great personal concessions or whether I should have taken the offensive all along the line, despite the absence of sufficient political grounds for such action. The fact is that I chose the first way and, in spite of everything, I do not regret it. There are victories that lead into blind alleys, and there are defeats that open up new avenues.[5]

On 15 May, Lenin was moved from his apartment in the Kremlin to the country house at Gorki. In July, his health recovered enough for him to take walks and to practise writing with his left hand. He was even able to visit the chairman of the local state farm and spend three days with him. Around 10 August, he was allowed to write. He received *Pravda* every day and later

Izvestia and other publications. He began to try to read books. However, it was Krupskaya who read the newspaper articles to him and passages from books, as he was still very ill.

With Lenin fighting for his life, the political differences soon began to surface in the Party, as Stalin and the triumvirate widened the conspiracy against Trotsky. Their confidence grew greater with every advance. Nevertheless, they had to act with caution as Trotsky still had enormous prestige within the Party. More seriously, there was always the possibility that Lenin might recover.

Within the Politburo, however, Trotsky found himself in an impossible position. It was one man against all the rest. The 'old Bolsheviks' now had their own faction (the Septemvirate) directed against Trotsky. They were all bound in vows of secrecy to act as one. There would be no polemics against one another. Everything was decided in advance and simply rubber stamped in the meetings. Similar factional centres were created in the localities. This conspiracy also included Kuibyshev, the chairman of the Supreme Council of National Economy.

The selection of pliable functionaries within the Russian Party was now being extended into the Comintern, as leaders were soon replaced. Removing people and replacing them with what Lenin described as 'obedient fools' was Zinoviev's speciality. The artificial selection concentrated greater power in the hands of the ruling faction. But the 'interregnum' created by Lenin's illness was only the first stage in a bitter struggle for power.

The Left Opposition

Developments internationally served to bring this clash in the leadership out into the open. Events in Germany had by now reached fever pitch. The French and Belgian occupation of the Ruhr in January 1923 had forced the German government to introduce a policy of 'passive resistance'. But this policy provoked a series of strikes against the occupation and raised the class war in Germany to new heights.

The policy of printing money to cover the widening state budget created a hyper-inflationary spiral, which saw prices rise exponentially. The inflation became so intense that workers would receive their wages in wheelbarrows, and they would be forced to spend them the same day before they became worthless.

The trade unions ceased to function and collapsed as the union dues became worthless. The middle class, with its reliance on fixed incomes, was

258. Gathering of workers in Essen outside a steel factory, 31 March 1923

on the verge of bankruptcy. The old parties began to lose support, except for the Communists, who gained enormously.

By the summer of 1923, a revolutionary situation had developed. The workers streamed towards the Communist Party, looking to the German revolution as a solution to their dire problems. The situation was not only ripe for a successful revolution, but over-ripe. In reality, it was much more favourable than Russia in 1917. But the leaders of the Communist Party were completely out of their depth. They vacillated, not knowing what to do.

Heinrich Brandler, the German Communist Party leader, came to Moscow to ask for advice. But Lenin was very ill, immobilised by paralysis, and Trotsky was away from Moscow. As a result, the German leaders looked to the other members of the leadership of the International. They met with Zinoviev and Stalin, who urged restraint on the German Communists, advising them to wait and allow the fascists to strike the first blow. "We should restrain the Germans", wrote Stalin to Zinoviev and Bukharin, "not spur them on."[6]

This showed just how far they were lagging behind events. In the midst of a revolutionary situation, where the seizure of power was on the order of the day, the leaders of the Comintern were acting as a brake on the German leadership. It was exactly the same conservatism that Zinoviev, Kamenev and Stalin had shown in 1917.

The movement of the working class is not like a water tap that can be opened and closed at will. When the decisive hour has struck and the workers are ready to act, they cannot be held in check for a long time without becoming disappointed and demoralised. They look to the Communists for a decisive lead. But if all they see is constant delaying, hesitation and prevarication, they lose all confidence in the leadership and lapse once more into feelings of apathy and indifference. They will say: 'We thought that the Communists were serious about taking power, but now we see that it was just empty talk – they are like all the others!'

In a revolutionary situation, decisive action is absolutely vital. The whole business can be settled in just a few days, one way or the other. This cowardly policy of Zinoviev and Stalin set the whole tone during these crucial weeks, and it effectively wrecked the German revolution.

When Trotsky heard what was happening, he urged the Party to take advantage of the revolutionary situation and make plans accordingly. They urgently needed to set a date for an insurrection. But the German leadership prevaricated and made some serious mistakes, resulting in the revolution being bungled and the opportunity lost. The Party let the revolution slip through its fingers. This tragedy came down to a failure of leadership: there was no one who was able to play the role that Lenin did in 1917. As Trotsky explained:

> Why then in Germany has there been no victory thus far? I think there can be only one answer: because Germany did not have a Bolshevik Party, nor did it have a leader such as we had in October… And one can say with full assurance that history will hardly create objective conditions any more favourable to the German proletariat than those of the latter half of the past year. What was lacking? A party with the tempering that our party has.[7]

The defeat of the German revolution had serious international repercussions, especially in Russia. It was a colossal blow to the Russian working class and led to an even greater mood of pessimism and despondency. A wave of disappointment swept the country. This served to strengthen the bureaucracy and, with it, the Stalin faction.

By October 1923, Trotsky could no longer delay matters and wrote an appeal to the Party membership regarding the economic situation and the "unhealthy regime within the party":[8]

> In view of the situation that has developed, I think it is not only my right but my duty to make the true state of affairs known to every party member...[9]

Within a week, forty-six prominent Party members issued a statement in support of Trotsky, which resulted in the emergence of the Left Opposition. These differences were now raised at the Central Committee Plenum in October. At this meeting, the triumvirate, who now felt secure, attacked the Opposition in no uncertain terms and a resolution was passed that stated:

> The plenums of the Central Committee and Central Control Commission and representatives of ten Party organisations resolutely condemn the statement of the forty-six as a factional and schismatic step; for that is its nature, whatever the intentions of those who signed it. That statement threatens to subject the entire Party in the coming months to an inner-Party struggle and thereby weaken the Party at a supremely important moment for the destinies of the world revolution.[10]

Stalin and the other faction members attempted to block the Opposition, but they were forced to open up the pages of *Pravda* for a debate in the Party. As a result, the circulation of *Pravda* doubled, as the support for the Opposition increased.

Trotsky's Left Opposition put forward a programme against bureaucracy, against the kulak menace, for industrialisation and socialist planning, for socialist internationalism and the restoration of workers' democracy in the Party, in trade unions and in the Soviets. This was followed by a series of articles by Trotsky written for *Pravda* outlining these ideas during December 1923, which were published separately as *The New Course*.

Such was the pressure that members of the triumvirate, along with Trotsky, voted for a resolution on internal Party democracy at the joint meeting of the Central Committee and Central Control Commission, held on 5 December. This included measures "to really put workers' democracy into practice" and "to fight against the bureaucratic perversion of the party apparatus..."[11] But this was simply a ploy by Stalin and his supporters.

It was then agreed to submit the resolution on 'Party democracy' to the Thirteenth Party Conference in January 1924. Again, this was simply a smokescreen, and the triumvirate was making preparations to rig the conference. Feeling somewhat constricted following this December meeting, Trotsky wrote another letter to the Party membership warning of the dangers of bureaucratic degeneration and calling on the youth – the Party's truest barometer – to act sharply against the Party bureaucracy. This resulted in an open breach. The knives were now out.

On 15 December, Stalin responded with a public attack on Trotsky, accusing him of duplicity. It was carried in *Pravda* and was a clear signal that the machine was already being mobilised for action. The tempo of the struggle now intensified.

Lenin's final struggle

The sick Lenin took a trip to the Kremlin on 18 October 1923, accompanied by Krupskaya and Maria Ulyanova. He visited his apartment, looked into the meeting hall of the Council of People's Commissars and visited his office. For some this visit was cause for alarm. Could it be a sign that the 'Old Man' was considering a return to work?

He stayed overnight at his flat and in the morning went for a short walk in the Kremlin grounds. He was then driven through the city, stopping for a short time at the Agricultural Exhibition. After some dinner, he returned to his office, remained silent for a long time, took some books from his bookcase, and headed back to Gorki. Lenin seemed to be very much alive. But this was to be his last ever visit to Moscow.

There seemed to be other promising signs. On 19 October, Lenin requested that the three volumes of Hegel and the works of Plekhanov be brought from his library in the Kremlin to Gorki. This interest in philosophy pointed in the direction of a certain recovery in his health, although everything was still very tentative.

Between 24 November and 16 December, a number of people visited him, including Bukharin, Preobrazhensky, Ivan Skvortsov-Stepanov, Krestinsky, Pyatnitsky and the editor of the *Krasnaya Nov*, Aleksandr Voronsky. They talked about current affairs and the latest news. Lenin listened attentively, but did not seem to have recovered the use of his speech. At the beginning of 1924, he even attended a Christmas party organised at the State Farm, where he greeted his guests with "friendly gestures".

Lenin must have been aware, either from his secretaries or Krupskaya, that Trotsky was coming under attack in the Party. But he was not in a position to do anything about it. While he was conscious and lucid, he was still unable to speak, and must have felt utterly helpless. All his life, he had been extremely

259. The final photograph of Lenin, Gorki, 1 January 1924

active and enjoyed the blessings of good health. To be reduced to a state of helplessness was the cruellest form of torture for such a man.

The debate about the Opposition's New Course was now to be held at the Thirteenth Party Conference, which was planned for 16 to 18 January 1924. The Opposition had attracted a growing layer of support in the Party, and in the Party cells in Moscow, they won a majority. One-third of the military Party cells in Moscow voted for the Opposition, including a majority of the students and the Communist youth. They also won majorities in Ryazan, Penza, Kaluga, Simbirsk and Chelyabinsk.

But in the end, this would count for little as the apparatus was now in the grip of Stalin and the triumvirate, who used their position to manipulate the choice of delegations. It marked a new and decisive stage in the struggle. It was now a vicious fight in which the old rules of Lenin's Party no longer applied.

At the Conference, there were 128 full delegates (222 with speaking rights), and there were two resolutions presented by the leadership: on 'Party Affairs' and 'Results of the Discussion and the Petty-Bourgeois Deviation in the Party'. In this way, the stage was set for a vicious all-out attack on the Opposition.

As the delegations had been hand-picked by Stalin's apparatus, the result was a foregone conclusion. The conference voted near unanimously to condemn the Opposition as a petty-bourgeois deviation from Bolshevism and recommended that the Central Committee republish Point 7 of the resolution 'On Party Unity' that banned factions, which had been adopted by the Tenth Congress.

Stalin also attacked the Georgian Bolsheviks for an alleged deviation to Georgian chauvinism, under the influence of Menshevism. Zinoviev and Kamenev wanted to expel Trotsky from the Party for violating the decision of the Tenth Congress on factions, but Stalin opposed the move for tactical reasons. He was clearly biding his time, waiting to see which way the wind was blowing.

At one point, he even made overtures to Trotsky. This is quite interesting, as an example of how Stalin operated. He was using Zinoviev and Kamenev against Trotsky for his own purposes. But if things turned out differently, and the balance swung in Trotsky's favour, he would not hesitate to ditch his erstwhile allies and temporarily seek a bloc with Trotsky against Zinoviev and Kamenev.

Stalin was keeping all his options open. He even reached out to suggest that Trotsky should give the speech at the Twelfth Congress. But Trotsky, sensing a manoeuvre, would have nothing to do with it. For Trotsky to deliver a political report in Lenin's place at this point would have been used to reinforce the whispering campaign branding him as a vain, ambitious man, eager to step into Lenin's shoes. He immediately rebuffed this cynical offer.

There is a revealing comment about this made by Boris Bazhanov, who attended a meeting of the Politburo:

> When I attended a session of the Politburo for the first time, the struggle between the triumvirs and Trotsky was in full swing. Trotsky was the first to arrive for the session. The others were late, they were still plotting... Next entered Zinoviev. He passed by Trotsky; and both behaved as if they had not noticed one another. When Kamenev entered, he greeted Trotsky with a slight nod. At last Stalin came in. He approached the table at which Trotsky was seated, greeted him in a most friendly manner and vigorously shook hands with him across the table.[12]

An excessive show of friendship by Stalin was a sure sign that he was preparing to crush his victim without mercy. In the same way, certain Roman emperors used to invite their intended victim for dinner at the palace, during which they were murdered by the Praetorian guard.

Yet again, fate took a hand in shaping events. Shortly before the Thirteenth Party Conference, Trotsky's health took a turn for the worse and he was advised by the doctors to take a two-month leave of absence and rest in Sukhum (modern-day Sukhumi), on the coast of the Black Sea in Georgia, where the weather was warmer. He was therefore not able to attend the Party Conference in person. As a result, the defence of the Opposition was left to Preobrazhensky, Radek, and Sapronov.

The absence of Trotsky may not have been a decisive factor at the Conference. In this game, the dice were already loaded to guarantee the result, whatever speeches were made, or not made. But it certainly weakened the hand of the Opposition.

Stalin gave the report on the immediate tasks in Party affairs. In the full knowledge that he had the firm backing of the Politburo, and the Party apparatus, and that the composition of the delegations ensured a favourable result, he felt supremely confident when he stood up to address the Conference. The time for prevarication was over. Now at last, the velvet gloves could be cast aside to reveal the iron fist hidden inside.

He immediately launched a sustained attack on the Opposition, ridiculing their position on Party democracy and their allegation of a degeneration in the Party. Stalin boasted that the leadership's "clear-cut resolution summed up the present discussion":

> We have declared: groups and factions cannot be tolerated, the Party must be
> united, monolithic, the Party must not be put in opposition to the apparatus,
> there must be no idle talk of our cadres being in danger of degeneration, for they
> are revolutionary cadres, there must be no searching for cleavages between these
> revolutionary cadres and the youth, which is marching in step with these cadres
> and will continue to do so in future.[13]

These attacks were extensively reported in the Party newspapers. In the end, such was the rigging of Conference delegates, the Opposition managed to gain only *three* votes for its position. The apparatus had triumphed. It put an abrupt end to the three-month discussion within the Party and gave an official stamp of approval to the self-appointed triumvirate. The age of unanimous votes, unconditional support for the leadership and the vilification and crushing of all opposition, was born right here. This represented a fundamental break with the traditions of Lenin's party, as EH Carr himself states:

> It had, however, a novel and disquieting character. It was the first representative party assembly at which it could be clearly seen that personalities rather than principles were at stake. To discredit the Opposition, not to secure the adoption or rejection of a policy, was the primary preoccupation of the Party leaders. The struggle for power had assumed a naked form.[14]

The previous tactic of avoiding an all-out clash was now reversed, and everything was done to identify the absent Trotsky with the Opposition. It was no longer necessary to manoeuvre. The Opposition and Trotsky needed to be clearly identified and crushed.

However, the plans of the Troika met with a setback: the unexpected news that Lenin was making a recovery. On 18 January, the day the Thirteenth Conference ended, it was reported that Lenin "felt wonderful". The following day, he even went out for a ride in a horse-drawn sleigh and followed a hunting expedition in the forest.

But it turned out to be short-lived. All of a sudden, his health began to rapidly decline. The day before his death, he became very agitated at the news that a resolution denouncing Trotsky was passed at the Party Conference. He sometimes asked questions by gestures. Certain points quite obviously caused him great anxiety, so his wife felt obliged to reassure him.

Krupskaya understood that this was the split that Lenin warned about in his *Testament*. To calm him, Krupskaya read selections from *Pravda*, probably inventing information for the purpose, and repeated that the Party was united at the Conference.[15] She also read to him a tract by Trotsky in which he compared Lenin's significance with that of Marx.

Krupskaya confirmed this point, but placed the reading somewhat earlier. A few days after Lenin's death, she wrote to Trotsky:

> Dear Lev Davidovich,
>
> I write to tell you that about a month before his death, as he was looking through your book, Vladimir Ilyich stopped at the place where you sum up Marx and Lenin, and asked me to read it over again to him; he listened very attentively, and then looked it over again himself. And here is another thing I want to tell you. The attitude of VI [Lenin] toward you at the time when you came to us in

London from Siberia has not changed until his death. I wish you, Lev Davydovich, strength and health, and I embrace you warmly.

N Krupskaya[16]

The Stalinist historians, unsurprisingly, give a totally different account of what Krupskaya is supposed to have said:

When Lenin appeared excited on Saturday, I told him the resolutions were passed unanimously. We spent Saturday and Sunday reading them. Lenin listened very attentively, and asked questions from time to time.[17]

The accompanying comment states:

During the discussion Lenin familiarised himself with the principal documents published in *Pravda* and literature dealing with it. There is every reason to assume that Krupskaya opposed the Trotsky line with Lenin's knowledge. After the conference opened, Lenin wanted the account of it read to him from beginning to end.[18]

But if Lenin was satisfied, why did he become so agitated at what was happening? The idea that Lenin, who had entered a bloc with Trotsky over the fight against bureaucracy, the monopoly of foreign trade, the Georgian question and other matters, was told that Trotsky's ideas had been condemned as a "petty-bourgeois deviation" by Stalin and the triumvirate, hardly fits with the picture put out by the Stalinists of a very "attentive" (and seemingly calm) Lenin.

This clearly does not fit the bill. Far more likely is that Krupskaya kept the news from Lenin and invented certain things so as not to agitate him. After all, Stalin's attack on Trotsky would only confirm Lenin's fears of a split – something he was anxious to avoid.

Lenin's death

On Monday 21 January, Vladimir Ilyich woke at 10.30 am and drank some coffee. Not feeling well, he went back to bed and was awake by 3 pm. He seemed a little better, but by 5.40 pm he felt the tremor of another attack, which occurred at 6 pm.

Just before 6.50 pm, Bukharin, who was apparently staying in an adjacent building in Gorki, heard a commotion and rushed to see what was happening. "When I ran into Ilyich's room, full of doctors and stacked with medicines", he wrote, "Ilyich let out a last sigh."[19] Lenin finally passed away at exactly 6.50 pm in the evening, dying at his rest home in Gorki.

According to his doctors, Lenin's death was brought on by "disseminated arterio-sclerosis of the vessels of the brain."[20] Lenin's death must have come as a relief, given the pain and suffering he was forced to endure. "Medical science proved impotent to achieve what was so passionately demanded by millions of human hearts", stated Trotsky, the day after his death. "Now Ilyich is no more. The Party is orphaned; and so is the working class."[21]

"Stalin, Kalinin, Zinoviev and Kamenev reached the villa at 11 pm", states a report in the *Daily Worker*.[22] Trotsky, who was ill, heard the news when on his way to Sukhum. When he contacted the Kremlin, he was told by Stalin that Lenin was to lie in state until Saturday 26 January, after which his body would be interred in the Kremlin Wall. Stalin advised Trotsky that since it was impossible for him to get back in time, he should remain and continue his treatment. Trotsky discovered later that the funeral had actually been held on Sunday, not Saturday, which meant he could have attended. Even in Lenin's death, Stalin had tricked Trotsky in order to keep him away from the funeral and enhance his own authority as the heir of Lenin.

On 23 January, Lenin's body was carried from Gorki to Moscow by train and he was laid to rest in the Hall of Columns of the Trade Union Club. He remained there for four days, allowing an innumerable multitude of people, who waited patiently in the freezing cold, overcome by a sense of irreparable loss and collective grief, to pay their last respects to their departed leader. An account from someone who was a young child at this time, has left us with a moving view of that fateful day:

> We joined one of the queues on the Mokhovaya Street. In front of us we could see only heads, and above them banners. The crowd is silent... The queue moves slowly and there are already many people behind us. Everybody feels cold. The frost pinches our feet, our hands, and faces.
>
> On a raised platform the red coffin and he in the coffin. One would give one's life to save him. No, that is impossible. The illness took what belonged to it. His face is yellowish, as if made of wax. The nose sharper, the expression severe. The beard exactly as in pictures, and the arms in repose as if he were alive. He is dressed in a green French* and on his breast the Order of the Red Banner.[23]

An incessant stream of hundreds of thousands of people came to Red Square and stood waiting for hours to pay their respects on that January day, in temperatures of 26 degrees below zero. It seemed as though the whole of Moscow was there. The *Daily Worker* reported:

---

* A kind of military jacket.

260. Lenin's coffin being transported from Gorki to Moscow

The farewell viewing of Lenin by the scores of thousands of mourners who filed past his bier was an impressive and solemn occasion such as never been seen in the metropolis. The crowd filed past, eight abreast, with the lines stretching out for half a mile outside.

The mournful farewell continued until late in the evening, while new crowds added themselves to the procession.[24]

A further report stated: "Thousands cried out 'Ilyich!' 'Ilyich!' as they passed the casket."[25]

On the day before Lenin's funeral, Saturday 26 January, the second All-Union Congress of Soviets held a solemn session with speeches about Lenin, given by Kalinin, Zinoviev, Krupskaya and Stalin. The latter gave his speech in the form of a liturgy:

> Departing from us, Comrade Lenin enjoined us to hold high and guard the purity of the great title of member of the Party.
>
> We vow to you, comrade Lenin, we shall fulfil your behest with honour!
>
> Departing from us, comrade Lenin enjoined us to guard the unity of our Party as the apple of our eye.

261. Lenin's funeral

We vow to you, comrade Lenin, we shall fulfil your behest with honour!

Departing from us, comrade Lenin, enjoined us to guard and strengthen the dictatorship of the proletariat.

We vow to you, comrade Lenin, we shall fulfil your behest with honour![26]

And so on, and so forth, like the monotonous drone of an Orthodox priest, delivering a homily to his congregation, who obediently provide the ritualistic answer. This grotesque parody carries the unmistakable imprint of the age-old church liturgy, faithfully learned by rote by Stalin in his seminarist past and now regurgitated at the funeral of the great materialist revolutionary.

A more indecent display of contempt for the memory of the lifelong militant atheist, Vladimir Ilyich Lenin, would be difficult to imagine. This whiff of stale incense must have seemed profoundly shocking to many of those present, but above all must have been deeply offensive to the widow and lifelong companion of Lenin.

But worse was soon to come. What pained Krupskaya most deeply was the decision, taken without her consent, to preserve the body of Lenin in a mausoleum, making it accessible to visitors. For the purpose, a mausoleum was to be constructed under the Kremlin Wall. Lenin's widow protested,

262. Stalin, Kamenev, Tomsky, Rudzutak, Molotov, Kalinin and Bukharin carrying
Lenin's coffin

saying: "All his life Vladimir Ilyich was against icons, and now they have
turned him into an icon."

This remark was very much to the point. The triumvirs meant to make
Lenin into a kind of Saint that people were supposed to worship, but without
paying any attention to the ideas that he really stood for. They mummified his
dead body while trampling his ideas underfoot. Monuments to Lenin were
erected in the principal cities of Russia and the name of Petrograd would be
changed to Leningrad. But genuine Leninism was dead, and buried by those
who claimed to be his sole heirs.

The protests of Krupskaya were ignored by the triumvirs. At 9 am on
Sunday 27 January, Lenin's body was carried to Red Square. Some said it
was the coldest day since 1812. At 4 pm, as his body was interred in the
mausoleum, cannons were fired, bells rang out everywhere, factory whistles
hooted and sirens let loose their noise. At that point, everything came to a
halt throughout Russia.

Only two days after Lenin's funeral, *Pravda* published a letter from
Krupskaya in response to the proposal to establish a Lenin Fund to build
monuments to him. She made the following appeal:

I wish to make a big request, don't let your grief for Ilyich run away into outward
regard for his personality. Don't build monuments to him, palaces in his name,

263. The Lenin Mausoleum in Red Square, Moscow

grand ceremonies in his memory and so on. When he was alive he had no time for such things, he found such things oppressive.[27]

She also protested quietly about the decision to rename Petrograd to Leningrad in his honour, taken by the Congress of Soviets on 26 January – no doubt under the direction of the Politburo – but she was ignored. This was followed by the struggle over Lenin's body.

The Lenin Mausoleum

Krupskaya and Lenin's family expected that Lenin would be buried. It was rumoured that it was Lenin's wish that he be buried alongside his mother in the Volkovskoe Cemetery in Petrograd, but this seems to be false. He wished to be buried with his comrades in the Kremlin wall. Krupskaya had even suggested Lenin be buried next to Inessa Armand in the Kremlin Wall, so as to keep the two families, who had been very close, together even in death. But all these suggestions were brusquely overruled by the Politburo.

The idea was initially raised in the ruling circles of preserving Lenin's dead body for a short time. But this 'short time' turned out to be of a permanent character. The Troika desperately needed to invent a cult of the dead Lenin, in order to conceal the fact that they were busy reversing everything he had stood for when he was alive. In particular, Stalin, all too conscious of his own mediocrity, felt the need to drape himself in the mantle of the dead body of Lenin to enhance his own prestige, while trampling on his wishes.

In order to excuse this monstrous aberration, they claimed that floods of workers had written urging the preservation of Lenin's body. Evidently, some of the ruling clique still had a few remaining qualms of conscience. But even if that were true, it would not provide any real justification for that macabre decision. In any case, it was not the 'floods of workers', but the Politburo that decided.

Krupskaya and Lenin's sisters and brother were vehemently opposed to the idea. Trotsky also raised his objections, but they too were dismissed. The Politburo then sent Bukharin and Zinoviev, who were closest to Krupskaya, to 'persuade' her of their proposal. Eventually, Krupskaya and the family were overruled and silenced.

In this way, the idea of the Lenin icon was born. Five years later, in July 1929, the Politburo decided to build a permanent stone structure, which became an inherent part of the cult of the personality promoted by Stalin, who soon transformed it into the even more abhorrent cult of the 'Father of the Peoples'. Such a thing is not only alien to Leninism – it is its complete antithesis.

Certain bourgeois historians accuse Lenin of being a 'tsar-god'. This slander would be amusing if it were not so utterly stupid and contrary to the facts. In reality, there was not a trace of any 'cult of personality' under the regime of Lenin and Trotsky. Quite the contrary, Lenin was vehemently opposed to any suggestion of a leadership cult, which was entirely alien and repugnant to him. In this, he was faithfully following the example of Marx and Engels. Marx wrote in a letter to Wilhelm Blos: "When Engels and I first joined the secret communist society, we did so only on condition that anything conducive to a superstitious belief in authority be eliminated from the Rules".[28]

When Lenin stood at the head of the Soviet state, he lived very modestly. His home was a small four-room flat at the end of a corridor in the Kremlin, which he shared with his wife and sister. A small room served both as a study and a bedroom.

Lenin's detestation of all pomp and ceremony is shown by the fact that he would not even allow pictures of himself to be displayed in the Kremlin. It is no accident that there were no photos of Lenin in either his office or any council room where he had meetings. "He thrust them away with indignation whenever he happened to come across one..." stated Fotieva.[29] The only picture that hung in his office was a single portrait of Marx, which was presented to him by the workers of Petrograd. It was only with great difficulty that he even allowed photographs to be taken of himself.

Lenin issued severe reprimands of anyone suggesting privileges. Wherever such tendencies arose – something inherent in a country on such a low cultural level – he strenuously opposed them. In September 1918, Lenin summoned a few leading comrades and told them:[30]

> I note with deep dissatisfaction that my person is being glorified. This is annoying and harmful. All of us know that personalities have nothing to do with it. It would be awkward for myself to prohibit that sort of thing. There would also be something ridiculous and pretentious about it. It is up to you to put the brakes on unobtrusively.[31]

He detested the kind of pompous displays of ceremony and 'loyalty', which the Stalinist bureaucracy used in order to cover up their crimes. Balabanoff writes:

> Lenin never spoke – except to his most intimate friends – of his loathing and disdain for official manifestations and diplomatic ceremonies. He usually found a way to avoid them, and his name never appeared in the news reports. When he considered such procedures useful and necessary he simply endured them.[32]

"You need to know Ilyich, he so hates every kind of ceremony", explained Kamenev.[33] While in the Kremlin, Lenin even avoided his own fiftieth birthday party. "When the laudatory speeches commenced, he got up and walked out, and telephoned every few minutes from his Kremlin office inquiring when the oratory would cease so he could return to the session."[34]

The great Russian poet Mayakovsky, who was a Bolshevik and who was opposed to the canonisation of Lenin, in the summer of 1924 wrote an editorial entitled 'Do Not Trade in Lenin' in the arts journal *Lef*:

> We insist:
> Don't stereotype Lenin.
> Don't print his portrait on placards,
> plates, mugs and cigarette cases.
> Don't bronze over Lenin,
> Don't take from him his living gait and human countenance.
> He is among the living.
> We need him as the living and not the dead.
> Therefore
> Learn from Lenin but don't canonise him.
> Don't create a cult in the name of the man, who all his life fought against all and
>   every cult.
> Don't trade in Lenin.

After Lenin's funeral, Krupskaya wrote a letter to Inessa Armand's twenty-five-year-old daughter, Inna, who was the daughter she never had:

> My very own dearest Inochka,
>
> We buried Vladimir Ilyich yesterday ... Lenin's death was the best outcome. Death had already been suffered by him so many times in the previous year... At this moment above all I want to think about Vladimir Ilyich, about his work and to read him.[35]

She wrote again to her:

> When the project arose among our people to bury VI in the Kremlin, I was filled with terrible indignation – what they should have done was bury him with his comrades so that they could lie beneath the Red Wall together.[36]

Afterwards, with her wish denied, she never again publicly mentioned the mausoleum, nor did she ever visit it or stand in it during Party processions. Furthermore, she refused to refer to the name of Leningrad in her letters, but only by its old nickname, 'Piter'.

Stalin's involvement

The question arises: was Stalin involved in Lenin's death? There is absolutely no doubt that it was especially convenient for Stalin. If Lenin had recovered and delivered his intended 'bombshell' at the Party Congress, the consequences would be fatal for Stalin. That was quite clear from the contents of his final letters and comments. Lenin's illness was, for Stalin, a stroke of good luck. It meant that Lenin was not able to finish the fight he had started, namely the struggle against Stalin and the bureaucracy, for the regeneration within the state and party. Particularly dangerous was the bloc that Lenin had formed with Trotsky. Stalin now saw Trotsky as the main enemy to be eliminated. But, if Lenin were to recover, that would be impossible. All his plans would be in ruins.

Stalin had motives – and very powerful ones – to ensure that the feared recovery of Lenin's health should not take place. And his power over the apparatus and even Lenin's doctors gave him unlimited opportunities to interfere in Lenin's medical treatment, and to do so silently and unobserved. And through his close contacts with Dzerzhinsky, he had access to an extensive arsenal of poisons that could only be traced with difficulty, if at all.

Another thing must be mentioned here. In the course of Lenin's illness, he suffered bouts of excruciating pain. In such moments, he had several discussions with Krupskaya that in the event of his situation becoming hopeless, he might decide to take his own life. Maria Ulyanova, Lenin's sister, revealed that Lenin had asked Stalin for cyanide if things got this bad, which Stalin promised to provide. According to Stalin, he did this to placate Lenin, but had no intention of carrying it out. This was a few days before Lenin's final rupture with Stalin. Stalin then informed members of the Politburo:

> On Saturday, 17 March in the strictest secrecy Comrade Krupskaya told me of "Vladimir Ilyich's request to Stalin", namely that I, Stalin, should take the responsibility for finding and administering to Lenin a dose of potassium cyanide. I felt it impossible to refuse him, and declared: "I would like Vladimir Ilyich to be reassured and to believe that when it is necessary I will fulfil his demand without hesitation."

Stalin added that he just could not do it:

> I do not have the strength to carry out Ilyich's request and I have to decline this mission, however humane and necessary it might be, and I therefore report this to the members of the Politburo.[37]

The Politburo was stunned. Kamenev remained silent, while Zinoviev was bewildered. Stalin stood before them with a sickly smile. "Naturally we cannot even consider carrying out this requisition!" exclaimed Trotsky. "Gaitier [the doctor] has not lost hope." They could never permit any thought of such an action while there was a chance of Lenin's recovery. After all, his doctors indicated that Lenin was improving, although slowly.

At this point, Lenin was walking with the aid of a stick and starting to read about Party discussions. By then, although weak, he felt strong enough to go for rides in the car and, as we have seen, even visited his office in the Kremlin. His state of mind, Krupskaya wrote later, changed completely. He "joked a lot, and laughed", and even hummed the *Internationale* and other revolutionary songs.

It is clear that Lenin at that moment was not wishing to die, but wanted to secure the fate of the Party. It is also clear that Stalin was manoeuvring behind the scenes. In other words, this show of loyalty in the Politburo seems to have been a ploy, all the better to be seen refusing to provide the poison, when actually doing so.

Stalin certainly had the character to undertake the 'task', as he called it. Krupskaya mentioned to Trotsky in 1926 that Stalin, "he" (Krupskaya did not call him by name, but nodded her head in the direction of Stalin's apartment) "is devoid of the most elementary honesty, the most basic honesty…"[38] Future events add credence to this supposition. Despite Stalin's assurance to the

Politburo, he certainly had the motive to eliminate Lenin and later years were to prove that he was absolutely ruthless. It is certain, for example, that Stalin had Maxim Gorky, the famous writer, and his son, Maxim Peshkov, poisoned in the mid-1930s. That was revealed in the trial of Yagoda, the chief of the secret police.

During the monstrous Moscow Trials between 1936-38, Stalin was to show that he had no qualms in ordering the murder of Kamenev, Zinoviev, Radek, Pyatakov, Sokolnikov, Bukharin, Rykov, Rakovsky, Krestinsky and many other Bolshevik leaders. In fact, all who were politically associated with Lenin were killed or disappeared. Stalin physically exterminated Lenin's party.

In these hideous trials, the accused were forced to confess their crimes by means of the most devilish tortures, many that were already familiar to the Spanish Inquisition. Stalin charged Bukharin (who Lenin called "the Party's favourite") in 1938 with having prepared the attempt on Lenin's life in 1918! He dispatched the cold-blooded assassin to murder Leon Trotsky in Mexico in 1940. Shortly before his assassination, Trotsky wrote that Stalin had indeed poisoned Lenin.

These victims of Stalin were Bolshevik leaders, members of Lenin's Politburo and Central Committee, who had served the cause of the working class and socialism all their lives. The only one to survive, after making her peace with Stalin, was Kollontai, who became a diplomat and died of natural causes.

Interestingly, new medical opinions concerning the reasons for the death of Lenin have emerged recently. According to a report in *The New York Times* of 7 May 2012, the University of Maryland's annual historical clinicopathological conference of doctors and medical students took place in Baltimore to re-examine the medical facts surrounding the death of Lenin. The question was raised of why a fatal stroke occurred in such a relatively young man, fifty-three years of age.

While the autopsy of Lenin revealed a near total obstruction of the arteries leading to the brain, he strangely did not have some of the traditional risk factors for strokes. He did not suffer from high blood pressure, did not smoke, only drank occasionally and did not have a brain infection or tumour.

It was felt that a clue was in his family history as his siblings had evidence of cardiovascular disease and Lenin's father seemed to have died from a disease described as similar to Lenin's. But according to Dr Harry Vinters, professor of neurology and neuropathology at the University of California, Lenin's seizures in the hours and days before he died were puzzling and were "quite unusual in a stroke patient." Significantly, he added, "almost any poison can cause seizures."[39]

In the view of Dr Lev Lurie, a Russian historian, from 1921 to his death in 1924, Lenin "began to feel worse and worse": "He complained that he couldn't sleep and that he had terrible headaches. He could not write, he did not want to work…"[40] In his opinion, poison was the most likely immediate cause of Lenin's death.

Furthermore, according to the National Library of Medicine, symptoms of poisoning, some of which Lenin had, are "unexplained anaemia, gastro-internal discomfort and abdominal cramps, as well as severe signs such as changes in behaviour and neurological status, nephropathy, and unexplained death…"

Although toxicology studies were done on others in Russia, there was an unusual order that no toxicology be carried out on Lenin's body. The information surrounding Lenin's death even today remains a closely guarded secret, hidden deep in the Party archives. Krupskaya's notes and Lenin's sister Maria's notes are held there. According to Volkogonov:

> Her [Krupskaya's] notes entitled 'The last six months of the life of VI Lenin', read together with the memoirs of Lenin's sister Maria, give the fullest account of that fateful period, and draw aside the veil on many hitherto unknown details, though neither of these women could reveal everything they knew, and their most informative reminiscences remain under lock and key in the Party archives.[41]

Unfortunately, he tells us nothing more. These accounts remain locked away and shrouded in secrecy.

By the time of Lenin's death, the machine was in complete control. Stalin had placed his representatives in the key posts. The Party apparatus, and therefore the key levers of the Party, were in the hands of the triumvirate. But in practice, they were in Stalin's hands.

'Testament' violated

Before the Thirteenth Party Congress,* on 18 May 1924, Krupskaya handed the envelope containing Lenin's 'Letter to the Congress' – his *Testament* – to the Central Committee. She writes:

> Some of these notes have been published (on the Workers' and Peasants' Inspection and about Sukhanov). The notes dated 24 and 25 December 1922, and 4 January 1923, are among the unpublished ones and contain character sketches of some Central Committee members. It was Vladimir Ilyich's express wish that these particular notes be submitted to the next Party Congress after his death.[42]

---

* Not to be confused with the earlier Thirteenth Party *Conference* that took place in January 1924.

At the Central Committee on 21 May, their contents were revealed. It was at this moment, following his return from convalescence, that Trotsky first heard of the *Testament*. Kamenev read out the text, but nobody was allowed to make any notes. Stalin apparently made a show of resigning, but twisted Lenin's words in the process.

> Yes, I am rude, comrades, in dealing with those who rudely and treacherously destroy and splinter the Party. I have not concealed this and do not conceal it.[43]

In fact, Lenin attacked Stalin for his rudeness not towards *enemies* of the Party, but to Party comrades who had a long and dedicated history in the movement.

But Zinoviev and Kamenev, the other two members of the triumvirate, "persuaded" Stalin to stay. As Zinoviev explained:

> Ilyich's last word is the highest law for us... but on one point at least the fears of Lenin have shown themselves to be unfounded. I wish to speak of that concerning our general secretary. You have all witnessed our common work during these last years and, like myself, have been happy to confirm that the fears of Ilyich have not been realised.[44]

Zinoviev, with Kamenev's support, was able to retain Stalin in his position, despite Lenin's wishes. All opposition was silenced. What Zinoviev and the others did not realise, was that this touching show of loyalty to the General Secretary was to be rewarded in future by their own death sentence.

Then, Lenin's request, made through Krupskaya, that his *Testament* be read to the Party's Thirteenth Congress was turned down by the Central Committee by thirty votes to ten. Instead, a peculiar arrangement was made to circumvent Lenin's wishes.

> They shall be read separately to the delegations with the provision that they are not reproduced. The documents shall be read to the delegations by members of the commission which studied Lenin's papers.[45]

Krupskaya pointed out that this procedure contradicted the will of Lenin, but again this was overruled.

The triumvirate had made sure beforehand that the provincial leaders at the Party Congress had been suitably prepared in advance. As the delegates arrived at the Congress on 24 May, the *Testament* was read to them in groups, but, again, under condition that no notes were to be taken. It was then agreed that the *Testament* would not be mentioned or referred to whatsoever during the plenary session of the Congress. In this way, Lenin last wish was violated, and his *Testament* quietly buried.

The Congress declared its support for the resolution of the Politburo, which had tactically included some of Trotsky's amendments, and which served to put an end to the controversy over the proposals of the 'New Course' resolution. This was simply a manoeuvre by Stalin and the other members of his faction.

Then Zinoviev shockingly demanded that the Opposition 'recant' its errors, the first time ever that Party dissidents were asked to disavow their ideas to escape censure. However, this was dismissed following an intervention from Krupskaya, who reminded the Congress that Lenin himself had been in a minority and was later proved correct. The proposal was "psychologically unacceptable", she said.[46]

Meanwhile, the mistakes that led to the German defeat were swept under the carpet, while all the blame was laid at the foot of Brandler, who was made the scapegoat for the fatal advice given by Zinoviev and Stalin.

In 1925, Max Eastman in the United States published the Lenin *Testament*, a copy of which had been sent abroad by an Oppositionist. On hearing this news, the Soviet press declared the publication a complete fabrication and slander against Lenin. Under pressure from the Politburo, Trotsky was forced to dissociate himself from Eastman.

The death of Lenin had transformed the situation. It unleashed the ambitions of the conspirators and allowed them to operate more openly. The conspiracy of 'Trotskyism' versus 'Leninism' was hatched, as was later revealed by Zinoviev and Kamenev, who had themselves actively participated in the conspiracy.

In the autumn of 1924, unable to express his opinions in public, Trotsky took the opportunity to write a preface to his intended collected works, entitled *Lessons of October*, which dealt with the October Revolution and drew parallels with what happened in the recent failure of the German Revolution. This served to bring the political differences behind the dispute out into the open. And this provoked an almighty reaction and ferocious campaign against the Opposition.

According to the official histories, 1924 was the year that the Communist International had become 'Bolshevised'. In fact, the campaign of so-called 'Bolshevisation' instigated by Zinoviev was used simply to bureaucratically purge those leaders of other sections who showed signs of any independent thought.

264. Politburo in 1924
Top row (left to right): Kamenev, Stalin, Trotsky
Bottom row: Rykov, Bukharin, Zinoviev, Tomsky

The struggle against 'Trotskyism' was ruthlessly stepped up. Zinoviev, who always nursed a vindictive streak, relished the task, especially towards Trotsky, who he regarded as a competitor.

While Zinoviev, Kamenev and Stalin led the attack, they pressed Krupskaya to join in, which she agreed to reluctantly, influenced by the ties of friendship with Zinoviev and his family formed in the years of exile. Krupskaya's criticisms against Trotsky were mild in comparison to the spiteful invective of the others. Often, she seems to speak half apologetically, as if wishing to excuse herself. "I do not know whether Comrade Trotsky has actually committed all the deadly sins of which he is accused – the exaggerations of controversy are inevitable".[47] Even in her conclusion, knowing full-well Lenin's opinions, she states:

> Comrade Trotsky devoted the whole of his powers to the fight for the Soviet power during the decisive years of the revolution. He held out heroically in his difficult and responsible position. He worked with unexampled energy and accomplished wonders in the interests of the safeguarding of the victory of the revolution. The Party will not forget this.[48]

However, as if she was being nudged in the back by the triumvirate, who were dissatisfied with her conciliatory words, she then adds the following passage, which has all the hallmarks of a statement added on by someone else:

> And when such a comrade as Trotsky treads, even unconsciously, the path of revision of Leninism, then the Party must make a pronouncement.[49]

When Zinoviev and Kamenev finally broke with Stalin in 1926, Krupskaya found herself briefly in the Opposition. She attempted in her own way to oppose the Stalin clique. However, frightened by a split, and under relentless pressure from Stalin, she soon surrendered, morally exhausted and broken in spirit. The ruling clique then did everything in their power to break her morally, submitting her articles to censorship, as we saw above, and abusing her authority. At one point, Stalin brutally warned her that, if she did not mend her ways, he could find another 'Lenin's widow to replace her'.

In his unofficial memoirs, Nikita Khrushchev, the general secretary of the Communist Party after Stalin's death and the undisputed leader of the Soviet Union until his removal in a coup d'etat in 1964, writes the following:

> I think Stalin's attitude toward Krupskaya was just another instance of his disrespect toward Lenin himself. Nothing was sacred to Stalin, not even Lenin's good name. Stalin never let himself breathe a word against Krupskaya in public, but in his inner circle he allowed himself to say all sorts of outrageous things about her. He wasn't just indulging in frivolous gossip, either. He wanted to influence us psychologically, to undermine our limitless love for Lenin, and to increase his own stature as the uncontested leader and great thinker of our era. To his end he cautiously but deliberately sprinkled into the consciousness of those around him the idea that privately he wasn't of the same opinion about Lenin that he professed publicly.

To illustrate this point, he cited the following outrageous example:

> Stalin used to tell his inner circle that there was some doubt as to whether Nadezhda Konstantinovna was really Lenin's widow at all, and that if the situation continued much longer we would begin to express our doubts in public. He said if necessary we would declare that another woman was Lenin's widow, and he named a solid and respected Party member.*[50]

* According to Alexander Orlov, a high-ranking NKVD officer who defected to the West, the substitute widow was to have been Elena Stasova, who later spent years in labour camps and was rehabilitated after Stalin's death.

265. The principal leaders of the Left Opposition in 1927
Front (from left to right): Serebryakov, Radek, Trotsky, Boguslavsky, Preobrazhensky
Back: Rakovsky, Drobnis, Beloborodov, Sosnovski

The triumvirate then used Lenin's death to announce a 'Lenin Levy'. This was a cynical measure designed to flood the ranks with raw, inexperienced members. The doors of the Communist Party were to be thrown open without any checks, and 240,000 new members joined the party between February and May 1924. Now only 1 per cent of members had been in the Party prior to March 1917. This meant that the voice of the old guard – those who remembered what the Bolshevik Party had been like before – was completely drowned out. The old traditions were erased from the collective memory and the Party of Lenin was crushed under an enormous dead weight.

All power was now concentrated in the hands of Stalin's apparatus. A new bureaucratic regime was emerging, where ideas and principles were reduced to empty slogans handed down from above, to be learned by rote and repeated mechanically, like the religious incantations chanted without thought by a servile congregation. This regime, so completely alien to Leninism, was soon accepted as normal by new members who had no knowledge or experience of the genuine democratic traditions of Bolshevism. The stage was now set for the wholesale abandonment of the genuine ideas and policies of Lenin.

It was, therefore, no accident that in the same year, Stalin first came forward with the theory of 'socialism in one country'. This was the very antithesis of proletarian internationalism and the Leninist programme of world revolution.

It is an elementary proposition of Marxist materialism that if an idea is put forward and gains significant support, that idea must be the expression – however vague and undeveloped – of the interests of a particular class, or subclass, in society. What did the 'theory' of socialism in one country represent? After the years of storm and stress, of war and civil war, of revolution and counter-revolution, there was a growing demand among a certain layer of society for peace and quiet.

But who are we talking about? Which layer of society was so satisfied with its position, that it longed for an end to all change, to an end of excitement and revolution? This layer was precisely the careerist social climbers who had managed to obtain a position in the state apparatus and longed for a quiet life. Their objective was neither communism nor socialism, but to get on with the practical business of running society and the state, and – why not? – to improve one's standard of living, to get a good job, a small apartment and a decent food ration. In short, this was a petty bourgeois reaction against October.

This demand for 'peace' and 'tranquillity' was a reflection of the interests of the 'educated classes', a layer made up of the intellectuals, clerks, managers, accountants, in a word, the bureaucracy that the October Revolution inherited from tsarism and anointed with a little Soviet oil. It was this alien layer that was the most vociferous in its denunciations of 'Trotskyism' and 'permanent revolution', which were really synonymous in their minds with the October Revolution itself.

Every counter-revolution in history always gathers around the same slogan: *order!* Let us put an end to this revolutionary madness! Let us have peace and stability. No more talk of revolution! No more agitation of the masses!

At this time, if a worker dared to complain about wages or conditions, or protest about the insolent conduct of arrogant officials, they would be quickly put in their place: 'What year do you think this is, comrade? Do you still think this is 1918?' Such were the social and class foundations of 'socialism in one country'. Such was the inner meaning of the ferocious campaign against 'Trotskyism'. These were the first hesitant but fateful steps of the Thermidorian counter-revolution.

Lenin's General Staff of 1917

STALIN, THE EXECUTIONER, ALONE REMAINS

RYKOV Shot	BUKHARIN Shot	SVERDLOV Dead	STALIN Survivor	ZINOVIEV Shot	KAMENEV Shot	TROTSKY In Exile	LENIN Dead
KOLLONTAI Missing?	URITSKY Dead	KRESTINSKY Shot	SMILGA Shot	NOGIN Dead	DZERZHINSKY Dead	BUBNOV Disappeared	SOKOLNIKOV In Prison
LOMOV ?	SHOMYAN Dead	BERZIN ?	MURANOV Disappeared	ARTEM Dead	STASSOVA Disappeared	MILIUTIN Missing	JOFFE Suicide

266. Gallery of the Bolshevik CC in 1917 and their fates published in the American *Socialist Worker* in March 1938, in response to Stalin's purges

The Soviet bureaucracy was still unsure of itself. It was feeling its way, looking fearfully over its shoulder. Yet these actions were to politically seal the fate of the Russian Revolution. They would end in a river of blood that would dramatically separate the regimes of Lenin and Stalin.

Suffice it to say that after the death of Lenin, the defence of genuine Marxism passed to Trotsky and the Left Opposition. They proudly took the name of Bolshevik-Leninists. They had come into existence, having originally formed a bloc with Lenin, in an implacable struggle against the bureaucratic degeneration of the Soviet state. They carried this fight through to the bitter end. Trotsky and his supporters were confronted by imprisonment, torture, concentration camps and firing squads, without flinching. They fell, one by one, victims to the most monstrous murder machine in history.

Leopoldo Trepper, the leader of the famous Red Opera, the anti-Nazi spy network in Western Europe during the Second World War, was a devoted Communist who was later imprisoned by Stalin. He describes the Stalinist Purges as follows:

Yugoslavs, Poles, Lithuanians, Czechs – all disappeared. By 1937, not one of the principal leaders of the German Communist Party was left, except for Wilhelm Pleck and Walter Ulbricht. The repressive madness had no limits. The

Korean section was decimated; the delegates from India had disappeared; the representatives of the Chinese Communist Party had been arrested. The shadow of October was being extinguished in the shadows of underground chambers. The revolution had degenerated into a system of terror and horror; the ideals of socialism were ridiculed in the name of a fossilised dogma which the executioners still had the effrontery to call Marxism.

And yet we all went along, sick at heart, but passive, caught up in machinery we had set in motion with our own hands. Mere cogs in the apparatus, terrorised to the point of madness, we became the instruments of our own subjugation. All those who did not rise up against the Stalinist machine are responsible, collectively responsible. I am no exception to this verdict.

But who did protest at the time? Who rose up to voice his outrage? The Trotskyists can lay claim to this honour. Following the example of their leader, who was rewarded for his obstinacy with the end of an ice-pick, they fought Stalinism to the death, and they were the only ones who did.

By the time of the great purges, they could only shout their rebellion in the freezing wastelands where they had been dragged in order to be exterminated. In the camps, their conduct was admirable. But their voices were lost in the tundra…

They did not 'confess', for they knew that their confession would serve neither the party nor socialism.[51]

Finally, in August 1940, Stalin succeeded in eliminating his greatest enemy: Lev Davidovich Trotsky, who was treacherously murdered by a Stalinist agent in Mexico. With his death, the last of the great revolutionary leaders of October passed into history.

One could say that this marked the end of Lenin's Party. But that is not at all the case. Trotsky knew that he could never prevail against the colossal power of Stalin and the bureaucracy. He was fighting for something far more important: to defend and preserve the authentic ideas of Lenin and the October Revolution. Right up to the moment of his death, he worked tirelessly to pass the spotless revolutionary banner on to the new generations, who are destined to carry out this fight to the very end.

40. Lenin's Revolutionary
Legacy

In his book *The Truth About Russia*, Arthur Ransome writes:

> Man does not live by his deeds so much as by the purpose of his deeds. We have seen the flight of the young eagles. Nothing can destroy that fact, even if, later in the day, the eagles fall to earth one by one, with broken wings.[1]

The centenary of Lenin's death gives us an opportunity to reflect on his extraordinary life and his contribution to the struggle of the working class to change society. However, a celebration of Lenin's life can only have real meaning for those who are in solidarity with his aims. It can only have meaning in the context of the struggle for the world socialist revolution today.

For the reformists and philistines of all kinds, the socialist revolution is an entirely alien or utopian concept, and the October Revolution is a matter of mere historical interest, nothing more. But for Marxists, it is the central issue of our time. And for us, the ideas of Lenin are as relevant today as they were then. In fact, they are even more relevant.

Role of the individual

Marxists have never denied the role of the individual in history. There are times when the actions of an individual can even alter the course of history. Under specific circumstances, great historical processes can be refracted through the actions of a single individual, who serves as the agent of a historical necessity. That was the case with Lenin.

That is not to say – as superficial historians do – that individuals are the principal, or the only moving force behind great historic events. This can initially appear to be the case. But on closer inspection, the determining role of great men and women turns out to be a mirage – or rather, a distorting mirror.

The view of history that concentrates on the personal characteristics of individuals, to the exclusion of everything else, can explain nothing because it reduces history to an infinite series of accidents. We are always left asking: what if? What if Julius Caesar had decided not to cross the Rubicon? What if Napoleon had never been born? And so on, and so forth. Following this approach, it is futile to seek any logic to history, since no logical explanations are possible. This fits in very nicely with the prejudices of postmodernism.

But this so-called philosophy represents a rejection of all rational thought in general. In reality, individuals can never act in isolation from the objective socio-economic conditions of the time. It is this that provides the context within which the historical drama is played out and sets definite limits on what any individual can, or cannot, achieve.

The same Lenin who undoubtedly played an absolutely key role in 1917, was condemned to spend most of his life in exile, struggling to maintain his forces together in the most difficult conditions. When the movement revived following the February Revolution, the objective situation changed rapidly. But even then, Lenin had to struggle (frequently against his own comrades) to keep the Party on a correct course. Let us not forget that, following the debacle of the July Days, he was compelled to take refuge in Finland in order to avoid arrest.

Nevertheless, at every major turning point, the role of Lenin proved to be absolutely decisive. Trotsky later stated – that without Lenin, the October Revolution would never have occurred. That is true. But it is equally correct that in the final period of his life, when the revolutionary tide had begun to ebb, Lenin proved powerless to halt the process of the bureaucratic degeneration of the revolution.

This means that, although the role of individuals constitutes a most important factor, and can be decisive under certain conditions, it can never be seen in isolation from powerful objective forces, which even the most able and most courageous people are powerless to alter or resist. One cannot set the individual actors apart from their social environment, which ultimately always plays the key role in history. The great German philosopher, Hegel, showed a profound understanding of the role of the dialectical relationship between the individual and broad historical processes:

The great man of the age is the one who can put into words the will of his age, tell his age what its will is, and accomplish it. What he does is the heart and essence of his age; he actualises his age.[2]

These profound words certainly apply to Lenin. Setting out from the basic ideological principles established by Marx and Engels, Lenin was compelled to translate these insights into concrete Russian conditions.

In order to fulfil the role he was destined to play, he had to prepare himself over a long and difficult period; to face up to the problems of revolutionary work in tsarist Russia; to learn how to apply the general theories of Marxism to the particular conditions of that country. In doing so, he learned the art of tactical flexibility and applied his knowledge to the concrete problems of building the Party in the decades prior to the Revolution. In this way, together with a thorough study of Marxist theory, he was able to acquire the necessary skills to guide the movement in the most critical moments.

In seventeenth century England, Oliver Cromwell built the New Model Army, which was the most indispensable instrument for carrying through the English bourgeois revolution. Several centuries later, Lenin built the Bolshevik Party, the greatest revolutionary party in history, which carried through the October Revolution. This was his greatest achievement. Without it, Lenin could not have carried out the role he played. EH Carr, in his book *What is History?*, explains:

> … the higher degree of creativity may perhaps be assigned to those great men who, like Cromwell or Lenin, helped to mould the forces which carried them to greatness, rather than to those who, like Napoleon or Bismarck, rode to greatness on the back of already existing forces.

> What seems to me essential is to recognise in the great man an outstanding individual who is at once a product and an agent of the historical process, at once the representative and creator of social forces which change the shape of the world and the thoughts of men.[3]

Under Lenin's leadership, a small party of about 8,000 members in February became a mass organisation, composed of hundreds of thousands of militants, with deep roots in the great mass of workers and peasants. His decisive role consisted in binding firmly together the class, party and leadership.

In the years that preceded the October Revolution, Lenin had accumulated great political authority within the Party. This political capital proved critical when sharp turns needed to be made. Of course, this did not mean that he got his way on all occasions, far from it. But in *decisive* matters, he tended to succeed. At a critical juncture of events, the subjective factor in history can become indispensable. Everything becomes completely focused on one critical factor, which can produce success or failure. This is just as true in the class struggle as it is in ordinary warfare. The difference between a good general and a bad one can mean the difference between victory and an absolute rout.

There are times when the greatest revolutionary party in history fails to keep up with events. Even in 1917, part of the Bolshevik leadership vacillated, lagging behind the ranks of the Party. But it is also true that the Party as a whole lagged behind the masses. At such times, Lenin's personal authority was a most decisive factor, overcoming the ingrained conservatism that is the product of routinism and galvanising the whole Party for action. Trotsky explains this very well:

> I know, and you know as well as I do, comrades, that the fate of the working class does not depend on individual personalities, but this does not mean that the individual personality is of no importance in the development of the working class. The individual cannot remould the working class after his own image and likeness, nor can he, at will, show the proletariat this or that road to follow, but he can help the accomplishment of the necessary tasks and speed up the attainment of the goal.[4]

One of Lenin's great strengths was his tremendous perspicacity, his ability to immediately grasp the essence of a given situation and act accordingly. He always seemed to know when to act, and how to act decisively. This ability, at first sight, appears to be a kind of intuition, a rather mysterious quality that is the prerogative of certain privileged individuals.

But in reality, there is nothing mysterious about it. Years of experience, a wealth of accumulated knowledge and a profound grasp of theory reached a point where they acquired the character of instinct. But what is instinct, but accumulated knowledge that is so concentrated and distilled that it becomes second nature, allowing one to grasp the essence of a given situation without the need for lengthy study and observation?

In 1917, this extraordinary ability played an essential role in leading the revolution to a successful conclusion, as Trotsky points out in his *Diary in Exile*:

> Had I not been present in 1917 in Petersburg, the October Revolution would still have taken place – *on the condition that Lenin was present and in command.*

> If neither Lenin nor I had been present in Petersburg, there would have been no October Revolution: the leadership of the Bolshevik Party would have prevented it from occurring – of this I have not the slightest doubt! If Lenin had not been in Petersburg, I doubt whether I could have managed to conquer the resistance of the Bolshevik leaders… But I repeat, granted the presence of Lenin the October Revolution would have been victorious anyway.[5]

Elsewhere, he explained Lenin's indispensable role in the following way:

> … under certain circumstances men can end up playing a decisive role. Without a mechanic, the machine will not run, without the spark plug's spark, the motor will not start even if every other part is working fine. *Lenin was the Russian Revolution's spark.*[6]

If Lenin had not been present, say, for example, if the German General Staff had refused Lenin and the others permission to travel through Germany, or if Lenin had been shot while trying to escape in July, then who would have occupied the leading role? The answer is clear: Kamenev, Zinoviev and Stalin. But the role they would have played is already known to us.

The revolution would still have broken out. Objective conditions were pushing in that direction and the events of February 1917 confirm this. But without Lenin, the 'old Bolshevik' leaders would have continued the policy of subordinating themselves to the moderate reformist leaders of the Soviet. The latter would have continued to subordinate themselves to the bourgeois Provisional Government, which, in turn, would have subordinated itself to the landowners and the imperialist Entente.

The discontent of workers, peasants and soldiers would have spent itself in a series of unplanned and leaderless uprisings, and the revolution would have been crushed in a sea of blood. The bourgeois historians now assert that the defeat of the revolution would have ended in the triumph of bourgeois democracy. This is absolute nonsense.

General Kornilov would have been able to overthrow Kerensky without any difficulty. And he certainly had no intention of establishing a Westminster-type parliamentary democracy. He would have made the workers pay a terrible price, to teach them a bloody lesson that they would never forget. A terrible massacre would have been followed by a brutal military dictatorship, accompanied by mass pogroms. Russian fascism would have made the regime of Mussolini look like an English vicar's tea party.

If this had been the case, university professors would have written many learned volumes explaining the reasons for the 'inevitable failure' of the

Bolsheviks, while the reformist traitors would hasten to draw the lesson that revolution always leads to violence and counter-revolution.

The fact that the Russian Revolution *did* succeed proves precisely the opposite. The working class, against all the odds, *did* come to power and created a workers' state. The Revolution *did* change the course of world history. And its repercussions are very much still felt today. Despite all the many attempts to rewrite history, the October Revolution is an undeniable fact of history.

Since the October Revolution, there have been many revolutionary situations where the working class could have easily taken power: Trotsky once remarked that the Spanish proletariat in the 1930s could have carried out *ten* revolutions. If they did not succeed, it was not because the objective conditions for revolution were absent. In fact, all the conditions were present – except for one: the presence of a genuine revolutionary party and leadership.

The same is true of many other cases: Germany (1918, 1923), Italy (1920), Britain (1926), China (1925-27), France (1934, 1968), Hungary (1956), Finland (1918), Ireland (1918-20), Spain (1936-37, and again during 1976-9), Portugal (1974-75), Greece (1974), Egypt (2011), Sri Lanka (2022) and so on – the list is endless.

Despite the countless examples of immense heroism and self-sacrifice, it was only in Russia that the working class took power and held on to it. The reason for this is the existence of the Bolshevik Party under the leadership of Lenin and Trotsky.

This fact stands out more sharply in the light of the many defeats cited above. Although the objective conditions were ripe for revolution in many countries, what was missing was the subjective factor. Trotsky described Lenin's qualities as inseparable from the Bolshevik Party in the following way:

> A revolutionist of Lenin's makeup and breadth could be the leader only of the most fearless party, capable of carrying its thoughts and actions to their logical conclusion. But genius in itself is the rarest of exceptions. A leader of genius orients himself faster, estimates the situation more thoroughly, sees further than others. It was unavoidable that a great gap should develop between the leader of genius and his closest collaborators. It may even be conceded that to a certain extent the very power of Lenin's vision acted as a brake on the development of self-reliance among his collaborators. Nevertheless, that does not mean that Lenin was 'everything', and that the Party without Lenin was nothing. Without the Party Lenin would have been as helpless as Newton and Darwin without collective scientific work… The leader of genius is important because, in shortening the

learning period by means of objective lessons, he enables the party to influence the developments of events at the proper moment.[7]

However, the exact course of history is not preordained. Lenin had to navigate his way through the events, adopting tactics that corresponded to the needs of the situation. He had, as we have seen, developed an instinctive feel for the situation and knew what to do and when. But, of course, he did make mistakes and was not afraid to admit them. You can see this throughout his numerous speeches and writings. Above all, he learned from these mistakes. That only served to strengthen the authority of his leadership. He explained in April 1920:

Defects, mistakes, blunders in such a new, difficult and great undertaking are inevitable. Those who are afraid of the difficulties of building socialism, those who allow themselves to be scared by them, those who give way to despair or cowardly dismay, are no socialists.[8]

And again:

It is not he who makes no mistakes that is intelligent. There are no such men, nor can there be. It is he whose errors are not very grave and who is able to rectify them easily and quickly that is intelligent.[9]

He retained this view throughout his life. Looking back on the past, Lenin even chuckled about the fact that he and the Bolsheviks had not only made mistakes but also not a few stupidities. But as Josef Dietzgen wrote:

An old man who desires to be able to start his life again, does not mean to repeat it, but to improve it. He recognises the ways he has walked as wrong ones, yet he cannot withhold the seemingly contradictory acknowledgement that they brought him wisdom.[10]

Vainglorious boasting, the desire for personal prestige, and any kind of pretentiousness were all completely alien to Lenin. If he made mistakes (and he made far fewer than most) he was always honest in recognising them and learning from them. He never treated Marxism as a ready-made set of formulas to be mechanically imposed on a given situation. He saw Marxist theory essentially as a guide to action, as he explained in November 1918:

The teaching of Marx and Engels is not a dogma to be learnt by heart. It must be taken as a guide to action. We have always stood by that, and I think we have acted consistently, never succumbing to opportunism, modifying our tactics. That is no departure from Marxism, and certainly cannot be called opportunism. I have said before, and I repeat once again, that this teaching is not a dogma, but a guide to action.[11]

Lenin and Marx

Working as an inseparable duo, Marx and Engels laid down the firm theoretical foundations of scientific socialism. After the death of Marx, it was Engels who became the real inheritor of the ideas of Karl Marx. And after him, it was Lenin who occupied the undisputed role of the standard bearer of Marxism. Throughout his life, Lenin kept the flame of Marx and Engels alive. He stood on the shoulders of the founders of scientific socialism.

While an important contribution was made in the early years by Plekhanov, 'the father of Russian Marxism', Lenin stands out, not only because he defended the ideas of Marx and Engels, but because he actually deepened the ideas of scientific socialism, making original contributions on the theory of the state, imperialism, and the national question, to name only a few.

But far more than that, Marx and Engels lived at a time when the conditions for socialist revolution were only beginning to ripen. The revolutions of 1848-9 were an anticipation, where the young and inexperienced forces of the working class made an early appearance, but were unable to set their stamp decisively upon events.

The Paris Commune, for the very first time, heralded the arrival of the revolutionary proletariat as a decisive force in world history. Although it ultimately suffered defeat, it acted as a glorious example, a kind of dress rehearsal for the future. In fact, without the experience of the Paris Commune, and the defeated Russian Revolution of 1905-6, the October Revolution would have been unthinkable.

But in the great events of 1848 and afterwards, Marx and Engels could never play a leading role. They were compelled by circumstances to play the role in the main of observers, commenting on revolutions, without ever having the possibility of intervening decisively in them. True, their commentaries and analyses, especially of the Commune, were immeasurably important for Lenin. But he lived at a later time and in a country where, despite all the difficulties, he could not only write about revolution, but participate actively in it.

Lenin's outstanding contribution was that he built the party that led the working class to the conquest of state power. From this assessment, however, it is possible to draw a radically false conclusion: namely, that

Marx may have been a great thinker, but Lenin translated Marx's words into deeds.

This false and one-sided view of Lenin as a 'practical' revolutionary, as opposed to a 'mere theoretician', is contradicted by the facts. From his early youth right throughout his life, Lenin paid the closest attention to the study of theory. He did not simply read Marx and Engels, but closely *studied and absorbed* these ideas. He conquered them for himself. Lenin's notebooks were full of quotations from the great teachers and the margins of his books were covered with numerous comments, as if he were engaged in a constant conversation, not just with the founders of scientific socialism but with Hegel and Aristotle, too. Reading these lively comments, one would think he was on first-name terms with them. For Lenin, theory was never a grey, lifeless abstraction, but something very much alive.

The Stalinists invented the myth of Lenin as an infallible being who never made mistakes. They needed this myth in order to justify the monstrous cult of Stalin as the all-seeing, all-knowing Leader who must never be questioned but obeyed blindly in all things. Any connection between this mythology and reality is purely accidental. Here, the real Lenin has disappeared entirely and replaced with a ridiculous fairy story. Lenin never claimed to be infallible or all-seeing. His wisdom was not the result of any divine inspiration, but was the result of years of painstaking study and experience.

Lenin's life can be characterised by a continually rising upward curve in his political development, punctuated with a series of crises and sharp turns. At each point, despite all the difficulties, he emerges stronger, taller, and more prepared. As a young man from a fairly well-to-do middle class family, the benefits of a very good education served him well. But Lenin was never satisfied. He continually extended his horizons, learned from others and, in doing so, drew himself up by degrees onto a higher plane. Moreover, his early life was punctuated by great personal tragedy and difficulties.

An important element in this equation was the peculiar conditions faced by the revolutionaries in tsarist Russia. Looking back on the movement's early period, Lenin pointed out that the revolutionary generation had gone through a hard school, tempered by the harshness of tsarist repression:

... Bolshevism, which had arisen on this granite foundation of theory, went through fifteen years of practical history (1903-17) unequalled anywhere in the world in its wealth of experience. During those fifteen years, no other country knew anything even approximating to that revolutionary experience, that rapid and varied succession of different forms of the movement – legal and illegal, peaceful and stormy, underground and open, local circles and mass movements, and parliamentary and terrorist forms, in so brief a period, such a wealth of forms, shades, and methods of struggle of all classes of modern society, a struggle which, owing to the backwardness of the country and the severity of the tsarist yoke, matured with exceptional rapidity, and assimilated most eagerly and successfully the appropriate 'last word' of American and European political experience.[12]

This provided the Russian movement with a unique experience compared to most other countries. This assisted in sharpening and clarifying ideas, and steeling its cadres in preparation for the events of 1905 and 1917. It gave Lenin a schooling as no other. He had been forced to learn many lessons, for example, how to combine propaganda and agitation, as well as legal and illegal work, the constant fight against opportunism and ultra-leftism, and finally the concrete tasks involved in an armed insurrection.

Yet, the mere recounting of these experiences is insufficient to explain Lenin's genius. Exactly the same conditions were faced by many others – some of them equally as intelligent and talented. The case of Martov immediately comes to mind. Yet they were not able to digest and assimilate their experiences, or to draw the necessary conclusions from them. For that, a particular character and mindset was necessary.

Strength of character

Throughout his life, Lenin was distinguished, on the one hand, by his clear-sightedness – his ability to see clearly what others failed to see and to correctly anticipate the road ahead. On the other hand, he had an iron determination that would sweep away all obstacles.

He began to acquire these characteristics already when, as a young man, he was confronted with all the difficulties faced by a persecuted family. The execution of his brother served to steel his will and fill him full of hatred for the oppressors. He was young, but the development of his character received a powerful impulse and he matured rapidly.

Lenin never lost a deep feeling for the sufferings of humanity, but that very feeling was accompanied by a fierce and lasting hatred of oppression and injustice of any kind. Harsh experience hardened him. From the trials of life, he derived a tremendous strength of character and great moral reserves. He understood better than anyone that revolution was a deadly serious matter. It was not for nothing that he admired the heroism and determination of the adherents of *Narodnaya Volya*. Indeed, he took their centralisation and iron discipline for a model, while rejecting their subjectivist philosophy and the methods of individual terrorism, which were the expression of the individualism of the petty bourgeois.

The proletarian revolution required other methods, based on collective mass action: strikes, general strikes, mass demonstrations and insurrection. In skilfully combining two different methods – centralism and democracy – he arrived at the idea of democratic centralism, which was the organisational backbone of Bolshevism.

He showed an unshakable confidence and determination in everything he did. But again, at all times, Lenin's experience was illuminated by a profound knowledge of Marxist theory. In the final analysis, his influence rested upon the power of his ideas. In explaining those ideas, he was simple and direct. The prolix and sometimes florid turns of phrase that were typical of Plekhanov were entirely foreign to him. He always expressed himself concisely and in concrete language, going straight to the heart of the matter and then sticking to it with the stubborn determination of a bulldog with a bone. On matters of political principle, Lenin was always like that: utterly implacable and unwilling to compromise. Plekhanov would take up a critic and subject him to a good shaking, but then put him down again. But once Lenin had his opponent between iron jaws, he would not let them go until they surrendered.

The polemics within Bolshevism could be very sharp, even brutal. This was especially the case in exile circles. Sometimes, in order to emphasise a point, Lenin presented his views in an exaggerated way and 'bent the stick too far', to use his own phrase. That was true when, in combatting the one-sided views of the Economists, he incorrectly asserted that the working class, left to itself, could only arrive at a 'trade union consciousness'. He later corrected this mistake and never repeated it, although every pseudo-Marxist sect in creation continues to repeat it.

Lenin did not mince his words when dealing with political deviations. His implacable attitude to theory recalls the words of Aristotle: "Plato is dear to me, but dearer still is truth." In a letter to Gorky about the period 1908-11, he said:

> But if they haven't understood it, if they haven't learned anything, then don't hold it against me: friendship is friendship, but duty is duty. Against attempts to abuse Marxism or to confuse the policy of the workers' party we shall fight without sparing our lives.[13]

In another letter to Inessa Armand in December 1916, Lenin complained:

There it is, my fate. One fighting campaign after another – against political stupidities, philistinism, opportunism and so forth.

It has been going on since 1893. And so has the hatred of the philistines on account of it. But still, I would not exchange this fate for 'peace' with the philistines.[14]

These words reveal Lenin's firmness when it came to defending his principles. On such questions, he was not prepared to bend. The leaders of the old Second International considered him obstinate. Those spineless opportunists naturally confused firmness on matters of principle with mere stubbornness. They themselves were always prepared to surrender. Their motto might have been: "Very well. If you don't like my principles, I'll change them."

But that 'obstinacy' was only one side of Lenin. There was another side that is not generally recognised but which was equally important, if not more so. He was firm, but never vengeful or spiteful, which were traits he regarded as alien. In polemics, he relied only on the strength of his ideas and argument to convince people.

Lenin was always open and honest, and whenever there was a dispute, he took the initiative to smooth things over wherever possible. He knew that the vanquished of today could very well be the friend and ally of tomorrow and therefore avoided unnecessarily burning bridges. For Lenin, intolerance was always the sign of an inward weakness. While fighting stubbornly to defend what he felt was essential, Lenin was capable of making the greatest organisational concessions so as to preserve the unity of the party. In this, he showed the greatest flexibility towards organisation and tactics.

One can say that Lenin combined elements of the great traditions of the Russian revolutionary movement of the nineteenth century with Marxism to create something radically new.

Among the circles of Party veterans, Lenin was affectionately known as *Starik* – the 'Old Man'. He was, after all, from an older generation compared to the rest of his collaborators, the composition of which had changed several times over the course of some fifteen or twenty years, up to and including 1917.

His initial close collaborators were Plekhanov and Martov. Following the split of 1903, they gave way to Bogdanov and Lunacharsky. But that layer succumbed to the pressures of ultra-leftism, leading to a sharp break with Lenin. When the Party finally recovered from the debacle of 1905, a new layer of young leaders – almost all of them former students – occupied leading positions. Foremost among these were Kamenev and Zinoviev. We have already described their role both during and after October.

Others, notably Bukharin, came to the fore during the First World War. For some years, Trotsky remained outside the ranks of the Bolsheviks. Although on all the major political questions he was always closer to the Bolshevik positions, he had illusions in the possibility of uniting Bolsheviks and left-wing Mensheviks, whose most outstanding representative was Martov.

It is not generally realised that Lenin himself dreamed of winning over Martov, with whom he had been united by close ties of friendship from his earliest days in St. Petersburg. On many occasions, Martov moved sharply to the left, but only to draw back at the decisive moment. In the end, he remained hopelessly encumbered by his involvement with Menshevism.

During the difficult years of the War, Trotsky's implacable defence of internationalism meant that his differences with the Bolsheviks virtually disappeared. At the time of the February Revolution, he immediately adopted the same position as Lenin, which was opposed by Stalin and Kamenev, along with other 'old Bolsheviks'.

On returning to Russia in 1917, he became a leading member of the Bolshevik Party, second only to Lenin himself. His firm stand against any conciliation with the Mensheviks caused Lenin to remark that there was 'no better Bolshevik'. And in his *Testament*, Lenin described him as the most outstanding member of the Central Committee.

For many reasons, Lenin and Trotsky stand head and shoulders above the other Party leaders, although among them there were not a few very talented people. But it was Lenin alone who would create a party that was like no other party in history – the party that was to lead the Russian workers to victory in October 1917.

The struggle for ideas

Lenin's entire life was one long and unbroken learning curve. Along this curve, there were many important turning points. The 1903 RSDLP Congress was certainly one from which he eventually emerged politically and organisationally strengthened. The 1905 Revolution was another, as was the outbreak of war in 1914.

The long fight that began with the struggle against the Economists, Mensheviks and revisionists, through to the rich experiences of the first Russian Revolution in 1905 and the subsequent battle against ultra-leftism and philosophical deviations, was the hard school that prepared Lenin for the main achievement of his life. Through these struggles, he gradually succeeded in creating the instrument that was needed to guarantee the success of the revolution.

At every moment of that long struggle, Lenin stood firmly on the sound theoretical foundation of Marxist theory. But Lenin always took care to write in such a way that would be easily understood by any intelligent worker. Lenin always had a good ear for the workers. He was attentive to their problems and struggles. In this way, he had a feel for the working class. After all, the task of Marxists, as he saw it, is to make conscious the unconscious yearnings of the masses to change society.

All his life, Lenin was fighting, not to discover a 'new and original' theory, but to defend the ideas of Marx and Engels against the revisionists like Bernstein and Kautsky. It was they, not he, who were always looking for 'new ideas', which, on closer inspection, are never new at all, but merely the regurgitation of very old and discredited theories in some new disguise.

Lenin did much to enrich the theories of Marxism, applying them to the concrete conditions of his own day: his analysis of the imperialist epoch of wars and revolution; of bourgeois democracy in the era of decaying capitalism; the role of insurrection; the role of the party; soviets and the trade unions in the epoch of proletarian revolution; the economic transition to socialism; and finally, the problems of bureaucracy and degeneration in a workers' state. These ideas, taken as a whole, constitute the extremely valuable heritage of Lenin's contribution to Marxism.

However, it is not strictly correct to speak of Leninism, as if one were referring to an entirely new theory, separate and apart from Marxism. That expression was never used during Lenin's lifetime, and he would have been horrified to have heard it spoken.

Lenin and culture

The long years in exile broadened his horizons and enabled him to acquire a sound knowledge of several European languages, notably German and French. This meant that he was able to read the works of Marx, Engels and Hegel in the original.

His thirst for theory was inexhaustible. Never content with merely skating over the surface of ideas, he took the trouble to study the works of Hegel, that master of dialectics who was the main source of philosophical inspiration for the young Marx and Engels. It is no accident that in the midst of the exploding bombs of the First World War, Lenin spent days on end sitting at a desk in the silence of a Swiss library reading room, devouring the pages of

Hegel's *Logic*. These works contain the most profound and brilliant insights, but they are not easy to read. Lenin once joked that reading *Logic* was 'the best way to get a headache'. But the unparalleled mastery of dialectics that Lenin acquired in this way provided the granite foundations upon which Bolshevism was built. Without it, there would have been no *Imperialism, the Highest Stage of Capitalism*, no *The State and Revolution*, and no victorious October Revolution.

Lenin did not confine his reading to politics. He was passionately interested in literature, especially the great European classics. He read widely, not only the works of Shakespeare and Goethe, but most of the great Russian writers. His works are frequently interspersed with quotes from Tolstoy, Gogol, Saltykov-Shchedrin, and above all, his favourite Chernyshevsky.

However, his tastes were somewhat conservative. He could never appreciate the modernistic style of Mayakovsky, but he was reconciled to it by the persuasive arguments of Lunacharsky, the first Soviet Commissar of Culture, who pointed out that Mayakovsky's poetry was very popular among the workers and youth.

Most of the other Bolshevik leaders were, like Lenin, men and women of culture. Like him, they could also speak foreign languages fluently. The exception was Stalin, who, apart from his native tongue, spoke only Russian, and that badly, with a thick Georgian accent.

The importance of theory

The superiority of Lenin and Trotsky was clear to everybody. That is why the Bolsheviks were popularly known as the Party of Lenin and Trotsky. These two men were, without any doubt, by far the most important theoreticians in the Party. Their strengths stand out all the more strikingly when compared with the other principal Party leaders.

Zinoviev was known for his skills as an agitator. However, the art of an agitator dies with the man, leaving no trace. The only book of his that is widely known is his *History of Bolshevism*, which can hardly be described as a theoretical work. It was a series of lectures delivered during the campaign against Trotsky, and was clearly motivated to boost Zinoviev's image as an 'old Bolshevik' and downplay the role of Trotsky. As a work of history, it is superficial, one-sided, and hardly worth the trouble of reading. Kamenev was a far more able man than Zinoviev, although he lacked his strength of character. He was more of a propagandist, but lacked any spark of originality. Who today knows or reads the works of Kamenev?

Preobrazhensky was noted as an Economist, and Rakovsky made some important contributions to the national question. But their scope in the field of theory was limited.

Of the other Bolshevik leaders, only Bukharin might qualify for the title of a theoretician. While his books still retain some interest, they suffer from a very serious defect. It was pointed out by Lenin in his *Testament*, where he correctly stated that Bukharin had never understood dialectics. This defect is present in all of his major works, which are marred by an extremely mechanical and formalistic method. It was precisely this formalism that explains the constant zig-zags and swings from left to right that characterise his entire political career and ultimately brought about his ruin.

As for Stalin, his claim to be a theoretician rests almost solely on one work: *Marxism and the National Question*, written in 1913, which he admitted had been basically dictated to him by Lenin. About the rest of his mercilessly few excursions into 'theory', the less said the better. This 100 per cent pure apparatchik had no use for theory, except as an afterthought and a source of convenient quotations to justify his latest about-turn.

Intellectually limited and narrow in outlook, Stalin was psychologically averse to broad generalisations. This creature of the apparatus was skilled in the black arts of intrigue and manoeuvre. For that narrow sphere, what was required were not general theories but only a grasp of the immediate facts and an intimate knowledge of the frailties of human nature and the weaknesses of individuals.

One can observe the workings of such a psychology on many levels of everyday life: the basest, most trivial and demeaning of human emotions, such as envy, jealousy, an all-consuming ambition to 'rise' in society – or at least in one's immediate social milieu. Such base feelings can, and do, arise not *just* in political parties, but even in a football club or an old ladies' knitting circle, giving rise to the most sordid and poisonous intrigues, backstabbing and an unhealthy competition for positions.

Such situations are too well known to require any further elaboration here. However unpleasant they may be, conflicts on a Lilliputian scale rarely cause any serious damage, save for hurt egos of individuals. But when they are replicated at the top layer of a mass party that stands at the head of a nation of over 150 million people, matters become far more dramatic.

Trotsky, in his *History of the Russian Revolution*, explains how the Bolshevik Party under Lenin's leadership resisted the colossal pressures bearing down upon it:

The necessary distance from bourgeois ideology was kept up in the party by a vigilant irreconcilability, whose inspirer was Lenin. Lenin never tired of working with his lancet, cutting off those bonds which a petty bourgeois environment creates between the party and official social opinion. At the same time Lenin taught the party to create its own social opinion, resting upon the thoughts and feelings of the rising class. Thus, by a process of selection and education, and in continual struggle, the Bolshevik Party created not only a political but a moral medium of its own, independent of bourgeois social opinion and implacably opposed to it. Only this permitted the Bolsheviks to overcome the waverings in their own ranks and reveal in action that courageous determination without which the October victory would have been impossible.[15]

In any genuine Marxist organisation, the chief guarantee against degeneration consists in the moral and political qualities of its leadership. Leaders who are sufficiently well grounded in the ideas of Marxism possess the confidence and authority to answer any criticisms whatsoever. They do not need to resort to organisational methods or underhand manoeuvres.

So it was in the Bolshevik Party. The colossal moral and political authority of Lenin and Trotsky was the strongest bulwark against political backsliding and the penetration of the Party by alien ideas and tendencies.

But with the death of Lenin, that bulwark was seriously weakened. This was a major factor in the process of the bureaucratic degeneration of the Party. The struggle against 'Trotskyism', which served as a convenient cover for an assault against everything that Lenin stood for, demolished the last remaining line of defence. Trotsky was isolated in the leadership, and the power of the apparatus – and therefore also of Stalin – grew irresistibly.

Of course, it would be a mistake to exaggerate the role of individuals in such a situation. Far more powerful factors were involved than the errors of omission or commission of different leaders. But what would have happened if Lenin had not died? That is an interesting question.

If Lenin had lived, the bureaucratic degeneration would have been much slower. The removal of Stalin would have postponed the process. That would have given time for Lenin and Trotsky to provide correct leadership to the Communist International, which could have helped the young Chinese Communist Party to carry out a successful revolution. That, in turn, would have served to inspire and reinvigorate the Soviet workers, potentially changing the course of history.

But this is a theory of a purely speculative character. Lenin did not survive and his death had a profound effect in accelerating the process of degeneration. Meanwhile, Stalin was quietly strengthening his hold on the Party apparatus. He made use of the services of Kamenev and Zinoviev as a cover for his own agenda.

While concealing his burning ambition under a false disguise of modesty, and affecting publicly the image of a 'practical' Party man, Stalin keenly felt his own inferiority beside other Party leaders. He secretly thirsted after the kind of authority they had as a result of a solid grasp of theory, which eluded him entirely. Due to this, he nursed a secret and deep resentment against all those who he knew were his moral and intellectual superiors. That included not only his immediate collaborators, Zinoviev and Kamenev, but every one of Lenin's closest companions. Insufficient as their understanding of Marxism may have been, Stalin's own primitive level was immeasurably lower.

Stalin must have been aware of the painful effect his seminarist homily at Lenin's funeral had made on the 'old Bolsheviks'. Naturally, they made no comments to his face, though he will have been the butt of numerous jokes behind his back. Zinoviev was particularly fond of impersonating Stalin's rough Georgian accent, for which Trotsky rebuked him, saying: 'one Stalin is enough'.

Stalin was well aware of how he was seen by the Party veterans. He felt slighted and underestimated by them. But for the time being, he kept silent and allowed them to believe that he was content to play the role of second fiddle in the orchestra. Sooner or later, he would make them all pay.

Stalin's struggle with Trotsky

Here, at first sight, we are faced with a paradox. How was it possible that a mediocre figure like Stalin could defeat a great revolutionary leader like Trotsky and rise to power? This seems like a mystery. However, on closer examination, there is nothing mysterious about it.

Superficial observers attempt to attribute Stalin's victory to his alleged greater 'realism' and superior grasp of tactics. In reality, this flies in the face of all the known facts. Stalin had no long-term plan, understood nothing, and foresaw nothing. His sole preoccupation at that time was the struggle to hold on to his position. Stalin proceeded empirically, always reacting to events and the ideas of other people.

The method he used in debating with the opposition was really very simple. If Trotsky said 'A', he would say 'B'. He would place a negative wherever the Left Opposition placed a positive, and vice versa. Thus, step by step, every one of the basic propositions of Bolshevism were annihilated, until finally not a *single trace* would be left of Lenin's ideas.

But to return to our initial question: how could such a hollow strategy succeed? Materialism teaches us that whenever an idea is put forward – however incorrect and absurd it may be – and gains mass support in society, that idea must somehow express the interests of a particular social class or stratum. Stalinism was the reflection, in political terms, of the reaction against October by a growing layer of officials who had climbed to positions of power and influence on the backs of a revolution in a period of retreat.

In periods of great historical upsurges like the Russian Revolution, leaders of a particular kind are required. Heroic periods demand heroic leaders: courageous and far-sighted men and women who provide necessary leadership to the revolution. But in periods when the revolutionary floodtide begins to ebb, such leaders are no longer required. Instead, a new breed emerges, a breed of unprincipled opportunists and careerists, mediocrities, and conformists, anxious to grab positions of power and hold onto them at all costs.

Such was the case in France when the Revolution was overthrown by the Thermidorian reactionaries. The heroic period of the French Revolution produced great revolutionary leaders. But with the exhaustion of the revolution, these were swept away one by one. At that point, in the place of great men and women, the dominant element became the 'Frogs of the Marsh', as they were appropriately baptised by the revolutionaries. These elements had kept their heads down, hiding under a stone in the days of storm and stress. Now they finally crawled out of the darkness to croak triumphantly over the dead body of the French Revolution.

An analogous process occurred in Russia when the revolutionary floodtide went into reverse. That tide was flowing strongly in the direction of counter-revolution by the time Lenin died. His last letters and speeches are filled with dire warnings of precisely this fact.

A courageous minority around Trotsky and the Left Opposition attempted to swim against the tide. They stubbornly defended the basic principles of Lenin and October, and showed great perspicacity and a profound understanding of the real situation, nationally and internationally. But even the most profound ideas are powerless in the face of overwhelming historical forces that sweep everything before them.

Many people, including many honest and devoted revolutionaries, were unable to stand against the current. Exhausted and disorientated, they bowed their heads and adapted themselves to the new conditions. All Stalin had to do was to wait patiently and go with the tide that, in effect, was sweeping him irresistibly towards power.

One by one, the 'old Bolshevik' leaders of the Party gave up the struggle and surrendered to Stalin. They proved to be too weak to resist the colossal pressures of alien classes – the kulaks, speculators, NEPmen and bureaucrats – that bore down on the Party from all sides. Trotsky alone remained firm in his opposition. All the others gave into these pressures, although they did so reluctantly and with considerable hesitation. It was Stalin, of all the Bolshevik leaders, who openly exulted in this degeneration.

Standing at the head of the bureaucracy, Stalin identified himself fully with it, became the mouthpiece for its interests and desires, and in effect was its personification. He alone expressed its prejudices and insolent demands in the most crude and brazen manner. In the person of Stalin, Bolshevism broke, not at its strongest, but at its weakest link.

The method of the usurpers

To add insult to injury, this new ideological concoction was baptised by the ruling clique as 'Marxism–Leninism'. That was really another name for Stalinism. The Stalinists used and distorted the ideas of Lenin, and claimed his legacy for their own cynical ends. Lenin himself had warned against this when he wrote:

> It has always been the case in history that after the death of revolutionary leaders who were popular among the oppressed classes, their enemies have attempted to appropriate their names so as to deceive the oppressed classes.[16]

So it was with Lenin. Stalin constantly appealed to the name of Lenin and 'Leninism' precisely when he was in the process of destroying Lenin's party, and burying the memory of Lenin under a heap of dirt.

There is nothing new about this. History has seen many examples of usurpers who attempt to conceal their usurpation by disguising themselves in the rhetoric of an earlier period. Stalin was merely following this well-trodden path of cynical usurpers. There are many examples of this phenomenon. Having overthrown the Roman Republic, Augustus and the early Roman emperors solemnly swore allegiance to an impotent and terrified senate. This ridiculous pretence was kept up until the emperor Caligula laid bare the real situation by declaring his intention to elevate his favourite horse to the rank of senator.

At a later period, Napoleon Bonaparte frequently spoke in the name of the Revolution at a time when he was trampling it underfoot to make himself absolute dictator. He continued this farce right up to the moment when he placed the imperial crown on his own head, proclaiming himself emperor.

The usual 'explanation' of Stalin's victory over the Opposition is based on the simple assumption that, since Stalin succeeded, he must have possessed a remarkable degree of intellectual acumen. But this is an explanation that explains nothing at all. It simply presupposes what has to be proved. It is also contradicted by many historical cases, not least in the present epoch.

The period of the senile decay of capitalism is also one in which mediocrity flourishes on all sides. It is sufficient to point to the mental coefficient of recent presidents of the United States, or British prime ministers, to prove the point. Whatever may have been the secret that propelled George W Bush or Joseph Robinette Biden into the White House, the powers of their intellect played no discernible role. Future historians may attempt to cast the Leaders of what is called the 'Free World' in a more favourable light than they rightly deserve. But whether their powers of understanding even reached the level of Caligula's horse must be a matter of some debate.

Thermidor

The real foundation for the defeat of the Left Opposition and the victory of Stalinism can be discovered, not in the machinations of individuals, but in the changed relationship of social forces. This, in turn, had a material base. Revolution, by its very nature, is a great devourer of human energy, both individual and collective. The workers, already exhausted by long years of war, revolution and civil war, were anxiously awaiting the victory of the international revolution to come to their aid.

This hope was dashed by the defeat in Germany in 1923. That was followed by the defeat of the British General Strike and then the Chinese Revolution of 1925-27. The Russian workers were gradually beginning to lose faith in the world revolution. The defeat of the revolutions in Germany and China led to the isolation of the Revolution in conditions of frightful economic and cultural backwardness.

These defeats dealt a series of hammer blows to the morale of the Soviet working class; moods of depression began to take hold, expressed in a growing apathy and political indifference. "Nothing in the world is so convincing as success and nothing so repelling as defeat for the large masses", as Trotsky observed.[17]

All of these factors played a role in weakening the social weight of the working class, and increasing that of the bourgeois and petty bourgeois elements that had grown stronger with the introduction of the New Economic Policy. They were striving to get control of the state itself – a danger that Lenin was constantly warning about in the last few years of his life. The formation of the bureaucracy was further boosted by the mass demobilisation of the Red Army. By the time of Lenin's death, a layer of privileged officials and careerists had risen up on the backs of the masses.

In 1926, alarmed by Stalin's conduct, Kamenev and Zinoviev suddenly broke with him, apparently over his adoption of the slogan 'socialism in one country'. They moved to form a bloc with Trotsky, which became known as the United Opposition.

For a time, they were joined by Krupskaya, who announced that: "If Vladimir Ilyich were alive today, he would be in one of Stalin's prisons." This was far truer than what she, or anyone else, could have thought possible at the time.

The 'old Bolsheviks' proved to be unequal to the problems posed by circumstances. They imagined that their past record would give them sufficient authority to stay afloat amidst the rising tide of bureaucratic reaction. They were mistaken.

One by one, they capitulated. Kamenev and Zinoviev broke with the opposition and threw themselves at Stalin's mercy, recanting their ideas in the most abject manner. They tried to manoeuvre, to prevaricate, in other words, to beat Stalin at his own game. But they were playing a dangerous game. They failed, and that failure was inevitable.

Before they finally capitulated to Stalin, Kamenev and Zinoviev attempted to persuade Trotsky that the best line of action was to pretend to retreat, to deceive Stalin into thinking he had won, and wait patiently for better times. Trotsky rejected this friendly advice and continued to fight for the genuine ideas of Lenin and October. He understood very well that it was impossible to deceive Stalin, for the simple reason that it was impossible to deceive history or outmanoeuvre powerful social processes.

In the given situation, the task of the Left Opposition was all but impossible: a fact of which Trotsky was well aware. He knew that he would be defeated. The forces ranged against him were too powerful. But by continuing the struggle, he was laying down an irreproachable tradition for future generations. History has proved that he was right. The colossal pressures of the objective situation, the defeats and the retreat of the world revolution, together with the bureaucratic reaction, bore down on individuals like Kamenev and Zinoviev.

They lacked both the moral fibre and solid grasp of theoretical principles to stand against the ebbing tide. They lost their bearings, and they gave up the fight. But this did not save them. Stalin had them arrested a few years later, put them on trial on trumped-up charges, and had them murdered in the cellars of the GPU.

The same fate awaited all those 'old Bolsheviks' whose only crime was to have been close to Lenin and who knew Stalin, and his weaknesses, all too well. They were a living reminder of what the Bolshevik Party used to look like. And that could not be tolerated. Only Trotsky and a handful of courageous followers continued to shout their defiance, like a voice crying in the wilderness. Trotsky explained:

> The revolution has its own laws: in the period of its culmination it pushes the most highly developed, determined, and far-seeing stratum of the revolutionary class to the most advanced positions. Yet the proletariat has not only a vanguard, but also a rearguard, and besides the proletariat there are the peasantry and the bureaucracy.
>
> Not one revolution up to now has brought all that was expected of it by the masses. Hence the inevitability of a certain disillusionment, of a lowering of the activity of the vanguard, and consequently of the growing importance of the rearguard. Stalin's faction has raised itself on the wave of reaction against the October Revolution. Look back at history – those who guided the revolution in the time of its culmination never kept their leading positions long after the turning point. In France, the leader of Jacobinism perished on the guillotine; with us, the change of leadership was achieved by means of arrest and banishment. The technique of the process is gentler, but its essence is the same.[18]

A river of blood

The process of bureaucratic degeneration that began even before Lenin's death ended in a political counter-revolution, and the monstrous deformation of the Soviet state under Stalin.

Bourgeois critics of Lenin and October claim that the degeneration had its origin and roots in Bolshevism. This blatant falsification, however, is contradicted by the facts. Far from being the legitimate heir of Bolshevism, Stalinism is its direct antithesis. The democracy of Lenin's Bolshevik Party was utterly destroyed.

The Stalinist bureaucracy could not tolerate dissent. Even the formal trappings of congresses were cast aside. In the seven years between the February Revolution in 1917 and the death of Lenin in January 1924, the Bolshevik Party held eight regular Party Congresses and seven Party Conferences, despite the ravages of civil war, blockade and the problems of reconstruction.

However, the Fifteenth Party Congress of December 1927 was held after a lapse of two years since the previous one. The Sixteenth Party Congress was held two-and-a-half years later. Between then and the Seventeenth Congress in January 1934, nearly four years were allowed to lapse.

The Stalinist counter-revolution reached its culmination with the monstrous Purge Trials of the 1930s. These were really a one-sided civil war against Bolshevism. Stalin used them to physically eliminate those with any ties to Lenin and the October Revolution. This fact alone is more than sufficient to prove that Bolshevism and Stalinism have nothing in common and are mortal enemies. A river of blood separates October from the grotesque, totalitarian caricature of Stalinism.

Stalin was, in a quite literal sense, the gravedigger of the October Revolution.

'Socialism in one country'

The same practice was applied to the Congresses of the Comintern. Originally they were held annually, but after the Fourth World Congress in November 1922, the Fifth was held eighteen months later in June 1924, while the Sixth was held in July 1928, and the last was the Seventh in July 1935. It never met again.

Stalin formally wound up the Communist International in 1943, although it had ceased to exist in reality long before this. Its dissolution was proclaimed by Stalin without any conference or congress. This was a gesture to the allies, Churchill and Roosevelt.

Every last trace of Lenin's policy was systematically expunged by Stalin, commencing with his introduction of the anti-Marxist 'theory' of 'socialism in one country'.

Trotsky explained that the adoption of the theory of 'socialism in one country' would mean the inevitable nationalist and reformist degeneration of the Communist International. Each party would now seek its own national road to socialism. The Comintern soon became transformed from the vanguard of the world proletarian revolution into an instrument to further the diplomatic and foreign policy aims of the Soviet bureaucracy.

This is exactly what happened. In one country after another, Stalin and his henchmen betrayed the revolution – in Germany, China, Spain and other countries – to serve the narrow national interest of the Soviet bureaucracy. These defeats allowed Stalin to consolidate his power and crush all opposition.

A political or social counter-revolution?

Here again, we find a parallel with the French Revolution, which went through a whole series of stages, in each of which the regime experienced dramatic changes.

Following the fall of the Bastille, we had the abolition of feudalism and the establishment of a constitutional monarchy. Invasion by the counter-revolutionary powers of Europe in league with the king provoked the storming of the Tuileries Palace, the overthrow of the monarchy and the declaration of a republic, but it was initially dominated by moderate bourgeois elements (the Girondists).

In order for the revolution to advance and to defeat its external enemies, power had to pass from the hands of the bourgeoisie to the more radical section of the petty-bourgeoisie (the Jacobins), who were prepared to lean on the semi-proletarian masses of Paris (the sans-culottes).

The Revolution reached its high point in 1793, but then entered into a series of severe internal contradictions, in which the strivings of the masses came into conflict with the property-owning classes who were beginning to recoil from the 'excesses' of the revolution.

As a result, there was the Thermidorian reaction, followed by the Directorate and the Consulate, and eventually the dictatorship of Napoleon Bonaparte. Finally, when Napoleon was defeated by the combined armies of the Monarchist reaction of Europe at the Battle of Waterloo, the victorious allies re-imposed the Bourbon monarchy upon a defeated France.

All these stages reveal striking differences. But throughout all of them, one thing remained constant. The abolition of feudalism and the seizure of the land by the peasants completely changed the social and economic physiognomy of France.

For that reason, we can see that although the political regime in France changed many times – even ending up with the restoration of the old Bourbon monarchy – the clock could not be put back, and the new social and economic relations remained, opening the way for the development of capitalism in the nineteenth century.

The regime established by Stalin had nothing whatsoever to do with Lenin's idea of a workers' state, which was democratic through and through. By democracy, of course, we do not refer to the hollow farce of formal bourgeois democracy, which is just another name for the dictatorship of the bankers and capitalists. Lenin's conception, as outlined in *The State and Revolution*, and clearly spelled out in the 1919 Party Programme, was based upon the model of the Paris Commune, in which the working people themselves control society from top to bottom.

Under Stalin, the Russian Revolution was thrown right back. Many of the worst features of the old regime were restored. However, the revolution was not thrown back to its starting point. The October Revolution had established an entirely new economic system which could not easily be destroyed. Nor, indeed, was it ever Stalin's intention to destroy it, since his power was ultimately dependent on it.

As we have explained, the Russian Revolution degenerated because it lacked the material basis for socialism. Stalinist totalitarianism completely destroyed the worker's democracy that had been established by the October Revolution. This was what Marxists call a political counter-revolution, as opposed to a social counter-revolution. The difference consists in the fact that a political revolution changes the regime, but does not alter the basic socio-economic conquests of the revolution, that is, the nationalised economy and planned production intact.

These were important gains that were worth preserving and defending, and they allowed the Soviet Union to make extraordinary progress, despite the appalling costs imposed by a corrupt bureaucratic administration. The remarkable gains made by the Soviet Union in a very short time remain a powerful testament to the advantages of a nationalised planned economy, even when it is hindered by the arbitrary and wasteful rule of a parasitic bureaucracy.

In the end, the potential was never fully allowed to realise itself. A nationalised planned economy requires democracy as the human body needs oxygen. The planned economy was fatally undermined by the rise of a parasitic bureaucracy, which slowly strangled the economy, wasted its resources and destroyed it.

However, the colossal potential of a nationalised planned economy was revealed by the unprecedentedly rapid transformation of a formerly backward, illiterate, semi-feudal country into one of the most advanced and highly educated nations in the world.

Lenin's legacy

The death of Lenin marked the passing of one of the great revolutionaries and teachers of Marxism. But the legacy that Lenin left behind for future generations is truly enormous. It constitutes a theoretical treasure for the new generation who are searching for the banner of communism, which has become increasingly attractive to those repelled by the crimes of capitalism and the extreme feebleness of the reformists, who limit themselves to tinkering with the system.

Communism is indelibly associated with the name of Lenin and the Russian Revolution, but the Communist Parties of today are 'communist' in name only. They long ago abandoned the ideas of Lenin and Bolshevism and instead adopted reformist perspectives and policies. It is our task to return the movement to its genuine origins, to break with cowardly revisionism and embrace the banner of Lenin.

In February 2023, an opinion poll from the Fraser Institute found that in Britain, "the level of total agreement for communism as an ideal economic system among those aged 18-34 years is disturbingly high", reaching a figure of 29 per cent of those polled. In the United States and in Australia it was 20 per cent. Moreover, the support for communism in Britain among the 25 to 34-year-olds was still higher at 32 per cent.

These figures indicate that the conditions for the socialist revolution are ripening rapidly. At the same time, the enormous advances in science and technology offer a tantalising picture of a world free from poverty, homelessness and hunger. The bankrupt capitalist system is in an impasse and is incapable of taking humanity forward. The entire world is plunged into an abyss of war, economic collapse and endless human suffering. Lenin's words are shown to be true: *capitalism is horror without end.*

The solution is obvious and within our grasp. The abolition of the dictatorship of the bankers and capitalists would allow the creation of an economy that is rationally planned to satisfy the needs of humanity, not the rapacious greed of a handful of billionaires. That is the only way to abolish hunger, poverty, wars and all the other ills of capitalism, and create a world fit to live in.

There is nothing utopian about communism. The material conditions for a new and higher human society already exist on a world scale. The scientists inform us that the development of artificial intelligence can serve to reduce the hours of work to the point where, ultimately, people will no longer have to work except out of personal choice. The abolition of the slavery of labour is precisely the material premise for a classless society. That is now entirely possible. But under capitalism, everything is turned into its opposite. In a system where all is subordinated to the profit motive, every advance of new technology signifies mass unemployment together with a lengthening of the working day, and an increase in exploitation and slavery.

There is a clear choice before humanity: *socialism or barbarism*. Today, the crisis facing humanity can ultimately be reduced to the crisis of leadership of the working class. What is required is a genuine Communist Party, which bases itself on the ideas of Lenin and the other great Marxist teachers, and an International on the lines of the Communist International during its first five years.

Vladimir Ilyich Lenin is no longer with us. But his ideas are very much alive and even more relevant today than they were one hundred years ago. The day after Lenin's death, Trotsky wrote movingly: "In each of us lives a small part of Lenin, which is the best part of each of us".[19] It is the duty of Marxists to continue to defend the immortal heritage of that great man and to continue to fight for his ideas, which alone provide a reliable compass and guide to the final victory of communism.

If this book has made a modest contribution to that cause, its publication will have been more than justified.

Appendices

Lenin Against 'Socialism in One Country'

Stalin put forward the theory of 'socialism in one country' in the autumn of 1924 as a policy that directly reflected the outlook of the bureaucracy. The idea of building socialism within the borders of backward Russia was, up until this point, regarded as a reactionary utopia, which contradicted the international perspective of Lenin. In fact, before this, Stalin had also opposed this very idea.

In April 1924 Stalin addressed students of the Sverdlov University in Moscow on the topic of the 'Foundations of Leninism'. In the first published edition of his speech, he is a firm *opponent* of 'socialism in one country':

> The overthrow of the power of the bourgeoisie and the establishment of a proletarian government in one country does not yet guarantee the complete victory of socialism. The main task of socialism, the organisation of socialist production, still lies ahead. Can this task be accomplished, can the victory of socialism in one country be attained without the joint efforts of the proletariat of several advanced countries? No, this is impossible... For the final victory of socialism, for the organisation of socialist production, the efforts of one country, particularly of such a peasant country as Russia are insufficient...[1]

However, a few months later, in a second edition, the text of the speech had been radically changed to say the exact opposite:

> But the overthrow of the power of the bourgeoisie and the establishment of the power of the proletariat in one country does not yet mean that the complete

victory of socialism has been assured. After consolidating power and leading the peasantry in its wake the proletariat of the victorious country can and must build a socialist society…[2]

The theory of 'socialism in one country' from then on became a cornerstone of Stalinism. Acceptance of the theory became a condition of Party membership. The whole justification for this was *a single* throwaway remark made by Lenin in 1915 on the *Slogan for a United States of Europe*:

> … the slogan of the United States of the World would hardly be a correct one, first, because it merges with socialism; secondly, it may be wrongly interpreted to mean that the victory of socialism in a single country is impossible, and it may also create misconceptions as to the relations of such a country to the others. […]
>
> Hence, the victory of socialism is possible first in several or even one capitalist country alone.[3]

What Lenin is referring to here as "the victory of socialism" is the elementary idea that the victory of the socialist revolution cannot surge up at the same time in all countries of the world, but must start in a few or even a single country. The "victory" Lenin is referring to is the conquest of power by the proletariat and the nationalisation of the means of production, and not in any shape the building of an isolated socialist state.

While the Bolsheviks referred more than once to the October Revolution as a great "victory of socialism", they saw it as the beginning of a new historical period which over generations would transform human society throughout the entire world.

It can be seen that throughout Lenin's works, in dealing with socialism, he *always* talked of the revolution in Russia succeeding only as part of the world revolution. Internationalism is the very essence of Leninism. Here is not *one* example, but *many*, to really explain his thoughts. Let Lenin speak for himself:*

*

8 November 1917

The Soviet is convinced that the proletariat of the West-European countries will help us to achieve a complete and lasting victory for the cause of socialism.[4]

*

---

* All dates are in the New Style. All emphasis is Lenin's.

17 November 1917

Comrade Lenin replies to the preceding speakers. He says no internationalist can use the expression: "The West is disgracefully silent." [...]

We believe in the revolution in the West. We know that it is inevitable, but it cannot, of course, be made to order. [...] We now see the same picture in Germany. There, too, there is a swelling undercurrent of dissatisfaction which will inevitably take the forms of a popular movement. We cannot decree a revolution, but we can help it along. We shall conduct organised fraternisation in the trenches and help the peoples of the West to start an invincible socialist revolution.[5]

*

5 December 1917

... we put our trust in the international solidarity of the working masses, who will surmount every obstacle and barrier in the struggle for socialism.[6]

*

27 December 1917

If socialism is not victorious, peace between the capitalist states will be only a truce, an interlude, a time of preparation for a fresh slaughter of the peoples. [...] We have now reached the stage of world economy that is the immediate stepping stone to socialism.

The socialist revolution that has begun in Russia is, therefore, only the beginning of the world socialist revolution. Peace and bread, the overthrow of the bourgeoisie, revolutionary means for the healing of war wounds, the complete victory of socialism – such are the aims of the struggle.[7]

*

14 January 1918

Comrades, I greet you as the living embodiment of the Russian proletariat's determination to fight for the triumph of the Russian revolution, for the triumph of its great slogans not only in this country, but also among the peoples of the whole world. [...] We must show that we are a force capable of overcoming every obstacle on the way to world revolution. [...] our army's ranks will soon be swelled by the proletarian forces of other countries and we shall no longer be alone.[8]

*

20 January 1918

That the socialist revolution in Europe must come, and will come, is beyond doubt. All our hopes for the final victory of socialism are founded on this certainty and on this scientific prognosis. [...]

In other words, the underlying principle of our tactics must not be, which of the two imperialisms it is more profitable to aid at this juncture, but rather, how the socialist revolution can be most firmly and reliably ensured the possibility of consolidating itself, or, at least, of maintaining itself in one country until it is joined by other countries.[9]

*

24 January 1918:

We are far from having completed even the transitional period from capitalism to socialism. We have never cherished the hope that we could finish it without the aid of the international proletariat. We never had any illusions on that score [...]

The final victory of socialism in a single country is of course impossible. Our contingent of workers and peasants which is upholding Soviet power is one of the contingents of the great world army, which at present has been split by the world war, but which is striving for unity [...]

We can now see clearly how far the development of the Revolution will go. The Russian began it – the German, the Frenchman and the Englishman will finish it, and socialism will be victorious.[10]

*

26 January 1918

You will not find a single worker in Europe today – either in Britain, France, Germany or any other country – who does not applaud news of the Russian revolution, because they all regard it with hope and see it as a torch that will light the flame all over Europe. [...]

The Russian people were the first to raise the torch of the socialist revolution, but they are aware that they are not alone in their struggle and that they will accomplish their task with the help of the most loyal comrades and friends.[11]

*

24 February 1918

Trotsky was right when he said: the peace may be a triply unfortunate peace [...]

The peace terms are intolerably severe. Nevertheless history will come into its own; to our aid will come – even if not so quickly as we should like – the steadily maturing socialist revolution in other countries. [...]

We have friends, supporters, very loyal helpers. They are late – owing to a number of conditions independent of their will – but they will come.[12]

*

28 February 1918

... that we must therefore devote our strength to helping the German workers, and must perish ourselves [...] to save a German revolution [...]

It is quite conceivable that, given these premises, it would not only be 'expedient' [...] but a downright *duty* to accept the possibility of defeat and the possibility of the loss of Soviet power.[13]

*

31 January 1918

We close this historic Congress of Soviets under the sign of the mounting world revolution, and the time is not far off when the working people of all countries will unite into a single world-wide state and join in a common effort to build a new socialist edifice. The way to this construction runs through the Soviets, as a form of the incipient world revolution.[14]

*

7 March 1918

International imperialism [...] could not, under any circumstances, under any conditions, live side by side with the Soviet Republic, both because of its objective position and because of the economic interests of the capitalist class embodied in it, because of commercial connections, of international financial relations. In this sphere a conflict is inevitable. This is the greatest difficulty of the Russian revolution, its greatest historical problem – the need to solve international problems, the need to evoke a world revolution, to effect the transition from our strictly national revolution to the world revolution. This problem confronts us in all its incredible difficulty [...]

Regarded from the world-historical point of view, there would doubtlessly be no hope of the ultimate victory of our revolution if it were to remain alone, if there were no revolutionary movements in other countries. When the Bolshevik Party tackled the job alone, it did so in the firm conviction that the revolution was maturing in all countries and that in the end – but not at the very beginning – no matter what difficulties we experienced, no matter what defeats were in store for us, the world socialist revolution would come – because it is coming; would mature – because it is maturing and will reach full maturity. I repeat, our salvation from all these difficulties is an all-European revolution. [...] But history has taught us a lesson. It is a lesson, because it is the absolute truth that without a German revolution we are doomed [...] At all events, under all conceivable circumstances, if the German revolution does not come, we are doomed.[15]

*

8 March 1918

The Congress considers the only reliable guarantee of consolidation of the socialist revolution that has been victorious in Russia to be its conversion into a world working-class revolution.[16]

*

8 March 1918

We have only just taken the first steps towards shaking off capitalism altogether and beginning the transition to socialism. We do not know and we cannot know how many stages of transition to socialism there will be. That depends on when the full-scale European socialist revolution begins...[17]

*

11 March 1918

Everywhere we issued the call for a world workers' revolution. [...]

Russia will become mighty and abundant if she abandons all dejection and all phrase-making, if, with clenched teeth, she musters all her forces and strains every nerve and muscle, if she realises that salvation lies *only* along that road of world socialist revolution upon which we have set out.[18]

*

14 March 1918

I am well aware, comrades, that the banner is in weak hands, I have said that outright several times already, and the workers of the most backward country will not be able to hold that banner unless the workers of all advanced countries come to their aid. [...]

...we shall wait until the international socialist proletariat comes to our aid and shall then begin a second socialist revolution that will be world-wide in its scope.[19]

*

23 April 1918

We shall achieve final victory only when we succeed at last in conclusively smashing international imperialism, which relies on the tremendous strength of its equipment and discipline. But we shall achieve victory only together with all the workers of other countries, of the whole world.[20]

*

29 April 1918

... we must exert all our strength to hold out as long as possible, until the Western revolution matures, the Western revolution which is maturing much more slowly than we expected and desired, but is undoubtedly maturing; it is undoubtedly absorbing and accumulating more and more inflammable material. [...]

And we say: it is better to endure and be patient, to suffer infinitely greater national and state humiliations and hardships, but to remain at our post as a socialist contingent that has been cut off by the force of events from the ranks of the socialist army and compelled to wait until the socialist revolution in other countries comes to its aid. And it is coming to our aid. It comes slowly but it is coming. [...]

... we are, strictly speaking, faced with two main lines – the proletarian line, which says that the socialist revolution is what is dearest and highest for us, and that we must take account of whether it will soon break out in the West, and the other line – the bourgeois line – which says that for it the character of the state as a Great Power and national independence are dearer and higher than anything else.[21]

*

30 April 1918

Therefore, the tactics of the Soviet Republic must be, on the one hand, to exert every effort to ensure the country's speediest economic recovery, to increase its defence capacity, to build up a powerful socialist army; on the other hand, in international policy, the tactics must be those of manoeuvring, retreat, waiting for the moment when the international proletarian revolution – which is now maturing more quickly than before in a number of advanced countries – fully matures.[22]

*

5 May 1918

In 1918 Germany and Russia have become the most striking embodiment of the material realisation of the economic, the productive and the socio-economic conditions for socialism, on the one hand, and the political conditions, on the other.

A successful proletarian revolution in Germany would immediately and very easily smash any shell of imperialism [...] and would bring about the victory of world socialism for certain.[23]

*

14 May 1918

To wait until the working classes carry out a revolution on an international scale means that everyone will remain suspended in mid-air. [...] It may begin with brilliant success in one country and then go through agonising periods, since final victory is only possible on a world scale, and only by the joint efforts of the workers of all countries.[24]

*

We workers, class-conscious workers, in all our agitation and propaganda, in every speech we deliver, in every appeal we issue, in our talks in the factories and at every meeting with peasants, must explain that the disaster that has befallen us is an international disaster and that there is no other way out of it except world revolution. Since we must pass through such a painful period in which we temporarily stand alone, we must exert all our efforts to bear the difficulties of this period staunchly, knowing that in the last analysis we are not alone, that the disaster which we are experiencing is creeping upon every European country, and that not one of these countries will be able to extricate itself except by a series of revolutions.[25]

*

... we never harboured the illusion that the forces of the proletariat and the revolutionary people of any one country, however heroic and however organised and disciplined they might be, could overthrow international imperialism. That can be done only by the joint efforts of the workers of the world. [...]

... we never deceived ourselves into thinking this could be done by the efforts of one country alone. We knew that our efforts were inevitably leading to a worldwide revolution, and that the war begun by the imperialist governments could not be stopped by the efforts of those governments themselves. It can be stopped only by the efforts of all workers; and when we came to power, our task [...] was to retain that power, that torch of socialism, so that it might scatter as many sparks as possible to add to the growing flames of socialist revolution.[26]

*

The workers of the world are looking hopefully towards us. We can hear their cry: "Hold on a little longer! You are surrounded by enemies, but we shall come to your aid, and by our joint effort we shall finally hurl the imperialist vultures over the precipice."[27]

*

20 August 1918

We are now, as it were, in a besieged fortress, waiting for the other detachments of the world socialist revolution to come to our relief. [...]

... we are invincible, because the world proletarian revolution is invincible.[28]

*

23 August 1918

We have been cut off from our comrades; but we had to act first because our country was the most backward. Our revolution was begun as a general revolution, and we shall tackle our tasks with the help of the workers and peasants of the world.[29]

*

28 August 1918

Our army has been formed from chosen people, from the class-conscious peasants and workers. Each of them goes to the front aware that he is fighting for the destiny of the world revolution as well as the Russian revolution; for we may rest assured that the Russian revolution is only a sample, only the first step in the series of revolutions in which the war is bound to end.[30]

*

22 October 1918

... our chief task is to carry on propaganda for a revolt in the Ukraine. That is correct from the standpoint of the world revolution because Germany is the main link in this chain, since the German revolution is already ripe; and the success of the world revolution most of all depends on it. [...]

That is why intelligent Ukrainian Communists say: "We must make every sacrifice for the victory of the world revolution, but we should realise that the future depends on us and we must march in step with the German revolution."[31]

*

6 November 1918

We are full of hope and assurance that we are fighting in the interests of the world socialist revolution as well as the Russian socialist revolution. [...]

We must realise what is lying in store for us, without in any way concealing the gravity of the situation. We shall go to meet it not alone but with the workers of Vienna and Berlin, who are moving into the same fight [...]

Our slogan must be: Put every effort into the fight once more, and remember that we are coming up to the last, decisive fight, not for the Russian revolution alone, but for the world socialist revolution.[32]

*

8 November 1918

Comrades, from the very beginning of the October Revolution, foreign policy and international relations have been the main questions facing us. Not merely because from now on all the states of the world are being firmly linked by imperialism into one, dirty, bloody mass, but because the complete victory of the socialist revolution in one country alone is inconceivable and demands the most active co-operation of at least several advanced countries, which do not include Russia. [...]

... we have never been so near to world proletarian revolution as we are now. We have proved we were not mistaken in banking on world proletarian revolution. [...]

Even if they can crush one country, they can never crush the world proletarian revolution, they will only add fuel to the flames that will consume them all.[33]

*

20 November 1918

... the transformation of our Russian Revolution into a socialist revolution was not a dubious venture but a necessity, for there was no other alternative: Anglo-French and American imperialism will inevitably destroy the independence and freedom of Russia if the world socialist revolution, world Bolshevism, does not triumph.[34]

*

18 March 1919

We are living not merely in a state, but in a system of states, and it is inconceivable for the Soviet Republic to exist alongside of the imperialist states for any length of time. One or the other must triumph in the end. And before that end comes there will have to be a series of frightful collisions between the Soviet Republic and the bourgeois states.[35]

*

19 March 1919

Comrade Podbelsky took exception to the fact that one of the clauses speaks of the *impending* social revolution. [...] This argument is obviously groundless, because the revolution referred to in our programme is the world socialist revolution.[36]

*

17 April 1919

Complete and final victory on a world scale cannot be achieved in Russia alone; it can be achieved only when the proletariat is victorious in at least all the advanced countries, or, at all events, in some of the largest of the advanced countries. Only then shall we be able to say with absolute confidence that the cause of the proletariat has triumphed, that our first objective – the overthrow of capitalism – has been achieved.

We have achieved this objective in one country, and this confronts us with a second task. Since Soviet power has been established, since the bourgeoisie has been overthrown in one country, the second task is to wage the struggle on a world scale, on a different plane, the struggle of the proletarian state surrounded by capitalist states.[37]

*

5 December 1919

Both prior to October and during the October Revolution, we always said that we regard ourselves and can only regard ourselves as one of the contingents of the international proletarian army [...] we always said that the victory of the socialist revolution therefore, can only be regarded as final when it becomes the victory of the proletariat in at least several advanced countries.[38]

*

26 November 1920

The Mensheviks assert that we are pledged to defeating the world bourgeoisie on our own. We have, however, always said that we are only a single link in the chain of the world revolution, and have never set ourselves the aim of achieving victory by our own means.[39]

*

6 December 1920

While capitalism and socialism exist side by side, they cannot live in peace: one or the other will ultimately triumph – the last obsequies will be observed either for the Soviet Republic or for world capitalism.[40]

*

22 December 1920

While our Soviet Republic remains the isolated borderland of the capitalist world, it would be absolutely ridiculous, fantastic and utopian to hope that we can achieve complete economic independence and that all dangers will vanish.[41]

*

6 February 1921

Ever since 1917, when we fought the bourgeois-republican governments in Russia, and ever since the power of the Soviets was established at the end of 1917, we have been telling the workers again and again that the cardinal task, and the fundamental condition of our victory is to spread the revolution to, at least, a few of the most advanced countries. And our main difficulties over the past four years have been due to the fact that the West European capitalists managed to bring the war to an end and stave off revolution.[42]

*

17 October 1921

You must remember that our Soviet land is impoverished after many years of trial and suffering, and has no socialist France or socialist England as neighbours which could help us with their highly developed technology and their highly developed industry. Bear that in mind! We must remember that at present all their highly developed technology and their highly developed industry belong to the capitalists, who are fighting us.[43]

*

End of February 1922

But we have not finished building even the foundations of socialist economy and the hostile powers of moribund capitalism can still deprive us of that. We must clearly appreciate this and frankly admit it; for there is nothing more dangerous than illusions [...] And there is absolutely nothing terrible, nothing that should give legitimate grounds for the slightest despondency, in admitting this bitter truth; for we have always urged and reiterated the elementary truth of Marxism – that the joint efforts of the workers of several advanced countries are needed for the victory of socialism.[44]

Krupskaya on Lenin

The first four pieces are from the appendices to
Krupskaya's *Memories of Lenin*; the final piece is from
Labour Monthly, No. 2, 1933

Lenin's Method of Work

No matter what work Vladimir Ilyich undertook, he did it extremely thoroughly. He himself did a tremendous amount of the ordinary routine work. The more importance he attached to any particular work, the more would he delve into all the details.

At the end of the nineties, Vladimir Ilyich saw how difficult it was to establish in Russia an illegal newspaper, appearing regularly. On the other hand, he attached tremendous organisational and agitational importance to an all-Russian newspaper that would elucidate from the Marxist standpoint all the events and facts of actual Russian life and the working-class movement that was beginning to develop more and more widely. He therefore selected a group of comrades, and decided to go abroad and organise the publication of such a newspaper there. *Iskra* was conceived by him and organised by him. Every number received exhaustive attention. Every word was thought out. And – what is a very characteristic detail – Vladimir Ilyich himself corrected the proofs of the whole paper. This was not because there was no one else to read the proofs (I quickly adapted myself to this work), but because he was anxious that no errors should slip in. First he read the proofs himself, then passed them to me, then looked them over again.

And it was the same with everything. He put in a great deal of work, studying and drawing up agrarian statistics. His notebooks contain a large number of carefully written-out tables. When he was dealing with figures that were of great importance, he even checked the additions, etc. of the printed tables. The careful verification of every fact and every figure was typical of Ilyich. He based his conclusions on facts.

This eagerness to base every conclusion on facts is plainly revealed in his early propaganda pamphlets, *The Law on Fines*, *On Strikes*, and *The New Factory Law*. He did not foist anything on the workers, but proved his contentions with facts. Certain people thought these pamphlets too long drawn-out. But the workers found them very convincing. Lenin's biggest work, written in prison – *The Development of Capitalism in Russia* – contains a tremendous amount of statistical material. Lenin, in whose life the reading of Marx's *Capital* played such a big role, remembered on what a great deal of statistical material Marx had based his work.

Lenin did not rely on his memory, although he had an excellent one. He never cited facts from memory, 'approximately', but always gave them with the greatest accuracy. He looked through piles of material (he read with extraordinary rapidity, just as he wrote), but whatever he wanted to remember he wrote down in his notebooks. A large number of these notes of his have been preserved. Once when looking over my brochure, *Organisation of Self-Education*, he said I was wrong in stating that notes should only be made on the most necessary things – his experience had been otherwise. He used to read over his notes several times, which is evident from the various remarks, underlinings, etc.

Sometimes, if the book were his own, he found it sufficient to make underlinings and marginal notes. On the cover he wrote the numbers of the pages marked, underlining them with one or several lines, according to the importance of the marked passages. He also re-read his own articles, making notes to them as well. Anything he noticed that led up to some new idea, he also underlined and noted the page on the cover. That was the way Ilyich organised his memory. He always remembered exactly what he had said, where, and in controversy with whom. In his books, speeches, and articles we find very few repetitions. It is true that over a period of years we encounter the same fundamental ideas in Ilyich's articles and speeches. This is because his utterances bear the imprint of a peculiar unity, a unique consistency. But we do not find just an ordinary repetition of something already uttered. The same fundamental idea is advanced but as applied to new conditions, in a new concrete setting, and treating the question from a new aspect. I remember a talk with Ilyich when he had already fallen ill. We were talking about the volumes of his complete works that had just appeared. We spoke of how they reflected the experience of the Russian Revolution, how important it was to make this experience accessible to foreign comrades. We agreed that the volumes published should be utilised to illustrate how the basic, cardinal idea must inevitably be treated in varying ways, dependent on the changing concrete historical environment. Ilyich commissioned me to find a comrade who would carry out this work.

That has not yet been done, however.

Lenin carefully studied the experiences of revolutionary struggle of the world proletariat. These experiences are brought out very clearly in the works of Marx and Engels. Lenin read and re-read these works over and over again. He re-read them at every new stage of our Revolution. Everyone knows what a tremendous influence Marx and Engels had on Lenin. But it would be of great value to examine where and how the study of their works helped Lenin in estimating the contemporary situation and the perspectives of development at each stage of our Revolution. Such a work of research has not yet been written. But it would reveal with unexampled clarity how the experience of the world revolutionary movement assisted Lenin's power of foresight. Such a work would be invaluable to whomever is interested in how Lenin worked, how he studied Marx and Engels, what guidance he derived from them in estimating our struggle. It would show what a great influence the experience of the revolutionary working class of the most industrially advanced countries had on the whole of our revolutionary movement. Such a book would also make it easier to realise that the Russian Revolution – all our struggle and constructive work – was part of the world proletarian struggle. It would show what Lenin took from international working-class experience, how he took it, and how he applied it. That is something particularly important to be learnt from Lenin.

As to *how* to utilise the international workers' struggle, Ilyich himself wrote on more than one occasion. I remember what he said about one of Kautsky's pamphlets in this connection. Kautsky wrote a pamphlet on the Russian Revolution of 1905 – *The Motive Forces and Perspectives of the Russian Revolution*. Ilyich was very pleased with this pamphlet. He immediately had it translated, himself corrected every phrase of the translation, and wrote a cordial preface to it. He asked me to see that it was printed without delay and to read the proofs myself. I remember how one big legal printing press worked three days, yet could not set up this small pamphlet, and how for three days there was nothing to do but to sit about in the printing works, waiting hours for the proofs. Ilyich was able to infect all those around him with his enthusiasm. Once he had spoken his mind in connection with Kautsky's pamphlet, once he had written the preface – it was obvious that I would have to leave all other work and sit there at the press until I succeeded in getting the pamphlet out. And now, more than twenty years after, it is strange how my memory associates Lenin's fervent speeches with the grey cover, the type-faces and the printing errors of that pamphlet born as it was in the labour-pangs of our then Russian technical inefficiency. I am also reminded of the concluding words in his preface to that pamphlet. He wrote:

> "In conclusion, a few words about 'authorities'. Marxists cannot adopt the viewpoint of the ordinary radical intellectual, with his allegedly revolutionary objectivity – 'no authorities'. No. The working class, leading a difficult and stubborn worldwide fight for complete emancipation, needs authorities; but it stands to reason, only in the sense that every young worker needs the experience of the old *fighters* against oppression and exploitation. He needs the experience of those who have been through manifold strikes, who have participated in the ranks of the Revolution, who have become learned in revolutionary traditions and a wide political vision. The authority of the world-wide proletarian struggles is needed by us in order to elucidate the programme and tactics of our Party. But such authority, of course, has nothing in common with the official authorities of bourgeois science and police policy. Our authority is the authority of the many-sided struggle in the ranks of the universal Socialist army.

In his preface to *The Motive Forces and Perspectives of the Russian Revolution*, Vladimir Ilyich wrote that Kautsky made a correct approach to an appreciation of the Russian Revolution in saying:

> We shall do well if we assimilate the idea that we are facing entirely new situations and problems, to which none of the old stock phrases will apply.

In his preface to the pamphlet, Ilyich fervently assailed the application of stock phrases to new situations. Yet, as we know, Kautsky himself, in his estimation of the 1917 Revolution, was unable to understand the new situations and the new problems, and for that reason turned renegade.

To be able to study new situations and problems, in the light of the experience of the revolutionary struggle of the world proletariat, to apply Marxist method to the analysis of new concrete situations – that is the special substance of Leninism. Unfortunately, this aspect of the matter has not been sufficiently elucidated by concrete facts, though a good deal has been written on the subject.

There has been still less illustration in the Press of another aspect of Lenin's approach in estimating revolutionary events, namely, the ability to perceive the concrete reality and to distinguish the collective opinion of the fighting masses. This, according to Lenin, is a decisive factor in practical and concrete questions of future policy.

* * *

Lenin on How to Write for the Masses

"There is nothing I would like so much, there is nothing that I have hoped for so much, as an opportunity to write for the workers" – wrote Vladimir Ilyich from his exile in Siberia to PB Axelrod, abroad (letter dated 16 July 1897).

But VI had written for the workers, already prior to 1897. In 1895 he wrote a pamphlet for workers, entitled *The Law on Fines*. That pamphlet was printed illegally in 1896 at the Lakhtinsky Press.

In 1895 the group of Petersburg Social Democrats afterwards known under the name of 'League of Struggle for the Emancipation of the Working Class', which included Lenin, Krzhizhanovsky, Starkov, Radchenko, Vaneyev Silvin, Yakubova and others, had as an object the publication of a working-class review, *Rabocheye Delo (Workers' Cause)*. When the first number was already prepared, arrests took place, Vaneyev was taken with all the manuscripts, and that number never saw light. Vladimir Ilyich wrote an article for that review, entitled 'What our Ministers are Thinking'.

Written with chemicals inside a book, Vladimir Ilyich sent out of prison two proclamations for workers: 'The Workers' Festival – The First of May' and 'To the Tsarist Government'.

Axelrod and Plekhanov gave a very good opinion of Ilyich's pamphlet, *The Law on Fines*.

In the above-mentioned letter to Axelrod, Ilyich wrote: "You and his (Plekhanov's) opinions on my literary attempts (for workers) have encouraged me tremendously."

Young workers, desirous of learning to write so as to be understood by the broad masses, should attentively study these works of Ilyich.

If we look at the pamphlet, *The Law on Fines*, we shall see that it is written in very simple language, but at the same time that it is far different from the superficial agitational material which is still issued in such abundance even in these days. The pamphlet contains absolutely no agitational phrases or appeals. But the choice of theme itself is very characteristic. It is a theme which greatly exercised the minds of the workers in those days – a theme they were intimate with. The pamphlet starts off from facts well known to the worker, and is based throughout on facts carefully selected from a multitude of sources, and clearly set out. It is not the words in the pamphlet, but the facts, that talk and convince. These facts are so telling and so convincing that the workers upon acquaintance with them draw their own conclusions. The plan of the pamphlet also shows it has been carefully thought out. This is how it was planned: (1) What are fines? (2) How were fines formerly inflicted and what caused the new law on fines? (3) On what pretexts can the factory owners inflict fines? (4) How big can fines be? (5) What is the procedure for inflicting fines? (6) Where should the fine-money go, according to the law? (7) Is the law on fines applicable to all workers? (8) Conclusion.

The concluding section briefly formulates the deductions that the worker himself will already have made from the facts cited in the preceding sections, and merely helps him to generalise and finally formulate these conclusions. These conclusions are simple, but of great importance for the workers' movement.

In the short article, 'What our Ministers are Thinking', Lenin maintains the same approach to the reader as in *The Law on Fines*. He takes the letter of the Minister for the Interior, Durnovo, to the High Procurator of the Holy Synod, Pobedonosstsev, examines in detail its meaning, and brings the workers to the conclusion:

Workers, you see how deadly our Ministers are of knowledge coming to the working people. Show everyone that no force can deprive the workers of their consciousness. Without knowledge the workers are defenceless; with knowledge they are a force.

The proclamation, 'The Workers' Festival – The First of May', written from prison, also relates to the year 1896. But even if we were unaware of the year of its origin, we should easily recognise it from the nature of the proclamation itself. It dealt with the international working-class festival and the international struggle of the workers; but it started with the actual position and the struggle of the workers in the big centres. The proclamation outlined the prospects of this struggle and made a direct appeal for strikes.

The proclamation appeared on 1 May 1896, and in June there were already 30,000 textile workers on strike in Petersburg.

The second proclamation, 'To the Tsarist Government', summed up the results of the strike and called for a further, more intense, struggle. The proclamation ended with the words:

> The strikes of 1895 and 1896 have not been in vain. They were of tremendous service to the Russian workers. They showed them the proper way to fight for their interests. They taught them to understand the *political position and the political needs of the working class.*

In the autumn of 1897, Vladimir Ilyich worked on his second pamphlet for workers, written on the same theme as the first. This was *The New Factory Law*. In 1899 he wrote the pamphlets *On Industrial Courts* and *On Strikes*.

Working on these pamphlets helped Lenin to learn still better to write and talk in such a way that his speeches and articles would be particularly intimate and comprehensible to the mass.

From whom did Lenin learn to speak and write in such a popular style? He learned from Pisarev, whose works he read much of at one time, and from Chernyshevsky. But he learnt most from the workers themselves. He talked with them for hours, inquiring about all the petty details of their life in the factory, listening carefully to their casual remarks, and to the questions they put. He adjusted his observation to their level of knowledge, so that he could find out just what they did not understand on any given question, and why. Workers tell of these interviews in their reminiscences of Lenin.

But while working hard to assure that he conveyed his ideas to the workers in the clearest and best possible form, Ilyich at the same time remonstrated against all vulgarisation, all attempts to narrow the question down for the workers, to simplify its substance. Ilyich wrote in *What Is to Be Done?* (1901-2):

> Attention, therefore, must be devoted *principally* to *raising* the workers to the level of revolutionaries; it is not at all our task *to descend* to the level of the 'working masses' as the Economists wish to do, or to the level of the 'average worker', as *Svoboda* desires to do (and by this ascends to the second grade of Economist 'pedagogics'). I am far from denying the necessity for popular literature for the workers, and especially popular (of course, not vulgar) literature for the especially

backward workers. But what annoys me is this constant confusion of pedagogics with questions of politics and organisation. You, gentlemen, who are so much concerned about the 'average worker', as a matter of fact, rather insult the workers by your desire *to talk down* to them when discussing working-class politics and working-class organisation. Talk about serious things in a serious manner; leave pedagogics to the pedagogues, and not to politicians and organisers! (*Collected Works of VI Lenin*, Vol. IV, English edn., p. 204)[1]

Ilyich deprecated all 'baby-talk' for workers, all substitution of serious arguments by *"adages or mere phrases."* (Ibid.)

In Lenin's speeches and articles the workers always saw that he was "talking seriously", as one worker put it. Three years later (in June 1905) Vladimir Ilyich returned to the question alluded to in *What Is to Be Done?* and wrote:

In the political activity of a social-democratic party there always is, and will be, a certain element of tutoring: it is necessary to train the entire class of employed workers in their role as fighters for the emancipation of entire humanity from all oppression. It is necessary continually to teach ever new strata of this class. We must be capable of approaching the rawest, undeveloped members of this class – those less touched by our science, and the science of life – in such a way as to get closer to them. We must be able, with restraint and patience, to educate them up to social-democratic consciousness. In doing so we must not turn our teaching into a dry dogma, we must instruct not by books alone, but also by participating in the day-to-day life-struggle of these very same raw, these very same undeveloped, strata of the proletariat. In this everyday activity there is, we repeat, an element of tutoring. A Social Democrat who forgot such activity would cease to be a Social Democrat. That is true. But in these days some of us often forget that a Social Democrat who reduces political tasks to those of a teacher alone, also – though for a different reason – ceases to be a Social Democrat. Whoever should think to make such 'tutorship' a special slogan – to oppose it to 'politics,' to build upon such a contra-position a special tendency, appealing to the masses in the name of this slogan against social-democrat politics' – whoever did this would immediately sink to the depths of demagogy. (Vol. VII, Russian edn., p. 308-9)

That is simply an elaboration of what was said earlier, and defines what Ilyich demanded in respect of popular literature.

In 1903, when spontaneous peasant risings broke out, Ilyich wrote a popular pamphlet, *To the Village Poor*, in which he explained to the poor peasants what the workers were fighting for, and why they should follow the workers.

In July 1905 Ilyich wrote his well-known leaflet, *Three Constitutions, or Three Systems of State Organisation*. (Vol. VII, Russian edn., pp. 377-8)[2] The leaflet compares an autocratic monarchy, a constitutional monarchy, and a democratic republic, both as regards their form, their content, and their aims. This leaflet is a model example of a lucid and popular style, but at the same time is an example of how to treat a question earnestly, how to 'talk seriously'.

At times of sharp and sudden turns in the situation, in the opinion of Ilyich, it is a special obligation to write and speak in a popular manner. At the April Conference, 1917, Vladimir Ilyich said:

> Many of us, including myself, have had to speak before soldiers, and I think that if everything is explained from the class standpoint, what will be the most unclear to them in our policy is how precisely we desire to end the war, how we consider it possible to end it. There exists among the broad masses a haze of misunderstandings, a complete lack of comprehension of our position. We must therefore speak as popularly as possible. (Vol. XIV, Part II, p. 416, old Russian edn.)[3]

In the same speech, Lenin said: "In speaking before the masses, we must provide concrete replies." There should be clarity of political meaning. "What is lacking in the slogan – 'fraternise' is clarity of political meaning." When saying that the proposed peace terms could not be put into effect without smashing the rule of the capitalists, Lenin insisted that this idea must be made clear to the masses.

> Once more I repeat: For the undeveloped masses of the people this truth demands intermediary channels, through which they may be introduced to the question. The error and the falseness of popular war literature consists in the fact that this question is avoided, is hushed up; things being represented as though there were no such thing as a class struggle, and as though two countries were living on friendly terms until suddenly one attacked the other and the latter defended itself. That is a vulgar interpretation which contains not a shade of objectivity. It is a conscious deception of the masses on the part of educated persons.

What are the conclusions to be drawn? Lenin attached great importance to the capacity to speak and write in a popular style. This is necessary in order to make Communism accessible and comprehensible to the masses, as their own cause. Popular speeches and popular literature should have a concrete object, one which urges to definite action. The political idea developed in a popular speech should be succinct and clear in its meaning. No vulgarisation, oversimplification, or departure from objectivity is permissible. The exposition should be planned in a lucid manner, should help the listener or reader himself to draw the conclusions, and only sum up and formulate these conclusions.

Statements should be based not on abstract arguments, but on facts closely concerning the listener or reader. These facts should be gradually explained, link by link, in connection with the most important questions of class struggle, with the most important questions of Socialist construction.

That is how Lenin taught us to speak and write popularly.

At the present moment popular literature is of particular importance. The sharpened class struggle makes it essential that the masses understand the situation as clearly as possible, that they understand how to link up the current facts of day-to-day life with the fundamental questions of the fight for Socialism. We have absurdly little of such literature. It is necessary to produce it. Both from Lenin and from the masses, we must learn to write in a popular style, must set ourselves to the collective work of improving this kind of writing, and must test in practice the success of our results.

* * *

Lenin and Chernyshevsky

I want to say a few words about the influence Chernyshevsky had over Vladimir Ilyich. In his articles and books, Vladimir Ilyich never spoke directly of this influence, but every time he spoke about Chernyshevsky it was with ardour. When one reads the works of Vladimir Ilyich, one sees that wherever he speaks of Chernyshevsky he does so with particular warmth. In Lenin's pamphlet, *What Is to Be Done?* there is an indirect allusion to Chernyshevsky's influence. Speaking of the period preceding the foundation of the Party, the period between 1894 and 1898, when the workers' movement was beginning to develop rapidly, and assume a mass character, Lenin pointed out that the youth belonging to this movement developed and were trained in the glamour of the revolutionary activity of the old revolutionaries. He pointed out that they had to pay the price of a big internal struggle in order to free themselves illogically from the influences of these revolutionary predecessors, and to follow a different path – that of Marxism. That characteristic contains an autobiographical element.

As a personality, Chernyshevsky influenced Vladimir Ilyich by his intransigence, his tenacity, and by the dignified and proud way he bore his unprecedentedly hard fate. Thus, everything Vladimir Ilyich said about Chernyshevsky breathes of a particular respect for his memory. During difficult moments, when we have experienced grave periods in our Party work, Vladimir Ilyich liked to repeat one passage from Chernyshevsky, where he said, "the revolutionary struggle is not the Nevsky Prospekt pavement." Vladimir Ilyich quoted that in 1917, when the reaction made itself particularly keenly felt, and when the Party had to make a retreat. In 1918 also, when all the difficulties confronting the Soviet Power became particularly threatening, when it was necessary to conclude the Brest-Litovsk peace and conduct a civil war – Ilyich recalled these words of Chernyshevsky. From the example of Chernyshevsky he gathered strength and often repeated that a revolutionary Marxist should always be ready for anything.

But Chernyshevsky influenced Lenin not merely as a personality. If we look at Vladimir Ilyich's first illegal composition – *Who are the Friends of the People?* – we see very clearly the influence Chernyshevsky had on Lenin.[4] The generation about whom Vladimir Ilyich spoke, the youth who belonged to revolutionary Social Democracy in 1894, grew up in an environment where there resounded – in literature, everywhere – only lip-service in regard to Peasant Reform. Chernyshevsky was able to appreciate this correctly, as Mikhail Nikolaevich (Prof. Pokrovsky) has said. And, as Vladimir Ilyich remarked: it needed all the genius of a Chernyshevsky, to give, in the very epoch of the Peasant Reforms, the estimation of Liberalism that he gave, to expose the treacherous role of this Liberalism, its class substance.

If we review Lenin's subsequent activity, we see that Chernyshevsky infected him with his intransigent attitude to Liberalism. Mistrust in Liberal phrases, in the whole position of Liberalism, runs like a red thread throughout all Lenin's activity. If we take the Siberian Exile and the protest against the *Credo*, if we take the break with Struve, and afterwards, the uncompromising attitude Lenin occupied towards the Cadets, towards the Menshevik-liquidators who were prepared to make a deal with the Cadets – we see that Vladimir Ilyich maintained the same intransigent line that Chernyshevsky adopted towards the Liberals who betrayed the peasantry at the time of the Reform of 1861. If we now survey this attitude of Lenin's, this uncompromising position of his, we see that it was thanks to this intransigence, which was also maintained by the Party, that the Party was able to be victorious. The question of the attitude towards the Liberal bourgeoisie is closely bound up with the question of democracy. In *Who are the Friends of the People?* Lenin wrote: "In Chernyshevsky's epoch, the fight for democracy and the fight for Socialism merged into one indivisible whole." Giving an estimation of bourgeois-Liberal democracy and the democracy of the Narodniks of the eighties who had fallen under the influence of the bourgeoisie and become reconciled with tsarism, Lenin opposed to it the democracy of revolutionary Marxism. Chernyshevsky gave an example of uncompromising struggle against the existing order, a struggle in which democracy was closely bound up with the fight for Socialism.

Lenin valued the activities of Chernyshevsky, his real democracy, for he perceived the harmony of this democracy with the Marxist attitude to the masses. The teachings of Marxism not only shed light on the economic struggle proceeding between the working class and the capitalists. Marxism took the phenomenon in its entirety; explained the whole system, giving an analysis of it and at the same time showing how to merge the fight for democracy and the fight for Socialism into one. If we observe how Marx opposed Lassalle, on what grounds they fought, how indignant Marx was that Lassalle did not understand the significance of the revolutionary initiative of the masses, we shall understand the Socialist substance of revolutionary Marxism. It was not understood at all, for instance, by the so-called Legal Marxists, who constantly shut their eyes to Marx's permanent orientation on the working class, on the masses. In Marxism, democracy and the fight for Socialism are indeed combined into one unbreakable chain. It is thus no mere chance that when Vladimir Ilyich referred to questions of democracy, he always remembered Chernyshevsky, from whom he first learnt of this combined struggle for democracy and Socialism. If we examine the teachings on Soviets, on the Soviet power, we see that precisely in these teachings on the Soviet system is the combination of the struggles for democracy and for Socialism put into force and most fully reflected. I remember when, in 1918, I was preparing to write a popular pamphlet on Soviets and the Soviet Power, Vladimir Ilyich once brought me a cutting from the French paper *L'Humanité* – I forget the name of the French comrade who wrote it – which said that the Soviet system was the most profoundly and consistently democratic system. On giving me that cutting, Vladimir Ilyich said it was precisely to that aspect of the question that I should draw particular attention. It was necessary to show the complete genuine democracy which is contained in the very structure of the Soviet system, where the proletariat is rising to a new and broader democracy.

Marx was translated into the Russian language as far back as in the sixties. But Marx had still to be translated into the language of Russian facts. Lenin did that in his book, *The Development of Capitalism in Russia*.[5] He was able to do it, thanks to Chernyshevsky's influence over him. Vladimir Ilyich several times reminded us how well acquainted Chernyshevsky was with actual Russian life, how well he knew the facts concerning the buying out of the peasantry, etc.

In the first period of his revolutionary activity, Vladimir Ilyich paid less attention to Chernyshevsky's philosophical convictions, although he was also acquainted with Plekhanov's little book, *On Chernyshevsky*, where particular attention was paid to the philosophical aspect. He was less interested, however, in this question. Only in 1908, when a big fight broke out on the philosophical front, only then did he once more re-read Chernyshevsky and talk of him as a great Russian Hegelian, a great Russian materialist. Later, in 1914, when the war began to draw nearer, and the national question assumed a particular topical importance, Vladimir Ilyich, in his article *National Self-Determination*, specially emphasised the fact that Chernyshevsky, like Marx, understood the whole meaning of the Polish insurrection.[6]

It is in the light of all these factors that we see what profound influence Chernyshevsky had over Lenin, over his entire revolutionary activity. Hence Lenin's attitude towards him is also comprehensible. In Siberia, Vladimir Ilyich had an album in which there were photographs of the writers who had a particularly strong influence on him. Next to Marx and Engels, and next to Hertzen and Pisarev, were two photos of Chernyshevsky, and also one of Myshkin, who tried to set Chernyshevsky free. And in recent times, in Lenin's study in the Kremlin, among the writers he permanently wished to have at hand, on the same shelves as Marx, Engels and Plekhanov, also stood the complete works of Chernyshevsky, which Vladimir Ilyich read again and again in his free moments.

In that same book, *Who are the Friends of the People?*, Vladimir Ilyich points out that Kautsky was right to say, in speaking of Chernyshevsky's epoch, that then every Socialist was a poet and every poet was a Socialist. Vladimir Ilyich read fiction, studied it and liked it. But there was one thing about Ilyich's novel-reading – he blended together the social approach with the artistic representation of life. He apparently did not separate these two things, and just as Chernyshevsky's sociological ideas are fully reflected in his works of fiction, so Vladimir Ilyich, when choosing a novel, had a special liking for books in which various social ideas were clearly reflected in the literary work.

What conversations we had together on the subject, I no longer remember. As years go by one forgets a great deal, every day something new happens, and we do not remember the particular words of a conversation, but only the gist.

I think, however, the books, articles and pamphlets of Vladimir Ilyich reflect sufficiently fully the great influence Chernyshevsky had over him.

* * *

The Kind of Fiction that Pleased Ilyich

The comrade who first introduced me to Vladimir Ilyich told me he was a very erudite man; that he exclusively read learned books, had never read a novel in his life, and never read poetry. I was astounded. When I was young myself I had read all the classics, knew by heart practically all Lermontov and the rest, while writers like Chernyshevsky, L Tolstoy, and Uspensky, seemed a very significant factor in my life. It seemed incredible to me that here was a man who had not the slightest interest in all that.

Later, when we worked together, when I came to know Ilyich more intimately, I found out his evaluation of people, observed his diligent study of life, and humanity; how he never substituted for the study of the living man the practice of dipping into books to see how people lived.

But life then was such that there never seemed to be an opportunity to talk on this theme. Later, when we were already in Siberia, I discovered that Ilyich had perused the classics no less than I had. For instance, not only had he read all Turgenev, but had re-read him more than once. He had an intimate knowledge of Nekrassov and Chernyshevsky. I took the works of Pushkin, Lermontov, and Nekrassov to Siberia with me. Vladimir Ilyich placed them by the side of his bed, along with Hegel, and read them in the evenings, over and over again. Pushkin he liked best of all; but he not only valued good style. For example, he liked Chernyshevsky's novel, *What Is to Be Done?* in spite of its not being a great example of literary art, and its naive form. I was surprised to see how attentively he read that novel, and how he took note of all the very fine nuances that are to be found in it. At one time Vladimir Ilyich read a great deal of Pisarev, and liked him immensely. In Siberia we also had Goethe's *Faust* in German, and a little volume of Heine's poems.

On returning to Moscow from Siberia, Vladimir Ilyich once went to a theatre to see *Henschel the Izvostchik*. He afterwards said he liked it very much.

In Munich, among the books Ilyich liked were Gerhardt's *Bei Mama* and *Büttnerbauer* (*The Peasant*) by Pollenz.

Later, during our second emigration, in Paris, Ilyich eagerly scanned Victor Hugo's poems, *Châtiments*, devoted to the 1848 Revolution. These were written by Hugo during the time he was outlawed, and secretly imported to France. These poems contain a good deal of naive bombast, but one nevertheless feels in them the breeze of the Revolution. Ilyich was very fond of going to various cafés and suburban theatres to listen to the revolutionary singers who sang in the working-class districts – about the peasants, who, while half-drunk, elect some carpet-bag agitator to the Chamber of Deputies; about child-education; about unemployment – indeed, about everything. Ilyich was particularly fond of Montègues. The son of a Communard, Montègues was a favourite in the working-class suburbs. It is true, his improvised songs – always on some vivid topical theme – expressed no definite ideology, but they contained a great deal of sincere feeling. Ilyich frequently sang his *Greetings to the Seventeenth Regiment* – who had refused to fire on strikers: *Salut, salut à vous, soldats du 17-me*. Ilyich once had a talk with Montègues at a Russian evening gathering, and it was curious to see these two extremely different people – when the war broke out, later, Montègues went over to the Chauvinists – confiding to one another their dreams of the World Revolution. That happens sometimes – people who hardly know each other meet in a railway-carriage, and to the music of the rushing train, talk about most cherished things, about things they would never speak of on other occasions. Then they part, never to meet again. It was the same on that evening. What is more, the conversation was in French, and in a foreign language one can talk day-dreams more easily than in one's own tongue. A French charwoman used to come to us for two hours a day. Ilyich once listened to her singing. It was an Alsatian nationalist song:

> *Vous avez pris Alsace et Lorraine:*
> *Mais malgré vous nous resterons français;*
> *Vous avez pu germaniser nos plaines*
> *Mais notre cœur – vous ne l'aurez jamais!*

> You have taken Alsace and Lorraine:
> But in spite of you we shall remain French;
> You could Germanise our plains
> But you shall never have our hearts!

This was in 1909 – the time of reaction. Our Party was broken up, but its revolutionary spirit was by no means smashed. And the spirit of that song was in keeping with Ilyich's mood. How triumphantly the words of the song resounded on his lips: *Mais notre cœur – vous ne l'aurez jamais!*

During those most difficult years of the reaction, years about which Ilyich always spoke with such pain, even when we were back in Russia – he sustained himself by dreaming; dreaming as he talked to Montègues, dreaming as he victoriously chanted that Alsatian song, and when during sleepless nights he read Verhaeren.

Later on, during the war, Vladimir Ilyich was fascinated by Barbusse's *Le Feu*, to which he attached immense significance. That book was in such concord with his feelings at that time.

We seldom went to a theatre. We might pay an occasional visit, but the inane nature of the play, or the artificiality of the acting, always jarred on Ilyich's nerves. Generally, we left the theatre after the first act. Comrades used to make fun of us for not taking our money's worth.

But once Ilyich did sit to the end. I think that was at the end of 1915, in Bern, when they were showing L Tolstoy's play, *The Living Corpse*. Although it was performed in German, the actor who took the part of the prince was a Russian, and knew how to interpret Tolstoy's ideas. Ilyich followed the play with intensity and excitement.

And, finally in Russia. The new art seemed foreign and incomprehensible to Ilyich. Once in the Kremlin we were invited to a concert arranged for Red Army men. Ilyich was placed in one of the front rows. The actress, Gzovskaya, was declaiming a Mayakovsky poem:

> Our god – the advance,
> Our heart – the drum

and she advanced straight on Ilyich. He sat there rather taken aback, and bewildered by this unexpected gesture. When Gzovskaya was followed by some actor who read Chekhov's *The Evil-doer*, he heaved a sigh of relief.

One evening Ilyich wanted to go and see how the Youth commune was living. We decided to pay a visit to our young art student, Varya Armand. I think that was the day of Kropotkin's funeral, in 1921. It was the famine year, but the youth were full of enthusiasm. They slept in the Commune almost on bare boards; they had no bread. "But we have some grain", said the art student who was on duty that day, with face beaming. They cooked some "kasha" (gruel) for Ilyich out of that grain, although there was no salt. Ilyich looked at the faces of these glowing boy and girl artists standing around him – and their joy was reflected on his face also. They showed him their naive drawings, explained their meaning, showered questions on him. But he smiled, and evading a reply, answered their questions by himself asking questions: "What do you read? Do you read Pushkin?" – "Oh, no!", someone blurted out. "He was a bourgeois. Mayakovsky for us." Ilyich smiled. "I think Pushkin is better." After that Ilyich somewhat took to

Mayakovsky. Whenever he heard that name it reminded him of those young art students, full of life and joy, ready to die for the Soviets, and, not finding in the contemporary language words to express themselves, sought this expression in Mayakovsky's rather obscure verse. Later, Ilyich once praised Mayakovsky for verses deriding Soviet bureaucracy. Of the modern writers I remember he liked Ehrenburg's novel describing the war. "You know that Ilya Lokhmaty (Ehrenburg's pseudonym) – well, he's made a fine job of it", he once eulogistically declared.

We went a few times to the Moscow Art Theatre. Once we saw *The Flood*. Ilyich liked it immensely. We wanted to go to the theatre again the next day. They were playing Gorky's *The Lower Depths*. Ilyich liked Alexei Maximovich (Gorky), as a man to whom he was already closely attracted as long ago as the London Congress. He liked him also as an artist, and considered that as an artist Gorky could express very much in a few words. He used to talk particularly frankly with Gorky. Therefore it went without saying that Ilyich was keenly critical of the acting of a Gorky play. He thought the production of this play too theatrical, and it irritated him. After *The Lower Depths* he gave up going to the theatre for a long time. I believe we went another time to see Chekov's *Uncle Vanya*. He liked it. And, finally, the last time we went to the theatre was in 1922, to see Dickens' *Cricket on the Hearth*. Ilyich was already bored after the first act. Dickens' middle-class sentimentality began to get on his nerves and when the dialogue commenced between the old toy-seller and his blind daughter, Ilyich could stand it no longer, and walked out in the middle of the act.

During the last months of his life, I used to read to him whatever literature he selected, usually at evening time. I read Shchedrin, and I read Gorky. He also loved listening to poetry, especially Demyan Bedny. But of Demyan's verses he preferred those with pathos to the satirical ones.

As I read him poetry, he would gaze musingly out of the window at the setting sun. I remember the poem ending with the words: "Never, never, will Communists be slaves."

In reading it, it was just as though I were repeating a vow to Ilyich – "Never, never, will we give up a single conquest of the Revolution…"

Two days before his death I read to him in the evening a tale of Jack London, *Love of Life* – it is still lying on the table in his room. It was a very fine story. In a wilderness of ice, where no human being had set foot, a sick man, dying of hunger, is making for the harbour of a big river. His strength is giving out, he cannot walk but keeps slipping, and beside him there slides a wolf – also dying of hunger. There is a fight between them: the man wins. Half dead, half demented, he reaches his goal. That tale greatly pleased Ilyich. Next day he asked me to read him more Jack London. But London's strong pieces of work are mixed with extraordinarily weak ones. The next tale happened to be of quite another type – saturated with bourgeois morals. Some captain promises the owner of a ship laden with corn to dispose of it at a good price: he sacrifices his life merely in order to keep his word. Ilyich smiled and dismissed it with a wave of the hand.

That was the last time I read to him…

* * *

How Lenin Studied Marx

Owing to the backwardness of industry in Russia, the workers' movement only began to develop in the nineties, when the revolutionary struggle of the working class was already taking place in a number of other countries. There had already been the experience of the great French Revolution, the experience of the Revolutions of 1848, the experience of the Paris Commune in 1871. The great ideological leaders of the workers' movement – Marx and Engels – were forged in the fire of the revolutionary struggle. The teachings of Marx showed the direction taken by social development, the inevitability of the disintegration of capitalist society, the replacement of this society by Communist society, the paths which will be taken by the new social forms, the path of the class struggle; they disclosed the role of the proletariat in this struggle, and the inevitability of its victory.

Our workers' movement developed under the banner of Marxism. It did not grow blindly, groping its way, but its aim and its path were plain.

Lenin did a tremendous amount to illuminate the path of struggle of the Russian proletariat with the light of Marxism. Fifty years have passed since the death of Marx, but for our Party Marxism is still the guide to action. Leninism is merely a further development of Marxism, a deepening of it.

It is therefore obvious why it is of so great an interest to illuminate the question of Lenin's study of Marx.

Lenin had a wonderful knowledge of Marx. In 1893, when he came to St. Petersburg, he astonished all of us who were Marxists at the time with his tremendous knowledge of the works of Marx and Engels.

In the nineties, when Marxist circles began to be formed, it was chiefly the first volume of *Capital* which was studied. It was possible to obtain *Capital*, although with great difficulties. But matters were extremely bad with regard to the other works of Marx. Most of the members of the circles had not even read *The Communist Manifesto*. I, for example, read it for the first time only in 1898, in German, when I was in exile.

Marx and Engels were absolutely prohibited. It is sufficient to mention that in 1897, in his article *The Characteristics of Economic Romanticism* written for the *New Word*, Lenin was compelled to avoid using the words 'Marx' and 'Marxism', and to speak of Marx in a roundabout way so as not to get the journal into trouble.[7]

Lenin understood foreign languages, and he did his best to dig out everything that he could by Marx and Engels in German and French. Anna Ilyinishna tells how he read *The Poverty of Philosophy* in French together with his sister, Olga. He had to read most in German. He translated into Russian for himself the most important parts of the works of Marx and Engels which interested him.

In his first big work, published illegally by him in 1894, *Who are the Friends of the People?*,[8] there are quotations from *The Communist Manifesto*, the *Critique of Political Economy*, *The Poverty of Philosophy*, *German Ideology*, the 'Letter of Marx to Ruge' in 1843, Engels' books *Anti-Dühring* and *The Origin of the Family, Private Property and the State*.

The *Friends of the People* tremendously widened the Marxist outlook of the majority of the then Marxists, who as yet had very little acquaintance with the works of Marx. It dealt with a number of questions in an entirely new way and was tremendously successful.

In the next work of Lenin, *The Economic Content of the Teachings of the Narodniki and a Criticism of Them in the Book of Struve*,[9] we find already references to *The Eighteenth Brumaire* and *The Civil War in France*, to the *Criticism of the Gotha Programme* and the second and third volumes of *Capital*.

Later, life in emigration made it possible for Lenin to become acquainted with all the works of Marx and Engels and to study them.

The biography of Marx written by Lenin in 1914 for the *Granat Encyclopaedia* illustrates better than anything else the wonderful knowledge of the works of Marx by Lenin.[10]

This is also shown by the innumerable extracts from Marx which Lenin constantly made when reading his works. The Lenin Institute has many notebooks with extracts from Marx.

Lenin used these extracts in his work, read them over and over and made notes on them. *Lenin not only knew Marx, but he also thought deeply on all his teachings.* In his speech at the Third All-Russian Congress of the YCL in 1920, Lenin said to the youth that it was necessary:

> ... to take the whole sum of human knowledge and to take it in such a way that Communism will not be something learned by heart but something which you have thought out yourselves, something which forms the inevitable conclusion from the point of view of modern education.

> If a Communist were to boast of Communism on the basis of ready-made conclusions, without doing serious, big and difficult work, without thoroughly understanding the facts towards which he must take a critical attitude, such a Communist would be a very poor one. (Volume XXV)[11]

Lenin not only studied the works of Marx but he studied what was written about Marx and Marxism by the opponents from the camp of the bourgeoisie and the petty bourgeoisie. In a polemic with them he explains the basic positions of Marxism.

His first big work was *Who are the Friends of the People and how they fight against the Social-Democrats* (a reply to an article in *Russian Wealth* against the Marxists), where he drew a contrast between the point of view of the Narodniki (Mikhailovsky, Krivenko, Yushakova) and the point of view of Marx.

In the article, *The Economic Content of the Teachings of the Narodniki, and the Criticism of Them in the Works of Struve*, he pointed out in what way the point of view of Struve was different from the point of view of Marx.

When examining the agrarian question, he wrote a book, *The Agrarian Question and the Criticism of Marx* (Volume IV),[12] where the petty-bourgeois point of view of the Social-Democrats David, Hertz, and the Russian critics, Chernov and Bulgakov was contrasted with the point of view of Marx.

De choc des opinions jaillit la vérité – truth arises from a conflict of opinions – says the French proverb. Lenin loved to carry it out. He constantly brought to light and contrasted class points of view on the basis of the questions of the workers' movement.

It is very characteristic how Lenin set forth various points of view side by side. A great deal of light is thrown on this by Volume XIX, or works where the extracts, conspects, plans for essays, etc. on the agrarian question for the period preceding 1917 are collected.

Lenin carefully recapitulates the *statements of the 'critics'*, selects and copies out the clearest and most characteristic phrases and counterposes them to the statements of Marx. In carefully analysing the statements of the 'critics', he tries to show the class essence of their statements, putting forward the most important and urgent questions in prominent relief.

Lenin very frequently *deliberately sharpened a question*. He considered that the tone was not the important thing. You may express yourself coarsely and bitingly. What is important is that you speak to the point. In the preface to the correspondence of FA Sorge, he gives a quotation from Mehring from his Correspondence with Sorge:

> Mehring is right in saying that Marx and Engels gave little thought to a "high tone". They did not stop long to think before dealing a blow, but they did not whine about every blow they received. (Volume XI)[13]

Incisiveness of form and style were natural to Lenin. He learned it from Marx. He says:

> Marx relates how he and Engels fought constantly against the "miserable" conducting of *Sozial-Demokrat* and often fought sharply ("*wobei oft scharf hergeht*"). (Volume XI)[14]

Lenin did not fear sharpness, but he demanded that objections should be to the point. Lenin had one favourite word which he frequently used: 'quibbling'. If a polemic began which was not to the point, if people began to pick at trifles or juggle with facts, he used to say: "that is mere quibbling." Lenin expressed himself with still greater force against polemics which had not the aim of bringing clearness into the question but of paying off small factional grudges. This was the favourite method of the Mensheviks. Concealing themselves behind quotations from Marx and Engels, taken out of their context, out of the circumstances in which they were written, they served factional aims entirely. In the preface to the correspondence of FA Sorge, Lenin wrote:

> To imagine that the advice of Marx and Engels to the Anglo-American workers' movement can be simply and directly adapted to Russian conditions means to utilise Marxism, not to elucidate his *method*, not to *study* the concrete historic peculiarities of the workers' movement in definite countries, but for petty factional grudges of the intelligentsia. (Volume XI)[15]

Here we arrive directly at the question of *how Lenin studied Marx*. This can partly be seen from the previous quotation: it is necessary to elucidate the method of Marx, to learn from Marx how to study the peculiarities of the workers' movement in definite countries. Lenin did this. For Lenin the teachings of Marx were a guide to action. He once used the following expression: "Who wants to consult with Marx?" It is a very characteristic expression. He himself constantly "consulted with Marx". At the most difficult turning points of the revolution, he once again turned to the reading of Marx. Sometimes when you went into his room, when everyone around was excited, Lenin was reading Marx and could hardly tear himself away. It was not to quieten his nerves, not to arm himself with belief in the power of the working class, belief in its ultimate victory. Lenin had sufficient of this faith. He buried himself in Marx so as to "consult" with Marx, to find a reply from him to the burning questions of the workers' movement. In the article 'F Mehring, on the Second Duma', Lenin wrote :

> The argumentation of such people is based on a poor selection of quotations. They take the general position on the support of the big bourgeoisie against the reactionary petty bourgeoisie and without criticism adapt it to the Russian Cadets and the Russian Revolution. Mehring gives these people a good lesson. *Anyone who wants to consult with Marx* (my italics – NK) on the tasks of the proletariat and the bourgeois revolution must take the reasoning of Marx which apply *precisely* to the epoch of the German bourgeois revolution. It is not for nothing that our Mensheviks so fearfully avoid this reasoning. In this reasoning we see the fullest and clearest expression of the merciless struggle against the *conciliatory* bourgeoisie which was carried on by the Russian 'Bolsheviks' in the Russian revolution. (Volume XI)[16]

Lenin's method was to take the works of Marx dealing with a *similar situation* and carefully analyse them, compare them with the current moment, discovering resemblances and differences. The adaptation to the Revolution of 1905 to 1907 illustrates best of all, how Lenin did this. In the pamphlet, *What Is to Be Done?*, in 1902, Lenin wrote:

> History now puts before us an immediate task which is the *most revolutionary* of all the *immediate* tasks of the proletariat of any other country. The carrying out of this task the destruction of the most powerful support not only for European but also (we may now say) Asiatic reaction would make the Russian proletariat the vanguard of the international revolutionary proletariat. (Volume IV)[17]

We know that the revolutionary struggle of 1905 raised the international role of the Russian working class, while the overthrow of the tsarist monarchy in 1917, really made the Russian proletariat into the vanguard of the international revolutionary proletariat, but this took place only fifteen years after *What Is to Be Done?* was written. When in 1905, after the shooting of the workers on 9 January, the revolutionary wave from the Dvortsoff Square began to rise higher and higher, the question urgently arose as to where the Party must lead the masses, what policy it must follow. And here Lenin consulted with Marx. He quotes with special, attention the works of Marx dealing with the French and German bourgeois-democratic revolutions of 1848: *The Class Struggle of 1848-50* and the third volume of *The Literary Heritage of Marx and Engels*, published by F Mehring and dealing with the German revolution.

In June – July 1905, Lenin wrote a pamphlet, *The Two Tactics of Social-Democracy and the Democratic Revolution*, where the tactic of the Mensheviks, who took the line of conciliation with the liberal bourgeoisie was contrasted to the tactics of the Bolsheviks, who called on the working class to carry on a most determined and irreconcilable struggle against the monarchy to the point of armed rebellion. It was necessary to put an end to tsarism, wrote Lenin in *Two Tactics*:

> The conference (of the new Iskraites – *NK*) also forgot that as long as the power remains in the hands of the Tsar, any decisions of any representatives remain empty talk and just as pitiful as the 'decisions' of the Frankfurt parliament which are famous in the history of the German Revolution of 1848. For this very reason Marx, in the *Neue Rheinische Zeitung*, mercilessly poured sarcasm on the liberal Frankfurt 'liberators' because they spoke excellent words, adopted all kinds of democratic 'decisions', 'established' all kinds of freedom, but in reality left the power in the hands of the monarchy, and did not organise the armed struggle against the troops of the monarchy. And while the Frankfurt liberators chattered, the monarchy bided its time, strengthened its military forces, and counter-revolution, relying on real force, overthrew the democrats with all their beautiful decisions. (Volume VIII)[18]

Lenin raises the question whether it would be possible for the bourgeoisie to destroy the Russian Revolution by an agreement with Tsarism, "or", as Marx said at one time, "settling with Tsarism in a 'plebeian' manner." "When the revolution decisively conquers, we shall settle with Tsarism in a Jacobine, or if you will, in a plebeian, manner."[19] The whole of French terrorism, wrote Marx in the famous *Neue Rheinische Zeitung* in 1848, was nothing else but the plebeian manner of settling with the enemies of the bourgeoisie with absolutism, feudalism, respectability. (See *Marx's Literary Heritage*, published by Mehring.)

Did those people who frightened the Social-Democratic Russian workers with the bogey of 'Jacobinism' in the epoch of the democratic revolution ever think of the meaning of these words of Marx? (Volume VIII)[20]

The Mensheviks said that their tactics were "to remain the Party of the extreme revolutionary opposition." And that this did not exclude partial seizures of power from time to time and the formation of revolutionary communes in one town or another. What do "revolutionary communes" mean? – asks Lenin, and replies:

The confusion of revolutionary thought leads them (the new Iskraites), as often happens, to *revolutionary phrase-mongering*. The use of the words "revolutionary commune" in the resolution of representatives of Social-Democracy is a revolutionary phrase and nothing more. Marx more than once condemned such phrases, when the tasks of the future are concealed behind soothing terms of the *dead past*. The fascination of terms which have played a role in history is converted in such cases into an empty and harmful tinsel, into a rattle. We must give to the workers and to the whole people a clear and unmistakeable idea of *why* we want to establish a provisional revolutionary government, *what changes exactly* we shall carry out if we decisively influence the power, even tomorrow, if the national revolt which has commenced is victorious. These are the questions which face the political leaders. (Volume VIII)[21]

These vulgarisers of Marxism never gave thought to the words of Marx on the necessity of replacing the weapon of criticism by criticism with weapons. Using the name of Marx everywhere, they in reality draw up a tactical resolution entirely in the spirit of the Frankfurt bourgeois cacklers, freely criticising absolutism, deepening democratic consciousness, and not understanding that the time of revolution is a time of action, above and below. (Volume VIII)[22]

"Revolutions are the locomotives of history", says Marx. By this reference to Marx, Lenin appraises the role of the revolution that was breaking out.

In his further analysis of the sayings of Karl Marx in the *Neue Rheinische Zeitung*, Lenin makes clear what the revolutionary democratic dictatorship of the proletariat and peasantry means. But in drawing the analogy, Lenin dwells also on the question in what way our bourgeois-democratic revolution differs from the German bourgeois-democratic revolution of 1848. He says:

Thus it was only in April 1849, after the revolutionary newspaper, *Neue Rheinische Zeitung* (which had been published since 1 June 1848) had existed almost a year, that Marx and Engels expressed themselves in favour of a separate labour organisation. Hitherto they simply conducted the "organ of democracy", which was not connected by any organisational link with an independent labour party. This fact – monstrous and improbable from our contemporary point of view – shows us clearly what an enormous difference there was between the then German and the present Russian Social-Democratic Labour Party. This fact shows us how much weaker (owing to the backwardness of Germany in 1848, economically and politically – absence of state unity) were the proletarian features of the movement in the German democratic revolution, the proletarian streak in it.[23]

Particularly interesting are Vladimir Ilyich's articles which refer to 1907 and are devoted to the correspondence and activity of Marx.

They are the foreword to the translation of *Marx's Letters to KL Kugelmann*,[24] 'Mehring on the Second Duma', and the foreword to the *Letters to FA Sorge*. These articles throw a particularly vivid light on the method by which Lenin studied Marx. The last article is of exceptional interest. It was written in the period when Lenin had taken up once more seriously the study of philosophy, in connection with his divergencies with Bogdanov, when the issues of dialectical materialism called for his special attention.

While studying simultaneously also the sayings of Marx that referred to questions analogous to those which sprang up among us in connection with the breakdown of the revolution, and questions of dialectical and historical materialism, *Lenin learned from Marx how to apply to the study of historical development the method of dialectical materialism.*

In the foreword to the *FA Sorge Correspondence*, he wrote:

A comparison of what Marx and Engels had to say on questions of the Anglo-American and German labour movements is very instructive. If one takes into consideration that Germany, on the one hand, and Great Britain and America, on the other, represent different stages of capitalist development, different forms of the rule of the bourgeoisie as a class in the whole political life of these countries, the said comparison assumes special significance. From the scientific point of view we have here a sample of materialist dialectic, ability to bring forward and emphasise different points, different sides of the question in their application to the concrete peculiarities of various political and economic conditions. From the point of view of practical politics and tactics of the worker's party, we have here a sample of the manner in which the creators of *The Communist Manifesto* defined the task of the struggling proletariat as applied to the various phases of the national labour movement of the various countries. (Free translation.)[25]

The Revolution of 1905 brought to the fore a whole series of new essential questions during the solution of which Lenin went more deeply into the works of Karl Marx. The Leninist method (Marxist through and through) of studying Marx was forged in the fire of the revolution.

This method of studying Marx armed Lenin for struggle against the distortions of Marxism with their emasculation of its revolutionary essence. We know what an important part Lenin's book *The State and Revolution* has played in the organising of the October Revolution and the Soviet Power. This book is entirely based on a deep study of Marx's revolutionary teachings about the state. There Lenin writes:

> Marx's doctrines are now undergoing the same fate which, more than once in the course of history, has befallen the doctrines of other revolutionary thinkers and leaders of oppressed classes struggling for emancipation. During the lifetime of great revolutionaries, the oppressing classes have invariably meted out to them relentless persecution, and received their teaching with the most savage hostility, most furious hatred, and a ruthless campaign of lies and slanders. After their death, however, attempts are usually made to turn them into harmless saints, canonising them, as it were, and investing their *name* with a certain halo by way of 'consolation' to the oppressed classes, and with the object of duping them, while at the same time emasculating and vulgarising the real *essence* of their revolutionary theories and blunting their revolutionary edge. At the present time the bourgeoisie and the opportunists within the labour movement are co-operating in this work of adulterating Marxism. They omit, obliterate, and distort the revolutionary side of its teaching, its revolutionary soul, and push to the foreground and extol what is, or seems, acceptable to the bourgeoisie. All the social-chauvinists are now 'Marxists' – don't laugh! And more and more do German bourgeois professors, erstwhile specialists in the demolition of Marx, now speak of the 'National-German' Marx, who, they claim, has educated the splendidly organised working class for the present predatory war. In these circumstances, when the distortion of Marxism is so widespread, our first task is to *resuscitate* the real nature of Marx's teachings on the subject of the State. (First page in *The State and Revolution*.)[26]

In *The Foundations of Leninism*, Comrade Stalin wrote:

> Not until the next phase, the phase of direct action, of proletarian revolution, when the overthrow of the bourgeoisie had become a question of practical politics, did the problem of finding reserves for the proletarian army (strategy) become actual, and the problem of the organisation of that army whether on the parliamentary or the extra-parliamentary field (tactics) clearly demand a solution. Not until this

phase had begun, could proletarian strategy be systematised and proletarian tactics be elaborated. *It was now that Lenin disinterred Marx's and Engels' masterly ideas on strategy and tactics, ideas which the opportunists of the Second International had buried out of sight.* (The italics are mine – *NK*)

But Lenin did not confine himself to re-establishing individual tactical propositions of Marx and Engels. He developed them further and supplemented them by new ideas and propositions, creating out of all this a system of rules and leading principles for the conduct of the class struggle of the proletariat. Such pamphlets of Lenin as *What Is to Be Done, Two Tactics, Imperialism, State and Revolution, Proletarian Revolution and the Renegade Kautsky*, and *'Left-Wing' Communism*, will no doubt be a most valuable contribution to the common treasure-house of Marxism, to its revolutionary arsenal. The strategy and tactic of Leninism is a science regarding the leadership of the revolutionary struggle of the proletariat. (J Stalin, *Questions of Leninism*)*

Marx and Engels said that their teaching "is not a dogma, but a guide to action." These words of theirs were continually repeated by Lenin. The method by which he studied the works of Marx and Engels, and revolutionary practice, all the circumstances of the epoch of proletarian revolutions, helped Lenin to convert just the revolutionary side of Marx into a real guide to action.

I shall dwell on a question which is of decisive significance. Not so long ago we celebrated the fifteenth anniversary of the Soviet Power. And in this connection, we recalled how the seizure of power was organised in October. It wasn't a spontaneous act; it was deeply thought out by Lenin who was guided by Marx's direct instructions regarding the organising of an uprising.

The October Revolution, by placing dictatorship into the hands of the proletariat, radically changed all the conditions of struggle, but only because Lenin was guided not by the letter of the teachings of Marx and Engels, but by their revolutionary essence, because he knew how to apply Marxism also to the building up of Socialism in the epoch of proletarian dictatorship.

I shall only dwell on a few points. Thorough research work is necessary here: select everything that was taken by Lenin from Marx and Engels, indicating in what periods and in connection with what tasks of the revolutionary movement. I have not even mentioned such important questions as the national question, imperialism, etc. The publication of Lenin's complete collected works makes this work easier. *Lenin's way of studying Marx in all the phases of revolutionary struggle from beginning to end*

---

* This quotation of Stalin was clearly made under the pressures of the time (1933), where references to Stalin had become increasingly obligatory, even for poor Krupskaya.

will help us to understand better and go deeper not only into Marx, but into Lenin himself, into his method of studying Marx and the method of converting Marx's teachings into a guide to action.

There is one more side of Lenin's study of Marx which must be mentioned owing to its great significance. Lenin did not only study what Marx and Engels wrote as well as what Marx's 'critics' wrote about him, *he also studied the way which led Marx to his various views, and the works and books which stimulated Marx's thoughts and drove them in a definite direction.* He studied, so to speak, the sources of Marxist philosophy, what and how precisely Marx took from this or that writer. He was especially concerned in making a deep study of the method of dialectical materialism. In 1922, in the article 'Meaning of Militant Materialism',[27] Lenin said that it was up to the contributors to the periodical, *Under the Banner of Marxism*, to organise the work for a systematic study of Hegel's dialectics from the materialist point of view. He believed that without a serious philosophical basis it is impossible to hold out in the struggle against the pressure of bourgeois ideas and the restoration of bourgeois philosophy. It was on the basis of his own experience that Lenin wrote about the manner of studying Hegel's dialectics from the materialist point of view. We give here the corresponding paragraph from Lenin's article 'On the Meaning of Militant Materialism':

> But in order to avoid reacting to such a phenomenon unintelligently, we must understand that no natural science, no materialism whatever, can hold out in the struggle against the onslaught of bourgeois ideas and the restoration of bourgeois philosophy without a solid philosophical basis. In order, to give aid to this struggle and help to carry it out to its successful conclusion, the natural scientist must be a modern Materialist, a conscious adherent of that Materialism which Marx represents, i.e. he must be a *dialectical* Materialist. To achieve this the staff of *Under the Banner of Marxism* must organise a systematic study of Hegelian dialectics from the Materialist point of view, i.e. the dialectics which Marx applied concretely in his *Capital* and used in his historical and political works…

> Basing ourselves on the manner in which Marx applied the materialist conception of Hegelian dialectics we can, and must, work out these dialectics from all sides. The magazine must publish excerpts from the principal works of Hegel, must interpret them materialistically, and give examples of how Marx applied dialectics, as well as examples of dialectics from the field of economic and political relations. Modern history, particularly modern imperialist war and revolution, provide innumerable examples of this kind. The editors and staff of *Under the Banner of*

Marxism should, I think, represent a sort of 'Association of Materialist Friends of Hegelian Philosophy'. Modern natural scientists will find (if they will seek and if we can learn to help them) in the materialist interpretation of Hegelian dialectics a number of answers to those brought forward to the front and which cause the intellectual admirers of bourgeois fashions to 'slip' into the reactionary camp. (*Lenin on Religion*, p. 41, Little Lenin Library, Volume VII)[28]

The IX and XII volumes of Lenin's collected works have already been published in the Soviet Union. They divulge the whole process of Lenin's thought when he was working through Hegel's chief works, they show how he applied the method of dialectical materialism to the study of Hegel, how closely he connected this study with a deep study of Marx's sayings, with the ability of converting Marxism into a guide to action in the most varied circumstances.

But Hegel was not the only object of Lenin's study. He read Marx's letter to Engels of November 1859, in which he criticises severely Lassalle's book, *The Philosophy of Heraclitus, the Dark, of Ephesus* (two volumes), and calls this work "amateurish". Lenin gives, to begin with, a brief formulation of Marx's criticism: "Lassalle simply *repeats* Hegel, he *describes* him, *ruminates* millions of times on certain sayings of Heraclitus, embellishing his work with a surfeit of most learned Gellertian ballast." But, nevertheless, Lenin plunges into the study of this work of Lassalle, makes conspects and extracts of it, writes notes to it, and sums it up thus: "Marx's criticism is on the whole correct. It isn't worthwhile to read Lassalle's book."[29] But the work over this book gave Lenin himself a deeper understanding of Marx: he understood why this book of Lassalle displeased Marx to such an extent.

In conclusion, I will mention one more form of Lenin's work over Marx – the popularisation of Marx's teachings. If the populariser takes his work 'seriously', if his aim is to give in a very simple and intelligible form an explanation of the very essence of this or that theory, this work will help him very much.

Lenin treated this work very seriously indeed. "There is nothing I would like so much as being able to write for the workers", he wrote from exile to Plekhanov and Axelrod.

He wanted to explain and bring near to the masses the teachings of Marx. In the nineties, when he worked in workers' circles, he endeavoured to explain to them first of all the first volume of *Capital*, and illustrated the propositions brought forward there by examples from the life of his hearers. In 1911, in the Party school in Lonjumeau (near Paris), where Lenin was working hard for the preparation of cadres of leaders for the budding revolutionary movement, he lectured to the workers on political economy, and tried to bring home to them as simply as possible the foundations of Marx's teachings. In his articles to *Pravda*, Ilyich tried to popularise various points from Marx's teachings. A sample of Leninist popularisation is his characterisation during the 1921 disputes on trade unions of the manner of studying the subject with the application of the dialectical method. Lenin said:

> To know the subject thoroughly, one must take hold of and study all its sides, all the connections and its proper place in the given situation. We shall never fully attain this, but the demand of many-sidedness will make us steer clear of errors and inertia. This comes first. Secondly, dialectical logic demands that the subject be taken in its development, in its 'self-motion' (as Hegel says) and its changes. Thirdly, human practice must concentrate on full 'definition' of the subject, as a criterion of truth, as well as a practical indicator of the *connection* of the subject with what man needs. Fourthly, dialectical logic teaches us that "there is no abstract truth, that truth is always concrete", as the late Plekhanov, who was a follower of Hegel, liked to say.[30]

These few lines are the quintessence of what Lenin came to as a result of long years of work over philosophical questions, in which he always made use of the method of dialectical materialism, "consulting" all the time, Marx. In a compressed form, these lines indicate all that is essential, that must be a guide to action, while studying phenomena.

The way in which Lenin worked over Marx is a lesson in how to study Lenin himself. His teaching is inseparably connected with the teaching of Marx, it is Marxism in action, it is the Marxism of the epoch of imperialism and proletarian revolutions.

Rosa Luxemburg provided a succinct evaluation of the October Revolution under the leadership of Lenin and Trotsky:

> Whatever a party could offer of courage, revolutionary farsightedness, and consistency in a historic hour, Lenin, Trotsky and the other comrades have given in good measure. All the revolutionary honour and capacity which western social democracy lacked were represented by the Bolsheviks. Their October uprising was not only the actual salvation of the Russian Revolution; it was also the salvation of the honour of international socialism. [...][31]

What is in order is to distinguish the essential from the non-essential, the kernel from the accidental excrescences in the policies of the Bolsheviks. In the present period, when we face decisive final struggles in all the world, the most important problem of socialism was and is the burning question of our time. It is not a matter of this or that secondary question of tactics, but of the capacity for action of the proletariat, the strength to act, the will to power of socialism as such. In this, Lenin and Trotsky and their friends were the *first*, those who went ahead as an example to the proletariat of the world; they are still the *only ones* up to now who can cry with Hutten,* 'I have dared!'[32]

---

* Ulrich von Hutten (1488-1523) – German imperial knight who advocated the dissolution of Germany's ties with the papacy. In 1520 he published 'Arouser of the German Nation', which opens with his motto, "I have dared to do it", in which announced his support of Martin Luther.

Timeline

22 April 1870 — Birth of Vladimir Ilyich Ulyanov in Simbirsk (modern-day Ulyanovsk)

24 January 1886 — Lenin's father, Ilya Nikolaevich dies

20 May 1886 — Lenin's brother, Alexander, is hanged for terrorism

End of June 1887 — Family moves to Kazan; Lenin enters university in August

6 December 1887 — Lenin expelled from Kazan University, with thirty-eight others

23 October 1889 — The family move to Samara; Lenin joins a study circle

29 May 1890 — Lenin registers at St. Petersburg University as external student

20 May 1891 — Olga, Lenin's sister, dies age nineteen

26 January 1892 — Lenin receives first-class degree in law and in the summer begins to practise

12 September 1893 — Lenin arrives in St. Petersburg

March – June 1894 — Lenin writes *What the 'Friends of the People' Are and How They Fight the Social-Democrats*

End of 1894 – beginning of 1895 — Lenin writes *The Economic Content of Narodism and the Criticism of it in Mr Struve's Book*

7 May 1895 — Lenin begins a trip to Europe; meets Plekhanov in Geneva, where the Emancipation of Labour Group is founded

5 August 1895	Engels dies in London
11 October 1895	Lenin returns to St. Petersburg
October 1895	The Union of Struggle for the Emancipation of the Working Class is established in St. Petersburg
20 December 1895	Lenin arrested
10 February 1897	All the arrested members of the Emancipation Group sentenced to three years 'administrative exile' in Siberia
20 May 1897	Lenin arrives in exile in Shushenskoe
13-15 March 1898	First Congress of the RSDLP held in Minsk
May 1898	Krupskaya joins Lenin in exile
22 July 1898	Lenin and Krupskaya are married
21 August 1898	Lenin finishes the draft of his book, *The Development of Capitalism in Russia*

1900

11 February	Lenin's term of exile in Siberia ends
First half of February	Lenin stops in Ufa, where Krupskaya remains until her exile finishes
29 July	Lenin goes abroad to meet Plekhanov and Axelrod
24 December	*Iskra* launched

1901

26-28 May	Lenin's 'Where to Begin' published in *Iskra* No. 4
December	Uses pseudonym 'Lenin' for first time

1902

March	Lenin's *What Is to Be Done? – Burning Questions of Our Movement* published in Stuttgart
April	Lenin and Krupskaya arrive in London
September	Lenin writes 'A Letter to a Comrade on Our Organisational Tasks'

1903

April	They leave London for Switzerland
17 July	Second Congress of the RSDLP opens in Brussels, but moves to London; Lenin is elected vice-chairman; the Congress ends in a split between Bolshevik and Menshevik factions
1 November	Lenin resigns from the Iskra editorial board after Plekhanov's defection to the Mensheviks

1904

19 May	Lenin publishes *One Step Forward, Two Steps Back*
2 September	Lenin and Krupskaya return to Geneva
2 November	Lenin announces formation of a Bureau of Majority Committees
22 December	Bolshevik paper *Vpered* (*Forward*) launched
December	Organising committee established to organise Third Party Congress

1905

22 January (9 January, Old Style)	Bloody Sunday in St. Petersburg; 1905 Revolution begins
25 April – 10 May	Third Congress of the RSDLP; solely a Bolshevik affair as Mensheviks refuse to attend and hold their own conference elsewhere
10 May	Launch of new paper, *Proletary*, with Lenin as editor-in-chief; first issue appears on 27 May
June – July	Lenin writes *Two Tactics of Social Democracy in the Democratic Revolution*
15-16 November	Lenin writes 'Our Tasks And the Soviet of Workers' Deputies', where he defines the Soviet as a provisional revolutionary government
20 or 21 November	Lenin arrives in St. Petersburg, following government amnesty of political exiles

November	Participates in *Noyaya Zhizn*, but it is closed the following month
25-30 December	Lenin attends the First Bolshevik Conference in Tammerfors, Finland

1906

23 April – 8 May	Fourth (Unity) Congress of RSDLP meets in Stockholm
May	Lenin begins to write articles for *Vperyod*, a new legal Bolshevik daily published in St. Petersburg; it lasted until the end of June, when it was closed down; after that a new paper, *Ekho*, is launched

1907

January – April	Lenin moves to Kokkala in Finland
13 May – 1 June	Fifth (London) Congress of the RSDLP, attended by Lenin, Plekhanov, Martov, Trotsky, Rosa Luxemburg, Gorky and others; Lenin elected to the Central Committee and onto the International Socialist Bureau
3-5 August	Lenin attends the Third Conference of the RSDLP in Finland
August – September	Lenin elected as editor-in-chief of Party paper, *Sotsial-Demokrat*
18-25 November	Lenin attends the Fourth Conference of the RSDLP in Finland

1908

7 January	Lenin arrives in Geneva with Krupskaya, the beginning of their second period of emigration
February	Lenin begins writing *Materialism and Empirio-criticism*; in May he goes to the British Museum in London to research philosophy
19 April – 1 May	Lenin visits Gorky on the Island of Capri
17 May	*Materialism and Empirio-criticism* published in Moscow

18 August	Lenin declines to speak at a school in Capri, which he regards as a factional school, but invites the students to come to Paris to attend Bolshevik lectures
11 October	Lenin attends the International Socialist Bureau, where British Labour Party affiliation is discussed
End of November	Lenin and Krupskaya move to Paris; *Proletary* also published there; he works in the Sorbonne Library

1909

End of November	Lenin delivers lectures in Paris to five students who were expelled from the Capri school
End of December	Lenin works in the Sorbonne library on questions related to philosophy

1910

15 January – 5 February	Lenin attends the Plenum of the Central Committee of RSDLP; moves a draft resolution against liquidationism and otzovism
1-13 July	Lenin stays with Gorky at Capri
26 August	Lenin arrives in Copenhagen for Eighth Congress of the Second International and the International Socialist Bureau
12 November	Lenin announces the founding of *Rabochaya Gazeta*, together with Plekhanov
December	Lenin writes for first issue of *Mysl*, a legal Bolshevik magazine

1911

Spring and summer	Lenin and Krupskaya live in Longjumeau, near Paris, and establish a Party school
23-24 September	Lenin attends meeting of the International Socialist Bureau in Zurich; defends Rosa Luxemburg's opposition to opportunism in German SPD
3 December	Lenin delivers a speech at the funeral of Paul and Laura Lafargue

1912

18-30 January	The Sixth (Prague) Conference of the RSDLP takes place, where the split between Bolsheviks and Mensheviks is finalised; the Bolsheviks assume the name of RSDLP
5 May	*Pravda* is launched as a legal Bolshevik daily
9 May	Lenin reports on the Lena shootings and strikes in Russia
Early June	Lenin moves from Paris to Kraków to establish closer ties with Russia
December	Lenin holds meeting of the Central Committee and Bolshevik deputies to discuss the Bolshevik group in the Fourth Duma

1913

25 January	Writes to *Pravda* demanding a reorganisation of its editorial board
6 May	Lenin and Krupskaya move to Poronin, near Kraków, and establish a Party school
June	Lenin lectures in Zurich, Geneva, Lausanne
20 October	Lenin and Krupskaya return to Kraków

1914

February – March	Lenin writes *The Right of Nations to Self-Determination*
9 May	Lenin moves back to Poronin
4 August	First World War declared; German SPD vote for war credits triggering the collapse of the Second International
8 August	Lenin arrested; released 19 August
5 September	Lenin forced to leave Austria-Hungary for neutral Switzerland
September	Lenin begins collecting material on philosophy at the Bern Library
17 October	Lenin resumes publication of *Sotsial-Demokrat*

1915

Prior to August	Lenin arranges publication of *Socialism and War* in German
1 September	Lenin's *The Collapse of the Second International* published in *Kommunist*
5-8 September	Lenin attends Zimmerwald conference and launches Zimmerwald Left
December – January 1916	Lenin lives in Bern, Switzerland
December	Lenin writes preface to Bukharin's *Imperialism and the World Economy*

1916

10 February	Lenin moves to Zurich
January – June	Lenin writes *Imperialism, The Highest Stage of Capitalism*, which is completed 2 July
24-30 April	Lenin takes part in the Kienthal international conference
25 July	Lenin's mother dies in Petrograd
4 November	Lenin addresses the Swiss Social-Democratic Party Congress on behalf of the RSDLP
December – February 1917	Lenin works in the Zurich Library on the Marxist attitude to the state

1917

22 January	Lenin delivers a lecture on the 1905 Revolution at a youth meeting in Zurich
12 March	Nicholas II abdicates; Provisional Government formed
15 March	Lenin receives the first news of the February Revolution and takes measures to return to Russia
20 March	Writes the first of his *Letters from Afar*
21-22 March	Writes the second of his *Letters from Afar*
23-24 March	Writes the third of his *Letters from Afar*

25 March	Writes the fourth of his *Letters from Afar*
8 April	Writes the fifth of his *Letters from Afar* (unfinished)
9 April	Lenin and Krupskaya leave Bern for Zurich, where they begin their journey to Russia in the 'sealed train'
16 April	Lenin arrives at the Finland Station in Russia
20 April	Lenin's article 'The Tasks of the Proletariat in the Present Revolution' containing the *April Theses* is published in *Pravda*
27 April – 5 May	Petrograd City Conference of the RSDLP(B), with Lenin taking part
7-12 May	Seventh (April) All-Russia Conference of the RSDLP(B), with Lenin taking part
4 June	Lenin addresses the First All-Russia Congress of Peasant Deputies on the agrarian question
16 June – 7 July	Lenin attends the First All-Russia Congress of Soviets of Workers' and Soldiers' Deputies
17 July	Lenin addresses a crowd from balcony of Kshesinskaya Palace
16-20 July	July Days; Lenin forced into hiding and escapes to Finland
21 July	Kerensky becomes Prime Minister of the Provisional Government
20 July	Provisional Government orders Lenin's arrest
8-16 August	Sixth Congress of RSDLP takes place, where the Inter-District organisation is taken into membership and Trotsky formally joins the Bolshevik Party
August – September	Lenin writes *The State and Revolution*
10-13 September	Kornilov attempts a coup against the Provisional Government; Bolsheviks spearhead the struggle against his putsch
23-27 September	Lenin writes *The Impending Catastrophe and How to Combat it*
Prior to 30 September	Lenin lives in Helsingfors (modern-day Helsinki), then moves to Vyborg District

14 October	Lenin writes *Can the Bolsheviks Retain State Power?*
23 October	At the Central Committee Lenin tables a motion for an armed uprising; Zinoviev and Kamenev vote against
29 October	At the enlarged Central Committee Lenin again proposes an armed insurrection; again Zinoviev and Kamenev vote against
30 October	Zinoviev and Kamenev publicly reveal the plans for an insurrection; Lenin proposes their expulsion
Night of 6 November	The insurrection begins
7 November (25 October, Old Style)	At 10 am, on behalf of the Revolutionary Military Committee, Lenin announces the overthrow of the Provisional Government; Lenin drafts decrees on peace, land, and the formation of a Soviet government
8 November	Organisation of a new government of People's Commissars, exclusively of Bolsheviks
9 November	Kerensky moves on Petrograd with General Krasnov and a force of Cossacks
11 November	Unsuccessful uprising of Junkers in Petrograd
14 November	Kerensky flees and Krasnov captured, but released on promise of good behaviour
15 November	Victory of the revolution in Moscow; General Alekseev, former commander of the tsarist army, organises the 'Volunteer Army'; he is later joined by Kornilov, Denikin and other generals
17 November	Lenin refuses a coalition with those parties that opposed the revolution; several members of the government resign, also from the Central Committee
20 November	The Ukrainian Rada seizes power in Ukraine; allows Cossacks to pass through to the Don
1 December	Left SRs enter the Soviet government
5 December	Preliminary armistice signed with Germany
20 December	Establishment of the Cheka – All-Russian Extraordinary Commission to Fight Counter-revolution and Sabotage
22 December	Start of the Brest-Litovsk negotiations

| 31 December | Lenin hands Finnish government a decree recognising Finland's independence |

1918

5-13 January	Third Congress of Soviets
14 January	Lenin's car shot at by counter-revolutionaries
18 January	Constituent Assembly opens; dispersed the following day
21-22 January	The Central Committee votes in favour of Bukharin's revolutionary war proposal
8 February	Red Army occupies Kiev; the following day, Rada signs separate peace with Central Powers
10 February	Trotsky refuses to sign peace deal at Brest-Litovsk, but declares that the war is over
14 February	New Style Gregorian calendar adopted
18 February	Germans advance; evening session of Central Committee endorses Lenin's motion to sign immediately, after Trotsky gives support
19 February	Soviet government agrees to sign peace deal
20 February	Decree passed to form Red Army
21 February	Lenin's article 'The Revolutionary Phrase' published in *Pravda*; the following day he wrote an article 'The Itch', published that evening
22 February	Germans demand harsher peace deal; the following day, the Soviet government agrees to sign
2 March	Germans occupy Kiev and restore the Rada
3 March	Treaty of Brest-Litovsk signed
6-8 March	Seventh Party Congress; Lenin delivers the political report; Bolsheviks change name to Communists
10-11 March	Government transferred from Petrograd to Moscow
13 March	Trotsky appointed Commissar for War
15 March	Fourth Congress of Soviets ratifies the Peace of Brest-Litovsk; Left SRs resign from government over this question

29 April	Germans dismiss Ukrainian Rada and appoint General Skoropadsky as Ukrainian Hetman and dictator
5 May	Lenin writes *'Left-Wing' Childishness and the Petty-bourgeois Mentality*
25 May	Hostilities open between Soviets and the Czech Legion, who seize a number of towns
29 May	Soviet Executive Committee introduces partial conscription for Red Army
8 June	Czechs occupy Samara; anti-Bolshevik government created in Omsk, Siberia
11 June	Committees of Poor Peasants established
20 June	Assassination of Volodarsky by a Socialist-Revolutionary
28 June	Decree to nationalise all large-scale industry
6 July	German ambassador, Count Mirbach, assassinated by Left SRs; beginning of Left SR rebellion
16 July	Former Tsar and family members shot at Ekaterinburg
2 August	Allied occupation of Archangel and anti-Bolshevik government established there
6 August	Czechs and anti-Bolshevik forces capture Kazan
14 August	Small British force occupies Baku, which leaves and is then occupied by Turks
August	White 'Volunteer Army' occupies Ekaterinodar, then Novorossiysk, with opening to sea
30 August	Lenin shot by Left SR, Fanny Kaplan; Uritzky assassinated by SR
4 September	'Red Terror' against the bourgeoisie begins
10 September	Red Army led by Trotsky captures Kazan from the White Army
8 October	Red Army captures Samara
9 October	Lenin writes *The Proletarian Revolution and the Renegade Kautsky*, which he completes by 10 November
9 November	Revolution sweeps Germany; workers' and soldiers' committees established

| 16 November | Lenin takes part in the Central Committee for first time since he was shot |
| 18 November | Kolchak proclaimed supreme ruler after coup in Siberia after coup in Omsk |

1919

3 January	Red Army takes Riga and Kharkov
6 January	Red Army captures Kiev
15 January	Rosa Luxemburg and Karl Liebknecht assassinated by the Freikorps
2-7 March	First Congress of Communist International; Lenin delivers the opening speech
21 March	Soviet regime established in Hungary
April	Red Army takes Odessa, then Simferopol
1-3 May	Fall of Bavarian Soviet Republic
June	Red Army takes Ufa; Denikin captures Kharkov, then Tsaritsin, and Ekaterinoslav
1 August	Fall of Hungarian Soviet Republic, overthrown by counter-revolutionary troops
23 August	Denikin takes Odessa, then Kiev
11 October	Yudenich marches on Petrograd
14 October	Denikin occupied Orel
20 October	Red Army takes Orel; Yudenich forced back from Petrograd
14 November	Red Army takes Omsk
12 December	Red Army takes Kharkov, then Ekaterinoslav

1920

| January | Red Army occupies Tsaritsin, captures Rostov, and Denikin retreats south; Czechs hand over Kolchak to the Soviets and is he shot; Allies raise the blockade of Soviet Russia; marks the end of imperialist intervention |

10 February	'Labour armies' organised involving Red Army for reconstruction
19 February	Northern Government in Archangel falls
4 April	Denikin resigns command of White armies; General Wrangel appointed in his place
29 April – 5 May	Tenth Congress of the Party
April – May	Lenin writes *'Left-Wing' Communism – An Infantile Disorder*, published in June
6 May	Polish army enters Kiev
12 June	Red Army retakes Kiev
11 July	Red Army captures Minsk, then occupies Vilna
21 July – 6 August	Second Congress of the Communist International
15 August	Polish forces stage counter-offensive, as Red Army retreats
12 October	Preliminary peace treaty with Poland signed

1921

8-16 March	Tenth Congress of the Party, where the New Economic Policy is accepted, and factions are banned in the Party
1-18 March	Kronstadt rebellion
17 March – 1 April	'March Action' in Germany
26-28 May	Tenth All-Russia Conference of the Party
22 June – 12 July	Third Congress of the Communist International; following the 'March Action' in Germany, the Congress rejects the 'theory of the offensive'
13 July	Lenin takes a month's holiday on the advice of his doctors and goes to Gorki
27 September	Lenin writes 'Tasks of the Workers' and Peasants' Inspection and How They Are to be Understood and Fulfilled'
31 December	Politburo grants Lenin six weeks' leave from 1 January

1922

2 February	Politburo prolongs Lenin's leave until Eleventh Party Congress
3 March	Lenin demands the strengthening of the monopoly of foreign trade
27 March – 2 April	Eleventh Congress of the Party
23 April	Lenin undergoes surgery to remove a bullet at the Soldatenkov Hospital
15 May	Lenin writes to Stalin saying that any discussion on the monopoly of foreign trade be dropped
25 May	Lenin suffers his first stroke, is partially paralysed and loses ability to speak
September	Stalin's proposals for relations with Soviet republics rejected by the Georgian Central Committee; Lenin opposes Stalin's 'autonomisation' project and proposes creation of USSR
27 September	Stalin accuses Lenin of 'national liberalism' in a letter to the Politburo
2 October	Lenin returns to Moscow from Gorki and resumes work in the Kremlin
6 October	Politburo accepts USSR proposal; Lenin writes to Kamenev saying he is going to fight Great Russian chauvinism
11 October	Lenin meets Trotsky and discusses the monopoly of trade and their 'bloc' against bureaucracy
5 November – 5 December	Fourth Congress of the Communist International held in Moscow
20 November	Lenin's last public speech at session of Moscow Soviet
End of November	Ordzhonikidze physically strikes Kabanidze, a member of the Georgian leadership and Mdivani's supporter
7-12 December	Lenin on leave in Gorki
12 December	Lenin approaches Trotsky to defend their common position on monopoly of foreign trade
13 December	Lenin suffers two further strokes

15 December	Lenin writes to Stalin about steps to retire and how he has concluded an agreement with Trotsky on foreign trade
18 December	The Central Committee rescinds previous decision and reaffirms monopoly of foreign trade; the CC makes Stalin responsible for Lenin's medical supervision
21 December	Lenin sends Trotsky a letter of congratulation at their common victory at the Central Committee
22 December	Stalin calls Krupskaya and attacks her for having written a letter dictated by Lenin
Night of 22-23 December	Lenin again half paralysed
23 December	Lenin asks doctors for permission to dictate some notes; the next day he says he will refuse treatment if this is declined; the Politburo grants permission
23-31 December	Lenin dictates his *Testament*
30 December	Congress of Soviets proclaims creation of USSR

1923

January – February	Lenin dictates 5 articles: 'Pages from a Journal', 'On Cooperation', 'Our Revolution', 'On the Workers' and Peasants' Inspection' and 'Better Fewer, but Better'
4 January	Lenin adds a note to his *Testament* to remove Stalin as general secretary
25 January	Politburo endorses the Dzerzhinsky commission into the Georgian affair and whitewashes Ordzhonikidze and condemns the Georgian Central Committee; Lenin demands to see the dossiers of the commission
1 February	Dossiers on Georgia handed over and Lenin asks his secretaries to study them and gives instruction how this should be done
3 March	Lenin's private investigation submits its findings
5 March	Lenin writes to Trotsky asking him to take up the defence of the Georgians in both their names at the Central Committee; Lenin begins dictating a letter to Stalin demanding an apology for his treatment of Krupskaya

6 March	Finishes the letter to Stalin; also writes another to the persecuted Georgians stating he is taking up their defence against Stalin and Ordzhonikidze; Kamenev hears from Krupskaya that Lenin intends to crush Stalin politically; Lenin's health worsens
10 March	Lenin suffers another stroke that paralyses half his body and deprives him of speech
12 May	Lenin moved to Gorki

1924

| 21 January | Lenin dies from his fourth stroke at age fifty-three |

List of Images

20. Lenin's Response from Exile

21. Rearming the Bolsheviks

22. Revolutionary Petrograd

23. July Days

28. The Civil War Begins

29. Founding the Comintern

Image credits

David King Collection, purchased from David King by Tate Archive 2016:
Images 17, 22, 23, 26, 36, 40, 43, 47, 48, 49, 50, 53, 55, 56, 81, 96, 122, 125, 132,
    134, 133, 154, 175, 191, 192, 205, 206, 207, 208, 209, 225, 237, 242, 243, 253,
    262, 263, 265, 266

Walter Meakin, with the kind permission of his grandson:
Images 136, 137, 138, 153, 155, 156, 157, 169, 178, 179, 182, 183 194, 212, 217,
    218, 219, 220, 221

© IMAGO /
    Album: Image 1
    ZUMA Wire: Images 186, 241
    SNA: Image 261

© Alamy Stock Photo /
    Heritage Image Partnership Ltd: Image 39
    akg-images: Image 118

Wikimedia Commons, via
    Пауль Фюрст, вдова и наследники: Image 3
    Annenkoan: Image 32
    Karl Bulla, Finnish Heritage Agency: Image 107
    © by James G Howes, 1998: Image 111
    Kimdime (edited by Wellred Books): Image 113
    Yukof: Image 171
    RIA Novosti archive, image #6464 / RIA Novosti / CC-BY-SA 3.0: Image 172
    Bundesarchiv / CC-BY-SA 3.0 /
        B 145 Bild-P046271 / Weinrother, Carl: Image 174
        Bild 119-2303E: Image 236
    Památkové Pohlednice Svazu Přátel SSSR Československu: Image 226
    Lwlvlad931: Image 255

All other images are in the public domain

Glossary

Cadets – Acronym for Constitutional Democrats, the main bourgeois liberal party in Russia which emerged from the earlier Liberation (Osvobozhdeniye in Russian) League.

Duma – An ancient Russian word, virtually synonymous with soviet, meaning a council. During the reign of Nicholas II the State Duma was the name given to the national parliament. There were also local dumas, the equivalent of local councils.

Kulak – A rich peasant. The word actually means 'a fist', probably an ironic reference to the tightfistedness of these elements.

Muzhik – Russian name for a peasant. Sometimes used colloquially to mean 'a man'.

Okhrana – Short for Okhrananoye Otdyelyeniye or Department of Safety. It was the tsarist secret police, founded in 1881, which operated a vast network of spies, informers, and agents provocateurs who infiltrated the revolutionary movement and whose operations extended to many countries.

Pogrom – A racially motivated attack in which mobs, usually organised and directed by agents of the state, attack minorities. The victims were most often Jews, but also included other minorities, such as the Armenians in Azerbaijan.

Socialist-Revolutionaries (SRs) – A petty-bourgeois party, descended from the Narodniks, which advocated a kind of 'peasant socialism'. They split into a right and left in 1917. The Left supported the October Revolution and for a time were in a coalition government with the Bolsheviks.

Zemstvo (Russian plural, zemstva) – Semi-official local organs of self-government. Control of the zemstvos was in the hands of the rural gentry. They had virtually no powers and were dependent on the whims of the local governor, who was appointed by the central government.

A name glossary has been compiled for this book, available online at:

wellred-books.com/in-defence-of-lenin-glossary

References

Preface to the Second Volume

1. Santayana, *The Life of Reason*, p. 82
2. Quoted in Liebman, *Leninism Under Lenin*, p. 222
3. Ross, *The Russian Soviet Republic*, p. 3
4. Deutscher, *Stalin: A Political Biography*, p. 166

22. Revolutionary Petrograd

1. Quoted in Liebman, *The Russian Revolution*, p. 137
2. Krupskaya, *Memories of Lenin*, pp. 351-2
3. Trotsky, *History of the Russian Revolution*, Vol. 1, p. 17
4. Lenin, 'Lessons of the Revolution', July 1917, *Lenin Collected Works*, (henceforth referred to as *LCW*), Vol. 25, p. 229
5. Quoted in *The History of the Civil War in the USSR*, Vol. 1, p. 118
6. Quoted in Liebman, *The Russian Revolution*, p. 143
7. Rabinowitch, *The Bolsheviks Come to Power*, p. xvii
8. Ibid., p. xxi
9. Raskolnikov, *Kronstadt and Petrograd in 1917*, p. 67
10. Lenin, *The Tasks of the Proletariat in our Revolution*, 10 April 1917, *LCW*, Vol. 24, pp. 65-6, emphasis in original
11. Ibid., p. 66, emphasis in original
12. Lenin, *The Petrograd City Conference of the RSDLP(B)*, 'Report on the Present Situation and the Attitude Towards the Provisional Government', 14 (21) April 1917, ibid., pp. 144-5
13. Ibid., p. 145
14. Lenin, 'The Dual Power', *Pravda*, No. 28, 9 April 1917, ibid., p. 38, emphasis in original
15. Ibid., p. 39, emphasis in original
16. Ibid., pp. 39-40, emphasis in original
17. Ibid., p. 40, emphasis in original
18. Ibid., emphasis in original
19. Ibid., pp. 40-1, emphasis in original
20. Lenin, *The Tasks of the Proletariat in our Revolution*, 10 April 1917, ibid., p. 63, emphasis in original
21. Lenin, 'A Shameless Lie of the Capitalists', *Pravda*, No. 30, 11 (24) April 1917, ibid., pp. 110-1, emphasis in original
22. Lenin, 'Resolution of the Central Committee of the RSDLP (Bolsheviks) Adopted 21 April (4 May) 1917', *Pravda*, No. 38, 5 May (22 April) 1917, ibid., p. 201, emphasis in original
23. Quoted in Liebman, *The Russian*

Revolution, p. 146

24. Raskolnikov, *Kronstadt and Petrograd in 1917*, p. 181

25. Lenin, 'Lessons of the Crisis', *Pravda*, No. 39, 6 May (23 April) 1917, ibid., p. 216

26. Lenin, *The Seventh (April) All-Russia Conference of the RSDLP(B)*, 'Speech Winding Up the Debate on the Report on the Current Situation', 24 April (7 May) 1917, ibid., p. 244

27. Lenin, 'Lessons of the Crisis', *Pravda*, No. 39, 23 April (6 May) 1917, *LCW*, Vol. 24, p. 216

28. Lenin, 'How a Simple Question Can Be Confused', *Pravda*, No. 39, 23 April (6 May) 1917, ibid., p. 217, emphasis in original

29. Lenin, *The Petrograd City Conference of the RSDLP(B)*, 'Report on the Present Situation and the Attitude Towards the Provisional Government', 14 (21) April 1917, p. 146, emphasis added

30. Lenin, 'Infamy Justified', *Pravda*, No. 70, 14 (1) June 1917, ibid., p. 561, emphasis in original

31. Lenin, 'Icons Versus Cannons, Phrases Versus Capital', *Pravda*, No. 37, 4 May (21 April) 1917, p. 197, emphasis in original

32. Quoted in Liebman, *The Russian Revolution*, p. 153

33. Trotsky, *History of the Russian Revolution*, Vol. 1, p. 291

34. Available online at: https://www.marxists.org/history/ussr/government/1917/03/01.htm (accessed 14 December 2023)

35. Quoted in Liebman, *The Russian Revolution*, p. 156

36. Lenin, *First All-Russia Congress of Soviets of Workers' and Soldiers' Deputies*, 'Speech on the Attitude Towards the Provisional Government', 4 (17) June 1917, *LCW*, Vol. 25, pp. 20-1, emphasis in original

37. Quoted in Lenin, 'Confused and Frightened', *Pravda*, No. 79, 24 (11) June 1917, ibid., p. 71

38. Quoted in Liebman, *The Russian*

Revolution, p. 168

39. 'A Historic Meeting', *Pravda*, No. 80, 13 June 1917, quoted in *The History of the Civil War in the USSR*, pp. 202-3

40. Quoted in Liebman, *The Russian Revolution*, p. 179

41. Lenin, 'Speech on the Cancellation of the Demonstration, Delivered at a Meeting of the Petrograd Committee of the RSDLP(B)', 11 (24) June 1917, *LCW*, Vol. 25, p. 79

42. Quoted in Liebman, *The Russian Revolution*, p. 168

43. Lenin, 'Titbits for the "Newborn" Government', *Pravda*, No. 50, 19 (6) May 1917, *LCW*, Vol. 25, p. 364

44. Ibid.

23. July Days

1. Quoted in Liebman, *The Russian Revolution*, p. 169

2. Lenin, 'A Class Shift', Pravda No. 92, 10 July (27 June), *LCW*, Vol. 25, p. 131

3. Quoted in Liebman, *The Russian Revolution*, p. 181

4. Quoted in Sukhanov, *The Russian Revolution 1917*, p. 450

5. Ibid., p. 452

6. Quoted ibid., p. 455

7. Raskolnikov, *Kronstadt and Petrograd in 1917*, p. 178

8. Quoted in Rabinowitch, *The Bolsheviks Come to Power*, p. 19

9. Lenin, 'Slander and Facts', *Listok 'Pravdy'*, 5 (18) July 1917, *LCW*, Vol. 25, p. 163

10. Quoted in Rabinowitch, *The Bolsheviks Come to Power*, p. 28

11. Buchanan, *My Mission to Russia*, Vol. 2, pp. 156-8

12. Quoted in Trotsky, *History of the Russian Revolution*, Vol. 2, p. 631

13. Ibid., p. 645

14. Quoted in Rabinowitch, *The Bolsheviks Come to Power*, p. 23

15. Quoted in Trotsky, *On Lenin*, p. 75

16. Buchanan, *My Mission to Russia*, Vol. 2, p. 156-8

17. Polovtsev, *Days of Eclipse*, p. 143
18. Quoted in Deutscher, *The Prophet Armed*, p. 276
19. Lenin, 'The Political Situation – Four Theses', 10 (23) July 1917, *LCW*, Vol. 25, p. 178
20. Ibid., p. 179
21. Ibid., pp. 178-80
22. Lenin, *On Slogans*, mid-July 1917, ibid., pp. 186-7
23. Ibid., p. 187
24. Quoted in Rabinowitch, *The Bolsheviks Come to Power*, p. 62
25. Lenin, 'To Alexandra Kollontai', 17 February 1917', *LCW*, Vol. 35, p. 286
26. Lenin, 'Note to LB Kamenev', between 5-7 (18-20) July 1917, *LCW*, Vol. 36, p. 454
27. Lenin, *The State and Revolution*, August – September 1917, *LCW*, Vol. 25, p. 497
28. Lenin, *The Impending Catastrophe and How to Combat It*, 10-14 September 1917, ibid., pp. 327-8
29. Ibid., p. 333
30. Ibid., p. 357, emphasis in original
31. Raskolnikov, *Kronstadt and Petrograd in 1917*, p. 218
32. Ibid.
33. Krupskaya, *Reminiscences of Lenin*, p. 369
34. *The Sixth Congress of the RSDLP(B)*, August 1917, Moscow, 1934, p. 251
35. *The Bolsheviks and the October Revolution: CC Minutes*, p. 256, footnote
36. Lenin, 'From the Theses for a Report at the 8 October Conference of the St. Petersburg Organisation, and Also For a Resolution and Instructions to Those Elected to the Party Congress', 'Note to Thesis "On the List of Candidates for the Constituent Assembly"', *LCW*, Vol. 41, p. 447, emphasis in original
37. See *LCW*, Vol. 25, pp. 525-8
38. Quoted in Liebman, *The Russian Revolution*, p. 194
39. Quoted in Trotsky, *History of the Russian Revolution*, Vol. 2, p. 654
40. Quoted in *The History of the Civil War in the USSR*, Vol. 1, p. 290
41. Denikin, *Sketches of the Russian Revolt*, Vol. 2, 1922, p. 31
42. Quoted in Liebman, *The Russian Revolution*, p. 206
43. Buchanan, *My Mission to Russia*, Vol. 2, p. 185
44. Sukhanov, *The Russian Revolution 1917*, p. 508
45. Lenin, 'To the Central Committee of the RSDLP', 30 August (12 September) 1917, *LCW*, Vol. 25, p. 289
46. Ibid., pp. 289-90, emphasis in original
47. Ibid., p. 190, emphasis in original
48. Ibid., pp. 190-3, emphasis in original
49. Lenin, 'On Compromises', *Rabochy Put*, No. 3, 6 (19) September 1917, ibid., pp. 310-1, emphasis in original
50. Ibid., p. 311, emphasis in original
51. Ibid., emphasis in original
52. Lenin, 'The Russian Revolution and Civil War', *Rabochy Put*, No. 12, 29 (16) September 1917, *LCW*, Vol. 26, p. 41, emphasis in original
53. Lenin, 'The Tasks of the Revolution', ibid., *Rabochy Put*, Nos. 20-21, 9-10 October (26-27 September) 1917, ibid., p. 60
54. Ibid., p. 67
55. Lenin, 'Heroes of Fraud and the Mistakes of the Bolsheviks', *Rabochy Put*, No. 19, 7 October (24 September) 1917, ibid., p. 48
56. Lenin, 'From a Publicist's Diary', 23 September 1917, ibid., p. 57
57. Quoted in Liebman, *The Russian Revolution*, p. 228
58. Quoted ibid.
59. Lenin, 'The Bolsheviks Must Assume Power', 12-14 (25-27) September 1917, *LCW*, Vol. 26, p. 19, emphasis in original
60. Ibid., p. 21
61. Quoted in Liebman, *The Russian Revolution*, p. 235
62. Lenin, 'Letter to IT Smilga', 27 September (10 October) 1917, *LCW*, Vol. 26, p. 69
63. Ibid., p. 70, emphasis in original
64. Ibid., emphasis in original

65. Lenin, 'The Crisis has Matured', 29
September 1917, ibid., p. 82
66. Ibid.
67. Ibid., p. 84
68. Ibid., emphasis in original
69. Trotsky, *History of the Russian Revolution*, Vol. 3, p. 981

24. The October Revolution

1. Quoted in Liebman, *The Russian revolution*, pp. 242-3
2. Sukhanov, *The Russian Revolution 1917*, p. 557, emphasis in original
3. 'Statement by Kamenev and Zinoviev', 11 (24) October 1917, *The Bolsheviks and the October Revolution: CC Minutes*, p. 90, emphasis in original
4. Lenin, 'Letter to Comrades', 17 (30) October 1917, *LCW*, Vol. 26, pp. 195-6
5. Ibid., p. 203, emphasis in original
6. Ibid.
7. Ibid., pp. 212-3, emphasis in original
8. Ibid., p. 213
9. Lenin, 'Meeting of the Central Committee of the RSDLP(B)', 10 (23) October 1917, ibid., pp. 191-2
10. Ibid., p. 192
11. *The Bolsheviks and the October Revolution: CC Minutes*, p. 103
12. *Joseph Stalin*, p. 38
13. Lenin, 'Letter to Bolshevik Party Members', 18 (31) October 1917, *LCW*, Vol. 26, p. 217, emphasis in original
14. Lenin, 'Letter to the Central Committee of the RSDLP(B)', 19 October (1 November) 1917, ibid., p. 223
15. *The Bolsheviks and the October Revolution: CC Minutes*, p. 120
16. Ibid., p. 112
17. Price, *Dispatches From the Revolution*, p. 90
18. Lenin, 'Letter to Central Committee Members', 24 October (6 November) 1917, *LCW*, Vol. 26, p. 235
19. Sukhanov, *The Russian Revolution 1917*, p. 620
20. Ibid.
21. See Reed, *Ten Days that Shook the World*
22. Stalin, *Pravda*, No. 241, 6 November 1918, *The October Revolution*, p. 30
23. Stalin, *Pravda*, No. 269, 26 November 1924, *The October Revolution*, p. 72
24. Price, *Dispatches From the Revolution: Russia 1916-18*, p. 91
25. Quoted in Liebman, *The Russian Revolution*, p. 274
26. Quoted ibid.
27. Trotsky, *Lenin*, pp. 126-7
28. Reed, *Ten Days That Shook the World*, pp. 128-9, 132
29. See Luxemburg, 'The Russian Revolution', *Rosa Luxemburg Speaks*, p. 395
30. Trotsky, *On Lenin*, p. 114
31. Price, *Dispatches From the Revolution*, p. 94
32. Ibid.
33. Quoted in Liebman, *The Russian Revolution*, p. 285

25. Soviets in Power

1. Lockhart, *Memoirs of a British Agent*, pp. 196-7
2. Sukhanov, *The Russian Revolution 1917*, p. 632
3. Ibid.
4. Quoted in Liebman, *The Russian Revolution*, p. 286
5. Ibid., p. 290
6. Price, *Dispatches from the Revolution: Russia 1916-18*, p. 88
7. Ibid., p. 102
8. Lenin, 'To the Citizens of Russia!', *Rabochy i Soldat*, No. 8, 25 October (7 November) 1917, *LCW*, Vol. 26, p. 236
9. Lenin, *Second All-Russia Congress of Soviets of Workers' and Soldiers' Deputies*, 'Decree on Peace', 26 October (8 November) 1917, ibid., pp. 249-51
10. Ibid., 'Decree on Land', p. 258
11. Quoted in Hill, *Lenin and the Russian Revolution*, p. 239
12. Quoted ibid.
13. Quoted ibid.

14. Lenin, ibid., 'Report on Land', p. 260
15. Ibid., p. 261
16. Lenin, 'From a Publicist's Diary –
    Peasants and Workers', *Rabochy*, No. 6,
    11 September (29 August) 1917, *LCW*,
    Vol. 25, p. 285, emphasis in original
17. Reed, *Ten Days that Shook the World*,
    p. 137
18. Lenin, 'Draft Regulations on Workers'
    Control', 26 or 27 October (8 or 9
    November) 1917, *LCW*, Vol. 26, p.
    264, emphasis in original
19. Lenin, 'Resolution on Measures
    to Cope with the Economic
    Disorganisation', *Sotsial-Demokrat*, No.
    64, 25 May (7 June) 1917, *LCW*, Vol.
    24, pp. 513-4
20. Lenin, 'To the Population', *Pravda*, No.
    4, 19 (6) November 1917, *LCW*, Vol.
    26, p. 298
21. Quoted in Reed, *Ten Days That Shook
    the World*, p. 231
22. Carr, *The Bolshevik Revolution, 1917-
    1923*, Vol. 1, p. 272
23. Akhapkin, *First Decrees of Soviet Power*
    and also 'Decrees and documents of
    the Russian Revolution, 1917-1918',
    Marxist Internet Archive, available
    at marxists.org/history/ussr/events/
    revolution/documents/index.htm
    (accessed 14 December 2023)
24. Peter Roberts and Weston, *Women,
    Family and the Russian Revolution*, p. 21
25. Lenin, *Eighth Congress of the RCP(B)*,
    'Report of the CC', 18 March 1919,
    LCW, Vol. 29, p. 155
26. Trotsky, *On Lenin*, p. 127
27. Ibid, p. 115
28. Quoted in Carr, *The Bolshevik
    Revolution, 1917-1923*, Vol. 1, p. 242
29. Quoted in Trotsky, *The Stalin School of
    Falsification*, p. 110
30. Lenin, 'Speech at the Fourth
    Conference of Gubernia Extraordinary
    Commissions', 6 February 1920, *LCW*,
    Vol. 42, p. 167
31. Lockhart, *Memoirs of a British Agent*,
    p. 241
32. Ibid., p. 247
33. Ibid., p. 256
34. Reed, *Ten Days That Shook the World*,
    p. 232
35. Ibid., p. 185, emphasis in original
36. Lockhart, *Memoirs of a British Agent*,
    p. 237
37. Ransome, *Six Weeks in Russia in 1919*,
    p. 68
38. *The Bolsheviks and the October
    Revolution: CC Minutes*, p. 132
39. Ibid., p. 129
40. Sukhanov, *The Russian Revolution 1917*,
    p. 636
41. Quoted in Trotsky, *The Stalin School of
    Falsification*, p. 110
42. Quoted ibid, p. 119
43. Lenin, 'Ultimatum From the Majority
    of the Central Committee of the
    RSDLP(B) to the Minority', 3 (16)
    November 1917, *LCW*, Vol. 26, p. 282
44. Lenin, 'From the Central Committee
    of the RSDLP(B)', *Pravda*, No. 182, 7
    (20) November 1917, *LCW*, Vol. 26,
    pp. 305-6
45. Ibid., p. 306
46. Ibid.
47. Ibid.
48. Ibid., p. 308, emphasis in original
49. Lenin, *Third All-Russia Congress of
    Soviets of Workers', Soldiers' and Peasants'
    Deputies*, 'Report on the Activities of
    the Council of People's Commissars',
    11 (24) January 1918, ibid., p. 473

26. Brest-Litovsk

1. Lenin, 'Speech on the Dissolution of
   the Constituent Assembly Delivered
   to the All-Russia Central Executive
   Committee', 6 (19) January 1918,
   LCW, Vol. 26, p. 439
2. Lenin, *The Proletarian Revolution
   and the Renegade Kautsky*, October –
   November 1918, *LCW*, Vol. 28, p. 248,
   emphasis added
3. Ibid., pp. 272-3, emphasis in original
4. Ibid., pp. 247-9, emphasis in original
5. Quoted in Liebman, *The Russian
   Revolution*, p. 315
6. Quoted in Hill, *God's Englishman*, pp.
   131-2

7. Carr, *The Bolshevik Revolution, 1917-1923*, Vol. 1, pp. 111-2

8. Ransome, *Six Weeks in Russia in 1919*, p. 44

9. Trotsky, *My Life*, p. 327

10. Ransome, *Six Weeks in Russia in 1919*, p. 47

11. Lenin, 'Theses on the Question of the Immediate Conclusion of a Separate and Annexationist Peace', 7 (20) January 1918, *LCW*, Vol. 26, p. 444

12. Ibid., p. 447

13. Quoted in Volkogonov, *Lenin*, p. 183

14. Lenin, 'Theses on the Question of the Immediate Conclusion of a Separate and Annexationist Peace', 7 (20) January 1918, *LCW*, Vol. 26, pp. 447-8

15. Ibid., p. 448

16. Ibid.

17. Quoted in Volkogonov, *Lenin*, p. 184

18. Lenin, 'Theses on the Question of the Immediate Conclusion of a Separate and Annexationist Peace', 7 (20) January 1918, *LCW*, Vol. 26, p. 450

19. Quoted in Carr, *The Bolshevik Revolution, 1917-1923*, Vol. 3, p. 33

20. Lenin, *Meeting of the Communist Group of the All-Russia Central Council of Trade Unions*, 'Reply to the Debate on the Report on Concessions', 11 April 1921, *LCW*, Vol. 42, p. 293

21. Price, *Dispatches From the Revolution: Russia 1916-18*, p. 110

22. Lenin, 'Afterword to the Theses on the Question of the Immediate Conclusion of a Separate and Annexationist Peace', 8-11 (21-24) January 1918, *LCW*, Vol. 42, pp. 451-2

23. *The Bolsheviks and the October Revolution: CC Minutes*, p. 178

24. Ibid., p. 179

25. Ibid., p. 180

26. Ibid., p. 213

27. Ibid., p. 215

28. Ibid., p. 215, emphasis in original

29. Lenin, 'The Revolutionary Phrase', *Pravda*, No. 31, 21 February 1918, *LCW*, Vol. 27, p. 20

30. Lenin, 'The Itch', *Pravda*, No. 33, 22 February 1918, ibid., p. 37, emphasis in original

31. Lenin, 'Peace or War?', *Pravda*, No. 34, 23 February 1918, ibid, p. 41

32. Lenin, 'Speeches at a Meeting of the CC of the RSDLP(B)', 23 February 1918, *LCW*, Vol. 36, p. 479

33. *The Bolsheviks and the October Revolution: CC Minutes*, p. 218

34. Lenin, 'A Painful But Necessary Lesson', *Pravda*, No. 35, 25 February 1918, *LCW*, Vol. 27, pp. 64-5, emphasis in original

35. Ibid., p. 65, emphasis in original

36. Quoted in Lenin, 'Strange and Monstrous', *Pravda*, Nos. 37 and 38, 28 February and 1 March 1918, ibid., p. 68

37. Ibid.

38. Quoted ibid., p. 69

39. Lenin, 'Political Report of the Central Committee', 7 March 1918, *Extraordinary Seventh Congress of the RCP(B)*, ibid., p. 95

40. Ibid., p. 97

41. Ibid., p. 101

42. Ibid., p. 98

43. Lenin, 'Reply to the Debate on the Political Report of the Central Committee', 8 March 1918, ibid., p. 111

44. Ibid., p. 113

45. Trotsky, *How the Revolution Armed*, Vol. 1, pp. 66-7

27. Fighting for Survival

1. Lenin, *Extraordinary Fourth All-Russia Congress of Soviets*, 'Reply to the Debate on the Report on Ratification of the Peace Treaty', 15 March 1918, *LCW*, Vol. 27, p. 196

2. Lenin, 'Speech in the Moscow Soviet of Workers', Peasants' and Red Army Deputies', 12 March 1918, ibid., p. 166

3. Price, *Dispatches From the Revolution*, p. 119

4. Serge, *Year One of the Russian Revolution*, p. 236

5. Quoted in Serge, *Year One of the*

Russian Revolution, p. 185

6. Ibid., p. 188

7. Ibid., p. 191

8. Lenin, 'The Chief Task of Our Day', 11 March 1918, *LCW*, Vol. 27, p. 161, emphasis in original

9. Lenin, 'Speech Delivered at the First (Inaugural) All-Russia Congress of Mineworkers', April 1920, *LCW*, Vol. 30, p. 500

10. Lenin, 'Moscow Party Workers' Meeting', 'Report on the Attitude of the Proletariat to Petty-bourgeois Democrats', 27 November 1918, *LCW*, Vol. 28, p. 216

11. Lenin, *Extraordinary Seventh Congress of the RCP(B)*, 'Political Report of the Central Committee', 7 March, ibid., p. 95

12. Lenin, *The State and Revolution*, August – September 1917, *LCW*, Vol. 25, p. 486, emphasis in original

13. Lenin, *Eighth Congress of the RCP(B)*, 'Report on the Party Programme', 19 March 1919, *LCW*, Vol. 29, p. 183, emphasis in original

14. Lenin, *Extraordinary Seventh Congress of the RCP(B)*, 'Report on the Review of the Programme and on Changing the Name of the Party', 8 March 1918, *LCW*, Vol. 27, pp. 131-3

15. Lenin, 'Moscow Party Workers' Meeting', 'Report on the Attitude of the Proletariat to Petty-bourgeois Democrats', 27 November 1918, *LCW*, Vol. 28, p. 215

16. Lenin, 'Report at the Second All-Russia Trade Union Congress', 20 January 1919, ibid., pp. 424-5

17. Lenin, *The Achievements and Difficulties of the Soviet Government*, 17 April 1919, *LCW*, Vol. 29, pp. 69-73

18. Lenin, *Eighth Congress of the RCP(B)*, 'Report on Work in the Countryside', 23 March, ibid., p. 208

19. Lenin, *The Immediate Tasks of the Soviet Government*, March – April 1918, ibid., p. 248, emphasis in original

20. Lenin, *'Left-Wing' Childishness and the Petty-bourgeois Mentality*, *Pravda*, Nos.

88-90, 9-11 May, ibid., pp. 349-50, emphasis in original

21. Lenin, *Eighth Congress of the RCP(B)*, 'Report of the CC', 18 March 1919, *LCW*, Vol. 29, p. 156

22. Ibid.

23. Lenin, *The Immediate Tasks of the Soviet Government*, March – April 1918, *LCW*, Vol. 27, p. 275

24. Lenin, 'Telegram to Samarkand Communists', 27 June 1921, *LCW*, Vol. 45, pp. 195-6, emphasis in original

25. Lenin, *Third All-Russia Congress of Soviets of Workers', Soldiers' and Peasants' Deputies*, 'Report on the Activities of the Councils People's Commissars', 11 (24) January 1918, *LCW*, Vol. 26, pp. 467-8

26. Quoted in Liebman, *Leninism Under Lenin*, p. 335

27. Lenin, *Session of the All-Russia CEC*, 'Report on the Immediate Tasks of the Soviet Government', 29 April 1918, *LCW*, Vol. 27, p. 297

28. Quoted in Avrich, *The Russian Anarchists*, p. 164

29. Lenin, *Eighth Congress of the RCP(B)*, 'Report of the CC', 18 March 1919, *LCW*, Vol. 29, p. 154

30. Ibid., pp. 154-5

31. Lenin, *Extraordinary Seventh Congress of the RCP(B)*, 'Political Report of the Central Committee', 7 March 1918, *LCW*, Vol. 27, p. 106

32. Lenin, *'Left-Wing' Childishness and the Petty-bourgeois Mentality*, *Pravda*, Nos. 88-90, 9-11 May, ibid., p. 340, emphasis in original

33. Ibid.

34. Lenin, *'Left-Wing' Childishness and the Petty-bourgeois Mentality*, *Pravda*, Nos. 88-90, 9-11 May, ibid., pp. 335-6

35. Ibid., p. 336, emphasis in original

36. Ibid., p. 337, emphasis in original

37. From *Seventeen Moments in Soviet History*, www.marxists.org/history/ussr/events/revolution/documents/1918/05/13.htm (accessed 14 December 2023)

38. Lenin, *Joint Session of the All-Russian*

Central Executive Committee, the
Moscow Soviet of Workers', Peasants'
and Red Army Deputies and the Trade
Unions, 'Report on Combating the
Famine', 4 June 1918, *LCW*, Vol. 27,
pp. 425-31

39. Ibid., p. 435
40. Quoted in Liebman, *Lenin Under
Leninism*, p. 284
41. Lenin, *Fifth All-Russia Congress of
Soviets of Workers', Peasants', Soldiers'
and Red Army Deputies*, 'Report of the
Council of People's Commissars', 5 July
1918, *LCW*, Vol. 27, p. 526
42. Lenin, *Extraordinary Seventh Congress
of the RCP(B)*, 'Political Report of the
Central Committee', 7 March 1918,
ibid., p. 105
43. Lenin, *The Tax in Kind*, 21 April 1921,
LCW, Vol. 32, p. 339, emphasis in
original
44. Lenin, *Session of the All-Russia CEC*,
'Reply to the Debate on the Report on
the Immediate Tasks', 29 April 1918,
LCW, Vol. 27, p. 310, emphasis in
original
45. Ibid., p. 309
46. Carr, *The Bolshevik Revolution, 1917-
1923*, Vol. 2, pp. 110-1
47. Quoted in Souvarine, *Stalin*, p. 169
48. Lenin, *Session of the All-Russia CEC*,
'Report on the Immediate Tasks of the
Soviet Government', 29 April 1918,
LCW, Vol. 27, p. 303
49. Ibid., p. 299

28. The Civil War Begins

1. Quoted in Serge, *Year One of the
Russian Revolution*, pp. 231-2
2. Trotsky, *Diary in Exile, 1935*, p. 80
3. Ibid., pp. 80-1, emphasis in original
4. Lockhart, *Memoirs of a British Agent*,
p. 304
5. Lockhart, *Diaries*, Vol. 1, p. 39
6. Quoted in Montefiore, *The Romanovs*,
p. 630
7. Ibid.
8. Serge, *Memoirs of a Revolutionary,
1901-1941*, p. 121

9. Carr, *The Bolshevik Revolution, 1917-
1923*, Vol. 2, p. 99
10. Brailsford, *The Russian Workers'
Republic*, p. 18
11. Serge, *Year One of the Russian
Revolution*, p. 262
12. Price, *Dispatches From the Revolution*,
p. 128
13. Ibid., p. 141
14. Ibid.
15. Ransome, *Six Weeks in Russia in 1919*,
p. 51
16. Lenin, *Extraordinary Seventh Congress
of the RCP(B)*, 'Political Report of the
Central Committee', 7 March, *LCW*,
Vol. 27, p. 99
17. Trotsky, *On Lenin*, pp. 102-3
18. Ibid., p. 103
19. Quoted in Fotieva, *Pages from Lenin's
Life*, p. 124
20. Quoted in Krausz, *Reconstructing Lenin*,
p. 69
21. See Lenin, *'Left-Wing' Communism: An
Infantile Disorder*, *LCW*, Vol. 31, p. 37
22. Quoted in Shub, *Lenin*, p. 362
23. Trotsky, *Terrorism and Communism*,
pp. 78-9
24. Quoted in Serge, *Year One of the
Russian Revolution*, p. 288
25. Lenin, 'Letter to American Workers',
Pravda, No. 178, 20 August 1918,
LCW, Vol. 28, p. 71, emphasis in
original
26. Quoted in Serge, *Year One of the
Russian Revolution*, p. 290
27. Trotsky, *How the Revolution Armed*,
Vol. 1, p. 310
28. Lenin, 'To YM Sverdlov and LD
Trotsky', 1 October 1918, *LCW*, Vol.
35, pp. 364-5, emphasis in original
29. Lenin, 'Telegram to All Soviets of
Deputies, To Everyone', 10 November
1918, *LCW*, Vol. 28, p. 179
30. *The German Revolution and the Debate
on Soviet Power*, p. 15

29. Founding the Comintern

1. Quoted in Wollenberg, *The Red Army*,
p. 103

2. Quoted in Braunthal, *History of the International*, Vol. 2, p. 165

3. Quoted in Carr, *The Bolshevik Revolution, 1917-1923*, Vol. 3, p. 128

4. Ransome, *Six Weeks in Russia in 1919*, pp. 169-70

5. Lenin, *First Congress of the Communist International*, 'Speech at the Opening Session of the Congress', 2 March 1919, *LCW*, Vol. 28, p. 455

6. Ibid., 'Theses and Report on Bourgeois Democracy and the Dictatorship of the Proletariat', 4 March, p. 471

7. Ibid., p. 474

8. Ransome, *Six Weeks in Russia in 1919*, pp. 167-8

9. Ibid., pp. 120-1

10. Quoted in Read, *The World on Fire*, p. 58

11. Quoted in Sewell, *In the Cause of Labour*, p. 158

12. Quoted in Serge, *Year One of the Russian Revolution*, p. 212, emphasis in original

13. Quoted in *Lenin*, Progress Publishers, p. 366

14. Lenin, 'All Out for the Fight Against Denikin!', *Bulletin of the CC, RCP(B)*, No. 4, 9 July 1919, *LCW*, Vol. 29, p. 452

15. Ibid., pp. 452-3, emphasis in original

16. Lenin, *Extraordinary Plenary Meeting of the Moscow Soviet of Workers' and Red Army Deputies*, 'Resolution on the Report on the Domestic and Foreign Situation of the Soviet Republic', 3 April 1919, p. 272

17. Lenin, *First All-Russia Congress on Adult Education*, 'Deception of the People with Slogans of Freedom and Equality', 19 May 1919, p. 364, emphasis in original

18. Stites, *Revolutionary Dreams*, p. 140

19. Lenin, 'The Salaries of High-ranking Office Employees and Officials', 20 November (3 December) 1917, *LCW*, Vol. 42, pp. 37-8

20. Liebman, *Leninism Under Lenin*, p. 352

21. Ibid.

22. Lenin, *Session of the Petrograd Soviet*, 'Replies to Written Questions', 12 March 1919, *LCW*, Vol. 29, p. 35

23. Ibid.

24. Zagorsky, *Wages and Regulation of Conditions of Labour in the USSR*, pp. 176-8

25. Lawton, *Economic History of Soviet Russia*, Vol. 2, pp. 359-61

26. Serge, *Memories of a Revolutionary, 1901-1941*, p. 79

27. Stites, *Revolutionary Dreams*, p. 142

28. Serge, *Memories of a Revolutionary, 1901-1941*, p. 101

29. Zetkin, *Reminiscences of Lenin*, p. 10

30. Balabanoff, *Impressions of Lenin*, p. 13

31. Quoted in *Lenin*, Progress Publishers, p. 72

32. Quoted ibid., p. 69

33. Stites, *Revolutionary Dreams*, p. 142

34. Lenin, 'Telegram to the Kursk Extraordinary Commission', 6 January 1919, *LCW*, Vol. 36, p. 499

30. The Red Army

1. Lenin, *Eighth Congress of the RCP(B)*, 'Report of the CC', 18 March 1919, *LCW*, Vol. 29, p. 152

2. Ibid., p. 153

3. Trotsky, *My Life*, p. 386

4. Quoted in Deutscher, *The Prophet Armed*, p. 412

5. Trotsky, *How the Revolution Armed*, Vol. 1, pp. 74-5

6. Trotsky, *My Life*, pp. 394-5

7. Radek, 'The Organiser of Victory', 1923, *Military Writings of Leon Trotsky*, p. 11

8. Serge, *Year One of the Russian Revolution*, pp. 310-1

9. Lockhart, *Memories of a British Agent*, p. 242

10. Ibid., p. 248

11. Trotsky, *Writings on Britain*, p. 518-9

12. Quoted in Volkogonov, *Lenin*, p. 202

13. Read, *The World on Fire*, p. 13

14. Quoted ibid.

15. Ibid., p. 23

16. Quoted in Gilley, 'Beyond Petliura: The Ukrainian National Movement and the

1919 Pogroms', *East European Jewish Affairs*, Vol. 47, No. 1, 2017, pp. 52-3

17. Babel, *Complete Works*, p. 275

18. Astashkevich, *Gendered Violence: Jewish Women in the Pogroms of 1917 to 1921*, p. 63

19. Quoted ibid., p. 64

20. Quoted ibid.

21. Quoted in Serge, *Year One of the Russian Revolution*, p. 305

22. Churchill, 'Zionism Versus Bolshevism', *Illustrated Sunday Herald*, 8 February 1920

23. Serge, *Year One of the Russian Revolution*, p. 307

24. Figes, *A People's Tragedy*, p. 649, all quotes, emphasis added

25. Krausz, *Reconstructing Lenin*, p. 239

26. Ibid.

27. Ibid., pp. 240-1

28. Quoted in Serge, *Year One of the Russian Revolution*, p. 298

29. *Joseph Stalin*, pp. 47-8, emphasis in original

30. Popov, *Outline History of the CPSU*, Vol. 2, pp. 78-9

31. Gorky, *Vladimir Ilyich Lenin*, also quoted in Deutscher, *The Prophet Armed*, p. 430

32. Balabanoff, *Impressions of Lenin*, p. 119

33. Lenin, 'Reply to a Peasant's Question', *Pravda*, No. 35, 15 February 1919, *LCW*, Vol. 36, p. 500

34. Quoted in Trotsky, *My Life*, p. 415

35. Quoted ibid., pp. 415-6

36. Quoted ibid., p. 416

37. *The Errors of Trotskyism*, CPGB, p. 5

38. Volkogonov, *Lenin*, p. 253

31. War Communism

1. Lenin, *Eleventh Congress of the RCP(B)*, 'Political Report of the CC', 27 March 1922, *LCW*, Vol. 33, p. 302

2. Ransome, *The Crisis in Russia*, p. 16

3. Brailsford, *The Russian Workers' Republic*, p. 16

4. Lenin, 'Letter to the Workers and Peasants Apropos of the Victory over Kolchak', *Pravda*, No. 190, 24 August

1919, *LCW*, Vol. 29, p. 555

5. Ransome, *The Crisis in Russia*, p. 21

6. Carr, *The Bolshevik Revolution, 1917-1923*, Vol. 2, p. 195

7. Quoted in Liebman, *Leninism Under Lenin*, p. 347

8. Lenin, *Tenth Congress of the RCP(B)*, 'Summing-up Speech on the Report of the CC', 9 March 1921, *LCW*, Vol. 32, p. 199

9. Goldman, *My Disillusionment in Russia*, pp. 8-9

10. Brailsford, *The Russian Workers' Republic*, pp. 23-4

11. Lenin, *Seventh All-Russia Congress of Soviets*, 'Report of the All-Russia CEC and the Council of People's Commissars', 5 December 1919, *LCW*, Vol. 30, p. 228

12. Meakin, 'Labour Mission in Russia', 11 June 1920, in 'The Russian Revolution as Never Seen Before', 5 November 2021, *In Defence of Marxism*

13. Brailsford, *The Russian Workers' Republic*, p. 27

14. Ransome, *Six Weeks in Russia in 1919*, p. 73

15. Quoted in Serge, *Year One of the Russian Revolution*, p. 355

16. Lenin, 'Fourth Anniversary of the October Revolution', *Pravda*, No. 234, 14 October 1921, *LCW*, Vol. 33, p. 58

17. Lenin, *Eleventh Congress of the RCP(B)*, 'Political Report of the CC', 27 March 1922, ibid., pp. 304-5

18. Lenin, *Ninth Congress of the RCP(B)*, 'Opening Speech', 29 March 1920, *LCW*, Vol. 30, p. 442

19. Lenin, 'Report of the CC', 29 March 1920, ibid., p. 443

20. Ibid., p. 450

21. See *LCW*, Vol. 31, p. 516

22. Ibid., p. 454

23. Quoted in Read, *The World on Fire*, p. 329

24. Lenin, *Tenth Congress of the RCP(B)*, 'Report on the Political Work of the CC', 8 March 1921, *LCW*, Vol. 32, p. 173

25. Carr, *The Bolshevik Revolution, 1917-*

1923, Vol. 1, p. 170

26. Quoted ibid., pp. 171-2, both quotes

27. Quoted ibid., p. 172

28. Brailsford, *The Russian Workers' Republic*, pp. 111-2

29. Ransome, *Six Weeks in Russia*, pp. 161-2

30. Carr, *The Bolshevik Revolution, 1917-1923*, Vol. 1, p. 175

31. Brailsford, *The Russian Workers' Republic*, p. 116

32. Lenin, *Extraordinary Plenary Meeting of the Moscow Soviet of Workers' and Red Army Deputies*, 'Report on the Domestic and Foreign Situation of the Soviet Republic', 3 April 1919, *LCW*, Vol. 29, p. 263, both quotes

33. Ibid., p. 264

34. Lenin, 'Letter to American Workers', *Pravda*, No. 178, 20 August 1918, *LCW*, Vol. 28, p. 74

35. Ibid., pp. 71-2

36. Ibid., pp. 72-3, emphasis in original

37. Ibid., p. 75, emphasis in original

38. Lenin, 'Letter to the British Workers', *Pravda*, No. 130, 30 May 1920, *LCW*, Vol. 31, p. 142

39. Quoted in Carr, *The Bolshevik Revolution, 1917-1923*, Vol. 1, pp. 349-50

40. Lenin, 'Telegram to the Revolutionary Military Council of the 11th Cavalry Army', 10 March 1921, *LCW*, Vol. 35, p. 479

32. A School of Communism

1. Brailsford, *The Russian Workers' Republic*, p. 148

2. Rosmer, *Lenin's Moscow*, p. 49

3. Lenin, *The Second Congress of the Communist International*, 'Report on the International Situation and the Fundamental Tasks of the Communist International', 19 July 1920, *LCW*, Vol. 31, pp. 217-8

4. Ibid., p. 219

5. Ibid., p. 222

6. Ibid., p. 224

7. Ibid., p. 226

8. Ibid., p. 227

9. Ibid.

10. Ibid., p. 234

11. Lenin, *'Left-Wing' Communism: An Infantile Disorder*, April – May 1920, ibid., p. 22, emphasis in original

12. Ibid., p. 24, emphasis in original

13. Ibid., pp. 25-6, emphasis in original

14. Ibid., p. 34, emphasis in original

15. Ibid., p. 38

16. Ibid., p. 39

17. Ibid., p. 53

18. Ibid., p. 56

19. Ibid., p. 58, emphasis in original

20. Ibid., p. 61

21. Ibid., pp. 63-4

22. Ibid., pp. 79-80, emphasis in original

23. Ibid., p. 88, emphasis in original

24. Ibid.

25. Lenin, *The Second Congress of the Communist International*, 'Speech on the Role of the Communist Party', 23 July 1920, ibid., pp. 238-9

26. 'Session 2. Role and structure of the Communist Party, part 1, 23 July', *Workers of the World and Oppressed Peoples, Unite! Proceedings and Documents of the Second Congress of the Communist International*, Vol. 1, pp. 160-1

27. Lenin, *The Second Congress of the Communist International*, 'Speech on Affiliation to the British Labour Party', 6 August 1920, *LCW*, Vol. 31, pp. 257-8

28. Ibid., p. 260, emphasis added

29. Lenin, *'Left-Wing' Communism: An Infantile Disorder*, April – May 1920, ibid., p. 88, emphasis in original

30. Lenin, *The Second Congress of the Communist International*, 'Speech on Affiliation to the British Labour Party', 6 August 1920, p. 260

31. Ibid., p. 263

32. Gallacher, *Revolt on the Clyde*, p. 251-3

33. Lenin, 'The Terms of Admission into the Communist International', July 1920, *LCW*, Vol. 31, p. 206

34. Ibid.

35. Ibid., p. 207

36. Ibid., p. 563, footnote
37. 'Session 14. Statutes, Evening, 4 August', *Workers of the World and Oppressed Peoples, Unite! Proceedings and Documents of the Second Congress of the Communist International*, Vol. 2, p. 696
38. Lenin, *The Second Congress of the Communist International*, 'Report of the Commission on the National and the Colonial Questions', 26 July 1920, p. 244
39. Ibid.

33. Limits of War Communism

1. Brailsford, *The Russian Workers' Republic*, pp. 204-5
2. Lenin, 'The Party Crisis', *Pravda*, No. 13, 21 January 1921, *LCW*, Vol. 32, p. 43, both quotes
3. Quoted in Carr, *The Bolshevik Revolution, 1917-1923*, Vol. 2, p. 222
4. Lenin, *Tenth Congress of the RCP(B)*, 'Report on the Political Work of the CC', 8 March 1921, *LCW*, Vol. 32, p. 176
5. Trotsky, 'The New Course', *The Challenge of the Left Opposition*, p. 82
6. Carr, *The Bolshevik Revolution, 1917-1923*, Vol. 2, pp. 219-20
7. Ibid., p. 374
8. Lenin, *The Eighth All-Russia Congress of Soviets*, 'Report on the Work of the Council of People's Commissars', 22 December 1920, *LCW*, Vol. 31, pp. 510-1
9. Lenin, *The Eighth All-Russia Congress of Soviets*, 'Reply to the Debate on the Report on Concessions', 21 December 1920, *LCW*, Vol. 42, p. 241
10. Lenin, *The Eighth All-Russia Congress of Soviets*, 'Report on the Work of the Council of People's Commissars', 22 December 1920, *LCW*, Vol. 31, p. 509
11. Brailsford, *The Russian Workers' Republic*, p. 69
12. Lenin, *The Eighth All-Russia Congress of Soviets*, 'Report on the Work of the Council of People's Commissars', 22 December 1920, *LCW*, Vol. 31, p. 517

13. Lenin, *Second All-Russia Congress of Political Education Departments*, 'The New Economic Policy and the Tasks of the Political Education Departments', 17 October 1921, *LCW*, Vol. 33, pp. 65-6
14. Ibid., p. 69
15. *The Case of Leon Trotsky*, p. 473
16. Lenin, *Tenth Congress of the RCP(B)*, 'Report on the Political Work of the CC of the RCP(B)', 8 March 1921, *LCW*, Vol. 32, p. 183
17. Serge, *Memoirs of a Revolutionary 1901-1941*, pp. 128-9
18. *Lenin – A Biography*, p. 310
19. Lenin, *Eleventh Congress of the RCP(B)*, 'Political Report of the CC', 27 March 1922, *LCW*, Vol. 33, p. 306
20. Ibid., p. 307
21. Lenin, 'To AD Tsyurupa', 24 January 1922, *LCW*, Vol. 35, p. 535
22. Schapiro, *The Communist Party of the Soviet Union*, p. 245
23. Lenin, 'To DI Kursky', 17 January 1922, *LCW*, Vol. 35, p. 534
24. Lenin, 'To the Presidium of the Supreme Economic Council', 16 October 1922, ibid., p. 556
25. Lenin, 'To AD Tsyurupa', July 1918, *LCW*, Vol. 44, p. 121
26. Lenin, 'To AD Metelev', 30 November 1921, *LCW*, Vol. 45, pp. 390-1, emphasis in original
27. Lenin, 'To DI Kursky', before 5 April 1919, *LCW*, Vol. 44, emphasis in original
28. Quoted in *Lenin: A Biography*, Progress Publishers, 1965, p. 68
29. Lenin, 'To AD Tsyurupa', 24 January 1922, *LCW*, Vol. 35, p. 537, emphasis in original
30. See Lenin, 'The International and Domestic Situation of the Soviet Republic', *LCW*, Vol. 33, p. 223

34. New Economic Policy and its Implications

1. Lenin, 'To Clara Zetkin and Paul Levi', 16 April 1921, *LCW*, Vol. 45, p. 125

2. Lenin, 'Notes for a Speech at the Tenth Congress of the RCP(B)', March 1921, *LCW*, Vol. 36, p. 535

3. Lenin, *Tenth Congress of the RCP(B)*, 'Report on the Substitution of a Tax in Kind for the Surplus Grain Appropriation System', 15 March 1921, *LCW*, Vol. 32, p. 215

4. Ibid., pp. 215-6

5. Ibid., p. 219

6. Lenin, 'Notes for a Speech at the Tenth Congress of the RCP(B)', March 1921, *LCW*, Vol. 36, p. 536, emphasis in original

7. Trotsky, *The Revolution Betrayed*, p. 15

8. Lenin, *Tenth Congress of the RCP(B)*, 'Report on the Substitution of a Tax in Kind for the Surplus Grain Appropriation System', 15 March 1921, *LCW*, Vol. 32, p. 225

9. Lenin, 'To the Russian Colony in North America', 14 November 1922, *LCW*, Vol. 42, p. 426

10. Quoted in Carr, *The Bolshevik Revolution, 1917-1923*, Vol. 2, p. 286

11. Lenin, *Tenth Congress of the RCP(B)*, 'Report on the Political Work of the CC of the RCP(B)', 8 March 1921, *LCW*, Vol. 32, p. 179

12. Ibid., 'Summing-up Speech on the Report of the CC of the RCP(B)', 9 March 1921, p. 199

13. Ibid., 'Report on Party Unity and the Anarcho-Syndicalist Deviation', 16 March 1921, p. 252

14. Ibid., 'Summing-up Speech on Party Unity and the Anarcho-Syndicalist Deviation', 16 March 1921, p. 258

15. Lenin, *Sochineniya*, Vol. 43, p. 403, quoted in Peter Roberts and Weston, *Women, Family and the Russian Revolution*, p. 393

16. Lenin, *Tenth Congress of the RCP(B)*, 'Report on the Political Work of the CC of the RCP(B)', 8 March 1921, *LCW*, Vol. 32, p, 178

17. Ibid., p. 177

18. Ibid., 'Preliminary Draft Resolution of the Tenth Congress of the RCP on Party Unity', p. 244

19. Carr, *The Bolshevik Revolution, 1917-1923*, Vol. 1, p. 201

20. Quoted ibid., p. 200

21. Lenin, *Tenth Congress of the RCP(B)*, 'Summing-up Speech on Party Unity and the Anarcho-Syndicalist Deviation', 16 March 1921, *LCW*, Vol. 32, p. 257

22. Carr, *The Bolshevik Revolution, 1917-1923*, Vol. 1, p. 188

23. Ibid., p. 192

24. Lenin, 'The Party Crisis', *Pravda*, No. 13, 19 January 1921, *LCW*, Vol. 32, p. 52

25. Lenin, *Tenth Congress of the RCP(B)*, 'Remarks on Ryazanov's Amendment to the Resolution on Party Unity', 16 March 1921, *LCW*, Vol. 32, p. 261, emphasis added

26. Ibid., emphasis added

27. Trotsky, *Writings, 1935-36*, pp. 185-6

28. Quoted in Medvedev, *Let History Judge*, p. 17

29. Quoted in Trotsky, *Lenin's Fight Against Stalinism*, p. 42, also Souvarine, *Stalin*, p. 285

30. Quoted in Trotsky, *Writings, 1929*, p. 40

35. The Impact of World Events

1. Trotsky, *The First Five Years of the Communist International*, p. 306

2. Lenin, *Third Congress of the Communist International*, 'Theses for a Report on the Tactics of the RCP', *LCW*, Vol. 32, p. 457-8, emphasis in original

3. *The Communist International*, Vol. 1, p. 218

4. Lenin, 'To Clara Zetkin and Paul Levi', 16 April 1921, *LCW*, Vol. 45, p. 124, emphasis in original

5. Quoted in Zetkin, *Reminiscences of Lenin*, p. 23

6. *Minutes of the Politburo of the CPSU*, 18 March 1926, quoted in Trotsky, *The Stalin School of Falsification*, pp. 33-4

7. Lenin, 'To GY Zinoviev', 10 June 1921, *LCW*, Vol. 42, pp. 319-21, emphasis in original

8. Ibid., p. 321, emphasis in original

9. Ibid., pp. 322-3, emphasis in original
10. Lenin, *Third Congress of the Communist International*, 'Speech in Defence of the Tactics of the Communist International', 1 July 1921, *LCW*, Vol. 32, p. 468
11. Ibid., pp. 469-70
12. Lenin, 'To Clara Zetkin and Paul Levi', 16 April 1921, *LCW*, Vol. 45, pp. 124-5
13. Quoted in Zetkin, *Reminiscences of Lenin*, p. 25
14. Lenin, *Third Congress of the Communist International*, 'Speech in Defence of the Tactics of the Communist International', 1 July 1921, *LCW*, Vol. 32, p. 470
15. Trotsky, *The First Five Years of the Communist International*, p. 343
16. Zetkin, *Reminiscences of Lenin*, p. 31
17. Quoted ibid., p. 24
18. Lenin, 'A Letter to the German Communists', 14 August 1921, *LCW*, Vol. 32, pp. 522-3
19. Ibid., pp. 513-5
20. Ibid., p. 515

36. Bureaucratic Deformations

1. Lenin, 'The Party Crisis', 19 January 1921, *LCW*, Vol. 32, p. 48
2. The 'Question of Nationalities or "Autonomisation"', 30 December 1922, p. 605
3. Ibid., p. 25
4. Lenin, *Eighth Congress of the RCP(B)*, 'Report on the Party Programme', 19 March 1919, *LCW*, Vol. 29, p. 183
5. Lenin, *Session of the Petrograd Soviet*, 'Replies to Written Questions', 12 March 1919, ibid., pp. 32-3
6. Ibid., p. 33
7. Lenin, *Second All-Russia Congress of Political Education Departments*, 'The New Economic Policy and the Tasks of the Political Education Departments', 17 October 1921, *LCW*, Vol. 33, p. 72
8. Lenin, *The Achievements and Difficulties of the Soviet Government*, 17 April 1919, *LCW*, Vol. 29, p. 58

9. Lenin, 'Purging the Party', 20 September 1921, *LCW*, Vol. 33, p. 40
10. Brailsford, *The Russian Workers' Republic*, p. 99
11. Lenin, 'Speech Delivered at a Meeting of the Moscow Soviet of Workers' and Red Army Deputies', 6 March 1920, *LCW*, Vol. 30, pp. 415-6
12. Lenin, *Tenth Congress of the RCP(B)*, 'Report on the Political Work of the CC', 8 March 1921, *LCW*, Vol. 32, p. 191
13. Ibid., 'Speech on the Trade Unions', 14 March 1921, p. 213
14. Lenin, 'New Times and Old Mistakes in a New Guise', *Pravda*, No. 190, 20 August 1921, *LCW*, Vol. 33, p. 26
15. Ibid.
16. Lenin, 'Tasks of the Workers and Peasants' Inspection', 27 September 1921, ibid., p. 42
17. Ibid., p. 44, emphasis added
18. Lenin, 'To AL Sheinman', 28 February 1922, *LCW*, Vol. 36, p. 567, emphasis in original
19. Lenin, 'To N Osinsky', 12 April 1922, ibid., p. 578
20. Lenin, 'To AD Tysurupa', 21 February 1922, ibid., p. 566
21. Quoted in Trotsky, *Stalinism and Bolshevism*, in *Classics of Marxism: Volume Two*, p. 237
22. Lenin, *Eleventh Congress of the RCP(B)*, 'Political Report of the CC', 27 March 1922, *LCW*, Vol. 33, p. 286
23. Ibid.
24. Ibid., pp. 286-7, emphasis added
25. Ibid., p. 288
26. Ibid.
27. Ibid., pp. 288-9
28. Lenin, 'Outline of Speech at the Tenth All-Russia Congress of Soviets', December 1922, *LCW*, Vol. 36, pp. 588-9, emphasis in original
29. Lenin, *Eleventh Congress of the RCP(B)*, 'Political Report of the CC', 27 March 1922, *LCW*, Vol. 33, p. 304
30. Lenin, 'To GY Sokolnikov', 22 February 1922, *LCW*, Vol. 35, p. 549
31. Lenin, 'To Members of the Collegium

of the People's Commissariat for Workers' and Peasants' Inspection', 21 August 1922, *LCW*, Vol. 36, p. 580, emphasis in original

32. *The Trotsky Papers, 1917-1922*, Vol. 2, p. 647

33. Quoted in Service, *Lenin*, p. 439

34. Trotsky, *My Life*, p. 419

35. Lenin, 'To Lydia Fotieva', *LCW*, Vol. 45, p. 560, emphasis in original

37. The Growing Menace of the Bureaucracy

1. Lenin, 'The Trade Unions, the Present Situation and Trotsky's Mistakes', 30 December 1920, *LCW*, Vol. 32, p. 32

2. Lenin, 'To JV Stalin and MI Frumkin', 15 May 1922, *LCW*, Vol. 45, p. 549

3. *Lenin, A Biography*, Progress Publishers, 1966, p. 517

4. Lenin, 'Letter to JV Stalin for Members of the CC, RCP(B) Re the Foreign Trade Monopoly', 13 October 1922, *LCW*, Vol. 33, p. 375

5. Ibid., p. 377

6. Lenin, 'On the Establishment of the USSR – Letter to LB Kamenev for Members of the Politbureau', 26 September 1922, *LCW*, Vol. 42, p. 421

7. *Lenin, A Biography*, Moscow, 1966, p. 525

8. Lenin, 'Memo to the Political Bureau on Combating Dominant Nation Chauvinism', 6 October 1922, *LCW*, Vol. 33, p. 372, emphasis in original

9. Lenin, *Fourth Congress of the Communist International*, 'Five Years of the Russian Revolution and the Prospect of the World Revolution', 13 November 1922, *LCW*, Vol. 33, p. 418

10. Ibid., p. 421

11. Ibid., pp. 421-2

12. Ibid., p. 424

13. Lenin, *Fourth Congress of the Communist International*, 'Five Years of the Russian Revolution and the Prospects of the World Revolution', 13 November 1922, *LCW*, Vol. 33, pp. 428-9

14. Ibid., p. 430

15. Lenin, 'To LD Trotsky', 13 December 1922, *LCW*, Vol. 45, p. 601

16. Lenin, 'Re the Monopoly of Foreign Trade – To Comrade Stalin for the Plenary Meeting of the CC', 13 December 1922, *LCW*, Vol. 33, p. 457

17. Ibid., p. 458

18. Lenin, 'To JV Stalin for Members of the CC, RCP(B)', 15 December 1922, ibid., p. 460

19. Ibid., pp. 460-1

20. Lenin, 'To LD Trotsky', 15 December 1922, *LCW*, Vol. 45, p. 604

21. Lenin, 'To LD Trotsky', 15 December 1922, ibid., pp. 604-5

22. Ibid., p. 605

23. Lenin, 'To LD Trotsky', 21 December, 1922 p. 756, footnote

24. Lenin, ibid., p. 606

25. Quoted in Buranov, *Lenin's Will*, p. 23

26. Quoted ibid., p. 23, emphasis added

27. Lenin, 'Letter to the Congress', 23 December 1922, *LCW*, Vol. 36, p. 593

28. Lenin, 'Granting Legislative Functions to the State Planning Commission', 27 December 1922, ibid., pp. 598-9

29. Ibid., p. 29

30. Lenin, 'How We Should Reorganise the Workers' and Peasants' Inspection', 23 January 1923, *LCW*, Vol. 33, p. 481

31. Ibid.

32. Lenin, 'Better Fewer, But Better', *Pravda*, No. 49, 2 March 1923, ibid., pp. 487-9

33. Ibid., pp. 490-1

34. Ibid., p. 498

35. Ibid., p. 499

36. Lenin, 'The Question of Nationalities or "Autonomisation"', 30 December 1922, *LCW*, Vol. 36, p. 605

37. Ibid.

38. Ibid.

39. *Journal of Lenin's Duty Secretaries*, Entry by Lydia Fotieva, 30 January 1923, *LCW*, Vol. 42, p. 484

40. Lenin, 'The Question of Nationalities or "Autonomisation"', 30 December 1922, *LCW*, Vol. 36, p. 606

41. Ibid.

42. Ibid.

43. Ibid., p. 606-7
44. Ibid., p. 606
45. Ibid., p. 610

38. Clash with Stalin

1. Trotsky, *The Stalin School of Falsification*, p. 74
2. Lenin, 'Better Fewer, But Better', 2 March 1923, *LCW*, Vol. 33, p. 494
3. Rosmer, *Lenin's Moscow*, p. 169
4. Lenin, *Fourth Congress of the Communist International*, 'Five Years of the Russian Revolution and the Prospects of the World Revolution', 13 November 1922, *LCW*, Vol. 33, pp. 428
5. Lenin, 'Letter to LB Kamenev, AI Rykov and AD Tsyurupa', 13 December 1922, *LCW*, Vol. 42, pp. 432-3
6. Quoted ibid., pp. 608-9, footnote
7. Quoted in Lewin, *Lenin's Last Struggle*, p. 40
8. Quoted in 'Khruschev's 'Secret Speech' to the Twentieth Party Congress in 1956', in *Moscow Trials Anthology*, New Park, p. 16
9. Ibid.
10. Quoted in *Lenin: A Biography*, Progress Publishers, p. 447
11. *Journal of Lenin's Duty Secretaries*, Entry by LA Fotieva, 12 February 1923, *LCW*, Vol. 42, pp. 492-3
12. Ibid., 16 December 1922, p. 481
13. Ibid., Entry by MA Volodicheva, 23 December 1922, p. 481
14. Quoted in, *Lenin: A Biography*, p. 446
15. *Journal of Lenin's Duty Secretaries*, Entry by MA Volodicheva, 24 December 1922, *LCW*, Vol. 42, p. 482, emphasis in original
16. Lenin, 'Letter to the Congress', Part 2, 24 and 25 December 1922, *LCW*, Vol. 36, p. 594
17. Ibid., pp. 594-5
18. Ibid., 4 January 1923, p. 596
19. Trotsky, *My Life*, p. 426
20. *Journal of Lenin's Duty Secretaries*, Entry by LA Fotieva, 30 January 1923, *LCW*, Vol. 42, p. 484
21. Ibid., p. 620, footnote

22. Ibid., p. 621, footnote
23. Ibid., Entry by LA Fotieva, 30 January 1923, p. 484
24. Quoted in Lewin, *Lenin's Last Struggle*, p. 95
25. *Journal of Lenin's Duty Secretaries*, Entry by LA Fotieva, 30 January 1923, *LCW*, Vol. 42, p. 485
26. Ibid., Entry by MA Volodicheva, 2 February 1923, p. 486
27. Ibid., Entry by MI Glyasser, 5 February 1923, p. 489
28. Ibid., Entry by MA Volodicheva, 6 February 1923, p. 489-90
29. Ibid., Entry by LA Fotieva, 7 February 1923, p. 490
30. Ibid., Entry by LA Fotieva, 10 February 1923, p. 492
31. Ibid., Entry by MA Volodicheva, 5 March 1923, p. 493
32. Lenin, 'To LD Trotsky', 5 March 1923, *LCW*, Vol. 45, p. 607
33. Quoted in Trotsky, *The Stalin School of Falsification*, p. 69
34. Quoted in Trotsky, *My Life*, p. 429
35. *Journal of Lenin's Duty Secretaries*, Entry by MA Volodicheva, 5 March 1923, *LCW*, Vol. 42, p. 493
36. Lenin, 'To JV Stalin', 5 March 1923, *LCW*, Vol. 45, p. 607-8
37. Quoted in Trotsky, *The Stalin School of Falsification*, p. 71
38. Lenin, 'To PG Mdivani, FY Makharadza and Others', 6 March 1923, *LCW*, Vol. 45, p. 608
39. Quoted in Liebman, *Leninism Under Lenin*, p. 424
40. Quoted in Volkogonov, *Lenin*, p. 424
41. Fotieva, *Pages From Lenin's Life*, p. 193
42. *Journal of Lenin's Duty Secretaries*, Entry by MA Volodicheva, 6 March 1923, *LCW*, Vol. 42, p. 494
43. Quoted in Trotsky, *The Stalin School of Falsification*, p. 70

39. Fighting for His Life

1. Volkogonov, *Lenin*, p. 418
2. Lenin, 'Letter to the Congress', Part 2, 24 and 25 December 1922, *LCW*, Vol.

36, p. 594

3. Marx, *The Class Struggles in France, 1848 to 1850, MECW*, Vol. 10, p. 99
4. Quoted in Trotsky, *My Life*, p. 429
5. Trotsky, *Writings, 1929*, pp. 41-2
6. Sewell, *Germany 1918-1933: Socialism or Barbarism*, pp. 266-1
7. Trotsky, *The Challenge of the Left Opposition, 1923-25*, p. 165
8. Ibid., p. 52
9. Ibid., p. 58
10. Quoted in Stalin, *On the Opposition*, Peking, 1974, p. 74
11. Trotsky, *The Challenge of the Left Opposition, 1923-25*, p. 409
12. Quoted in Deutscher, *Stalin*, p. 275
13. Stalin, *Works*, Vol. 6, pp. 23-4
14. Carr, *The Interregnum, 1923-1924*, p. 340
15. See Lewin, M, *Lenin's Last Struggle*, pp. 175-6
16. Trotsky, *My Life*, p. 452
17. *Lenin: A Biography*, Moscow, 1965, p. 467
18. Ibid., pp. 466-7
19. Quoted in Service, *Lenin*, p. 479
20. Carr, *The Interregnum, 1923-1924*, p. 352
21. Trotsky, *On Lenin*, p. 203
22. *Daily Worker*, US edition, Thursday 24 January 1924
23. Trotsky, *On Lenin*, p. 186
24. *Daily Worker*, US edition, 25 January 1924
25. *Daily Worker*, US edition, 29 January 1924
26. Stalin, 'On the Death of Lenin', *Works*, Vol. 6, pp. 47-8
27. Quoted in Volkogonov, *Lenin*, p. 440
28. Marx, 'To Wilhelm Blos', 10 November 1877, *MECW*, Vol. 45, p. 288
29. Fotieva, *Pages From Lenin's Life*, p. 99
30. Schapiro, *The Communist Party of the Soviet Union*, p. 250
31. *Izvestia*, No. 38, 14 February 1960, in Lunacharsky, *Remembrances*
32. Balabanoff, *Impressions of Lenin*, p. 5
33. Raskolnikov, *Kronstadt and Petrograd in 1917*, p. 68
34. Fischer, *Life of Lenin*, p. 414

35. Quoted in Service, *Lenin*, p. 482
36. Quoted ibid., p. 483
37. Quoted in Gina Kolata, 'Lenin's Stroke: Doctor Has a Theory (and a Suspect)', *The New York Times*, 7 May 2012
38. Trotsky, *Stalin*, p. 524
39. Quoted in Gina Kolata, 'Lenin's Stroke: Doctor Has a Theory (and a Suspect)', *The New York Times*, 7 May 2012
40. Quoted ibid.
41. Volkogonov, *Lenin*, p. 35
42. Quoted in *Lenin – A Biography*, p. 459
43. Quoted in Medvedev, *Let History Judge*, p. 28
44. Broué, *The Bolshevik Party (CP) of the USSR*, translation by John Archer, p. 48
45. *Lenin – A Biography*, p. 459
46. Quoted in Broué, *The Bolshevik Party (CP) of the USSR*, translation by John Archer, p. 48
47. Krupskaya, 'The Lessons of October' in *The Errors of Trotskyism*, p. 365
48. Ibid., p. 370
49. Ibid., p. 371
50. Trepper, *The Great Game*, pp. 55-6

40. Lenin's Revolutionary Legacy

1. Ransome, *The Truth About Russia*, in *Six Weeks in Russia in 1919*, pp. 29-30
2. Hegel, *Philosophy of Right*, p. 295
3. Carr, *What is History?*, p. 55
4. Trotsky, *On Lenin*, p. 193
5. Trotsky, *Diary in Exile, 1935*, pp. 53-4
6. Trotsky, *Writings, 1932*, p. 316, emphasis in original
7. Trotsky, *Stalin*, pp. 259-60
8. Lenin, 'From the Destruction of the Old Social System to the Creation of the New', *Kommunistichesky Subbotnik*, 8 April 1920, *LCW*, Vol. 30, pp. 517-8
9. Lenin, *'Left-Wing' Communism: An Infantile Disorder*, April – May 1920, pp. 35-6, footnote
10. Dietzgen, *Philosophical Essays*, pp. 182-3
11. Lenin, *Moscow Party Workers' Meeting*, 'Reply to the Discussion of Report of the Attitude of the Proletariat to Petty-

bourgeois Democrats', 27 November 1918, *LCW*, Vol. 28, p. 217

12. Lenin, *'Left-Wing' Communism: An Infantile Disorder*, April – May 1920, pp. 25-6

13. Lenin, 'To Maxim Gorky', before 8 January 1913, *LCW*, Vol. 35, p. 71

14. Lenin, 'To Inessa Armand', 18 December 1916, ibid., p. 259

15. Trotsky, *History of the Russian Revolution*, Vol. 3, p. 1016

16. Lenin, 'Imperialism and the Split in Socialism', October 1916, *LCW*, Vol. 23, p. 118

17. Trotsky, *Writings, 1938-39*, p. 252-3

18. Trotsky, *Writings, 1932*, p. 289

19. Trotsky, *On Lenin*, p. 204

Lenin Against 'Socialism in One Country'

1. Stalin, *Lenin and Leninism*, p. 40, also in *The Theory and Practice of Leninism*, Communist Party of Great Britain, pp. 45-6

2. Stalin, *Works*, Vol. 6, p. 110

3. Lenin, 'On the Slogan for a United States of Europe', *Sotsial-Demokrat*, No. 44, 23 August 1915, *LCW*, Vol. 21, p. 342

4. Lenin, 'Meeting of the Petrograd Soviet of Workers' and Soldiers' Deputies', *Izvestia*, No. 207, 26 October (7 November) 1917, *LCW*, Vol. 26, p. 242

5. Lenin, Meeting of the All-Russia CEC', 'Speech and Resolution on the Resignation of a Group of People's Commissars from the Council of Peoples' Commissars', 4 (17) November 1917, *Izvestia*, No. 218, *LCW*, Vol. 26, pp. 292-3

6. Lenin, 'Speech at the First All-Russia Congress of the Navy', *Izvestia*, No. 235, 22 November (5 December) 1917, *LCW*, Vol. 26, p. 346

7. Lenin, 'For Bread and Peace', 14 (27) December 1917, *LCW*, Vol. 26, p. 386

8. Lenin, 'Speech at the Send-off of the Socialist Army's First Troop Trains', *Pravda*, No. 3, 1 (14) January 1918, *LCW*, Vol. 26, p. 420

9. Lenin, 'On the History of the Question of the Unfortunate Peace', 7 (20) January 1918, *LCW*, Vol. 26, p. 443-5, emphasis in original

10. Lenin, *Third All-Russia Congress of Soviets of Workers', Soldiers' and Peasants' Deputies*, 'Report on the Activities of the Council of People's Commissars', 11 (24) January 1918, *LCW*, Vol. 26, pp. 465-72

11. Lenin, *Extraordinary All-Russia Railwaymen's Congress*, 'Report of the Council of People's Commissars', 13 (26) January 1918, *LCW*, Vol. 26, p. 492

12. Lenin, 'An Unfortunate Peace', *Pravda*, No. 34, 24 February 1918, *LCW*, Vol. 27, pp. 51-2

13. Lenin, 'Strange and Monstrous', *Pravda*, Nos. 37-38, 28 February and 1 March 1918, *LCW*, Vol. 27, p. 72, emphasis in original

14. Lenin, *Third All-Russia Congress of Soviets of Workers', Soldiers' and Peasants' Deputies*, 'Summing-up Speech', 18 (31) January 1918, *LCW*, Vol. 26, p. 482

15. Lenin, *Extraordinary Seventh Congress of the RCP(B)*, 'Political Report of the CC', 7 March 1918, *LCW*, Vol. 27, pp. 92-8

16. Lenin, *Extraordinary Seventh Congress of the RCP(B)*, 'Resolution on War and Peace', 8 March 1918, *LCW*, Vol. 27, p. 119

17. Lenin, *Extraordinary Seventh Congress of the RCP(B)*, 'Report on the Review of the Programme and on Changing the Name of the Party', 8 March 1918, *LCW*, Vol. 27, p. 131

18. Lenin, 'The Chief Tasks of our Day', *Izvestia VTsIK*, No. 46, 11 March 1918, *LCW*, Vol. 27, pp. 160-1, emphasis in original

19. Lenin, *Extraordinary Fourth All-Russia Congress of Soviets*, 'Report on Ratification of the Peace Treaty', 14 March 1918, *LCW*, Vol. 27, pp. 188-90

20. Lenin, 'Speech in the Moscow Soviet of Workers' Peasants' and Red Army

Deputies', 23 April 1918, *LCW*, Vol. 27, p. 231

21. Lenin, *Session of the All-Russia CEC*, 'Report on the Immediate Tasks of the Soviet Government', 29 April 1918, *LCW*, Vol. 27, p. 290-3

22. Lenin, 'Six Theses on the Immediate Tasks of the Soviet Government', written between 30 April and 3 May 1918, *LCW*, Vol. 27, p. 314

23. Lenin, '"Left-Wing" Childishness and the Petty-bourgeois Mentality', *Pravda*, Nos. 88-90, 5 May 1918, *LCW*, Vol. 27, p. 340

24. Lenin, *Joint Meeting of the All-Russia CEC and the Moscow Soviet*, 'Report on Foreign Policy', 14 May 1918, *LCW*, Vol. 27, pp. 372-3

25. Lenin, *Fourth Conference of Trade Unions and Factory Committees of Moscow*, 'Report on the Current Situation', 27 June 1918, *LCW*, Vol. 27, p. 464

26. Lenin, 'Speech at a Joint Session of the All-Russia CEC, The Moscow Soviet, Factory Committees and Trade Unions of Moscow', 29 July 1918, *LCW*, Vol. 28, pp. 24-5

27. Lenin, 'Speech at a Meeting in Sokolniki District', 9 August 1918, *LCW*, Vol. 28, p. 53

28. Lenin, 'Letter to American Workers', *Pravda*, No. 178, 20 August 1918, *LCW*, Vol. 28, p. 75

29. Lenin, 'Speech at a Meeting in the Alexeyev People's House', *Izvestia*, No. 182, 23 August 1918, *LCW*, Vol. 28, pp. 77-8

30. Lenin, 'Speech at the First All-Russia Congress of Education', 28 August 1918, *LCW*, Vol. 28, p. 87

31. Lenin, 'Report at a Joint Session of the All-Russia CEC, The Moscow Soviet, Factory Committees and Trade Unions', 22 October 1918, *LCW*, Vol. 28, p. 123

32. Lenin, *Extraordinary Sixth All-Russia Congress of Soviets of Workers', Peasants', Cossacks' and Red Army Deputies*, 'Speech on the Anniversary of the Revolution', 6 November 1918, *LCW*, Vol. 28, pp. 145-50

33. Ibid., 'Speech on the International Situation', 8 November 1918, pp. 151-64

34. Lenin, 'The Valuable Admissions of Pitirim Sorokin', *Pravda*, No. 252, 20 November 1918, *LCW*, Vol. 28, p. 188

35. Lenin, *Eighth Congress of the RCP(B)*, 'Report of the CC', 18 March 1919, *LCW*, Vol. 29, pp. 153

36. Ibid., 'Speech Closing the Debate on the Party Programme', 19 March 1919, p. 187, emphasis in original

37. Lenin, *The Achievements and Difficulties of the Soviet Government*, 17 April 1919, *LCW*, Vol. 29, p. 58

38. Lenin, *Seventh All-Russia Congress of Soviets*, 'Report of the All-Russia CEC and the Council of People's Commissars', 5 December 1919, *LCW*, Vol. 30, pp. 207-8

39. Lenin, 'Speech Delivered at a Meeting of Cells' Secretaries of the Moscow Organisation of the RCP(B)', 26 November 1920, *LCW*, Vol. 31, p. 431

40. Lenin, 'Speech Delivered at a Meeting of Activists of the Moscow Organisation of the RCP(B), 6 December 1920, *LCW*, Vol. 31, p. 457

41. Lenin, *Eighth All-Russia Congress of Soviets*, 'Report on the Work of the Council of People's Commissars', 22 December 1920, *LCW*, Vol. 31, p. 493

42. Lenin, 'Speech Delivered at the Fourth All-Russia Congress of Garment Workers', 6 February 1921, *LCW*, Vol. 32, p. 113

43. Lenin, 'The New Economic Policy and the Tasks of the Political Education Departments', 17 October 1921, *LCW*, Vol. 33, p. 72

44. Lenin, 'Notes of a Publicist', written at the end of February 1922, *LCW*, Vol. 33, p. 206

Krupskaya on Lenin

1. Lenin, *What Is to Be Done?*, 1901-2, *LCW*, Vol. 5, pp. 470-1

2. Lenin, *Three Constitutions or Three Systems of Government*, June-July 1905, *LCW*, Vol. 8, pp. 557-9

3. Lenin, *LCW*, Vol. 24, p. 232

4. Lenin, *What the 'Friends of the People' Are and How They Fight the Social-Democrats*, 1894, *LCW*, Vol. 1, pp. 129-332

5. Lenin, *LCW*, Vol. 3

6. Lenin, *The Right of Nations to Self-Determination*, April-June 1914, *LCW*, Vol. 20, p. 433, footnote

7. Lenin, *A Characterisation of Economic Romanticism*, April-July 1897, *LCW*, Vol. 2, pp. 129-266

8. Lenin, *What the 'Friends of the People' Are and How They Fight the Social-Democrats*, 1894, *LCW*, Vol. 1, pp. 129-332

9. Lenin, *The Economic Content of Narodism and the Criticism of it in Mr Struve's Book*, 1895, *LCW*, Vol. 1, pp. 333-508

10. Lenin, *Karl Marx*, 1915, *LCW*, Vol. 21, pp. 43-91

11. Lenin, 'The Tasks of the Youth Leagues', 5-7 October 1920, *LCW*, Vol. 31, p. 288

12. Lenin, *The Agrarian Question and the 'Critics of Marx'*, 2-3 December 1901, *LCW*, Vol. 5, pp. 103-222

13. Lenin, 'Preface to *Friedrich Sorge Correspondence*', 1907, *LCW*, Vol. 12, p. 370

14. Ibid., p. 367

15. Ibid., p. 373

16. Lenin, 'Franz Mehring on the Second Duma', 1907, *LCW*, Vol. 12, pp. 387-8

17. Lenin, *What Is to Be Done?*, 1901-2, *LCW*, Vol. 5, p. 373

18. Lenin, *Two Tactics of Social-Democracy in the Democratic Revolution*, July 1905, *LCW*, Vol. 9, pp. 33-4

19. Ibid., p. 58

20. Ibid., p. 59

21. Ibid., p. 80

22. Ibid., p. 96

23. Ibid., pp. 137-8

24. Lenin, 'Preface to *Marx's Letters to Dr Kugelmann*', 1907, *LCW*, Vol. 12,
104-12

25. Lenin, 'Preface to *Friedrich Sorge Correspondence*', 1907, *LCW*, Vol. 12, p. 362

26. Lenin, *The State and Revolution*, 1917, *LCW*, Vol. 25, pp. 390-1

27. Lenin, 'On the Significance of Militant Materialism', 12 March 1922, *LCW*, Vol. 33, pp. 227-36

28. Ibid., pp. 233-4

29. Lenin, 'Conspectus of Lassalle's Book *The Philosophy of Heraclitus the Obscure of Ephesus*', 1915, *LCW*, Vol. 38, p. 341 and p. 354

30. Lenin, 'Once Again on the Trade Unions, the Current Situation and the Mistakes of Trotsky and Bukharin', 30 December 1920, *LCW*, Vol. 32, p. 94

31. Luxemburg, 'The Russian Revolution', *Rosa Luxemburg Speaks*, p. 375

32. Ibid., p. 395

Bibliography

Akhapkin, Yuri, *First Decrees of Soviet Power*, Lawrence & Wishart, 1970

Alexievich, Svetlana, *Second-hand Time*, Juggernaut Books, 2016

Ali, Tariq, *The Dilemmas of Lenin*, Verso, 2017

Arnot, Robin Page, *A Short History of the Russian Revolution*, Victor Gollancz, London, 1937

Astashkevich, Irina, *Gendered Violence: Jewish Women in the Pogroms of 1917 to 1921*, Academic Studies Press, 2018

Avrich, Paul, *The Russian Anarchists*, AK Press, 2005

Babel, Isaac, *Complete Works of Isaac Babel*, WW Norton & Co., 2002

Badayev, Alexei Y, *Bolsheviks in the Tsarist Duma*, Bookmarks, 1987

Balabanoff, Angelica, *Impressions of Lenin*, University of Michigan Press, 1964

Beer, Max, *Fifty Years of International Socialism*, Unwin Brothers, 1937

Brailsford, Henry Noel, *The Russian Workers' Republic*, George Allen & Unwin, 1921

Braunthal, Julius, *History of the International*, Thomas Nelson, 1967

Broué, Pierre, *The German Revolution*, Merlin Press, 2006
— *Le Parti bolchevique, historie du PC de l'URSS*, Les Editions de Minuit, 1971

Bryant, Louise, *Six Red Months in Russia*, Journeyman Press, 1982

Buchanan, George, *My Mission to Russia: And Other Diplomatic Memoirs*, Little, Brown & Co., 1923

Bukharin, Preobrarazhensky, *The ABC of Communism*, Penguin Classics, 1970

Buranov, Yuri, *Lenin's Will*, Prometheus, 1994

Carlyle, Thomas, *Cromwell's Letters and Speeches*, Harper & Brothers, 1860

Carr, Edward Hallett, *The Bolshevik Revolution, 1917-1923*, Macmillan, 1950
— *The Interregnum, 1923-1924*, MacMillan, 1954
— *What is History?*, Penguin, 1965

Chaplin, Charlie, *My Trip Abroad*, Harper & Brothers, 1922

Churchill, Winston, *The World Crisis: The Aftermath*, Thornton Butterworth, 1929

Clark, Ronald William, *Lenin: The Man Behind the Mask*, Faber & Faber, 1988

Clausewitz, Carl von, *On War*, Penguin Classics, 1983

Cliff, Tony, *Building the Party: Lenin, 1983-1914*, Bookmarks, 1986
— *Revolution Besieged: Lenin, 1917-1923*, Bookmarks, 1987
— *All Power to the Soviets: Lenin, 1914-1917*, Bookmarks, 1985

Degas (ed.), Jane, *The Communist International*, Routledge, 1971

Denikin, Anton, *Sketches of the Russian Revolt*, Paris, 1922

Deutscher, Isaac, *Lenin's Childhood*, Oxford University Press, 1970
— *Stalin: A Political Biography*, Oxford University Press, 1961
— *The Prophet Armed*, Oxford University Press, 1976
— *The Prophet Unarmed*, Oxford University Press, 1970

Dietzgen, Josef, *Philosophical Essays*, Social-Democratic Philosophy, Chicago, 1917

Dutt, Palme, *Lenin*, Hamish Hamilton, 1933

Erich, Wollenberg, *The Red Army*, New Park, 1978

Figes, Orlando, *A People's Tragedy: The Russian Revolution, 1891-1924*, Pimlico, 1996

Fischer, Louis, *Life of Lenin*, Harper & Row, 1964

Foner, Philip, *The Bolshevik Revolution: Its Impact on American Radicals, Liberals and Labor*, International Publishers, 1967

Fotieva, Lydia, *Pages from Lenin's Life*, Progressive Publishers, 1960

Gallacher, Willie, *Revolt on the Clyde*, Lawrence & Wishart, 1949

Goldman, Emma, *My Disillusionment in Russia*, Doubleday, Page & Co, 1923

Gorky, Maxim, *Days with Lenin*, Martin Lawrence, 1933
— *Vladimir Ilyich Lenin*, Leningrad: State Publishing House, 1924

Grant, Ted, *Russia: From Revolution to Counter-revolution*, Wellred Books, 2023
— *The Unbroken Thread*, Fortress, 1989

Grant, Ted and Silvermanm Roger, *Bureaucratism or Workers' Power*, 1967

Harding, Neil, *Lenin's Political Thought*, Vol. 1, MacMillan, 1977

Hegel, Georg Wilhelm Friedrich, *Hegel Selections*, The Modern Student's Library, 1929

Henderson, Robert, *The Spark that Lit the Revolution: Lenin in London and the Politics that Changed the World*, IB Tauris, 2020

Hill, Christopher, *God's Englishman*, Pelican, 1979
— *Lenin and the Russian Revolution*, Hodder & Stoughton, 1947

Hollis, Christopher, *Portrait of a Professional Revolutionary*, Longmans Green & Co., 1938

Horne, Alistair, *The Fall of Paris: The Siege and the Commune 1870-71*, Penguin, 1990

James, Cyril Lionel Robert, *World Revolution, 1917-1936*, Martin Secker & Warburg, 1937

Kershaw, Ian, *Personality and Power: Builders and Destroyers of Modern Europe*, Allen Lane, 2022

Kerzhentsev, Platon, *Life of Lenin*, Cooperative Publishing Society of Foreign Workers in the USSR, 1937

Krausz, Tamás, *Reconstructing Lenin: An Intellectual Biography*, Monthly Review Press, 2015

Krupskaya, Nadezhda, *Memories of Lenin*, Martin Lawrence, 1930
— *Reminiscences of Lenin*, International Publishers, 1979

Khrushchev, Nikita, *Khrushchev Remembers*, London, 1971

Lawton, Lancelot, *Economic History of Soviet Russia*, Macmillan, 1932

LeBlanc, Paul, *Lenin and the Revolutionary Party*, Haymarket Books, 1993

Lenin, Vladimir Ilyich, *Lenin Collected Works*, Lawrence & Wishart, 1960

Lenin, Vladimir Ilyich and Gorky, Maxim, *Letters, Reminiscences, Articles*, Progress Publishers, 1974

Lewin, Moshe, *Lenin's Last Struggle*, Pluto Press, 1973

Liebman, Marcel, *Leninism Under Lenin*, Merlin, 1980
— *The Russian Revolution*, Vintage Books, 1972

Lockhart, Robert Hamilton Bruce, *Memoirs of a British Agent*, Pan Books, 2002
— *Diaries*, Macmillan, 1973

Lukomsky, Alexander, *Reminiscences: Archives of the Russian Revolution*, Otto Kirchner & Co, 1922

Lunacharsky, Anatoly, *Revolutionary Silhouettes*, Allen Lane, 1967

Luxemburg, Rosa, 'Organisational Questions of the Russian Social Democracy' (later retitled 'Leninism or Marxism?'), Pathfinder Press, 1971
— *Rosa Luxemburg Speaks*, Pathfinder Press, 1970

Maclean, John, *In the Rapids of Revolution*, Allison & Busby, 1978

McLachan, Donald, *In The Chair: Barrington-Ward of 'The Times', 1927-1948*, Weidenfeld and Nicolson, 1971

Marx, Karl and Engels, Friedrich, *Marx and Engels Collected Works*, Lawrence & Wishart, 1975
— *Marx and Engels Selected Correspondence*, Progress Publishers, 1965

Maxton, James, *Lenin*, Daily Express Publications, 1932

Medvedev, Roy, *Let History Judge*, MacMillan, 1972

Milton, Nan, *John Maclean*, Pluto Press, 1973

Montefiore, Simon Sebag, *The Romanovs*, Weidenfeld & Nicolson, 2017
— *Young Stalin*, Phoenix, 2008

Payne, Robert, *The Life and Death of Lenin*, Pan Books, 1967

Piatnitsky, Osip, *Memoirs of a Bolshevik*, International Publishers, 1926

Pipes, Richard, *The Russian Revolution, 1899-1919*, Harvill Press, 1997

Plekhanov, Georgi, *Selected Philosophical Works*, Progress Publishers, 1974

Polovtsev, Peter Alexandrovich, *Days of Eclipse*, Paris

Popov, Nicolai, *Outline History of the Communist Party of the Soviet Union*, Cooperative Publishing Society of Foreign Workers in the USSR, 1934

Price, Morgan Philips, *Dispatches From the Revolution: Russia 1916-18*, Pluto Press, 1997
— *My Three Revolutions: Russia, Germany, Britain, 1917-69*, Allen & Unwin, 1969

Rabinowitch, Alexander, *The Bolsheviks Come to Power: The Revolution of 1917 in Petrograd*, NLB, 1979

Ransome, Arthur, *Six Weeks in Russia in 1919*, Redwoods, 1992
— *The Crisis in Russia*, Redwords, 1992

Rappaport, Helen, *Conspirator: Lenin in Exile*, Windmill Books, 2010

Raskolnikov, Fyodor, *Kronstadt and Petrograd in 1917*, New Park, 1982

Read, Anthony, *The World on Fire: 1919 and the Battle with Bolshevism*, Jonathan Cape, 2008

Reed, John, *Ten Days That Shook the World*, Penguin, 1970

Rimlinger, Gaston V, *The Management of Labor Protest in Russia: 1870-1905*, Cambridge University Press, 1960

Roberts, John Peter and Weston, Fred, *Women, Family and the Russian Revolution*, Wellred Books, 2023

Rosmer, Alfred, *Lenin's Moscow*, Pluto Press, 1971

Ross, Edward Alsworth, *The Russian Soviet Republic*, George Allen & Unwin, 1923

Rogovin, Vadim Z, *1937: Stalin's Year of Terror*, Mehring Books, 1998

Rothstein, Andrew, *Lenin in Britain*, Communist Party of Great Britain, 1970

Rubenstein, Joshua, *Leon Trotsky: A Revolutionary Life*, Yale University Press, 2011

Russell, Bertrand, *Autobiography*, George Allen & Unwin, 1968
— *The Practice and Theory of Bolshevism*, Allen & Unwin, 1921

Santayana, George, *The Life of Reason*, Scribner, 1953

Schapiro, Leonard, *The Communist Party of the Soviet Union*, Methuen, 1964

Serge, Victor, *From Lenin to Stalin*, Monard Press, 1973
— *Memories of a Revolutionary, 1901-1941*, Oxford University Press, 1963
— *Year One of the Russian Revolution*, Allen Lane, 1972

Service, Robert, *Lenin: A Biography*, Macmillan, 2000
— *Lenin: A Political Life – Volume 3: The Iron Ring*, Palgrave Macmillan, 1995

Sewell, Rob, *In the Cause of Labour*, Wellred Books, 2003
— *Socialism or Barbarism: Germany 1918-1933*, Wellred Books, 2018

Shlyapnikov, Alexander, *On the Eve of 1917*, Allison & Busby, 1982

Shub, David, *Lenin: A Biography*, Penguin, 1969

Shulgin, Vasily, *Days of the Russian Revolution: Memoirs From the Right*, Russian
    Thought, Prague, 1922

Souvarine, Boris, *Stalin: A Critical Survey of Bolshevism*, Secker & Warburg, 1939

Stalin, Joseph, *Lenin and Leninism*, Foreign Languages Press, 1977
— *On the Opposition*, Foreign Language Press, 1974
— *The October Revolution*, Lawrence & Wishart, 1936
— *Works*, Foreign Languages Publishing House, 1954

Steffens, Lincoln, *The Autobiography of Lincoln Steffens*, Harcourt Brace Jovanovich, 1958

Stites, Richard, *Revolutionary Dreams: Utopian Vision and Experimental Life in the
    Russian Revolution*, Oxford University Press, 1989

Sukhanov, Nikolai Nikolaevich, *The Russian Revolution 1917*, Oxford University
    Press, 1955

Trepper, Leopold, *The Great Game*, Michael Joseph, 1977

Trotsky, Leon, *1905*, Penguin, 1973
— *Crisis of the French Section*, Pathfinder Press, 1977
— *Diary in Exile, 1935*, Faber and Faber, 1958
— *History of the Russian Revolution*, Wellred Books, 2022
— *How the Revolution Armed*, New Park, 1981
— *In Defence of Marxism*, Wellred Books, 2019

— *Lenin*, George G Harrap & Co., 1925
— *Lenin's Fight Against Stalinism*, Pathfinder, 1975
— *Military Writings of Leon Trotsky*, Merit Publishers, 1969
— *My Life: An Attempt at an Autobiography*, Wellred Books, 2018
— *Notebooks 1933-1935*, Columbia University Press, 1986
— *On Lenin: Notes Towards a Biography*, George Harrap, 1971
— *Our Political Tasks*, New Park, 1979
— *Our Revolution: Essays on Working-class and International Revolution, 1904-
     1917*, Henry Holt & Co., 1918
— *Political Profiles*, New Park, 1972
— *Stalin: An Appraisal of the Man and His Influence*, Wellred Books, 2016
— *Terrorism and Communism*, New Park, 1975
— *The Case of Leon Trotsky*, Merit Publishers, 1969
— *The Challenge of the Left Opposition*, Pathfinder, 1981
— *The First Five Years of the Communist International*, Wellred Books, 2020
— *The Living Thoughts of Karl Marx*, Fawcett Publications, 1963
— *The Permanent Revolution & Results and Prospects*, Wellred Books, 2020
— *The Revolution Betrayed*, Wellred Books, 2015
— *The Stalin School of Falsification*, Pioneer Publishers, 1937
— *The War and the International*, Colombo, 1971
— *The Young Lenin*, David & Charles, 1972
— *Their Morals and Ours*, New Park, 1968
— *Writings of Leon Trotsky*, Pathfinder Press, 1969
— *Writings on Britain*, Wellred Books, 2023

Valentinov, Nikolay, *Encounters with Lenin*, Oxford University Press, 1968

Vodovozov, V, *Moe Znakomstvo s Leninym*, Prague, 1925

Volkogonov, Dmitri, *Lenin: A New Biography*, Free Press, 1994

Watt, Richard, *The Kings Depart*, The Literary Guild, 1969

Wells, Herbert George, *A Short History of the World*, The Labour Publishing
     Company, 1924
— *Russia in the Shadows*, Hodder & Stoughton, 1920

Wicks, HM, *Eclipse of October*, Holborn Publishing Company, 1957

Williams, Albert Rhys, *Lenin: The Man and His Work*, Scott and Seltzer, 1919

Wilson, Edmund, *To the Finland Station: A Study in the Writing and Acting of
     History*, The Fontana Library, 1968

Wolfe, Bertram David, *Three Who Made a Revolution*, Stein & Day, 1984

Wollenburg, Erich, *The Red Army*, New Park, 1978

Woods, Alan, *Bolshevism: The Road to Revolution*, Wellred Books, 2017
— *The First World War: A Marxist Analysis of the Great Slaughter*, Wellred Books, 2019

Woods, Alan and Grant, Ted, *Lenin and Trotsky: What They Really Stood For*, Wellred Books, 2000

Zagorsky, S, *Wages and Regulation of Conditions of Labour in the USSR*, Geneva, 1930

Zbarsky, Ilya, and Hutchinson, Samual, *Lenin's Embalmers*, Vintage, 1999

Zetkin, Clara, *Reminiscences of Lenin*, International Publishers, 1934

Zinoviev, Grigory, *History of the Bolshevik Party: A Popular Outline*, New Park, 1973
— *Lenin*, Socialist Labour League, 1966

Minutes and collections

1903: Second Congress of the RSDLP, New Park, 1978

Classics of Marxism: Volume Two, Wellred Books, 2015

Founding the Communist International, Riddell (ed.), Pathfinder, 1987

History of the Communist Party of the Soviet Union (Short Course), Foreign Languages Publishing House, 1948

Joseph Stalin: A Short Biography, Foreign Languages Publishing House, 1940

Lenin: A Biography, Progress Publishers, 1965

Lenin Through the Eyes of the World, Progress Publishers, 1969

Lenin and Trotsky on Kronstadt, Monad Press 1979

Lenin's Economic Writings, Desai (ed.), Lawrence & Wishart, 1989

Lenin's Fight Against Stalinism, Pathfinder, 1975

Lenin's Struggle for a Revolutionary International, Riddell (ed.), Monad Press, 1984

Moscow Trials Anthology, New Park, 1967

Not by Politics Alone: The Other Lenin, Deutscher, Tamara (ed.), Allen & Unwin, 1973

The German Revolution and the Debate on Soviet Power, Riddell (ed.), Pathfinder, 1986

The Age of Permanent Revolution: A Trotsky Anthology, Deutscher (ed.), Dell Publishing, 1964

The Bolsheviks and the October Revolution: Minutes of the Central Committee of the Russian Social-Democratic Labour Party (Bolsheviks), August 1917 to February 1918, Bone (trans.), Pluto Press, 1974

The Errors of Trotskyism: A Symposium, Communist Party of Great Britain, 1925

The History of the Civil War in the USSR, Lawrence & Wishart, 1937

The Trotsky Papers, 1917-1922, Meijer (ed.), The Hague, 1971

The Theory and Practice of Leninism, Communist Party of Great Britain, 1925

The Sixth Congress of the RSDLP(B), August 1917, Moscow, 1934

Workers of the World and Oppressed Peoples, Unite! Proceedings and Documents of the Second Congress of the Communist International, 1920, Riddell (ed.), Pathfinder, 1991

Papers and periodicals

East European Jewish Affairs
Encyclopedia Britannica
Financial Times
In Defence of Marxism
Manchester Guardian
New York Evening Call
The New Leader
The Russian Review
The Wire

Index

Titles by Wellred Books

Wellred Books is a publishing house specialising in works of Marxist theory. Among the titles we publish are:

In Defence of Marxism, Leon Trotsky

In the Cause of Labour, Rob Sewell

Ireland: Republicanism and Revolution, Alan Woods

Lenin and Trotsky: What They Really Stood For, Alan Woods & Ted Grant

Lenin, Trotsky & the Theory of the Permanent Revolution, John Roberts

Marxism and Anarchism, Various authors

Marxism and the USA, Alan Woods

Materialism and Empirio-criticism, VI Lenin

My Life, Leon Trotsky

Not Guilty, Dewey Commission Report

The Origin of the Family, Private Property & the State, Friedrich Engels

The Permanent Revolution and Results & Prospects, Leon Trotsky

Permanent Revolution in Latin America, John Roberts & Jorge Martin

Reason in Revolt, Alan Woods & Ted Grant

Reformism or Revolution, Alan Woods

Revolution and Counter-Revolution in Spain, Felix Morrow

The Revolution Betrayed, Leon Trotsky

The Revolutionary Legacy of Rosa Luxemburg, Marie Frederiksen

The Revolutionary Philosophy of Marxism, John Peterson (Ed.)

Russia: From Revolution to Counter-Revolution, Ted Grant

Spain's Revolution Against Franco, Alan Woods

Stalin, Leon Trotsky

The State and Revolution, VI Lenin

Ted Grant: The Permanent Revolutionary, Alan Woods

Ted Grant Writings: Volumes One and Two, Ted Grant

Thawra hatta'l nasr! - Revolution until Victory!, Alan Woods & others

What Is Marxism?, Rob Sewell & Alan Woods

What Is to Be Done?, VI Lenin

Women, Family and the Russian Revolution, John Roberts & Fred Weston

Writings on Britain, Leon Trotsky

To make an order or for more information, visit wellred-books.com, email books@wellred-books.com or write to Wellred Books, 152-160 Kemp House, City Road, London, EC1V 2NX, United Kingdom.

Printed in the USA
CPSIA information can be obtained
at www.ICGtesting.com
CBHW010734280424
7593CB00114B/1459